Evaluating Mental Workload for Improved Workplace Performance

Arturo Realyvásquez-Vargas
Instituto Tecnológico de Tijuana, Mexico

Karina Cecilia Arredondo-Soto
Universidad Autónoma de Baja California, Mexico

Guadalupe Hernández-Escobedo
Instituto Tecnológico de Tijuana, Mexico

Jorge González-Reséndiz
Instituto Tecnológico de Tijuana, Mexico

A volume in the Advances in Psychology, Mental Health, and Behavioral Studies (APMHBS) Book Series

IGI Global
DISSEMINATOR OF KNOWLEDGE

Published in the United States of America by
IGI Global
Medical Information Science Reference (an imprint of IGI Global)
701 E. Chocolate Avenue
Hershey PA, USA 17033
Tel: 717-533-8845
Fax: 717-533-8661
E-mail: cust@igi-global.com
Web site: http://www.igi-global.com

Library of Congress Cataloging-in-Publication Data

Names: Realyvasquez, Arturo, 1984- editor. | Arredondo-Soto, Karina Cecilia, 1983- editor. | Hernández-Escobedo, Guadalupe, 1971- editor. | González-Reséndiz, Jorge, 1966- editor.
Title: Evaluating mental workload for improved workplace performance / Arturo Realyvásquez-Vargas, Karina Cecilia Arredondo-Soto, Guadalupe Hernández-Escobedo, Jorge González-Reséndiz, editors.
Description: Hershey, PA : Medical Information Science Reference, [2020] | Includes bibliographical references and index. | Summary: "This book provides comprehensive research on mental workload and the effects, both adverse and positive, that it can have on employee populations as well as strategies for decreasing or deleting it from the labor sector"--Provided by publisher.
Identifiers: LCCN 2019024767 (print) | LCCN 2019024768 (ebook) | ISBN 9781799810520 (hardcover) | ISBN 9781799810537 (ebook)
Subjects: MESH: Workload--psychology | Work Performance | Total Quality Management--methods | Employee Performance Appraisal--methods
Classification: LCC RA972 (print) | LCC RA972 (ebook) | NLM BF 481 | DDC 362.11068/3--dc23
LC record available at https://lccn.loc.gov/2019024767
LC ebook record available at https://lccn.loc.gov/2019024768

This book is published in the IGI Global book series Advances in Psychology, Mental Health, and Behavioral Studies (APMHBS) (ISSN: 2475-6660; eISSN: 2475-6679)

British Cataloguing in Publication Data
A Cataloguing in Publication record for this book is available from the British Library.

For electronic access to this publication, please contact: eresources@igi-global.com.

Advances in Psychology, Mental Health, and Behavioral Studies (APMHBS) Book Series

Bryan Christiansen
Global Research Society, LLC, USA
Harish C. Chandan
Argosy University, USA

ISSN:2475-6660
EISSN:2475-6679

Mission

The complexity of the human mind has puzzled researchers and physicians for centuries. While widely studied, the brain still remains largely misunderstood.

The **Advances in Psychology, Mental Health, and Behavioral Studies (APMHBS)** book series presents comprehensive research publications focusing on topics relating to the human psyche, cognition, psychiatric care, mental and developmental disorders, as well as human behavior and interaction. Featuring diverse and innovative research, publications within APMHBS are ideally designed for use by mental health professionals, academicians, researchers, and upper-level students..

Coverage

- Developmental Disorders
- Personality Disorders
- Emotional Health
- Addiction
- Cognition
- Anxiety
- Socialization
- Treatment & Care
- Neurological Disorders
- Human Behavior

IGI Global is currently accepting manuscripts for publication within this series. To submit a proposal for a volume in this series, please contact our Acquisition Editors at Acquisitions@igi-global.com or visit: http://www.igi-global.com/publish/.

The Advances in Psychology, Mental Health, and Behavioral Studies (APMHBS) Book Series (ISSN 2475-6660) is published by IGI Global, 701 E. Chocolate Avenue, Hershey, PA 17033-1240, USA, www.igi-global.com. This series is composed of titles available for purchase individually; each title is edited to be contextually exclusive from any other title within the series. For pricing and ordering information please visit http://www.igi-global.com/book-series/advances-psychology-mental-health-behavioral/110200. Postmaster: Send all address changes to above address.

Titles in this Series

For a list of additional titles in this series, please visit:
https://www.igi-global.com/book-series/advances-psychology-mental-health-behavioral/110200

Mental Health Intervention and Treatment of First Responders and Emergency Workers
Clint A. Bowers (University of Central Florida, USA) Deborah C. Beidel (University of Central Florida, USA) and Madeline R. Marks (University of Central Florida, USA)
Medical Information Science Reference • © 2020 • 372pp • H/C (ISBN: 9781522598039) • US $255.00

The Psychology and Dynamics Behind Social Media Interactions
Malinda Desjarlais (Mount Royal University, Canada)
Information Science Reference • © 2020 • 477pp • H/C (ISBN: 9781522594123) • US $195.00

Multifaceted Approach to Digital Addiction and Its Treatment
Bahadir Bozoglan (IF Weinheim Institute for Systemic Education and Development, Germany)
Information Science Reference • © 2019 • 388pp • H/C (ISBN: 9781522584490) • US $225.00

Media Models to Foster Collective Human Coherence in the PSYCHecology
Stephen Brock Schafer (Pacific Rim Enterprises, USA)
Information Science Reference • © 2019 • 307pp • H/C (ISBN: 9781522590651) • US $195.00

Developing and Sustaining Play Therapy Clinics
Erin M. Dugan (LSU Health New Orleans, USA) Krystal Vaughn (LSU Health New Orleans, USA) and Kellie Camelford (LSU Health New Orleans, USA)
Medical Information Science Reference • © 2019 • 316pp • H/C (ISBN: 9781522582267) • US $265.00

Ethical Problem-Solving and Decision-Making for Positive and Conclusive Outcomes
Penelope D. Keough (National University, USA)
Information Science Reference • © 2019 • 326pp • H/C (ISBN: 9781522575825) • US $195.00

Chronic Stress and Its Effect on Brain Structure and Connectivity
Ana Starcevic (University of Belgrade, Serbia)
Medical Information Science Reference • © 2019 • 318pp • H/C (ISBN: 9781522575139) • US $225.00

Analyzing the Role of Cognitive Biases in the Decision-Making Process
Verónica Juárez Ramos (International University of Rioja, Spain)
Information Science Reference • © 2019 • 262pp • H/C (ISBN: 9781522529781) • US $190.00

IGI Global
DISSEMINATOR OF KNOWLEDGE

701 East Chocolate Avenue, Hershey, PA 17033, USA
Tel: 717-533-8845 x100 • Fax: 717-533-8661
E-Mail: cust@igi-global.com • www.igi-global.com

Table of Contents

Detailed Table of Contents

Companies are in constant search of greater productivity and better use of resources; however, they have neglected the human being. In this regard, it is important to analyze the presence of the psychosocial factors to which workers are exposed at all levels. These factors exert both a positive and a negative influence and indeed turn into a risk when they are not in balance with worker capabilities. This literature review aims to provide a comprehensive understanding of the psychosocial factors present in the manufacturing industries. The methodology consisted of conducting a search in two databases in addition to government pages. A combination of keywords was used for the search, and each publication was classified according to the factors analyzed, the type of evaluation, and the area of application. Out of all 2,468 publications found, eight were selected. Finally, work-related psychosocial factors were found to be the most analyzed.

Chapter 3
Relationships Between Mental Workload, Burnout, and Job Performance: A Research Among Academicians 49
Meltem Akca, Alanya Alaaddin Keykubat University, Turkey
Mübeyyen Tepe Küçükoğlu, Trakya University, Turkey

Mental workload is a popular topic for ergonomics, psychology, and organizational behavior-related studies. Difficulties and differences in defining and measurement of mental workload engage the attention of scholars to the concept. Furthermore, the importance of mental workload on performance and burn out increases attention to the topic for empirical studies. In this chapter, the authors reveal the relations between mental workload, burnout, and job performance. Data were obtained from 144 academicians in Turkey. Results demonstrated that mental workload has a 1) positive impact on burn out and 2) negative impact on job performance of academicians. Moreover, it was found that burn out and job performance are negatively correlated. Finally, findings reported that there are differences among some demographic variables in accordance with mental workload, burn out, and job performance.

Chapter 4
All-in-One Academics: Mental Workload in Turkish Academic Employment 69
Nazlı Ayşe Ayyıldız Ünnü, Ege University, Turkey
Burcu Şentürk, Ege University, Turkey

The changing nature of higher education systems and academic work all around the world generally and in Turkey specifically highlight the need for academics to use, analyze, and process so much information simultaneously, and deliver results at a specific period of time, which cause them mental workload. Thus, this chapter addresses the problem of understanding and exploring the dynamics of mental workload in Turkish academic setting. The main data for the analysis comes from a wide field research, including 505 questionnaires and 45 in-depth interviews with academics in various universities of Turkey. The mixed methods research revealed that growing publication pressures, administrative work, teaching and supervision hours, the unpredictability of academic positions, the curse of flexibility, and the bureaucratic nature of universities are some of the factors, leading to mental workload in Turkish academia. The other dynamics, such as academic incentive system, demanding nomination/promotion criteria, lack of family-work life balance, were also explored.

considering their physical, social, and mental environment, to respond to the Mexican Official Norm NOM-035-STPS and the ILO guidelines. The methodology consisted of applying to 125 workers a questionnaire of 74 items with 10 factors. The answers were assigned a score of 0 to 4 to later determine the risk level of each factor. The results revealed that the factors with the highest risk are working hours (93%), workload (71%), and lack of control over work (34%). It is concluded that the higher risk factors affect the mental workload of workers in the metalworking industry and associated with the characteristics of the tasks they perform.

The main objective is to evaluate the techno stress perception in the Chilean higher education system professors, a system with a strong market orientation regarding the career's free choice and professional orientation, which is mainly offered in face-to-face mode. In the techno-stress levels identification, it is important to distinguish if these are such that they can affect the teaching performance. For this, techno-tensors and factors are used that determine the technology impact levels in academic stress, in the components: skepticism, fatigue, anxiety and inefficacy. A quantitative approach methodology and non-random design is used, with a snowball sampling obtaining the 190 academics' opinions from Chilean universities. Detecting in general low techno-stress levels with the fatigue slightly higher in comparison to the other three components.

In this chapter, the authors propose the application of artificial intelligence (namely expert system and neural network) for estimating the mental workload of air traffic controllers while working at different control centers (sectors): terminal control center, approach control center, area control center. At each air traffic control center, air traffic controllers will perform the following procedures: coordination between units, aircraft transit, climbing, and descending. So with the help of the artificial intelligence (AI) and its branches expert system and neural network, it is possible to estimate the mental workload of dispatchers for a different number of aircraft, compare the workload intensity of the air traffic control sectors, and optimize the workload between sectors and control centers. The differentiating factor of an AI system from a standard software system is the characteristic ability to learn, improve, and predict. Real dispatchers, students, graduate students, and teachers of the National Aviation University took part in these researches.

Section 3
Performance Evalutation

At present, the manufacturing industries require the implementation of more efficient and flexible fabrication processes to offer high-quality products. The changeover methodologies can be used to reduce the setup times, allowing the industries to be more competitive. The application of changeover methodologies is mainly influenced by the 4Ps model, which is composed of organizational and design factors, such as people, practices, product, and processes. However, this model is not useful in determining the relationship between each one of the Ps and the changeover activities. In this chapter, the authors have developed an exhaustive review of the references to establish the indicators to design an instrument composed of 79 items and divided into the five constructs of the 4P model, which was statistically validated using the Kendall W indicator and the Cronbach´s alpha indicator.

At the global level, the service industry represents a critical component for the economy and its growth trend is above of the other sectors. This sector alone is responsible for 63% of the gross domestic product and 45.5% of labor occupation worldwide. Despite its role in modern economies, the sector receives very little attention. In the literature, the authors have found the efforts that have been made to increase the efficiency and productivity of this type of organizations: adapting philosophies, tools, and/or techniques that were born to achieve this goal in the manufacturing industry, such as Lean manufacturing, total quality management, six sigma, lean six sigma, among others. The objective of this study is to perform an exhaustive literature review of the critical success factors reported in diverse studies of the implementation of these tools or philosophies in the service sector, as well as their differences, similarities, and results.

Foreword

The book *Evaluating Mental Workload for Improved Workplace Performance*, edited by Doctors Arturo Realyvásquez-Vargas, Karina Cecilia Arredondo-Soto, Guadalupe Hernández-Escobedo and Jorge González-Reséndiz offers and important contribution to the field of mental workload, within the science of Ergonomics. The book contains 12 chapters provided by authors from six countries, and it is divided into three sections named Theoretical Contributions to Mental Workload, Mental Workload Evaluation, and Performance Evaluation.

Information provided in this book will help to understand the importance of mental workload level and its effects on employees in different productive or services sectors. Also, it will help promote ergonomic interventions in more countries and industrial sectors from a cognitive approach. In some countries, such as Mexico, mental workload represents a topic that is ignored by middle and top management in most of the companies in different labor sectors. Moreover, this topic is not included in most of the educational programs of undergraduate or graduate. Therefore, students and academicians unknow how to evaluate it and the effects it may cause on employees' health. In addition, there are relatively few people that research and publish about mental workload. This situation makes mental workload is unknown for the middle and top management of companies. This book can help fill that gap both in educational institutions and in companies from different sectors of work.

All chapters include topics that presently represent challenge in different industrial sectors for enterprises of all sizes that try to improve employees' health and optimize their organizational performance. The book contains theory, assessment methods and case studies that readers can apply in similar situations. People interested in Ergonomics will benefit from the content of this book, which deserves to be in libraries and bookstores that deal with the topic of Ergonomics, and more specifically with mental workload.

Yolanda Báez-López
Universidad Autónoma de Baja California, Mexico

Preface

INTRODUCTION

Mental workload is defined as the amount of effort involved in performing a particular task. Currently, employees of different labor sectors (agriculture, aviation, manufacturing, education, services, among others) are involved in different projects in the company for which they work. This fact leads to employees have to use, analyze, and process so much information at a same time, which cause them mental workload. Moreover, employees are pressed to deliver results at a specific period of time, which increase the mental workload. Therefore, there exists a need for an edited collection of original research in the area of mental workload, its causes and effects, methods to evaluate it, strategies to decrease it or control it, and different case studies in any labor sector from around the world.

The general objective of this book is to increase knowledge about mental workload, its causes, effects, methods of evaluation, case studies, and strategies to decrease it or delete it in any labor sector (agriculture, manufacturing, bank, supermarket, education, aviation, construction, etc.). Specific objectives include developing of new theories, applying specific methods to evaluate mental workload, or developing new ones. Another specific objective is promoting the adoption of strategies to decrease or delete mental workload.

The target audience of this book will be composed of professors, managers, employers, ergonomists, researchers and students working in the field of Ergonomics of any labor sector. More specifically, the target audience include ergonomists, manufacturing engineers, agricultural engineers, aviation engineers, industrial engineers, industrial designers, researchers, industry practitioners, research scientists, academics, and any employee that manages information at any level.

ORGANIZATION THE BOOK

This book is the result of the research and applications of different colleagues located in six different countries: Arab Emirates, Chile, India, Mexico, Turkey, and Ukraine. The Mental Workload plays a very important role in the productive processes and in the investigations of the different areas such as theoretical contributions, assessment methods, and performance evaluation.

Section 1: Theoretical Contributions to Mental Workload

Chapter 1 presents information about the methods that combine physical and mental workload/fatigue during ergonomic evaluation. The methods were identified through a systematic literature review. The search criteria were done through a literature search in databases like SciFinder, SciELO, ScienceDirect, etc. As result, the following methods described: Global Load Scale, Multivariate Workload Assessment, Subjective Fatigue Symptoms Test, Fatigue Assessment Scale, Scale of Recovery for Exhaustion of Occupational Fatigue, Scale of Estimated Fatigue-Energy Points, Swedish Occupational Fatigue Inventory, NASA-TLX, Combined Cognitive and Physical Assessment, Laboratory Method of Economics and Sociology of Work, OWL Method, Ergonomic Checklist Method, RENAULT Method, Joyce Method, NERPA Method, ARBAN Method, and MAPFRE Method. As a conclusion, it is possible to affirm that there are some evaluation methods that provide better elements for an accurate evaluation and others lack of basic elements, which causes an incomplete/not accurate evaluation.

Chapter 2 aims to provide a comprehensive understanding of the psychosocial factors present in the manufacturing industries. The methodology consisted of conducting a search in two databases in addition to government pages. A combination of keywords was used for the search, and each publication was classified according to the factors analyzed, the type of evaluation, and the area of application. Out of all 2468 publications found, eight were selected. Finally, work-related psychosocial factors were found to be the most analyzed.

Chapter 3 reveals the relations between mental workload, burnout and job performance. Data's were obtained from 144 academicians in Turkey. Results demonstrate that mental workload has a 1) positive impact on burn out and 2) negative impact on job performance of academicians. Moreover, it was found that burn out and job performance are negatively correlated. Finally, findings reported that there are differences among some of demographic variables accordance with mental workload, burn out and job performance.

Chapter 4 addresses the problem of understanding and exploring the dynamics of mental workload in Turkish academic setting. The main data for the analysis comes from a wide field research, including 505 questionnaires and 45 in-depth interviews with academics in various universities of Turkey. The mixed methods research revealed that growing publication pressures, administrative work, teaching and supervision hours, the unpredictability of academic positions, the curse of flexibility, and the bureaucratic nature of universities are some of the factors, leading to mental workload in Turkish academia. The other dynamics, such as academic incentive system, demanding nomination/promotion criteria, lack of family-work life balance were also explored.

Chapter 5 is spotting a correlation in the planning stage process-centered approach and its effect on employees workload design. The quality definition is the fitness for use or purpose at the most economical level. Literature suggests that many organizations have realized both savings and growth by implementing Total Quality Management as an evolution that contributed to the development of principles and practices, the tools, and techniques for continual improvement to partners as employees, customers, suppliers, and owners.

Section 2: Mental Workload Evaluation

Chapter 6 aims to know the mental workload level and its effects on middle and senior managers in manufacturing companies. The chapter aims to know the mental workload level related to gender, age range, civil status, number of children, years of experience, and worked hours per week. As method, the NASA-TLX method was implemented. This method measures mental workload based on six dimensions: mental demand, physical demand, temporal demand, effort, performance, and frustration level. Data was collected by applying an online questionnaire. Results indicated that some dimensions contributed to mental workload in the following decreasing order: mental demand, temporal demand, effort, performance, frustration level, and physical demand. Similarly, results from mental workload level varied from 55.73 to 64.10. Nevertheless, there was no clear relationship between the gender, age range, civil status, number of children, years of experience, worked hours per week, and mental workload level. Finally, employees manifested mental workload mainly due to stress, mental fatigue, and headache.

The International Labour Organization (ILO) considers mental workload one of the most important psychosocial risk factors associated with the characteristics of the task and is paramount in the metalworking industry. The objective of Chapter 7 was to analyze the levels of risk of the psychosocial factors that workers present, considering their physical, social and mental environment, to respond to the Mexican Official Norm NOM-035-STPS and the ILO guidelines. The methodology consisted of applying to 125 workers a questionnaire of 74 items with 10 factors. The answers were assigned a score of 0 to 4, to later determine the risk level of each factor. The results revealed that the factors with the highest risk are working hours (93%), workload (71%) and lack of control over work (34%). It is concluded that the higher risk factors affect the mental workload of workers in the metalworking industry and associated with the characteristics of the tasks they perform.

The main objective of Chapter 8 is to evaluate the techno stress perception in the Chilean higher education system professors, a system with a strong market orientation regarding the careers free choice and their professional orientation, which is mainly offered in face-to-face mode. In the techno-stress levels identification it is important to distinguish if these are such that they can affect the teaching performance. For this, techno-tensors and factors are used that determine the technology impact levels in the academics stress, in the components: skepticism, fatigue, anxiety and inefficacy. A quantitative approach methodology and non-random design is used, with a snowball sampling obtaining the 190 academics opinion from Chilean universities. Detecting in general low techno stress levels, being the fatigue slightly higher in comparison to the other three components.

In Chapter 9, the authors propose the application of Artificial Intelligence (namely Expert System and Neural Network) for estimating the mental workload of air traffic controllers while working at different control centers (sectors): Terminal Control Center, Approach Control Center, Area Control Center. At each air traffic control center, air traffic controllers will perform the following procedures: coordination between units, aircraft transit, climbing, and descending. So with the help of the Artificial Intelligence (AI) and its branches Expert System and Neural Network, it is possible to estimate the mental workload of dispatchers for a different number of aircraft, compare the workload intensity of the air traffic control sectors and optimize the workload between sectors and control centers. The differentiating factor of an AI system from a standard software system is the characteristic ability to learn, improve, and predict. Real dispatchers, students, graduate students and teachers of the National Aviation University took part in these researches.

Section 3: Performance Evaluation

In Chapter 10, the authors have developed an exhaustive review of the references to establish the indicators to design an instrument composed of 79 items and divided into the five constructs of the 4P model, which was statistically validated using the Kendall W indicator and the Cronbach´s alpha indicator.

The objective of Chapter 11 is to perform an exhaustive literature review of the critical success factors reported in diverse studies of the implementation of these tools or philosophies in the service sector, as well as their differences, similarities, and results.

Chapter 12 focusses on Six Sigma (SS) will be shown, a strategy used in companies to achieve competitive objectives, continuously improving processes. In this sense, it is considered important to identify and know the main factors that are involved in its implementation. Likewise, the organizations are presenting a culture towards the sustainability and the environmental care, derived from this, the methodology used to develop a measurement instrument that allows to identify the CSF in the implementation of SS, the sustainable benefits that can be achieve with correct implementation, the procedure used for the validation of the content of the instrument, the validity of internal consistency and the obtained results.

Acknowledgment

Sincerely, editors want to acknowledge to all participants, researchers, academicians and students who contribute with their chapter to achieve this book. The book includes 14 chapters that provides theory, methods and case studies of mental workload. Authors of book chapters are from six different countries (Arab Emirates, Chile, India, Mexico, Turkey, Ukraine) and from 15 institutions of affiliation.

Institutions to which editors are affiliated deserve special acknowledgement: Tecnológico Nacional de México/Instituto Tecnológico de Tijuana and Universidad Autónoma de Baja California. These institutions provided their facilities and services to develop this book. In addition, editors want to acknowledge to the National Council of Science and Technology (CONACYT) and PRODEP, since these organizations have provided support to perform researches.

Editors also want to express their sincere acknowledgement to the editorial IGI Global Publishing for the opportunity to edit and promote this book. Finally, editors want to recognize the effort of all those people who contributed to the development of this book with their valuable reviews of chapters, and to the researcher who contributed with the foreword.

Section 1

Theoretical Contributions to Mental Workload

Chapter 1
Combined Methods for Physical and Mental Workload:
Fatigue Evaluation – A Systematic Literature Review

Ángel Fabián Campoya Morales
https://orcid.org/0000-0002-2920-1186
Universidad Autónoma de Ciudad Juárez, Mexico

Juan Luis Hernández Arellano
https://orcid.org/0000-0002-8612-5132
Universidad Autónoma de Ciudad Juárez, Mexico

Elvia Luz González-Muñoz
https://orcid.org/0000-0003-0353-1723
Universidad de Guadalajara, Mexico

ABSTRACT

This chapter presents information about the methods that combine physical and mental workload/fatigue during ergonomic evaluation. The methods were identified through a systematic literature review. The search criteria were done through a literature search in databases like SciFinder, SciELO, ScienceDirect, etc. As result, the following methods are described: Global Load Scale, Multivariate Workload Assessment, Subjective Fatigue Symptoms Test, Fatigue Assessment Scale, Scale of Recovery for Exhaustion of Occupational Fatigue, Scale of Estimated Fatigue-Energy Points, Swedish Occupational Fatigue Inventory, NASA-TLX, Combined Cognitive and Physical Assessment, Laboratory Method of Economics and Sociology of Work, OWL Method, Ergonomic Checklist Method, RENAULT Method, Joyce Method, NERPA Method, ARBAN Method, and MAPFRE Method. As a conclusion, it is possible to affirm that there are some evaluation methods that provide better elements for an accurate evaluation, and others lack basic elements, which causes an incomplete/not accurate evaluation.

DOI: 10.4018/978-1-7998-1052-0.ch001

INTRODUCTION

The changes in job processes and work design happened in the last decades were, predominantly, demographic, economic, political, and technological (Bailey & Iqbal, 2008). These changes have caused that the current work must be performed developing physical and mental efforts in a combined and/or simultaneous way (Gil-Monte, 2012). Currently, modern technology has involved new changes in industrial work, especially in decision-making involving high levels of mental load (Demands & De, 2018). As a result, the mental workload is one of the most researched concepts in ergonomics and human factors and represents an issue of increasing importance (Ayaz, 2012). In work environments, more and more cognitive demands are imposed on operators, while physical demands decrease in tasks, understanding how the mental workload affects performance is increasingly critical (Hernandez Arellano, Serratos Perez, Alcaraz, & Maldonado Macias, 2018; Young, Brookhuis, Wickens, & Hancock, 2015).

Due to high levels of mental load, levels of stress and fatigue are being generated and affecting the worker's performance, organizational productivity as well as health problems (Arce & Silvia, 2012). Stress is shown in the physiological plane altering indexes such as the reactivity of the heart rate and the increase in blood pressure. In the behavioral level, the effects of stress are revealed in problems of smoking, alcoholism, drug abuse, antisocial, and aggressive acts, which leads to a possible tendency to accidents and errors, as well as problems of relationships at work (González Muñoz & Gutiérrez Martinez, 2006).

The physical workload is the set of physical requirements that the person required during his working day (Moreno, 2015). A physical job occurs when the type of activity required by the task is primarily physical or muscular. On the contrary, the mental workload is the amount of deliberate mental effort that must be made to achieve a specific result, and it is linked to the need for information processing and decision making for the execution of the task (O'Donnell & Eggemeier, 1986).

The mental workload is used in tasks involving mainly cognitive processes, information processing and affective aspects (Arquer de, 1999). All jobs require a certain level of physical load and mental load. However, the working conditions can affect the mental load of the people (Ceballos Vásquez, Paravic Klijn, Moreno, & Barriga, 2014). For example, in work on production lines (application of adhesives, sewing, welding of electronic parts, insertion of components, etc.), transport of materials (manual or automated), and manual assembly lines (assembly of harnesses, automobiles, components electronic, etc.), are some of the jobs where there are high levels of physical and/or mental load. To assess the workload, both physical and mental aspects must be evaluated, so there are different techniques for evaluation. Similarly, physiological, behavioral and subjective changes should be considered. Some physiological measures evaluate the effect of the increase or decrease of the workload, examples of these are heart rate, heart rate variability, eye movement and brain activity (Stanton, Hedge, Brookhuis, Salas, & Hendrick, 2005). However, the number of methods that combined both kinds of efforts are limited in contrast to the great number of methods, tools, and techniques to evaluate physical or mental factors during an occupational task.

Ergonomic Evaluation

Over time, ergonomic studies have been carried out on the workload, theoretical discussions, and reviews of past investigations (Hart & Staveland, 1988; Lysaght, Ouellette-Kuntz, & Lin, 2012). A growing number of different approaches and techniques for measuring workloads have been discussed, developed, and used. Subjective techniques seem to proliferate, this creates an opportunity and a problem for professionals and researchers of human factors. More recent studies (Hart & Staveland, 1988; Lysaght et al., 2012; Moray, 1979) have taken into account the current situation and perspective of the future on occupational stress, as well as the techniques of study for the workload in laboratories (Piñeda Geraldo and Montes Panice 2014). Studies are still being carried out where a high workload is identified and continuous improvements are sought to reduce the mental workload and improve workers' performance (Kakushi & Évora, 2014).

There are many tools that have been developed for a wide variety of situations, and human factors specialists face the choice of the most appropriate tool or tools to be able to find the information needed to make a choice and consequently causes a problem to choose the right tool (Hill et al., 1992). The ergonomic evaluation aims to determine the level of presence of risk factors in workplaces, which can generate physical health problems in workers. There are two types of analysis: that of working conditions to identify risks and risk assessment if they exist. For each factor, there are different methods that help to evaluate the level of risk associated (Asensio-Cuesta, Bastante Ceca, & Diego Más, 2012).

Combined Physical and Mental Workload

The workload is a concept that involves the capacity of the human being in complex systems considering the equipment, the training offered, the organizational, and environmental constraints. Also, it implies diverse perceptions and responses by the Workers (Jung & Jung 2001). More often, we find jobs that require the individual to attend multiple tasks at the same time, make decisions, and solve problems effectively in stable and emergency situations. The growing role of technology and the use of complex procedures have led to greater demand imposed on the worker (Stanton et al., 2005). The workload produced by an activity that responds to the requirements of a task is composed of physical load and mental load. In the next section, combined methods to assess physical and mental workload are presented in chronological order.

Objective

The objective of this research is, through a systematic review of the literature, to identify and describe the methods to evaluate physical and mental workload in a combined way.

METHODOLOGY

Step 1. Search Criteria

The identification of the combined evaluation methods presented in this article arises from a literature review, using scientific databases and journals such as SciFinder, ScienceDirect, SciELO, Dialnet, Sage Journals, Research Gate, MDPI and Springer. During the search, the selecting area of knowledge was: Ergonomics and human factors. To identify the results, the following keywords were used: "Method, Ergonomics, Combined, Mental, Physical, Study, Scale, Evaluation, Workload, Human, Factors."

Step 2. Identification of Related Papers

During the literature research using the search criteria, more than 200 related papers where found. All of them were read and separated to classify those that would be useful for research.

Step 3. Selection of Relevant Papers

In the final step, 17 relevant papers we had selected, each paper was used to integrate the information and methods included in this article.

RESULTS: COMBINED METHODS IDENTIFIED

The combined methods in this article were selected based on the most used during investigations and ergonomic evaluations in articles. A total of 17 methods were identified, as shown in Table 1.

Table 1. Combined methods identified

Method	Paper	Author, year	Country	Citation
MAPFRE Method	Practical Ergonomics	(MAPFRE, 1975)	Spain	106
Laboratory Method of Economics and Sociology of Work (LEST)	For an analysis of the working conditions of the worker in the company	(Guelaud, Beauchense, Gautrat, & Roustrang, 1977)	France	95
RENAULT Method	Job profiles "method of analysis of working conditions"	(Renault, 1977)	France	84
Subjective Fatigue Symptoms Test (SFST)	Three characteristic patterns of subjective fatigue symptoms	(Yoshitake, 1978)	Japan	267
ARBAN Method	ARBAN: A new method for analysis of ergonomic effort. Applied Ergonomics	(P. Holzmann, 1982)	Sweden	78
Global Load Scale (GLS)	Absolute Magnitude Estimation and Relative Judgement Approaches to Subjective Workload Assessment.	(Vidulich, Field, & Tsang, 1987)	USA	70
NASA- TLX (Task Load Index)	Development of NASA-TLX (Task Load Index): Results of Empirical and Theoretical Research.	(Hart & Staveland, 1988)	USA	9034
Joyce Method	Applied Industrial Ergonomics Reference Manual	(Joyce Institute Training Design Team, 1992)	USA	3
Swedish Occupational Fatigue Inventory (SOFI)	Perceived quality of fatigue during different occupational tasks Development of a questionnaire Elizabeth Åhsberg	(Ahsberg, Garnberale, & Kjellberg, 1997)	Sweden	168
OWL Method	Establishment of overall workload assessment technique for various tasks and workplaces	(Jung & Jung, 2001)	South Korea	90
Multivariate Workload Assessment (MWE)	Multivariate workload evaluation combining physiological and subjective measures.	(Miyake, 2001)	Japan	165

continues on following page

Table 1. Continued

Method	Paper	Author, year	Country	Citation
Fatigue Assessment Scale (FAS)	Fatigue Assessment Scale (FAS)	(Michielsen, H. J., De Vries, J., & Van Heck, 2003)	Netherlands	204
The Scale of Recovery for Exhaustion of Occupational Fatigue (OFER)	Development and validation of a scale to measure work-related fatigue and recovery: The Occupational Fatigue Exhaustion/Recovery Scale (OFER).	(Winwood, Winefield, Dawson, & Lushington, 2005)	Australia	169
The Scale of Estimated Fatigue-Energy Points (SEFEP)	The fatigue-energy dimension as an indicator of presentism: validity of a scale in Mexican workers.	(Juárez-García, 2007)	Chile	18
NERPA Method	Novel Ergonomic Postural Assessment Method (NERPA) Using Product-Process Computer-Aided Engineering for Ergonomic Workplace Design.	(Sanchez-Lite A, Garcia M, Domingo R, 2013)	Spain	21
Combined Cognitive and Physical Assessment (CCPA)	CCPE: Methodology for a combined evaluation of cognitive and physical ergonomics in the interaction between humans and machines.	(Bligård & Osvalder, 2014)	Sweden	17
Ergonomic Checklist Method	Influences on the use of observational methods by practitioners when identifying risk factors in physical work.	(Diego-Mas, Poveda-Bautista, & Garzon-Leal, 2015)	Spain	26

Source: Own creation with data collected in databases.

DESCRIPTION OF THE METHODS

MAPFRE Method

This method, also called the method of ergonomic analysis of the workplace, aims to be a simplified ergonomic assessment, in which, from a general analysis of the conditions of the position, it can be addressed deeper and specific studies of the aspects considered as negative. This method carries out a triple evaluation: descriptive, of the work position (machines and materials used, description of the tasks that are carried out).

The valuation of each factor ranges from 1 (very favorable condition) to 5 (an unfavorable condition that needs to be corrected). The second part is the evaluation, where the factors to be considered are established, covering aspects related to the physical environment (noise, temperature, etc.), the physical load (manual lifting of loads, main posture, etc.), nervous load (operations mental and level of attention) and psychological (individual autonomy, cycle repeatability, schedules). The third part is dedicated to correction measures, technical improvements to be made in the analyzed jobs, all showed in Table 2. Because it is a mixed-method, in each one of the factors, an assessment of the conditions by the worker is introduced, also in five qualitative grades: (++) very acceptable, (+) acceptable, (•) neutral, (-) un-favorable, (-) very unfavorable (MAPFRE, 1975).

Table 2. Items considered in the MAPFRE method

Items
Job Position. Equipment. Space Layout.
Static Physical Load
Dynamic Physical Load
Attention Sensory-Motor Coordination
Complexity Content of Work
Autonomy and Decisions
Monotony and Repetitive
Communications and Social Relations
Shifts. Schedules Pause.
Accident Risks
Chemical Contaminants
Noises and Vibrations
Thermal Conditions
Lighting. Chromatic Environment
Radiation. Other Environmental Factors

Source: (MAPFRE, 1975)

Laboratory Method of Economics and Sociology of Work (LEST)

Aims to evaluate the working conditions in the most objective and global way possible, establishing a final diagnosis that indicates whether each of the situations considered in the position is satisfactory, annoying or harmful. It is a global method that considers each aspect of the job in a general way, providing a first assessment that allows establishing if a deeper analysis with specific methods is required.

The objective is, according to the authors, to evaluate the set of factors related to the content of the work that can have an impact both on the health and on the personal life of the workers. Before the application of the method must have considered and resolved the occupational risks related to Health and Safety at Work since they are not contemplated by the method. To determine the diagnosis, the method considers 16 variables grouped into 5 aspects (dimensions): physical environment, physical load, mental load, psychosocial aspects and work time (Diego-Mas et al., 2015).

The evaluation is based on the scores obtained for each of the 16 variables considered, shown in Table 3. The simplified variables are the thermal environment, light environment, noise, vibrations, attention, and complexity.

Evaluate the mental load based on four indicators:

- Time constraint
- Complexity - Speed
- Attention
- Thoroughness (Guelaud et al., 1977).

Table 3. Items considered in the laboratory method of economics and sociology of work (LEST)

Items				
Physical Environment	Physical Load	Mental Load	Psychosocial Aspects	Work Time
Thermal Environment	Static Charge	Time Constraint	Initiative	Working Time
Noise	Dynamic Load	Complexity	Social Status	
Illumination			Communications	
Vibrations			Relationship with the Command	

Source: (Guelaud et al., 1977)

RENAULT Method

It aims to make an assessment from an objective point of view. This method has been made from an industrial experience started in the 1950s by specialists in working conditions and production of the R.N.U.R. (Regie Nationale des Usines Renault (National Director of the Renault Factories)) and is mainly applicable to repetitive short-cycle jobs. It intends to make an assessment from an objective point of view. This method has been compiled from an industrial experience begun in the fifties by specialists working conditions and production of the R.N.U.R. and it is mainly applicable to repetitive, short-cycle jobs, as is the case of assembly lines in automobile manufacturing. For this, the analysis of eight factors that are evaluated through 23 criteria is considered, showed in Table 4, to which are added four other factors related to the Global Conception of the Post (Renault, 1977).

Table 4. Items considered in the RENAULT method

Items							
Security	Physical Environment	Physical Load	Mental Load	Autonomy	Independent Work Relationships	Repeatability	Contented of The Work
	Thermal Environment	Main Posture	Mental Operations	Individual Autonomy	Dependents of Work	Repeatability of The Cycle.	Potential
	Sound Environment	Work Effort	Level of Attention	Group Autonomy			Responsibility
	Artificial Lighting	Work Posture					Interest of Work
	Vibrations	Effort					
	Industrial Hygiene	Maintenance Posture					
	The Appearance of the Position						

Source: (Renault, 1977)

Subjective Fatigue Symptoms Test (SFST)

The Subjective Fatigue Symptoms Test (SFST) was developed by the Industrial Fatigue Research Committee of the Industrial Health Association of Japan (Yoshitake, 1978), and it is composed of 30 items showed in Table 5, that explore the presence of symptoms of fatigue. Originally, the SFST classified the items into three groups: physical, mental, and neurosensory (Saito, 1970). However, (Saito, Kogi, & Kashiwagi, 1970) subjected the instrument to factorial validity obtaining three factors: drowsiness and heaviness, projection of physical discomfort, and difficulty concentrating. Yoshitake, (1978) related the first factor with undifferentiated work, the second with physical work and the third with mental work. Additionally, Yoshitake proposed the qualification of the test through the percentage of affirmative answers. In addition, it determined that, if a person answers affirmatively to 6 of the 10 questions of one of the analyzed dimensions, it can be considered that this dimension presents as a symptom of fatigue.

ARBAN Method

It is a method for the ergonomic analysis of work, which includes work situations that involve very different postures and body loads. The idea of the method is that all the phases of the analysis process that imply a specific knowledge about ergonomics are taken by the film crew and a computer routine. All the tasks that the researcher must carry out in the analysis process are designed in such a way that they appear as evident using systematic common sense.

The ARBAN analysis method contains four steps: 1. Recording of the workplace situation in video or film. 2. Coding of the posture and the situation of the load in a series of "frozen" situations very close. 3. Computerization. 4. Evaluation of the results. When evaluating the film, the human body is regarded as a conglomerate of functional units, based on the logical coordinated sequence of movements achieved by most human beings while working.

Table 5. Items considered in the subjective fatigue symptoms test (SFST)

Items		
Group A (General)	**Group B (Mental)**	**Group C (Physical)**
1. Feel heavy in the head	1. Find difficulty in thinking	1. Have a headache
2. Feel tired in the whole body	2. Become weary while talking	2. Feel stiff in the shoulder
3. Feel tired in the legs	3. Become nervous	3. Feel pain in the waist
4. Give a yawn	4. Unable to concentrate attention	4. Feel constrained in breathing
5. Feel the brain hot or muddled	5. Unable to have an interest in thinking	5. Feel thirsty
6. Become drowsy	6. Become apt to forgot things	6. Have a husky voice
7. Feel strained in the eyes	7. Lack of self-confidence	7. Have dizziness
8. Become rigid or clumsy in motion	8. Anxious about things	8. Have a spasm of the eyelids
9. Feel unsteady while standing	9. Unable to straighten up in a posture	9. Have a tremor in the limbs
10. Want to lie down	10. Lack of patience	10. Feel ill

Source: (Yoshitake, 1978)

The intervals between the analyzed frames depend on the properties of the work situation and dividing the cycle time into 100-200 equal time intervals is often enough for simple tasks. It provides a representative sample of the working postures throughout the job and allows a quick evaluation procedure. However, the intervals should normally not exceed a few seconds, to avoid loss of information. This method is used to offer a simple and easily handled procedure with a broad field of application. Such methods normally contain two sources of error - the man and the system and is designed to enable both man and machine to do what they can best accomplish, thus reducing the risk of error. Even persons with limited knowledge of ergonomics will be able to use the method after a few hours of training.

The computer calculates the figures for total ergonomic tension throughout the body, as well as in different parts of the body separately, shown in Table 6. They are presented as 'Ergonomic tension/time curves', where heavy load situations occur as curve peaks. The work cycle can also be divided into different tasks, where the stress and duration patterns can be compared. The integral of the curves are calculated for the comparison of a single figure of different tasks, as well as different work situations. The results of the analysis make it possible to identify critical phases of the studied work and to compare different working conditions. The method allows the analyzer to work in a correct ergonomic sequence so that his efforts produce the best result. Subtasks that do not require the comprehension of the human brain or exceed its capabilities are handled by technical equipment such as video and computers (P. Holzmann, 1982).

Global Load Scale (GLS)

It was proposed by Vidulich, Field & Tsang (1987) for the evaluation of the mental load experienced by individuals. GLS is a bipolar scale from 0 to 100, with intervals of 5 units, where the 0 represents a very low mental load and 100 very high mental load. This scale has been used, for example, in the study by Zeitlin, (1995) whose objective was to evaluate the mental load associated with driving a car under different situations (urban or rural environment) and combinations of additional tasks. In Table 7, it shows two rating scale techniques employing an absolute magnitude estimation method were compared to a relative judgment method for assessing subjective workload. The absolute estimation techniques used was a unidimensional Overall Workload scale and the other was the multidimensional NASA-Task Load Index technique. The techniques were used to assess the subjective workload of various single and dual tracking conditions. Thomas Saaty's Analytic Hierarchy Process was the unidimensional relative judgment method used. The validity of the techniques of this method was defined as their ability to detect

Table 6. Items considered in the ARBAN method

Items
Head - neck
Right shoulder - arm
Left shoulder - arm
Trunk – back
Right leg
Left leg

Source: (P. Holzmann, 1982)

the same phenomena observed in the tracking performance. Reliability is assessed by calculating test-retest. The Saaty Analytic Hierarchy Process was found to be superior in validity and reliability using this method. These findings suggest that the relative judgment method would be an effective addition to the currently available subjective workload assessment techniques. An equally used evaluation modality is that of binary comparisons, a method that essentially consists of comparing two to two the mental load associated with the tasks that make up a certain activity, so that for each task it can be calculated in a matrix double entry the load index resulting from the average of the times that people attribute a greater value with respect to the other tasks considered (Vidulich et al., 1987).

NASA- TLX (Task Load Index)

This procedure developed by Hart & Staveland (1988) distinguishes six dimensions of mental load (mental demand, physical demand, temporal demand, yield, effort, and level of frustration), from which it calculates a global index of mental load. In various laboratory investigations, it has been proven that it is sensitive to a variety of tasks and that each of the six subscales, showed in Table 8 who provides independent information about its structure.

The application of this instrument is carried out in two phases: a weighting phase, at the time prior to the execution of the task and another phase immediately after the execution, called the scoring phase. It is part of the base that the specific sources of load imposed by the different tasks are determinant in the experience of load and the subjective feeling of load, therefore the prerequisite is that the subjects themselves make a weighting in order to determinate the extent to which each of the six factors on each specific task or subtask.

The objective of this phase is to define the load sources. It consists in presenting to the people the definitions of each one of the dimensions in order to compare them by pairs (binary compares) and choose for each pair, which is the element that is perceived as a greater source of the load. From this election you get a weight for each dimension, depending on the number of times you have been chosen.

These weights can take values between 0 (for the dimension that has not been chosen on any occasion and therefore is not considered relevant) and 5 (for the dimension that has always been chosen and therefore is the most important source). The same set of weights can be used for variations of the same task or for a group of subtasks. In Addition, the weights give diagnostic information about the nature of the workload imposed by the task as they provide data about two sources of interpersonal variability:

A. The interpersonal differences in the definition of the workload in each task considered.
B. Differences in workload sources between different tasks. The second requirement is to award value for each factor, which represents the magnitude of each factor in a given task.

Table 7. Scores considered in the global load scale (GLS)

Scores
Overall Workload Scale – OW
Nasa-Task Load Index (TLX)
Saaty's Analytic Hierarchy Process

Source: (Vidulich et al., 1987)

In this scoring phase, people value the task or subtask they have just done in each of the dimensions, marking a point on the scale presented to them. Each factor is presented in a line divided into 20 equal intervals (a score that is reconverted to a scale over 100) and bipolarly limited by some descriptors (for example: high/low and bearing in mind the definitions of the dimensions. One of the main advantages of this method is its applicability in the real labor framework as people can directly and quickly rate the task done either right after its execution or retrospectively. A video recording can be useful to improve the memory of the activity, stop if necessary, in each segment of the task. In experiences carried out on retrospective valuations, it has been found that there is a high correlation between the data obtained and the scores obtained in a way Immediate (Archer & Nogare, 2001).

Joyce Method

It is a method for the ergonomic evaluation of jobs, whose objective is to eliminate or minimize the causes of Damage due to Accumulated Trauma (DTA's) related to work. The method allows identifying the jobs that present or are susceptible to present problems of this type, as well as to determine the associated risk to be able to initiate actions that resolve them. It consists of five steps, shown in Table 9.

Table 8. Items considered in the NASA- TLX (Task Load Index)

Items	
Subscales	**Subscales for rating**
Mental Demand	Mental Demand: How much mental and perceptual activity was required? Was the task easy or demanding, simple or complex?
Physical Demand	Physical Demand: How much physical activity was required? Was the task easy or demanding, slack or strenuous?
Temporal Demand	Temporal Demand: How much time pressure did you feel due to the pace at which the tasks or task elements occurred? Was the pace slow or rapid?
Performance	Overall Performance: How successful were you in performing the task? How satisfied were you with your performance?
Effort	Effort: How hard did you have to work (mentally and physically) to accomplish your level of performance?
Frustration	Frustration Level: How irritated, stressed, and annoyed versus content, relaxed, and complacent did you feel during the task?

Source: (Hart & Staveland, 1988)

Table 9. Items considered to the Joyce method

Items
Data collection
Data evaluation
Problem prioritization
Solution design
Validation

Source: (Joyce Institute Training Design Team, 1992)

The risk estimation is done with the checklist during the data collection and its evaluation, the possible results of this estimation are jobs of low, medium or high risk, which facilitates the prioritization of problems. Once the evaluation list is applied, a list of possible situations that could cause damage to workers' health is made. This method is very complete to detect potentially risky jobs in developing DTA's, but it does not detect physical fatigue or metabolic expense which are important processes in the ergonomic evaluation and the worker's involvement is only done if a detailed analysis is necessary (Joyce Institute Training Design Team, 1992).

Swedish Occupational Fatigue Inventory (SOFI)

Swedish Occupational Fatigue Inventory (SOFI) is an instrument composed of 25 items (expressions) showed in Table 10, that evaluates five dimensions of fatigue: lack of energy, physical fatigue, physical discomfort, lack of motivation, and drowsiness, all of them related to physiological, cognitive, motor, and emotional responses.

According to Ahsberg, Garnberale, & Kjellberg (1997), the underlying structure of the instrument corresponds to a new qualitative and quantitative description of the physical (physical exertion and physical discomfort) and mental (lack of motivation and sleepiness) dimensions of perceived fatigue. Together with these, the factor ''lack of energy'' corresponds to a fatigue dimension with both physical and mental characteristics.

The subject must respond to the extent to which these expressions describe how he usually feels at the end of his workday using a scale of the analogous visual type of 11 response points, where 0 is interpreted as "nothing at all" and 10 as "in a high degree". The first version of this instrument was made in Sweden by Ahsberg et al., (1997) and was subsequently revised by Ahsberg, (2000) using confirmatory factorial analysis, and the number of expressions in each dimension was reduced to four (the questionnaire finally consisted of 15 elements). Previously, in accordance with the information from earlier research, two of the original expressions had been replaced by new ones. Finally, the response scale was changed to one with seven points (González Gutiérrez, Jiménez, Hernández, & López, 2005).

OWL Method

It was developed to evaluate the level of general workload (OWL) by introducing sets of variables and application of the hierarchical analysis process (AHP) to estimate the external workload imposed on

Table 10. Factors and items considered in the Swedish occupational fatigue inventory (SOFI)

	Factors of fatigue				
	Lack of energy	**Physical exertion**	**Physical discomfort**	**Lack of motivation**	**Sleepiness**
Items	Overworked	Sweaty	Tense muscles	Uninterested	Sleepy
	Worn out	Breathing heavily	Stiff joints	Passive	Falling asleep
	Exhausted	Palpitations	Numbness	Listless	Drowsy
	Spent	Warm	Hurting	Indifferent	Yawning
	Drained	Out of breath	Aching	Lack of involvement	Lazy

Source: (Ahsberg et al., 1997)

a human operator in systems man-machine. The number of factors considered as potential sources of occupational workload is seemingly limitless. For this, a five-point linguistic variable set scale was constructed, and their hierarchical prioritization procedures were set up (weight of load: 'very light,' 'light,' 'medium,' 'heavy,' 'very heavy,'). Whether the source of an imposed workload is physical or mental in an industrial environment, it may influence an operator's health, performance, or productivity. of the task and the workplace variables (e.g., physical job demand, environmental, postural, and mental demand workloads) which can capture the operator's perception of a workload are introduced as a value of variables.

It must be pointed out that some factors (i.e., task and workplace variables) might be sources of workloads for some individuals but not for others. These differences can arise from various individual characteristics of a physical, mental, attitudinal, or emotional nature. Individual differences in such characteristics might be reflected, for example, in everyone's differences in capacities to adjust or adapt to different external conditions. In addition, a person's perception of his or her own ability to deal with specific job requirements and its external features could cause some people to experience workload but not others.

The task and workplace variables (e.g., physical, environmental, postural, and mental job demand workloads), showed in Table 11, which can obtain the operator's perception of the workload are selected as workload factors and the AHP technique is used to collect different weights. Since there exist various perceptions and responses to a workload by different individuals, the analytic hierarchy process (AHP) is introduced to collect different weighting factors. It organizes basic rationality by breaking down a problem into its smaller constituent parts and then guides subjects through a series of pairwise comparison judgments to express the relative strength or intensity of impact on a subject's workload in the hierarchy. This approach calculates the ratio of the subjective judgment from each type of workload and weighs each workload based on the impact on the subject's perception. Finally, OWL is calculated using a computer-assisted system to determine the level of overall workload impinged on an operator. The OWL was implemented in an actual industrial environment from a physiological and epidemiological viewpoint to determine the validity of the model (Jung & Jung, 2001).

Multivariate Workload Assessment (MWE)

The multivariate workload assessment, which integrates physiological parameters and one subjective parameter through Principal Components Analysis (PCA), was proposed to characterize task-specific

Table 11. Items considered in the OWL method

Items			
Physical job demand	Environment factors	Postural Discomfort	Mental Job Demand
Weight	Working Climate	Standing	
Frequency	Light	Stooping	
Duration	Noise	Squatting	
Distance	Vibration	Twisting	
	Exposure to Chemicals		

Source: (Jung & Jung, 2001)

responses and individual differences in response patterns to mental tasks (Miyake, 2001). With the aim of integrating in the workload measurement parameters with different origin in a single index, the multivariate workload assessment (MWE) allows to mix physiological parameters, showed in Table 12 (heart rate variability, changes in the sanguine pressure of the fingers of the hands and the perspiration) with subjective parameters (mental demands, temporary demand and global effort) by means of the technique of PCA.

This method employs three subscales: mental demand, temporal demand, and effort out of six subscales in the NASA-Task Load Index were used as subjective scores. These parameters were standardized within each participant and then combined. It was possible to assess workload using this method from two different aspects, i.e. physiological and subjective, simultaneously. As a result of this combination, a workload index with a range of 0 to 1 is obtained (Miyake, 2001).

Fatigue Assessment Scale (FAS)

The Fatigue Assessment Scale (FAS) is a method designed to assess the total fatigue using 10 items showed in Table 13, which is divided into two dimensions: physical fatigue and mental fatigue. The final score of the total fatigue is obtained by adding the values of the 10 items included in the questionnaire. In the same way, the physical and mental fatigue score is obtained.

A five-point Likert scale is used. An answer to every question must be given, even if the person does not have any complaints. Where 1 means "never", 2 "sometimes", 3 "regularly", 4 "almost always" and 5 "always". Scores on question 4 and 10 should be recorded (1=5, 2=4, 3=3, 4=2, 5=1). Subsequently, the total FAS score can be calculated by adding the scores on all questions (recorded scores for questions 4 and 10). The total score ranges from 10 to 50. A total FAS score < 22 indicates no fatigue, a score ≥ 22 indicates fatigue. All online versions of the FAS calculate the FAS scores automatically: a total score, as well as mental and physical score, will be provided (Michielsen, H. J., De Vries, J., & Van Heck, 2003)

Table 12. Items considered in the multivariate workload assessment (MWE)

Items
Heat rate variability
Finger plethysmography amplitude
Perspiration
Mental demand
Temporal demand
Effort

Source: (Miyake, 2001)

Table 13. Items considered in the fatigue assessment scale (FAS)

Items
1. I am bothered by fatigue
2. I get tired very quickly
3. I don't do much during the day
4. I have enough energy for everyday life
5. Physically, I feel exhausted
6. I have problems to start things
7. I have problems to think clearly
8. I feel no desire to do anything
9. Mentally, I feel exhausted
10. When I am doing something, I can concentrate quite well

Source: (Michielsen, H. J., De Vries, J., & Van Heck, 2003)

Used in conjunction with other techniques of inquiry, FAS is valuable for the study of the physical and cognitive demands of different types of work processes. This method is now available in more than 15 languages. FAS is quick and easy to complete and not time-consuming. It is also helpful for physicians and other health care workers in the follow-up of their patients in addition to the regular functional tests such as lung function tests. The FAS has proven to be a valid questionnaire to assess fatigue in patients with ILD, but also in many other patients with chronic diseases and it was used few times for industrial use (Cano-Climent, Oliver-Roig, Cabrero-García, de Vries, & Richart-Martínez, 2017).

The Scale of Recovery for Exhaustion of Occupational Fatigue (OFER)

The Occupational Fatigue Exhaustion Recovery Scale (OFER) is a method designed to assess the recovery that a worker requires after their activities, it was developed by Winwood, Winefield, Dawson, & Lushington (2005) in the Netherlands. The 20-item scale showed in Table 14, has been developed and validated using data from three study populations specifically to measure work-related fatigue and possesses robust, gender-bias free psychometric characteristics. The three subscales identify and distinguish between chronic work-related fatigue traits, acute end-of-shift states, and effective fatigue recovery between shifts and analyze fatigue in 3 dimensions (called fatigue states): Chronic Fatigue (CF), acute fatigue (AF), and recovery between work shifts (RT).

The rating scale used in this method is Likert type from 0 to 6, where 0 is "strongly disagree", 1 is "disagree", 2 "little disagree", 3 "no opinion (neutral)", 4 " bit of agreement ", 5" agree "and 6" totally agree." This scale is suggested as a potentially valuable new tool for use in work-related fatigue research (Winwood et al., 2005).

The Scale of Estimated Fatigue-Energy Points (SEFEP)

The Scale of Estimated Fatigue-Energy points (SEFEP) allows relating fatigue with the energy that a worker uses when performing a specific task (Juárez-García, 2007). Whose methodology of application requires the evaluation at the beginning and at the end of the working day; an estimated point (average) is obtained from the objective and subjective items, shown in Table 15.

SEFEP contains 10 levels of punctuation and its interpretation is inverse to the Borg scale (0-10) (Borg, 1985). Consider the score of 10 as the best on the scale, that is, it is interpreted as extremely strong, animated and full of energy and level 1 is interpreted as extremely exhausted and exhausted. As concurrent criteria, several objectives and subjective indicators were used (Juárez-García, 2007).

NERPA Method

It is a novel method for the ergonomic postural evaluation method, fit for product-process design, which was developed with the help of a digital human model together with a 3D CAD tool. NERPA is widely used in the aeronautic and automotive industries. The power of 3D visualization and the possibility of studying the actual assembly sequence in a virtual environment can allow the functional performance of the parts to be addressed. NERPA works as a modified version of the method of rapid evaluation of upper extremities (RULA), showed in Table 16, this tool was developed for use in typical industrial manual assembly tasks in the automotive industry. The effectiveness of RULA and NERPA was compared by a real manufacturing process.

Table 14. Items considered in the fatigue assessment scale (FAS)

Items
1. "I use a lot of my spare time recovering from work"
2. "I often feel at the end of my rope with my work"
3. "I often dread waking up to another day of my work"
4. "I often wonder how long I can keep going at my work"
5. "I feel most of the time I'm living to work"
6. "My head feels dull/heavy a lot of the time"
7. "I often feel exhausted at work"
8. "Too much is expected of me at my work"
9. "My working life takes all my energy from me"
10. "I feel exhausted all the time"
11. "I usually have lots of energy to give my family or friends"
12. "I wish I had more 'get up and go' generally"
13. "I have the energy for my hobbies/relaxing activities in my spare time"
14. "I have plenty of reserve energy when I need it"
15. "I can't recover my energy completely between work shifts"
16. "I fully rested at the start of each workday/shift"
17. "Worrying about work issues makes it hard to relax at home"
18. "I usually recover my energy within a few hours of getting home from work"
19. "I usually feel fully relaxed by the time I go to bed"
20. "I don't get enough time between work shifts to recovery my energy fully"

Source: (Winwood et al., 2005)

Table 15. Items considered in the scale of estimated fatigue-energy points (SEFEP)

Items	
Objective	**Subjective**
Simple visual	Yoshitake's fatigue scale
Auditory	Maslach's MBI-GS emotional exhaustion sub-scale
Discriminatory time reaction tests	
Precision	
Speed of psychomotor performance test	

Source: (Juárez-García, 2007)

Table 16. Items considered in the NERPA method

Items
Stature
Eye height
Mid-shoulder height
Elbow height
Wrist height

Source: (Sanchez-Lite A, Garcia M, Domingo R, 2013)

The NERPA method, which modifies the evaluation of some joint ranges while maintaining the same evaluation structure as the RULA method, presents significant differences with respect to RULA. For the working conditions in which it was used, this method can detect positions with ergonomic risk and is more sensitive to the detection of an ergonomic improvement than the RULA method. The two methods lead to significantly different results. Under the methodological concept presented in this document, other ergonomic risk factors could be added to the NERPA method, which would allow the development of a general risk assessment methodology for industrial production within the framework of risk prevention (Sanchez-Lite A, Garcia M, Domingo R, 2013).

Combined Cognitive and Physical Assessment (CCPA)

It has a proactive and analytical approach to assess the imbalances in the interaction between the human being and the artifact. The CCPA methodology is based on the methods of cognitive assessment and predictive analysis of human errors. These methods have been further developed into four new methods: enhanced cognitive assessment, predictive use error analysis, predictive ergonomic error analysis, and generic task specification.

In addition to the changes that avoid the weaknesses and deficiencies identified in the original methods, the most important aspect of the CCPA methodology is that it deals with cognitive and physical ergonomics together. The objective of CCPA is to predict presumed discrepancies in the interaction of the human-machine, such as physical and mental workload, use of errors, usability problems and ergonomic errors, using a process that supports the cognitive processes of the evaluators. The purpose of examining the problems of physical and cognitive usability and errors of use in this interaction is to achieve a more comprehensive global assessment. In addition, this results in a more cost-effective evaluation of what would be the case if separate methods of cognitive and physical ergonomic assessment were used. CCPA also has a deep theoretical base in both areas.

CCPA is a task-based methodology that uses a structured and systematic questioning process to look for imbalances at each step of the interaction, as well as at a more general level of the system, showed in Table 17. The methodology was developed during work on product development projects in the industry and the academic world, where it was judged that existing evaluation methods did not provide enough information on interaction problems. The research was driven by problems and was conducted as action research. During and after development, CCPA and its methods were used in a series of evaluations in which the methodology predicted, identified and presented supposed imbalances in a structured manner. The strength of CCPA is that its development was iterative and based on reality, as well as on a solid theoretical basis.

The greatest strength of CCPA is the structured and systematic search for imbalances and the integration of cognitive and physical factors. The main weakness of CCPA is that it is more cumbersome and complicated to learn and use than the original methods, as well as compared to other individual HFE methods. However, CCPA generates a more complete result, which is presented in clear descriptions, than in the case of other methods. CCPA also contributes to consensus and knowledge transfer in the evaluation group in a product development project. To conclude, this thesis has resulted in a methodology to predict, identify and present presumed differences in the interaction between the human being and the artifact. However, more work is needed to evaluate the reliability of the methodology and to develop computer aids to simplify its use (Bligård & Osvalder, 2014).

Ergonomic Checklist Method

Developed by the International Labor Office & International Association of Ergonomics (1991), the ergonomic risk checklist is a tool whose main objective is to contribute to a systematic application of ergonomic principles. It was developed with the purpose of offering practical and low-cost solutions to ergonomic problems, particularly for small and medium enterprises. It aims to improve working conditions in a simple way, through the improvement of safety, health, and efficiency. It is a particularly suitable tool to carry out a basic level assessment (or initial risk identification) prior to the advanced level assessment.

Table 17. Items considered in the combined cognitive and physical assessment (CCPA)

Items			
Task Demands	Automation Levels	Mental Workload	Physical Workload
Task Type (TT)	Power (P)	Mental Processing Type (MPT)	Force Resources (FR)
Task Category (TC)	Data Collection (DC)	Attention Resources (AR)	Fine Motor Resources (MR)
Performance/Accuracy (P/A)	Data Analysis (DA)	Memory Resources (R)	Speed Resources (SR)
Time Pressure (TP)	Decision Making (DM)	Processing Resources (PrR)	Body Loads (BL)
Performance Shaping Factors (PSF)	Control (CO)	Frustration and Stress (FS)	Body Contact (BC)
Frustration	Execution (EX)	Superimposed Mental Activities (SMA)	
	Supervision (S)		

Source: (Bligård & Osvalder, 2014)

Table 18. Items considered in the ergonomic checklist method

Grouped Items
Material Handling and Storage
Manual tools
Safety of Production Machinery
Drawing of the Workstation
Illumination
Locals
Environmental risks
Hygienic and Local Rest Services
Individual Protection Equipment
Organization of Work

Source: (Diego-Mas et al., 2015)

The ergonomic checklist performs an analysis of ten different areas in which ergonomics influence working conditions. In Table 18, it shows the grouped items who contains from 10 to 20 checkpoints. In its entirety, the list consists of 128 points. Each checkpoint indicates an action. Options and some additional indications are given for each of the actions. In this way, there is the possibility to select the checkpoints that are applicable to a specific workplace and use the action proposals as an adapted checklist.

The way of using the list is as follows:

- Define the work area that will be inspected. In the case of a small company, it can be the entire work area.
- Know the most important characteristics and factors of the workplace that will be analyzed, such as, for example, the different products and processes that are carried out, the number of workers, shifts, breaks, overtime and any problems or incident that may exist in the workplace.

- Use the checklist to select and apply the checkpoints that are relevant in the workplace.
- Read each item carefully to know how to apply it, in case of doubt, ask the bosses or employees.
- Organize a discussion group using the user-specific checklist as a reference material. A group of people can examine the workplace to conduct a field study.
- Mark at each checkpoint, in the section "Do you propose any action?", A "YES", if the checkpoint is being met. If you think it should be fulfilled and it is not, mark a "NO". Use the Observations section if you wish to add any suggestions or locations.
- Once finished, re-analyze the items marked "NO". Select those whose improvements seem more important and mark them as a priority.

During the group discussion, existing information on "preventive actions" and "recommendations" could be useful as additional information to the selected checkpoints. In addition, good working practices and conditions should also be specified, where they are observed (Diego-Mas et al., 2015).

CONCLUSION

Through the review, using the information gathered in the research conducted in the databases, it was possible to conclude that there are combined evaluation methods most used than others because of the wide variety of tasks and the ease of obtaining results of the evaluation of tasks, where some methods quickly allow the accomplishment of the evaluations of the tasks. With the 17 methods explained in this research, it was found the three most used evaluations methods: NASA- TLX (Task Load Index), Subjective Fatigue Symptoms Test (SFST) and Fatigue Assessment Scale (FAS) with 9034, 267 and 204 citations respectively.

There are ergonomic evaluation methods that work differently from one another, some work with questionnaires, others with factors captured from observation or measurement of data, all have the goal to make an accurate assessment. Some methods work quickly, and others work slower, as there are some that in the evaluation does not consider more important items. Where a better evaluation is facilitated using physical load factors, mental load factors and other factors like ambient factors, which over time has been validated in different investigations.

According to this, it is recommendable to determine criteria to do a proper evaluation, using and compare the different methods considering the evaluated task and factors available against criteria for suitability and application of different ergonomic methods to do an accurate evaluation.

REFERENCES

Ahsberg, E. (2000). Dimensions of fatigue in different working populations. *Scandinavian Journal of Psychology*, *41*(3), 231–241. doi:10.1111/1467-9450.00192 PMID:11041305

Ahsberg, E., Garnberale, F., & Kjellberg, A. (1997). Perceived quality of fatigue during different occupational tasks Development of a questionnaire Elizabeth Åhsberg, Francesco Garnberale. *Anders Kjellberg.*, *20*, 121–135.

Arce, A., & Silvia, R. (2012). Factores organizacionales causantes del estrés en el trabajo y estrategias para afrontarlo. *Revista Venezolana de Gerencia (RVG), 17*(60), 611–634.

Arquer de, M. I. (1999). NTP 534: Carga mental de trabajo: factores. *Instituto Nacional de Seguridad e Higiene En El Trabajo*, 1–6. Retrieved from http://www.insht.es/InshtWeb/Contenidos/Documentacion/FichasTecnicas/NTP/Ficheros/501a600/ntp_534.pdf

Asensio-Cuesta, S., Bastante Ceca, M. J., & Diego Más, J. A. (2012). *Evaluación ergonómica de puestos de trabajo*. Retrieved from https://books.google.com.mx/books/about/EVALUACIÓN_ERGONÓMICA_DE_PUESTOS_DE_TR.html?id=v5kFfWOUh5oC&redir_esc=y

Ayaz, H., Shewokis, P. A., Bunce, S., Izzetoglu, K., Willems, B., & Onaral, B. (2012). Optical brain monitoring for operator training and mental workload assessment. *NeuroImage, 59*, 36–47.

Bailey, B. P., & Iqbal, S. T. (2008). Understanding changes in mental workload during execution of goal-directed tasks and its application for interruption management. *ACM Transactions on Computer-Human Interaction, 14*(4), 1–28. doi:10.1145/1314683.1314689

Bligård, L. O., & Osvalder, A. L. (2014). CCPE: Methodology for a combined evaluation of cognitive and physical ergonomics in the interaction between human and machine. *Human Factors and Ergonomics in Manufacturing, 24*(6), 685–711. doi:10.1002/hfm.20512

Borg, G., Ljunggren, G., & Ceci, R. (1985). The increase of perceived exertion, aches and pain in the legs, heart rate and blood lactate during exercise on a bicycle ergometer. *European Journal of Applied Physiology and Occupational Physiology, 54*(4), 343–349. doi:10.1007/BF02337176 PMID:4065121

Cano-Climent, A., Oliver-Roig, A., Cabrero-García, J., de Vries, J., & Richart-Martínez, M. (2017). The Spanish version of the Fatigue Assessment Scale: Reliability and validity assessment in postpartum women. *PeerJ, 5*, e3832. doi:10.7717/peerj.3832 PMID:28970968

Ceballos Vásquez, P., Paravic Klijn, T., Moreno, M. B., & Barriga, O. (2014). Validación De Escala Subjetiva De Carga Mental De Trabajo En Funcionarios/As Universitarios Validation of Subjective Mental Workload Scale in Academics Staff. *Ciencia y Enfermería, 20*(2), 73–82. doi:10.4067/S0717-95532014000200008

de Arquer, I., & Nogareda, C. (2001). *Estimación de la carga mental de trabajo: el método NASA TLX*. Retrieved from http://www.prevencionintegral.com/Ntps/contenidoNTPS/ntp_544.pdf

Demands, J., & De-, J. (2018). *Job Demands, Job Decision Latitude, and Mental Strain : Implications for Job Redesign Administrative Science Quarterly, 24*(2), 285–308.

Diego-Mas, J. A., Poveda-Bautista, R., & Garzon-Leal, D. C. (2015). Influences on the use of observational methods by practitioners when identifying risk factors in physical work. *Ergonomics, 58*(10), 1660–1670. doi:10.1080/00140139.2015.1023851 PMID:25735462

Gil-Monte, P. R. (2012). Riesgos psicosociales en el trabajo y saud ocupacional. *Revista Peruana de Medicina Experimental y Salud Pública, 29*(2), 237–241. doi:10.1590/S1726-46342012000200012 PMID:22858772

González Gutiérrez, J. L., Jiménez, B. M., Hernández, E. G., & López, A. L. (2005). Spanish version of the Swedish Occupational Fatigue Inventory (SOFI): Factorial replication, reliability and validity. *International Journal of Industrial Ergonomics*, *35*(8), 737–746. doi:10.1016/j.ergon.2005.02.007

González Muños, E., & Gutiérrez Martinez, R. E. (2006). 2_Factor De Riesgo En Industria Electronica. *Revista Latinoamericana de Psicología*, *38*(2), 259–270. Retrieved from http://www.scielo.org.co/scielo.php?script=sci_arttext&pid=S0120-05342006000200003&lng=en&nrm=iso

Guelaud, F., Beauchense, M. N., Gautrat, J., & Roustrang, G. (1977). *Pour une analyse des conditions du travail ouvrier dans l'entreprise* (Vol. 11). Paris: Espirit.

Hart, S. G., & Sta, L. E. (1988). *Human Mental Workload* (A. Hancock & N. Meshkati, Eds.). Elsevier Science Publishers.

Hart, S. G., & Staveland, L. E. (1988). Development of NASA-TLX (Task Load Index): Results of Empirical and Theoretical Research. *Advances in Psychology*, *52*(C), 139–183. doi:10.1016/S0166-4115(08)62386-9

Hernandez Arellano, J. L., Serratos Perez, J. N., Alcaraz, J. L. G., & Maldonado Macias, A. A. (2018). Assessment of Workload, Fatigue, and Musculoskeletal Discomfort Among Computerized Numerical Control Lathe Operators in Mexico. *IISE Transactions on Occupational Ergonomics and Human Factors*, *5*(2), 65–81. doi:10.1080/24725838.2017.1317301

Hill, S. G., Iavecchia, H. P., Byers, J. C., Bittner, A. C. Jr, Zaklade, A. L., & Christ, R. E. (1992). Comparison of Four Subjective Workload Rating Scales. *Human Factors: The Journal of the Human Factors and Ergonomics Society*, *34*(4), 429–439. doi:10.1177/001872089203400405

Juan, P., Hernández, A., Hernández, R. G., Yokasta, A., Vela, D. L. S., Valdés, E. S., … Robledo, A. L. (2016). *Ergonomía cognitiva . Resultados cognitive ergonomics . Results De Un Taller De Capacitación Of A Training Workshop, 17*(3), 49–56.

Juárez-García, A. (2007). La dimensión de fatiga-energía como indicador de presentismo: Validez de una escala en trabajadores mexicanos. *Ciencia & Trabajo*, *9*(24), 55–60. Retrieved from http://bases.bireme.br/cgi-bin/wxislind.exe/iah/online/?IsisScript=iah/iah.xis&src=google&base=LILACS&lang=p&nextAction=lnk&exprSearch=489174&indexSearch=ID

Jung, H. S., & Jung, H. S. (2001). Establishment of overall workload assessment technique for various tasks and workplaces. *International Journal of Industrial Ergonomics*, *28*(6), 341–353. doi:10.1016/S0169-8141(01)00040-3

Kakushi, L. E., & Évora, Y. D. M. (2014). Direct and indirect nursing care time in an Intensive Care Unit. *Revista Latino-Americana de Enfermagem*, *22*(1), 150–157. doi:10.1590/0104-1169.3032.2381 PMID:24553716

Lysaght, R., Ouellette-Kuntz, H., & Lin, C. J. (2012). Untapped potential: Perspectives on the employment of people with intellectual disability. *Work (Reading, Mass.)*, *41*, 409–422. doi:10.3233/WOR-2012-1318 PMID:22495411

MAPFRE. (1975). *Ergonomía Práctica*. Retrieved from https://machete2000.files.wordpress.com/2012/05/mapfre-ergonomc3ada-prc3a1ctica.pdf

Michielsen, H. J., De Vries, J., & Van Heck, G. L. (2003). Fatigue Assessment Scale (FAS). *Springer Science+Business Media, 5*, 1–406. doi:10.1007/978-1-4419-9893-4

Miyake, S. (2001). Multivariate workload evaluation combining physiological and subjective measures. *International Journal of Psychophysiology, 40*(3), 233–238. doi:10.1016/S0167-8760(00)00191-4 PMID:11228350

Moray, N. (1979). Models and Measures of Mental Workload. Mental Workload. doi:10.1007/978-1-4757-0884-4_2

Moreno, B. (2015). Ergonomía y Psicosociología. *Programa Técnico En Prevención de Riesgos Laborales - UGT, 1*, 1689–1699. doi:10.1017/CBO9781107415324.004

O'Donnell, R. D., & Eggemeier, F. T. (1986). Handbook of Perception and Human Performance: Vol. 49. Workload Assesment Methodology. Academic Press.

P., H. (1982). ARBAN: A new method for analysis of ergonomic effort. *Applied Ergonomics, 13*(2), 82–86. Retrieved from http://ovidsp.ovid.com/ovidweb.cgi?T=JS&PAGE=reference&D=emed1a&NEWS=N&AN=1982164797

Piñeda Geraldo, A., & Montes Paniza, G. (2014). ERGONOMÍA AMBIENTAL: Iluminación y confort térmico en trabajadores de oficinas con pantalla de visualización de datos. *Rev. Ingeniería. Matemáticas y Ciencias de La Información, 1*(2), 49–71.

Renault, U. (1976). *Método Renault*. Retrieved from https://books.google.com.mx/books/about/Lesœ_profils_de_postes.html?id=TrcYvwEACAAJ&redir_esc=y

Saito, Y., Kogi, K., & Kashiwagi, S. (1970). Factors Underlaying Subjective Feelings of Fatigue. *J Sci Lab, 46*(4), 204–224.

Sanchez-Lite,, A., Garcia,, M., & Domingo,, R. A. S. M. (2013). Novel Ergonomic Postural Assessment Method (NERPA) Using Product-Process Computer Aided Engineering for Ergonomic Workplace Design. *PLoS One, 12*. doi:10.1371/journal.pone.0072703 PMID:23977340

Stanton, N., Hedge, A., Brookhuis, K., Salas, E., & Hendrick, H. (2005). Handbook of Human Factors and Ergonomics Methods. doi:10.1201/9780203489925

Team, T. J. I. T. D. (1992). *Estimación del riesgo al usar métodos de evaluación ergonómica de puestos de trabajo*. Academic Press.

Vidulich, M. A., Field, M., & Tsang, P. S. (1987). Absolute magnitude estimation and relative judgement approaches to subjective workload assessment. *Proceedings of the Human Factors Society-31st Annual Meeting*, 1057–1061.

Winwood, P. C., Winefield, A. H., Dawson, D., & Lushington, K. (2005). Development and validation of a scale to measure work-related fatigue and recovery: The Occupational Fatigue Exhaustion/Recovery scale (OFER). *Journal of Occupational and Environmental Medicine*, *47*(6), 594–606. doi:10.1097/01.jom.0000161740.71049.c4 PMID:15951720

Yoshitake, H. (1978). Three characteristic patterns of subjective fatigue symptoms. *Ergonomics*, *21*(3), 231–233. doi:10.1080/00140137808931718 PMID:27351

Young, M. S., Brookhuis, K. A., Wickens, C. D., & Hancock, P. A. (2015). State of science: Mental workload in ergonomics. *Ergonomics*, *58*(1), 1–17. doi:10.1080/00140139.2014.956151 PMID:25442818

Zeitlin, L. R. (1995). Estimates of Driver Mental Workload: A Long-Term Field Trial of Two Subsidiary Tasks. *Human Factors: The Journal of the Human Factors and Ergonomics Society*, *37*(3), 611–621. doi:10.1518/001872095779049327

Chapter 2
Work Stress and Psychosocial Factors in the Manufacturing Industry:
A Literature Review

Mónica Gabriela Gutiérrez Hernández
Instituto Tecnológico de Ciudad Juárez, Mexico

Rosa María Reyes Martínez
Instituto Tecnológico de Ciudad Juárez, Mexico

Aide Aracely Maldonado-Macias
https://orcid.org/0000-0002-4959-161X
Instituto Tecnológico de Ciudad Juárez, Mexico

Jaime Sánchez Leal
https://orcid.org/0000-0002-6324-2379
Instituto Tecnológico de Ciudad Juárez, Mexico

Jorge De La Riva Rodríguez
Instituto Tecnológico de Ciudad Juárez, Mexico

ABSTRACT

Companies are in constant search of greater productivity and better use of resources; however, they have neglected the human being. In this regard, it is important to analyze the presence of the psychosocial factors to which workers are exposed at all levels. These factors exert both a positive and a negative influence and indeed turn into a risk when they are not in balance with worker capabilities. This literature review aims to provide a comprehensive understanding of the psychosocial factors present in the manufacturing industries. The methodology consisted of conducting a search in two databases in addition to government pages. A combination of keywords was used for the search, and each publication was classified according to the factors analyzed, the type of evaluation, and the area of application. Out of all 2,468 publications found, eight were selected. Finally, work-related psychosocial factors were found to be the most analyzed.

DOI: 10.4018/978-1-7998-1052-0.ch002

INTRODUCTION

Currently, companies are looking for a better use of resources in order to increase their productivity. However, they are neglecting the most important resource which is the human element. As years go by, high market competitiveness and globalization have caused changes in the work environment, which have resulted in greater demands on workers. Such demands are placed by the need to execute more complex tasks in stressful work environments, with a high mental workload, and in the face of harassment and work violence among other factors. Such conditions are known as psychosocial work factors, and their importance has begun to be recognized throughout organizations because of their impact on the performance of workers and companies. However, the study and evaluation of such factors involve challenges that countries must recognize in order to face and evaluate them, and to develop strategies for their better management and prevention. Indeed, psychosocial factors are highly complex and, thus, difficult to understand as they depend on workers' perceptions and include aspects that range from individual characteristics to the social situations in which they operate outside of work hours. Thus, one way to facilitate the analysis of psychosocial factors is by grouping them into categories or areas; for example, they can be classified as personal aspects, factors inherent in work tasks, and organizational factors, among others, to try to explain the nature of their interactions and effects on health (International Labor Office, 1984).

In this regard, it is normal to observe that workers in the manufacturing industries are exposed to psychosocial factors as well as psychosocial factor risks. The International Labor Organization deemed the workplace as an important source of psychosocial risks by identifying that human beings spend most of their life at work. Consequently, it presented the workplace as the ideal place to treat workers and to look after their health and well-being. On the other hand, that organism affirmed that the psychosocial risk factors that take place in the world, and particularly in Mexico require effective government participation that supports the increase of health and safety in the workplace. Government must promote and help providing healthy working environment that allows workers to achieve honest or decent work through policies, strategic lines of action and projects with a preventive focus, so that work centers with safe and healthy conditions can prevail (Secretaría del Trabajo y Previsión Social - STPS, 2016).

This present era is one in which the population is being affected by stress due to the excessive, and perhaps self-imposed, pace of life and work. Workers are continually exposed to situations that create an imbalance on a personal and work level, placing them in a state of vulnerability to diseases associated with nervousness, stress and unjustified fear (Lupien, McEwen, Gunnar, & Heim, 2009). These constant changes in the work environment are perceived by workers as threats and could lead to chronic stress, acting as backdrops for health disorders. The risk factors generated by the organization at the workplace lead to physiological, emotional, cognitive and behavioral responses that result in disease under certain conditions of intensity, frequency and duration (Trade Union Institute of Labor, Environment and Health - ISTAS, 2010). Finally, after analyzing the increase in these diseases, the World Health Organization has signaled 2020 as the year when chronic stress-related depression will be the second cause of disability in the world (Organización Mundial de la Salud- OMS, 2012).

Based on the foregoing, it can be affirmed that identifying and assessing psychosocial risks is an important task in this investigation due to the great impact they have on the workers' health and on their performance in the company, specifically in manufacturing companies. This work's main objective, then, is to determine the state of the art on the psychosocial factors present in manufacturing companies, as well as the instruments that are used to identify and evaluate them. Another important objective is to analyze the instrument provided by the Ministry of Labor and Social Security (STPS) through the standard NOM-035-STPS-2018, which is mandatory for all work centers located in the country. Finally, other goals are to make recommendations on the usefulness of evaluating psychosocial factors and to offer suggestions for further research.

Background

Psychosocial factors are present in all work areas without exception, thereby the importance of their analysis. Currently, different ways to refer to psychosocial aspects are being used; therefore, it is important to point out their differences. Psychosocial factors are concerned to conditions in the individual, in the non-work environment and the intra-work environment, which depending on the intensity and duration can have a positive and negative impact on a worker, groups of workers or entire organizations (Oficina Internacional del Trabajo - OIT, 1986). While psychosocial risk factors are those that are likely to negatively, influence the workers' health and well-being (Benavides, *et al.,* 2002).

Worldwide, occupational health and occupational medicine perform a wide variety of studies aiming to ensure health and well-being of the worker (Kawakami & Tsutsumi, 2010, Siegrist, 2008, Van Vegchel, De Jonge, Bosma, & Schaufeli, 2005). As a result of globalization and technological advances, there have been created work environments with high cognitive, emotional and psychological demands, with little control over the task, under low social support and poor quality of leadership (International Labor Office, 2012).

In relation to the above, there is evidence to affirm that these work characteristics are strongly related to cardiovascular risk factors with a high probability of cerebrovascular events and ischemic heart disease (Belkic, 2004, Hausser, Mojzisch, Niesel, & Schulz-Hardt, 2010; Juárez, 2007; Smith, Roman, Dollard, Winefield, & Siegrist, 2005; Steptoe & Kivimäki, 2012). Likewise, there is significant relationship between psychosocial risk factors in the workplace and different types of disorders, such as musculoskeletal injuries (Palliser, Firth, Feyer, & Paulin, 2005), work stress (Shultz, Wang, Crimmins, & Fisher, 2010; Valverde, 2007; Wang, Schmitz, Dewa, & Stansfeld, 2009), absenteeism (Darr & Johns, 2008; Gartner, Nieuwenhuijsen, Van Dijk, & Sluiter, 2010), the increase in work-related accidents (International Labor Office (ILO), International Program on Safety and Health at Work and the Environment & International Occupational Safety and Health Information Center, 2007), interference in the work-family relationship (Kawakami & Tsutsumi, 2010; Kinman & Jones, 2008), sleep disorders (Heponiemi, *et al.*, 2009; Kudielka, Von Kanel, Gander, & Fischer, 2004; Yang, Ge, Hu, Chi, & Wang, 2009) and alterations in mental health (Bourbonnais, *et al*, 2006; Burr, Albertsen, Rugulies, & Hannerz, 2010; Wang, Schmitz, Dewa, & Stansfeld, 2009; Griffin, Greiner, Stansfeld, & Marmot, 2007; Kirchhof, *et al.*, 2009; Laurent, Pinte, Gerard-Guery, Wehrly, & Pamart, 2009: Lehr, Hillert, & Keller, 2009; Silva, De Souza, Borges, & Fischer, 2010) as affective-depression disorders (Lehr, *et al.*, 2009; Rugulies, Bultmann, Aust, & Burr, 2006; Ylipaavalniemi, *et al.,* 2005) and anxiety disorders (Griffin *et al.*, 2007). This evidence provide theoretical frame that emphasize the relevance of psychosocial factors at work. Developing countries such Mexico are recognizing this importance by releasing initiatives and normative standards that can contribute to their detection and prevention. In this chapter, some of this normative is commented and described.

PSYCHOSOCIAL FACTORS AND THEIR ASSESSMENT

As previously mentioned, in the workplace and especially in the manufacturing industries, workers are exposed to a great variety of psychosocial factors that can influence their health. Thus, it should be considered that work conditions ought to ensure the safety and health of the worker at the workplace in addition to seeking to provide them with free time to rest. Another aspect that should be allowed for should be the opportunity to collaborate with society and to engage in the search for self-realization. According to the International Labor Office (2012), the presence of psychosocial risk factors is becoming more evident in both developed and developing countries, affecting all workers. These factors have a severe impact on workers' health, absenteeism and performance. One of the main reasons is that the pace of life is getting faster each day, and technological changes are occurring more rapidly. Companies, then, should look for an optimal way to identify, assess and effectively deal with such factors. A starting point should be to define the characteristics that a work center should show to promote health:

1. Incorporate safety and health measures at work, reinforcing the quality of work life as well as the worker's (physical and mental) health.
2. Support workers so that they develop the capacity to face work, personal or family-related problems that may affect their health and work performance.
3. Encourage workers ability to handle their chronic conditions, so that they become proactive in caring for their health and seeking a better quality of life.
4. Promote health from a collective point of view as it looks to improve task organization, working conditions, and the environment while encompassing both the family and the social contexts.
5. Consider a balance between its demands and workers' capabilities.
6. Consider that workers learn at the workplace, and learning is ongoing.
7. Consider aspects on which the worker can make decisions.
8. Realize the need for a certain degree of social support and recognition at the workplace.
9. Understand that workers must be able to establish a relationship between what they do or produce and social life.
10. Workers must be motivated by perceiving that their job leads to some kind of desirable future.

Regarding the previous points, the ecological model (see figure 1) consists of analyzing the psychosocial factors considering aspects ranging from the personal to the social. The reason in that it recognizes that there is a wide variety of factors that influence the health of the worker and that not all of them necessarily belong to the workplace, considering that human beings are a part of a complex system of interrelations that can influence them both positively and negatively.

When analyzing the ecological model, it is evident that risk factors can be present at work, at home or in the social environment, and each environment could contain one or more stress factors. Because it is highly difficult to achieve a separation between them, the presence of risk factors in any given environment tends to affect the others. Below is a description of each of the environments and their stress-vulnerable points.

Figure 1. Ecological model (Source: Oficina Internacional Del Trabajo, 2012)

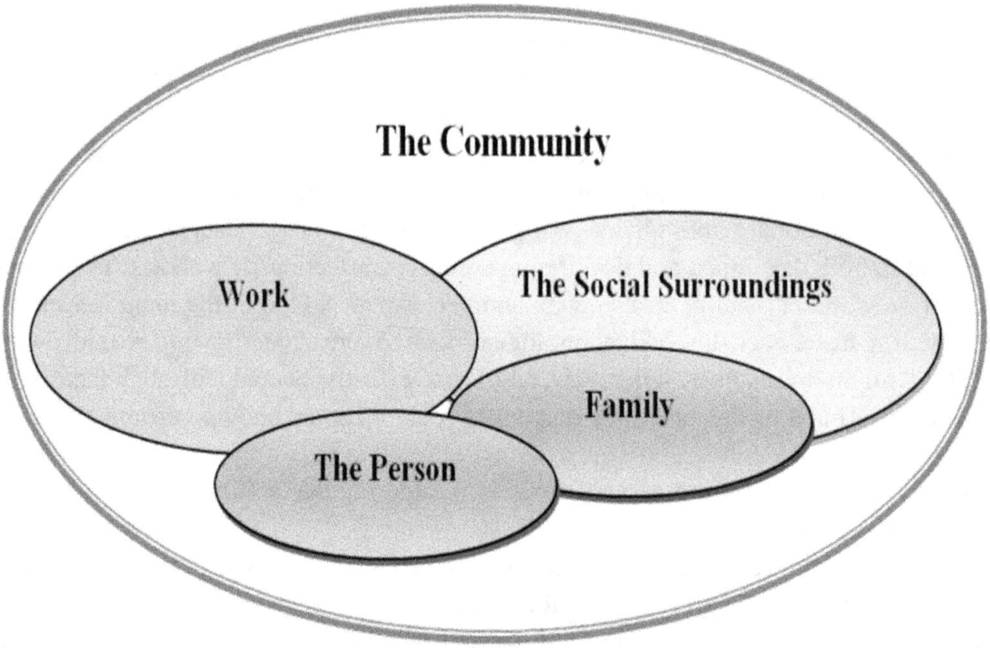

The Person

In individual terms, aspects such as age, gender, some type of disability and socioeconomic status are related to the presence of stress, and most times stress results from a combination of factors. For example, the relationship between gender, work and stress is a highly complex one. The reason is that women play a fundamental role in caring for the family. In this sense, the daily work load for women who have a full-time job outside the home is usually greater than that of men as regardless of the working day, they must still fulfill family responsibilities at home.

The Family

One of stress triggers can be the work-family relationship, especially when both parents work. It is difficult for workers to balance the different schedules and shift durations while keeping in mind the lack of control they have over their work.

The Community

The ability to socialize is often key in the stress levels. This environment considers the ease with which people establish good communication and support with their family members, or friends. These relationships range from frequent family gatherings to belonging to sports groups, both of which promote adequate handling of problems.

Social Surroundings

This environment can have both positive and negative effects on psychosocial risks. For instance, the social environment can contribute with aspects such as regulations that allow a better response to potential stressors such as addictions. Likewise, if the society in which people operate has good public transportation, sports facilities, social support such as workshops to help them better cope with problems, and good medical service, people will be able to face stress factors more effectively as the situations that represent a threat to their stability are reduced.

The Workplace

Technological changes and constant competition worldwide promote new forms of work organization where the intensity of work, hours and shift durations, new forms of employment (partial or temporary contracts), hiring requirements (age, experience, and training), among others, stand out. Consequently, the workplace has become the most important source of risk, having the greatest impact on the balance between work and private life. The workplace can help to prevent stress by matching workers' capabilities to the workload and tasks assigned to them. It is certainly recognized that the level of stress can serve as essential motivation to boost performance and create a bond with work. However, there can be a point where that initial stress becomes excessive.

Also, it is possible to classify the psychosocial factors according to the place where they originate. This literature review focused on the psychosocial factors to which workers at the workplace are exposed. These refer to the organizational conditions that can be both positive and negative (Minztberg, 1993). There is a great variety of them, and they are classified according to what one wishes to analyze. These factors facilitate work, job growth and job satisfaction, and increase workers' productivity and motivation (Kalimo, El-Batawi, & Cooper, 1988). For example, Table 1 shows Roozeboom, Houtman and Van den Bossche's (2008) classification of the factors that can be observed in an organization.

Table 1. List of organizational factors

ORGANIZATIONAL FACTORS		WORK FACTORS	
Organization's Philosophy and Policies	Work-family relationship Human resources management Health and Safety policies Corporate social responsibility Commercial strategies	Work Conditions	Type of contract Salary Career design
Organizational Culture	Work relationships policies Organizational Information Organizational Communication Organizational Justice Supervision / Leadership	Job Design	Staff turnover Group work
Industrial Relationships	Work climate Trade Union representation Collective agreements	Work Quality	Use of personal skills Job demands Autonomy and capacity to control Physical safety at work Social support Work hours Teleworking

In addition, psychosocial factors become psychosocial risks when they begin to negatively affect workers' health and performance. Just as there is a great variety of psychosocial factors, the number of risk or stress factors is also quite broad. Cox and Griffiths (1996) state that each of the psychosocial factors can lead to a number of risks. Table 2 lists some of them.

In general, it is appropriate to say that the purpose of most of the instruments is to analyze the psychosocial factors related to intra-labor conditions, which are associated with the work and organization characteristics that influence the health and well-being of people. The work environment-related psychosocial factors can be grouped into the following four categories: work demands, control over work, presence of leadership and reward or recognition of worker's performance.

Work Demands

These encompass the work demands imposed on the individual. Among them are the following:

1. The amount of work that must be done during a work day turns into a risk when the time available to carry it out is insufficient; this results in accelerated work rates and in having to work overtime to achieve the expected objectives.
2. Mental requirements are defined by the quantity of information and its complexity as well as by whether the task requires considerable memory, attention or concentration efforts.
3. Emotional demands occur when workers must understand other people's situations and/or feelings and exert self-control over their own emotions so as not to affect their work performance.
4. There is high degree of responsibility, for example, when workers must answer for the results of their work area or section.

Table 2. Psychosocial stress factors

Work content	Lack of variety at work, short work cycles, fragmented and pointless work, low use of skills, high uncertainty, intense relationships.
Overload and pace	Excess of work, work pace, high temporary pressure, urgent completion deadlines.
Schedules	Changing shifts, night shift changes, inflexible schedules, unpredictable work schedule, long work hours or without time for interaction.
Control	Low participation in decisión-making, low capacity to control the work load, and other work factors.
Environment and teams	Poor working conditions, inadequate work teams, lack of equipment maintenance, lack of personal space, poor lighting or excessive noise.
Organizational Culture and functions	Poor internal communication, low levels of support, lack of task definition or not in accordance with organizational objectives.
Interpersonal relationships	Physical or social isolation, scarce relationship with bosses, interpersonal conflicts, lack of social support.
Role in the organization	Role ambiguity, role conflicts and responsibility for others.
Career development	Uncertainty or halts in the professional career, poor remuneration, contract insecurity.
Work-family relationship	Conflicting demands between work and family, low family support. Dual career problems.
Contract safety	Dangerous work, temporary work, uncertainty regarding work future. Insufficient remuneration.

5. Environmental and physical demands are considered a risk factor when workers must perform their work under unsafe or unhealthy conditions which also require a great amount of physical effort.
6. The type of shift becomes an important aspect to analyze since there is evidence that when working on night shifts, for long hours or during rest days, workers experience a greater toll on their health (Tucker & Rutherford, 2005).

Control Over Work

It refers to the individual's ability to influence and make decisions regarding some of the aspects involved in the performance of their work. These aspects occur more frequently when workers have the ability to adapt to the challenges of the workplace and when the task fosters the application of the worker's knowledge along with the development of new knowledge and skills. In this sense, it is essential to consider the workers' ability to establish the sequence of their activities as well as their work pace.

Leadership and Social Relations at Work

Leadership refers to a type of social relationship that occurs between the hierarchical levels in descending manner, whose characteristics influence the way of working and the work environment. Thus, it is important for leaders to establish a good relationship with their workers (subordinates) to achieve the expected results. Likewise, they must find the best way to approach conflict resolution and must be in constant pursuit of motivation, support and good communication with their collaborators. This is achieved when leaders offer their subordinates effective feedback, one that allows them to identify their strengths and their areas of opportunity to improve their performance.

Reward

This term deals with the recognition that workers obtain in exchange for their performance. This category includes various types of remuneration: financial (economic compensation for work), esteem (psychological compensation, which includes recognition of the social group and fair treatment at work) and opportunities for promotion and safety at work. Receiving these rewards from the organization boosts workers' feelings of pride and the perception of job stability, as well as their feeling of self-realization.

IMPACT OF PSYCHOSOCIAL FACTORS

Several authors affirm that the presence of psychosocial factors in the work environment is closely related to stress as most of the factors become a risk when they create working conditions that exert higher demands on workers. In this regard, Palmer, Cooper, & Thomas (2003) affirm that stress is triggered when the demands or the pressure perceived by workers exceed their ability to cope with them. It is also noteworthy that stress is a natural defense mechanism that contributes to human survival. However, it is also a cause for stress when either a single worker's or a group's knowledge and ability to resist, face and overcome difficulties does not match the expectations of a company's organizational culture. Moreover, as technology advances, people spend 24 hours a day connected to their phone, email, internet and other means of electronic communication, which allows them to be able to deal with job issues outside their work schedule. Thus, the boundaries separating work from domestic life are increasingly blurred as the workplace is set by the multiple and instant types of communication and the high level of global competition.

When speaking of work, both formal and informal types of work are considered. In the case of the latter, it can be even more difficult to separate work demands from those of everyday life since its financial survival depends on an enormous amount of workload and highly unpredictable working conditions.

On the other hand, the workers' perceived need to keep working to ensure a steady income can lead to many personal concessions resulting in physical, psychological or behavioral reactions caused by stress. When these demands are maintained for a prolonged time, some workers tend to suffer from anxiety disorders, emotional exhaustion, and severe depression, which gives rise to a loss of interest first in their work and then in life in general. The World Health Organization (WHO) affirms that more than 300 million people in the world suffer from depression, a disorder that is the main current cause for disability. At the same time, many of them also suffer from anxiety symptoms. According to a recent study conducted by the WHO, depression and anxiety disorders cost the world economy one billion dollars per year in lost productivity (Organización Mundial de la Salud - OMS, 2017). In Mexico, 40% of employees suffer from work-related stress. This stress is associated with pressure from supervisors and clients, lack of work stability, and excessive workloads (Oficina Internacional del Trabajo, 2012). On the other hand, as Figure 2 shows, an analysis of the presence of depression in households showed that the percentage of household members who are 12 years old or older and who have felt depression at various times during the year has increased. When researching the information a bit further, it was found that during the year 2017, 60% of the people who suffered from this disorder were women. (Instituto Nacional de Estadística y Geografía - INEGI, 2017)

Figure 2. Percentage of household members who experience feelings of depression at various times during the year

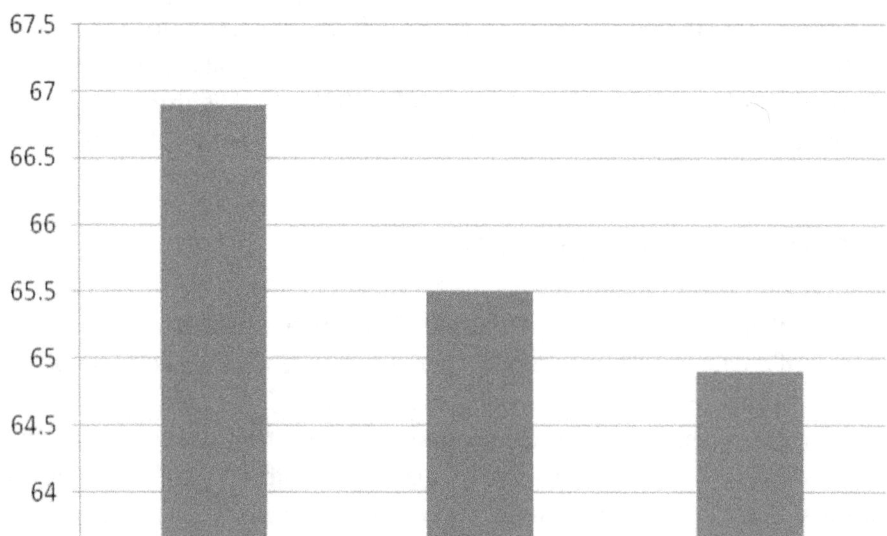

As can be seen, the main consequence of psychosocial risk is stress, whose most frequent symptoms range from irritability to depression and are generally accompanied by physical and mental exhaustion. Likewise, stress directly affects workers' performance, which results in low productivity and affects work comfort. The reason for the above is that a person undergoing a large amount of pressure is incapable of making correct decisions, and his/her creativity decreases notably as the mind is unable to find the multiple solutions required for successful performance. Güilgüiruca, Meza, Góngora, & Moya (2015) pose that a company with many stressed people usually features a poor work environment. Based on the above, it is important for employers to understand that poor intervention leads to a decrease not only in productivity but in the quality of life of those suffering from stress, which may even be a reason for permanent sick leave.

Human beings are complex by nature, and since they are an organization's most important resource, they represent a constant challenge for the future of companies. Thus, there is an important need to incorporate processes that understand and address both the human and the work dimensions of the people that make up each company. Doing so will allow companies to identify the influence that psychosocial and organizational factors have on productivity, as well as to work on strategies that allow for continuous improvement. Along these lines, work policies worldwide are establishing wellbeing programs which are based on the analysis and evaluation of the factors that affect mental health, such as the standard of living and the working conditions, while preventing and promoting health, including mental health. This is done through activities that reduce stigma and discrimination and improve health services, including occupational health services, to expand the access to scientifically proven care.

Issues, Controversies, Problems

Immersed in a constant change due to technological development and communications, in new forms of organization with more automated production processes, and in the search for global competitiveness in the midst of an economic crisis, companies remained unaware that it would be necessary to create new profiles for job positions as the task demands on workers increased, taking a toll on both workers' health and company productivity. The Ministry of Labor and Social Welfare in Mexico, through the National Program for Emotional Wellbeing and Human Development at Work (PRONABET) began to investigate the possible causes for psychological resignation, high rates of absenteeism, staff turnover, lack of loyalty, increase in sick-leave days, costs due to accidents, and employees' low sense of belonging. An important point in this research was that the above-mentioned problems were observed even in those companies that complied with the current regulations, which focus on safeguarding workers' safety and health within the work area. In this sense, it has been observed that neglecting to factor in the psychosocial factors to which workers are exposed can create problems for both the company, such as low work performance, and the workers' health.

The International Labor Office (2012) states that in the long term, stress at work can be a factor in the presence of musculoskeletal disorders, hypertension, cardiovascular diseases and overall poor health. Likewise, stress could alter immunological functions, thus allowing for the development of cancer. In addition, work-related stress can contribute to an inability to cope with work and to a decrease in job opportunities and prospects.

It can also indirectly cause problems inside and outside the workplace, such as violence; drug, tobacco and alcohol abuse; tension in family relationships; depression and even suicide. These are potentially enormous costs, both in terms of personal loss and economic burdens. Upon considering the above, the need arose to evaluate psychosocial risks in a context of major social, political, economic and technological transformations, all of which have an impact on the workplace. It has been shown that working conditions take a toll on workers' health and that stress is known to be one of the main causes of occupational diseases. Consequently, there is increasing political interest in safeguarding workers' health and well-being (The International Labor Office, 2012; Secretaría del Trabajo y Previsión Social - STPS, 2016; Organización Mundial de la Salud - OMS, 2017). By reflecting on the wide variety of instruments available and taking into account that the identification of psychosocial factors for their evaluation requires a very different analysis from that of traditional assessments, it is not possible to establish one general instrument as either ideal or invalid. Rather, it is necessary to choose an instrument that allows for a precise diagnosis of the real conditions of a specific organization -one that takes into account the particular characteristics of the economic sector to which the organization belongs. Likewise, it is important to ensure that the choice of instrument does not obey any private interests of the organization other than to determine the tool that is the most convenient for each company and always respecting the legal guidelines established in each country.

Juarez (2008) holds that evaluation instruments or methods can be grouped into three categories: a) environment-centered models, which focus on the realities of work in the search for risks or potentially inconvenient conditions; b) individual-centered models that explore workers' traits, characteristics or internal conditions as well as the way in which these can adversely affect their health, well-being or performance; and c) models centered on exploring the effects of individuals' interactions with their context. He concludes that in structuring psychosocial models, one of the universal principles should be the consideration of these three dimensions. In Mexico and Colombia, the development of instruments is more recent. However, in many of the cases it is decided to use instruments created in other countries, although it is not always possible to obtain the evidence that these instruments have psychometric properties. It is important that developing countries have validated instruments, since with societies with different labor characteristics and that must face strong changes at the economic and social level; propitiating the presence of work stress problems (Gómez, 2010). Although this field contains abundant literature reporting results on the effect of work conditions on health (Uribe, 2008, Whaley, Morrison, Payne, Fritschi, & Wall, 2005, Tucker & Rutherford, 2005), there is still a lot to examine to attain clear knowledge on the subject. In this regard, it is important to mention, for example, the studies on work stress, psychological exhaustion, psychosomatic disorders or psychopathological problems and more specific issues such as depression, anxiety, or low back pain, to name a few. In all these cases, evidence has been shown of the relationship between work conditions and these effects.

METHODOLOGY

As shown in Figure 3, the methodology followed in the conduction of this work consists of five stages: a) selection of the database and government pages to be used, b) selection of keywords, c) sorting out of the results, d) final selection and e) selection of the instruments for the evaluation of psychosocial factors.

Selection of Database and Government Pages

Database selection was done by identifying those that showed a greater number of indexed journals and focused mainly on the areas of engineering, social sciences and public health.

Figure 3. Methodology stages

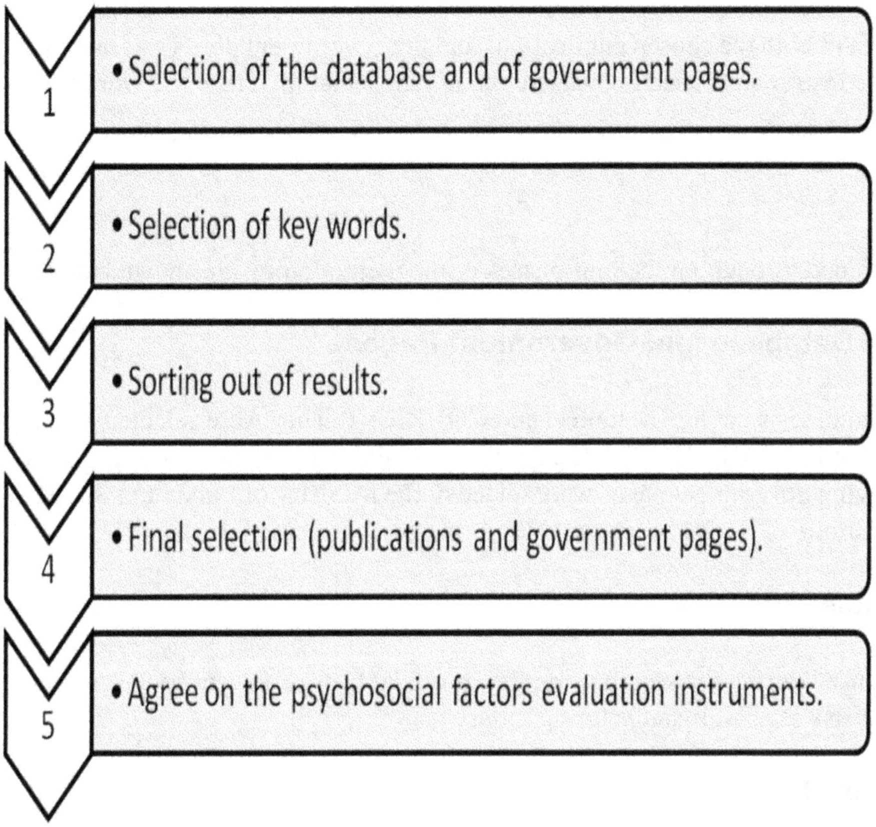

Key Word Selection

Once databases were selected, key words were chosen according to the search characteristics of each one.

Sorting out of Results

After the results of the databases advanced searches were obtained, they were exported and analyzed to then be sorted out. The results were classified according to the following criteria: Psychosocial factors background, psychosocial factors assessment instrument, and application sector (manufacturing, health centers, education, others). Both the publications that did not yield information on these criteria and duplicates were eliminated.

Final Selection

After this first sorting out, the articles centering on the analysis of psychosocial factors from their context and those focusing on analysis within the manufacturing area were preselected. Next, their whole content was analyzed. Those articles showing the entire content and those whose research, application and/or development took place inside the manufacturing companies were identified.

Compilation of the Psychosocial Factors Assessment Instruments

Once the content of both the chosen publications and the government pages was analyzed, a compilation was made of the instruments used to evaluate the psychosocial factors at the workplace.

RESULTS

The results obtained throughout the four phases of the methodology are shown below.

Selection of Database and Government Pages

The selected databases were ScienceDirect and CONRICyT. They were selected because they feature a large number of indexed journals. Besides, they focus mainly on the manufacturing sectors. On the other hand, the following government pages were selected: the Ministry of Labor and Social Welfare (STPS), the Mexican Institute of Social Security (IMSS), and the International Labor Office (OIT).

Key Word Selection

The key words used during the search were: Psychosocial factors, Psychosocial risk factors, Evaluation of psychosocial risk factors, manufacturing industry.

Sorting out of Results

During the first search, a total of 2468 publications was found. In the "firs search" column, Table 3 shows the number of articles obtained per database. The next step consisted of classifying those articles into either literature review or application of a psychosocial factors-evaluation instrument according to the information they contained. Once this classification took place, the number of articles was reduced to 22.

Final Selection

Finally, out of the 22 publications that met the established criteria, only those that could be freely accessed were selected, yielding an end total of 8 articles (see Table 3). Two of the studies described methodologies for psychosocial factors assessment, three consisted of literature review, and 3 addressed the use of a psychosocial assessment instrument at the workplace (see Table 4).

Psychosocial Factors Assessment Instruments and Techniques

The Ministry of Labor and Social Welfare (2018) states that psychosocial factors prevention and control measures, which also foster a favorable organizational environment, should be established at three levels: a) The organizational plane, where the necessary policies and measures to foster a favorable environment are established; b) The group plane, in which workers' interrelations, time of work, sharing of information to worker, and provision of the necessary courses to promote awareness of what the company's goals are fostered; and c) The individual plane, when it is confirmed that there are health alteration symptoms.

Table 3. Number of items found by database

Database	Number of items			
	First search	First selection	Second selection	Final selection
ScienceDirect	2063	20	10	7
CONRICyT	405	2	1	1
TOTAL	2468	22	11	8

Table 4. Classification used for publication selection

Publication types	Amount	References
Methodology to assess psychosocial factors	2	(Toro, Londoño Londoño, Sanin Posada, & Valencia Jáuregui, 2010; Instituto Nacional de Seguridad e Higiene en el Trabajo (INSHT), 2015)
Literature review on psychosocial factors	3	(Moreno Jiménez & Baéz León, 2010; OFICINA INTERNACIONAL DEL TRABAJO GINEBRA, 1984; Herazo, Ospina Serna, & Ramírez Henao, 2013)
Application of psychosocial factors assessment instruments	3	(Luceño Moreno, Martín García, Jáez Díaz, & Díaz Ramiro, 2005; Blanch, Sahagún, & Cervantes, 2010; Vaquero Álvarez, Álvarez Theurer, & Romero Saldaña, 2018)

Because psychosocial risk factors depend mostly on the workers' perception, they need to be evaluated systematically as it has been difficult to prevent them. Several authors hold that such difficulty stems from the methodologies used since risk factors assessment differs from the traditional physical, ergonomic and other types of assessments (Blanch, Sahagún, & Cervantes, 2010; National Institute of Safety and Health at Work -INSHT, 2004; Villalobos, 2005; Tejada & Gómez, 2009). Another difficulty lies in the lack of standardization among some of the questionnaires and diagnostic methods as they do not have psychometrically reliable data (Guardia, Peró, & Barrios, 2008, Ministerio de la Protección Social, 2009).

On the other hand, Guardia, Peró and Barrios (2008) consider that an important cause for the difficulty in addressing psychosocial risk factors is that organizations tend to perform very simple and general systems, focusing on survey application as their only option to address such risks while ignoring other indices such as occupational health and job position evaluation, among others, which could be very useful.

Meliá indicates that any psychosocial risks evaluation instrument must be based on research, an index of reliability, (construct and content) validity tests, an item quality psychometric analysis and standardization processes for the specific application to be done (Ministerio de la Protección Social, 2009). In addition, the instrument confidentiality must be ensured, and the participants must receive guarantee of anonymity and confidentiality through the use of an informed consent. That is why currently, many companies in the search for results that are as close as possible to reality hire an external person to, first, explain what the study consists of and, then, continue with the study, including the analysis of both the surveys and of the afore-mentioned indices.

Furthermore, Rodríguez, González and Carbonen (2007) point out that, even if doing so results in the organization's using more resources (time and money), it is highly important for questionnaires to be adapted to the organization being analyzed as this aspect has an impact on the instrument's reliability.

The most widely used psychosocial factors identification and assessment instruments are listed below. Table 5 shows a compilation of them. The instruments are arranged chronologically and are accompanied by their country of origin, year of creation, aspects they evaluate, and the number of items that make up the instrument.

Table 5. Instruments for the assessment of psychosocial risks at work. Improved from (Charria, Sarsosa, & Arenas, 2011)

Name	Author	Country of origen	Year	Evaluated aspects	Number of items
Psychosocial factors identification guide	Mexican Institute of Social Security (IMSS, 1986)	México	1986	• Task-dependent psychosocial factors. • Work system-related. • Social interaction-dependent . • Organization related.	56
Job Content Questionnaire (JCQ)	Karasek, R.A., Pieper, C. & Schwartz, J (1993).	United States	1985/ 1993	• Psychological demands • Control over one's work • Social support (peer support and supervisor support)	29
Bocanument	Guillermo Bocanument	Colombia	1993	• Work performance-derived psychic and biological alterations • Mental load • Interpersonal relations • Work organization • Staff administración • Job's specific content.	47
Effort Reward Imbalance Questionnaire [ERI]	Siegrist, J. (2000)	Germany	1996	• Effort • Reward • Overcommitment	23
Assessment Method of Psychosocial Factors FPSICO	National Institute of Safety and Health at Work	Spain	1997	• Mental load • Temporary autonomy • Job content • Supervision and participation • Role definition • Concern for the worker • Personal relationships	75
Copenhaguen Psychosocial Questionnaire (CoPsoQ – Istas 21)	Denmark's National Institute of Occupational Health – Adapted for Spain by the Union's Institute for Work Environmnet and Health [ISTAS]	Denmark	2000	• Doble presence • Psychological demands (quantitative, sensorial, cognitive, emotional) • Active work and skill development (influence over work, possibilities for development, control over working time, sense of work, integration in the company) • Leadership and social relationships at the company (predictability, clearity and role conflict, leadership, reinforcement, social support, opportunites for social relationships, group feeling) • Lack of compensations (job insecurity and esteem).	Long version 133 Medium 99 Short 38

continues on following page

Table 5. Continued

Name	Author	Country of origen	Year	Evaluated aspects	Number of items
Psychosocial Factors Assessment Questionnaire	Navarro Institute of Work Health in Spain (2002)	Spain	2002	• Participation, implication and responsibility (autonomy, team work, initiative, control over task, control over employee, staff turnover, supervision, task enrichment) • Formation, information and communication (communications flows, welcoming, person-work adjustment, acknowledgement, training, job description, isolation). • Time management (Work pace, time constraints, work load, temporary autonomy, fatigue). • Group cohesion (Social climate, conflict management, cooperation, work environment).	30
Multidimensional Questionnaire DECORE	Luceño, L., Martín, J., Miguel, J. & Jaén, M. (2005).	Spain	2005	• Cognitive demands (quantitative y qualitative) • Control (command over task, work place, decisions) • Rewards (salary y safety) • Organizational support (relationship with bosses, relationship with peers).	44
MCMutual - UB Battery	University of Barcelona – MC Mutual Corporation	Spain	2005-2006	• Organization of the work time. • Communication • Training and development • Social and group effects • Participation • Job content • Task and work environmnet requirements	46
Survey of work, employment, health and occupational safety conditions of Quebec (EQCOTESST)	National Institute of Public Health of Quebec	Canada. Chilean adaptation.	2008/2010	• Psychological demands • Control • Effort-reward balance • Social support from superiors • Stress Scale • Use of psichotropics • Depression symptoms	
Work Conditions Questionnaire	Blanch, J. Sahagún, M. Cervantes, G. (2010)	Spain	2010	• Organization and method (Regulation and development) • Organization and environment (material environment and social environment) • Organization and Person (organization-person adjustment)	44

continues on following page

Table 5. Continued

Name	Author	Country of origen	Year	Evaluated aspects	Number of items
Battery for Psychosocial Factors Assessment Instruments	Ministry of Social Protection	Colombia	2010	*Intra-labor Conditions* o Work demands (quantitative, mental load, emotional, job responsibility, environmental demands and physical efforts, work day duration, role consistency, influence of work environment over outside of work environment). o Control (work autonomy, opportunities for development and use of skills and abilities, participation y handling of change, role clarity, training) o Leadership and social relations at work (leadership characteristics, social relations at work, feedback on performance, relation with subordinates) o Reward (Acknowledgement and compensation, sense of belonging towards company and work) *Out of work conditions* o Time out of work o Family relationships o Communication and interpersonal relations o Family group's financial situation o Living conditions and environment characteristics o Influence of the out-of-work environment over work o Home-work-home commuting. *Individual Conditions* o Sociodemographic information o Occupational information	Intralaboral forma A 123 Forma B 97 Extralaboral 31
Questionnaires to identify psychosocial risk factors and to assess the organizational environment at work centers.	Ministry of Labor and Social Welfare (STPS, 2018)	México	2018	• Work environment • Activity-inherent factors o Work loads o Control over work • Organization of the working time o Work day duration o Work-family relation • Leadership and work relations at the workplace. o Leadership o Work relations o Work violence • Organizational environment o Acknowledgement of work performance o Sense of belonging and work instability	72

As can be seen, there is a wide variety of instruments, most of which most were developed in Spain. On the other hand, Mexico has two instruments; the first one consists of the Psychosocial Factors Identification Guide, created by the Mexican Institute of Social Security (IMSS) in 1986, and the second one created by the Ministry of Labor and Social Welfare (STPS) in 2018. Moreover, all the questionnaires take into account the task's different demands as well as an assessment of the work relations.

DISCUSSION

The interest in identifying and assessing psychosocial risk factors has increased considerably in recent years, and its purpose has been to achieve a favorable work environment in all productive sectors. When considering the instruments analyzed above, it can be seen that out of the last two, one corresponds to the Battery of psychosocial risk factors assessment instruments, prepared by the Ministry of Social Protection in Colombia. This is one of the few instruments that show evidence of compliance with the necessary psychometric tests to back up the instrument's validity (Albarrán, *et al.,* 2018). The other and more recent questionnaire is the one proposed by the Secretariat of Labor and Social Welfare in Mexico. However, unlike the Colombian battery, this instrument does not yet show evidence of having been administered at the workplace, and therefore, there is no evidence of its validity. It must be highlighted that despite the fact that the work centers in much of northern Mexico belong to the manufacturing sector, at the time when this research was conducted, no evidence was found of studies related to psychosocial factors to which employees were exposed at work, this revealing the scarce amount of existing research on this subject in the manufacturing or industrial sector.

Currently, Mexico is undergoing a process of adaptation. The reason is that on October 23, 2018, through government organizations, Mexican Official Standard NOM-035-STPS-2018 was accepted. Its objective goes beyond identifying and assessing psychosocial risk factors as it aims to foster favorable organizational environments in the workplace, considering aspects such as leadership and work relations, control over work, social support, violence at the workplace and workloads. It is worth mentioning that this norm will be auditable as of October 23, 2019 (Secretaría Del Trabajo y Previsión Social-STPS, 2018).

FURTHER RESEARCH SUGGESTIONS

It is important to recognize that due to the databases constraints, some articles may not have been considered. However, by the date of publication there were no records of administration of the instrument not only in the manufacturing industry, but in any work center. Thus, it is of essence to carry out research on psychosocial factors in any field, but mainly in industry as it is one of the sectors with the highest task demands on workers. Likewise, it would be ideal to conduct studies on the impact of psychosocial risk factors on organizational goal achievement.

As was mentioned in the discussion section, there is no evidence of the suggested questionnaire having been administered by the Secretariat of Labor and Social Welfare at the different work centers, nor of its validation. Therefore, it is important to consider that because the tool is part of an auditable standard whose purpose is to ensure workers' health and welfare, certainty of its validity is paramount.

CONCLUSION

From the information covered in this chapter, it can be concluded that the effects related to psychosocial risk factors are multicausal as they result from the interaction of intra-labor, individual and outside-of-work conditions. Therefore, the interventions carried out should consider the working conditions and provide older people with tools to face the situations that arise, thus fostering a work/non-work life balance. This type of interventions mixing the organizational and the individual level have proven to be the most effective for both companies and people (Organización Mundial de la Salud - OMS, 2017). Furthermore, this chapter analyzes the lack of consideration of the psychosocial factors at the workplace and of the importance of their identification, assessment and prevention in the workplace worldwide. In doing so, it highlights the main psychosocial factors to which workers are exposed as well as some of the instruments used for their identification and assessment. It also shows evidence of the psychosocial risk factors impact both on the health of the worker and on the productivity of the company. According to Moreno and Baéz (2010) the psychosocial risk factors to which workers are exposed greatly influence their health (creating physical and mental issues, substance use and psychosomatic disorders) as well as their performance and attitudes towards the organization (their job satisfaction, involvement, commitment and counterproductive behaviors), causing organizations to show high rates of staff turnover, presenteeism, sick leave, work accidents, and low performance and productivity.

Despite the exhaustive literature review, the number of research articles found was insufficient. Thus, the field of research on psychosocial factors in the manufacturing industry presents an opportunity for researchers to work further in the area. In addition, a precise approach for the identification, measurement and assessment of psychosocial risk factors poses the most important challenge for the implementation of the 035 standard and its consideration in companies wishing to achieve a favorable organizational environment that contributes to workers' health care and welfare since much of life is spent at the workplace. Finally, among the psychosocial risk factors identification and assessment instruments, not only are the tools in Colombia the second most recent, but they also feature validation data, which offers a considerable advantage over the other instruments.

ACKNOWLEDGMENT

We thank Leslie Yaratzed Cedeño Castillo for her outstanding support translating and improving this work.

REFERENCES

Albarrán, V., Geldres, V., Paredes, P., Ramírez, O., Ruiz, F., & Palomino, J. C. (2018). Validación de la batería de instrumentos para la evaluación de factores de riesgo psicosocial. *Horiz Med*, *18*(1), 59–67. doi:10.24265/horizmed.2018.v18n1.09

Belkic, K., Landsbergis, P. A., Schnall, P. L., & Baker, D. (2004). Is job strain a major source of cardiovascular disease risk? *Scandinavian Journal of Work, Environment & Health*, *30*(2), 85–128. doi:10.5271jweh.769 PMID:15127782

Benavides, F., Gimeno, D., Benach, J., Martínez, J. M., Jarque, S., Berra, A., & Devesa, J. (2002). Descripción de los factores de riesgo psicosocial en cuatro empresas. *Gaceta Sanitaria, 16*(3), 222–229. doi:10.1016/S0213-9111(02)71665-8 PMID:12057177

Blanch, J., Sahagún, M., & Cervantes, G. (2010). Estructura factorial del cuestionario de condiciones de trabajo. *Revista de Psicología del Trabajo y de las Organizaciones, 26*(3), 175–189. doi:10.5093/tr2010v26n3a2

Bourbonnais, R., Brisson, C., Vinet, A., Vezina, M., Abdous, B., & Gaudet, M. (2006). Effectiveness of a participative intervention on psychosocial work factors to prevent mental health problems in a hospital setting. *Occup Environ Med, 63*(5), 335-342. Doi:10.1136/oem.2004.018077

Burr, H., Albertsen, K., Rugulies, R., & Hannerz, H. (2010). Do dimensions from the Copenhagen Psychosocial Questionnaire predict vitality and mental health over and above the job strain and effort-reward imbalance models? *Scandinavian Journal of Public Health, 38*, 59-68. DOI: . doi:10.1177/1403494809353436

Charria, V., Sarsosa, K., & Arenas, F. (2011). Factores de riesgo psicosocial laboral; métodos e instrumentos de evaluación. *Rev. Fac. Nac. Salud Pública, 29*(4), 380–391.

Cox, T., & Griffiths, A. J. (1996). The assessment of psychosocial hazards at work. In M.J. Schabracq, J. A. M. Winnubst, & C. L. Cooper (Eds.), Handbook of Work and Health Psychology (pp. 127-146). Academic Press.

Darr, W., & Johns, G. (2008). Work strain, health, and absenteeism: A meta-analysis. *Journal of Occupational Health Psychology, 13*(4), 293–318. doi:10.1037/a0012639 PMID:18837626

Gartner, F. R., Nieuwenhuijsen, K., Van Dijk, F. J., & Sluiter, J. K. (2010). The impact of common mental disorders on the work functioning of nurses and allied health professionals: A systematic review. *International Journal of Nursing Studies, 47*(8), 1047–1061. doi:10.1016/j.ijnurstu.2010.03.013 PMID:20444449

Gómez, V. (2010). Assessment of Psychosocial Stressors at Work: Psychometric Properties of the Spanish Version of the ERI (Effort-Reward Imbalance) Questionnaire in Colombian Workers. *Revista de Psicología del Trabajo y de las Organizaciones, 26*(2), 147–156. doi:10.5093/tr2010v26n2a6

Griffin, J. M., Greiner, B. A., Stansfeld, S. A., & Marmot, M. (2007). The effect of self-reported and observed job conditions on depression and anxiety symptoms: A comparison of theoretical models. *Journal of Occupational Health Psychology, 12*(4), 334–349. doi:10.1037/1076-8998.12.4.334 PMID:17953493

Guardia, J., Peró, M., & Barrios, M. (2008). Propiedades psicométricas de la batería de evaluación de riesgos psicosociales en la medianan y pequeña empresa. *Psicothema, 20*(4), 939–944. PMID:18940107

Güilgüiruca, M., Meza, K., Góngora, R., & Moya, C. (2015). Factores de riesgo psicosocial y estrés percibido en trabajadores de una empresa eléctrica en Chile. *Medicina y Seguridad del Trabajo, 61*(238).

Hausser, J. A., Mojzisch, A., Niesel, M., & Schulz-Hardt, S. (2010). Ten years on: A review of recent research on the job demand-control (-support) model and psychological well-being. *Work and Stress, 24*(1), 1–35. doi:10.1080/02678371003683747

Heponiemi, T., Kouvonen, A., Vanska, J., Halila, H., Sinervo, T., Kivimäki, M., & Elovainio, M. (2009). The Association of distress and sleeping problems with physicians' intentions to change profession: The moderating effect of job control. *Journal of Occupational Health Psychology*, *14*(4), 365–373. doi:10.1037/a0015853 PMID:19839657

Herazo, R. C., Ospina Serna, M., & Ramírez Henao, S. (2013). Factores psicosociales y organizacionales que afectan la productividad. Medellín: Universidad De Medellín: Facultad De Ciencias Econ0micas Y Administrativas Especializaci0n en Gesti0n Del Talento Humano Y La Productividad.

Instituto Nacional de Estadística y Geografía (INEGI). (2017). ENH - Encuesta Nacional de los Hogares. Author.

Instituto Nacional de Seguridad e Higiene en el Trabajo (INSHT). (2015). Algunas orientaciones para evaluar los factores de riesgo psicosocial (edición ampliada 2015). Madrid: Instituto Nacional de Seguridad e Higiene en el Trabajo (INSHT).

Instituto Nacional del Seguridad e Higiene en el Trabajo (INSHT). (2004). *El programa de ayuda al empleado (EAP): Intervención individual en la prevención de los riesgos psicosociales*. Madrid: Instituto Nacional del Seguridad e Higiene en el Trabajo.

Instituto Sindical de Trabajo. Ambiente y Salud (ISTAS). (2010). Manual del método CoPsoQ-istas21 (versi0n 1.5) para la evaluación y prevenci0n de los riesgos psicosociales. Barcelona: Instituto Sindical de Trabajo, Ambiente y Salud.

International Labour Office (ILO). International Programme on Safety and Health at Work and the Environment & International Occupational Safety and Health Information Centre. SafeWork bookshelf. Geneva: ILO.

Juárez, A. (2007). Psychosocial work factors associated to blood pressure and cardiovascular symptoms among Mexican nurses. *Salud Pública Mex*, *49*(2), 109-117.

Juárez, A. (2008). Percepción del control en la salud y bienestar laboral: Desarrollo de un modelo psicosocial. In J. F. Uribe (Ed.), Facultad de Psicología UNAM.

Kalimo, R., El-Batawi, M., & Cooper, C. L. (1988). *Los factores psicosociales en el trabajo y su.* Ginebra: OMS.

Kawakami, N., & Tsutsumi, A. (2010). Job stress and mental health among workers in Asia and the World. *Journal of Occupational Health*, *52*(1), 1–3. doi:10.1539/joh.editorial1001 PMID:20154466

Kinman, G., & Jones, F. (2008). Effort-reward imbalance, over-commitment and work-life conflict: Testing an expanded model. *Journal of Managerial*, *23*(3), 236–251. doi:10.1108/02683940810861365

Kirchhof, A. L., Magnago, T. S., Camponogara, S., Griep, R. H., Tavares, J. P., Prestes, F. C., & Paes, L. G. (2009). Working conditions and social-demographic characteristics related to the presence of minor psychic disorders in nursing workers. *Texto & Contexto Enfermagem*, *18*(2), 215–223. doi:10.1590/S0104-07072009000200003

Kudielka, B. M., Von Kanel, R., Gander, M. L., & Fischer, J. E. (2004). Effort - reward imbalance, overcommitment and sleep in a working population. *Work and Stress*, *18*(2), 167–178. doi:10.1080/02678370410001731785

Laurent, P., Pinte, S., Gerard-Guery, S., Wehrly, S., & Pamart, B. (2009). Use of the mos sf-36 questionnaire for carrying perceived health study among 4476 workers. Study carried out between 2007 and 2008. *Archives des Maladies Professionnelles et de l'Environnement*, *70*(5), 525–538. doi:10.1016/j.admp.2009.03.002

Lehr, D., Hillert, A., & Keller, S. (2009). What can balance the effort? Associations between effort-reward imbalance, overcommitment, and affective disorders in German teachers. *International Journal of Occupational and Environmental Health*, *15*(4), 374–384. doi:10.1179/oeh.2009.15.4.374 PMID:19886348

Luceño Moreno, L., Martín García, J., Jáez Díaz, M., & Díaz Ramiro, E. M. (2005). Evaluación de factores psicosociales en el entorno laboral. *EduPsykhé:Revista de Psicología y Psicopedagogía*, *4*(1), 19–42.

Lupien, S., McEwen, B. S., Gunnar, M. R., & Heim, C. (2009). Effects of stress throughout the lifespan on the brain, behavior and cognition. *Nature Reviews. Neuroscience*, *10*(6), 434–445. doi:10.1038/nrn2639 PMID:19401723

Ministerio de la Protección Social. (2009). *Resolución 2566, Julio 7 del 2009: pro el cual se adopta la Tabla de Enfermedades Profesionales*. Bogotá: El Ministerio.

Minztberg, H. (1993). *Structure in fives: designing effective organizations*. London: Prentice-Hall International.

Moreno Jiménez, B., & Baéz León, C. (2010). *Factores y riesgos psicosociales, formas, consecuencias, medidas y buenas práctica* . Madrid: Universidad Autónoma de MAdrid.

Oficina Internacional del Trabajo. (2012). *Guía del Formador SOLVE: Integrando la promoción de la salud a las políticas de SSt en el lugar de trabajo*. Ginebra: Valentina Forastieri.

Oficina Internacional del Trabajo Ginebra (OIT). (1984). *Factores Psicosociales en el Trabajo: Naturaleza, incidencia y prevención*. Ginebra: Oficina Internacional del Trabajo.

Oficina Internacional del Trabajo (OIT). (1984). *Factores psicosociales en el trabajo: naturaleza, incidencia y prevención*. Ginebra: OIT.

Oficina Internacional del Trabajo (OIT). (1986). *Factores psicosociales en el trabajo: reconocimiento y control*. Ginebra: OIT.

Organización Mundial de la Salud (OMS). (2012). *Informe general por el Día Mundial de la Salud 2012: La buena salud añade vida a los años*. OMS.

Organización Mundial de la Salud (OMS). (2017). *Salud Mental*. Obtenido de https://www.who.int/mental_health/in_the_workplace/es/

Palliser, C. R., Firth, H. M., Feyer, A. M., & Paulin, S. M. (2005). Musculoskeletal discomfort and work-related stress in New Zealand dentists. *Work and Stress*, *19*(4), 351–359. doi:10.1080/02678370500421064

Palmer, S., Cooper, C., & Thomas, K. (2003). *Creating a balance: managing stress.* Londres: British Library.

Rodríguez, I., González, G., & Carbonen, S. (2007). El modelo AMIGO y la metodología PREVENLAB-Psicosocial. Aportaciones y retos en la prevención de los riesgos psicosociales. *Seguridad y Salud en el Trabajo*, *42*, 18–25.

Roozeboom, M. B., Houtman, I., & Van den Bossche, S. (2008). Monitoring Psychosocial Risks at work. In S. Leka & T. Cox (Eds.), The European Framework for psychosocial Risk, (pp. 17-36). Academic Press.

Rugulies, R., Bultmann, U., Aust, B., & Burr, H. (2006). Psychosocial work environment and incidence of severe depressive symptoms: prospective findings from a 5-year follow-up of the Danish work environment cohort study. *J Epidemiol*, *163*(10), 877-887. Doi:10.1093/aje/kwj119

Secretaría del Trabajo y Previsión Social (STPS). (2016). *Proyecto de Norma Oficial Mexicana Proy-Nom-035-Stps-2016.* Factores de Riesgo Psicosocial- Identificación Y Prevención.

Secretaría del Trabajo y Previsión Social (STPS). (2018). *Norma oficial mexicana NOM-035-STPS-2018: Factores de Riesgo Psicosocial en el Trabajo-Identificación, análisis y prevención.* STPS.

Shultz, K. S., Wang, M., Crimmins, E. M., & Fisher, G. G. (2010). Age differences in the demand-control model of work stress an examination of data from 15 european countries. *Journal of Applied Gerontology*, *29*(1), 21–47. doi:10.1177/0733464809334286 PMID:20948986

Siegrist, J. (2008). Effort-reward imbalance and health in a globalized economy. *Scandinavian Journal of Work, Environment & Health*, 163–168.

Silva, A. A., De Souza, J. M., Borges, F. N., & Fischer, F. M. (2010). Health related quality of life and working conditions among nursing providers. *Revista de Saude Publica*, *44*(4), 718–725. doi:10.1590/S0034-89102010000400016 PMID:20676562

Smith, L., Roman, A., Dollard, M. F., Winefield, A. H., & Siegrist, J. (2005). Effort-reward imbalance at work: The effects of work stress on anger and cardiovascular disease symptoms in a community sample. *Stress and Health*, *21*(2), 113–128. doi:10.1002mi.1045

Steptoe, A., & Kivimäki, M. (2012). Stress and cardiovascular disease. *Nat Rev Cardiol.* DOI: . doi:10.1038/nrcardio.2012.45

Tejada, P., & Gómez, V. (2009). Factores psicosociales y laborales asociados al Burnout de psiquiatras en Colombia. *Revista Colombiana de Psiquiatría*, (38), 488–512.

Toro, Á. F., Londoño Londoño, M. E., Sanin Posada, A., & Valencia Jáuregui, M. (2010). Modelo Analítico de Factores Psicosociales en Contextos. *Revista Interamericana de Psicología Ocupacional*, *29*(2), 95–137.

Tucker, P., & Rutherford, C. (2005). Moderators of the relationship between long work hours and health. *Journal of Occupational Health Psychology*, *10*(4), 465–476. doi:10.1037/1076-8998.10.4.465 PMID:16248693

Uribe, J. F. (2008). *Psicología de la Salud Ocupacional en México.* UNAM.

Valverde, M. (2007). Radiografía de los riesgos psicosociales. *Gestión práctica de riesgos laborales: integración y desarrollo de la gestión de la prevención*, *34*, 32-35.

Van Vegchel, N., De Jonge, J., Bosma, H., & Schaufeli, W. (2005). Reviewing the effort-reward imbalance model: Drawing up the balance of 45 empirical studies. *Social Science & Medicine*, *60*(5), 1117–1131. doi:10.1016/j.socscimed.2004.06.043 PMID:15589679

Vaquero Álvarez, M., Álvarez Theurer, E., & Romero Saldaña, M. (2018). Influencia de las condiciones de trabajo sobre la incapacidad temporal por contingencias comunes. *Atencion Primaria*, *50*(4), 238–246. doi:10.1016/j.aprim.2017.03.011 PMID:28623010

Villalobos, G. (2005). *Diseño de un sistema de vigilancia epidemiológica de factores de riesgo psicosocial en el trabajo (Tesis doctoral)*. La Habana: Doctorado en Ciencias de la Salud, Escuela Nacional de Salud Pública.

Wang, J. L., Schmitz, N., Dewa, C., & Stansfeld, S. (2009). Changes in perceived job strain and the risk of major depression: Results from a population-based longitudinal study. *American Journal of Epidemiology*, *169*(9), 1085–1091. doi:10.1093/aje/kwp037 PMID:19318611

Whaley, W. J., Morrison, D. L., Payne, R. L., Fritschi, L., & Wall, T. D. (2005). Chronicity of psychological strain in occupational settings and the accuracy of the General Health Questionnaire. *Journal of Occupational Health Psychology*, *10*(4), 310–319. doi:10.1037/1076-8998.10.4.310 PMID:16248682

Yang, X., Ge, C., Hu, B., Chi, T., & Wang, L. (2009). Relationship between quality of life and occupational stress among teachers. *Public Health*, *123*(11), 750–755. doi:10.1016/j.puhe.2009.09.018 PMID:19883926

Ylipaavalniemi, J., Kivimäki, M., Elovainio, M., Virtanen, M., Keltikangas-Jarvinen, L., & Vahtera, J. (2005). Psychosocial work characteristics and incidence of newly diagnosed depression: A prospective cohort study of three different models. *Social Science & Medicine*, *61*(1), 111–122. doi:10.1016/j.socscimed.2004.11.038 PMID:15847966

KEY TERMS AND DEFINITIONS

Favorable Organizational Environment: It is the one in which workers have a sense of belonging to the organization. Among other aspects, it features an adequate method for the performance of tasks, clear responsibilities, and proactive participation of workers, in accordance with the Federal Labor Law, as well as performance evaluation and recognition.

Ministry of Labor and Social Welfare (STPS): The Ministry of Labor and Social Welfare, as a Federal agency, is in charge of the performance of the powers attributed to it by the Organic Law of the Federal Public Administration, the Federal Labor Law, and other laws and treaties, as well as regulations, decrees, agreements and orders of the President of the country.

NOM-035-STPS-2018: It is a norm that came into force in October 2018, aiming to outline the elements by which to identify and prevent psychosocial factors and promote a favorable organizational environment in the workplace.

PRONABET: It is a public policy focused on creating a new occupational health culture in Mexico by promoting emotional care at work and the prevention of psychosocial risk factors that affect workers' welfare.

Psychosocial Risk Factors: These are organizational conditions that are likely to adversely affect the physical and psychological health of the worker.

Psychosocial Risks: They are those conditions inherent in the workplace, which relate to 1) work organization and its social environment, 2) work content and task performance, and which have the capacity to affect the workers' performance and health (physical, mental or social).

Social Support: These are actions to improve social relations in the workplace, in which the mutual support for the solution of work problems among the workers themselves is promoted.

Work Loads: They refer to the work demands imposed on workers, exceeding their capacity. They can be of different types such as quantitative, mental, emotional, and responsibility-related, among others.

Chapter 3
Relationships Between Mental Workload, Burnout, and Job Performance:
A Research Among Academicians

Meltem Akca
https://orcid.org/0000-0001-5544-5929
Alanya Alaaddin Keykubat University, Turkey

Mübeyyen Tepe Küçükoğlu
https://orcid.org/0000-0002-3717-4165
Trakya University, Turkey

ABSTRACT

Mental workload is a popular topic for ergonomics, psychology, and organizational behavior-related studies. Difficulties and differences in defining and measurement of mental workload engage the attention of scholars to the concept. Furthermore, the importance of mental workload on performance and burn out increases attention to the topic for empirical studies. In this chapter, the authors reveal the relations between mental workload, burnout, and job performance. Data were obtained from 144 academicians in Turkey. Results demonstrated that mental workload has a 1) positive impact on burn out and 2) negative impact on job performance of academicians. Moreover, it was found that burn out and job performance are negatively correlated. Finally, findings reported that there are differences among some demographic variables in accordance with mental workload, burn out, and job performance.

INTRODUCTION

At the present time, the business work environment is becoming more volatile and competitive. The development of information technologies, rapid changes in organizational structures, changeable customer attitudes are more important for today's organizations. These features of the marketplace direct organi-

DOI: 10.4018/978-1-7998-1052-0.ch003

zations to be in search of new methods to achieve and maintain sustainable performance. Leadership, employee's favorable work behaviors, technological investments are some of the interesting methods to provide continuity of the organization's existence. Moreover, today's work atmosphere is shaped with several elements of organizational behavior. These elements such as job satisfaction, organizational culture, organizational commitment, empowerment, organizational trust etc. have strong or weak relationships with each other. Furthermore, according to the results of studies in the literature these elements have positive effects on job performance or organizational performance (Akyol, 2014; Campbell et al., 1990; Kirkman & Rosen, 1999; Robbins & Judge, 2011; Spector, 1997; Viswesvaran & Ones, 2000). On the other hand, there exist some elements such as high mental workload, job stress or burnout that result with negative impact on organizational outcomes as productivity loss, reduced performance or lower organizational commitment.

In the last four decades, assessment of the mental workload also takes place in academic studies related with organizational behavior, occupational psychology and ergonomics (Wickens, 2017). Moreover, workload is considered as a major determinant for physical and psychological symptoms (stress, anxiety, sleep problems) occurrence in human's life that catches the scholars' attention to the concept.

In the literature, most part of the workload related empirical studies have been implemented in aviation, transportation, automation related samples (Demerouti et al., 2019; Keser & Yılmaz, 2014; Lee et al., 2015). In this study it is aimed to analyze high-education employees' mental workload, burnout and performance relations to fill the gap about academicians related studies based on mental workload.

It is well known that being an academician needs to show cognitive effort and attention in the work environment (Borghini et al, 2014). Academicians have a multitasking work structure. In addition to teaching courses in their professional areas, they have the duty of conducting academic researches and making the result of these researches useful publications. They also take on administrative duties in various positions in university. For research purposes academicians need to make long hours of search and reading. Moreover, they have to maintain a balance not only between all tasks but also work and life. Therefore, an academician's mental workload issue and circumstances of this subject are worth to investigate. For this reason, in this book chapter it is targeted to measure mental workload level of academicians. It is also aimed to investigate the differences of mental workload, burn out and performance accordance to the demographic groups. In the first part, workload, burnout and job performance were identified detailed. Moreover, studies in the literature related to these variables were summarized. In addition to these, academicians related studies were also evaluated reference to the literature. Then, research model, hypothesis and aims of the study were mentioned. Finally, findings were discussed with the perspective of similar results in the literature.

BACKGROUND

Mental Workload

Mental workload concept goes back to the Cognitive Load Theory (Sweller, Merrienboer &Paas, 1998) that deals with the relations between human mind and its limitations (Wickens, 2008). Accordance to the theory, if human is overloaded or low loaded, learning new things or performing tasks are influenced negatively (Longo, 2018). In this context, Hart (2006) identified mental workload as the adaptation and interaction between work requirements and employee's perception, talents, abilities and emotions. For this reason, if two person perform the same tasks but the outputs are different, mental workload may be evaluated one of the reason of performance deficit (Vidulich & Tsang,2012). On the other side, amount of the information while performing a task is also related to mental workload. Furthermore, information memory capabilities may influence the balance between task demands and cognitive resources (Parasuraman, Sheridan & Wickens, 2008). Comparably, O'Donnel and Eggemeier (1986) stated that mental workload is a portion of employee's limited mental capacity which is required for balancing tasks' supply and demand. Colle and Reid (1999) also defined that mental workload is considered as the average level of mental work. Otherwise, when job demand is covered with time pressure and task complexity, perception of the workload increases (Young et al, 2015). In a such case, mental workload related strains like stress generally impact human behaviors (Schlegel, 1993).

In literature, Spector (1997) classified workload in two general aspects as: qualitative workload and quantitative workload. Qualitative workload is related with difficulty of tasks in physical and mental perspective. Qualitative workload related time pressure, precipitance and multi tasks cause stress and burnout that impact human's life negatively (Schmoldt et al,1994). Otherwise, quantitative workload also defines as the amount of completed tasks by employees (Che et al,2017). On the other hand, Vidulich and Tsang (2012) expressed that mental workload is comprised of exogenous task demands and endogenous supplies of resources. Task priority, task difficulty, situational contingencies are classified under exogenous task demands while updating, perceiving memory, decision making, planning and processing is related with endogenous factors (Vidulich&Tsang, 2012). Moreover, workload is evaluated as a cumulative result of different demands for the job. Therefore, it is hard to identify it shortly (Cain, 2007). In addition to these explanations, mental workload is connected with three main dimensions as: characteristics of the tasks, employee's skills and abilities and environmental features of the workplace and the organization (Young et al., 2015). Cognitive demands for doing tasks also trigger mental workload perception of employees. In this context, mental workload is considered with the complexity of the tasks that are required to perform for daily activities (Young et al., 2015). Furthermore, Vidulich and Tsang (2012) described workload as an interaction between employee's capacity and task requirements. Deviations between structure of the required tasks and human's capabilities affect the occurrence of the workload. In such a case, if there is not a balance between task demands and employee capacity, mental workload comes to exist.

Finally, Longo (2018) defined that cognitive load is generally preferred to measure human's mental workload. Besides, mental workload assessment is important in today's human-machine interacted work environment to provide effectiveness. (Ortiz-Solis et al,2018). For this reason, human factor is an important issue for the betterment of work's sustainability (Soto et al, 2016). In this context, mental workload needs to be evaluated in some periods to prevent unexpected job outcomes for minimizing risk factors. Longo (2018) also stated that mental workload can be measured in three types as: self-assessment measures (subjective ratings-self reports), task performance measures and physiological measures. It is often uses self-report measures to assess perception about workload of employees. Moreover, Longo (2018) pointed out that subjective measures are easy to obtain and analyze data's for evaluating mental workload. For these reasons, in this chapter it was also used subjective ratings to measure mental workload.

Understanding the Burnout

Burnout is one of the most important concept of employee perception related studies. Burnout was firstly mentioned in organizational behavior literature by Freudenberger (1974) and Maslach (1976). According to the scholars, main characteristics of burnout are listed as an overwhelming exhaustion; feelings of frustration, anger, and cynicism; and a sense of ineffectiveness and failure (Maslach & Goldberg, 1998). Besides, burnout is generally defined as a state of physical, emotional and mental exhaustion that contains loss of energy, idealism, perspective and purpose, and causes constant stress, hopelessness, helplessness and trapped situation (Pines & Aronson, 1988).

Maslach and Jackson (1981) explained the burnout syndrome in three stages as; emotional exhaustion, depersonalization and reduced personal accomplishment. First one is defined as increased feelings of emotional exhaustion such as emotional resources of person are depleted. Sometimes, work overload or personal conflicts at work may cause such results. This component is basic stress dimension of burnout. Then, negative and cynical attitudes and feelings are developed to other people in contact. This situation is also called interpersonal dimension of burnout and often includes loss of idealism. Last aspect is feeling unhappy and dissatisfied about the job accomplishments and contains inability to cope with demands of job. This situation represents the self-evaluation dimension of burnout (Maslach & Goldberg, 1998). In summary, the principal dimensions of job burnout are listed as: stress component (emotional exhaustion), interpersonal relations (depersonalization), and self-evaluation (personal accomplishment) (Kim, Shin, & Umbreit, 2007).

According to Demerouti and colleagues (2002) burnout may be found in any occupational context and seen both within and outside the human services. Early theories of burnout focused mainly on work-related factors; however recent researchers explain that environmental and individual factors also have an effect on burn out syndrome (Çiçek Sağlam, 2011; Demerouti et al., 2019; Gezer et al., 2009; Kim et al., 2007; Maslach&Goldberg, 1998).

Burnout often occurs as a consequence of a complicated interaction between individual characteristics and factors in the work environment (Kokkinos, 2007). Some existing studies reveal out that causes of burnout with a focus on the work environment implying role stressors, organizational structures, and job characteristics (Kim et al., 2007). It also seems important to take into account individual characteristics in analyzing the relationships between burnout and job performance (Lazaro, Shinn, & Robinson, 1984). In other words, what is stressful for one may not be stressful for another (Kim et al., 2007).

Burnout syndrome has different outcomes than short-term effects of strain. Mainly, burnout develops after repeated, prolonged and unsuccessful confrontations of undesirable working conditions (Demerouti vd., 2002). According to Karabay, Tezergil and Köse (2014) initiators of burnout syndrome among people are mainly work related stress factors. These factors trigger the existence of burnout situations at work and then create damaging circumstances. Besides, burn out related these factors also influence performance of employees at work and result with low productivity.

Job Performance

Performance is considered as a concept that is fulfilled in the direction of completing the task and accomplishing the purpose in a way to meet the pre-determined criteria within the framework of the task (Pugh, 1991). Employee's job performance is generally defined as an effort of individual that serves for organizational performance (Akyol, 2014). According to Campbell and colleagues (1990), efforts contribute organizational goals through the appraisal of an employee's performance on job-related attitudes and outcomes in comparison with her/his colleagues. In today's business environment, organizations need highly performing employees: i) to achieve their goals ii) to sustain daily activities, iii) to have a competitive advantage (Sonnentag & Frese, 2002). In this context, job performance is evaluated as a key factor for researchers as well as for organizations, managers and employees. In order for organizations to get their corporate goals and gain competitive advantage (Soto et al, 2018) in the industry they are in, they need high performance employees (Realyvásquez et al,2015). High business performance is also important for employees as well as for organizations. Completing their duties as required and show high success in their work, as a source of pride, skill and satisfaction for employees; is the basic condition of many work results that are important for individuals such as job performance, higher income, better career and social reputation (Sonnentag & Frese, 2002).

In competitive working environment, individuals have a big portion in the success of organizations. In some cases, if employees succeed in achieving success through effective and efficient work, rewarding them may be necessary to ensure continuity of performance. On the other hand, it is important to motivate employees who do not have the same performance as their colleagues (Erdoğan, 2011).

According to Borman and Motowidlo (1993), there are two main components of business performance which are called as task performance and contextual performance. The task performance deals with the main technical processes or on going activities in a company. For example; production operations, delivery operations of finished goods, material supplying, and relationships with subordinates or service operations. On the other side, contextual performance includes behaviors that develop and contribute organizational culture and climate which affect employees who carry out daily activities in company. It includes trust building, calming hostility and conflict situations (Bang & Reio, 2017).

Shortly, performance is a concept about achieving tasks and responsibilities that contribute to the manufacture or service production or management duties. As a multidimensional concept, employee performance includes both accomplishment of task and positive organizational citizenship behavior that contains avoiding counterproductive behaviors for a good performance outcome (Robbins & Judge, 2011; Viswesvaran & Ones, 2000).

In addition to the upper explanations, job performance is considered as one of the most important organizational outcome incorporated with burnout concept (Brandes et al., 2008; Wright & Cropanzano, 1998). In literature, there are some researches which investigate the impact of burnout on performance. Actually, results of burnout have serious impacts on organizational performance. Reference to the literature, burnout causes higher turnover and absenteeism, diminished organizational commitment, health problems, poor quality etc (Gandi et al., 2011; Kar&Suar, 2014; Keratepe&Uludağ, 2008; Lazaro et al., 1984; Liu&Lo, 2018). Some job characteristics also trigger burnout syndrome such as workload, time pressure, lack of support and control, autonomy (Keser & Yılmaz, 2014). Wright and Bonett (1997) also found that emotional exhaustion leads to subsequent poor performance. According to Maslach and Jackson (1981), as a consequence of burnout syndrome, a person feels himself unhappy and unsatisfied due to the his/her job accomplishment.

Studies About Mental Workload, Burnout and Job Performance

Mental workload get attention for being a significant occupational risk factor in the workplace that leads to loss of performance, productivity, welfare and well-being (Keser&Yılmaz, 2014; Liu&Lo, 2018). Moreover, high workload negatively impacts job satisfaction that causes burnout, health problems and intention to quit (Rubio-Valdehita et al,2017). Hancock and Caird (1993) also emphasized that mental workload is an indicator of job performance. However, he noticed that performance failure also may rises up the perception of the workload. On the other side, it was expressed that mental workload is connected with mental fatigue (Demerouti et al., 2002). Overload and fatigue speed up to make errors and failures in the job (Brookhuis & de Waar, 2010). Moreover, it is often believed that when mental workload increases, control variability and errors pick up but individual performance tends to decrease (Huey and Wickens, 1993). Especially, when time pressure merges with capacity problems, variations in the performance enhances (Wickens, 2017). All in all, when mental workload is one of the important elements of employee performance.

Studies About Burnout, Personal Characteristics and Job Performance

In recent years, researchers pay attention to antecedents and consequences of burnout syndrome. Numerous studies have been made during the past decades. Regarding burnout there are studies focused on different populations such as doctors (Turgut et al., 2016), nurses (Gandi et al., 2011) and other health staff (Portoghese et al., 2014; Yıldırım & İçerli, 2010), hotel staff (Keratepe & Uludag, 2008; Kim vd., 2007), insurance company employees (Schaufeli & Bakker, 2004), call-center employees (Keser & Yılmaz, 2014), teachers (Çapri, 2006; İnce & Şahin, 2015; Kokkinos, 2007) academicians (Ardıç, 2008; Çavuş, Gök, & Kurtay, 2007; Gezer, Yenel, & Şahan, 2009; Toker, 2011) and students (Schaufeli et al.; Tümkaya, Çam, & Çavuşoğlu, 2009).

In early studies, Lazaro and colleagues (1984), investigated the relationship of burnout and job performance. Moreover, scholars also worked on individual characteristics in a sample of child care workers in residential programs for youths. According to the findings, burnout was associated with job performance; however individual characteristics were unrelated to most of the indicators of burnout and job performance. Keratepe and Uludağ (2008) also analysed the effect of burnout on job performance. Results showed that only reduced personal accomplishment has a significant negative effect on job performance.

Kokkinos (2007), analyzed the relationships between burnout, personality characteristics and job stressors in primary school teachers and revealed out that relative contribution of these variables on the three dimensions of burnout – emotional exhaustion, depersonalization and reduced personal accomplishment. Furthermore, Turgut and colleagues (2016) searched for correlation between burnout and years of residency among residents. Scholars reported that burnout syndrome is a common problem during residency period and there are significant relationships between some dimensions of burnout and years of residency.

Lee, An and Noh (2015) made a research among 230 flight attendants of a global airline company in South Korea. Scholars aimed to find out the impacts of emotional display rules on the emotional labor strategies, burnout and work performance. They suggested important outcomes to improve performance and reduce burnout. Another study was performed with airline pilots to investigate work characteristics and outcomes which are related to burnout of this occupation. First of all, scholars pointed out that high amount of pilots (%40) were suffering from burnout syndrome that effects negatively pilots' happiness with life. Scholars also highlighted the significance of psychosocial factors in the existence of the burnout syndrome (Demerouti, Veldhuis, Coombes, & Hunter, 2019).

Furthermore, Mo and Shi (2017) performed a research in a pharmaceutical retail chain company. Their study was consisted of 45 team leaders and 247 employees to measure the impact of ethical leadership on employee burnout, deviant behavior and task performance. As a result, researchers found significantly positive relationships between ethical leadership and employee burnout, deviant behavior and task performance. Moreover, Virgolino, Coelho and Ribeiro (2017) analyzed the impact of burnout syndrome on the employee's individual performance with using survey method to obtain data from 407 employees.

Interestingly, the first two dimensions of burnout as emotional exhaustion and depersonalization on individual performance were not significant. On the other hand, there was a negative relationship between the reduced personal accomplishment and individual performance. Findings of the study indicated that when reduced personal accomplishment increases, individual performance also decreases.

Nevertheless, burnout and performance relationship with career path gap was investigated in another study with the participation of 210 employees from four different technology companies. According to results, burnout level was the lowest degree when employee experiences career path fit. However, performance level was also the lowest degree among employees who were currently on the technical career path but would prefer the managerial path (Biron & Eshed, 2017).

Studies Among Academicians and Students Regarding Academic Burnout

In literature, there are plenty of researches from different populations regarding burnout syndrome. Different sectors with various reasons create stress, emotional fluctuations and depression on employees. Therefore, researchers aim to introduce burnout concept and its relationship with other organizational behavior elements or company specific outcomes from different point of view. One of these areas is academic population. There are many papers discussing burnout of academicians as calling the subjects as "academic burnout". On the other hand, "academic burnout" is searched among students ranging from college to postgraduate degree. This section refers to some of mentioned studies.

Academicians have multi-tasks in the workplace that sometimes lead to workload. Course preparation, article writing, consultation of students, international coordination about cooperation, committee tasks, teaching, administrative duties, invigilation are some of academicians' daily works in the workplace (Mustapha, 2013; Porter &Umbach,2000). Rahayu and colleagues (2012) also pointed out that lecturers' tasks are comprised of education, teaching, consultation, mentoring and academic working. For this reason, it was emphasized that mental intensity and workload is generally observed because of the job's nature. In addition to these duties, in some countries as Turkey, period of courses for one lecturer is on the average of standard values. As a result when course period increases load of academician tends to pick up. Moreover, student number for one academician is also high in Turkey. Consultancy duties have also major role on overloading of academicians. And finally, administrative jobs related faculties impact academicians workload. Lack of administrative staff play a significant role in this situation. There is a common problem in Turkey about employment policies and appointments in administrative staff. For this reason, it is assumed that mental workload of academicians in Turkey is high. In this context, in this study it is focused on academicians and mental workload related literature is summarized below.

Ardıç (2008), aimed i) to determine burnout levels of academic staff at Gaziosmanpaşa University in Turkey and ii) to reveal out the relationship between burnout levels and some variables. In the study with the participation of 202 academicians, some personal characteristics and their impact on burnout were analyzed. Moreover, in the light of the data obtained from the research, it was tried to offer solution suggestions to prevent burnout of academic staff. Iraz and Ganiyusufoğlu (2011) also conducted a study with 151 academicians to examine perceptions of burnout sub-dimensions in terms of gender, age, marital status, seniority and title. Similar studies were performed to determine whether burnout levels of academic staff differ according to some socio-demographic variables (Budak & Sürgevil, 2005; Çiçek Sağlam, 2011; Gezer et al., 2009; Toker, 2011). Interestingly, emotional exhaustion score of the teaching staff varied significantly by geographic region. On the other hand, personal achievement scores differed significantly in terms of age, administrative task, academic level and geographical region. There was no significant difference between the depersonalization scores and the personal and professional characteristics of the lecturers (Gezer et al., 2009). The results showed that research assistants had higher scores on emotional exhaustion than professors. Besides, research assistants had higher levels of desensitization than associate professors and lower personal performance scores than other academicians. However, marital status and age of demographic variables had a significant relationship with occupational burnout, gender did not have a significant relationship with burnout (Toker, 2011).

Naktiyok and Kaygın (2012) investigated the relationships between workaholism and physical, mental and emotional exhaustion. The findings showed that the rise in the level of occupational activity also increases mental, physical and emotional exhaustion. Researchers also performed another study to determine the levels of burnout and job satisfaction of academic staff. They found negative relationship between burnout and job satisfaction (Naktiyok & Kaygın, 2012). In another study, the burnout levels of the academic staff working in the vocational schools were examined according to some variables by Çavuş and colleagues (2007). Emotional exhaustion and depersonalization scores of the academic staff were low and the personal success score was high. Reference to the results of the study, significant relationships were found between emotional exhaustion and some organizational behavior elements as; administrative task, total course load, job satisfaction and between personal achievement and satisfaction from work. Furthermore, burnout and performance relationship was examined with master students as naming the concepts academic burnout and academic performance. Data from 361 students were analyzed and researchers found significant and negative relationships of emotional exhaustion and depersonalization with student's academic performance. Reference to the findings, when burnout of students increases then learning and performance degree tends to decrease (Rana, 2016). Similar studies realized among students by scholars (Kutsal & Bilge, 2012; Nikodijević, Labrović, & Đoković, 2012; Rostami, et al., 2013). Scholars pointed out that high expectations from students cause stress and burnout and resulted with less concentration, decreased attention and low grade levels.

METHODOLOGY

Gopher and Donchin (1986) noticed that there is not a unique and universal method for measurement of workload. Wierwille and Casali (1983) also explained that if workload is not able to measure easily, it should be focused on its impact on individual's behaviors and psychological strains. Therefore, evaluation of mental workload of academicians is preferred to measure with individual outcomes.

Reference to the summarized studies in the first part, research model and methodology designed in detail to find out the relationship between mental workload, burnout and job performance of academicians. Shortly, in this book chapter it is aimed to explain these relationships between variables. For this purpose, research model of study is shown below in Figure 1.

The sample of this study is comprised of academicians in Turkey, city of Edirne. Respondents of sample comes exist from Trakya University's academicians. Trakya University was established as a state university in the northwest of Turkey and has a growing profile as a regional leader in the Balkans in higher education, research and technology. It has a multitasking structure with different disciplines and there are 12 faculties, 5 institutes, 6 collages and 10 vocational schools, 30 research and application centers. There exist almost 1700 academicians from various branches. Therefore, Trakya University offers an opportunity with its academic staff diversification in order to research about mental workload, burnout and job performance. It was also preferred to use convenience sampling method for the study

Figure 1. Research model

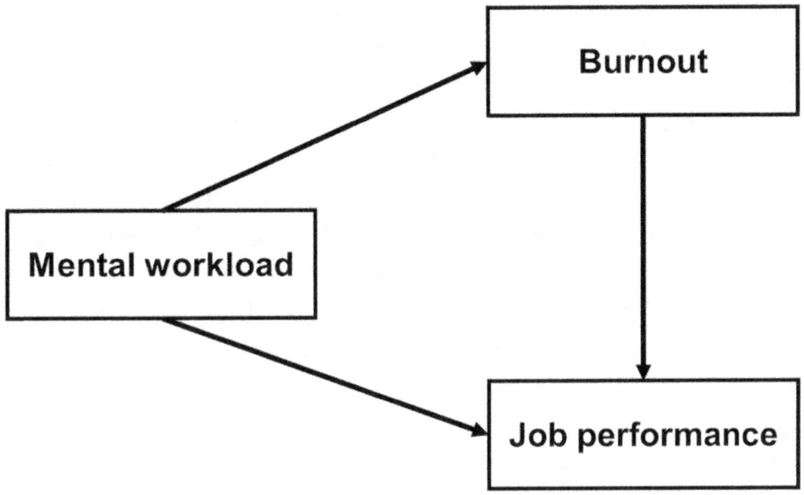

and the questionnaires sent to public university academician. Ease of distribution and collection of questionnaires, cost and schedule advantage impact to choose of this public university for the empirical study. Population of this research becomes from academicians who are research assistant, lecturer and faculty members, which are assistant professor, associated professor or professor. Academician numbers were obtained from university web-site and activity report. It was stated that there was 1804 academician in the university by May 2019. According to the sample size formulation (Mendenhall, Sincich& Boundreau, 1996) with error margin 0.10 it was calculated that 96 questionnaires is suitable for the study. Error margin preferred as 0.10 due to the academicians sometimes may not intended to participate about work related studies. Because they have some hesitations that questionnaire answers may be analyzed by managers. 250 questionnaires distributed to the faculties in line with the ratio of academicians in each department. Finally, it was obtained 144 valid questionnaires to use in statistical analyses.

Survey items for each variable derived from literature. In this book chapter, it was used CarMen-Q Questionaire (Rubio-Valdehita et al., 2017) to measure perception of mental workload cognitive demands with 10 items. Moreover, Maslach Burnout Scale (Maslach & Jackson, 1981) was preferred to measure emotional exhaustion with 9 items. Finally, Employee Performance Scale (Kirkman & Rosen, 1999) was used to assess job performance with 7 items. All items within the survey were scored on a 5-point Likert scale with an agree/disagree continuum (1= strongly disagree, 2= disagree, 3= neither agree nor disagree, 4= agree, 5= strongly agree). Survey also had some demographical items such as gender, age, job experience and academic position of respondents.

Reference to the literature and research model hypotheses of this study are listed below as;

H1: Mental workload (cognitive demands) has a significant impact on burnout (emotional exhaustion).
H2: Mental workload (cognitive demands) has a significant impact on job performance.
H3: Burnout (emotional exhaustion) has a significant impact on job performance.

Data gathered from 144 academicians were analyzed with IBM SPSS 21.00 Statistical Program. First part of survey includes some descriptive information of respondents. According to the descriptive analyses, information about respondents is shown in Table 1 below.

Second, third and fourth parts of survey have mental workload, burnout and job performance items respectively. For each variable, validity and reliability analyses were made. Moreover, construct validity of scales was tested with Factor Analyses. Findings reported that all scales have good Kaiser-Meyer-Olkin and Bartlett values that show sample size is suitable and statistically significant for Factor Analyses. Thereby, mental workload scale explained %64.842 of total variance. No items were deleted and in total 10 items presented the scale. Cronbach's alpha value of scale was 0.937. Burnout scale also explained %65.99 of total variance with 9 items in total. According to reliability analysis Cronbach's alpha value was found as 0.930. Job performance scale explained %76.295 of total variance with 7 items. Cronbach's alpha value was obtained as 0.746 of this scale.

When the average values of each variable in the research model were examined, the average value of the mental workload variable was obtained as 4.1444. In addition to this, the average value of the burnout variable was calculated as 2.4630 and the average value of the job performance variable was achieved as 3.9325. Reference to the findings, it is observed that academicians' mental workload and job performance values are around 4.00 and burnout level is under the average value of 3.00.

In the next step, the relationships between variables were examined. The relationships between variables in the study were investigated by Pearson Correlation Analyses. Findings showed that there is a

Table 1. Descriptive information

Descriptive information	Frequency	Percent (%)
Gender		
Female	64	44,4
Male	80	55,6
Age		
26-35	62	43,1
36-45	52	36,1
>45	30	20,8
Total job experience		
<3 years	8	5,6
3-5 years	12	8,3
6-8 years	28	19,4
9-11 years	30	20,8
>11 years	66	45,8
Current workplace experience		
<3 years	36	25
3-5 years	28	19,4
6-8 years	32	22,2
9-11 years	18	12,5
>11 years	30	20,8
Academic rank		
Research assistant	20	13,9
Lecturer	30	20,8
Assistant professor	42	29,2
Associated professor	16	11,1
Professor	10	6,9
No answer	26	18,1

Table 2. Results of Pearson correlation analysis

	Mental workload	Burnout	Job performance
Mental workload	1	0,242**	-0,195*
Burnout		1	-0,381**
Job performance			1

**Correlation is significant at the 0,01 level (2-tailed)
*Correlation is significant at the 0,05 level (2-tailed)

poor and positive correlation between mental workload and burnout while there is a poor and negative correlation between mental workload and job performance. On the other hand, there is a medium-level and negative correlation between burnout and job performance. It is important to note that all correlation values were statistically significant.

In order to test first hypothesis "Mental workload (cognitive demands) has a significant impact on burnout (emotional exhaustion)" regression analysis was performed. According to the results of regression analysis, the effect of mental workload on burnout was found statistically significant. ($p = 0{,}003 < 0{,}05$). Moreover, it was obtained that just % 5.2 of the change in burnout levels of academicians was explained by mental workload. Moreover, positive impact coefficient was similar with correlation coefficient (Beta) as 0.242. In accordance with the findings, H_1 hypothesis was accepted.

Reference to the regression analysis to test the second hypothesis, the effect of mental workload on job performance was found statistically significant ($p=0{,}019<0{,}05$). Accordingly, the hypothesis "Mental workload (cognitive demands) has a significant impact on job performance" was accepted. Moreover, negative impact coefficient is similar with correlation coefficient (Beta) as -0.195.

According to regression analysis that performed for the third hypothesis "Burnout (emotional exhaustion) has a significant impact on job performance" and burnout explained %13.9 of the change in job performance level ($p=0{,}000<0{,}005$). Besides, negative impact coefficient was similar with correlation coefficient (Beta) as – 0,381. By this, H_3 hypothesis was also accepted.

It was also used Independent T-Tests and One Way Analysis of Variance Tests (Anova) to find out any difference on research variables for gender, age, academic rank, total job experience and current job experience. According to the findings, there was no significant difference for gender on mental workload, burnout and job performance variable. Secondly, Anova analysis for age groups of academicians was made. There was also no significant difference for age groups on research variables. Third control variable was the academic rank of respondents for difference analysis. Academic rank referred to the academic degree of university staff and includes research assistant, lecturer, assistant professor, associated professor and professor ($p<0{,}05$). For burnout, there was difference between associate professor and professor and burnout level of professor was more than associate professor (Burnout; Aveasso. prof.=2,0833, Aveprof.=3,1556). Also for job performance it was found several statistically significant differences ($p<0{,}05$). There was difference between assistant professor and other groups and the average value of assistant professor was more than other groups (JobPerformance; Aveasst.prof.=4,1905, Averes.ast.=3,6714, Aveprof.=3,3714). Furthermore, current workplace experience was also asked to the respondents. For this control variable there was no statistically significant difference for both mental workload and burnout ($p>0{,}05$), on the other hand, for job performance there was difference between <3 years with 3-5 years and 6-8 years' groups; between >11 years' group with 3-5 years and 6-8 years' groups (p<0,05). Average values of <3 years and >11 years' groups were less than mentioned groups (JobPerformance.; Ave<3=3,6746, Ave3-5=4,2653, Ave6-8= 4,0982, Ave>11=3,6476).

Another and last control variable was the total job experience of academicians. For mental workload variable there was significant difference between <3 years and the other groups (3-5 years, 6-8 years, 9-11 years and >11 years groups; p<0,05). Average value of <3 years group was found less than the other groups (MentalWL.; Ave<3=2,6750, Ave3-5=3,9667, Ave6-8=4,0573, Ave9-11=4,3133, Ave>11=4,3152). For burnout, <3 years' group had significant difference with other groups (3-5 years, 6-8 years' groups; p<0,05) and average value of <3 years' group was less than these groups (Burnout; Ave<3=1,4444, Ave3-5=3,0370, Ave6-8=3,0238). Also difference was found between 6-8 years and >11 years' group (p<0,05; (Burnout; Ave6-8=3,0238, Ave>11=2,2727). Lastly, for job performance there were differences between groups of <3 years and the other groups (9-11 years and >11 years' groups; p<0,05). Average value of <3 tears group is less than other two groups (Job Perf.; Ave<3=3,2143, Ave9-11=4,1429, Ave>11=3,9870).

FUTURE RESEARCH DIRECTIONS

In this chapter, it was aimed to demonstrate the relationships between perceived mental workload and i) burn out and ii) job performance. Moreover, it was tested the relationship between burnout and job performance. It was also mentioned about differences among demographic variables accordance with mental workload, burnout and job performance. In future researches, it is advised to use other sampling methods and comprehensive sample size. Besides, in coming studies testing relations with stepwise regression analysis will explain better results.

As this study was performed among academicians, in order to generalize results of this study for the other organizations, same study should be made in the future as including respondents from different industries. Moreover, it will be beneficial to repeat this research for other organizational behavior subjects.

Limitations

Selection of only one university is one of the main limitation of this study. Besides, convenience sampling method may be sometimes considered as a limitation. Sample size is also required to rise up in next studies.

Practical Implications

According to findings, it was revealed out that mental workload has a positive and significant impact on burnout (β=0,242) while has negative and significant impact on job performance (β= -0,195). Furthermore, it was found that burnout also affect job performance negatively (β= -0,381). Results demonstrate that H_1, H_2 and H_3 were accepted.

Moreover, it was deduced that there is not a significant differences between age and gender groups in the basic workload, burnout and job performance. Likewise, it was seen that burnout level rise up with the increase of academic rank. Assistant professors' job performance is also higher than other groups. Besides, it was revealed out that increase of job experience raise the mental workload of academicians. Finally, it was found that academicians who have less than 3 years of experience have less burnout and job performance than other groups. Reference to the upper findings, it is important to emphasize some issues about academicians in Turkey.

Generally, raise of academic rank triggers the administrative duties of academicians. Moreover, collateral duties increase with the experience and rise of academic title. In addition to that, consultancy for firms or coordinator roles in projects affect perception of workload of academicians. It is also significant to point out that academicians sometimes need to have duties as mentioned previous explanations to have extra incomes. Academician salary level is low in Turkey than other countries. For this reason, extra loads (teaching in private universities, special courses, weekend jobs, consultancy etc.) may trigger the perception of workload. Furthermore, competition in the academic life also have a major role on working of academicians. Besides, staff policies and condensation in universities also impress academicians. On the other side, new regulations for being an associate professor force assistant professors to study harder. Due to the things have changed for being an associate professor, assistant professors need to work intensively that may impress physical and mental workload. Therefore, it is estimated that performance of assistant professors may have higher than other groups.

CONCLUSION

Mental workload, burnout and job performance are main topics of this study and our research area. Literature on these subjects is quite fruitful and presents lots of research results. There are plenty of researches that investigate separately or together of some combinations of workload, burnout or job performance (as work outcomes, innovation performance, efficiency etc.). Specially, mental workload subject is a developing concept in social sciences. Moreover, these studies are lack of analysis about control variables such as age, gender, job experience, academic positions or university status.

Consequently, this study examined the relationships between mental workload, burnout and job performance. Accordance to the findings, statistically significant relationships were found between the related variables. Moreover, the impact of mental workload on burnout and also burnout's effect on job performance was confirmed. Besides, the results showed that mental workload has an effect on job performance. In this respect, all hypotheses of the study were accepted.

Findings of this study was found similar to the results of other studies. Naktiyok and Karabey (2005) reported that the rising of workaholic level increases mental, physical and emotional burnout. Liu and Lo (2018) confirmed relationship between workload and job burnout. Scholars also analyzed relationships of job burnout with job satisfaction and turnover intention which effects job performance. It was obtained that job burnout has negative correlation with job satisfaction and positive correlation with turnover intention. On the other side, Demerouti and colleagues (2002), examined short-term consequences of mental strain and burnout relationship. In their study, mental strain consists of mental fatigue, stress sensation, satiation and monotony. Moreover, scholars classified burnout as exhaustion and disengagement dimensions. They found that each burnout dimension was related to short-term consequences of mental strain. Similarly, Portoghese and colleagues (2014) found positive interactions between workload and exhaustion.

According to Maslach and Jackson (1981) and Arabacı (2010), if employees display symptoms of burnout, they reduce motivation for work and they stop making an effort altogether, hence decreasing their feelings of job competence and productivity (Kar & Suar, 2014; Siu, Cooper, & Phillips, 2014). Ahsan and colleagues (2009) also found that workload pressure, role ambiguity, performance pressure are related with academicians' job stress and dissatisfaction. Kamel (2009) stated that role overload of academicians leads job stress in the workplace. Furthermore, Panatik and colleagues (2012) revealed out that job demand of academicians positively related with turnover intention. Mustapha (2013) also expressed that huge job demands can lead academicians to burn out and intention to quit. Nevertheless, Mustapha (2013) found that there is a negative relationship between workload and job satisfaction of academicians. Besides, Shahzad and colleagues (2010) obtained that there is a negative relationship between workload and job satisfaction on lecturers. In another study with the participation of 294 employees it was found that burnout is related with mental strain. It was also reported that exhaustion is positively related with fatigue (Demeroutie et al, 2002).Finally, Rahayu and colleagues (2012) stated that mental components related health problems impact individual's performance. Otherwise, it was stated that to increase work performance and teaching abilities it is required to provide good workplace conditions and social support that lead better well-being of academicians.

Moreover, it seems valuable to control for individual characteristics in analyzing the relationships of burnout and job performance (Lazaro vd., 1984). Another result of the study is related to demographic variables. Possible differences in research variables were investigated in terms of gender, age group, work experience and academic titles. It was found no significant difference between male and female academicians and also among age groups for three research variables. Also Toker (2011) implied that gender did not have a significant impact on burnout. However, regarding academic degree, there were statistically significant differences for burnout and job performance. Also, for job performance variable according to current and total workplace experience groups, it was found significant differences. Khan and colleagues (2015) also obtained that young academicians had the highest burnout level. Moreover, it was stated that they found some differences about burnout based on age and experience groups of academicians however they could not find any significant difference based on gender and marital status about burnout.

Finally, it is advised that; workload related regulations need to be revised. Academicians' working conditions and income levels are also required to regulate detailed. Moreover, job related loads should be distributed to the academicians more balanced. Academicians also should be supported with stress, time management related workshops to minimize individual conflicts.

REFERENCES

Ahsan, N., Abdullah, Z., Fie, D. Y. G., & Alam, S. S. (2009). A Study of Job Stress on Job Satisfaction among University Staff in Malaysia: Empirical Study. *European Journal of Soil Science*, *8*(1), 121–131.

Akyol, H. (2014). The Measuring Effect of Employee Satisfaction of Academic Staff to Employee Performance. *Journal of Social and Administrative Sciences*, *1*(1), 18–33. doi:10.1453/jsas.v1i1.119

Arabacı, B. (2010). The effects of depersonalization and organizational cynicism levels on the job satisfaction of educational inspectors. *African Journal of Business Management*, *4*(13), 2802–2811.

Ardıç, K. (2008). Tükenmişlik Sendromu Akademisyenler Üzerine Bir Uygulama (GOÜ Örneği). *Gazi Üniversitesi İktisadi ve İdari Bilimler Fakültesi Dergisi*, *10*(2), 69–96.

Bang, H., & Reio, T. G. (2017). Análisis del papel del cinismo en la relación entre el burnout y el comportamiento de los trabajadores. *Revista de Psicología del Trabajo y de las Organizaciones, 33*(3), 217–227. doi:10.1016/j.rpto.2017.07.002

Biron, M., & Eshed, R. (2017). Gaps Between Actual and Preferred Career Paths Among Professional Employees: Implications for Performance and Burnout. *Journal of Career Development, 44*(3), 224–238. doi:10.1177/0894845316645664

Borghini, G., Astolfi, L., Vecchiato, G., Mattia, D., & Babiloni, F. (2014). Measuring neurophysiological signals in aircraft pilots and car drivers for the assessment of mental workload, fatigue and drowsiness. *Neuroscience and Biobehavioral Reviews, 44*, 58–75. doi:10.1016/j.neubiorev.2012.10.003 PMID:23116991

Borman, W. C., & Motowidlo, S. J. (1993). Expanding the criterion domain to include elements of contextual performance. In A. N. Schmitt & W. C. Borman (Ed.), Personnel selection in organizations (pp. 71–98). San Francisco: Jossey-Bass.

Brandes, P., Castro, S., James, M. S. L., Martinez, A. D., Matherly, T. A., Ferris, G. R., & Hochwater, W. A. (2008). The interactive effects of job insecurity and organiza- tional cynicism on work effort following a layoff. *Journal of Leadership & Organizational Studies, 14*(3), 233–247. doi:10.1177/1071791907311967

Brookhuis, K. A., & de Waard, D. (2010). Monitoring drivers' mental workload in driving simulators using physiological measures. *Accident; Analysis and Prevention, 42*(3), 898–903. doi:10.1016/j.aap.2009.06.001 PMID:20380918

Budak, G., & Sürgevil, O. (2005). Tükenmişlik ve Tükenmişliği Etkileyen Örgütsel Faktörlerin Analizine İlişkin Akademik Personel Üzerinde Bir Uygulama. *Dokuz Eylül Üniversitesi İİBF Dergisi, 20*(2), 95–108.

Cain, B. (2007). *A review of the mental workload literature*. Defence Research and Development Toronto.

Campbell, J. P., McHenry, J. J., & Wise, L. L. (1990). Modeling job performance in a population of jobs. *Personnel Psychology, 43*(2), 313–333. doi:10.1111/j.1744-6570.1990.tb01561.x

Çapri, B. (2006). Tükenmişlik Ölçeğinin Türkçe Uyarlaması: Geçerlik ve Güvenirlik Çalışması. *Mersin Üniversitesi Eğitim Fakültesi Dergisi, 2*(1), 62–77. doi:10.17860/EFD.24817

Çavuş, M. F., Gök, T., & Kurtay, F. (2007). Tükenmişlik: Meslek Yüksekokulu Akademik Personeli Üzerine Bir Araştırma. Ç.Ü. *Sosyal Bilimler Enstitüsü Dergisi, 16*(2), 97–108.

Che, X. X., Zhou, Z. E., Kessler, S. R., & Spector, P. E. (2017). Stressors beget stressors: The effect of passive leadership on employee health through workload and work–family conflict. *Work and Stress, 31*(4), 338–354. doi:10.1080/02678373.2017.1317881

Çiçek Sağlam, A. (2011). Akademik Personelin Sosyo-demografik Özelliklerinin Tükenmişlik Düzeyleri ile İlişkisi. *Mustafa Kemal Üniversitesi Sosyal Bilimler Enstitüsü Dergisi, 8*(15), 407–420.

Colle, H. A., & Reid, G. B. (1999). Double trade-off curves with different cognitive processing combinations: Testing the cancellation axiom of mental workload measurement theory. *Human Factors, 41*(1), 35–50. doi:10.1518/001872099779577327 PMID:10354805

Demerouti, E., Bakker, A., Nachreiner, F., & Ebbinghaus, M. (2002). From mental strain to burnout. *European Journal of Work and Organizational Psychology, 11*(4), 423–441. doi:10.1080/13594320244000274

Demerouti, E., Veldhuis, W., Coombes, C., & Hunter, R. (2019). Burnout among pilots: Psychosocial factors related to happiness and performance at simulator training. *Ergonomics, 62*(2), 233–245. doi:10.1080/00140139.2018.1464667 PMID:29648499

Erdoğan, E. (2011). *Etkili Liderlik, Örgütsel Sessizlik ve Performans İlişkisi.* Gebze Yüksek Teknoloji Enstitüsü.

Freudenberger, H. J. (1974). Staff Burn-Out. *The Journal of Social Issues, 30*(1), 159–165. doi:10.1111/j.1540-4560.1974.tb00706.x

Gandi, J. C., Wai, P. S., Karick, H., & Dagona, Z. K. (2011). The role of stress and level of burnout in job performance among nurses. *Mental Health in Family Medicine, 8*(3), 181–194. PMID:22942900

Gezer, E., Yenel, F., & Şahan, H. (2009). Öğretim Elemanlarının Tükenmişlik Düzeyleri ile Sosyodemografik Değişkenleri Arasındaki İlişki. *Uluslararası Sosyal Araştırmalar Dergisi, 2*(6), 243–250.

Glazer, G., & Henry, M. S. (1994). Approaches to Conducting Faculty Workload Studies: A Case Study at Kent State University. *New Directions for Institutional Research, 83*(83), 39–55. doi:10.1002/ir.37019948306

Gopher, D., & Donchin, E. (1986). *Workload: An examination of the concept.* Academic Press.

Hancock, P. A., & Caird, J. K. (1993). Experimental evaluation of a model of mental workload. *Human Factors, 35*(3), 413–429. doi:10.1177/001872089303500303 PMID:8244409

Hart, S. G. (2006). Nasa-Task Load Index (Nasa-Tlx). *20 Years Later. Human Factors and Ergonomics Society. Annual Meeting Proceedings, 50*(9), 904–908.

Huey, B. M., & Wickens, C. D. (1993). *Workload transition: Implications for individual and team performance.* National Research Council.

Idris, M.K. (2009). *Occupational Stress in Academic Life: A Study of Academics of Malaysian Public Universities* (PhD thesis). The University of Waikato, New Zealand.

İnce, N. B., & Şahin, A. E. (2015). Maslach Tükenmişlik Envanteri-Eğitimci Formu'nu Türkçe'ye Uyarlama Çalışması. *Eğitimde ve Psikolojide Ölçme ve Değerlendirme Dergisi, 6*(2), 385–399. doi:10.21031/epod.97301

Iraz, R., & Ganiyusufoglu, A. (2011). Örgütlerde Mesleki Tükenmişlik ve Akademisyenler Üzerinde Bir Uygulama. *SÜ İİBF Sosyal ve Ekonomik Araştırmalar Dergisi, 11*(21), 452–472.

Kar, S., & Suar, D. (2014). Role of burnout in the relationship between job demands and job outcomes among indian nurses. *Vikalpa, 39*(4), 23–37. doi:10.1177/0256090920140403

Karabay, M. E., Tezergil, S. A., & Köse, A. (2014). Does Motivation Mediate the Job Performance and Burnout? Evidence from Turkish Banking Sector. *American International Journal of Social Science, 3*(6), 98–108.

Kaygın, E., & Naktiyok, A. (2012). Tükenmişlik Ve İş Tatmini Arasındaki İlişki: Akademik Personel Üzerinde Bir Araştırma. *Çukurova Üniversitesi İktisadi ve İdari Bilimler Fakültesi Dergisi, 16*(1).

Keratepe, O. M., & Uludag, O. (2008). Role Stress, Burnout and Their Effects on Frontline Hotel Employees' Job Performance: Evidence from Northern Cyprus. *International Journal of Tourism Research, 10*(2), 111–126. doi:10.1002/jtr.645

Keser, A., & Yılmaz, G. (2014). Workload, Burnout, and Job Satisfaction Among Call Center Employees. *Sosyal Siyaset Konferansları Dergisi*, (66–67), 1–13.

Khan, F., Rasli, A., Yusoff, R., & Ahmad, A. (2015). Do Demographic Make a Difference to Job Burnout Among University Academicians? *International Journal of Economics and Financial Issues*, *5*(1), 229–237.

Kim, H. J., Shin, K. H., & Umbreit, W. T. (2007). Hotel job burnout: The role of personality characteristics. *International Journal of Hospitality Management*, *26*(2), 421–434. doi:10.1016/j.ijhm.2006.03.006

Kirkman, B. L., & Rosen, B. (1999). Beyond Self-Management: Antecedents and Consequences of Team Empowerment. *Academy of Management Journal*, *42*(1), 58–74.

Kokkinos, C. M. (2007). Job stressors, personality and burnout in primary school teachers. *The British Journal of Educational Psychology*, *77*(1), 229–243. doi:10.1348/000709905X90344 PMID:17411497

Kutsal, D., & Bilge, F. (2012). Adaptation of Maslach burnout Inventory-student Survey: Validity and Reliability study. *World Applied Sciences Journal*, *19*(9), 1360–1366.

Lazaro, C., Shinn, M., & Robinson, P. E. (1984). Burnout, Job Performance and Job Withdrawal Behaviors. *Journal of Health and Human Resources Administration*, *7*(2), 213–234.

Lee, C., An, M., & Noh, Y. (2015). The effects of emotional display rules on flight attendants' emotional labor strategy, job burnout and performance. *Service Business*, *9*(3), 409–425. doi:10.100711628-014-0231-4

Liu, H. L., & Lo, V. (2018). An integrated model of workload, autonomy, burnout, job satisfaction, and turnover intention among Taiwanese reporters. *Asian Journal of Communication*, *28*(2), 153–169. doi:10.1080/01292986.2017.1382544

Longo, L. (2018). Experienced mental workload, perception of usability, their interaction and impact on task performance. *PLoS One*, *13*(8), e0199661. doi:10.1371/journal.pone.0199661 PMID:30067747

Maslach, C. (1976). Burned-out. *Human Behavior*, *5*(9), 16.

Maslach, C., & Goldberg, J. (1998). Prevention of burnout: New perspectives. *Applied & Preventive Psychology*, *7*(1), 63–74. doi:10.1016/S0962-1849(98)80022-X

Maslach, C., & Jackson, S. E. (1981). The Measurement of Experienced Burnout. *Journal of Occupational Behaviour*, *2*(2), 99–113. doi:10.1002/job.4030020205

Mendenhall, W., Sincich, T., & Boudreau, N. S. (1996). *A second course in statistics: regression analysis* (Vol. 5). Upper Saddle River, NJ: Prentice Hall.

Mo, S., & Shi, J. (2017). Linking Ethical Leadership to Employee Burnout, Workplace Deviance and Performance: Testing the Mediating Roles of Trust in Leader and Surface Acting. *Journal of Business Ethics*, *144*(2), 293–303. doi:10.100710551-015-2821-z

Mustapha, N. (2013). Measuring Job Satisfaction from the Perspective of Interpersonal Relationship and Faculty Workload among Academic Staff at Public Universities in Kelantan, Malaysia. *International Journal of Business and Social Science*, *4*(15), 120–124.

Naktiyok, A., & Karabey, C. N. (2005). İşkoliklik ve Tükenmişlik Sendromu. *Atatürk Üniversitesi İktisadi ve İdari Bilimler Dergisi*, *19*(2), 179–198.

Naktiyok, A., & Kaygın, E. (2012). Tükenmişlik ve İş Tatmini Düzeylerini Belirlemeye Yönelik Akademik Personel Üzerinde Bir Uygulama. *Sosyal ve Beşeri Bilimler Dergisi, 4*(1).

Nikodijević, A., Labrović, J. A., & Đoković, A. (2012). Academic Burnout Among Students at Faculty of Organizational Sciences. *Management Journal for Theory and Practice Management*, (64), 47–53.

O'Donnell, R. D., & Eggemeier, F. T. (1986). Workload assessment methodology. In K. R. Boff, L. Kaufman, & J. P. Thomas (Eds.), (pp. 42-1–42-49). Handbook of perception and human performance New York: Wiley.

Ortiz-Solis, M., Maldonado-Macias, A. A., Barajas-Bustillos, M. A., Arredondo-Soto, K., & Carrillo-Gutiérrez, T. (2018). Human Error Identification and Mental Workload Index Setting During a Computer Power Source Change Task: A Case Study. In *International Conference on Applied Human Factors and Ergonomics* (pp. 427-438). Springer.

Panatik, S. S. B., Rajab, A., Shaari, R., Shah, I. M., Rahman, H. A., & Badri, S. K. B. Z. (2012). *Impact of Work-related Stress on Well-being among Academician in Malaysian Research University. 2012 International Conference on Education and Management Innovation*, Singapore.

Parasuraman, R., Sheridan, T. B., & Wickens, C. D. (2008). Situation awareness, mental workload, and trust in automation: Viable, empirically supported cognitive engineering constructs. *Journal of Cognitive Engineering and Decision Making*, *2*(2), 140–160. doi:10.1518/155534308X284417

Pines, A. M., & Aronson, E. (1988). *Career burnout: Causes and cures*. New York: Free press.

Porter, S. R., & Umbach, P. D. (2001). Analyzing Faculty Workload Data Using Multilevel Modeling. *Research in Higher Education*, *42*(2), 171–196. doi:10.1023/A:1026573503271

Portoghese, I., Galletta, M., Coppola, R. C., Finco, G., & Campagna, M. (2014). Burnout and workload among health care workers: The moderating role of job control. *Safety and Health at Work*, *5*(3), 152–157. doi:10.1016/j.shaw.2014.05.004 PMID:25379330

Pugh, D. (1991). Organizational Behaviour. London: Prentice Hall International (UK) Ltd.

Rahayu, S. N., Norazan, M. N., Az'lina, A. H., Adriana, I., Nornadiah, M. R., & Naslina, A. N. N. (2012). Determining the Significant Factors Affecting the Physical and Mental Components of Academicians Using Robust Linear Regression Models. *International Journal of Mathematical Models And Methods in Applied Sciences*, *7*(1), 30–37.

Rana, H. (2016). Impact of Student's Burnout on Academic Performance/Achievement. *Journal of Academic Research, 3*(2), 159–174.

Realyvásquez, A., Maldonado-Macías, A. A., García-Alcaraz, J. L., & Blanco-Fernández, J. (2015). Effects of organizational macroergonomic compatibility elements over manufacturing systems' performance. *Procedia Manufacturing*, *3*, 5715–5722. doi:10.1016/j.promfg.2015.07.807

Robbins, S. P., & Judge, T. A. (2011). *Organizational Behavior*. Pearson Education Inc.

Rostami, Z., & Abedi, M. R., B., S. W., Ahmadi, S. A., & Sadeghi, A. H. (2013). The Psychometric Characteristics of Maslach Burnout Inventory Student Survey: Among Students of Isfahan University. *Zahedan Journal of Researches in Medical Sciences*, *16*(9), 29–32.

Rubio-Valdehita, S., López-Núñez, M. I., López-Higes, R., & Díaz-Ramiro, E. M. (2017). Desarrollo del cuestionario CarMen-Q para evaluar la carga mental de trabajo. *Psicothema*, *29*(4), 570–576. doi:10.7334/psicothema2017.151 PMID:29048320

Schaufeli, W. B., & Bakker, A. B. (2004). Job demands, job resources, and their relationship with burnout and engagement: A multi-sample study. *Journal of Organizational Behavior*, *25*(3), 293–315. doi:10.1002/job.248

Schaufeli, W. B., Salanova, M., Gonzalez-Roma, V., & Bakker, A. B. (2002). The Measurement of Engagement and Burnout: A Two Sample Confirmatory Factor Analytic Approach. *Journal of Happiness Studies*, *3*(3), 71–92. doi:10.1023/A:1015630930326

Schlegel, R. E. (1993). Driver mental workload. *Automotive ergonomics*, 359-382.

Schmoldt, R. A., Freeborn, D. K., & Klevit, H. D. (1994). Physician burnout: Recommendations for

Shahzad, K., Mumtaz, H., Hayat, K., & Khan, M. A. (2010). Faculty Workload, Compensation Management and Academic Quality in Higher Education of Pakistan: Mediating Role of Job Satisfaction. European Journal of Economics. *Finance & Administrative Sciences*, *27*, 111.

Siu, O. L., Cooper, C. L., & Phillips, D. R. (2014). Intervention studies on enhancing work well-being, reducing burnout, and improving recovery experiences among Hong Kong health care workers and teachers. *International Journal of Stress Management*, *21*(1), 69–84. doi:10.1037/a0033291

Sonnentag, S., & Frese, M. (2002). Performance Concepts and Performance Theory. In S. Sonnentag (Ed.), *Psychological Management of Individual Performance*. John Wiley and Sons, Ltd. doi:10.1002/0470013419

Soto, K. C. A., Carrillo-Gutiérrez, T., Solís-Quinteros, M., & Hernández-Escobedo, G. (2018). A theoretical framework about the impact of human factors on manufacturing process performance. In *New Perspectives on Applied Industrial Tools and Techniques* (pp. 327–352). Cham: Springer. doi:10.1007/978-3-319-56871-3_16

Soto, K. C. A., Rivera, H. H., de la Riva Rodríguez, J., & Martínez, R. M. R. (2016). Effects of human factors in planning and production control activities in remanufacturing companies. In *Advances in Ergonomics of Manufacturing: Managing the Enterprise of the Future* (pp. 465–474). Cham: Springer. doi:10.1007/978-3-319-41697-7_41

Spector, P. E. (1997). *Job satisfaction: Application, assessment, causes, and consequences* (Vol. 3). Sage publications.

Sweller, J., Van Merrienboer, J. J., & Paas, F. G. (1998). Cognitive architecture and instructional design. *Educational Psychology Review, 10*(3), 251–296. doi:10.1023/A:1022193728205

Toker, B. (2011). Burnout Among University Academicians: An Empirical Study on the Universities of Turkey. *Doğuş Üniversitesi Dergisi, 12*(1), 114–127. doi:10.31671/dogus.2019.155

Tümkaya, S., Çam, S., & Çavuşoğlu, İ. (2009). Tükenmi̇şli̇k Ölçeği Kısa Versi̇yonunun Türkçe'ye Uyarlama, Geçerli̇k ve Güveni̇rli̇k Çalışması. Ç.Ü. *Sosyal Bilimler Enstitüsü Dergisi, 18*(1), 387–398.

Turgut, N., Karacalar, S., Polat, C., Kıran, Ö., Gültop, F., Kalyon, S. T., & Kaya, E. (2016). Uzmanlık Eğitimindeki Doktorlarda Tükenmişlik Sendromu. *Turk Anesteziyoloji ve Reanimasyon Dernegi Dergisi, 44*, 258–264. doi:10.5152/TJAR.2016.28000

Vidulich, M. A., & Tsang, P. S. (2012). Mental Workload and Situation Awareness. In G. Salvendy (Ed.), *Handbook of Human Factors and Ergonomics*. John Wiley and Sons, Ltd. doi:10.1002/9781118131350.ch8

Virgolino, A. I., Coelho, A., & Ribeiro, N. (2017). The Impact of Perceived Organizational Justice, Psychological Contract, and the Burnout on Employee Performance: The Moderating Role of Organizational Support, in the Portuguese Context. *International Journal of Academic Research in Business and Social Sciences, 7*(1), 241–263. doi:10.6007/IJARBSS/v7-i1/2604

Viswesvaran, C., & Ones, D. S. (2000). Perspectives on Models of Job Performance. *International Journal of Selection and Assessment, 8*(4), 216–226. doi:10.1111/1468-2389.00151

Wickens, C. D. (2008). Multiple resources and mental workload. *Human Factors, 50*(3), 449–455. doi:10.1518/001872008X288394 PMID:18689052

Wickens, C. D. (2017). Mental workload: assessment, prediction and consequences. In *International Symposium on Human Mental Workload: Models and Applications* (pp. 18-29). Springer.

Wierwille, W. W., & Casali, J. G. (1983). A validated rating scale for global mental workload measurement applications. In *Proceedings of the Human Factors society Annual Meeting* (Vol. 27, No. 2, pp. 129-133). Los Angeles, CA: Sage Publications. 10.1177/154193128302700203

Wright, T. A., & Bonett, D. G. (1997). The contribution of burnout to work performance. *Journal of Organizational Behavior, 18*(5), 491–499. doi:10.1002/(SICI)1099-1379(199709)18:5<491::AID-JOB804>3.0.CO;2-I

Wright, T. A., & Cropanzano, R. (1998). Emotional exhaustion as a predictor of job performance and voluntary turnover. *The Journal of Applied Psychology, 83*(3), 486–493. doi:10.1037/0021-9010.83.3.486 PMID:9648526

Yıldırım, M. H., & İçerli, L. (2010). Tükenmişlik Sendromu: Maslach ve Kopenhag Tükenmi̇şli̇k Ölçekleri̇ni̇n Karşılaştırmalı Anali̇zi̇. *Organizasyon ve Yönetim Bilimleri Dergisi, 2*(1), 1309–8039.

Young, M. S., Brookhuis, K. A., Wickens, C. D., & Hancock, P. A. (2015). State of science: Mental workload in ergonomics. *Ergonomics, 58*(1), 1–17. doi:10.1080/00140139.2014.956151 PMID:25442818

Chapter 4
All-in-One Academics:
Mental Workload in Turkish Academic Employment

Nazlı Ayşe Ayyıldız Ünnü
Ege University, Turkey

Burcu Şentürk
Ege University, Turkey

ABSTRACT

The changing nature of higher education systems and academic work all around the world generally and in Turkey specifically highlight the need for academics to use, analyze, and process so much information simultaneously, and deliver results at a specific period of time, which cause them mental workload. Thus, this chapter addresses the problem of understanding and exploring the dynamics of mental workload in Turkish academic setting. The main data for the analysis comes from a wide field research, including 505 questionnaires and 45 in-depth interviews with academics in various universities of Turkey. The mixed methods research revealed that growing publication pressures, administrative work, teaching and supervision hours, the unpredictability of academic positions, the curse of flexibility, and the bureaucratic nature of universities are some of the factors, leading to mental workload in Turkish academia. The other dynamics, such as academic incentive system, demanding nomination/promotion criteria, lack of family-work life balance, were also explored.

INTRODUCTION

Watson's (1968) account of the intense competition surrounding the discovery of DNA-structure, have tended to portray academic life and science as intensely competitive (Sullivan, 1975, p. 223). Since the time of Watson, the competition even get worse as it has been reported that there is keen competition among academics for positions, promotion, tenure, research grants, patents, benefits, academic prestige via peer reviewed publications and international scholarly awards such as the Nobel Prize (White, 2001, Ortaş, 2011; Dill, 2014).

DOI: 10.4018/978-1-7998-1052-0.ch004

Additionally, there has been a change of paradigm in higher education systems (Bruckmann & Carvalho, 2018; Hsieh & Huisman, 2017; Pinheiro, Geschwind, Ramirez, & Vrangbæk, 2016; Dill, 2014; Huisman & Kaiser, 2002; Huisman, Adelman, Hsieh, Shams, & Wilkins, 2012; Pavlenko & Bojan, 2014), leading to increase in rivalry among academics. Humboldtian idea of the university (see Humboldt, 1970), where knowledge seeking and sharing was a value on its own, has been questioned and transformed from traditional model into various university ideas, such as "research university model" (Perkins, 1973), which focuses mainly on research activities and "the entrepreneurial university model" (Clark, 2001, 2004), which strives for professionalized management, diversification of activities, proactiveness rather than "reactiveness" to changes and opportunities (Pavlenko & Bojan 2014, p. 99). This transformation has ended up with a model, clearly closer to private sector organizations (Bruckmann & Carvalho, 2018, p. 630).

Public research funding is now increasingly allocated through competitive processes, rather than long-term institutional block grants (Heinze, Shapira, Rogers, & Senker, 2009, p. 610). Thus, most of the leading OECD countries are allocating some portion of their general university funds competitively for designated purposes, such as research doctoral students, distinguished faculty chairs, grants for research infrastructure, research centers of excellence, graduate or research schools and funds to achieve institutional "world-class" status (Dill, 2014, p. 4).

In the light of this growing evidence, universities no longer provide the low stress working environments that they once did due to increase in and variety of workload. Stress in university staff in different countries are widely researched, such as Winefield & Jarrett (2001); Winefield et al. (2003) in Australia; Tytherleigh, Jacobs, Webb, Ricketts, & Cooper (2007); Bradley & Eachus (1995) in England; Essiam, Mensah, Kudu, & Gyamfi (2015) in Ghana; Ahsan, Abdullah, Fie, & Alam (2009) in Malaysia; Taris, Schreurs, & Van Iersel-Van Silfhout (2001) in the Netherlands; Biron, Brun, & Ivers (2008) in Canada; Akinmayowa & Kadiri (2016) in Nigeria; Blix, Cruise, Mitchell, & Blix (1994); Richard & Krieshok (1989) in the United States; Yeşiltaş & Ekici (2017); Akın, Baloğlu, & Karslı (2014); Yıldırım & Taşmektepligil (2011); Üzüm, Yalçın, Özen, & Yüktaşır (2014) in Turkey. Most of these studies have found that work-related stress has become a cause for concern as a result of increased competition, workload, work pressures, and reduced support.

As well as that there are a lot of studies reporting the relationship between workload and stress (Schif & Leip, 2019; Goh, 1997; Glaser, 1999; Hart & Warren, 2015; Conard & Matthews, 2008; Desai 1993; Birhanu, Gebrekidan, Tesefa, & Tareke, 2018). However, only a few studies focus on of the effects, causes and nature of mental workload in academic setting (Seaberg, 1998; Duze, 2011) although it is a critical factor in the life of academics. Not only does it dictate the amount of time and effort academicians must invest in their work, but it also has implications for their continuance in an academic work setting, such as to attain tenure, to meet standards for performance in the areas of teaching, scholarship, and service (Seaberg, 1998, p. 7).

In line with the global change in higher education systems and academic employment;

- the Bologna Process, which brought out many new issues, such as quality assurance, qualifications framework, student councils, leading to increase in administrative workload,
- Academic Incentive Allowance, which was introduced to increase the academic productivity of researchers by The Council of Higher Education (CoHE) in 2015,
- Recent regulations of Universities on Appointment and Promotion Criteria in parallel with "Mission Differentiation and Specialization Aimed at Regional Development Project" of CoHE,

- The dramatic increase in number of universities and students, leading to increase in teaching and supervison workloads of academics, whereas the challenges of shortage of positions and norm cadre practices

have lead to both multidimensional workloads and stress for academicians in Turkey, which needs to be examined thoroughly.

Thus, in this chapter, it is aimed to shed light on the dynamics of mental workload in the Turkish academic context by referring its effects on and links with family-work balance, academic promotion systems and changes in the nature of academic employment. The main data for this mixed methods research comes from a wider research on Turkish universities, including 505 questionnaires and 45 in-depth interviews with academics from 39 different universities located in 20 different cities of Turkey, which is highly representative.

The chapter consists of five sections. In this section, the general perspective and objectives of the chapter is stated. In the background section, an overview of the concept of mental workload is shared by referring to why mental workload should be studied in Turkish context generally and Turkish academia specifically. The current and changing state of Turkish academic employment is discussed as well to point out the importance of mental workload for Turkish academia. In the third section, the methodology of the study is presented. In the fourth, fifth, and sixth sections; findings and discussions, future research directions and conclusion parts are shared, respectively.

BACKGROUND

An Overview of the Concept of Mental Workload

"Workload" generally and "mental workload" specifically are multidimensional concepts with no clearly defined, universally accepted definitions. Despite of the ambiguity about the definition of workload, a growing literature seems to get an agreement on the following aspects of this concept: 1- the amount of work and number of things to do; 2- time and the particular aspect of time, one is concerned with; 3- the subjective psychological experiences of the human (Lysaght, Hill, Dick, Plamondon, & Linton, 1989; Rouse, Edwards, & Hammer, 1993; De Waard, 1996; Miller, 2001).

The same ambiguity is the case for the concept of mental workload (Kramer 1991, p. 279). In the 1980's, mental workload was defined as the interaction between the structure of systems and tasks on the one hand, and the capabilities, motivation, and state of the human operator on the other (Gopher & Donchin, 1986; Moray, 1989; Wickens & Kramer, 1985). In this context, mental workload was determined by characteristics of the "task" (e.g. demands, performance), "the operator" (e.g. skills, attention) and "the environmental context" in which the performance occurs.

In an attempt to bring each of these dimensions together and provide a recent definition of mental workload, Young and Stanton (2005) have suggested that mental workload reflects "the level of attentional resources required to meet both objective and subjective performance criteria, which may be mediated by task demands, external support, and past experience" (Young et al., 2015, p. 2). On the other hand according to Tsang and Vidulich (2006) mental workload is just a function of the supply and demand of attentional or processing resources (Hertzum & Due Holmegaard, 2013, p. 27). When the recent definitions of mental workload are considered, it is seen that they are even more diverse. As Young and Stanton (2002) states it is all "relative".

In this context, the following conceptual definition, which is derived from the concept analysis conducted by Van Acker, Parmentier, Vlerick, & Saldien (2018) is taken as a basis throughout this chapter. "*Mental workload is a subjectively experienced physiological processing state, revealing the interplay between one's limited and multidimensional cognitive resources and the cognitive work demands being exposed to.*" (Van Acker et al., 2018, p. 358).

Mental Workload in the Turkish Context

When the studies in the Turkish context are examined, it is seen that there isn't any study on the effects of mental workload on employees generally and on academics specifically. All of the studies investigate how to "measure" mental workload, in various sectors and groups such as; in information technologies sector (see Duru, Ermiş, Akay, & Kurt, 2005), in banking sector (see Seçkiner & Toraman, 2017), in elite and amateur sportsmen groups (see Koca & Duru, 2017), in hospital settings (see Emeç & Akkaya, 2018; Karadağ & Cankul, 2015a; Karadağ & Cankul, 2015b). However, it is important to understand and explain in more detail the "dynamics and effects" of mental workload in various settings generally and in academic contexts specifically, as the national and global higher education policy changes have affected the nature of academic employment dramatically.

The changing nature of higher education systems and academic work highlight the need for academics to use, analyze, and process so much information simultaneously, and deliver results at a specific period of time, which cause them mental workload. Thus, it is aimed to understand and explore the dynamics of mental workload in Turkish Universities, which have faced dramatic changes, especially recently due to the new emphasis on research intensive universities, norm cadre practices, academic productivity of researchers, mission differentiation and specialization of universities. These changes are discussed in details in the following part.

The Current and Changing State of Turkish Academic Employment

The Council of Higher Education (CoHE) is the main body responsible for higher education in Turkey. It decides and coordinates main administrative and financial issues (e.g. student intake, appointment and dismissal of academic staff, supervision of university budgets, disciplinary issues, etc.). The other national coordinating bodies are the Inter-University Council and the Ministry of National Education, with limited impact (Yağcı, 2010, pp. 588-589).

Turkish higher education system is based on a two-tier structure: 1) public universities 2) private universities. Faculty members include professors, associate professors and assistant professors and the other ranks are nominated as ancillary academic staff, such as research assistants, lecturers and instructors (Gürüz, 2012, pp. 298-299).

CoHE requires professional vacancies to be advertised in one of the five highest circulation daily newspapers. Both public and private universities are legally obliged to publicly announce the available posts in their institutions on the website of the CoHE. Candidates have to provide a portfolio including their CV's, details of their scientific publications, training and educational activities, supervision of research degrees and overall contribution to the current institution. However universities have a degree of freedom to add on extra criterion.

The remuneration of academic staff that has civil servant status in public universities and it is regulated by legislation, whereas in private universities pay scales are set by the university administration. So, in the public universities, there is no pay difference between men and women at the same position and title.

In public universities, assistant professorships are temporary positions whereas professors and associate professors have tenure. Private institutions usually function by calling part-time teaching staff members in public universities to work with them. They may also hire full-time teaching staff, with a different social insurance mechanism but the same career development structure. In general, private universities do not offer permanent positions.

For the research assistant position, which is the entry level, the candidates take two centrally organized exams (one is a Turkish version of GRE and the other is a foreign language exam). The title of associate professorship is given by a central authority, Inter-University Council, which is attached to CoHE, as a result of the review of the candidate's publication by a panel composed of professors. There are 3 conditions for promotion to full professorship: 1-Applicants should have served at least 5 years at associate professor grade, 2- A portfolio of original research publications produced at an international level, 3- To be selected for a professorial post.

When the current status of Turkish higher education system is considered, it is seen that the number of universities and students have been increasing consistently as well as the need for academicians. On the other hand, the number of academicians remain insufficient due to inadequate opportunities for scholarships and norm positions. Since becoming a Bologna Process country in 2001, the number of universities has increased from 77 to 206 in 2018 and the number of students in the first (including the associate degree) and second cycles has risen from 1,573,281 in 2000/2001 to 7,465,221 in 2017/2018. However, the total number of academicians, including both faculty members and ancillary staff is only 158.098. This leads to increase in teaching and supervison workloads and gives a teaching-oriented character to Turkish academy (Akyol & Tanrısevdi, 2018, pp. 135-136).

As well as that the Bologna Process, which aims to ensure more comparable, compatible and coherent systems of higher education in Europe with the creation of a European Higher Education Area (EHEA) also brought out many new issues, such as quality assurance; standardizing degrees into a three-cycle system (the short cycle is an associate degree; the first cycle is a bachelor's degree; the second cycle is a master's degree; and the third cycle is a doctoral degree); introducing a common credit system called the European Credit Transfer and Accumulation System; providing a Diploma Supplement, that refers to a document accompanying a usual diploma providing a standardized description of the studies completed by the diploma holder; increasing the mobility of students and portability of financial support; and encouraging the production of a National Qualifications Framework by each member country (EHEA, 2019). The Turkish government has voluntarily participated as a signatory country in 2001 and increased its commitment in 2008 by requiring the establishment of a Bologna Coordination Committee in every higher education institution to support the implementation of the aforementioned Bologna requirements (Arkan & Gürleyen, 2015). The Turkish government has also initiated a national framework since 2006, called National Qualifications Framework for Higher Education in Turkey (CoHE, 2010). Adopting this framework has become a legal requirement, since amendment to the Law on Higher Education in 2011 (Arkan & Gürleyen, 2015). In this sense, Turkey's integration into the Bologna Process has ended up with the need for the establishment of new units to meet the requirements of the Bologna process, thus leading to increase in administrative workload of academics.

Meanwhile, the shift from teaching-based universities to research-based ones all around the world and the concept of world-class university taking place in country's agenda due to globalization, university rankings and internationalization (Emil & Akşab, 2018) have ended up with a project of CoHE and the Ministry of Development, called "Mission Differentiation and Specialization Aimed at Regional Development" in 2015 (CoHE, 2018). According to CoHE there has been a tendency for Turkish universities to look alike, a problem that can be eliminated through differentiated mission and specialization (Emil & Kondakçı, 2017). Thus, CoHE initiated the classification of public universities under the categories such as Research, Education, Regional Development, Internationalization and University-Industry Cooperation within the scope of performance-based competition and institutional autonomy with flexible governance (Emil, 2018, p. 246). So, the major aim of the project is to increase the regional contribution of universities and promote them to specialize in specific fields by transforming into research based universities. Consequently, competitive allocation by government has lead to increasing concentration of resources in so-called "research intensive universities". Additionally, public universities have started to add on extra criterion for promotion to increase quality level of their academic staff and increased their efforts to be in the list of "research intensive universities". In parallel with that, recently announced norm cadre practices, which determine the quantity and quality of the optimal staff that a university and its units need in order to be able to carry out its previously determined tasks, put great pressure on both university management and academics and foster rivalry among academicians to get norm position.

In parallel with that, The Regulation on Academic Incentive Allowance was put into effect since 2015 to increase the academic productivity of researchers. Within the scope of the regulation prepared in accordance with the Higher Education Law, a maximum total of 100 points can be obtained, with a maximum of 30 points from each of the following activities: project, research, publication, design, exhibition, patent, citation, conference talks, and award. Starting from 2016, financial support has been provided to the academic staff at different levels and at the rates indicated in the regulation. An academician can get a maximum of 30 points on an activity and a maximum of 100 points in total from all activities. Evaluation commissions are established in every higher education institution to evaluate the studies of academicians, whereas the academicians are not always satisfied with the commission's practices (Yücel & Demir, 2018, p. 39).

In the light of these changes and developments, Turkish academics find themselves in a tense academic rivalry, while dealing with complex and multidimensional tasks. They face a critical dilemma of choosing between "dealing with consistently increasing teaching, supervision, administrative workloads" and "focusing on research activities", finally ending up with increased mental workload.

METHODOLOGY

The main data for this mixed methods research comes from a wider research on Turkish universities, including 505 questionnaires and 45 in-depth interviews with academics from 39 different universities located in 20 different cities of Turkey. Stratified sampling methods, in which the population is divided into small subgroups (strata), based on the similarity in such a way that the elements within the group are homogeneous and heterogeneous among the other subgroups formed. The prior information about the population of the academics in Turkish universities were gathered from the Student Selection and Placement Centre's (SSPC) annual report of Turkish Higher Education Statistics (see SSPC, 2013). The sample of the quantitative research is based on a representative distribution of gender, department, managerial experience, position, and development level of the city, where the universities are located. In surveys, a diverse group of academics were asked about their workload, family-work balance, opinions about academic promotion system and employment. In depth interviews were used along with the survey to have a better understanding of the given situation of the nature of academic employment in Turkey and the implications of quantitative data collected for this research. All interviews were conducted based on the consent of the respondents and an interview protocol, which guided the implementation of the interviews to ensure consistency between them was used to increase the reliability of the findings. Interviews lasted between 30 and 65 minutes and were audio-recorded with the permission of participants. They were fully transcribed by the authors. MAXQDA 12 was used for qualitative content analysis.

FINDINGS AND DISCUSSION

Teaching Hours

Lecturing appeared as the most time consuming academic activity, with a mean of 3.99, as the academics were asked to score a set of academic activities on a scale 1 through 5, score one indicates "never takes time" and five indicates "takes most of my time". In Turkish academic employment system, academics are not allowed to lecture before completing their PhD, and following their PhD the minimum hours for lecturing has to be 10 hours, meanwhile they are paid for each extra hours after 10 hours. In many of the cases, the academics are not able to decide their lecturing loads since the departments have to cover graduate and undergraduate programs with a limited number of academics. Our quantitative data clearly shows heavy teaching loads of academics as the average of the teaching is 15,61 hours a week, excluding the supervision hours.

323 out of 505 respondents were teaching at the time of the field research, and as it is shown in Table 1, almost one quarter of (%24,1) of the academicians teach more than 20 hours/week (supervision hours excluded). ANOVA test indicates a statistically significant difference of teaching hours among the different academic positions as seen in Table 2. Assistant professors appear as the academic positions, which have the largest number of weekly teaching hours. Professors and associate professors have tenure, meanwhile assistant professorships are employed on contractual basis. The contract is renewed based on publication performance and private universities set more demanding requirements for contract renewal. The title of associate professor is awarded by the Inter-University Council and the CoHE. In order to become associate professor or professor, a candidate needs to prepare a portfolio and receives a good

Table 1. Weekly teaching hours

		Frequency	Percent	Valid Percent	Cumulative Percent
Valid	Less than 10h/w	117	36,2	36,7	36,7
	10-15 h/w	67	20,7	21,0	57,7
	16-20 h/w	57	17,6	17,9	75,5
	More than 20 h/w	78	24,1	24,5	100,0
	Total	319	98,8	100,0	
Missing	System	4	1,2		
Total		323	100,0		

evaluation/report about it by a jury of three to five experts in a given discipline. The criteria to earn associate professorship title has been recently amended to incorporate scientific publications in highly ranked academic journals in order to meet international standards of quality by CoHE.

Although lecturers are not expected to have career advancements and their contract is not renewed based on the publication performance and they are only expected to teach predetermined hours a week, the research suggests that assistant professors have more teaching hours than lecturers. Table 3 also shows the allocation of teaching load to academic posts, clarify the heavy teaching hours for academics, especially those of assistants professors as 39,7% of them say that they teach more than 20 hours a week. A female professor, who hold a dean position at the time of the research, mentioned her years as a young assistant professor, who was preparing for associate professorship, as her toughest years in academia and she focused on teaching hours:

It was the year that I took associate professorship exam. My teaching load was 27 hours per week. I had no mornings and evenings. Well, I always have too many things to do in all my career, but those years were the toughest ones. No one can understand this.

A gradauate student working as a research assistant in a prestigous university, reported his observations about the teaching load of the faculty members in his department:

The sharp increase in students' number directly increase the teaching hours of the academics as there is faculty member shortage. I do not lecture for now, but I can observe my professors, they have too much teaching load and the more they teach, the more they get exhausted and their academic performance decrease.

A young lecturer used the term "mentally intensive" in explaining his teaching load:

I teach 19 hours a week. Most people might think that "you do not work 40 hours a week as others, but 19 hours". But, it is not only teaching... You have to get prepared for each and every class, prepare the exams and check the exam papers. You have to multiply 19 hours teaching by three. Labour intensive indicates manual work, may be ours is "mentally intensive." Some days I have 6 hours teaching in one day, and when I come home I become so exhausted and have left no energy to do anything and I am not able to even move in those days.

Administrative and Managerial Duties

30% of the respondents among the faculty members hold an administrative position and 32% of them said they used to have an administrative position in universities. Compulsory teaching hours, graduate students' supervision and responsibility of publication (especially if they are assistant or associate professors) remain for the faculty members, who hold administrative positions such as chair or vice chair of department, institute, college, research centers or faculties. Independent T-test is applied to understand the difference between academics, who hold an academic position and who does not hold in terms of weekly teaching hours. Descriptive analysis shows that academics with administrative positions have even more

Table 2. Average teaching hours of academic positions

	N	Mean	Std. Deviation	SD1	SD2	F	P (sig)
Professor	46	15,07	10,663	4	318	8,165	0,00
Associate Professor	61	16,26	7,113				
Assistant Professor	97	18,21	9,717				
Research Assistant	74	10,88	7,910				
Lecturer	45	17,49	7,754				
Total	323	15,61	9,147				

Table 3. Teaching hours - academic position crosstabulation

Teaching Hours * Academic Position Crosstabulation		Academic Position					Total
		Professor	Associate Professor	Assistant Professor	Research Assistant	Lecturer	
Less than 10h/w	Count	18	14	24	48	13	117
	% within Teaching Hours	15,4%	12,0%	20,5%	41,0%	11,1%	100,0%
	% within Academic Position	40,9%	23,0%	25,3%	64,9%	28,9%	36,7%
10-15 h/w	Count	15	17	20	10	5	67
	% within Teaching Hours	22,4%	25,4%	29,9%	14,9%	7,5%	100,0%
	% within Academic Position	34,1%	27,9%	21,1%	13,5%	11,1%	21,0%
16-20 h/w	Count	6	14	20	8	9	57
	% within Teaching Hours	10,5%	24,6%	35,1%	14,0%	15,8%	100,0%
	% within Academic Position	13,6%	23,0%	21,1%	10,8%	20,0%	17,9%
More than 20 h/w	Count	5	16	31	8	18	78
	% within Teaching Hours	6,4%	20,5%	39,7%	10,3%	23,1%	100,0%
	% within Academic Position	11,4%	26,2%	32,6%	10,8%	40,0%	24,5%
Total	Count	44	61	95	74	45	319
	% within Teaching Hours	13,8%	19,1%	29,8%	23,2%	14,1%	100,0%
	% within Academic Position	100,0%	100,0%	100,0%	100,0%	100,0%	100,0%

teaching hours in average (18 h/w) than those of not have (16 h/w) but there is no statistically significant difference (t (202)= 1,645, p>0,05) between them. Academics with administrative positions mentioned the difficulty of conducting research, making publications and teaching simultaneously with their administrative jobs. A faculty member, who is chairing a department and used to be a dean, declared that:

I have never whinned... But my toughest years of my career was the time that I hold the dean position. I have never stopped my academic research during administration roles but you have to protect of the rights of your faculty members, you have to solve many problems. They are all too many burdens on your shoulders.

An associate professor, who has been in different academic administrative positions, mentioned her self-exploitation in sharing time for her research beside her teaching and administrative job:

I completed my PhD in 2005 and became assistant professor in 2006. Since than I have been in administrative jobs such as vice chair of department and chair of department, vice-dean etc. I have always been too busy. When I go home, after tidying up the house and the children go to the bed, I turn on my computer and study whole night. During the day time at university, I am so busy with meetings and lectures. I can never do my academic jobs at the office, I always work on my publication at home. My parents and sisters told me that they had expected to see me more after I got the title of associate professor but your work never finished.

In depth interviews show that managerial duties are not considered among the main job duties of the academics and seem to be so time consuming and prevent academics to dedicate their times to research and students. A professor holding a dean position in a private university said that:

I did not dream of this when I thought of being an academics. But I see now that, rather than the science it is the politics, procedures, bureaucracy and managerial duties that shape the academic work. Since I am Vice Dean now, the majority of my job at office is bureaucratic work. I can do my academic job only at home. But before, even during my assistantship, I did not have time for academic work at workplace because of managerial duties and work given by the professors.

Academic Incentive System and Demanding Criteria

A set of questions were asked both in questionnaires and in depth interviews to understand the attitudes of academics towards recent Academic Incentive Allowance in Turkey. Academics seem to be skeptical about the overall result of this implementation while they consider this policy necessary. The majority of the academics (60%) believe that increase in salaries motivate academics to work more, 36% of them are hesitant about contribution of this implementation to the improvements of scientific knowledge production in Turkey and 20% of them disagree with the positive effects of this implementation to the scientific knowledge production in Turkey. One third of the sample declare their distrust to this implementation as a just performance system, meanwhile 25% consider it as a just performance system and the rest is hesitant. The in depth interviews and open ended questions about positive and negative effects of the implementation in the questionnaires are referred. In open ended questions, as an additional incentive for making publishing, Academic Incentive implementation is considered positively. On the other hand, considering the quality of publication, academics answers show their worries about that the recent incentive has the potential to decrease the quality of publication and reduce the academic job only to the number of publication regardless of the quality.

A young assistant professor stated her strong position against the implementation as such:

I did not think that it stands for a motivation source to direct us to produce more academic knowledge because the measuring tool is only based on quantity, not on quality. How many conferences do you attend a year? I can attend 30 conferences in a year with a same research by changing the title. Look at the reference gangs, I give reference to you, and you to me... It does not indicate the quality. Considering the majority of the publications in Turkey, I see lots of low quality papers, now with this implementation they are even rewarded by salary increase.

Revealing of the high levels of plagiarism and unethical publication among Turkish academics help understanding respondents' skepticism towards this implementation. CoHE made a recent release (see CoHE, 2019) about the predatory journals and conferences and the president of CoHE declared about an action taken against low quality production and that publications in predatory journals and conferences are not scored in academic promotion and incentive applications. In order to increase the place of Turkish universities in international university rankings, CoHE and individual universities started to demand academics to have publications in academic journals with higher impact factors.

Demanding criteria, combined with long hours of teaching and administrative and managerial jobs resulted in self exploitation of academics to make time for research and publication. 74.5% of the respondents said that they work on their research and publication in their homes as they do not have time since teaching and administrative roles and managerial duties take all their time during working hours at university. This ends up with a very limited time for social and family life and other activities. When academics are asked about their activities after their work, 44% of the academics said that they don't have time left for other things or people (such as household tasks, socio-cultural activities, activities with family members and/or friends, NGO activities, and etc.) due to their academic tasks.

FUTURE RESEARCH DIRECTIONS

The mixed methods research, which combines quantitative and qualitative research, has been identified as useful (see Johnson, Onwuegbuzie, & Turner, 2007) as combinations enable confirmation or corroboration of each other through triangulation. Besides, combinations are used to enable or to develop analysis in order to provide richer data and initiate new modes of thinking by attending to paradoxes that emerge from the two data sources (Rossman & Wilson, 1985). This aligned well with the authors' interest since there is little research on the nature of academic employment in Turkey generally and the dynamics of mental workload in the academic context specifically. Narrative accounts of the academics provide valuable and in depth information about the factors leading to mental workload, whereas more generalizable results are offered by numerical data. In order to complement this study, further analysis of suggestions to overcome the problems arising from time load, mental effort load and psychological stress in Turkish academic context could be explored. It would be useful to see whether the findings could be replicated in a study in other education contexts, such as privately held schools in Turkey, which are aggressive marketers and operate in line with the changing state of Turkish higher education system to have more students. The teachers and lecturers in such private primary, secondary and high schools may also face the challenges of mental workload in Turkey. Finally, the academics' administrative work, teaching and supervision hours, access to academic positions and research funds, and the nature of university management in "world-class" universities could be explored and compared with the findings of this study. In the context of these comparisons, "world-class" universities that perform well in the Global University Ranking, and the higher education systems, in which they operate could be comprehensively reviewed to suggest plans to restructure the Turkish higher education system, in order to decrease various forms of workload.

CONCLUSION

Competition in higher education, which influence and shape the management of universities, is a global phenomenon and this study attempts to follow the tracks of this competition and how it creates time load, mental effort load and psychological stress load, which is critical in explaining mental workload (Reid & Nygren, 1988) for academics in Turkey. The general trend of focus on research productivity and citation analysis impose demanding nomination, promotion and selection criteria of academics in Turkish universities. Despite promoting higher education institutions to become research universities by increasing their research capacity, the lack of division of research and teaching job, shortage of academic and managerial staff in universities remain and result in a combined activities of research, teaching and management for academic staff. Currently, academics are required to compete with their global colleagues in publishing high rank journals and getting the research funds along with their stable teaching, supervising and managerial duties.

Growing publication pressures, administrative work, teaching and supervision hours, the unpredictability of academic positions, the curse of flexibility, and the bureaucratic nature of universities are reported as some of the factors, leading to mental workload in Turkish academia. Surveys and in-depth interviews clearly suggest that, academics, regardless of their department, university and academic post, have to limit their social and family life for the aim of fulfilling the publishing requirements as they have apparently no time for to do so in work hours since their daily agenda is filled with teaching, supervision and administrative tasks.

The research data indicates that the largest workload on academics is in their early to mid-careers. Assistant professors, who are legally required to teach at least ten hours at graduate and undergraduate levels, are found to teach 18,21 hours a week on average excluding their supervision hours. Adding their managerial duties, such as working in diverse commissions in universities, preparing documents to keep up with Bologna process, assistant professors do not have time to work on research and publish in high rank journals and accomplish the demanding nomination and promotion criteria. This imposes a high pressure on academics, who are also expected to prepare a portfolio of their publications and apply for associate professorship to preserve their jobs, as assistant professorship is contract based. Time restrictions and dealing with partial work prevent academics in their early to mid-careers to focus on research and publications, and the nature of academic job, which is based on mental work, directly result in mental overload for them. Almost all of the interviewees state that the multidimensional workloads and changing nature of academic work increase their stress levels.

The research conducted by 505 academics in different universities in Turkey show that the academics with administrative jobs do not have less teaching hours than who are not occupied with this kind of duties as expected. Administrative and managerial duties are counted for neither nomination/promotion criteria nor academic incentive allowance and therefore considered as a major time consuming activity for academics.

Recently introduced academic incentive allowance, which does not recognize the managerial duties and teaching workload in rewarding academics exacerbate the situation for academics, especially for those who have more teaching hours and administrative tasks. Exclusion of teaching and managerial duties by academic nomination/promotion and academic incentive allowance criteria conflict with the long teaching hours and time consuming administrative duties. This increases the stress level of academics, who are obliged to cope with the pressure of publications along with their courses and administrative jobs, which are not counted for their promotion and academic incentive application. Moreover, introduction of an extra salary reward by academic incentive reward is not considered as a tool for increasing academic quality by the respondents due to the focus on quantity of the publication rather than the quality.

Consequently, global competition forces the Turkish universities to accomplish the quality standards in research and it is resulted by highly demanding criteria for academic nomination and promotion. On the other hand, global aspirations of Turkish universities did not make a change in academic employment system, in which academics are equally responsible for teaching, researching and administrative/managerial jobs. Academics' efforts to accomplish all their responsibilities simultaneously, as suggested by the respondents, bring in lowering quality of teaching and research.

ACKNOWLEDGMENT

This research is supported by Ege Universitesi Scientific Research Projects Commission.

The second author, Burcu Şentürk, is the corresponding author.

REFERENCES

Ahsan, N., Abdullah, Z., Fie, D. G., & Alam, S. S. (2009). A study of job stress on job satisfaction among university staff in Malaysia: Empirical study. *European Journal of Social Sciences, 8*(1), 121-131.

Akın, U., Baloğlu, M., & Karslı, M. D. (2014). Türkiye'deki Kadın Üniversite Yöneticilerinin Stres ve Kaygı Düzeylerinin İncelenmesi. *Eğitim ve Bilim, 39*(174), 160–172.

Akinmayowa, J. T., & Kadiri, P. A. (2016). Stress Among Academic Staff in a Nigerian University. *Covenant Journal of Business and Social Sciences, 6*(1), 73–91.

Akyol, B., & Tanrisevdi, F. (2018). Academicians in Turkey: An Evaluation of Current Status of Academic Staff in Higher Education. *Higher Education Studies, 8*(4), 129–138. doi:10.5539/hes.v8n4p129

Arkan, Z., & Gürleyen, I. (2015). Europeanization of Education in Turkey. In A. Güney & A. Tekin (Eds.), *Europeanization of Turkish Public Policies* (pp. 164–177). London: Routledge. doi:10.4324/9781315733005-11

Birhanu, M., Gebrekidan, B., Tesefa, G., & Tareke, M. (2018). Workload Determines Workplace Stress among Health Professionals Working in Felege-Hiwot Referral Hospital, Bahir Dar, Northwest Ethiopia. *Journal of Environmental and Public Health, 2018*, 1–8. doi:10.1155/2018/6286010 PMID:30598668

Biron, C., Brun, J. P., & Ivers, H. (2008). Extent and sources of occupational stress in university staff. *Work (Reading, Mass.), 30*(4), 511–522. PMID:18725713

Blix, A. G., Cruise, R. J., Mitchell, B. M., & Blix, G. G. (1994). Occupational stress among university teachers. *Educational Research, 36*(2), 157–169. doi:10.1080/0013188940360205

Bradley, J., & Eachus, P. (1995). Occupational stress within a UK higher education institution. *International Journal of Stress Management, 2*(3), 145–158. doi:10.1007/BF01740300

Bruckmann, S., & Carvalho, T. (2018). Understanding change in higher education: An archetypal approach. *Higher Education*, *76*(4), 629–647. doi:10.100710734-018-0229-2

Capano, G., & Piattoni, S. (2011). From Bologna to Lisbon: The Political Uses of the Lisbon 'script' in European Higher Education Policy. *Journal of European Public Policy*, *18*(4), 584–606. doi:10.1080/13501763.2011.560490

Clark, B. R. (2001). The Entrepreneurial University: New Foundations for Collegiality, Autonomy, & Achievement. *Higher Education Management*, *13*(2), 9–24.

Clark, B. R. (2004). *Sustaining Change in Universities: Continuities in case studies & concepts*. London: SRHE/OUP.

CoHE. (2010). *National Qualifications Framework for Higher Education in Turkey*. Retrieved from https://tyyc.yok.gov.tr/?pid=31&dil=eng

CoHE. (2019). *"Yağmacı" Dergi Yayınlari Akademik Yükseltmelerde Kullanılamayacak*. Retrieved from https://www.yok.gov.tr/Sayfalar/Haberler/yagmaci-dergi-yayinlarina-onlem.aspx

Conard, M. A., & Matthews, R. A. (2008). Modeling the stress process: Personality eclipses dysfunctional cognitions and workload in predicting stress. *Personality and Individual Differences*, *44*(1), 171–181. doi:10.1016/j.paid.2007.07.023

De Waard, D. (1996). *The measurement of drivers' mental workload*. Groningen University, Traffic Research Center.

Desai, T. P. (1993). Stress and mental workload: A study in an industrial organisation. *Indian Journal of Industrial Relations*, *28*(3), 258–273.

Dill, D. D. (2014). Public policy design and university reform: Insights into academic change. In C. Musselin & P. Teixeira (Eds.), *Reforming higher education* (pp. 21–37). Dordrecht: Springer. doi:10.1007/978-94-007-7028-7_2

Duru, H. A., Ermiş, A., Akay, D., & Kurt, M. (2005). Bilgisayar Sektöründe Öznel Bir Yöntemle (Nasa-Tlx) Zihinsel İş Yükünün Ölçülmesi. *Teknoloji*, *8*(2), 173–180.

Duze, C. (2011). Job Stress, Workload, Academic Freedom and Quality Research in Nigerian Universities. *Academic Leadership: The Online Journal*, *9*(2), 1–10.

EHEA. (2019). *European Higher Education Area and Bologna Process*. Retrieved from http://www.ehea.info/page-home-page

Emeç, Ş., & Akkaya, G. (2018). Sağlık Sektöründe Zihinsel İş Yükü Değerlendirmesi ve Bir Uygulama. *Ergonomics*, *1*(3), 156–162.

Emil, S. (2018). Can world-class universities really exist in Turkey. In M. Rabossi, K. M. Joshi, & S. Paivandi (Eds.), *Pursuit of World-Class Universities: A Global Experience* (pp. 239–269). Studera Press.

Emil, S., & Akşab, Ş. (2018). Türkiye Yükseköğretiminde Araştırma Üniversitesi Kavramını Anlamak: Karşılaştırmalı Analiz. In C.T. Uğurlu, K. Beycioğlu, S. Koşar, H. Kahraman, & F. Köybaşı Şemin (Eds.), 13. Internatıonal Congress On Educational Administration E-Book (pp. 1-11). Sivas: Cumhuriyet Üniversitesi Yayıncılık.

Essiam, J. O., Mensah, M. E., Kudu, L. K., & Gyamfi, G. D. (2015). Influence of job stress on job satisfaction among university staff: Analytical evidence from a public university in Ghana. *International Journal of Economics. Commerce & Management*, *3*(2), 1–15.

Glaser, D. N., Tatum, B. C., Nebeker, D. M., Sorenson, R. C., & Aiello, J. R. (1999). Workload & social support: Effects on performance and stress. *Human Performance*, *12*(2), 155–176. doi:10.1080/08959289909539865

Goh, T. Y. (1997). *Workload as a Stressor: Teachers' Perceptions of Work-related Stress and Its Sources* (Unpublished doctoral dissertation). International Islamic University, Malaysia.

Gopher, D., & Donchin, E. (1986). Workload-an examination of the concept. In K. Boff, L. Kaufman, & J. Thomas (Eds.), *Handbook of Perception and Performance* (pp. 1–49). New York: Wiley.

Gürüz, K. (2012). Remuneration of Academic Staff in Turkish Universities. In P. G. Altbach, L. Reisberg, M. Yudkevich, G. Androushchak, & I. F. Pacheco (Eds.), *Paying the Professoriate: A Global Comparison of Compensation & Contracts* (pp. 297–307). New York: Routledge.

Hart, S. M., & Warren, A. M. (2015). Understanding nurses' work: Exploring the links between changing work, labour relations, workload, stress, retention and recruitment. *Economic and Industrial Democracy*, *36*(2), 305–329. doi:10.1177/0143831X13505119

Heinze, T., Shapira, P., Rogers, J. D., & Senker, J. M. (2009). Organizational & institutional influences on creativity in scientific research. *Research Policy*, *38*(4), 610–623. doi:10.1016/j.respol.2009.01.014

Hertzum, M., & Holmegaard, K. D. (2013). Perceived Time as a Measure of Mental Workload: Effects of Time Constraints & Task Success. *International Journal of Human-Computer Interaction*, *29*(1), 26–39. doi:10.1080/10447318.2012.676538

Hsieh, C. C., & Huisman, J. (2017). Higher education policy change in the European higher education area: Divergence of quality assurance systems in England and the Netherlands. *Research Papers in Education*, *32*(1), 71–83. doi:10.1080/02671522.2015.1129645

Huisman, J., Adelman, C., Hsieh, C. C., Shams, F., & Wilkins, S. (2012). Europe's Bologna Process & Its Impact on Global Higher Education. In D. K. Deardorff, H. d. Wit, J. Heyl, & T. Adams (Eds.), *The Sage Handbook of International Higher Education* (pp. 81–100). Thousand Oaks, CA: Sage. doi:10.4135/9781452218397.n5

Huisman, J., & Kaiser, F. (2002). A Comparative View on Policy Trends in Western European Higher Education. *German Policy Studies*, *2*(3), 1–23.

Johnson, R. B., Onwuegbuzie, A. J., & Turner, L. A. (2007). Toward a definition of mixed methods research. *Journal of Mixed Methods Research*, *1*(2), 112–133. doi:10.1177/1558689806298224

Kageyama, T., Matsuzaki, I., Morita, N., Sasahara, S. I., Satoh, S., & Nakamura, H. (2001). Mental health of scientific researchers I. Characteristics of job stress among scientific researchers working at a research park in Japan. *International Archives of Occupational and Environmental Health, 74*(3), 199–205. doi:10.1007004200000200 PMID:11355294

Karadağ, M., & Cankul, İ. (2015b). Hemşirelerde Zihinsel İş Yükü Değerlendirmesi. *Anadolu Hemşirelik ve Sağlık Bilimleri Dergisi, 18*(1), 26–34.

Karadağ, M., & Cankul, İ. H. (2015a). Hekimlerde Zihinsel İş Yükü Değerlendirmesi. *The Journal of Academic Social Science Studies, 35*, 361–370.

Koca, E. I., & Duru, D. G. (2017). Relationship between mental workload and photoplethysmography in the effect of physical performance. In *2017 Medical Technologies National Congress (TIPTEKNO)* (pp. 1-4). IEEE. 10.1109/TIPTEKNO.2017.8238094

Kramer, A. F. (1991). Physiological metrics of mental workload: A review of recent progress. In D. L. Damos (Ed.), *Multiple-task performance* (pp. 279–328). London: Taylor & Francis.

Lysaght, R. J., Hill, S. G., Dick, A. O., Plamondon, B. D., & Linton, P. M. (1989). *Operator workload: Comprehensive review & evaluation of operator workload methodologies (No. TR-2075-3)*. Analytics Inc. Willow Grove Pa. doi:10.21236/ADA212879

Maykut, P., & Morehouse, R. (1994). *Beginning qualitative research: A philosophic & practical guide*. London: Falmer Press.

Miller, S. (2001). *Workload measures*. National Advanced Driving Simulator. Retrieved from http://www.nads-sc.uiowa.edu/publicationstorage/200501251347060.n01-006.pdf

Moray, N. (1989). Mental workload since 1979. *International Reviews of Ergonomics, 2*, 123–150.

Ortaş, İ. (2011). Ohio State Üniversitesinde Eğitim ve Araştırma. *Yükseköğretim Dergisi, 1*(1), 45–50.

Pavlenko, S., & Bojan, C. (2014). Reclaiming the Idea of the University as a Possible Solution to Today's Crisis. *Center for Educational Policy Studies Journal, 4*(2), 91–104.

Perkins, J. A. (1973). Organisation & Function of the University. In J. A. Perkins (Ed.), *The University as an Organisation* (pp. 3–14). New York: McGraw Hill.

Pinheiro, R., Geschwind, L., Ramirez, F. O., & Vrangbæk, K. (Eds.). (2016). *Towards a comparative institutionalism: Forms, dynamics and logics across the organizational fields of health care & higher education*. Emerald Group Publishing Limited. doi:10.1108/S0733-558X201645

Reid, G. B., & Nygren, T. E. (1988). The subjective workload assessment technique: A scaling procedure for measuring mental workload. *Advances in Psychology, 52*, 185–218. doi:10.1016/S0166-4115(08)62387-0

Richard, G. V., & Krieshok, T. S. (1989). Occupational stress, strain, and coping in university faculty. *Journal of Vocational Behavior, 34*(1), 117–132. doi:10.1016/0001-8791(89)90068-7

Rossman, G. B., & Wilson, B. L. (1985). Numbers and words: Combining quantitative and qualitative methods in a single large-scale evaluation study. *Evaluation Review, 9*(5), 627–643. doi:10.1177/0193841X8500900505

Rouse, W. B., Edwards, S. L., & Hammer, J. M. (1993). Modeling the dynamics of mental workload and human performance in complex systems. *IEEE Transactions on Systems, Man, and Cybernetics*, *23*(6), 1662–1671. doi:10.1109/21.257761

Schiff, M., & Leip, L. (2019). The Impact of Job Expectations, Workload, & Autonomy on Work-Related Stress Among Prison Wardens in the United States. *Criminal Justice and Behavior*, *46*(1), 136–153. doi:10.1177/0093854818802876

Seaberg, J. R. (1998). Faculty Reports of Workload. *Journal of Social Work Education*, *34*(1), 7–19. do i:10.1080/10437797.1998.10778901

Seçkiner, S. U., & Toraman, N. (2017). Bilişsel İşyükünü Belirlemek İçin Yeni Bir Model. *Mühendislik Bilimleri ve Tasarım Dergisi*, *5*(1), 365–381.

SSPC. (2013). *Yüksek öğretim istatistikleri, 2012-2013 öğretim yılı lisans eğitimi veren yükseköğretim programlarında görevli öğretim elemanlarının öğretim alanlarına göre sayıları*. Retrieved from http://www.osym.gov.tr/dosya/1-69402/h/13ogretimalanlisansogrencisay.pdf

Stén, J. C. E. (2018). The Petersburg Academy of Sciences as Seen by the Finnish Mathematician Anders Johan Lexell. *Transcultural Studies*, *14*(2), 226–247. doi:10.1163/23751606-01402008

Sullivan, D. (1975). Competition in bio-medical science: Extent, structure, and consequences. *Sociology of Education*, *48*(2), 223–241. doi:10.2307/2112477

Taris, T. W., Schreurs, P. J., & Van Iersel-Van Silfhout, I. J. (2001). Job stress, job strain, and psychological withdrawal among Dutch university staff: Towards a dualprocess model for the effects of occupational stress. *Work and Stress*, *15*(4), 283–296. doi:10.1080/02678370110084049

Tsang, P. S., & Vidulich, M. A. (2006). Mental workload and situation awareness. In G. Salvendy (Ed.), *Handbook of human factors & ergonomics* (pp. 243–268). New York, NY: Wiley. doi:10.1002/0470048204.ch9

Tytherleigh, M. Y., Jacobs, P. A., Webb, C., Ricketts, C., & Cooper, C. (2007). Gender, Health and Stress in English University Staff—Exposure or Vulnerability? *Applied Psychology*, *56*(2), 267–287. doi:10.1111/j.1464-0597.2006.00254.x

Üzüm, H., Yalçın, H. B., & Özen, G. B., & Yüktaşır. (2014). Akademik Yaşam ve Örgütsel Stresin Kaynakları. *Gazi Beden Eğitimi ve Spor Bilimleri Dergisi*, *19*(1-4), 23–35.

Van Acker, B. B., Parmentier, D. D., Vlerick, P., & Saldien, J. (2018). Understanding mental workload: From a clarifying concept analysis toward an implementable framework. *Cognition Technology and Work*, *20*(3), 351–365. doi:10.100710111-018-0481-3

von Humboldt, W. (1970). On the spirit & the organisational framework of intellectual institutions in Berlin. *Minerva*, *8*(2), 242–250.

Watson, J. D. (1968). *The Double Helix*. New York: Atheneum.

Westerheijden, D. F., Stensaker, B., Rosa, M. J., & Corbett, A. (2014). Next Generations, Catwalks, Random Walks & Arms Races: Conceptualising the Development of Quality Assurance Schemes. *European Journal of Education, 49*(3), 421–434. doi:10.1111/ejed.12071

White, M. (2001). *Rivals: Conflict As the Fuel of Science*. London: Secker & Warburg.

Wickens, C. D., & Kramer, A. (1985). Engineering Psychology. *Annual Review of Psychology, 36*(1), 307–348. doi:10.1146/annurev.ps.36.020185.001515

Winefield, A. H., Gillespie, N., Stough, C., Dua, J., Hapuarachchi, J., & Boyd, C. (2003). Occupational stress in Australian university staff: Results from a national survey. *International Journal of Stress Management, 10*(1), 51–63. doi:10.1037/1072-5245.10.1.51

Winefield, A. H., & Jarrett, R. (2001). Occupational stress in university staff. *International Journal of Stress Management, 8*(4), 285–298. doi:10.1023/A:1017513615819

Yağcı, Y. (2010). A different view of the Bologna process: The case of Turkey. *European Journal of Education, 45*(4), 588–600. doi:10.1111/j.1465-3435.2010.01456.x

Yeşiltaş, M. D., & Ekici, E. (2017). İş Akış Deneyiminin Kişilik Özellikleri Ve İş Stresi İle İlişkisi: Akademik Personel Üzerine Bir Araştırma. *Çukurova Üniversitesi Sosyal Bilimler Enstitüsü Dergisi, 26*(1), 1-11.

Yıldırım, Y., & Taşmektepligil, M. Y. (2011). Beden eğitimi ve spor yüksekokullarındaki görevli akademisyen personelin örgütsel stres ve tükenmişlik düzeyleri arasındaki ilişkinin incelenmesi. *Spormetre Beden Eğitimi ve Spor Bilimleri Dergisi, 9*(4), 131–140.

Young, M. S., Brookhuis, K. A., Wickens, C. D., & Hancock, P. A. (2015). State of science: Mental workload in ergonomics. *Ergonomics, 58*(1), 1–17. doi:10.1080/00140139.2014.956151 PMID:25442818

Young, M. S., & Stanton, N. A. (2002). It's all relative: Defining mental workload in the light of Annett's paper. *Ergonomics, 45*(14), 1018–1020. doi:10.1080/00140130210166816 PMID:12569059

Young, M. S., & Stanton, N. A. (2005). Mental workload. In N. A. Stanton, A. Hedge, K. Brookhuis, E. Salas, & H. W. Hendrick (Eds.), *Handbook of Human Factors & Ergonomics Methods* (pp. 390–400). London: Taylor & Francis.

Yücel, A. G., & Demir, S. B. (2018). Academic Incentive Allowance: Scientific Productivity, Threats, Expectations. *International Online Journal of Educational Sciences, 10*(1), 39–55.

ADDITIONAL READING

Arimoto, A. (2011). The changing nature of academic work from an international comparative perspective. *Higher Education Forum*, 8, 1-22.

Comm, C. L., & Mathaisel, D. F. (2003). A case study of the implications of faculty workload and compensation for improving academic quality. *International Journal of Educational Management, 17*(5), 200–210. doi:10.1108/09513540310484922

Currie, J., & Vidovich, L. (2009). The changing nature of academic work. The Routledge International Handbook of Higher Education, 441-452.

Karwowski, W. (2006). Mental workload: theory, measurement, and application. In W. Karwowski (Ed.), *International Encyclopedia of Ergonomics and Human Factors* (pp. 866–869). USA: Set CRC Press.

Megaw, T. (2005). The definition and measurement of mental workload. In J.R. Wilson, & N. Corlett (Eds.), Evaluation of Human Work (pp. 530-556). 3. Edition, CRC Press. doi:10.1201/9781420055948.ch18

Reznichenko, G., Musingwini, C., Yilmaz, H., & Cawood, F. (2008). A perspective on university academic workload measurement. *Acta Academica*, *40*(2), 153–179.

Soliman, I., & Soliman, H. (1997). Academic workload and quality. *Assessment & Evaluation in Higher Education*, *22*(2), 135–157. doi:10.1080/0260293970220204

Taberner, A. M. (2018). The marketisation of the English higher education sector and its impact on academic staff and the nature of their work. *The International Journal of Organizational Analysis*, *26*(1), 129–152. doi:10.1108/IJOA-07-2017-1198

KEY TERMS AND DEFINITIONS

Academic Incentive Allowance: A financial support system, which was prepared in accordance with the Higher Education Law and put into effect since 2015, to increase the productivity of academic staff at different levels in Turkey.

Council of Higher Education: The main body, which is responsible for higher education in Turkey. It decides and coordinates the administrative and financial issues (e.g., student intake, appointment and dismissal of academic staff, supervision of university budgets, disciplinary issues, etc.).

MAXQDA: A program designed to facilitate and support qualitative, quantitative and mixed methods research projects. It enables to import, organize, analyze, and visualize various forms of data such as interviews, surveys, tables, pictures, etc.

Ministry of Development: An organization, which plans and guides Turkey's developmental processes with a macro approach and focuses on the coordination of policies and strategy development.

Mission Differentiation and Specialization Aimed at Regional Development: A project of CoHE and the Ministry of Development to increase the regional contribution of universities and promote them to specialize in specific fields by transforming into research-based universities in Turkey.

Mixed Methods Research: A form of research, which combines quantitative and qualitative research as such combinations enable confirmation or corroboration of each other through triangulation.

Norm Cadre: The quantity and quality of the optimal staff that a university and its units need in order to carry out its tasks.

Triangulation: The use of multiple methods, theories, data and/or researchers in the research process.

Chapter 5
Quality Management Approach to Workload and Performance Evaluation:
Interdependencies for Fair Measures

Eman A. Zabalawi
https://orcid.org/0000-0003-4948-7684
Higher Colleges of Technology, UAE

ABSTRACT

Literature suggests that many organizations have realized both savings and growth by implementing total quality management as an evolution that contributed to the development of principles and practices, the tools, and techniques for continual improvement to partners as employees, customers, suppliers, and owners. This chapter is spotting a correlation in the planning stage process-centered approach and its effect on employee workload design.

INTRODUCTION

Total Quality Management (TQM) is an evolution that contributed to the development of principles and practices of business strategic planning and operations. The tools and techniques for continual improvement to the partnership will all stakeholders to maximization trust and loyalty by setting a healthy business environment set by top management. That grants conforming outcome to expectations (Hornsby *et al.*, 2009) find a correlation between top management supports between the organizational culture with the extent of use of quality management (QM) practices created in the planning stage of the business.

Setting directions for the interrelationship between assets that contains employees' competencies, technology, corporate culture, and performance drivers in the growth perspective is the responsibility of a leader. Each of these assets cannot be seen separated from one another. Employee competencies, for instance, depending on the technology available in the organization, the same rarely on skills, expertise, or corporate culture. The efficient leader of organizational assets is impossible without understanding

DOI: 10.4018/978-1-7998-1052-0.ch005

the interrelationships and interdependencies of such interrelationship assets. Therefore workload and performance evaluation set by a leader and evaluated by an assessor who understands the mapping of dependencies used for value creation is needed to validate business inputs and outputs.

Below points outline how a leader develop a value creation culture through processes relationships designing a strategy map from the organizational objectives, mission, and vision and the assets that are interdependent on value drivers are identified. The performance dimensions, with its relative importance. the interactions between the different assets as well as their overall links to performance will be visualized expressing the level of importance, and how they interact to deliver value, in this case, visualize the workload. Stress at work is a relatively new phenomenon in a concern of the management to drastic changes at rapid speed in the market retained by their workforce. To become a universal organization or to survive the local competition. Employers today are critically affected by workload and its impact over employment turnover.

In successful businesses, workforce inputs are the most costly inputs. The focus on team cooperation and dynamics, especially the early signaling of problems via a continual improvement cycle (Deming, 1993) implementation is core in quality management (QM) business setup converge with sustainability and transparency initiatives. QM practices examine the direct and indirect effects of these practices on various performance levels, update the process accordingly, improve the excursion and its expected outcomes as a perceived quality tied to successful and comprehensive planning regimes. Quality management is expressed as the organizational goals and aspirations stated in the business scope. From policies and processes, with the availability of support to resources across different stages of project delivery, a clarity in workload and expectations of outcomes is a necessary measure to human capital needs. The alignment of workload and performance evaluation with resource availability is on employed. The alignment focus on aspects of human capital, business value creation in a healthy work culture promoted by leaders to meet business scope in cognitive processes. Business culture is driven through ethics in operational control and tolerance to differences keeping corporate crime to the minimum due to implementation of talent management program by using well-designed software set to value employees inputs to successful outputs avoiding bias or subjective workload and performance evaluation.

HUMAN CAPITAL DRIVEN ECONOMY

Knowledge-based is the economic drive to the market in the form of abilities to carry tasks successfully that contribute to the market corporates performance by reducing the risks and increasing return on investments (Hayton and Kelley, 2006). Therefore, besides its direct effect on firm performance, human capital resource act as a moderator to facilitate roles in the attempts to designing, developing, and improving products and services they also influence the economic success. Scholars' studies this decisive role of human capital reference to Edelman *et al.* (2002) with emphasis on the firm's strategic directions to be in line with its human resources are innovative performance setup. Hitt *et al.* (2001) mentioning that substantial resources and strategy interact to produce positive returns conclude that human resource moderates the strategy and performance relationship as a moderator role in a different set of outcomes (Selvarajan *et al.*,2007). The human capital interacting with social capital increases radical, innovative capability which purports that human capital plays a moderator role in innovative performance. We may assess the drivers to establishing and sustaining healthy corporate for the healthy economy of knowledge as an essential driver to improvement and implementation, rewards, good managerial relations, discretionary power, etc., would create a better work environment. If organizations with quality management support human capital development due to the precise task and, time allocations, processes and procedures guidance, resource support, and managerial encouragements, tolerance, ethics, discretion, rewards, etc. the performance increase.

However, on the other hand, since human capital development practice connects to synergetic increase in this personal ethics, cultural differences, and self-actualization threats among work individuals. Instead, implementing quality management culture could minimize differences through set processes across the business. In a TQM context described by Bushe (1988) as a total quality culture clarifying norms, values, and reward procedures that emphasize holistic behavior oriented toward cooperation with fellow organizational members. Work performance (Meeus and Oerlemans, 2000) in such a culture would tend to be defined broadly to include innovative accomplishment of tasks and taking initiatives to the best duty, and sharing information with and helping co-workers for improvement purpose in a written procedures of tasks clearing roles and relationships with the direct and interactive effects of organizational expectations to successful outcome meeting policies and procedures that concludes a healthy job workload.

Leadership support is accomplished by generating and developing new business models, allocation of time, organizational structures, decision-making process, rewards, and tolerance in cases of creative undertakings or risky project implementations (Dess *et al.*, 2008) suggest that tolerance for failure improving work is among the sound organizational practices, the claim is that decision-making autonomy may make poor decisions while some others may be productive depending on the mental ability to handle unplanned actions or workload pressure. One could argue that increased demand would cause an increased workload. In the comparison of traditional to a quality management system, an employee performance journey efficiency calculation ratio is used to set out needed resources in a system process-focused approach during different stages of project management. At the other hand, work performance behavior has been criticized in traditional management organizations for being too narrow in focus and involving too few antecedent variables reference to (Campbell, 1990) in attempting to model work performance, omitted opportunity factors of the job.

VALUE CREATION STRUCTURE

In the dilemma of workload and performance evaluation, performance measures vary among studies. Some studies performance only at operating levels, while others like Douglas and Judge (2001) measure only financial performance; and still others as do Das et al. (2000), measure performance at multiple levels. The framework used to investigate the relation between TQM and performance, which TQM practices have direct and indirect effects on various levels of performance.

The team-based structure is organized around teams in quality management organizations that work on different processes for different types of outcomes. The advantages and challenges of team-based and network structures using processes as a grouping method can create substantial improvements in organizations by allowing people to work across teams avoiding traditional structure. Nonetheless, changing to a process-based organization is neither simple nor easy, which leads to not conforming to the traditional employee's performance evaluation. It takes much thought because it means taking the organization apart and putting it back again without aligning the efforts and other soft factors effects the employee mental health.

A crucial but challenging point often stems from an internal focus and the creation of teams to reduce the number of hierarchical layers from traditional management to quality management organization. Several layers of middle management are also eliminated (making it flatter). Redesigning an organizational structure is virtually impossible without considering its impacts on employees' workload and performance measures. High-performance work is designed by skill sharing, flexibility, innovation, knowledge, exceeding customer needs in fast-changing business needs, and marketplace requirements in a continue improvement cycle. The consideration of soft skills and soft knowledge are not yet impeded into the planning stage in a task action, an evaluation measure. This chapter intends to put a spotlight on areas that could be the determinants performance evaluation at are not yet put in a measurable process neither in traditional management nor in quality management driving the world economies.

Structuring an organization has significant implications for staff and productivity, with control forming the fundamental link between desired outcomes and actual processes. Organization structure is the outline how the company is doing business, guidelines operations, and decision making by stating span of control, number of employees, chain of command and control to achieve a profitable and productive employment relationship.

Quality management organizations apply a flat organization structure that supports higher productivity. Flat organizations focus on empowerment rather than a focus on the chain of command. Flat structures designed with a less controlling level in groups. On the contrary, traditional management tends to have a tall organization structure that sets challenging span of control and slows decision making, slow flow of work, managers' form many ranks, and each has a narrow area of control which could lead to lower performance that effects on employees health, happiness, and performance due to its workflow and centralization of process and its outcomes. In this relation, Bandura (1998, p. 56) notes that "evidence shows that human accomplishments and positive well-being require an optimistic sense of personal efficacy to override the numerous impediments to success." In assessing the similarities and differences between traditional and quality management, notes that goal based cognitive process operates whenever an outcome is perceived as adding value." the optimism was found Snyder (2002, p. 257) to have a significant relationship with the rated performance and their job satisfaction and work happiness.

Quality management structure aims at decentralization of the structure to solve problems by collaboration in a less overhead cost between the teams assigned for the task completion based on their set of skills and talent. During the closure of the project cycle, management review all decisions made to improve the process for the next project cycle and align all outcomes with workload consideration, policies, and job design to available resources. This approach is based on a matrix structure that combines elements of the functional and divisional models. It groups employees into functional departments of specialization, then further separates them into divisional projects and products. In a matrix structure, the team members take responsibility for their work following the precise process supported by procedures and outcome expectations set before the project startup. Also, the employee is involved in a cross-departmental improvement process review in granting effective outcomes. This type of organizational structure takes lots of planning and effort, making it appropriate for companies that have the management information systems as a strategic planning tool Excellency model framework.

Size of the organization and the nature of the processes influence employees who contributes to a given process. One of the inadequacies of traditional management that it inhibits process improvement due to lack of organizational unit or function that has control over the whole process, although processes involve quite many functions but carried out by one department. This is because the breakup of the organization into functions is unrelated to the processes used to deliver an outcome which creates wasteful processes and a lost opportunity to improve, as people do things in one area that must be undone or redone in another area, this case extra workload with externality of efforts on employees production or improvement in a measured approach as an aspect of that job that have essential implications in motivation of behavior The traditional structure may not appreciate efforts made to integrate or cross work amount department. Which otherwise in quality setup up of a business, must be internally consistent and designed to encourage firm-value-increasing behavior across all roles and levels on the structure regardless of the size of the organization.

The design of organizational structures focuses on processes and talent involved within the process, structured by size rather than function in the modern Excellency Management models that are based on process focus (Hornsby et al., 2002) as fundamental principles of TQM. Processes that drive the organization and have an enormous impact on the strategic goals of an organization. These are called value creation processes which are the most important to maintaining or achieving a sustainable competitive advantage for internal and external customers by putting external customers first, recognize internal customers, team structures and engagement model stated by procedures of tasks with the calculated workload to expected, planned outcomes.

Advantages and challenges of quality management team based and network structures using processes as a grouping method can create substantial improvements in organizations by allowing people to see and change procedures they could not see or change in the traditional functional structure. Nonetheless, changing to a process-based organization is neither simple nor easy. It takes much thought because it means taking the organization apart and putting it back again by the top strategic leaders applying quality allocation to all outcomes. A crucial but challenging point often stems from a structural change from an internal focus and the creation of process teams is the reduction in the number of hierarchical layers in the organization. Several layers of middle management are often eliminated (making it flatter). Redesigning an organizational structure is virtually impossible without considering its impacts on work systems and its required awareness efforts among employees in the design and application of work systems to achieve high performance in a calculated workload assigned into each team task aligned with availability of efficient information systems prior start of the project stage were leaders must recognize internal customers efforts who outreach external customers in a process factual culture of excellence approach .

The learning organization: motivating employees by integrating QM philosophy in a supportive organizational culture. (Pool, 2000)

A healthy organizational culture is known as a culture of excellence. Culture is about shared values, beliefs, and behaviors. The word "shared" is critically important. The structure is the necessary work of how business should be carried on. It is clear now that quality must be a principal value in an organization that wants to achieve excellence. Values are those things that most matter to people, to what is precious to them. Behaviors are those actions that can be seen that show how people act. Building a culture of excellence is vital to have an organization looking for excellence. Culture influence the behaviors of employees at different levels, which begins with the senior leadership commitment to the workforce categorized in:

- The main reason is that a culture of high performance leads to successful results for the employee as a personal outcome that adds to their experience, and for the organization.
- Teams often provide the infrastructure for high-performance work systems.

- Employees understand the customer and actions to satisfy them, and responsibilities to achieve agreed outcomes.
- Leading organizations with a commitment to people explicit in the vision, mission, and values within a robust system in place to factually understand what matters to all partners.
- A culture of excellence is characterized by respect, aligned values, shared purpose, clear expectations, communication, and trust considering internal customers' needs in the planning and improving stages of each process.

LEADERSHIP

The leadership system refers to how leadership is exercised, formally, and informally, throughout an organization. These elements include how decisions are made, communicated, and carried out at all levels. Strategic leaders effects of the performance dimensions in many ways (Antoncic and Zorn, 2004) by stating the organizational model, identification of the customers and their needs, innovative performance measures (Hagedoorn and Cloodt, 2003), set of communication, and the human capital management as the moderators and internal customers to meet external customers' needs prior start of the project, developing directions with policies and regulations in a structured process that yield healthy work environment. Reference to Deming (1986) that a mean performance level reflects merely a system's overall capability.

Variation factors are highly influential in determining performance evaluation outcome within an organization system. Quality management introduces a holistic approach to organizational design in a systematic factual approach. It suggests that wellbeing of employees in continue to improve businesses, the compatibility to construct job design is required with each improvement of a product or service. If leaders lack holistic support in documentation such as ethical, and cultural differences embedded into a common framework. Employees will face work challenges that lead to negative performance due to its hidden influence, and therefore, it causes low morale as facts are not being collected within the process. It is postulated that improving the well-being of workers will simultaneously improve organizational outcomes. Quality management model moves beyond personal inputs by providing a system structure of work and combination of methods to progress any organizational success due to the high intensive planning efforts put to direct each action within the organizations presented in the table below that include opportunity factors, or environmental influences beyond an individual's control, as determinants of performance.

Table1 represents a basic framework and roles of different managerial actions in the planning stage. Each stage involves performance measure, feedback, and improvement set by Deming the quality management guru (Abell & Oxbrow, 2002). The framework clarify business priorities effectively; the establishment of a process to map the people against the needs is an action outcome required for each task (Project Management Institute, 2008). Positive psychological feedback on planning motivation of employees to produce positive performance is the strategic planners must lead one action. Also, performance represents critical influences on a variety of subsequent determinants that influence the outcomes and possibly a bias evaluation. If the performance evaluation is not systematic to develop informed understanding of the performance rating and components measured within given time and resources provided within the expected outcome, then the whole process could be lacking structural or factual approach of evaluation, which will affect the employee self-esteem and self-actualization negatively (Landy and Farr, 1980).

Table 1. Quality management presented in the Deming cycle

Deming cycle vs. roles	Outcomes
(PLAN) Support (top management)	(Scope, Customers and market differentiation, Resources availability, People, Infrastructure, Operational Environment, Monitoring & Measurement Tools, Organizational Knowledge, commitment to people, internal communication (employees, ethics, culture),external communication(customers, partners), opportunities and motivation, objectives, change,resource availability, selection of partners,infrastructure, monitoring and measures)
(DO) Product & Service Development (Middle Management and employees)	(Operational Planning & Control, Customer and Employee Requirements, Design & Development, Control of Suppliers & External Processes, Production & Service Provision.
(CHECK) Performance Evaluation	(Customer and Employee Satisfaction, Analysis, and evaluation to Internal Audit, Management Review, Inputs solutions, Outputs corrective action and documentation update)
(ACT) Improvement (ALL)	(Non-conformity & Corrective Action, Product, Policy, Procedure, Process, Communicate corrective documentation)

Deming (1986)

SETTING PROJECT SCOPE AND RESOURCES

It is the project manager responsivity to employ the initiative, identify the project goals, and communicate business objectives. Also, develop a milestone list and communicate it along with the plan progress with the operations leadership in addition to the measurable objectives along with contextual and cognitive barriers to outstanding performance. Communication within the dedicated team brings understandable deliverables to the set of objectives set with tasks dependencies within the timeframe, people, and their workload, and interrelationship to determinants of less performing. The benefits of this effort are to familiarize with a structured approach communicated with the team. The team will value the processes, a measurable reality to the expectations involved with a reduced pressure due to a foresight leading to positive outcomes.

The impact of quality management include reduced errors and improved quality in an individual's immediate work environment, researchers have included the role of leadership processes (Yukl, 1989), job design person/system fit with situational constraints.

Quality Management leadership method of providing direction, implementing plans, and motivating people in an organizational structure that focuses on processes as a fundamental principle of quality management. The processes that drive the creation of products and services are critical to the organization and have a significant impact on the strategic goals of an organization through the empowerment and high involvement of employees. These are called value creation processes, which are the most important to maintaining or achieving sustainable competitive advantage.

Empirical studies have shown that positive emotions enhance resilience in the face of adverse events, which reflect its state to potential quality. Individuals may either become resilient or effects their mental health to an adverse situation each time they get across similar previous setback. Such reactions have been found in studies of emotions to either success or failure to situations (Fredrickson, 2001). Those studies propose that interaction, optimism, self-efficacy, self-esteem, team support, pressure, and past experiences may vary in the level of resilience or confusion (Richardson, 2002). For example, "Success usually comes through renewed effort after failed attempts. It is the personal efficacy that counts." This is where the role of the project manager to direct attempts to success through continues improvement in quality management approach. However, in a traditional management Luthans et al. (2012) did find a significant relationship between the resilience of the Chinese workers who were undergoing significant change and transformation and their rated performance; found that hardy, resilient employees in a firm undergoing a massive downsizing affected their health, happiness, and performance.

COGNITIVE PROCESSES

Embedding components such as noise, urgency, out of scope, unplanned task, late shift allocation, finish time, count of served customers per hour, historical data, etc are components that provides comprehensive investigation incorporating several cognitive processes within the excursive of employee performance evaluation (DeNisi 1996) which either creates recognition or possibly job loss according to how the evaluation incorporated the cognitive aspects influences the workload outcome. Mainly the contextual elements surrounding the outcome must be planned as one of the roles of leadership in the planning stage in quality management-oriented organizations. Communicate to understand what work is allocated with specific contextual or cognitive situation upon delivery is crucial. The aim is to be able to see the best-measured outcomes of human capital (Subramaniam and Youndt, 2005) where the project management regulates its measure of performance considering the contextual and cognitive elements.

The drive is to reduce risks within the journey to all stakeholders' by proactively removing potential barriers understanding its bias effect, and waste. The check opportunity is to identify a repeated, operational process, track operations in the process conducted on an ongoing basis, if a lack of standardization that led to more extended work hours, reactive maintenance, or change of material, a revised and improvement is a high priority. In response to this operational need, the project manager must take the opportunity to empower the employees in charge to create an improved standardized process to support ongoing operations with less workload. Proactive communication leads to improvement and appreciated outcomes, and it becomes the responsibility of all employees.

The whole purpose of performance evaluation in quality management check phase in table 1 is to evaluate the fitness of the process. Start to determine what in their processes need to be measured, how and when to measure these aspects of the process, and finally, when to analyze and evaluate the measurements. By doing this, employees can continually monitor the critical aspects of a process. This can inform the process owner (employee) whether the process is functioning well (workload).

Analysis and evaluation of the data collected are critical to making sure the processes are functioning as per the requirements. This analysis is an important part of the process; if it is not done, then employees are just carrying on jobs, collecting data without improvement, which is an expense that will do no good for the business quality management system. In addition, the ISO 9001 is an example of quality management system requirements identify customer satisfaction as a critical performance indicator for the company that an organization needs to monitor, analyze, and evaluate. The employee role is to put the process to practice, and records for each process as an evident reference to internal audit is an important part of evaluating the performance of business quality management system processes effectively implemented and maintained. This is one of your best tools to identify the need for corrective actions, but also to identify opportunities for continual improvement, followed by management review to ensure that the processes are effectively integrated together as an indicator that top management can see where the system is functioning well and where it needs improvement, and assign the necessary resources to create the improvements needed to maintain and modify system outcomes. Internal audit, and management review eventually care to assess the efficiency of workload as the most important aspect influencing the human capital economy to gather the necessary information required to make decisions based on facts, not conjecture.

By properly gathering and analyzing the real data, business to make real improvements rather than subjective employee performance evaluation. It will also allow you to determine if the changes made worked to provide sustained benefits for the organization and stakeholders rather than building success based on individual efforts not based on a structured based on continues improvement system.

ETHICS IN OPERATIONAL CONTROL

To increase the likelihood that individuals will behave in desired ways in their roles as employees and managers, the firm's organizational architecture can be structured to encourage those behaviors If the organizational ethics and cultural performance is low, then either the quality of human resources or the level of the organizational support will be applied professionally, human resources will be challenged considering the internal and external recruitment pool of resources talent, otherwise the system can result in the utter failure of well-practiced policies, where managerial misconduct and tolerance for unethical variation becomes low. Nevertheless, considering the industry in which they operate, it should not be expected to t significantly identify unethical behavior that contradicts with the planned processes, procedures, and regulations. Therefore, a significant input of planning and clarifying the misconduct within each procedure, and its negative effect is mandatory in the planning stage. It is risky to run a business in a reactive approach. Strategic leaders can forecast the incremental advancements in each work process and procedures both the quality of the human resources workload, organizational structure, and culture of excellence provided to employees to increase excellent performance. The effects of work overload lead to conflicts at work and personal social network. Employees who have heavy workloads and are unable to establish balance roles become emotionally exhausted. Such employees, in turn, are less embedded in their jobs and display poor performance in the service delivery process (Osman and Karatepe, 2013). Organizations norm is to set up for ethical culture, but catastrophes would happen if employees feel forced or overloaded. Reference to the Former Federal Prosecutor:

When I first began persecuting corruption, I expected to work into rooms and see the vilest people. I was shocked to find ordinarily good people I could have had coffee with that morning. They were still good people who made terrible choices. (Vash, 2019).

Corporate Crime

Corporate crime scholars find that the "climate" (Coleman, 1985) reference to the organizational culture exercises a powerful influence on unethical behavior in organizations. Clinard (1983) concluded from his study that corporate crime determines top managers who push their subordinates tacitly necessary to survive illegal practices. Clinard (1988) concludes that lawbreaking is a product of operating in a corporate lack of systematic support "socialize" their members into patterns of obedience.

A recent analysis of disasters concludes that corporate cultures were an essential piece (Werhane, 1991; Vaughan, 1990). The ethics of organizations suffer at least the same difficulties whether the organization has moral status, an existence or even a good intent independent of its members, are questions that have received considerable attention (French, 1984; Ewin, 1991). Managers are confronting flawed organizational ethics and the authoritative culture that requires fixing. Reference to Murphy's "that ethical business practices stem from an ethical corporate culture" (1989, p. 81) leads to cultivating culture.

Tolerance

Other managerial implication (Robin *et al.*, 1998) is related to the direct and combined effects of correlations, support, and tolerance to the individual are found-to-be-related to work discretion and time allocation. On the other hand, factors that the project manager could manipulate or variate its tolerance still exerted significant effects on the employees' performance and indirect workload constraints that yet need consideration within a quality management process and procedures. Thus, top managers should invest in building such an organizational ethical culture where first, support tolerance, understanding other's needs, and measure fairness across the hierarchy. The employee should feel and have ethical policies discourage judgments and threats are forbidden at all stages of the project; they will not be punished or penalized indirectly to their suggestions. Feedback is an action that must be encouraged to drive innovative improvements.

Fears of failure seem to be essential burdens on the way to start and implement healthy project work environment, an internal environment (Kuratko *et al.*, 1992) promising support and tolerance will be an excellent remedy for continual improvement and development of the business. In brief, we can suggest that organizations should spend less time and money on rewards and empowerment, and more on recruiting and training managers to be supportive and hold a philosophy that ethical behavior and failure tolerance are a stepping-stone to success considering workload pressure and other personal goals for human capital economic outcome with shaped policies of right and wrong that govern the exchanges of members of the organization when they are engaged in organizational activities that measure the ethics exhibited by organizational members.

Measures to Quality of Ethics

Another challenge in the formation of ethics developing organizational culture is determining how the quality of ethics is to be measured in standards of operation, or in routine decision-making practices, which include ethical considerations of workplace practices and processes of reflection. This should measure the outcomes and how they are resolved? (Jackson, 1992). Organizational culture then requires serious attention by strategic leaders, an examination of organizational culture offers a plausible explanation for the incidence of unethical behavior and the causes of such action followed by corrections and provisional design to all input cycles. As a result of changes and trends of employment, due to an evolving international workforce that is represented by a skilled and increasing highly diverse labor force, that is growing in nonstandard forms of employment (Plummer and Taylor, 2004), they reveal that corporate culture is a significant driver for regional economic growth.

TALENT MANAGEMENT

Understanding resources are more than how many people are involved. It is the capability of the resources. The differentiation of skills, experience, and responsibilities as a component of workload planning, this is easier said than done. This is not a list prioritized by the manager. The customer segment will prioritize this list of job design of support needed for production processes and systems. The customers generally state the level of staffing based on the service level the strategic leader identified the organization strategic planning stage. In almost all organizations, the support of processes and systems is a top priority. Resource mapping for each project and the timeframe for when each project starts and ends is a planning stage phase to grant successful implementation at all stages of the project. The workload scheduling process is expected in Table 1. It is based on a systematic approach based on client prioritization, as well as the right staff pool.

Every person in the organization, who is related to the realization of the product, must have a job description. Every employee is doing something related to the production of business goals. Whether if it is a production worker or the CEO. A job description specifies the daily tasks and objective of a role. The job description organizes the list of responsibilities and authorities for each role and instructs each task responsibility for positive, fair outcomes (ISO 9001:2015) standard documentation is necessary in order to validate the job description for the chosen Quality Management System (QMS) implemented. A documented job description should include title of the role, the function, specifications of responsibilities that combine the activities and tasks to its deliverables of the job, specifications of authorities along the processes where the function is authorized to make decisions that are linked to external qualifications such as the degree and credentials related to the job.

Moreover, all internal qualifications initiated by the organization required for the job such as working procedure training, system training, IT procedures, and lunch break hours, the organizational tour is the responsibility of the project manager initiation. The ISO 9001 standard handles this subject (requirements of chapter 6 –Management of Resources). It is essential that all job description must correspond with the list of working procedures to provide a leading indicator of consumer satisfaction is leading to loyalty. System generated "customer satisfaction data" is the most frequently collected indicators used to appreciate employee's efforts, and dissemination of data is used for tending to customers reactions to the service provided, expected outcome is a positive experience with the company's ethical and services.

Job analysis is crucial to internal and external customers, individuals develop an awareness of their careers, organizations develop a talent pool of human resource in order to maximize product and service differentiation, and subordinates understand each other supporting service and product development. The outcomes of job analysis are critical to designing responsibilities and workload, developing performance interventions, and improving processes. Job analysts are typically industry experiences or psychologists of human resource who have been trained by and are acting under the supervision of leaders setting procedures linked to a job. Information technology experts have presented different systems to accomplish job analysis that has become increasingly detailed over the decades and mandatory in quality management culture. However, the root purpose of job analysis in quality management is to understand the behavioral requirements of concerning the job workload job environment, and customer segment's needs. Scholars study customer satisfaction has an active emotional (Fedorikhin et al. 2008), a component that customer satisfaction jointly influences each other over time (Kolowich 2015). The transactional satisfaction experienced with each interaction can cumulate the satisfaction of the customer, and the employees' that evolves in the organizational structure communication to perform specific duties which are packaged into a job. In a quality management corporate context, an employee is a partner who is hired to provide services to a company regularly in exchange for the agreed package of compensation. Increased workload, the particular assignment from the board, and the high demand period could be misleading factors that influence a healthy spread of workload. Employers could misuse the employee need for a job and maneuver round hidden job obstacles that are not written in the contract, not stated in the job briefing.

Webster's dictionary defines partnership using the phrase "close cooperation" and "specified rights and responsibilities." these phrases partially capture the relationships essential to successful systems development projects in a Total Quality Management company within a systematic approach of implementation.

Working Relationships. The system development plan for partnerships is known as working relationships based on equality outcome because the traditional development of subordinate and superior roles relationship moderating the interactions of business in matrix management in the modern business. Matrix management works through sharing talents and skills across departments in a system allowing individuals from all different functions to work on different project outcomes under the leadership of different manager to create something new and unique. This gives the team the ability to draw upon diverse skill sets from multiple disciplines, which strengthens the overall outcome of the team and organization. As matrix approaches projects are typically less expensive than establishing dedicated project teams, and the diversity of the team members makes them gain experience and able to innovate, but at the other hand it creates extra workload and influence performance evaluation negatively if not set in a holistic approach taking into consideration the assigned load with no coordination from multi-managers in matrix management.

Quality management recommends that each of the project partners has different needs, skills, and will, each partner fills different roles at different stages of the project. Therefore, critical elements as a mutual dependency and shared success in modem matrix management.

Workload Planning. The workload planning process is to distribute and to manage work across teams efficiently. When workload is successfully planned, workload management maximizes employee performance in a systematic rewarding, teams and the project manager satisfaction at the end of each working day. Employees will be confident presuming their work, its load volume, and deliver higher quality work at a faster pace due to clear written expectations to each task carried within a well-planned time frame. Once the outcome is not matching the process expectations, it is time to run an improvement cycle to the task and reassess the support of resources linked to the task. Improvement suggestion goes to management review. Management reviews policies, IT systems, resources, and workload within the work process and job descriptions for an update and amendment to the improvement of the process. This will allow holistic improvement to every action in the job design internally and externally. The improvement process is carried out by the involved employees being engaged with the process and experienced the gaps benchmarked with outcome expectations. The strategic leader's role is to amend load to available resources or amend salaries to match outcome expectations reference to workloads.

Resource Allocation is defined in the Project Management Dictionary as activities scheduled to link with resources required to meet the organization goal in a time frame of delivery to each activity stage (Smartsheet, 2019). Resource allocation aims to assign a company's available resources in the most economical way for best project performance; the resource allocation process initiation phase is by project manager starts with three crucial determinants such as:

Motivators. How behavior selection of the employee is chosen according to the desired outcome, "how the processes elements will motivate outcomes." The top management sets the motivator depending on the level of importance of each process and its workload to set the mental processes regarding choice or choosing to fulfill a job in a quality management setup. It explains the processes that an individual decision making and choices to fulfill personal needs and goals.

Deliverable. What are the client's issues, problems, needs, and wants? It is the manager responsibility to determine the deliverables and the scope of work. Having clearly defined deliverables is what a manager wants to form the teams to strive for when they build their project requirements and project schedule divide them into smaller units. The method to identify project deliverables, identify owners, and get estimates of time, identify risk, and maintain an attainable outcome (Enterprise-project-managemen, 2019).

Time. What are the client's deadlines? It is the manager responsibility to allow the time available to get the project achieved, which then clarifies the relation to deliverables and workload with clear expectations.

Workload. How many people will the project need? What is the task force needed for each task? Are they available? If not, what action to make that resource available? Determining the human resources availability precise tasks with an informed time limit is best done before delegating workload (Hayton, J.C., 2005). After which, the manager can move on to formulating the best people-tasks combination to maximize performance and workforce usage in a proactive approach. The workload allocation part is divided into three actions delegation, documentation, and cross-checking.

Delegation by resource allocation. The project management expert asserts that determining the resource needs to determine who the perfect people are for the job, check their availability, and book them.

Documentation is by communicating the progress of the work using professional software designed to monitor project outcomes, workload management organization is one component of the software. By having a visual representation, the business can share and allow for better project and workload analysis allowed employees empowerment and job enhancement.

Cross-checking. Project management (Enterprise-project-managemen, 2019) defines cross-checking as one of the techniques to improve workload management. It is a cross-check to critical tasks against the workforce's workload and schedules. It is the manager responsivity to continuously review, re-evaluate, and replant to adjust workloads in a given project, where workload software will clarify productivity by teams which are most likely could occur in handover stages and multiple deadlines within the project.

SOLUTIONS AND RECOMMENDATIONS

Traditional and quality management businesses are yet in the exploration of new ground to setting workloads and performance evaluation because job performance is more than just the execution of specific tasks and that it involves a comprehensive array of critical organizational activities. It also involves potential bias use of supervisory ratings and recognition that three subjective appraisal instruments.

The Value of an Individual. The workload is likely to vary substantially depending on the job (Lawler 1990) as a traditional perspective that the major contributor of employees worth to the organization is through work behavior and ultimately, performance. The fact that one employee could not explicitly deal with the job individually and performance evaluation do not consider team performance and an influencing factor to the success of the individual (Guzzo & Dickson 1996). Awareness that it is essential for individuals to develop and possess skills that facilitate teamwork that is distinct and are different from the specific on-task performance is also consistent with this theme (McIntyre & Salas 1995). Likewise, there is a growing recognition that counterproductive behaviors that detract from organizational goals should also be specified and treated as aspects of performance perhaps as conditions of employment.

Multi-layered Relationship. Supervisors use subjective/personal information to evaluate subordinates' performance to allocate rewards, but supervisors are not themselves the residual claimants of subordinates' output that is based on preferences and biases that manipulating the appraisal system.

Force of the Internal Environment. The designs of compensation systems are designed to serve the interests to suppress information to serve beyond the apparent financial incentive on payments and budgeting but for either downsizing or unannounced the strategic plan. Behaviors that are typically treated as rating errors would be seen as adaptive responses to forces of internal environment before attempting to analyze or evaluate the effectiveness, or accuracy, of performance ratings.

The Behavior of the Individual and the System. Cardy & Dobbins (1994) discussed the relationships between concepts from research on Total Quality Management (TQM) and performance appraisal. They noted that performance is determined by both the system build and how the individual behaves to achieve it. Likewise, Waldman (1994a,b) suggested an integration of TQM principles with performance appraisal/management and noted that an adequate theory of performance should contain both person and system components.

Personal Competencies. The nature of work is changing and therefore, different definitions of what jobs and job performance are changing. Employees required to perform various work roles and jobs rather than a narrow review of specific tasks and duties inherent in fixed jobs and work roles. Hedge&Borman (1995) suggested that different rater types (i.e., peers, self, subordinates) will capture different and valued perspectives in measuring performance, not only the supervisor. In a matrix organizational chart, the employee works across functions, changing roles, and inputs.

Contextual Performance. The task proficiency in a job should be rated. Borman & Motowidlo (1993) suggested that task performance relates to the proficiency with which incumbents perform core technical activities that are important for the jobs, whereas contextual performance is defined as extra task proficiency that contributes more to the organizational, social, and psychological environment to help accomplish organizational goals. These contextual factors include such aspects as persisting with enthusiasm and extra effort, volunteering to carry out duties not formally part of a job, and endorsing and supporting organizational objectives (Borman & Motowidlo 1993). Organizational citizenship behavior; prosocial behavior as discussed by Brief & Motowidlo (1986); and organizational spontaneity (George&Brief 1992). All these labels refer to constructs contributing to organizational goals and reflect the opposites of constructs of employee deviance and counter productivity that detract from organizational goals. Such contextual behaviors serve to facilitate communications, lubricate social communications, and reduce tension and/or disruptive emotional responses and are viewed as essential and contributing to organizational goals. Research suggesting that performance consists of both task-oriented and contextually oriented facets has led to the question of whether the attributes that lead some applicants to excel in specific aspects of performance (e.g., performing individual job tasks) might be different from those that lead some applicants to excel in other aspects of job performance (e.g., working well with others). Several studies suggest that there are differences in the variables that predict task vs. contextual performance (Borman et al. 1997). The cognitive abilities might be more relevant for predicting task performance, whereas personality variables might be more critical for predicting contextual performance. Arvey et al. (1997) hypothesized that constructs associated with individual differences in emotionality might also predict contextual aspects of performance.

Performance Measures Across Time. Another issue explored in terms of the definition of performance is the work by Hofmann et al. (1993), who discussed the dynamic nature of performance measures across time by addressing the issue of emphasis should be placed on decomposing change of inter-individual differences in observed change. The age-performance relationship is a popular topic of research, has not received much attention within the past few years (Waldman & Avolio, 1986)

Gender Fairness. The relationship between gender and performance has received little recent investigation. One exception is the study by Pulakos et al. (1989), which found that males were rated significantly higher than females by peers. The study noted earlier by Woehr & Roch (1996) showed that females tend to receive relatively lower ratings compared with males when being rated after the evaluation of a low-performing ratee (either male or female).

Job Interviewers and Performance Evaluators Training. Recent research has examined the process impact of the evaluator to the performance. To reach higher performance evaluation is to train raters/ evaluators to share and use the modern conceptualizations of performance when making evaluations (Woehr&Huffcutt, 1994). Several recent studies have explored the mechanics of training improves rater accuracy and understanding or the process, and will be demonstrated through improved ratings using different indices of accuracy (i.e., differential elevation, differential accuracy) as dependent variables.

Handling Wide Skills Gaps. Some people are comfortable only in a traditional organizational hierarchical in which control and rewarding are not factual, aspects of systems development based on individual decision making. Other factors have superb technical skills but lack the interpersonal skills necessary to function as a member of a team, not pro setting accurate performance indicators, or they are against change due to personal reasons. No amount of training will erase these behavioral gaps.

Quality management strategic implementation could cause discomfort to exist employees; the change should occur as quickly as possible. Speed not only benefits the organization as a whole, but it is even preferable to the employees who will be replaced because it erases the uncertainty that accompanies periods of change and allows them to continue their careers in measurable outcomes. Although company policies vary widely, many companies provide outsourcing assistance as well as severance payments to employees who no longer meet the company's profile of successful quality management professional.

Although the transition can be painful, mainly when long-term employees are unable to meet new standards, developing a fully qualified, trained staff is necessary for successful systems development in a TQM company. Failure to recognize the need for staffing changes or delaying their implementation creates additional problems and slows the development of a fully qualified, trained staff.

Workload Software Management. The software allows managers to monitor the team's load visually and steer resource conflicts. Once a resource is allocated, the employee becomes unavailable for other tasks as a short term or projects in the long term. Project management software functionality forecast capability of the management actions that affect all other project outcomes, as well as resource pools to help and appreciate efforts supported by data statistical, factual approach (Millhollan, 2009). Project management standardization builds relationships with operations, fostering an appreciation for partners within the business success. Identifying that employees are the core of strategic business planning, but it is an unpleasant fact that not all employees will make the transition from traditional company structures to the total quality enterprise.

CONCLUSION

The hierarchical management employs a mechanism to guarantee inputs and outputs efficiency. Top managers have strong incentives to monitor their subordinates. Moreover, competition among managers for these top jobs provides incentives for lower managers to monitor senior executives. This mutual monitoring imposes constraints on an individual manager's ability to cheat on quality. Oversight of the firm's CEO is the responsibility of its board of directors. Board structure provides valuable monitoring of the internal management team monitored by outside board members. Management and the board adopt a set of policies that make themselves better off, yet reduce the value of the firm. By including an individual whose career choices indicate that maximizing income is not that individual's most important goal, the firm makes a believable promise to focus on value-maximizing policies when the board meets behind closed doors.

The existence of opportunities for bias raises not only the issue of how should firms and workers respond to bias but the rational, how, and when a supervisor provide feedback? However, bias and lack of trust influence future effort and propensity to performance and continuous improvement. As a cause, the employee decides to deviate from accepting performance review to improve business outcome to intentions to leave has been one of the recent disrupt.

Job workload exhaustion, measuring performance without linking the measures to the workload, style of communication, workplace environment, policies, forward planning, daily assignments are given, salary, the benefits received, sleeping problems and anxiety during tight dateline are interdependencies required as rating factors upon performance evaluation and feedback. Performance evaluation is done to measure the fitness of procedures rather than the employees' application to the procedures for the purpose of continues improvement.

REFERENCES

Abell, A., & Oxbrow, N. (2002). *Competing with knowledge*. London: Library Association Publishing.

Antoncic, B., & Zorn, O. (2004). The mediating role of corporate entrepreneurship in the organizational support-performance relationship: An empirical examination. *Managing Global Transitions*, *2*(1), 5.

Arvey, R. D., Renz, G., & Watson, T. (1997). Individual differences in emotionality as predictors of job performance. In *Research in Personnel and Human Resources Management* (Vol. 15). Greenwich, CT: JAI.

Borman WC, Hanson M, Hedge J. (1997). Personnel selection. *Annu. Rev. Psychol.*, *48*, 299-337.

Borman, W. C., & Motowidlo, S. J. (1993). Expanding the criterion domain to include elements of contextual performance. Academic Press.

Bushe, G. R. (1988). Cultural contradictions of statistical process control in A. *Journal of Management*, *14*(1), 19–31. doi:10.1177/014920638801400103

Campbell, P. J. (1990). Modeling the performance prediction problem in industrial and organizational psychology. Handbook of Industrial and Organizational Psychology.

Cardy, R. L., & Dobbins, G. H. (1994). *Performance Appraisal: Alternative Perspectives*. Cincinnati, OH: Southwest.

Deming, W. E. (1982). Quality productivity and competitive position. Massachusetts Institute of Technology.

DeNisi, A. S. (1997). *A Cognitive Approach to Performance Appraisal: A Program of Research*. London: Routledge.

DeNisi, A.S., & Peters, L.H. (1996). Organization of the information in memory and the performance appraisal process: Evidence from the field. *J. Appl. Psychol., 81*(6), 717-37.

Dess, G., Lumpkin, G. A., & Eisner, A. (2008). *Strategic Management*. New York, NY: McGraw-Hill.

Edelman, L. F., Brush, C. G., & Manolova, T. S. (2002). The impact of human and organizational resources on small firm strategy. *Journal of Small Business and Enterprise Development, 9*(3), 236–244. doi:10.1108/14626000210438562

Enterprise-project-management. (2019). *Enterprise project management*. Retrieved from CIO: https://www.cio.com/article/3277972/epmo-enterprise-project-management-office-explained.html

Ewin, R. (1991). Moral Status of the Corporation. *Journal of Business Ethics, 10*(10), 749–756. doi:10.1007/BF00705709

Fedorikhin, A., Park, C. W., & Thomson, M. (2008). Beyond fit and attitude: The effect of emotional attachment on consumer responses to brand extensions. *Journal of Consumer Psychology, 18*(4), 281–291. doi:10.1016/j.jcps.2008.09.006

Fredrickson, B. L. (2001). The role of positive emotions in positive psychology: The broaden-and-build theory of positive emotions. *The American Psychologist, 56*(3), 218–226. doi:10.1037/0003-066X.56.3.218 PMID:11315248

George, R. A., & Brief, A. P. (1992). Feeling good doing good: A conceptual analysis of the mood at work-organizational spontaneity relationship. *Psychological Bulletin, 112*(2), 310–329. doi:10.1037/0033-2909.112.2.310 PMID:1454897

Guzzo, R. A., & Dickson, M. W. (1996). Teams in organizations: Recent research on performance and effectiveness. *Annual Review of Psychology, 47*(1), 307–338. doi:10.1146/annurev.psych.47.1.307 PMID:15012484

Hagedoorn, J., & Cloodt, M. (2003). Measuring innovative performance: Is there an advantage in using multiple indicators? *Research Policy, 32*(8), 1365–1379. doi:10.1016/S0048-7333(02)00137-3

Harung, H. S., Heaton, D. P., & Alexander, C. N. (1999). Evolution of organizations in the new millennium. *Leadership and Organization Development Journal, 20*(4), 198–206. doi:10.1108/01437739910277000

Hayton, J. C. (2005). Competing in the new economy: The effect of intellectual capital on corporate entrepreneurship in high-technology new ventures. *R & D Management, 35*(2), 137–155. doi:10.1111/j.1467-9310.2005.00379.x

Hayton, J. C., & Kelley, D. J. (2006). A competency-based framework for promoting corporate entrepreneurship. *Human Resource Management, 45*(3), 407–427. doi:10.1002/hrm.20118

Hayton, J. C., & Zahra, S. A. (2005). Venture team human capital and absorptive capacity in high technology new ventures. *International Journal of Technology Management, 31*(3/4), 256–274. doi:10.1504/IJTM.2005.006634

Hedge, J. W., & Borman, W. C. (1995). Changing conceptions and practices in performance appraisal. In The Changing Nature of Work. San Francisco: Jossey-Bass.

Hitt, M. A., Bierman, L., Shimizu, K., & Kochhar, R. (2001). Direct and moderating effects of human capital on strategy and performance in professional service firms: A resource-based perspective. *Academy of Management Journal*, *44*(1), 13–28.

Hornsby, J. S., Kuratko, D. F., Shepherd, D. A., & Bott, J. P. (2009). Managers' corporate entrepreneurial actions: Examining perception and position. *Journal of Business Venturing*, *24*(3), 236–247. doi:10.1016/j.jbusvent.2008.03.002

Hornsby, J. S., Kuratko, D. F., & Zahra, S. A. (2002). Middle managers' perception of the internal environment for corporate entrepreneurship: Assessing a measurement scale. *Journal of Business Venturing*, *17*, 253.

Hornsby, J. S., Naffziger, D. W., Kuratko, D. F., & Montagno, R. V. (1993). An interactive model of the corporate entrepreneurship process. *Entrepreneurship Theory and Practice*, *24*(2), 9–24. doi:10.1177/104225879902400202

ISO. (2012). *Quality management principles*. ISO.

Jackson, S. E. (1992). Consequences of group composition for the interpersonal dynamics of strategic issue processing. *Advances in Strategic Management*, *8*, 345–382.

Jackson, S. E. (1992). *Diversity in the Workplace: Human Resources Initiatives*. New York: Guilford.

Jackson, S. E., Brett, I. F., Sessa, V. I., Cooper, D. M., Julin, J. A., & Peyronnin, K. (1991). Some differences make a difference: Individual dissimilarity and group heterogeneity as correlates of recruitment, promotions, and turnover. *The Journal of Applied Psychology*, 675–689.

Jackson, S. E., & Dutton, J. E. (1988). Discerning threats and opportunities. *Administrative Science Quarterly*, *33*(3), 370–387. doi:10.2307/2392714

Karatepe, O. M. (2013). The effects of work overload and work-family conflict on job embeddedness and job performance: The mediation of emotional exhaustion. *International Journal of Contemporary Hospitality Management*, *25*(4), 614–634. doi:10.1108/09596111311322952

Kolowich, L. (2015). *12 of the best marketing and advertising campaigns of all time*. Retrieved from Blog.hubspot.com

Kuratko, D. F., Hornsby, J. S., & Goldsby, M. G. (2004). Sustaining corporate entrepreneurship: Modeling perceived implementation and outcome comparisons at organizational and individual levels. *International Journal of Entrepreneurship and Innovation*, *5*(2), 77–89. doi:10.5367/000000004773863237

Kuratko, D. F., Montagno, R. V., & Hornsby, J. S. (1990). Developing an intrapreneurial assessment instrument for effective corporate entrepreneurship. *Strategic Management Journal*, *11*(5), 49–58.

Lawler, E.E., III, & Jenkins, G.D., Jr. (1992). *Strategic reward systems*. Academic Press.

Luthans, F., & Doh, J. (2012). *International Management: Culture, Strategy, and Behavior*. New York: McGraw-Hill.

McIntyre, R. M., & Salas, E. (1995). Measuring and managing for team performance: Emerging principles from complex environments. In R. A. Guzzo & E. Salas (Eds.), *Team effectiveness and decision making in organizations*. San Francisco: Jossey-Bass.

Meeus, M. T. H., & Oerlemans, L. A. G. (2000). Firm behavior and innovative performance: An empirical exploration of the selection-adaptation debate. *Research Policy*, *29*, 41–58. doi:10.1016/S0048-7333(99)00032-3

Millhollan, C. (2009). *The journey to an enterprise project management office*. Paper presented at PMI® Global Congress 2009—North America, Orlando, FL.

Pinchot, G. (1985). *Intrapreneuring: Why You Do not Have to Leave the Corporation to Become an Entrepreneur*. New York, NY: Harper, and Row.

Plummer, P., & Taylor, M. (2004). Entrepreneurship and human capital. *Journal of Small Business and Enterprise Development*, *11*(4), 427–439. doi:10.1108/14626000410567071

Pool, S. W. (2000). The learning organization: Motivating employees by integrating TQM philosophy in a supportive organizational culture. *Leadership and Organization Development Journal*, *21*(8), 373–378. doi:10.1108/01437730010379276

Pulakos, E. D., White, L. A., Oppler, S. H., & Borman, W. C. (1989). Examination of race and sex effects on performance ratings. *The Journal of Applied Psychology*, 74.

Robin, D. P., Giallourakis, M., David, F. R., & Moritz, T. E. (1989). A Different Look at Codes of Ethics. *Business Horizons*, *32*(1), 66–73. doi:10.1016/0007-6813(89)90028-1

Selvarajan, T. T., Ramamoorthy, N., Flood, P. C., & Gutherie, J. P. (2007). The role of human capital philosophy in promoting firm innovativeness and performance: A test of a causal model. *International Journal of Human Resource Management*, *18*(8), 1–70. doi:10.1080/09585190701502588

Smartsheet. (2019). *The Complete Glossary of Project Management Terminology*. Retrieved from Smart Sheet: https://www.smartsheet.com/complete-glossary-project-management-terminology

Subramaniam, M., & Youndt, M. A. (2005). The influence of intellectual capital on the types of innovative capabilities. *Academy of Management Journal*, *48*(3), 450–463. doi:10.5465/amj.2005.17407911

Vash, S. (2019). *Why ethical people make unethical choices*. Retrieved from Harvard Business Review: https://oregonaudits.org/

Waldman, D. A. (1994a). Contributions of total quality management to the theory of work performance. *Academy of Management Review*, *19*(3), 510–536. doi:10.5465/amr.1994.9412271811

Waldman, D. A. (1994b). Designing performance management systems for total quality implementation. *Academy of Management Review*.

Woehr, D. J., & Roch, S. G. (1996). Context effects in performance evaluation: The impact of ratee sex and performance level on performance ratings and behavioral recall. *Journal of Management*, 705–720.

Yukl, G. (1989). Managerial Leadership: A Review of Theory and Research. *Journal of Management*, *15*(2), 251–289. doi:10.1177/014920638901500207

KEY TERMS AND DEFINITIONS

Policy: Prudence or wisdom in the management of affairs. a high-level overall plan embracing the general goals and acceptable procedures especially of a governmental body.

Procedure: A particular way of accomplishing something or of acting. A traditional or established way of doing things.

Process: A series of actions or operations conducing to an end, especially a continuous operation for an output.

Process-Centered: A holistic business view build-in to provide value into every process and its improvement by integrating best practices of analysis,design, change management, and deploying a value-driven culture.

Quality Management: The actions to maintain the desired level of excellence set in the project scope. This includes the determination of a quality policy, implementing quality planning and assurance, control of production, measures of process, and improvement to each outcome value.

Scope: Is a statement that states the specific work included in a project, define the completion stage with the high-level deliverables and its resource with metrics measurement to determine the success level.

Value Creation: Managers focus capital and talent on the most profitable opportunities for growth. Value creation differs by industry, major categories of intangible profit include technology, innovation, intellectual property, alliances, management capabilities, employee relations, customer relations, community relations, and brand value.

Workflow: The sequence of steps involved in moving from the beginning to the end of a working process.

Section 2

Mental Workload Evaluation

Chapter 6
Mental Workload Assessment and Its Effects on Middle and Senior Managers in Manufacturing Companies

Arturo Realyvásquez-Vargas
https://orcid.org/0000-0003-2825-2595
Tecnológico Nacional de México, Instituto Tecnológico de Tijuana, Mexico

Emigdio Z-Flores
https://orcid.org/0000-0002-1442-5320
Tecnológico Nacional de México, Instituto Tecnológico de Tijuana, Mexico

Lilia-Cristina Morales
Tecnológico Nacional de México, Instituto Tecnológico de Tijuana, Mexico

Jorge Luis García-Alcaraz
https://orcid.org/0000-0002-7092-6963
Autonomous University of Ciudad Juarez, Mexico

ABSTRACT

This chapter aims to know the mental workload level and its effects on middle and senior managers in manufacturing companies. The chapter aims to know the mental workload level related to gender, age range, civil status, number of children, years of experience, and worked hours per week. As method, the NASA-TLX method was implemented. This method measures mental workload based on six dimensions: mental demand, physical demand, temporal demand, effort, performance, and frustration level. Data was collected by applying an online questionnaire. Results indicated that some dimensions contributed to mental workload in the following decreasing order: mental demand, temporal demand, effort, performance, frustration level, and physical demand. Similarly, results from mental workload level varied from 55.73 to 64.10. Nevertheless, there was no clear relationship between the gender, age range, civil status, number of children, years of experience, worked hours per week, and mental workload level. Finally, employees manifested mental workload mainly due to stress, mental fatigue, and headache.

DOI: 10.4018/978-1-7998-1052-0.ch006

INTRODUCTION

Nowadays, the scientific and technological advances that have been developed in the last hundred years have facilitated the daily life in several aspects, decreased the physical effort in the tasks, as well as work-related activities that require greater technical and intellectual skills for their implementation. In fact, this affects the way in which occupational diseases have evolved as well as the Ergonomics approach by applying theoretical principles, data, and methods to design which are used to optimize the human well-being and overall work system performance (Dul et al., 2012; International Ergonomics Association (IEA), 2018).

Specifically, Ergonomics is both a scientific discipline and a profession. From a scientific discipline perspective, and according to several authors, Ergonomics involves the understanding of interactions among human beings and other elements of a system. On the other hand, from a professional perspective, Ergonomics applies theoretical principles, data, and methods to design in order to optimize the well-being and overall performance (Dul et al., 2012). In addition, to achieve its objectives, Ergonomics applies knowledge from different sciences, such as Medicine, Physiology, Physics, Psychology, among others.

Therefore, Ergonomics is a multidisciplinary science (International Ergonomics Association (IEA), 2018). According to the object of study, Ergonomics is divided into Physical Ergonomics and Cognitive Ergonomics. Physical Ergonomics focuses on physical aspects of work and human capabilities, such as force, repetitive movements, and body postures (Choppin, Roth-McDuffie, Drake, & Davis, 2018), the design of working environments to fit human physical abilities, i.e., Physical Ergonomics deals with physical variables that can affect human beings: repetitive movements, body postures, physical load, and environmental conditions (Goonetilleke & Karwowski, 2018). In order to achieve its main goal of optimizing the human well-being and the work systems performance, Ergonomics applies different assessment methods. For instance, methods of Physical Ergonomics include Rapid Upper Limb Assessment (RULA), the Rapid Entire Body Assessment (REBA), the National Institute for Occupational Safety and Health (NIOSH) lifting equation, Occupational Repetitive Action tool, and the Job Strain Index (JSI) (Otto & Battaïa, 2017).

However, the cognitive Ergonomics domain comprises mental and psychological variables, such as perception, information processing, decision-making, action-taking, memory, reasoning, and mental workload (Belkic, 2003), as they affect interactions among human beings and other elements of a system (Wung & Schatz, 2018). This last variable, mental workload, focuses in activities that are mental or cognitive in nature and may comprise physical coordination, but excludes physical activities (Jin, Zheng, Pei, & Li, 2017). Currently, it is presented in most of employees from different labor sectors (agriculture, aviation, manufacturing, services, education, among others) (Claxton Bomme & Fendley, 2018; Jin et al., 2017; Li, Cao, Lin, Braithwaite, & Greaves, 2017; McLean, Abry, Taylor, Jimenez, & Granger, 2017). As a result, it is urgent to promote research on the causes, effects, and methods of evaluation, as well as the generation of new knowledge concerning the mental workload in different labor sectors. Also, cognitive Ergonomics includes methods, such as NASA Task Load Index (NASA-TLX), Systematic Human Error Reduction and Prediction Approach (SHERPA), Subjective Workload Assessment Technique (SWAT), Cognitive Work Analysis (CWA), and Task Analysis for Error Identification (TAFEI) (Stanton, Salmon, Walker, Baber, & Jenkins, 2018). All these methods help reduce or eliminate occupational risk factors, provide well-being to workers, and improve the organizational performance in companies (Khani Jazani, Salehi Sahlabadi, & Mousavi, 2018).

Furthermore, the mental workload impact varies from one individual to another, for this reason, the authors of this chapter propose a research to determine the level of mental workload in middle and senior management from the manufacturing industry in Tijuana, Mexico. Also, it is intended to acknowledge those factors that may affect the level of mental workload, such as age, civil status, the number of children, just to a few aspects. At the same time, authors also seek to know the effects that mental workload may have on middle and senior management in the manufacturing industry; such effects may include mental fatigue, work errors, memory loss, irritability, among others.

Finally, in order to measure the level of the mental workload, the authors applied the NASA-TLX method, which is one of the most popular worldwide method.

LITERATURE REVIEW

Mental Workload

Mental workload is defined as the amount of effort involved in performing a particular task (Boet et al., 2017). Currently, employees from different labor sectors (agriculture, aviation, education, manufacturing, among others) are involved in several projects in the company where they work for. This fact leads employees to use, analyze, and process too much information at the same time, which cause them a mental workload. Additionally, employees are under frequent pressure to deliver results at a specific period of time, which increase the mental workload. For instance, in the agricultural sector several authors, such as Jin et al. (2017) have stated that recently agricultural vehicles have new features, which may lead mental workload to seem to be a critical problem. Similarly, Bashiri and Mann, (2015) point out that the increasing trend of automation in agricultural vehicles raises some concerns about the drivers' mental workload in such vehicles. These authors performed a case study using a tractor driving simulator, where they found that reaction time and number of errors made by drivers both decreased as the automation level increased.

Moreover, they found that there is a correlation among performance parameters and subjective mental workload reported by the drivers. Regarding the field of aviation, Young, Brookhuis, Wickens, & Hancock (2015) found that this field is the second one with more research on mental workload; only after driving field. Some other authors have focused on the decision-making and performance of pilots (Moriarty & Jarvis, 2014; Salas & Maurino, 1988; Wiegmann & Shappell, 2017). In fact, some studies have indicated that impaired situational awareness (SA) resulting from an excessive mental workload significantly degrades the quality of decision-making (Endsley & Garland, 2000; Lee & Liu, 2003; Salas & Maurino, 1988). Several authors mention that workload of pilots and air traffic controllers are heavy during landing, which leads to a stressful management of mental workload (Loft, Sanderson, Neal, & Mooij, 2007; Moriarty & Jarvis, 2014). Excessive mental workload in pilots may cause communication conflicts and accidents. For instance, Mosier et al. (2013) documented that 52% of communication conflicts occurred during the approach phase. Another study reported that communication errors were involved in 37% of aircraft accidents (Plane Crash Info, 2013).

Several authors have found that education is another labor sector in which employees suffer from high levels of mental workload. For instance, Xiao et al. (2015) study the effects of mental workload in the work ability in primary and secondary school teachers. They measure the mental workload levels and the work ability by applying the National Aeronautics and Space Administration-Task Load Index

(NASA-TLX) and Work Ability Index (WAI) questionnaires, respectively. Also, these authors found that primary and secondary school teachers work ability reached the highest level at a certain level of mental workload (55.73 < mental workload ≤ 64.10). When the teachers' mental workload was lower than the level, their work ability had a positive correlation with the mental workload, i.e., their work ability increased or continuous stable with the increasing mental workload. Also, these authors found that the percentage of teachers with good work ability increased, while teachers with a moderate work ability decreased. These authors concluded that too high or low mental workload will result in the decrement of primary and secondary school teachers' work ability, whereas moderate mental workload (55.73~64.10) will benefit the maintaining and stabilization of their work ability. Likewise, Mohammadian, Malekpour, Malekpour, Zoghipour, and Malalekpour (2015) analyzed the rate of mental workload on teachers and its correlation with their quality of life (QOL). As in the previous study, these authors applied the NASA-task load index (TLX) tool, and a questionnaire of QOL (SF36). They found that the median from mental workload between the teachers with two jobs and single job was significantly different (P < 0.05). Also, it was found that in the median between mental workload and dimensions of QOL (activity limitation due to emotional problems as well as social performance and general health) there was a significant negative correlation (P < 0.5). The median of the mental workload score was higher among teachers, which can negatively impact teachers' life quality, and the quality and quantity of their education. Some other authors that have done research on mental workload in teachers are Pimenta et al. (2015), who point out that long or demanding tasks are often performed in an educational context, which causes teachers feel exhausted with a performance degradation. In addition, Gray, Wilcox, and Nordstokke (2017) studied mental workload on teachers; they mention that teachers are in a profession with high demands, since they work to meet the diverse learning needs of their students. Consequently, many teachers experience high levels of stress contributing to fatigue, and unfortunately, many of them quit.

Furthermore, other labor sector where employees have experienced high levels of mental workload is the manufacturing industry. Choe, Tew, and Tong (2015) mention that operators who work in the material handling system must perform physical and cognitive tasks. These cognitive tasks include supervision, decision making, and control based on the available information. Thus, the automation of cognitive activities has become as significant as the automation of mechanical activities in today's material handling systems. These authors claim that a high level of cognitive automation may improve the operators' performance and decrease their mental workload. As a result, an increased level of cognitive automation and improved information flow can provide a better support material-handling operator, thereby enhancing manufacturing flexibility. Similarly, Zhao, Hsu, Chang, and Li (2016) state that the increasing complexity of products variety can increase mental workload in manufacturing activities. These authors also mention that mental workload can improve product quality and guarantee the efficiency simultaneously. However, minimal research has been done for balancing the quality production and efficiency, which is based on the mental workload effect and complexity in manufacturing activities. Therefore, these authors proposed a mathematical model to formulate the multi-objective problem in an assembly line, where the genetic algorithm for problem solving due to the computational complexities was applied. Their results showed that by incorporating the impact of mental workload on performance may consider the rolled throughput yield (RTY) and efficiency balance when designing an assembly line.

Based on the previous backgrounds, it is declared that mental workload influences employees' health and performance. This chapter focuses on measure mental workload in middle and senior management from manufacturing companies in Tijuana, Mexico. Also, this chapter provides descriptive information on several characteristics of employees, their level of mental workload, as well as the effects it causes on them. Such characteristics include age, civil status, number of children, gender, years of experience, among others.

Effects of Mental Workload

As it was mentioned before, mental workload is presented continuously in activities from different industrial sectors. When these activities demand high levels of mental workload, several negative effects may be visible on employees. For instance, Pimenta et al. (2015) mention that mental workload can lead employees to suffer mental fatigue, mental health problems (i.e. chronic fatigue syndrome or depression), performance degradation, lack of attention in tasks, errors, and accidents. Similarly, several authors mention that high levels of mental workload may cause occupational stress on employees (Hong, Zhijian, & Baohua, 2003; Mohammadian et al., 2015), bad quality of life (Mohammadian et al., 2015), physical health problems (Babazono, Mino, Nagano, Tsuda, & Araki, 2005; Gholamreza, 2006; Lederer, Weltle, & Weber, 2001; Mohammadian et al., 2015; Stansfeld & Candy, 2006), occupational discomfort (Babazono et al., 2005; Lederer et al., 2001; Mohammadian et al., 2015; Stansfeld & Candy, 2006), anxiety (Babazono et al., 2005; Forcella et al., 2007; Maslach, Schaufeli, & Leiter, 2001; Mohammadian et al., 2015; Schaufeli & Greenglass, 2001; Unterbrink et al., 2008) and hypertension (Babazono et al., 2005; Forcella et al., 2007; Maslach et al., 2001; Mohammadian et al., 2015; Schaufeli & Greenglass, 2001; Unterbrink et al., 2008). Different authors have pointed out that both low and excessive mental workload levels result in poor operation performance of employees (Xiao et al., 2015; Zhao et al., 2016). Therefore, a medium mental workload level (55.73~64.10 with the NASA-TLX) is appropriate.

Table 1 portrays a literature review summary of mental workload effects. It is relevant to notice that 19 negative effects are listed in Table 1, therefore, it is important that senior managers pay attention to the mental workload they assign to their employees.

Methods to Evaluate Mental Workload

There are several methods to evaluate mental workload. The following sections explain some of these methods.

NASA Task Load Index (NASA-TLX)

The NASA Tsk Load Index (NASA-TLX) is the most widely used method for measuring mental workload (Galy, Paxion, & Berthelon, 2018; Rizzo & Longo, 2017; Ruiz-Rabelo et al., 2015; Tubbs-Cooley, Mara, Carle, & Gurses, 2018). This method is a subjective validated workload assessment scale that was developed initially as a tool for subjective evaluation of individual workload in air traffic control, flight simulation, and vigilance, which has been increasingly applied to other sectors (Hart & Staveland, 1988; Ruiz-Rabelo et al., 2015; Tubbs-Cooley et al., 2018), such as nuclear energy, transportation, health care (Hart, 2006; Hart & Staveland, 1988; Hwang et al., 2008; Jacobson et al., 2011; Mazur et al., 2012; Tubbs-Cooley et al., 2018), transportation, cognitive psychology, and human computer interaction (Longo, 2012; Rizzo & Longo, 2017). It comprises six dimensions (mental demand, physical demand, time demand, performance, effort, and frustration), which are evaluated based on a 20-point scale ranging from 0 (very low) to 20 (very high) (Galy et al., 2018). These dimensions are also esti-

Table 1. Literature review of mental workload effects (The Authors, 2019)

Reference	Effects of mental workload
(Pimenta et al., 2015)	Mental fatigue
(Pimenta et al., 2015)	Chronic fatigue syndrome
(Pimenta et al., 2015)	Depression
(Mohammadian et al., 2015; Pimenta et al., 2015)	Performance degradation
(Pimenta et al., 2015)	Lack of attention from tasks
(D'Addona et al., 2018; Pimenta et al., 2015)	Errors
(Pimenta et al., 2015)	Accidents
(Hong et al., 2003; Mohammadian et al., 2015)	Occupational stress
(Mohammadian et al., 2015)	Bad quality of life
(Babazono et al., 2005; Gholamreza, 2006; Lederer et al., 2001; Mohammadian et al., 2015; Stansfeld & Candy, 2006)	Physical health problems
(Lederer et al., 2001; Mohammadian et al., 2015)	Early retirement / abandonment of work
(Babazono et al., 2005; Lederer et al., 2001; Mohammadian et al., 2015; Stansfeld & Candy, 2006)	Occupational discomfort
(Babazono et al., 2005; Forcella et al., 2007; Maslach et al., 2001; Mohammadian et al., 2015; Schaufeli & Greenglass, 2001; Unterbrink et al., 2008)	Anxiety
(Babazono et al., 2005; Forcella et al., 2007; Maslach et al., 2001; Mohammadian et al., 2015; Schaufeli & Greenglass, 2001; Unterbrink et al., 2008)	Hypertension
(Babazono et al., 2005; Forcella et al., 2007; Maslach et al., 2001; Mohammadian et al., 2015; Schaufeli & Greenglass, 2001; Unterbrink et al., 2008)	Headache
(Babazono et al., 2005; Forcella et al., 2007; Maslach et al., 2001; Mohammadian et al., 2015; Schaufeli & Greenglass, 2001; Unterbrink et al., 2008)	Psychosomatic disorders
(Babazono et al., 2005; Forcella et al., 2007; Maslach et al., 2001; Mohammadian et al., 2015; Schaufeli & Greenglass, 2001; Unterbrink et al., 2008)	Cardiovascular diseases
(Hong et al., 2003; Mohammadian et al., 2015)	Lower quality of life
(Hong et al., 2003; Mohammadian et al., 2015)	Life expectancy

mated through a paired comparison procedure. In this procedure, participants are required to decide, for each paired comparison (there are 15 paired comparisons among the 6 dimensions), which aspect out of the two contributes the most to mental workload during a task (Rizzo & Longo, 2017). This procedure provides an overall index of mental workload as well as the relative contributions of each dimension (Ruiz-Rabelo et al., 2015). The overall index is the sum of the relative contributions of each dimension, and it is intended to measure the total of the mental workload experienced by an individual during a specific time, event, or situation (Hart, 2006; Tubbs-Cooley et al., 2018). The weights w represent the number of preferences for each dimension (i.e. the number of times each dimension was chosen) in the 15 paired comparisons. Therefore, the preferences range is from 0 (not significant) to 5 (more significant than any other attribute). The final mental workload score is estimated as a weighted average, considering the subjective rating of each attribute d_i (for the 6 dimensions), and the corresponding weights w_i (Equation 1) (Rizzo & Longo, 2017).

$$NASA-TLX = \frac{1}{15}\sum_{1}^{6} d_i w_i \quad (1)$$

Stanton et al., (2018) point out that the NASA-TLX has several advantages and disadvantages; the advantages are the following:

1. The NASA-TLX provides a quick and simple technique for estimating operator workload.
2. The NASA-TLX sub-scales are generic, therefore, the technique can be applied to any domain.
3. The NASA-TLX has been tested thoroughly in the past and has also been the subject of several validation studies.
4. There is a software package from the NALSA-TLX, however, for those who cannot acquire the software, the method format is also available in a handwriting form.
5. This is probably the most widely used technique for estimating employee workload.
6. The NASA-TLX is a multi-dimensional approach for workload assessment.
7. Different studies have shown the NASA-TLX is better than the SWAT technique.
8. When post-trial is performed the approach is non-intrusive to primary task performance.
9. The NASA-TLX has demonstrated sensitivity to demand manipulations in numerous flight experiments.

Similarly, the disadvantages of this method are the following:

1. When it is performed on-line, the NASA-TLX can be intrusive to primary task performance.
2. When it is performed after the fact, participants may have forgotten high workload aspects of the task.
3. Workload ratings may be correlated with task performance i.e. subjects who performed poorly on the primary task may rate their workload as very high and vice versa.
4. The sub-scale weighting procedure is diligent and adds more time to the procedure.

Other Methods

Stanton et al., (2018) mention that there are different methods to evaluate mental workload, such as Subjective Workload Assessment Technique (SWAT), and Subjective Workload Dominance Technique (SWORD), to mention few. Also, these authors point out the corresponding advantages and disadvantages. Table 2 provides a summarize about the other methods that can be used to evaluate mental workload, as well as their advantages and disadvantages.

Table 2. Methods to evaluate mental workload and their advantages and disadvantages (Stanton et al., 2018)

Method	Advantages	Disadvantages
Modified Cooper Harper Scales (MCH)	1. It is easy and quick to use, and it requires minimal training. 2. Non-intrusive measure of workload. 3. It has been widely used to measure workload in a variety of domains. 4. It is accessible, unobtrusive, easily to performed and easily transferable. 5. High face validity. 7. It has been successfully applied to workload assessment in different flight simulation experiments incorporating demand manipulations. 8. The data obtained when using uni-dimensional tools is simpler to analyze than when using multi-dimensional tools.	1. It is a dated approach. 2. It was developed originally to rate controllability of aircraft. 3. It is limited to manual control tasks. 4. Data is collected post-trial, which is a subject for different problems, such as correlation with performance. Also, participants are restricted when reporting past mental events. 5. It is uni-dimensional.
Subjective Workload Assessment Technique (SWAT)	1. It offers a quick, simple, and low-cost procedure for estimating participant mental workload. 2. Its dim can be applied to any domain. 3. It is one of the most widely used and well-known subjective workload assessment technique available. 4. The Pro-SWAT variation allows the technique to be used to predict operator workload. 5. It is a multidimensional approach to workload assessment. 6. This technique has demonstrated a sensitivity to demand manipulations in flight environments.	1. It can be intrusive if it is performed on-line. 2. Different validation studies have reported that the NASA-TLX is superior to SWAT in terms of sensitivity, particularly for low mental workloads. 3. It has been constantly criticized for having a low sensitivity to mental workloads. 4. It is time consuming and diligent. 5. The post-trial collection of mental workload data has several associated disadvantages, including a potential correlation between mental workload ratings and task performance, and participants may be forgetting different parts of a task when workload was especially low.
Subjective Workload Dominance Technique (SWORD)	1. It offers a quick, simple use, and a low-cost approach for assessing mental workload. 2. It is especially useful when comparing the mental workload imposed by different tasks of devices. One potential evaluation would be for the evaluation of the mental workload imposed by different design concepts. 3. It is performed by post-trial, therefore is non-intrusive to task performance. 4. It has high face validity. 5. It has been demonstrated to have a sensitivity to mental workload variations.	1. The post-trial collection of mental workload data has several associated disadvantages, including a potential correlation between mental workload, ratings, and task performance, and participants may be forgetting different parts of a task when workload was especially low. 2. Only limited validation evidence is available in the literature review. 3. It has not been as widely used as other mental workload assessment techniques, such as SWAT and NASA-TLX. 4. The SWORD output does not offer a rating for participant mental workload as it is; only a rating list of what type of tasks or devices imposed greater mental workload than others.
Dra Workload Scales (Draws)	1. It offers a quick, simple use, and low-cost approach for assessing mental workload. 2. Data is obtained on-line during task performance, therefore, the problems of collecting posttrial mental workload data is discarded. 3. It has high face validity. 4. Sensitivity to workload variation has been demonstrated. 5. The workload dimensions used in the DRAWS technique were validated in several studies during the development of the technique. 6. Although its application was developed for the aviation domain, the workload dimensions are generic, allowing the technique to be applied in any domain.	1. It is intrusive to primary task performance. 2. There are limited applications reported in the literature review. 3. The workload ratings may correlate highly with task performance when it is implemented. 4. There is limited validation evidence available in the literature review. 5. The technique requires further validation.

continues on following page

Table 2. Continued

Method	Advantages	Disadvantages
Malvern Capacity Estimate (MACE)	1. It offers a quick, simple, and low-cost approach for assessing participant spare capacity. 2. The output is potentially useful, indicating when operators are experiencing mental overload and mental underload. 3. It provides a direct measure of operator capacity. 4. On-line implementation removes the problems associated with the collection of mental workloads posttrial (i.e. correlation with performance, forgetting certain parts of a task, etc.).	1. The technique is totally dependent on the participant's ability to estimate their remaining capacity. 2. The technique remains largely unvalidated. 3. The reliability and accuracy of this technique is questionable. 4. The MACE technique has only been used in simulators; it would be an intrusive technique if it is applied on-line during task performance in the 'real-world'.
Workload Profile Technique	1. The technique is based on sound underpinning theory (Multiple Resource Theory). 2. It is quick and easy to use, requiring minimal analytical training. 3. It also offers an overall task workload rating; the output also provides a workload rating for each of the eight workload dimensions. 4. It is a multi-dimensional mental workload assessment technique. 5. As the technique is applied post-trial, it can be applied in real-world settings.	1. It may be difficult for participants to rate workload on a scale of 0 to 1. 2. A more sophisticated scale may be required in order to obtain a more appropriate workload measure. 3. The post-trial collection of mental workload data has several associated disadvantages, including a potential correlation between mental workload ratings and task performance, as well as participants may be 'forgetting' different parts of a task when workload was especially low. 4. There is minimal evidence of the actual usage of the technique. 5. There is limited validation evidence associated with the technique. 6. Participants require an understanding of mental workload and multiple theory resources. 7. The dimensions used by the technique may not be fully understood by participants with limited experience on psychology and human factors. In a study comparing the NASATLX, SWAT, and workload profile techniques, it was found that there were problems with some of the participants understanding the different dimensions used in the workload profile technique.
Bedford Scales	1. It is very quick and easy to use, requiring minimal analytical training. 2. Its scale is generic; therefore, the technique can be easily applied in different domains. 3. It may be useful when it is applied along with other mental workload assessment techniques. 4. It has low intrusiveness.	1. There is minimal evidence of actual implementation of this technique. 2. There is limited validation evidence associated with the technique. 3. It offers limited output. 4. Participants are not efficient at reporting mental events 'after the fact.'
Instantaneous Self-Assessment (ISA)	1. ISA is a simple technique that it is easy to learn and use. 2. The output allows a workload profile for a task under analysis to be constructed. 3. ISA is very quick on its application as data collection occurs during the trial. 4. It has been used extensively in several domains. 5. It does not require too much resources. 6. While the technique is obtrusive to the primary task, it is probably the least intrusive of the on-line workload assessment techniques. 7. It is a low-cost technique.	1. ISA is intrusive to primary task performance. 2. There is a limited validation evidence associated with the technique. 3. ISA is a simplistic technique, offering only a limited assessment of operator workload. 4. Participants are not very efficient at reporting mental events.

continues on following page

Table 2. Continued

Method	Advantages	Disadvantages
Cognitive Task Load Analysis (CTLA)	1. The technique is based on sound theoretical underpinning. 2. It can be used during the design of systems and processes to highlight tasks or scenarios that impose especially high cognitive task demands. 3. It seems to be suitable for analyzing control room type of tasks or scenarios.	1. The technique seems to be quite complex. 2. This technique would be very time consuming when it is applied. 3. A high-level of training would be required. 4. There is no guidance on the rating of cognitive task load; it would be difficult to give a task load a numerical rating based on the underlying model. 5. Initial data collection would be time consuming. 6. The CTLA technique requires validation. 7. Evidence of its implementation is limited.
Pro-Sword – Subjective Workload Dominance Technique	1. It is easy to learn and use. 2. It is non-intrusive. 3. It has high face validity. 4. SWORD has been demonstrated to have a sensitivity to workload variations. 5. It is very quick in its application.	1. Data is collected post-task. 2. SWORD is a dated approach to workload assessment. 3. Workload projections are more accurate when domain experts are involved. 4. Further validation is required. 5. The SWORD technique has not been as widely used as other workload assessment techniques, such as SWAT, MCH, and the NASA TLX.
Primary and Secondary Task Performance Measures	1. When using a battery of mental workload assessment techniques for mental workload assessment, the data obtained can be crosschecked for reliability purposes. 2. Primary task performance measures offer a direct index of performance. 3. Primary task performance measures are particularly effective when measuring workload in tasks that are long in duration. 4. Primary task measures are also useful when measuring operator overload. 5. It requires no further effort besides the analyst to set up and record the data; as primary task performance is normally measured anyway. 6. Secondary task performance measures are effective at discarding tasks when no difference was observed while assessing performance alone. 7. Primary and secondary task performance measures are easy to use, as a computer typically records the required data.	1. Primary task performance measures isolated may not distinguish between different levels of workload; particularly minimal ones. Different operators may still achieve the same performance levels under completely different workload conditions. 2. It is suggested that primary task performance is not a reliable measure when it is used isolated. 3. Secondary task performance measures have been known to be only sensitive to gross changes in mental workload. 4. Secondary task performance measures are intrusive to primary task performance. 5. Considerable attention is required during the design and selection of the secondary task to be used. The analyst must confirm that the secondary task is having the same resources as the primary task. The secondary task must be carefully designed in order to be an appropriate measure of spare attentional capacity. 6. Extra work and resources are required in developing the secondary task performance measure. 7. The techniques are required to be implemented together to be effective. 8. Using primary and secondary task performance measures may be expensive, as simulators and computers are required.
Physiological Measures	1. Several physiological techniques have demonstrated a sensitivity to task demand variations. 2. When using physiological techniques, data is recorded continuously throughout task performance. 3. Physiological measurements can often be taken in a real-world setting, removing the need for a simulation of the task. 4. Advances in technology have resulted in an increased accuracy and sensitivity of the several physiological measurement tools. 5. Physiological measurement does not interfere with primary task performance.	1. The data is easily mistaken by foreign interference. 2. The equipment that is used to measure physiological responses is typically physically obtrusive. 3. The equipment is also typically expensive to be acquired, temperamental, and difficult to perform. 4. Physiological data is highly difficult to obtain and analyze. 5. In order to use physiological techniques effectively, the analyst(s) require a full understanding about physiological responses to workload. 6. It may be difficult to use certain equipment in the field i.e. brain and eye examination equipment.

METHODOLOGY

Instruments

Authors rely on the following instruments to perform the research on mental workload:

- **Computer equipment:** Laptop Toshiba Satellite C645d and Dell Inspiron 7567
- **Google forms**
- **Microsoft Excel®**

Method

The method presented in this chapter is divided into some phases. Figure 1 shows the different phases.

Phase 1: Contacting manufacturing companies. It is carried out in two ways: 1) students working in the manufacturing industry, and 2) the educational institution liaison office. In the first case, several students have a senior or middle job position, and/or interact with manufacturing employees who have these positions. Once students are contacted, they receive an explanation about the project and its objective, and if there are doubts, they are clarified. In the case of the liaison office, a similar explanation is given, and then, the office contact ex-students who have a senior or middle job position in the manufacturing industry. Once ex-students are contacted, the same explanation is given to them.

Phase 2: Applying the mental workload questionnaire. Once manufacturing companies are contacted and employees are willing to participate in this research, a mental workload questionnaire is applied to them. The original questionnaire is written in Spanish and it is applied online through a Google form. The questionnaire contains items, such as job position that the employee currently has, gender, age, and number of children he/she has, to mention few. The Appendix, Figure 17 shows the English version of the mental workload questionnaire.

Figure 1. Methodology applied to obtain mental workload on senior and middle managers in manufacturing companies

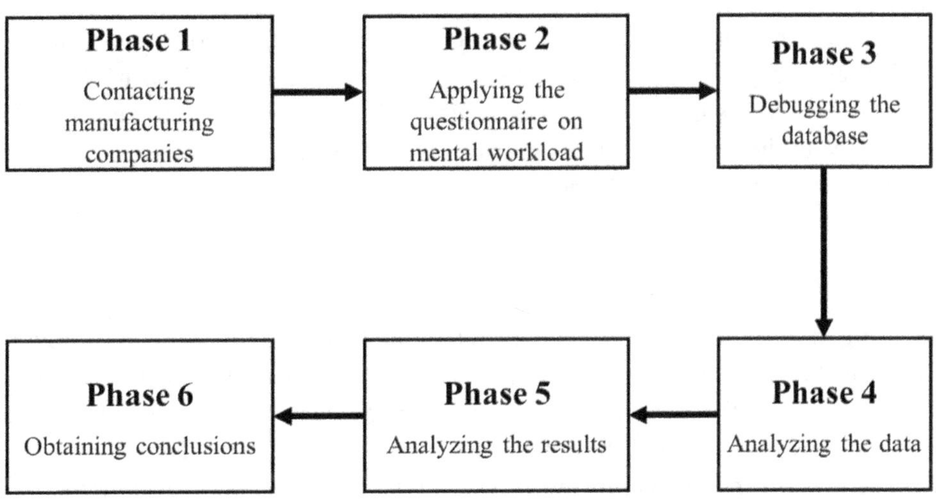

Phase 3: Debugging the database. Once employees answered the questionnaire, the information is registered automatically in an Excel® file, generating a database. From this information, some answers are removed from the database. For instance, if a participant answers that he/she is currently an operator, all the responds provided by this participant are removed from the database, since operator is not a senior or middle job position in manufacturing companies. The same happens if incoherent answers are given to other items.

Phase 4: Analyzing the data. Once the database is ready, the data is analyzed. This analysis is performed for all the companies in a general way. The analysis includes a comparison of the responses for each item with the mental workload level. This in order to determine the variables, and their levels, which can facilitate the increase or decrease of the mental workload. Mental workload is estimated by applying Equation (1).

Phase 5 Obtaining results. After the data analysis is finished, the results are obtained. These results are illustrated through graphs or tables for each item.

Phase 6: Analyzing results. Results are analyzed to stablish conclusions about the impact of each variable on the mental workload level in middle and senior management in manufacturing companies. As a summary, variables are arranged in a decreasing order according to their contribution level to mental workload.

RESULTS

Phase 1

Results from phase 1 indicated that 62 companies were contacted. Figure 2 shows the distribution of these companies by industrial sector. It is important to notice that most of the companies belonged to the Electrical/Electronic sector, with 16 companies, representing 25.8% out of the 62 companies. On the other hand, only one company was in the Paper sector, this represents only 1.6% out of the 62 companies. Other sectors included Automotive, Medical, Food, Textile, Wood, Metallic products, Plastic and rubber, and Other.

Phase 2

From the 62 manufacturing companies, 193 employees belonging to the middle and senior management were surveyed. The company with most surveyed employees was Company 53, with 29 employees, which represents 15.03% of the 193 surveyed employees. Most of the companies (39, i.e. 62.9%) contributed with only 1 employee to the research. One employee represents 0.52% of the total participants. Figure 3 presents the number of surveyed employees by company.

Phase 3

From the debugging of the database, it was obtained that the 62 originally surveyed companies, only 55 companies continued towards the final analysis of mental workload. Company 6, Company 16, Company 21, Company 26, Company 39, Company 51, and Company 57 were discarded from the database due to incorrect answers, such as omission of the company's name, the job position does not belong to middle and senior management, or that the company did not belong to the manufacturing field.

Figure 2. Distribution of the surveyed companies by industrial sector

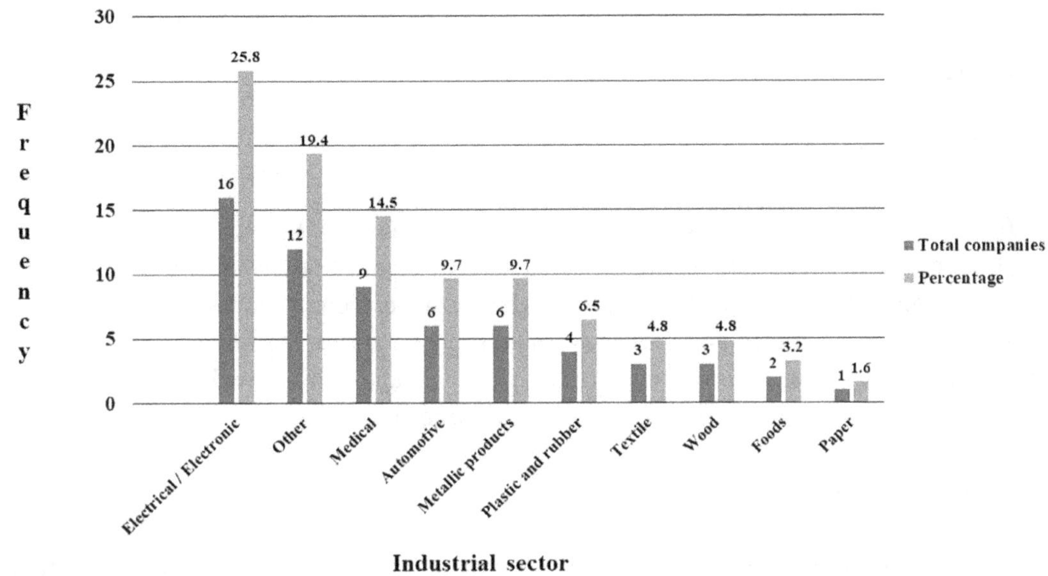

Figure 3. Surveyed employees by company

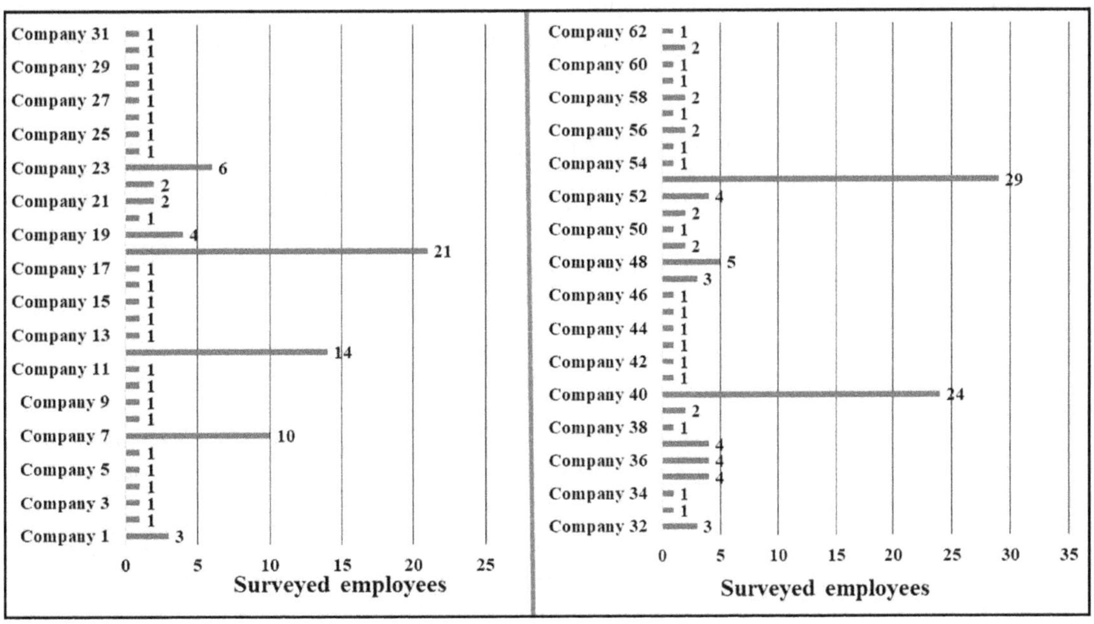

Specifically, from the 193 surveyed employees, only the data of 167 employees were acceptable in the database for further analysis.

Final Results

Mental Workload According to Gender

From the 167 surveyed employees, 99 were men while 68 were women. In both, mental demand was the dimension that impacted the most on mental workload, with values of 60.6 and 57.9 in men and women respectively. The second dimension that impacted the most on mental workload level was the time demand, with a value of 37 in men and 38.1 in women. Figure 4 shows the impact on mental workload level of the six dimensions, both in men and women. The average mental workload level for men was 65.1, whereas for women was 66.4. Figure 5 displays these results.

Mental Workload According to Age Range

As in the case of mental workload by gender, mental demand was the dimension that more impacted on the mental workload by age range, followed by effort and time demand. Again, the dimension of physical demand was the dimension that has the lowest impact on mental workload. Figure 6 shows the impact on mental workload of the six dimensions according to the age range. Results of mental workload level according to the age range indicated that employees between 18-20 years old had the lowest level of mental workload with a value of 55.1. However, from the 21-25 age range to the range of 36-40 years

Figure 4. Impact of the six dimensions on the mental workload level in men and women

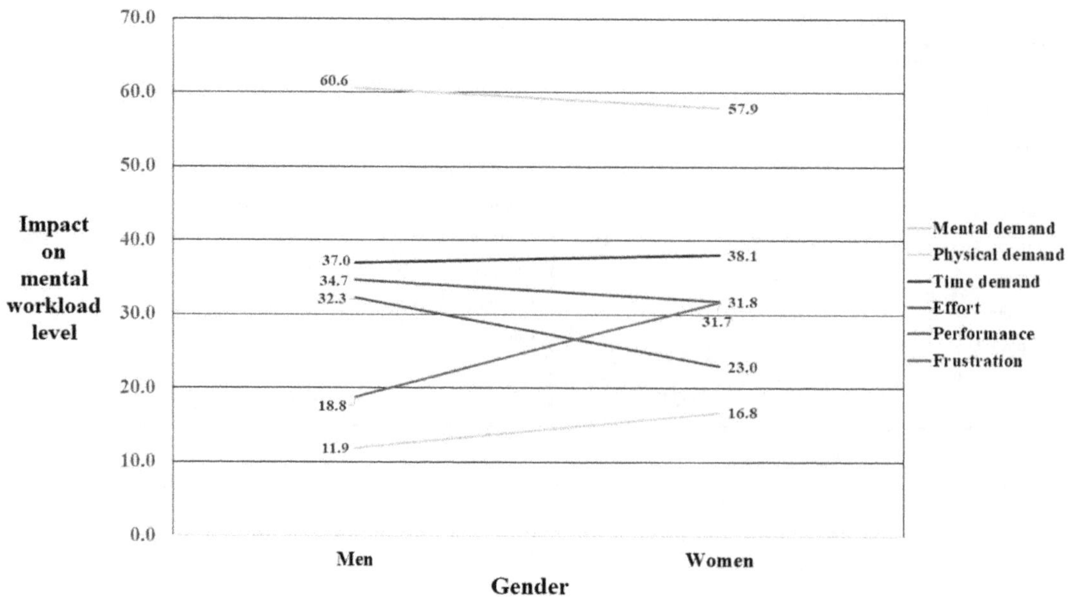

Figure 5. Mental workload level in men and women

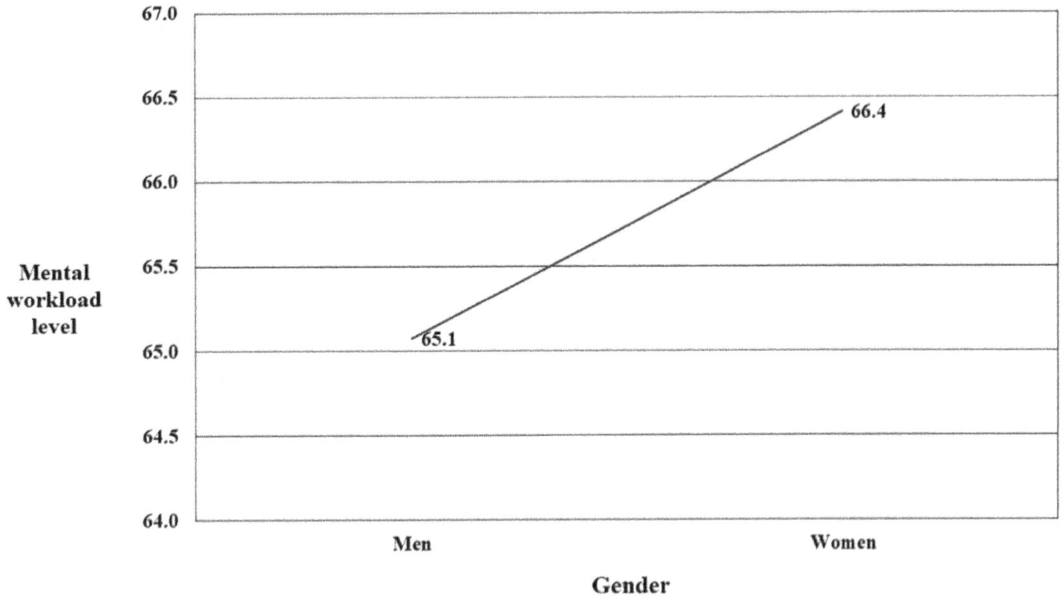

old, results indicated that there is an increasing trend on the mental workload level, being employees in this last age range who presented the highest mental workload level with a value of 71.1. From employees between 41 and 60 years old, mental workload level varied from 61.7 to 64.6. Figure 7 shows these results.

Mental Workload According to Civil Status

Results of mental workload based on the civil status from surveyed employees showed that the dimension of mental demand was the one that impacted the most on the general mental workload level, followed by the dimensions of time demand and effort. On the other hand, dimensions of physical demand and frustration had the lowest impact on the general level of mental workload. Figure 8 presents the impact on mental workload of the six dimensions according to civil status.

Regarding the mental workload level, results indicated that married employees had the highest one, with a value of 66.9, whereas employees in free union had the lowest mental workload level, with a value of 63.2. Figure 9 shows the results of mental workload level according to civil status.

Mental Workload According to Number of Children

Results from mental workload, according to the number of children that employees have, indicated that the dimension of frustration had the lowest impact on the mental workload level, since for employees with ˃ 4 children, this dimension had a value of zero. The second dimension with the lowest impact on mental workload was the effort. On the other hand, it is repeated that the dimension of mental demand had the highest impact on the mental workload, followed by the effort and time demand. Figure 10 shows the impact of the six dimensions on the mental workload level according to the number of children. Similarly, Figure 11 presents the general mental workload level of surveyed employees according to the number of

Figure 6. Impact of the six dimensions on the mental workload level according to age range

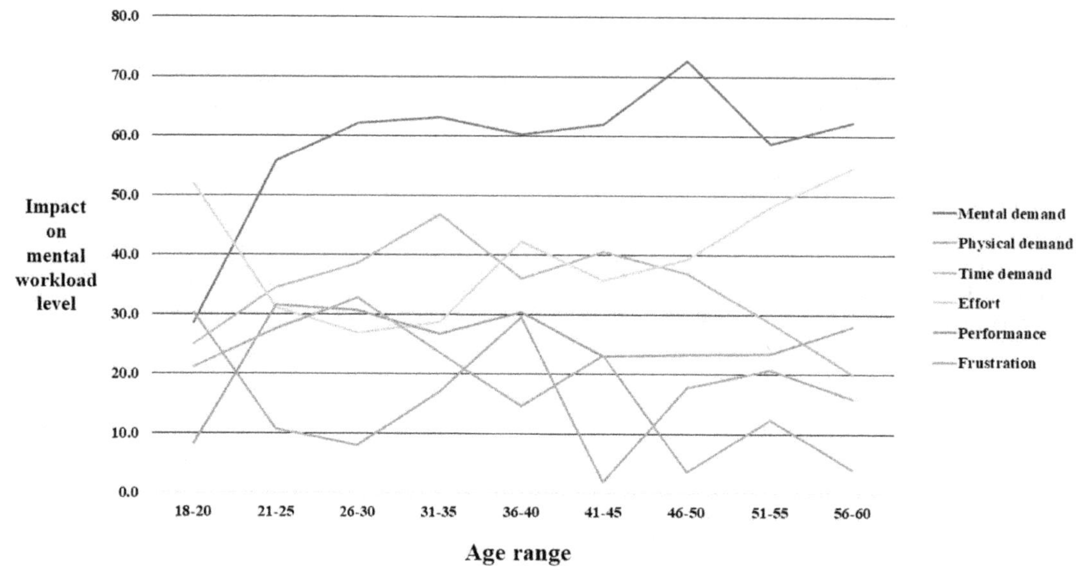

Figure 7. Mental workload level according to age range

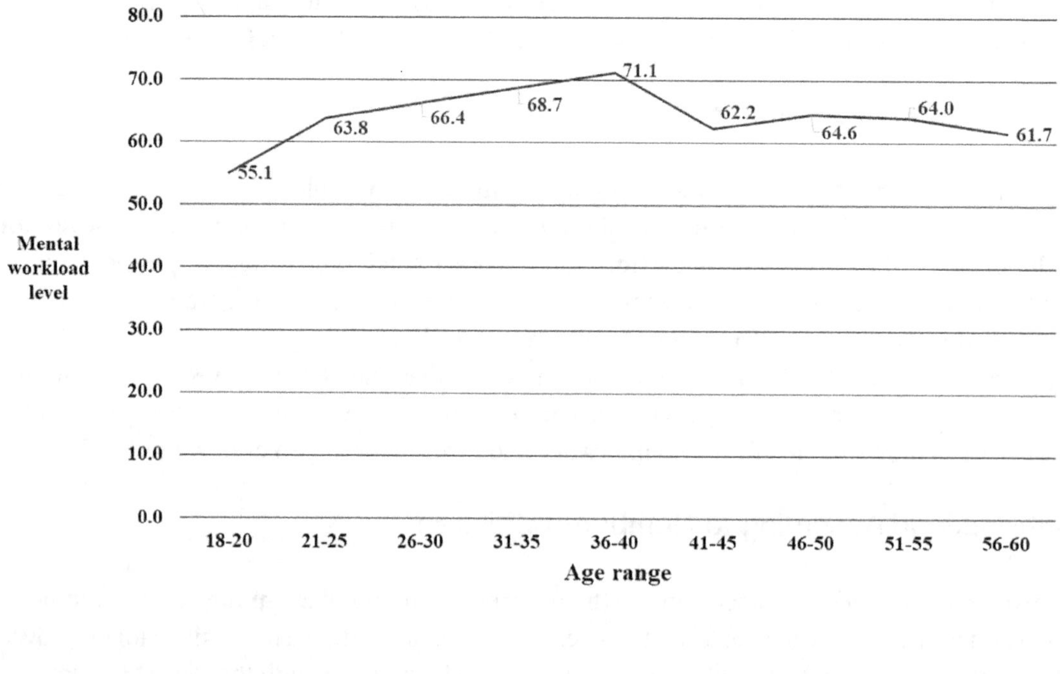

Figure 8. Impact of the six dimensions on the mental workload level according to civil status

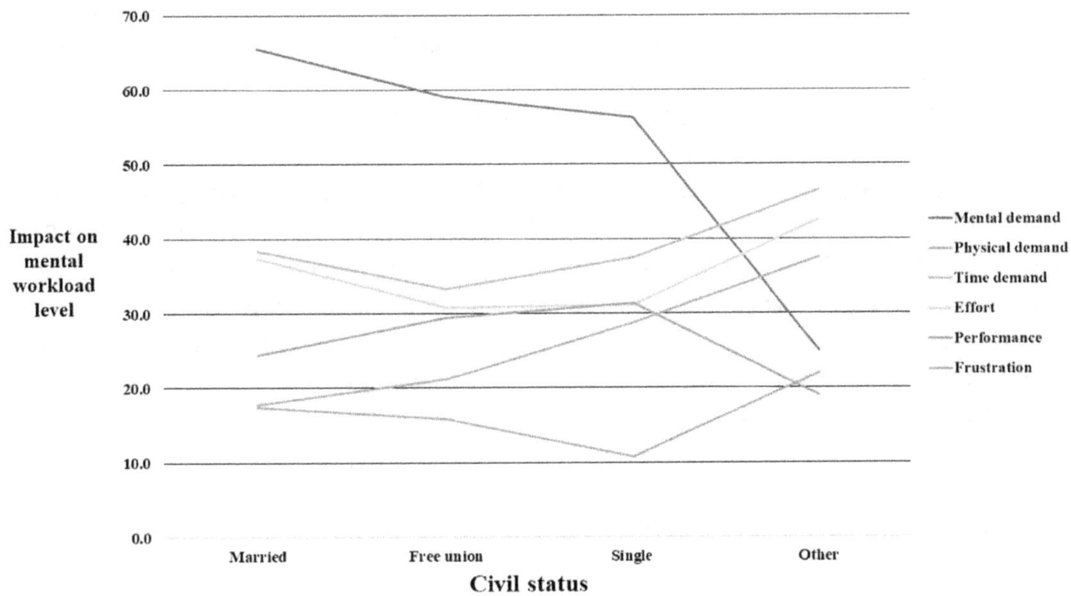

Figure 9. Mental workload level according to civil status

children they have. Notice that the employees with only one child had the lowest mental workload level, with a value of 61.4, whereas employees with 3-4 children had the highest mental workload level with a value of 61.4. Employees with no children had a medium level of mental workload, with a value of 65.8.

Mental Workload According to Years of Experience

Once again, results indicated that mental demand was the dimension that contributed the most to the mental workload level, this time according to years of experience. Effort and time demand were the other two dimensions that contributed the most to the mental workload level. On the other hand, frustration, physical demand, and performance had the lowest impact on the mental workload level. These results are shown in Figure 12. Regarding the mental workload level, employees between ˃ 25-30 years of experience had the lowest level of mental workload, with a value of 55.4, whereas employees between ˃ 30-35 had the highest mental workload level, with a value of 76. Figure 13 shows all the results of mental workload level according to the years of experience.

Mental Workload According to Worked Hours per Week

As in all other results, mental demand was the dimension that contributed the most to the mental workload according to the hours employees work per week. The other two dimensions that contributed the most to the mental workload level related to the worked hours per week, were time demand and performance. The lowest impact on mental workload was due to the dimensions from physical demand, frustration, and effort; Figure 14 shows these results. Regarding the mental workload level, employees that work between ˃ 30-35 hours per week had the lowest level of mental workload, with a value of 62.4. On the other hand, employees that work between ˃ 25-30 hours per week had the highest level of mental work-

Figure 10. Impact of the six dimensions on the mental workload level according to number of children

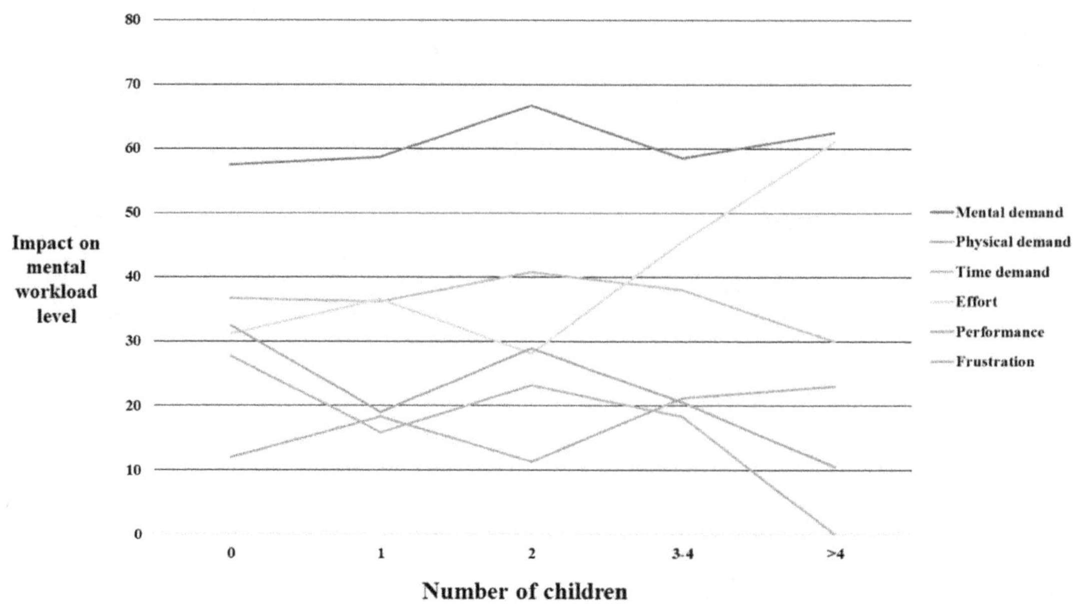

Figure 11. Mental workload level according to number of children

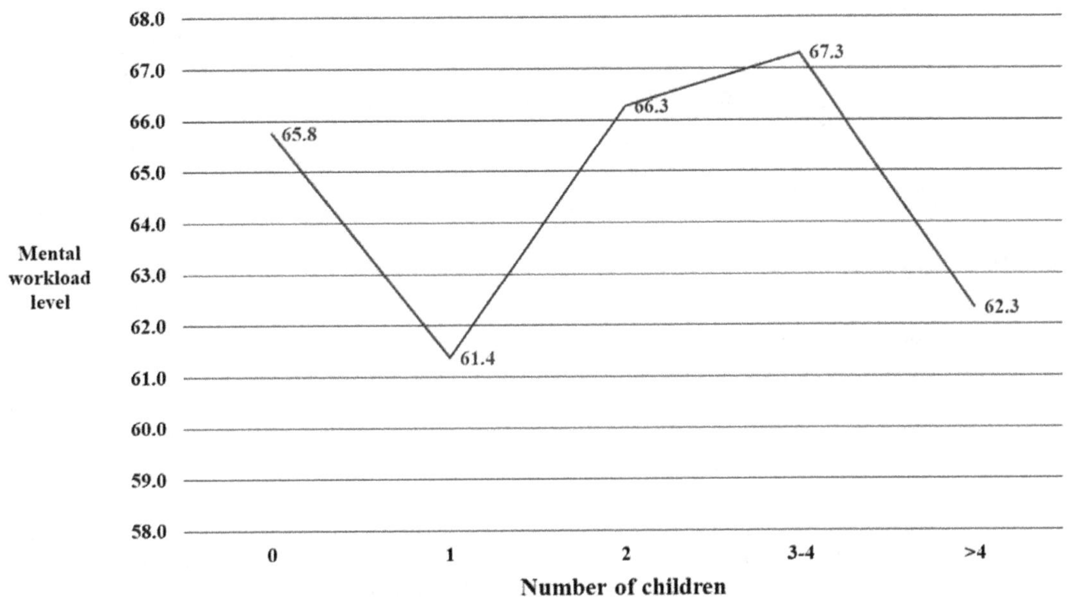

Figure 12. Impact of the six dimensions on the mental workload level according to years of experience

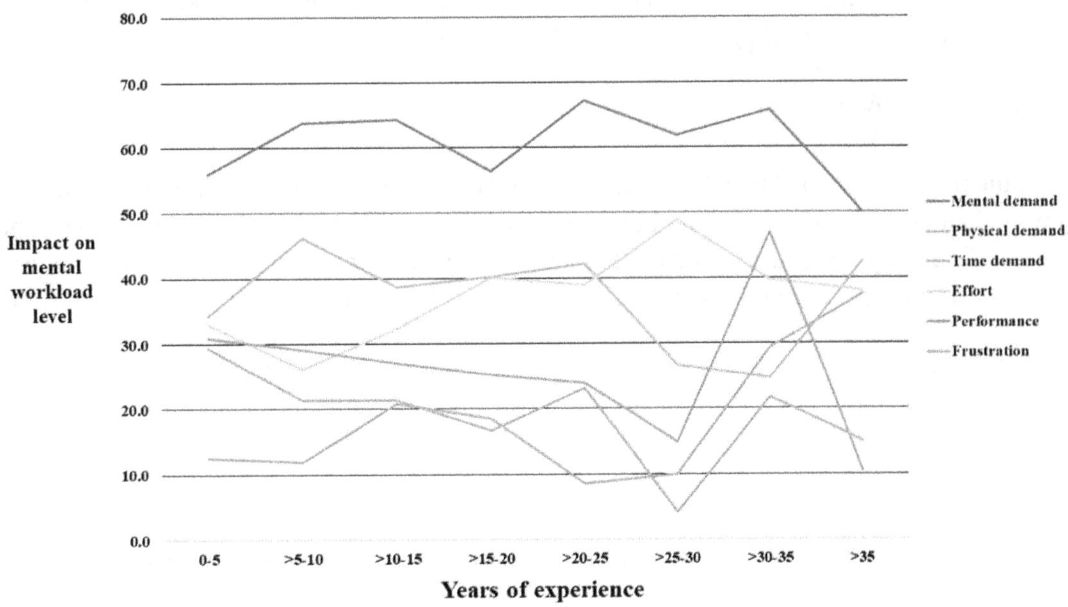

Figure 13. Mental workload level according to years of experience

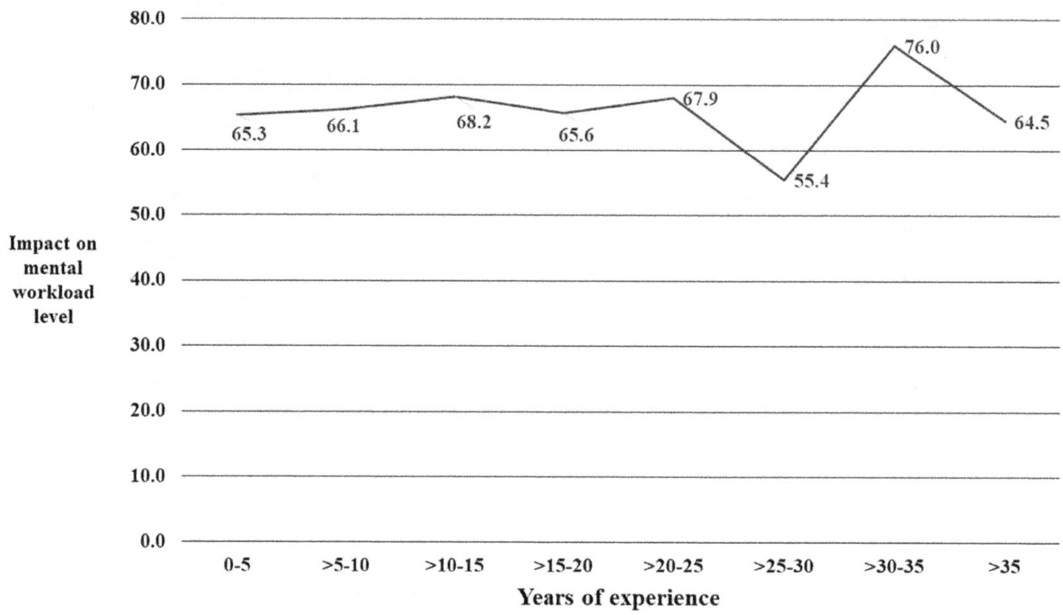

load, with a value of 73. Figure15 displays the level of mental workload according to the worked hours per week. Notice that in these results, as in the other ones, there is no trend that indicates that the mental workload level increases according to the value of a specific variable.

Effects of Mental Workload

Regarding the mental workload effects, results indicated that employees have suffered from stress, headache, physical and mental fatigue, irritability, depression, work errors, loss of memory, social problems, and increment on body weight. The most frequent effects were stress and mental fatigue, whereas the less frequent effects were social problems, depression, and loss of memory. Figure 16 shows these effects and their frequency.

FUTURE WORK

As a matter of fact, while considering the present research, including not only the results, but also the data, there is an opportunity to perform a deeper investigation on the causes and effects of the mental workload. Therefore, it is suggested to propose specific hypotheses and create a hypothetical causal model. Consequently, performing a statistical analysis through a structural equation modelling (SEM) will help obtain more precise results concerning the effects of age range, civil status, number of children, years of experience, and worked hours per week over the mental workload level of middle and senior management employees in manufacturing companies. Similarly, future research will help to know the mental workload effects and their significance on this type of employees. Specifically, such effects may

Figure 14. Impact of the six dimensions on the mental workload level according to the worked hours per week

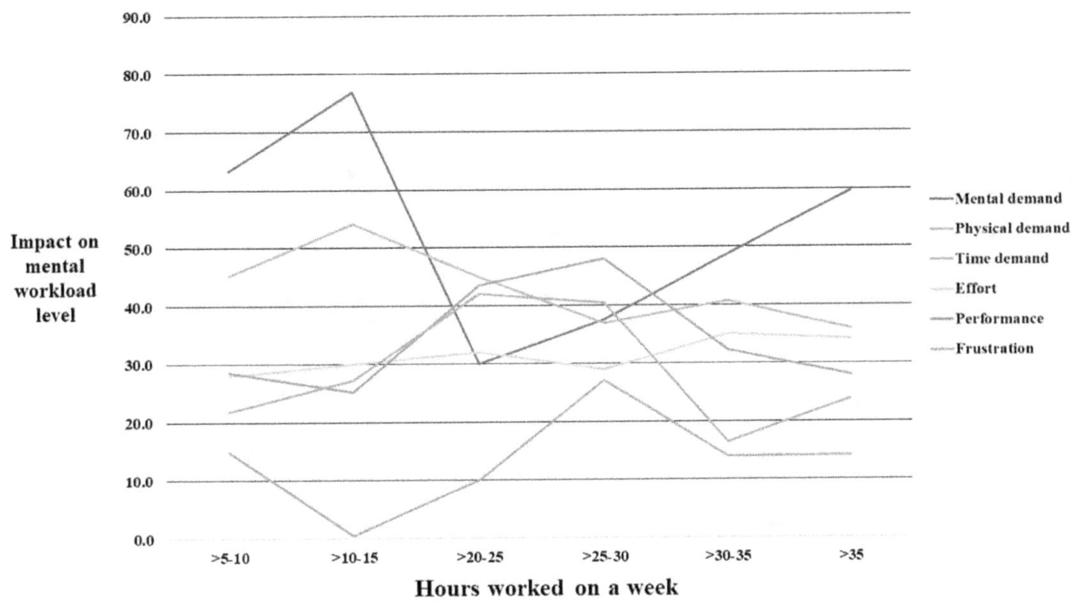

Figure 15. Mental workload level according to the worked hours per week

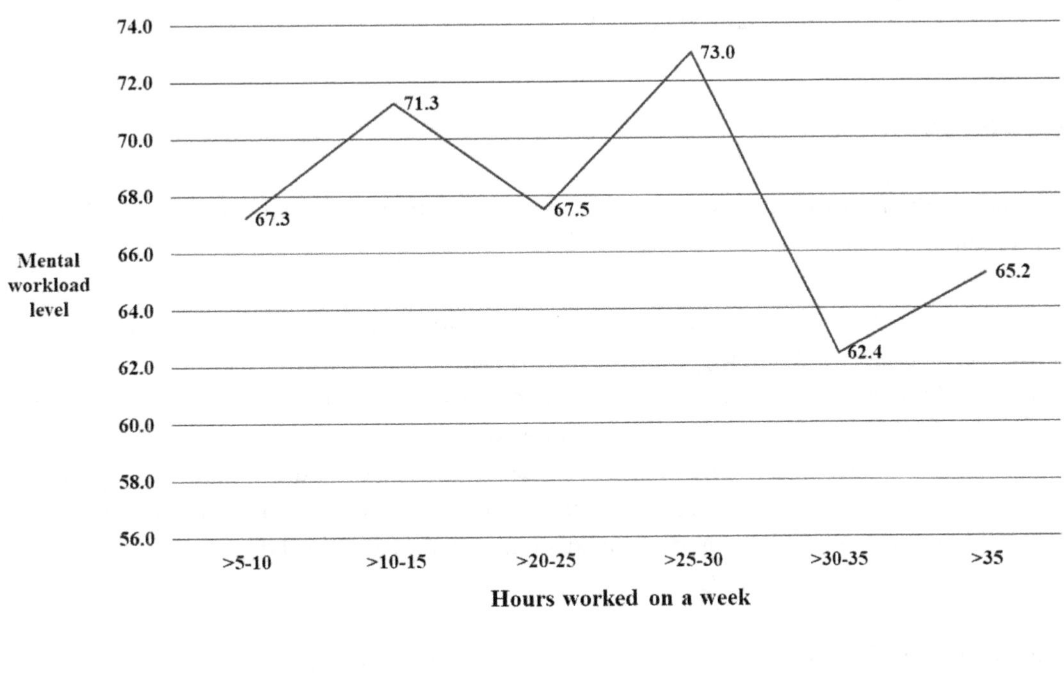

Figure 16. Effects of mental workload and their frequency

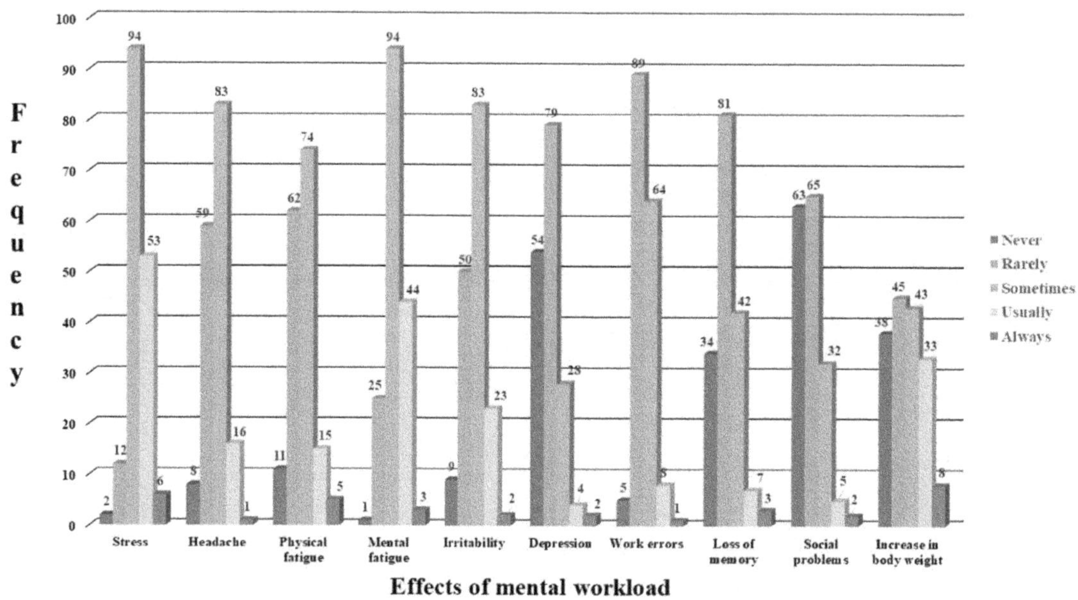

include those presented in Figure 16, i.e., stress, mental fatigue, headache, depression, just to mention few. This future research will allow to apply statistical tools to acknowledge concretely if there is a relationship among the variables analyzed in this chapter.

CONCLUSION

Based on the results previously presented, following conclusions are established about the six dimensions from mental demand:

- Mental demand is the dimension that contribute the most to the mental workload level in middle and senior management employees in manufacturing companies.
- Temporal demand and effort are the second and third dimensions that contribute the most to the mental workload level in the mentioned employees.
- On the other hand, physical demand is the dimension that contribute the least to the mental workload level in middle and senior management employees in manufacturing companies.
- Similarly, frustration level and performance are the second and third dimension that contribute the least to their mental workload level.

These conclusions lead a general conclusion, which is the following:

- Middle and senior management employees in manufacturing companies are exposed to high mental demand tasks, which is not a physical demand, as they feel pressured by the time, consequently, it leads them to maximize their effort to finish the tasks on time. Despite this, they meet the required expectations and feel satisfied with their performance.

Similarly, results lead to the following conclusions regarding the mental workload level:

- There is no significant different between the mental workload level in men and women.
- There is no relationship between the mental workload level and the age of the employees.
- There is no relationship between the mental workload level and the civil status of the employees.
- There is no relationship between the mental workload level and the number of children employees have.
- There is no relationship between the mental workload level and the years of experience employees have.
- There is no relationship between the mental workload level and the worked hours per week employees have.

As it can be seen, results of the mental workload level varied from 55.1 to 76.0. Considering that Xiao et al. (2015) mention that there is a better work ability when mental workload level varies from 55.73 to 64.10, the mental workload level of middle and senior management employees in manufacturing companies are out of this range, which may cause some effects, such as mental fatigue, stress, headache, just to mention few, as it is presented in Figure 16.

REFERENCES

Babazono, A., Mino, Y., Nagano, J., Tsuda, T., & Araki, T. (2005). A Prospective Study on the Influences of Workplace Stress on Mental Health. *Journal of Occupational Health*, *47*(6), 490–495. doi:10.1539/joh.47.490 PMID:16369111

Bashiri, B., & Mann, D. D. (2015). Impact of Automation on Drivers' Performance in Agricultural Semi-Autonomous Vehicles. *Journal of Agricultural Safety and Health*, *21*(2), 129–139. doi:10.13031/jash.21.10977 PMID:26204788

Belkic, K. (2003). *The Occupational Stress Index: An Approach Derived from Cognitive Ergonomics and Brain Research for Clinical Practice*. Cambridge International Science Publishing.

Boet, S., Sharma, B., Pigford, A.-A., Hladkowicz, E., Rittenhouse, N., & Grantcharov, T. (2017). Debriefing decreases mental workload in surgical crisis: A randomized controlled trial. *Surgery*, *161*(5), 1215–1220. doi:10.1016/j.surg.2016.11.031 PMID:28104293

Choe, P., Tew, J. D., & Tong, S. (2015). Effect of cognitive automation in a material handling system on manufacturing flexibility. *International Journal of Production Economics*, *170*, 891–899. doi:10.1016/j.ijpe.2015.01.018

Choppin, J., Roth-McDuffie, A., Drake, C., & Davis, J. (2018). Curriculum ergonomics: Conceptualizing the interactions between curriculum design and use. *International Journal of Educational Research*, *92*, 75–85. doi:10.1016/j.ijer.2018.09.015

Claxton Bomme, S., & Fendley, M. (2018). A theoretical framework for evaluating mental workload resources in human systems design for manufacturing operations. *International Journal of Industrial Ergonomics*, *63*, 7–17. doi:10.1016/j.ergon.2016.10.007

D'Addona, D. M., Bracco, F., Bettoni, A., Nishino, N., Carpanzano, E., & Bruzzone, A. A. (2018). Adaptive automation and human factors in manufacturing: An experimental assessment for a cognitive approach. *CIRP Annals*, *67*(1), 455–458. doi:10.1016/j.cirp.2018.04.123

Dul, J., Bruder, R., Buckle, P., Carayon, P., Falzon, P., Marras, W., ... van der Doelen, B. (2012). A strategy for human factors/ergonomics: Developing the discipline and profession. *Ergonomics*, *55*(4), 377–395. doi:10.1080/00140139.2012.661087 PMID:22332611

Endsley, M. R., & Garland, D. J. (2000). *Situation Awareness Analysis and Measurement.* CRC Press. Retrieved from https://books.google.com.mx/books?id=WrJGDsjJakcC&lr=&hl=es&source=gbs_navlinks_s

Forcella, L., Di Donato, A., Coccia, U., Tamellini, L., Di Giampaolo, L., Grapsi, M., … Boscolo, P. (2007). Anxiety, job stress and job insecurity among teachers with indefinite or definite time contract. *Giornale Italiano Di Medicina Del Lavoro Ed Ergonomia, 29*(3 Suppl), 683–686. Retrieved from http://www.ncbi.nlm.nih.gov/pubmed/18409903

Galy, E., Paxion, J., & Berthelon, C. (2018). Measuring mental workload with the NASA-TLX needs to examine each dimension rather than relying on the global score: An example with driving. *Ergonomics*, *61*(4), 517–527. doi:10.1080/00140139.2017.1369583 PMID:28817353

Gholamreza, K. (2006). *Stress and anxiety for individuals and organizations.* Tehran: Reflections Publication.

Goonetilleke, R. S., & Karwowski, W. (Eds.). (2018). *Advances in Physical Ergonomics & Human Factors.* Orlando, FL: Springer; doi:10.1007/978-3-319-60825-9

Gray, C., Wilcox, G., & Nordstokke, D. (2017). Teacher mental health, school climate, inclusive education and student learning: A review. *Canadian Psychology*, *58*(3), 203–210. doi:10.1037/cap0000117

Hart, S. G. (2006). Nasa-Task Load Index (NASA-TLX); 20 Years Later. *Proceedings of the Human Factors and Ergonomics Society Annual Meeting*, *50*(9), 904–908. doi:10.1177/154193120605000909

Hart, S. G., & Staveland, L. E. (1988). Development of NASA-TLX (Task Load Index): Results of Empirical and Theoretical Research. *Advances in Psychology*, *52*, 139–183. doi:10.1016/S0166-4115(08)62386-9

Hernández-Arellano, J. L., Aguilar-Duque, J. I., & Gómez-Bull, K. G. (2018). Methodology to Determine Product Dimensions Based on User Anthropometric Data. In J. L. García-Alcaraz, G. Alor-Hernández, A. A. Maldonado-Macías, & C. Sánchez-Ramírez (Eds.), New Perspectives on Applied Industrial Tools and Techniques (pp. 373–385). Cham, Switzerland: Springer International Publishing. doi:10.1007/978-3-319-56871-3_18

Hong, S., Zhijian, J., & Baohua, M. (2003). Research on life-span of the population of intellectuals in Harbin Chinese. *Chin J Hosp Stat, 10*, 8–16.

Hwang, S.-L., Yau, Y.-J., Lin, Y.-T., Chen, J.-H., Huang, T.-H., Yenn, T.-C., & Hsu, C.-C. (2008). Predicting work performance in nuclear power plants. *Safety Science*, *46*(7), 1115–1124. doi:10.1016/j.ssci.2007.06.005

International Ergonomics Association (IEA). (2018). *Definition and Domains of Ergonomics | IEA Website*. Retrieved November 2, 2018, from http://www.iea.cc/whats/

Jacobson, C. J. Jr, Bolon, S., Elder, N., Schroer, B., Matthews, G., Szaflarski, J. P., ... Horner, R. D. (2011). Temporal and subjective work demands in office-based patient care: An exploration of the dimensions of physician work intensity. *Medical Care*, *49*(1), 52–58. doi:10.1097/MLR.0b013e3181f53542 PMID:21164325

Jin, X., Zheng, B., Pei, Y., & Li, H. (2017). A Method to Estimate Operator's Mental Workload in Multiple Information Presentation Environment of Agricultural Vehicles. In D. Harris (Ed.), *Engineering Psychology and Cognitive Ergonomics: Performance, Emotion and Situation Awareness* (pp. 3–20). Vancouver: Springer; doi:10.1007/978-3-319-58472-0_1

Khani Jazani, R., Salehi Sahlabadi, A., & Mousavi, S. S. (2018). Relationship Between Lean Manufacturing and Ergonomics. In S. Trzcielinski (Ed.), *Advances in Ergonomics of Manufacturing: Managing the Enterprise of the Future. AHFE 2017. Advances in Intelligent Systems and Computing* (pp. 162–166). Cham: Springer; doi:10.1007/978-3-319-60474-9_15

Lederer, P., Weltle, D., & Weber, A. (2001). Illness-related premature unfitness for work among civil servants in Bavaria - an evaluation in the social medical field. *Gesundheitswesen (Bundesverband der Arzte des Offentlichen Gesundheitsdienstes (Germany))*, *63*(8–9), 509–513. doi:10.1055-2001-16688 PMID:11561198

Lee, Y., & Liu, B. (2003). Inflight workload assessment: Comparison of subjective and physiological measurements. *Aviation, Space, and Environmental Medicine*, *74*(10), 1074–1084. Retrieved from https://www.ingentaconnect.com/content/asma/asem/2003/00000074/00000010/art00011 PMID:14556571

Li, W.-C., Cao, J., Lin, J.-H., Braithwaite, G., & Greaves, M. (2017). The Evaluation of Pilot's First Fixation and Response Time to Different Design of Alerting Messages. In D. Harris (Ed.), *Engineering Psychology and Cognitive Ergonomics: Performance, Emotion and Situation Awareness* (pp. 21–31). Vancouver: Springer; doi:10.1007/978-3-319-58472-0_2

Loft, S., Sanderson, P., Neal, A., & Mooij, M. (2007). Modeling and Predicting Mental Workload in En Route Air Traffic Control: Critical Review and Broader Implications. *Human Factors: The Journal of the Human Factors and Ergonomics Society*, *49*(3), 376–399. doi:10.1518/001872007X197017 PMID:17552304

Longo, L. (2012). Formalising Human Mental Workload as Non-monotonic Concept for Adaptive and Personalised Web-Design. In J. Masthoff, B. Mobasher, M. Desmarais, & R. Nkambou (Eds.), *User Modeling, Adaptation, and Personalization* (pp. 369–373). Berlin: Springer. doi:10.1007/978-3-642-31454-4_38

Maslach, C., Schaufeli, W. B., & Leiter, P. M. (2001). Job burnout. *Annual Review of Psychology*, *53*(1), 397–422. doi:10.1146/annurev.psych.52.1.397 PMID:11148311

Mazur, L. M., Mosaly, P. R., Jackson, M., Chang, S. X., Burkhardt, K. D., Adams, R. D., ... Marks, L. B. (2012). Quantitative Assessment of Workload and Stressors in Clinical Radiation Oncology. *International Journal of Radiation Oncology*Biology*Physics, 83*(5), e571–e576. doi:10.1016/J.IJROBP.2012.01.063

McLean, L., Abry, T., Taylor, M., Jimenez, M., & Granger, K. (2017). Teachers' mental health and perceptions of school climate across the transition from training to teaching. *Teaching and Teacher Education, 65*, 230–240. doi:10.1016/j.tate.2017.03.018

Mohammadian, Y., Malekpour, F., Malekpour, A., Zoghipour, S., & Malalekpour, K. (2015). Study on Mental Workload of Teachers and Its Correlation with Their Quality of Life. *J. Educ. Manage. Stud, 5*(2), 144–149. Retrieved from www.science-line.com

Moriarty, D., & Jarvis, S. (2014). A systems perspective on the unstable approach in commercial aviation. *Reliability Engineering & System Safety, 131*, 197–202. doi:10.1016/j.ress.2014.06.019

Mosier, K. L., Rettenmaier, P., McDearmid, M., Wilson, J., Mak, S., Raj, L., & Orasanu, J. (2013). Pilot–ATC Communication Conflicts: Implications for NextGen. *The International Journal of Aviation Psychology, 23*(3), 213–226. doi:10.1080/10508414.2013.799350

Otto, A., & Battaïa, O. (2017). Reducing physical ergonomic risks at assembly lines by line balancing and job rotation: A survey. *Computers & Industrial Engineering, 111*, 467–480. doi:10.1016/j.cie.2017.04.011

Pimenta, A., Goncalves, S., Carneiro, D., Fde-Riverola, F., Neves, J., & Novais, P. (2015). Mental workload management as a tool in e-learning scenarios. In *2015 International Conference on Pervasive and Embedded Computing and Communication Systems (PECCS)* (pp. 25–32). Angers, France: Academic Press.

Plane Crash Info. (2013). *Accident statistics*. Retrieved February 1, 2019, from http://planecrashinfo.com/cause.htm

Rizzo, L., & Longo, L. (2017). Representing and Inferring Mental Workload via Defeasible Reasoning: a Comparison with the NASA Task Load Index and the Workload Profile. In *1st Workshop on Advances In Argumentation In Artificial Intelligence* (pp. 126–140). Bari, Italy: Academic Press. Retrieved from https://arrow.dit.ie/scschcomcon/216

Ruiz-Rabelo, J. F., Navarro-Rodriguez, E., Di-Stasi, L. L., Diaz-Jimenez, N., Cabrera-Bermon, J., Diaz-Iglesias, C., ... Briceño-Delgado, J. (2015). Validation of the NASA-TLX Score in Ongoing Assessment of Mental Workload During a Laparoscopic Learning Curve in Bariatric Surgery. *Obesity Surgery, 25*(12), 2451–2456. doi:10.100711695-015-1922-1 PMID:26459432

Salas, E., & Maurino, D. (1988). *Human Factors in Aviation* (2nd ed.). San Diego, CA: Gulf Professional Publishing. Retrieved from https://books.google.com.mx/books?hl=es&lr=&id=Fi2Bqh_6fW4C&oi=fnd&pg=PT1&ots=wMOh3QytxD&sig=x3dUbOAfTX75N0IMXgX1faEwdxo&redir_esc=y#v=onepage&q&f=false

Schaufeli, W. B., & Greenglass, E. R. (2001). Introduction to special issue on burnout and health. *Psychology & Health, 16*(5), 501–510. doi:10.1080/08870440108405523 PMID:22804495

Stansfeld, S., & Candy, B. (2006). Psychosocial work environment and mental health--a meta-analytic review. *Scandinavian Journal of Work, Environment & Health, 32*(6), 443–462. doi:10.5271jweh.1050 PMID:17173201

Stanton, N. A., Salmon, P. M., Walker, G. H., Baber, C., & Jenkins, D. (2018). *Human Factors Methods. A Practical Guide for Engineering and Design*. New York: Routledge.

Tubbs-Cooley, H. L., Mara, C. A., Carle, A. C., & Gurses, A. P. (2018). The NASA Task Load Index as a measure of overall workload among neonatal, paediatric and adult intensive care nurses. *Intensive & Critical Care Nursing, 46*, 64–69. doi:10.1016/j.iccn.2018.01.004 PMID:29449130

Unterbrink, T., Zimmermann, L., Pfeifer, R., Wirsching, M., Brähler, E., & Bauer, J. (2008). Parameters influencing health variables in a sample of 949 German teachers. *International Archives of Occupational and Environmental Health, 82*(1), 117–123. doi:10.100700420-008-0336-y PMID:18535835

Wiegmann, D. A., & Shappell, S. A. (2017). *A Human Error Approach to Aviation Accident Analysis. The Human Factors Analysis and Classification System*. London: Routledge; doi:10.4324/9781315263878

Wung, S.-F., & Schatz, M. R. (2018). Critical Care Nurses' Cognitive Ergonomics Related to Medical Device Alarms. *Critical Care Nursing Clinics of North America, 30*(2), 191–202. doi:10.1016/j.cnc.2018.02.002 PMID:29724438

Xiao, Y., Li, W., Ren, Q., Ren, X., Wang, Z., Wang, M., & Lan, Y. (2015). Effects of mental workload on work ability in primary and secondary school teachers. *Chinese Journal of Industrial Hygiene and Occupational Diseases, 33*(2), 93–96. Retrieved from http://www.ncbi.nlm.nih.gov/pubmed/25916354 PMID:25916354

Young, M. S., Brookhuis, K. A., Wickens, C. D., & Hancock, P. A. (2015). State of science: Mental workload in ergonomics. *Ergonomics, 58*(1), 1–17. doi:10.1080/00140139.2014.956151 PMID:25442818

Zhao, X., Hsu, C.-Y., Chang, P.-C., & Li, L. (2016). A genetic algorithm for the multi-objective optimization of mixed-model assembly line based on the mental workload. *Engineering Applications of Artificial Intelligence, 47*, 140–146. doi:10.1016/j.engappai.2015.03.005

KEY TERMS AND DEFINITIONS

Effort: It refers to the degree in which a worker must expend energy, either physical or mental, to achieve the objectives of the company.

Frustration Level: It refers to the level at which employees feel insecure, dissatisfied, stressed out, and unmotivated when they perform a task.

Mental Demand: It refers to the amount of work where the execution of a specific task requires that employees perform mental processes, such as thinking, deciding, calculating, remembering, analyzing, searching, observing, to mention few.

Mental Workload: It refers to the resources demanded by a specific task. It may be influenced by effort, frustration, mental demand, physical demand, performance, and temporal demand.

NASA-TLX: It is the most widely used method to evaluate the mental workload in a specific task. It is based on six dimensions: effort, frustration level, mental demand, physical demand, performance, and temporal demand

Physical Demand: It refers to the physical effort required by a specific task, i.e. pushing, pulling, controlling, activating, and turning.

Temporal Demand: It refers to the time pressure that employees feel when performing a specific task.

APPENDIX: MENTAL WORKLOAD QUESTIONNAIRE

Figure 17. Mental workload questionnaire

EVALUATION OF THE MENTAL WORKLOAD AND ITS EFFECTS IN MIDDLE AND SENIOR MANAGEMENT EMPLOYEES FROM MANUFACTURING COMPANIES

SECTION I. PERSONAL INFORMATION

Name and signature: ______________________

E-mail: ______________________

Company where you work ______________________

Current job position: ______________________

Date, City, State: ______________________

SECTION II. DESCRIPTIVE DATA

Instructions: Carefully read each question and select the option that best suits your reality.

1. Gender*
   - ◯ Male
   - ◯ Female

2. Age*__________

3. Civil status*
   - ◯ Single
   - ◯ Married
   - ◯ Free union
   - ◯ Other

4. Number of children*
   - ◯ 0
   - ◯ 1
   - ◯ 2
   - ◯ 3-4
   - ◯ >4

5. Sector of the manufacturing industry where you work*
   - ◯ Automotive
   - ◯ Medical
   - ◯ Electrical/Electronic
   - ◯ Food
   - ◯ Textile
   - ◯ Wood
   - ◯ Paper
   - ◯ Chemistry
   - ◯ Plastic and rubber
   - ◯ Metallic products
   - ◯ Computer equipment, ICTs
   - ◯ Other

6. Years of experience in the manufacturing industry*
   - ◯ 0-5
   - ◯ >5-10
   - ◯ >10-15
   - ◯ >15-20
   - ◯ >20-25
   - ◯ >25-30
   - ◯ >30-35
   - ◯ >35

7. Number of worked hours per week*
   - ◯ 0-5
   - ◯ >5-10
   - ◯ >10-15
   - ◯ >15-20
   - ◯ >20-25
   - ◯ >25-30
   - ◯ >30-35
   - ◯ >35

SECTION III. EVALUATION OF MENTAL WORKLOAD WITH THE NASA-TLX METHOD

Instructions: Next, dimensions and scales that the NASA-TLX method uses to measure the mental workload are mentioned. Please select, for each dimension, the value that best represents your work, where 1 is Low and 20 is High*.

Dimension	Scale																			
Mental demand: How much mental demand and perceptual activity is required to perform your work (for example, thinking, deciding, calculating, remembering, searching, etc.)? 1 = Low, 20 = High	1																			20
Physical activity: From 1 to 20, how much physical activity is required, for example pushing, pulling, turning, controlling, activating, etc., to carry out their work? 1 = Low, 20 = High	1																			20
Temporal demand: From 1 to 20, how much time pressure do you feel due to the speed or pace at which tasks or task elements occur? 1 = Low, 20 = High	1																			20
Effort: From 1 to 20, how hard do you have to work (mentally and physically) to achieve your level of performance? 1 = Low, 20 = High	1																			20
Performance: From 1 to 20, how satisfied are you with your performance in achieving your objectives? 1 = Good, 20 = Poor	1																			20
Frustration level: From 1 to 20, how insecure, discouraged, irritated, stressed and upset you feel while performing your tasks? 1 = Low, 20 = High	1																			20

Chapter 7
Psychosocial Factor Evaluation in Metal-Mechanic Workers With Particular Reference to Mental Load:
A Case in Ensenada, Baja California

Julio Cesar Cano Gutierrez
Autonomous University of Baja California, Mexico

Jesús Everardo Olguín Tiznado
https://orcid.org/0000-0002-6205-0973
Autonomous University of Baja California, Mexico

Claudia Camargo Wilson
https://orcid.org/0000-0001-7803-6706
Autonomous University of Baja California, Mexico

Juan Andrés López Barreras
https://orcid.org/0000-0002-5477-033X
Autonomous University of Baja California, Mexico

ABSTRACT

The International Labour Organization (ILO) considers mental workload one of the most important psychosocial risk factors associated with the characteristics of the task and paramount in the metal-working industry. The objective was to analyze the levels of risk of the psychosocial factors that workers present, considering their physical, social, and mental environment, to respond to the Mexican Official Norm NOM-035-STPS and the ILO guidelines. The methodology consisted of applying to 125 workers a questionnaire of 74 items with 10 factors. The answers were assigned a score of 0 to 4 to later determine the risk level of each factor. The results revealed that the factors with the highest risk are working hours (93%), workload (71%), and lack of control over work (34%). It is concluded that the higher risk factors affect the mental workload of workers in the metalworking industry and associated with the characteristics of the tasks they perform.

DOI: 10.4018/978-1-7998-1052-0.ch007

BACKGROUNDS

Ergonomics is a scientific discipline of a multidisciplinary nature, which studies the relationships between man, the activity he performs and the elements of the system in which he is immersed, in order to reduce the physical, mental and psychological burdens of the individual and to adapt the products, systems, jobs and environments to the characteristics, limitations and needs of its users; seeking to optimize its efficiency, safety, comfort and overall system performance (IEA, 2000), So the fields of knowledge of engineering, sociology, physiology, psychology, economics and legislation, among others, participate in it (Mondelo, Cremades Oliver, & Montoya Taborda, 2015).

In addition, González y Gutiérrez (2007) y Vedder (2013) the factors associated with the scope of Ergonomics can be classified into: 1. The physical load; 2. Mental workload; 3. Environmental conditions; 4. Work organization. (González-Muñoz & Gutiérrez-Martínez, 2007; Vedder & Laurig, 2013).

Psychosociology is the discipline that applies and discovers information about the psychological mechanisms underlying the individual-workplace-organization interaction, and the negative consequences, which have repercussions on occupational health, for the application of the knowledge and techniques developed with the intervention, prevention and promotion of Occupational Health Labor (Steven L., M. Lawrence & Levi, 2001).

In this sense, a large part of the well-being of the worker lies in the quality of the physical and mental working conditions, from which comes the relevance of identifying, analyzing and evaluating psychosocial factors. The evaluation of psychosocial factors, as well as the evaluation of risks, is a complex process that is still under development, particularly in workplaces (Mélan & Cascino, 2014; Osorio-Escobar, 2011) due to the difficulty that exists to evaluate them, the lack of improvement in the adoption of techniques in the multiple organizational contexts, the confusion in the concepts of some variables and even the difficulty that is presented when trying to establish a direct causal relation between a risk factor and a health condition, since the loss of health due to an inadequate psychosocial situation cannot be explained by a direct cause-effect relationship, but has a multicausal origin (Instituto Nacional de Seguridad e Higiene en el Trabajo (INSHT), 2003).

It is proposed that psychosocial factors at work consist of interactions between work, its environment, job satisfaction and organizational conditions, on the one hand, and on the other, the worker's capabilities, needs, culture and personal situation outside of work, all of which, through perceptions and experiences, can influence health, performance and job satisfaction (Comité Mixto OIT-OMS, 1984; Mélan & Cascino, 2014; Rodríguez, Sánchez-Gómez, Dorado, & Ramírez, 2015)

Psychosocial factors are perceived characteristics of the work environment that have an emotional connotation for workers and managers (Carayon, Smith, & Haims, 2007). They are also considered as aspects of work, organization and labor management, and their social and organizational contexts (Cox & Griffiths A, 1996). They are also defined as those conditions that are present in a labor situation and that are directly related to the organization, the content of the work and the performance of the task, as well as having the capacity to affect both the well-being or health (physical, psychic or social) of the worker and consequently his performance at work (Pérez Bilbao & Nogareda Cuixart, 2012).

Work psychosocial factors are organizational conditions that as such can be positive or negative (Cox & Griffiths A, 1996). Their number is very wide and their classification and organization depends on the theoretical approach chosen. When such conditions are adequate, they facilitate work, the development of personal job skills and high levels of job satisfaction, business productivity and states of motivation in which workers achieve greater experience and professional competence. The right forms of corporate culture, leadership and work climate, general psychosocial conditions, positively affect health generating individual development, personal and organizational well-being (Berniker & Mintzberg, 2006). Psychosocial factors would be defined as organizational factors that can give rise to both positive and negative consequences. Psychosocial risk factors refer when the organizational and psychosocial factors of workplaces and organizations are dysfunctional, i.e., they provoke maladaptive responses, stress responses, psychophysiological stress responses become psychosocial risk or stress factors (El-Batawi, Kalimo, & Cooper, 1988). The psychosocial factors when they are factors with probability of negatively affecting the health and well-being of the worker are risk factors (Benavides et al., 2002), that is to say, when they act as triggers of tension and labor stress. From this approach, psychosocial risk or stress factors would be defined as organizational factors with the risk of having negative effects on health (Beltrán, Moreno, López, Estrada, & Torres, 2011; Peiro, 2013).

Just as the number of psychosocial factors is very large, so is the number of psychosocial risk or stress factors (Magana CG, Hovey JD., Magana C.G., Magaña, & Hovey, 2003). The psychosocial risk factors that are identified as those factors coming from the organization and human interaction that can affect the health of the worker, are mainly the content of the work, physical and mental workload, monotony and repetitiveness, schedules, workday, control, autonomy, leadership, supervision, conditions in the environment and teams, organizational and functional culture, interpersonal relationships, role in the organization, career development, work-family relationship, contractual security, salary, labor demands, security, social support, violence, recognition of performance and sense of belonging (Beltrán et al., 2011; Moreno, 2015; Sarsosa-Prowesk, Charria-Ortiz, & Arenas-Ortiz, 2014).

From this point of view, psychosocial factors can positively or negatively affect health, psychosocial risk factors can negatively affect health, usually to a lesser extent, and psychosocial risks generally have important consequences for health (Sarsosa-Prowesk et al., 2014). In the present work, we will analyze in a general way, the psychosocial risk factors that are presented in the workers of a work center of the metal-mechanic sector and in particular, the workload as a factor that evaluates the mental workload.

Workload

The workload has a partial or total relationship with the mental workload. It has been difficult to construct a satisfactory definition in this regard, however for practical purposes, Hart and Staveland (1988a) establish that workload can be understood as the perceived relationship between mental processing capacity and the amount of that capacity required for the task (Hart & Staveland, 1988a; Mélan & Cascino, 2014).

Ergonomic scales evaluate the level of workload according to posture, external load, repeatability and duration. A variety of measurement methods, easy to use and providing quantitative workload assessments, are the OCRA, RULA and REBA methods (Cain, 2004). However, most methods focus on only a few aspects of the workload factors involved. For example, RULA and REBA evaluate the workload of the entire body, while OCRA focuses on the upper body only; REBA and RULA consider the static load, while OCRA considers the repetitiveness of the workload and the duration. Most methods define body posture quantitatively by the angle of the joints involved, but differ in their range of values, therefore evaluating the same workload with different methods can lead to different results. So it is important to use subjective workload measurement methods that complement objective methods, such as NASA TLX, COPSOQ, ISTAS21, FPSICO, LEST, RNUR, ANACT, EWA and MPF, to name a few (Yu et al., 2019).

In any workplace, the worker has to put into operation both physical and mental mechanisms or processes (Cinaz, Arnrich, La Marca, & Tröster, 2013). These are the mechanisms that determine the workload, which we can define as "the set of psychophysical requirements to which the worker is subjected throughout his working day". In the labor reality we are not going to find purely physical jobs or purely mental jobs, but in any type of activity both aspects are going to be present. However, from a theoretical point of view, physical work is differentiated from mental work, according to the type of activity that predominates. That is to say, when the activity developed is predominantly physical, we will speak of physical or muscular work and, therefore, of physical load, and when, on the contrary, the activity implies a greater intellectual effort, we will speak of mental load. The workload, both physical and mental, could therefore be considered as a danger or risk factor present in all work activities and in any type of work center (Arquer de, 1999).

Mental Workload

The ISO 10075 Standard: Ergonomic principles related to mental workload, in its 1st part, defines the terms related to mental workload, with the fundamental objective of clarifying concepts and promoting the use of a common terminology among experts and professionals in the field of Ergonomics. This 1st part talks about mental stress and strain and defines them in the following way:

- Mental stress: the total of all the valuable influences that affect a human being.
- Mental strain: the immediate effect of mental pressure on the individual (not the long-term effect), which depends on his usual and current preconditions, including individual coping styles.

In this International Standard the expression "mental" is used to refer to any of the processes to which human experience and behavior are related, i.e. cognitive, information and emotional processes in the human being. These aspects are interrelated and in practice should not be treated separately. The Standard states that any activity, even a predominantly physical one, can impose mental pressure. Such mental pressure leads to processes of increasing or decreasing mental tension in human beings. The consequences of pressure can differ in form and intensity depending on the conditions, both of the situation and individual (Aoki, 2011).

However, until now there is no consensus among specialists on the precise definition of the concept of mental workload (Young, Brookhuis, Wickens, & Hancock, 2015). Mental workload has been defined as the amount of intellectual effort that must be invested to develop a labor task, different and complementary to the physical effort required to develop a manual task.

The change in manufacturing processes and the current lifestyle require a transformation in the way in which the factors of occupational risk and, consequently, mental workload is determined. The most accepted approach to the concept of mental workload alludes "to the difference between the resources of the worker and the demands of work, produce problems in the performance and health of workers" (Valdehita, Ramiro, García, & Moreno, 2010).

One of the first works that mention mental workload is that carried out by Moray (1982), in this pioneering work there was still not enough empirical work volume to give clarity about the meaning of the term, although it was already warned as a phenomenon that involved the performance of the worker in one or several tasks depending on the mental workload that these tasks suppose (Moray, 1982). A little later, Reid and Nygreen (1988) propose that the concept of mental load is a construct of subjective nature, with perceptual, multidimensional character, that can be explained by three main components or factors: (1) the burden of time, (2) the burden of mental effort and (3) the burden of psychological stress (Reid & Nygren, 1988).

Reid and Nygreen (1991) develop a three-level scale for mental workload from the three factors they explain. For the time burden factor, he suggests that the lowest level of burden is associated with the worker having free time and when he does not perceive that there are interruptions or overlapping of the activities he performs. At the intermediate level of the time factor, it states that the worker occasionally has free time and interruptions occur frequently; the highest level is detected when he almost never has free time and interruptions or overlaps of activities occur all the time (Nygren, 1991).

As for the second factor, or mental effort load, the lowest level is when the activity can be performed with very little or no conscious effort or concentration, requiring little or no attention. At the intermediate level of this factor, mental effort or mental concentration is moderate and the worker perceives the activity with moderate complexity, due to the insecurity to perform it or because he feels unfamiliar with the task so it requires a lot of attention. The highest level of mental effort occurs when the worker demands all his attention or concentration due to the complexity of the task (Nygren, 1991).

In the factor called psychological stress load, at the lowest level the worker perceives little confusion, risk, frustration or anxiety to which he can easily accommodate. At the second level, moderate stress is perceived because confusion, anxiety or frustration adds to the workload. The last level of this factor is distinguished because the stress is now high to very intense due to confusion, frustration or anxiety; at the same time it perceives a high to extreme determination and self-control required (Reid & Nygren, 1988).

The notions of the Raid and Naygren model (1988), were applied in a variety of instruments, whose revisions provided by (Cain, 2004), suggest a diversity of views (Byrne et al., 2010; Castor et al., 2003; Oppold, Rupp, Mouloua, Hancock, & Martin, 2012; Young et al., 2015).

One of the main criticisms of mental workload assessment techniques and instruments is that it cannot be observed directly during the worker's interaction with the task or tasks he performs and must be inferred indirectly (Matthews, Reinerman-Jones, Barber, & Abich, 2015), but despite problems with assessment instruments and their interpretation, for different work sectors it is important to have this information, since all human activity is subject to the effects of the workload (Dillard et al., 2014; Jung & Jung, 2001), so it is important to detect vulnerabilities in processes within the work environment in time, especially those that require high precision in the performance of the task, such as air traffic controllers, pilots, surgeons, operators in the assembly of machinery, among other areas (Byrne et al., 2010; Dillard et al., 2014; Ma & Kaber, 2005).

RELATIONSHIP BETWEEN MENTAL WORKLOAD AND PSYCHOSOCIAL FACTORS

For Gracia-Camón (2003), the workload from the analysis of psychosocial and organizational factors can also be designated as mental workload (Gracia-Camón, 2003). In this same sense, Artazcoz (2001), proposes that psychosocial risk factors can be synonymous of mental load, although the term, psychosocial risk factors, comes from two approaches. The first seen from the scope of psychology and the sociology of work, focusing on the study of the work relation and health; instead, if the term is interpreted from the cognitive ergonomics, then it alludes to the interactions between the intellectual processes and the capacities of the subject to develop a task (Artazcoz, 2001). That is why it is very important to take into account which approach to the analysis of psychosocial factors is being considered in order to properly analyze mental workload.

The workload derived from psychosocial and organizational factors can be called mental workload. Psychosocial and organizational risks, according to the National Institute of Safety and Hygiene at Work, refer to those conditions that are present in a labor situation and are directly related to the organization, the content of the work and the performance of the task, and that have the capacity to affect both the well-being or the physical, psychic or social health of the worker as well as the development of the work (Moreno-Jiménez & Báez León, 2010). Therefore, the manifestation of unfavorable psychosocial conditions is at the origin of the appearance of certain inappropriate behaviors and attitudes in the course of work, as well as of certain harmful consequences for the health and well-being of the worker. According to the International Labor Organization, psychosocial risks are interactions between the content, organization and management of work, and environmental conditions, on the one hand, and the functions and needs of workers, on the other. From these definitions it can be deduced that psychosocial risks can arise from a wide variety of causes. These causes can be ergonomic, social, emotional, task-related and many others. For this reason, in order to evaluate psychosocial risks, we have chosen to evaluate ergonomic, architectural, task derived, communication derived and other risk factors (Ángel & Camón, 2003).

Psychosocial risk factors continue to become synonymous with mental workload, which is partly due to the vague definition of these terms that come from different disciplines (Cinaz et al., 2013). If the concept of psychosocial risk factors comes from the field of psychology and the sociology of work and is framed in the study of the relationship between work and health, mental workload is a concept of cognitive ergonomics that describes the interaction between cognitive and energetic processes (Byrne et al., 2010; Oppold et al., 2012). The aim of cognitive ergonomics is to investigate the capacities and limitations of the human being as an information processing system (Artazcoz, 2001).

Mental workload as an important element of workload and psychosocial risk factors can be assessed through subjective methods, since workload assessment can have high levels of sensitivity, set minimum implementation requirements, be accepted by workers, and have adequate levels of validity and internal reliability, indispensable requirements for such purpose. However, both subjective methods, based on cognitive psychology, and objective (physiological) methods should be used to obtain more complete information for the understanding of working conditions and the physical and mental effort made by workers (Wickens, Gordon, & Liu, 2004).

Subjective assessment methods have been developed for use that contemplate the study of mental workload, such as the NASA TLX method (Sandra G Hart & Staveland, 1988), Copenhagen Psychosocial Questionnaire (COPSOQ) (Kristensen & Borg, 2003), ISTAS21 (Moncada, Llorens, Navarro, & Kristensen, 2005), FPSICO (Nogareda Cuixart & Pérez Bilbao, 2012b), by Laboratoire de Economie et Sociologie du Travail (LEST) (Guelaud, F., Beauchesne, M.N., Gautrat, 1975), the method of the Régie Nationale des Usines Renault (RNUR) (nationale des usines Renault, 1976), the method of the Agence nationale pour l'Amélioration des Conditions de Travail (ANACT) (Piotet, F., & Mabile, 1984), Ergonomic Workplace Analysis Method (EWA) (Sharan, 2012), the Mini Psychosocial Factors (MPF) method for psychosocial risks (Ruíz García E. Idoate García, 2005), the Battery of instruments for the evaluation of psychosocial risk factors (Charria, Sarsosa, & Arenas, 2011), Psychosocial Factors: evaluation methodology (Nogareda Cuixart & Pérez Bilbao, 2012a) and the Guide III of the NOM035 of the STPS Psychosocial risk factors at work, identification, analysis and prevention (Secretaría del Trabajo y Previsión Social, 2018). Retrieved text from (A. J. Callejón-Ferre, Pérez-Alonso, Carreño-Ortega, & Velázquez-Martí, 2011).

The instrument Guide III of the NOM035 of the STPS Psychosocial risk factors at work, identification, analysis and prevention used in this work, is recently adopted in Mexico and constitutes an adaptation of the Colombian and Spanish experience mainly (Lahera & Nogareda, 2009; Ministerio de la Protección Social, 2010; Nogareda Cuixart & Pérez Bilbao, 2012a), is composed of 72 items in a five-level Likert scale, grouped into ten factors: conditions in the work environment, workload, lack of control over work, workday, interference in the work-family relationship, leadership, work relations, violence, recognition of performance and insufficient sense of belonging and instability.

There are concerns in the workplaces of the industrial sector in Mexico, related to the need to incorporate better manufacturing technology, which has led to the replacement of traditional machines with those using Computer Numeric Control (CNC). As a result, workers have experienced new levels of workload and fatigue levels that have not been investigated in depth. However, it is known that nighttime sleep, weight and height of workers are variables that should be considered in the design of tasks, so it is desirable to develop and improve production schedules when operating CNC machines. With the introduction of new and more sophisticated machinery, commonly classified as Advanced Manufacturing Technology (AMT), workers in the industrial sector must increasingly make both physical and mental efforts, often simultaneously (Hernandez-Arellano, Garcia-Alcaraz, Serratos-Perez, & Maldonado-Macías, 2016). Likewise, the studies on the workload for office workers since the 1990s, with the acceleration of the restructuring process, the adoption of new technologies, management methods and poor working relations, has generated an increase in the prevalence of occupational diseases that can cause risks in the worker due to individual, biomechanical, organizational, psychosocial and environmental factors, due to physical, mental, mechanical and ergonomic workloads, which triggers the development of physical and psychological disorders in workers who develop office activities (Sontag et al., 2012).

Therefore, this paper focuses on an objective physiological perspective of the analysis of psychosocial risk factors associated with working conditions, workload, lack of control over work, working hours, interference in the work-family relationship, leadership, work relations, violence, recognition of performance and insufficient sense of belonging and instability, as psychosocial factors that may affect the mental workload in workers. In particular, the workload factor is analyzed as that psychosocial risk factor that refers to quantitative burdens, accelerated work rhythms, mental burdens, emotional psychological burdens, high responsibility burdens and contradictory or inconsistent burdens.

SETTING THE STAGE

Given the characteristics of the objective methodological approach on which this study was based, a modification to the instrument proposed by Official Mexican Standard NOM-035-STPS was used. The modification was considering the context variables such as age, seniority in the work area and the anonymity of the worker. However, the details of the validation are not added to the present.

Three stages were necessary to develop this study. First, the size and composition of the representative sample of participating workers were determined, then the questionnaire was applied and finally an analysis of the responses was carried out. To determine the sample, it was calculated based on section III.1 of Standard 035 of the Ministry of Labor and Social Security of Mexico (NOM-035-STPS) according to the following expression:

$$n = \frac{0.9604N}{0.0025(N-1)+0.9604}$$

where:

N is the total number of workers in the workplace.

n is the number of workers to whom the questionnaires should be applied.

Participating workers were randomly selected considering the activities of the job or work area. Subject to informed consent, the sample was distributed proportionally between men and women according to the composition of each gender in the workplace and the number of workers in each of the workplace areas.

The questionnaire used was the one suggested by NOM-035-STPS, which contemplates the identification of the factors of psychosocial risk and favorable organizational environment. This questionnaire is made up of 72 items with five levels of response (never, almost never, sometimes, almost always and always). This paper only presents the analysis of the 10 psychosocial risk factors: workload, lack of control over work, workday, interference in the work-family relationship, leadership, work relations, violence, recognition of performance and insufficient sense of belonging and instability.

The questionnaire was applied by people outside the workplace within the working day. Ten workers formed each group per shift and area, in a space with noise, temperature, humidity and reduced lighting, problems, there was no responsibility for the work center during the application. Care was taken at all times to give clear instructions on: how to respond to the questions in the different sections; that the questionnaire be answered completely; that there are no correct or incorrect answers; that concentration is necessary; that the working conditions of the last two months be considered, and that your opinion is the most important reason why you are asked to answer sincerely, and above all to start the application in the following order: firstly, the questionnaire on psychosocial risk factors, and finally, the completion of the general data sheet on the worker, such as seniority, work area and job position, given that the questionnaires were considered anonymous, so there is no general data on the worker based on the agreements made for this study.

The questionnaires were graded based on the recommendations of NOM-035-STPS, using the Likert scale and the evaluation of the answers answered by the worker considered in each item, as shown in Table 1. It was very important to be careful when assigning the corresponding scores to the scale, depending on whether the items were shown with positive or negative affirmations as detailed in Table 1.

To determine the risk levels of each factor, the responses of each of the workers were captured in a spreadsheet and the scores obtained for each of the factors were calculated, adding the score of the items that make up the factor, as detailed in Table 2.

Table 1. Qualifications of the answers of the items of the questionnaire (NOM035, 2018)

Items	Qualification of response options				
	Always	Almost always	Sometimes	Almost never	Never
1, 4, 23, 24, 25, 26, 27, 28, 30, 31, 32, 33, 34, 35, 36, 37, 38, 39, 40, 41, 42, 43, 44, 45, 46, 47, 48, 49, 50, 51, 52, 53, 55, 56, 57	0	1	2	3	4
2, 3, 5, 6, 7, 8, 9, 10, 11, 12, 13, 14, 15, 16, 17, 18, 19, 20, 21, 22, 29, 54, 58, 59, 60, 61, 62, 63, 64, 65, 66, 67, 68, 69, 70, 71, 72	4	3	2	1	0

Table 2. Structure of the questionnaire (NOM035, 2018)

Factor	Characteristics	Item number
Conditions in the working environment	Hazardous and unsafe conditions	1, 3
	Poor and unhealthy conditions	2, 4
	Dangerous work	5
Workload	Quantitative loads	6, 12
	Accelerated work rates	7, 8
	Load mental	9, 10. 11
	Emotional psychological burdens	65, 66, 67, 68
	Loads of high responsibility	13, 14
	Contradictory or inconsistent loads	15, 16
Lack of control over work	Lack of control and autonomy over work	25, 26, 27, 28
	Limited or no possibility of development	23, 24
	Insufficient participation and change management	29, 30
	Limited or no training	35, 36
Working day	Extended working days	17, 18
Interference in the work-family	relationship Influence of work outside the workplace	19, 20
	Influence of family responsibilities	21, 22
Leadership	Clarity of functions	31, 32, 33, 34
	Leadership characteristics	37, 38, 39, 40, 41
Relations at work	Social relations at work	42, 43, 44, 45, 46
	Poor relationship with supervised collaborators	69, 70, 71, 72
Violence	Violence in the workplace	57, 58, 59, 60, 61, 62, 63, 64
Recognition of performance	Little or no feedback on performance	47, 48
	Little or no recognition and compensation	49, 50, 51, 52
Insufficient sense of belonging e instability	Limited sense of belonging	55, 56
	Job instability	53, 54

The evaluation of the risk level of the workers with respect to each factor was established using the sum obtained with Table 2 and contrasting the scores based on the ranges presented in Table 3, which range from null, low, medium, high and very high.

Once the scores and risk level for each factor had been determined for each of the workers who participated in the study, the general evaluation of the workplace and the evaluation of each factor were carried out. For the first case and given the importance of knowing the overall risk level of the workers, the scores of all the items of each one of the workers were added together and the risk level of the worker was determined by comparing the score obtained with the score referred to in the traffic light in Table 4.

With respect to the global evaluation of each factor, given the relevance of knowing the psychosocial factors with the highest level of risk in the workplace, the median of the workers' responses in each item was determined and subsequently, the sum of the median of the items corresponding to each of the factors was calculated, considering the scores in Table 4. Likewise, the analysis by work area was made to determine the psychosocial factors that present the highest level of risk in the workers.

Table 3. Ranges of ratings to evaluate the level of risk by factor (NOM035, 2018)

Factor result	Null	Low	Medium	High	Very high
Conditions in the working environment	$C_{factor}<5$	$5\leq C_{factor}<9$	$9\leq C_{factor}<11$	$11\leq C_{factor}<14$	$C_{factor}\geq 14$
Workload	$C_{factor}<15$	$15\leq C_{factor}<21$	$21\leq C_{factor}<27$	$27\leq C_{factor}<37$	$C_{factor}\geq 37$
Lack of control over work	$C_{factor}<11$	$11\leq C_{factor}<16$	$16\leq C_{factor}<21$	$21\leq C_{factor}<25$	$C_{factor}\geq 25$
Working day	$C_{factor}<1$	$1\leq C_{factor}<2$	$2\leq C_{factor}<4$	$4\leq C_{factor}<6$	$C_{factor}\geq 6$
Interference in the work-family	$C_{factor}<4$	$4\leq C_{factor}<6$	$6\leq C_{factor}<8$	$8\leq C_{factor}<10$	$C_{factor}\geq 10$
Leadership	$C_{factor}<9$	$9\leq C_{factor}<12$	$12\leq C_{factor}<16$	$16\leq C_{factor}<20$	$C_{factor}\geq 20$
Relations at work	$C_{factor}<10$	$10\leq C_{factor}<13$	$13\leq C_{factor}<17$	$17\leq C_{factor}<21$	$C_{factor}\geq 21$
Violence	$C_{factor}<7$	$7\leq C_{factor}<10$	$10\leq C_{factor}<13$	$13\leq C_{factor}<16$	$C_{factor}\geq 16$
Recognition of performance	$C_{factor}<6$	$6\leq C_{factor}<10$	$10\leq C_{factor}<14$	$14\leq C_{factor}<18$	$C_{factor}\geq 18$
Insufficient sense of belonging e instability	$C_{factor}<4$	$4\leq C_{factor}<6$	$6\leq C_{factor}<8$	$8\leq C_{factor}<10$	$C_{factor}\geq 10$

Table 4. Traffic light for risk level assessment (NOM035, 2018)

LEVEL OF RISK				
Very high	High	Medium	Low	Null
$C_{final}\geq 140$	$99\leq C_{final}<140$	$75\leq C_{final}<99$	$50\leq C_{final}<75$	$C_{final}<50$

RESULTS

A total of 125 workers made up the final sample, 92% men and 8% women and the average age per area was 5 years or more (Table 5). Based on the scores of the qualifications obtained for each worker, the results presented below are grouped by factor.

Table 6 shows the level of risk by number and percentage of workers for each of the factors evaluated. It can be seen that the factors that present a majority proportion of workers with medium, high or very high risk levels refer to the "Workload" factors with 71% (88) and "Workday" with 93% (116).

The factors "Lack of control over work" 34% (43), "Interference in the work-family relationship" 26% (32), "Conditions at work" 23% (29), "Recognition of performance" 12% (15), "Leadership" 11% (14), "Violence" 7% (9), "Insufficient sense of belonging and instability" 2% (3) and "Relations at work" 2% (2) resulted in a lower proportion of workers. Therefore, the psychosocial risk factors of greatest presence in workers are "Workday", "Workload" and "Lack of control over work".

Overall, the levels of risk associated with psychosocial risk factors present in workers reflect that 28% (35) of workers have a medium risk level, 7% (9) of workers have a high risk level and 1% (1) have a very high risk level, as shown in Table 7. The majority of workers 64% (80) present low or no risk levels.

Figure 1 summarizes the center's overall assessment of psychosocial risk factors that constitutes the case study of this paper. The average results per factor are shown, highlighting that the risk factors with a medium level evaluation are "Workload" and with a high level evaluation is "Workday", with values of 25 ($21\leq$Cfactor<27) and 4 ($4\leq$Cfactor<6), respectively.

Table 5. Sample of workers by area (own elaboration)

#	Area	N	n	Seniority Average in years
1	Administration	32	30	1 a 3
2	Spare parts warehouse	5	3	More than 5
3	Warehouse finished product	16	15	3 a 5
4	Quality	8	4	More than 5
5	Decorated	35	33	1 a 3
6	Electrical	7	6	More than 5
7	Molding	22	20	More than 5
8	Chemical process and ecology	7	5	More than 5
9	Appliance and tooling workshop	6	4	More than 5
10	Transportation	7	5	More than 5

Table 6. Evaluation of the level of risk by factor - number and % of workers (Own elaboration)

	LEVEL OF RISK					
FACTOR	**Measurement**	**Very high**	**High**	**Medium**	**Low**	**Null**
(F1) Conditions in the working environment	Number	1	5	23	52	44
	%	1%	4%	18%	42%	35%
(F2) Workload	Number	2	32	54	29	8
	%	**2%**	**26%**	**43%**	23%	6%
(F3) Lack of control over work	Number	3	9	31	42	40
	%	**2%**	**7%**	**25%**	34%	32%
(F4) Working day	Number	10	55	51	4	5
	%	**8%**	**44%**	**41%**	3%	4%
(F5) Interference in the work-family	Number	2	6	24	39	54
	%	2%	5%	19%	31%	43%
(F6) Leadership	Number	4	4	6	16	95
	%	3%	3%	5%	13%	76%
(F7) Relations at work	Number	0	0	2	2	121
	%	0%	0%	2%	2%	97%
(F8) Violence	Number	1	3	5	8	108
	%	1%	2%	4%	6%	86%
(F9) Recognition of performance	Number	0	2	13	27	83
	%	0%	2%	10%	22%	66%
(F10) Insufficient sense of belonging e instability	Number	0	0	3	40	82
	%	0%	0%	2%	32%	66%

Table 7. Overall assessment of the level of risk - number and % of workers (Own elaboration)

LEVEL OF RISK					
Measurement	**Very high**	**High**	**Medium**	**Low**	**Null**
Number	1	9	35	56	24
%	1%	7%	28%	45%	19%

The "workload" factor draws attention, where the characteristics are synthesized: Quantitative loads of accelerated work rhythms, mental load, emotional psychological loads, high responsibility loads and contradictory or inconsistent loads, present a medium risk. Also the factor "working day" where characteristics are condensed such as the possibility of momentarily absent from one's job or taking voluntary rest breaks in the development of one's work or situations in which one must prolong one's working day, as can be seen in the items of the questionnaire applied.

With respect to the evaluation of the risk level of the psychosocial factors by area, as visualized in Table 8, the areas of "Decoration", "Chemical process and ecology", "Workshop of apparatus and tools" and "Transportation" present a high level of risk in "Workload" and "Workday", likewise, the areas of "Electrical" and "Transportation" present levels of high or medium risk in three psychosocial factors:

Figure 1. Overall assessment of the level of risk by factor (Own elaboration)

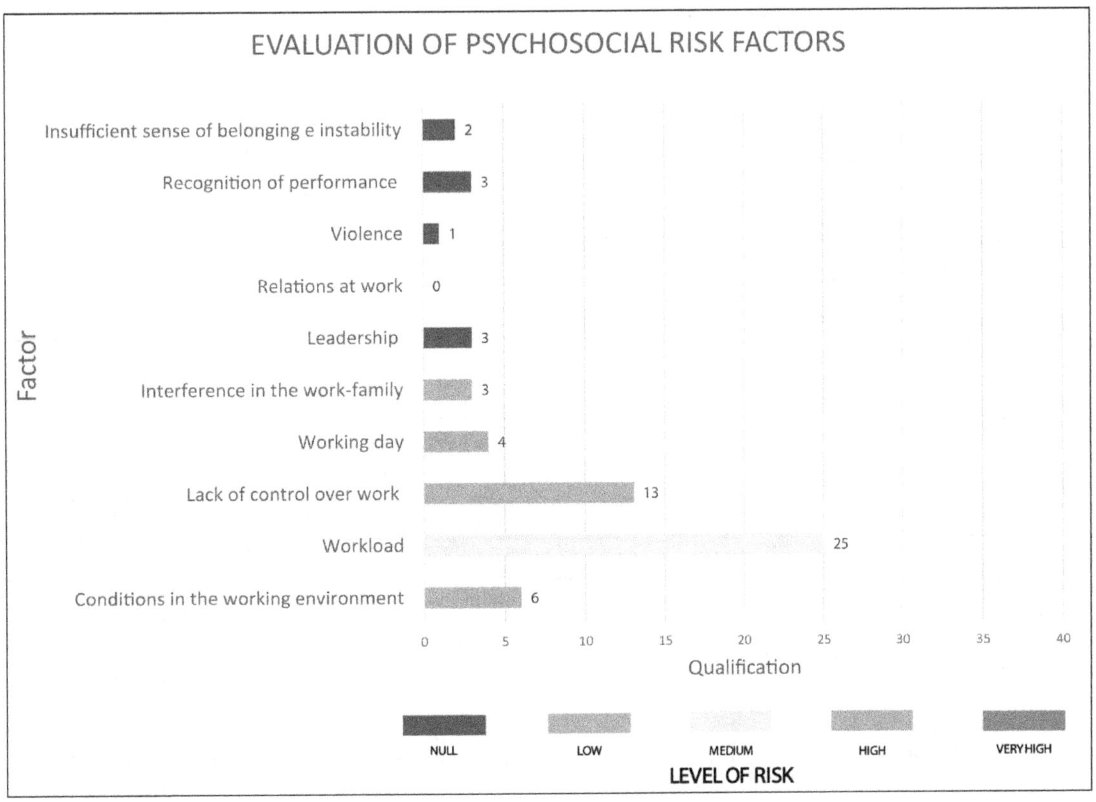

"Workload", "Lack of control over the work". Workday" and "Interference in the work-family relationship". All areas present at least one psycho-social factor the average risk level, in general, associated with "Workload" and "Workday".

DISCUSSION

There are three reasons that may explain why the factors: Conditions at work, Interference in the work-family relationship, Leadership, Relationships at work, Violence, Recognition of performance, and Insufficient sense of belonging and instability resulted in little or no risk in most areas of work. The first may be due to the fact that the workplace under analysis has adequate facilities and clear health and environmental safety policies, so that the worker perceives low or no risks (Iavicoli, Cesana, Dollard,

Table 8. Evaluation of the level of psychosocial risk by factor of the work center (global) and of each of the areas (Own elaboration)

		Psychosocial risk factors									
	Total evaluation in the work center	**F1**	**F2**	**F3**	**F4**	**F5**	**F6**	**F7**	**F8**	**F9**	**F10**
GLOBAL	Global	6	25	13	4	3	3	0	1	3	2
		Low	Medium	Low	High	Null	Null	Null	Null	Null	Null
WORK AREA	Administration	2.5	25.5	12.5	3	5	4.5	1	2	3	1
		Null	Medium	Low	Medium	Low	Null	Null	Null	Null	Null
	Spare parts warehouse	5	20	8	4	1	0	0	1	0	4
		Low	Low	Null	High	Null	Null	Null	Null	Null	Low
	Finished product warehouse	6	21	11	3	3	0	4	3	3	2
		Low	Medium	Low	Medium	Low	Null	Null	Null	Null	Null
	Quality	3.5	20	18	3	4.5	7	1	4.5	6	2
		Null	Low	Medium	Medium	Low	Null	Null	Null	Null	Null
	Decoration	7	25	14	4	3	5	0	2	4	2
		Low	Medium	Low	High	Null	Null	Null	Null	Null	Null
	Electrical	6	25.5	18.5	3.5	4	11.5	5.5	4.5	5.5	5
		Low	Medium	Medium	Medium	Low	Low	Null	Null	Null	Low
	Molding	6	24	11	3	3	0	0	1	1	3
		Low	Medium	Low	Medium	Null	Null	Null	Null	Null	Null
	Chemical process and ecology	4	20	3	4	1	0	0	0	0	3
		Null	Low	Null	High	Null	Null	Null	Null	Null	Null
	Apparatus and tooling workshop	7.5	29	8.5	3.5	2	0	1	0.5	2	3
		Low	High	Null	Medium	Null	Null	Null	Null	Null	Null
	Transportation	8	24	13	4	7	4	1	1	3	2
		Low	Medium	Low	High	Medium	Null	Null	Null	Null	Null

Leka, & Sauter, 2015; Leka, Van Wassenhove, & Jain, 2015; Schütte et al., 2014). Another viable explanation for low levels of these factors is the worker's access to a precise description of the procedures corresponding to the activity in the different jobs, which facilitates congruence between performance and job satisfaction in terms of leadership and work relations (Çakmak, Öztekin, & Karadağ, 2015; Macdonald & Levy, 2016; Petty, McGee, & Cavender, 2011; Pollock, Whitbred, & Contractor, 2006). The third and final proposal of explanation for a zero or low level of risk for these psychosocial factors is the existence of schemes within the industry that favor a good organizational environment (Raziq & Maulabakhsh, 2015; Tsai, 2011).

Notwithstanding the above, it has also been pointed out that a zero or low level of risk perceived by workers in psychometric instruments can be attributed to the fear of losing a job, or to the emotions associated with responding to each of the psychosocial factors, as expressed by Leka et al. (2015): "Perhaps the most difficult obstacle to overcome in managing psychosocial risk is fear and resilience..........the way psychosocial risks and psychosocial risk management are perceived and understood.... as an employee, manager, policy maker, as an individual. The answer will depend on the context in which each of us finds ourselves, the associated pressures, needs and values" (Leka et al., 2015).

In the questionnaire on psychosocial factors applied to the case of the work center analyzed, the "workload" section was found to be the section with the highest risk (Figure 1). Some authors have established that in the evaluation of psychosocial factors at work is immersed the evaluation of mental workload (Aoki, 2011; Galy, Cariou, & Mélan, 2012). Aspects such as the requirements of mental concentration, memorization of information, speed in decision making as well as the multiplicity of tasks to attend at the same time, place the workload as an important reference in the instrument of psychosocial factors, as already expressed by Jung and Jung (2011), those who affirm that either in the assignment of multiple tasks or in that of a single task that requires the memorization of multiple details, the relational complexity of the cognitive task increases and therefore the mental load as a relevant aspect of the workload (S G Hart, Staveland, Hancock, & Meshkati, 1988; Jung & Jung, 2001), which reinforces the assertion of (Rubio Valdehita, Díaz Ramiro, Martín García, & Luceño Moreno, 2010), who clearly establish mental workload as one of the most important psychosocial risk factors associated with the characteristics of the task.

The assessment of mental workload has been considered from two methodological perspectives. The first is situated in psychometry (Nygren, 1991) and the second in cognitive psychology (Young et al., 2015). The present work is approached from psychometry, using a modification of the instrument to evaluate psychosocial factors proposed by Standard 035 of the STPS, where the module called "Workload", involves to a great extent what is related to the "mental workload". As far as our knowledge goes, it is the first time that an evaluation of these characteristics is applied in the Mexican population, especially in the metal-mechanic industry. Some similar evaluations have been carried out in Mexico (Álvarez, 2012; Beltrán, Gónzalez, & Barraza Salas, 2013; Beltrán et al., 2011; De Castro, Place, Billings, Rivera, & Frongillo, 2015; De, Preciado-Serrano, Pozos-Radillo, Plascencia-Campos, & Colunga-Rodríguez, 2016; Garcia-Rojas, Choi, & Krause, 2015a, 2015b; González-Forteza & C., A. Juárez-López, L. Jiménez, U. Montejo-León, 2017; Guerrero, Jiménez, Ferrer, & Rivera, 2016; Negrete & Garcia-Aurrecoechea, 2008; Orozco-Solis et al., 2017; Salazar-Estrada & Romero, 2013; Shete & Wilkinson, 2017; S Unda et al., 2016; Sara Unda et al., 2016), in other countries such as Germany (Chirico, 2017; Niedhammer, Sultan-Taïeb, Chastang, Vermeylen, & Parent-Thirion, 2012; Nübling, Stößel, Hasselhorn, Michaelis, & Hofmann, 2006), Spain (Benavides et al., 2002; Á. J. Callejón-Ferre, Montoya-García, Pérez-Alonso, & Rojas-Sola, 2015; A. J. Callejón-Ferre et al., 2011; Gil-Monte, Lopez-Vilchez, Luis Llorca-Rubio, &

Sanchez Piernas, 2016; Moral & Suárez, 2016; Vega Perez, Vargas Ramos, Amores Guevara, & Arias Tapia, 2017), United States (Farnacio, Pratt, Marshall, & Graber, 2017; Macdonald & Levy, 2016; Yang et al., 2016), and in the Latin American region: Chile (Acevedo, Sánchez, Farias, & Fernández, 2013; Ansoleaga Moreno & Toro, 2010; Bones et al., 2014; Palomo-vélez, Carrasco, Bastías, Doris, & Jiménez, 2015; Rubén, Marchetti, Villalón, Hirmas, & Pastorino, 2010) and Colombia (Calderón Hernández, Serna Gómez, & Zuluaga Soto, 2013; Charria et al., 2011; Muñoz Rojas, Orellano, & Hernández Palma, 2018; Rodríguez et al., 2015), to name a few. However, Artazcoz (2001), Valdehita et al. (2010), Aoki (2011) and Galy, Cariou, and Mélan, (2012) are the ones who establish that instruments of this type can be useful for assessing mental workload (Aoki, 2011; Artazcoz, 2001; Galy et al., 2012; Valdehita et al., 2010).

Increased seniority may be an indication of a good degree of well-being in the workplace (Galy et al., 2012), which may partly explain why the area best evaluated with respect to psychosocial risks were: Spare Parts Store, Transportation and Chemical Process and Ecology, given that the workers presented a low or zero risk level with more than five years of seniority; followed by the areas of Quality, Training and Equipment and Tools Workshop where workers with medium, low or zero risk were presented, it coincides that in these areas of the workplace are those in which there is less staff turnover (Table 1).

CONCLUSION

The workload section of the questionnaire applied corresponding to NOM035-STPS largely contemplates aspects related to mental workload from a psychometric perspective, although it would be advisable to complement the information with an instrument that analyzes the cognitive vision of this indicator.

The areas that were best evaluated with respect to psychosocial risks were the following: Warehouse of Spare Parts, Chemical Process and Ecology and Transportation, given that the workers presented a low or zero risk level. In the areas of Quality, Training and Workshop of Apparatus and Tools, workers with medium, low or no risk were presented. In contrast, the areas where there were workers with high risk were Management, Finished Product Warehouse and Electrical. It should be noted that the only area where the case of a worker with very high risk was presented was the Decoration area.

Those areas where there were workers with high risk were the Administration, Finished Product and Electrical Warehouse. It should be noted that the only area where the case of a worker with very high risk was presented was the Decoration area. Of the areas analyzed in the company, the risk factors that occurred most frequently in the different areas were workload, lack of control over the work and workday; followed by factors such as: conditions in the work environment, interference in the work-family relationship, leadership and violence.

Very infrequent in the workplace areas were the factors: relationships at work, recognition of performance and insufficient sense of belonging and instability. Specifically, in the Spare Parts Warehouse area, where only one factor was presented, which was the working day, in contrast to the Decoration area in which most of the factors were present.

In relation to the general evaluation of the work center, it is important to point out that the majority of workers do not present psychosocial risks, or present a very low level, although it is necessary to consider that in order to attend to the proportion of personnel who have a medium risk, it is necessary to revise some work center policies aimed at the prevention of those risks that require intervention at the organizational level; for those who turned out to be at high risk, it will be necessary to review some group strategies focused on personal interrelations, information from the work center toward the work areas and others that are considered second level. On the other hand, for the minority that turned out to be at very high risk, it will be necessary to consider intervention one by one, directly with those cases of specific workers that require it.

REFERENCES

Acevedo, G., Sánchez, J., Farias, M., & Fernández, A. (2013). Riesgos Psicosociales en el Equipo de Salud de Hospitales Públicos de la Provincia de Córdoba. *Ciencia & Trabajo*, *15*(48), 140–147. doi:10.4067/S0718-24492013000300006

Álvarez, C. (2012). Riesgo psicosocial intralaboral y "burnout" en docentes universitarios de algunos países latinoamericanos. *Cuadernos de Administración, 28*(48), 118–133. Retrieved from http://search.ebscohost.com/login.aspx?direct=true&db=fua&AN=86056250&lang=es&site=ehost-live

Ángel, D., & Camón, G. (2003). *Criterios objetivos para la evaluación de la carga de trabajo derivada de factores psicosociales y organizacionales*. Academic Press.

Ansoleaga Moreno, E., & Toro, J. P. (2010). Factores psicosociales laborales asociados a riesgo de sintomatología depresiva en trabajadores de una empresa minera. *Salud Trab, 18*(1), 7–16.

Aoki, K. (2011). International Activity and Topics on "Ergonomic Principles related Mental Work Load (ISO 10075). *The Japanese Journal of Ergonomics*. doi:10.5100/jje.29.supplement_54

Arquer de, M. (1999). NTP 534: Carga mental de trabajo: factores. *Instituto Nacional de Seguridad e Higiene En El Trabajo*.

Artazcoz, L. (2001). Factores de riesgo psicosocial y carga mental : ¿ estamos midiendo lo mismo o son conceptos diferentes? *Archivos de Prevencion de Riesgos Laborales*, *4*(3), 91–92.

Beltrán, C., Gónzalez, J., & Barraza Salas, J. (2013). Factores psicosociales y síndrome de burnout en trabajadores de la industria de la transformación de la masa, Tepic, México. *Revista Colombiana de Psiquiatría*, *42*(2), 167–172. doi:10.1016/S0034-7450(13)70003-9 PMID:26572811

Beltrán, C., Moreno, M., López, T., Estrada, J., & Torres, J. (2011). Factores psicosociales y patologías laborales en trabajadores de un sistema de transporte público urbano, México. *Revista Colombiana de Psiquiatría*, *40*(2), 266–278. doi:10.1016/S0034-7450(14)60123-2

Benavides, F., Gimeno, D., Benach, J., Martínez, J., Jarque, S., Berra, A., & Devesa, J. (2002). *Descripción de los factores de riesgo psicosocial en cuatro empresas*. Gaceta Sanitaria / S.E.S.P.A.S.; doi:10.1016/S0213-9111(02)71665-8

Berniker, E., & Mintzberg, H. (2006). Structure in Fives: Designing Effective Organizations. *Administrative Science Quarterly*. doi:10.2307/2393181

Bones, K., Muntaner, C., Solar, O., Borrell, C., Bernales, P., & González, M., … Vallebuona, C. (2014). Social class, psychosocial occupational risk factors, and the association with self-rated health and mental health in Chile. *Cadernos de Saude Publica*. doi:10.1590/0102-311X00176213

Byrne, A., Oliver, M., Bodger, O., Barnett, W. A., Williams, D., Jones, H., & Murphy, A. (2010). Novel method of measuring the mental workload of anaesthetists during clinical practice. *British Journal of Anaesthesia, 105*(6), 767–771. doi:10.1093/bja/aeq240 PMID:20846966

Cain, B. (2004). A Review of the Mental Workload Literature. *NATO RTO-TR-HFM-121-Part-II*, (1998), 4-1-4–34. doi:10.14339/RTO-TR-HFM-121-Part-II

Çakmak, E., Öztekin, Ö., & Karadağ, E. (2015). The effect of leadership on job satisfaction. In Leadership and Organizational Outcomes: Meta-Analysis of Empirical Studies. doi:10.1007/978-3-319-14908-0_3

Calderón Hernández, G., Serna Gómez, H., & Zuluaga Soto, J. (2013). Liderazgo y relaciones sociales en el trabajo como factor de riesgo psicosocial : Su incidencia sobre gestión humana en las Organizaciones. *Revista Diversitas - Perspectivas Psicológicas, 9*(2), 409–423. Retrieved from http://aplicacionesbiblioteca.udea.edu.co:3628/ehost/detail/detail?vid=7&sid=9d93b370-38eb-4567-baeb-4c2cee3ce91f%40sessionmgr4002&hid=4209&bdata=Jmxhbmc9ZXMmc2l0ZT1laG9zdC1saXZl#AN=98258180&db=fua

Callejón-Ferre, Á., Montoya-García, M., Pérez-Alonso, J., & Rojas-Sola, J. (2015). The psychosocial risks of farm workers in south-east Spain. *Safety Science, 78*, 77–90. doi:10.1016/j.ssci.2015.04.015

Callejón-Ferre, A., Pérez-Alonso, J., Carreño-Ortega, A., & Velázquez-Martí, B. (2011). Indices of ergonomic-psycholsociological workplace quality in the greenhouses of Almería (Spain): Crops of cucumbers, peppers, aubergines and melons. *Safety Science, 49*(5), 746–750. doi:10.1016/j.ssci.2010.12.009

Carayon, P., Smith, M. J., & Haims, M. C. (2007). Work Organization, Job Stress, and Work-Related Musculoskeletal Disorders. *Human Factors: The Journal of the Human Factors and Ergonomics Society*. doi:10.1518/001872099779656743

Castor, M., MacLeod, I., Hanson, E., Svensson, E., Nählinder, S., Le Blaye, P., … Hilburn, B. (2003). GARTEUR Handbook of mental workload measurement. GARTEUR, Group for Aeronautical Research and Technology in Europe, Flight Mechanics Action Group FM AG13.

Charria, V., Sarsosa, K., & Arenas, F. (2011). Factores de riesgo psicosocial laboral : métodos e instrumentos de evaluación. *Revista Facultad Nacional de Salud Pública, 29*, 380–391. Retrieved from http://www.redalyc.org/articulo.oa?id=12021522004%5CnRevista

Chirico, F. (2017). The forgotten realm of the new and emerging psychosocial risk factors. *Journal of Occupational Health, 59*(5), 433–435. doi:10.1539/joh.17-0111-OP PMID:28819083

Cinaz, B., Arnrich, B., La Marca, R., & Tröster, G. (2013). Monitoring of mental workload levels during an everyday life office-work scenario. *Personal and Ubiquitous Computing, 17*(2), 229–239. doi:10.100700779-011-0466-1

Comité Mixto, O. I. T.-O. M. S. (1984). Factores psicosociales en el Trabajo: naturaleza, incidencia y prevención. *Oficina Internacional Del Trabajo, 1*, 1–85. Retrieved from http://biblioteca.uces.edu.ar/MEDIA/EDOCS/FACTORES_Texto.pdf

Cox, T., & Griffiths, A. (1996). The assessment of psychosocial hazards at work. In Handbook of work and health psychology. Academic Press.

De, M., Preciado-Serrano, L., Pozos-Radillo, E., Plascencia-Campos, A., & Colunga-Rodríguez, C. (2016). The Association of Psychosocial Risk Factors with the Burnout Syndrome in Dentists in Guadalajara, Jalisco Mexico. *Advances in Applied Sociology*, *6*(6), 81–89. doi:10.4236/aasoci.2016.63008

De Castro, F., Place, J., Billings, D., Rivera, L., & Frongillo, E. A. (2015). Risk profiles associated with postnatal depressive symptoms among women in a public sector hospital in Mexico: The role of sociodemographic and psychosocial factors. *Archives of Women's Mental Health*, *18*(3), 463–471. doi:10.100700737-014-0472-1 PMID:25416532

Dillard, M., Warm, J., Funke, G., Funke, M., Finomore, V., & Matthews, G. … Parasuraman, R. (2014). The Sustained Attention to Response Task (SART) does not promote mindlessness during vigilance performance. *Human Factors*. doi:10.1177/0018720814537521

El-Batawi, M., Kalimo, R., & Cooper, C. (1988). Los factores psicosociales en el trabajo y su relación con la salud. *Organización Mundial de La Salud*, 1–106. Retrieved from http://apps.who.int/iris/bitstream/10665/37881/1/9243561022_spa.pdf

Farnacio, Y., Pratt, M., Marshall, E., & Graber, J. (2017). Are Workplace Psychosocial Factors Associated with Work-Related Injury in the US Workforce?: National Health Interview Survey, 2010. *Journal of Occupational and Environmental Medicine*, *59*(10), e164–e171. doi:10.1097/JOM.0000000000001143 PMID:28991808

Galy, E., Cariou, M., & Mélan, C. (2012). What is the relationship between mental workload factors and cognitive load types? *International Journal of Psychophysiology*, *83*(3), 269–275. doi:10.1016/j.ijpsycho.2011.09.023 PMID:22008523

Garcia-Rojas, I., Choi, B., & Krause, N. (2015). Psychosocial job factors and biological cardiovascular risk factors in Mexican workers. *American Journal of Industrial Medicine*, *58*(3), 331–351. doi:10.1002/ajim.22410 PMID:25678459

Gil-Monte, P., Lopez-Vilchez, J., Luis Llorca-Rubio, J., & Sanchez Piernas, J. (2016). Prevalence of psychosocial risks in the justice administration staff of the valencian community (Spain). *Liberabit-revista de psicologia*.

González-Forteza, C., Juárez-López, C. E., Jiménez, A., Montejo-León, L., Rodríguez-Santisbón, U. R., & Wagner, F. A. (2017). Suicide behavior and associated psychosocial factors among adolescents in Campeche, Mexico. *Preventive Medicine*, *105*, 206–211. doi:10.1016/j.ypmed.2017.09.011 PMID:28917950

González-Muñoz, E., & Gutiérrez-Martínez, R. (2007). Contribution of mental workload to job stress in industrial workers. *Work (Reading, Mass.)*, *28*(4), 355–361. Retrieved from http://www.ncbi.nlm.nih.gov/pubmed/17522456 PMID:17522456

Gracia-Camón, Á. (2003). *Criterios objetivos para la evaluación de la carga de trabajo derivada de factores psicosociales y organizacionales*. Academic Press.

Guelaud, F., Beauchesne, M. N., & Gautrat, J. Y. R. G. (1975). Pour une Analyse des Conditions du Travail Ouvrier dans l'Entreprise. *Economics and Politics*, *114/116*(257).

Guerrero, M., Jiménez, J., Ferrer, B., & Rivera, A. (2016). Un análisis psicosocial de la confianza en los grupos policiales: El caso de Cuernavaca (México). *Perfiles Latinoamericanos*, *24*(47), 151–174. doi:10.18504/pl2447-009-2016

Hart, S., & Staveland, L. (1988). Development of NASA-TLX (Task Load Index): Results of Empirical and Theoretical Research. *Advances in Psychology*, *52*, 139–183. doi:10.1016/S0166-4115(08)62386-9

Hart, S., Staveland, L., Hancock, P., & Meshkati, N. (1988). *Human mental workload. Human mental workload* (Vol. 2). Retrieved from https://www.elsevier.com/books/human-mental-workload/hancock/978-0-444-70388-0

Hernandez-Arellano, J., Garcia-Alcaraz, J., Serratos-Perez, J., & Maldonado-Macías, A. (2016). Assessment of Workload, Fatigue, and Musculoskeletal Discomfort among Advanced Manufacturing Technology Operators in Mexico. A preliminary study. *IIE Transactions on Occupational Ergonomics and Human Factors*.

Iavicoli, S., Cesana, G., Dollard, M., Leka, S., & Sauter, S. (2015). Psychosocial Factors and Workers' Health and Safety. *BioMed Research International*, *2015*, 1–3. doi:10.1155/2015/628749 PMID:26634211

IEA. (2000). *Definition of ergonomics*. International Ergonomics Association.

Instituto Nacional de Seguridad e Higiene en el Trabajo (INSHT). (2003). *NTP 702: El proceso de evaluación de los factores psicosociales*. Insituto Nacional de Seguridad e Higiene en el Trabajo.

Jung, H., & Jung, H. (2001). Establishment of overall workload assessment technique for various tasks and workplaces. *International Journal of Industrial Ergonomics*, *28*(6), 341–353. doi:10.1016/S0169-8141(01)00040-3

Kristensen, T., & Borg, V. (2003). Copenhagen Psychosocial Questionnaire. *Mental Health*. doi:10.1177/1403494809353652

Lahera, M., & Nogareda, C. (2009). El método del INSL para la identificación y evaluación de factores psicosociales, 1–6. Retrieved from papers3://publication/uuid/A9400361-817C-47B4-862D-9A95C1DC28D9

Leka, S., Van Wassenhove, W., & Jain, A. (2015). Is psychosocial risk prevention possible? Deconstructing common presumptions. *Safety Science, 71*(Part A), 61–67. doi:10.1016/j.ssci.2014.03.014

Ma, R., & Kaber, D. (2005). Situation awareness and workload in driving while using adaptive cruise control and a cell phone. *International Journal of Industrial Ergonomics*, *35*(10), 939–953. doi:10.1016/j.ergon.2005.04.002

Macdonald, J., & Levy, S. (2016). Ageism in the Workplace: The Role of Psychosocial Factors in Predicting Job Satisfaction, Commitment, and Engagement. *The Journal of Social Issues*, *72*(1), 169–190. doi:10.1111/josi.12161

Magana, C., Hovey, J., Magana, C., Magaña, C., & Hovey, J. (2003). Psychosocial stressors associated with Mexican migrant farmworkers in the Midwest United States. *Journal of Immigrant Health*.

Matthews, G., Reinerman-Jones, L., Barber, D., & Abich, J. IV. (2015). The psychometrics of mental workload: Multiple measures are sensitive but divergent. *Human Factors*, *57*(1), 125–143. doi:10.1177/0018720814539505 PMID:25790574

Mélan, C., & Cascino, N. (2014). A multidisciplinary approach of workload assessment in real-job situations: Investigation in the field of aerospace activities. *Frontiers in Psychology*. doi:10.3389/fpsyg.2014.00964 PMID:25232346

Ministerio de la Protección Social. (2010). *Batería de instrumentos para la evaluación de factores de riesgo psicosocial*. Retrieved from http://www.riesgopsicosocial.com.co/Bateria-riesgo-psicosocial.compressed.pdf

Moncada, S., Llorens, C., Navarro, A., & Kristensen, T. S. (2005). ISTAS21: Versión en lengua castellana del cuestionario psicosocial de Copenhague (COPSOQ). *Arch Prev Riesgos Labor.*

Mondelo E., Barrau P. Ergonomía, P. R. (1999). *Edicions UPC Aula Politècnica / Etseib. Ergonomía 1 Fundamentos*. doi:10.1186/1748-717X-2-28

Moral, M., & Suárez, C. (2016). Factores de riesgo en el uso problemático de Internet y del teléfono móvil en adolescentes españoles. *Revista Iberoamericana de Psicología y Salud*, *7*(2), 69–78. doi:10.1016/j.rips.2016.03.001

Moray, N. (1982). Subjective mental workload. *Human Factors*, *24*(1), 25–40. doi:10.1177/001872088202400104

Moreno, B. (2015). Summary for Policymakers. In Intergovernmental Panel on Climate Change (Ed.), Climate Change 2013 - The Physical Science Basis (pp. 1–30). Cambridge, UK: Cambridge University Press. doi:10.1017/CBO9781107415324.004

Moreno-Jiménez, B., & Báez León, C. (2010). *Psychosocial factors and risks, forms, consequences, measures and good practices*. Instituto Nacional de Seguridad e Higiene En El Trabajo. doi:10.1016/0277-9536(85)90255-2

Muñoz Rojas, D., Orellano, N., & Hernández Palma, H. (2018). Riesgo psicosocial: Tendencias y nuevas orientaciones laborales. *Psicogente*, *21*(40), 532–544. doi:10.17081/psico.21.40.3090

Negrete, B., & Garcia-Aurrecoechea, R. (2008). Psychosocial risk factors for illicit drug use in a sample of Mexican high school students. *Revista Panamericana de Salud Publica*, *24*(4), 223–232. PMID:19133170

Niedhammer, I., Sultan-Taïeb, H., Chastang, J., Vermeylen, G., & Parent-Thirion, A. (2012). Exposure to psychosocial work factors in 31 European countries. *Occupational Medicine*, *62*(3), 196–202. doi:10.1093/occmed/kqs020 PMID:22394680

NOM035. S. (2018). *DOF: 23/10/2018*. Retrieved from https://www.dof.gob.mx/nota_detalle.php?codigo=5541828&fecha=23/10/2018&print=true

Nogareda Cuixart, C., & Pérez Bilbao, J. (2012a). Factores Psicosociales: metodología de evaluación. *Notas Técnicas de Prevención*, 1–5. Retrieved from http://www.insht.es/InshtWeb/Contenidos/Documentacion/NTP/NTP/926a937/926w.pdf

Nogareda Cuixart, C., & Pérez Bilbao, J. (2012b). *NTP 926. Factores Psicosociales: metodología de evaluación*. Notas Técnicas de Prevención.

Nübling, M., Stößel, U., Hasselhorn, H., Michaelis, M., & Hofmann, F. (2006). Measuring psychological stress and strain at work - Evaluation of the COPSOQ Questionnaire in Germany. *Psycho-Social Medicine*. PMID:19742072

Nygren, T. E. (1991). Psychometric properties of subjective workload measurement techniques: Implications for their use in the assessment of perceived mental workload. *Human Factors, 33*(1), 17–33. doi:10.1177/001872089103300102

Oppold, P., Rupp, M., Mouloua, M., Hancock, P., & Martin, J. (2012). *Design considerations to improve cognitive ergonomic issues of unmanned vehicle interfaces utilizing video game controllers*. Work. doi:10.3233/WOR-2012-0896-5609

Orozco-Solis, M., Colunga-Rodríguez, C., Preciado-Serrano, M., Ángel-González, M., Vázquez-Colunga, J., & Colunga-Rodríguez, B. (2017). Representación del autocuidado de la salud en el trabajo de conductores de autobús urbano de Guadalajara, México. *Cadernos de Saude Publica, 33*(3), e00139815. doi:10.1590/0102-311x00139815 PMID:28380145

Osorio-Escobar, M. (2011). El trabajo y los factores de riesgo psicosociales: Qué son y cómo se evalúan. *Revista CES Salud Pública, 2*(1), 74–79. Retrieved from http://revistas.ces.edu.co/index.php/ces_salud_publica/article/viewFile/1450/892

Palomo-vélez, G., Carrasco, J., Bastías, Á., Doris, M., & Jiménez, A. (2015). Factores de riesgo psicosocial y satisfacción laboral en trabajadoras estacionales de Chile. *Revista Panamericana de Salud Pública, 37*(7), 301–307. PMID:26208200

Peiro, J. (2013). *Desencadenantes del estrés laboral*. Universidad de València.

Pérez Bilbao, J., & Nogareda Cuixart, C. (2012). *Factores psicosociales : metodología de evaluación*. Instituto Nacional de Seguridad e Higiente En El Trabajo.

Petty, M., McGee, G., & Cavender, J. (2011). A Meta-Analysis of the Relationships Between Individual Job Satisfaction and Individual Performance. *Academy of Management Review*. doi:10.5465/amr.1984.4277608

Piotet, F., & Mabile, J. (1984). *Conditions de travail, mode d'emploi ANACT [Agence nationale pour l'amélioration des conditions de travail]*. Academic Press.

Pollock, T., Whitbred, R., & Contractor, N. (2006). Social information processing and job characteristics. *Human Communication Research, 26*(2), 292–330. doi:10.1111/j.1468-2958.2000.tb00759.x

Raziq, A., & Maulabakhsh, R. (2015). Impact of Working Environment on Job Satisfaction. *Procedia Economics and Finance, 23*, 717–725. doi:10.1016/S2212-5671(15)00524-9

Reid, G., & Nygren, T. (1988). The Subjective Workload Assessment Technique: A Scaling Procedure for Measuring Mental Workload. *Advances in Psychology, 52*, 185–218. doi:10.1016/S0166-4115(08)62387-0

Renault, R. (1976). Les profils de postes. Méthode d'analyse des conditions de travail. *Services Des Conditions de Travail.*

Rodríguez, E., Sánchez-Gómez, J., Dorado, H. A., & Ramírez, J. M. (2015). Factores de Riesgo Psicosocial Intralaboral y Grado de Estrés en Docentes Universitarios. *Revista Colombiana de Salud Ocupacional, 4*(2), 12–17. Retrieved from http://revistasojs.unilibrecali.edu.co/index.php/rcso/article/view/111

Rubén, A., Marchetti, N., Villalón, M., Hirmas, M., & Pastorino, M. S. (2010). Adaptación y análisis psicométrico de un cuestionario para evaluar riesgos psicosociales en el trabajo en Chil: Versión media del CoPsoQ. *Revista Chilena de Salud Pública, 13*(1), 7–16. doi:10.5354/0717-3652.2009.652

Rubio Valdehita, S., Díaz Ramiro, E. M., Martín García, J., & Luceño Moreno, L. (2010). La carga mental como factor de riesgo psicosocial. Diferencias por baja Laboral TT - Mental workload as a psychosocial risk factor. Differnces based on sick leave. *Ansiedad y Estrés.*

Ruíz García, E. (2005). *Idoate García.* MPF Cuestionario de Factores Psicosociales. Mini Psychosocial Factors.

Salazar-Estrada, J., & Romero, N. (2013). Factores psicosociales del trabajador en la industria manufacturera en México. *Trabajo y Sociedad (Santiago del Estero), 20,* 119–129. Retrieved from http://www.unse.edu.ar/trabajoysociedad/20 SALAZAR ROMERO trabajador manufactura mexico.pdf

Sarsosa-Prowesk, K., Charria-Ortiz, V., & Arenas-Ortiz, F. (2014). Caracterizaci??n de los riesgos psicosociales intralaborales en jefes asistenciales de cinco cl??nicas nivel III de Santiago de Cali (Colombia). *Revista Gerencia y Politicas de Salud, 13*(27). doi:10.11144/Javeriana.rgyps13-27.crpi

Schütte, S., Chastang, J., Malard, L., Parent-Thirion, A., Vermeylen, G., & Niedhammer, I. (2014). Psychosocial working conditions and psychological well-being among employees in 34 European countries. *International Archives of Occupational and Environmental Health, 87*(8), 897–907. doi:10.100700420-014-0930-0 PMID:24526111

Secretaría del Trabajo y Previsión Social. (2018). *NORMA Oficial Mexicana NOM-035-STPS-2018, Factores de riesgo psicosocial en el trabajo-Identificación, análisis y prevención.* Author.

Sharan, D. (2012). Ergonomic workplace analysis (EWA). In Work. doi:10.3233/WOR-2012-0821-5366

Shete, S., & Wilkinson, A. (2017). Identifying demographic and psychosocial factors related to the escalation of smoking behavior among Mexican American adolescents. *Preventive Medicine, 99,* 146–151. doi:10.1016/j.ypmed.2017.02.018 PMID:28235542

Sontag, A., Vilagra, J., Moreira, H., Moro, A., Cruz, R., Reis, P., & Galvão, I. (2012). *Identification of the mental workload of public employees in the administrative sector at a public university.* Work. doi:10.3233/WOR-2012-0965-5828

Steven L., M. Lawrence, J., & Levi, L. (2001). Factores psicosociales y de organización. *O.I.T. Enciclopedia de Salud y Seguridad En El Trabajo.*, (2–3), 88.

Tsai, Y. (2011). Relationship between organizational culture, leadership behavior and job satisfaction. *BMC Health Services Research, 11*(1), 98. doi:10.1186/1472-6963-11-98 PMID:21569537

Unda, S., Uribe, F., Jurado, S., García, M., Tovalín, H., & Juárez, A. (2016). Construction of a scale for assessing at work psychosocial risk factors in professors. *Revista de Psicología del Trabajo y de las Organizaciones*, *32*(2), 67–74. doi:10.1016/j.rpto.2016.04.004

Unda, S., Uribe, F., Jurado, S., García, M., Tovalín, H., & Juárez, A. (2016). Elaboración de una escala para valorar los factores de riesgo psicosocial en el trabajo de profesores universitarios. *Revista de Psicología del Trabajo y de las Organizaciones*, *32*(2), 67–74. doi:10.1016/j.rpto.2016.04.004

Valdehita, S., Ramiro, E., García, J., & Moreno, L. (2010). La Carga Mental Como Factor De Riesgo Psicosocial. Diferencias Por Baja Laboral. *Ansiedad y Estrés*.

Vedder, J., & Laurig, W. (2013). *Ergonomía: Herramientas Y Enfoques*. Enciclopedia de Salud y Seguridad En El Trabajo.

Vega Perez, J., Vargas Ramos, M., Amores Guevara, P., & Arias Tapia, S. (2017). Psychosocial risks and industrial safety in the textile laundries of pelileo canton. *Revista de comunicacion de la SEECI*. doi:10.15198eeci.2017.43.135-149

Wickens, C., Gordon, S., & Liu, Y. (2004). *An introduction to human factors engineering*. Pearson.

Yang, H., Hitchcock, E., Haldeman, S., Swanson, N., Lu, M., & Choi, B. … Baker, D. (2016). Workplace psychosocial and organizational factors for neck pain in workers in the United States. *American Journal of Industrial Medicine*. doi:10.1002/ajim.22602

Young, M., Brookhuis, K., Wickens, C., & Hancock, P. (2015). State of science: Mental workload in ergonomics. *Ergonomics*, *58*(1), 1–17. doi:10.1080/00140139.2014.956151 PMID:25442818

Yu, Y., Li, H., Umer, W., Dong, C., Yang, X., Skitmore, M., & Wong, A. Y. L. (2019). Automatic Biomechanical Workload Estimation for Construction Workers by Computer Vision and Smart Insoles. *Journal of Computing in Civil Engineering*, *33*(3), 04019010. doi:10.1061/(ASCE)CP.1943-5487.0000827

Chapter 8
Evaluating Technostress to Improve Teaching Performance: Chilean Higher Education Case

Alejandro Vega-Muñoz
https://orcid.org/0000-0002-9427-2044
Universidad Autónoma de Chile, Chile

Carla Estrada-Muñoz
https://orcid.org/0000-0002-4657-8751
Universidad de Concepción, Chile

ABSTRACT

The main objective is to evaluate the techno stress perception in the Chilean higher education system professors, a system with a strong market orientation regarding the career's free choice and professional orientation, which is mainly offered in face-to-face mode. In the techno-stress levels identification, it is important to distinguish if these are such that they can affect the teaching performance. For this, techno-tensors and factors are used that determine the technology impact levels in academic stress, in the components: skepticism, fatigue, anxiety and inefficacy. A quantitative approach methodology and non-random design is used, with a snowball sampling obtaining the 190 academics' opinions from Chilean universities. Detecting in general low techno-stress levels with the fatigue slightly higher in comparison to the other three components.

INTRODUCTION

According to an International Labor Organization (ILO) a fundamental resolution issued in 1975 must not only respect the worker's life and health and leave them free time for rest and leisure but must also allow them to serve society and achieve their self-realization by developing their abilities. (Sauter, Murphy, Hurrell, & Levi, 1998). Molina-Sabando and García-Lucas (2018), add that in the last decade the labor demands imposed by the Higher Education supervisory bodies encourage a high level of anxiety in

DOI: 10.4018/978-1-7998-1052-0.ch008

university teachers who must fit into different roles, which involve greater participation in management procedures and decision making inherent into the teaching - learning process.

Conditions and work nature have changed rapidly in recent decades. Thus, today's work environments are characterized by a growing emphasis on knowledge and information-based activities and an increasing trust in new technologies. A situation that has generated new demands to assume the new teaching role and education challenges with new pedagogical, technological and methodological approaches. (García, Iglesias, Saleta & Romay, 2016).

Thus the increase in labor demands in recent decades imposed by the Higher Education supervisory bodies, have forced university academics to join different roles that involve greater participation in management procedures and decision making inherent into the teaching - learning process, adding the increase of administrative jobs that are not contemplated within the classroom hours and adding to these the mental waste. Resulting in teachers with high workloads, a performance in line with their monotonous routines, lack of initiative and interest in innovating on their work. The above results in academics subjected to strong work pressure and therefore suffering occupational high levels of stress, affecting negatively their satisfaction, performance, productivity and health, leading to psychosomatic symptoms and diseases that gradually develop and accumulate, causing Exhaustion or Burnout syndrome. (Molina-Sabando & García-Lucas, 2018).

García (2017, 2017b), stands out as the main characteristics of the work performed by university teachers in contemporary times: the tensions between teaching and research, work intensification, academic productivism, commodification, competition, quantitative assessment, the individual versus the collective, and the bureaucratization of research activities.

The term stress was used in 1926 by Hans Selye when he noticed in laboratory mice that they experienced glandular abdominal changes due to a hormone injection. Who defined this a nonspecific response of body to any request for change, a decade later (1936) in his article "A Syndrome produced by Diverse Nocuous Agents" published in Nature (Seyle, 1936, p. 32). This non-specific stress response is considered a mental state, that is, a relationship between an individual and a threatening context that exceeds their coping resources, which in the technical and computer-related work, specific case reveal several medical consequences in employees, because they experience an increase in the adrenaline and noradrenaline levels in their body, the excessive secretions of adrenal glands increase the stress stimulus, accelerate the pulse, increase blood pressure, increase the conductivity skin level and increase the effort jaw muscle. (Alam, 2016, Molina-Sabando & García-Lucas, 2018).

Already in 2003, Salanova-Soria realized that terms such as the Internet, mobile connectivity, automation, telework, among others that emerged with the information society are increasingly familiar, even forming our private and public life. In this way, the incorporation of these technological changes in the workplace, revealed not only technical challenges but also human and social challenges of deep debate, given the consequences they imply for both people and organizations. Adding a demand for prevention and counseling to the potential risks and negative technological impact effects on the effectiveness of companies and workers' psychosocial needs. A scenario in which technostress or stress derived from the new technologies introduction at work becomes important. Nowadays, with the greatest growth and development of information technologies, people can take care of their work in a ubiquitous way, in the distance and even after working hours using mobile devices connected in a network, compared to a traditional labor compliance method in which his work is carried out within a limited time and space of his life. (Seong-Tak & Park, 2016).

Molina-Sabando & García-Lucas (2018), added, based on their study in the Humanistic and Social Sciences Faculty of the Manabí Technical University, the relationship existence in work stress and the university teacher's affectivity (based to a Woodworth Test adaptation). As for lower work stress levels, lower is the difficulty of affectivity.

Although it is necessary to clarify that the simple exposure to IT is not the cause of negative psychosocial effects, but some variables that mediate and modulate that relationship, such as the experience assessment with the IT use, attitudes and assessment regarding technology, and self-efficacy beliefs about the technology use. It has an attention point when workers come to point out that they are subject to work demands that exceed the time available to be able to get performing tasks on time. This work overload, which can be quantitative (too much work to do in the time available) or qualitative (things too complex that exceed the competences to perform them), is constituted by emotional demands based on the rhythm of work impose: coworkers, supervisors, users or customers, to which others could undoubtedly add. In many cases corresponds to a mental overload for the work with IT caused by the work pace imposed by "the machines", the ubiquity and speed of information technologies work, given that the increase in mental demands at work is directly related to the IT implementation in organizations. (Salanova-Soria, 2003).

On the other hand, according to Chu & Kuo (2015) the motivation importance is relevant in the areas of human resources management, industrial and organizational psychology, and organizational behavior. Increasing the importance on modern management, and a need for organizations to understand what motivates their employees and the reasons why employees are motivated, to know what are the internal and external forces that influence the action choice of its employees. And in this way manage compliance with hygiene factors, which although they are not a motivation direct source, it is necessary to avoid their dissatisfaction because this causes the labor efficiency to decrease, the product of an unfavorable work environment that leads to lower labor participation and involvement in educational processes. Typical hygienic factors consider: the company policy and administration, job security feelings, financial remuneration (salary/wages), the supervision quality, the interpersonal relationship quality and, working conditions.

So, Camargo-Mayorga (2016), provides an example from the teaching exercise in higher education, studying the university teacher's motivation in Bogotá, based on the results achieved in academic objectives terms, and the teacher motivation analysis in the function of hygienic factors and motivating factors that influence work. Concluding that in the universities studied, the academics are motivated, and satisfied with their full-time dedication, regardless of the dissatisfaction received by other factors, to the extreme point that a low remuneration of the labor market of higher education does not weaken their motivation to continue dedicated to education. But it is recognized that the motivators influence the teacher and have an impact on their work, highlighting the motivation power as a pedagogical and didactic tool in teaching practice, a subject not so much worked in research in education and, therefore, it is important to follow the works, from the interpretative approach of teaching subjectivities in higher education.

Regardless of the current work type, it is unavoidable that this involves some advanced technology kind, and therefore employees face technological stress. Understanding this as an inability adaptive syndrome to cope with an optimistic technological change, it is necessary to highlight that technological stress has a nonconstructive impact on the individual attitude and response that originates directly or indirectly from technology and smog-data, one of the growing problems related to excess of information. (Alam, 2016). Thus, the demands of the environment do not correspond to the individual capacity, or the opportunities offered by the environment and are not up to the needs and expectations of the individual being as major psychosocial stressors that cause stress at work or elsewhere, this Poor "person-environment adjustment" in interaction with genetic factors. (Sauter, Murphy, Hurrell, & Levi, 1998).

Arquero & Donoso (2013) indicate that universities have their psychosocial risks, as an interaction result that occurs between institutional characteristics, demands and working conditions, with the needs, abilities and the university professors' expectations. Considering the possibility of the varied roles: teaching, extension, research, administration and technical assistance. They point out that university professors are under pressure to try to respond to an enormous demand's diversity, such as new study plans implementation, teaching methodologies modification, permanent university teaching activity assessment, research quality evaluation, etc. These multiple demands present an imbalance, with lack of time being the most consistent stress cause over time for university professors. The current university context is far from diminishing this pressure since it is in an important process of structural and teaching change that will require additional efforts from its academics in all aspects (teaching, research and management) with dwindling resources. As from now, it is not enough to do well, also it is necessary to do a lot. (Vega, Martinez & Morales, 2017, Vega, Rojas & Salazar, 2018, Vega, Valdés & Cruz, 2019).

The above, emphasizes that the job demands should be assigned in a balanced way, since the excessive workload that affects particularly some people should be avoided to prevent work stress due to difficult deadlines and an unfair workload distribution within a team, requiring close cooperation between senior positions and workers. (International Labour Office, 2014). Especially because the markets economic globalization processes, such as liberation, internalization, competitiveness, techno-scientific advances, privatization and the social programs' adjustment have promoted changes in work and the working class, particularly on their labor management, which are characterized by a great demand for workers, a greater emphasis on mental work, the organizational structures flexibility, the services outsourcing or the virtual work environments use, among others. Besides that, the changes that are registered in the social and organizational environment influence the new psychosocial risks appearance in the work: sociodemographic conditions, regulations and legislation, population culture, technological conditions and the work conception. (Unda, et al., 2016).

Another reason originated in the growing awareness that work stress implies secondary costs that are avoidable and health promotion, through the proper configuration jobs, can constitute a considerable advantage for the countries that apply it in the growing globalized competition. Ideas reinforced in recent knowledge obtained from psychobiological stress research and socio-medical studies (epidemiological), which emphasize the importance for the corporal and spiritual psycho mental health and socio-emotional situations specific to the stressful conditions of active working life. Underlining the importance of these stressful psychosocial experiences in the paid work, substantial transformations that have taken place in the societies developed during the last decades, as a the technical progress result of: automation, greater IT incorporation and the production dematerialization; progress that entails an increase in control activities (Fernández-López, Siegrist, Rödel & Hernández-Mejía, 2003).

Several reasons are those that motivate the contemporary study in the work conditions for university professors in Latin America. With emphasis such as the work conditions identification in university academics in Mexico and their relationship with the stress prevalence (Palacios-Nava & Montes de Oca-Zavala, 2017), establishing the relationship between stress levels in university teachers in the Ecuador public sector with the presence and psychological violence intensity, workplace harassment and socio-demographic labor factors (gender, age, marital status, dedication time and formation level) (Lara-Sotomayor & Pando-Moreno, 2014), occupational fatigue influence verification in professors' work ability of the Biological Sciences and Health Center from a Higher Education Public Institution (HEPI) in Brazil (Amorim-Santino, Ferreira-Tomaz & Gomes de Lucena, 2017), prevalence measurement of six generic psychosocial risk categories (psychological demands, control over work, social support and leadership quality, double presence, esteem and insecurity about the future) in a teacher sample belonging to a public university in Argentina (Pujol-Cols & Arraigada, 2017), psychosocial risk intra-occupational factors identification in full-time teachers of a public university in Colombia (Ortiz-Doncel, 2017),work participation attenuating function exploration in the relationship between the perceived exposure to psychosocial risks and academic affective job satisfaction from a public university in Argentina (Pujol-Colsa & Lazzaro-Salazar, 2018), direct and interactive effects on examination of the core self-evaluations (CSE) and autonomy on the three dimensions that make up the work engagement (physical, cognitive and emotional involvement) (Pujol-Cols, 2018), evaluation of relationship between psychosocial risk factors and work stress in the engineering and architecture faculty of a private university in Peru. But these studies, in no case confronts the technology factor with the academics working conditions.

Despite the above, a small number of studies about online education, generate a cross between stress and technology used in education in the Latin American region. Thus, Kruel-Goebel and Carlotto (2019) publication, was able to identify the predictive power of socio-demographic, labor and psychosocial variables (occupational stressors, contextual stressors and techno-stress dimensions) on the Burnout Syndrome dimensions in distance education teachers in Brazil. Also Vergara-Mendoza, Carabajo-Romero and Leal-Maridueña (2017) give an account of the stress level in the Ecuadorian university teachers with distance component, which turns out to be elevated mainly by the variety of activities that develop in fulfilling with teaching expectative, as well as the radical change proposed by the national higher education quality assurance council, the development of research projects and links with society, as well as the changes suggested by the university authorities themselves. Resulting in symptomatology on professors, among which are anxiety, inability to concentrate, irritability, eating disorders, physical fatigue, headache, up to depression, cardiovascular disorders, respiratory and immune system disorders, which has influenced an increase in permits that affects the learning process of students and increases the stress load given the need to recover classes.

And on the other hand, Pereira, Grützmann, and Novello (2019) realize that the research related to the technostress study is deficient in Brazil, although it represents a relevant topic to the teaching today context. What becomes an incentive to study on this subject, as it contributes to the development of strategies and the well-being of teachers in the digital age.

EVALUATING TECHNOSTRESS TO IMPROVE PERFORMANCE

Evaluating Technostress

The stress impact on health varies according to each individuals' response to meet these adaptation requirements for which he has not developed previous capacities. Although higher stress levels can contribute to developing health disabilities, which include mental and behavioral disorders (exhaustion, anxiety and depression), as well as physical disorders (cardiovascular diseases and musculoskeletal disorders). Increasing attention is also paid to the new coping behaviors impact (alcohol and drug abuse, smoking, unhealthy diet, poor sleep), as well as the relationship with increased accident rates in the workplace and non-communicable diseases. But in the expert's opinion, the prior competencies development to address work stress, could be a good measure if they are achieved: psychosocial risk management capabilities, adequate key stakeholders' knowledge, relevant and reliable information to support the decision-making, effective and easy-to-use tools and availability of methods, and competent support structures (International Labour Organization, 2016).

There is much literature that supports the work stress as a disease promoter idea, which puts the workers at social risk and psychological health and damages their social, professional and affective lives, generating a variety of negative results for both physical health and mental health, including depression and anxiety, along with maladaptive behaviors such as smoking and drinking. This is followed by poor performance at work, a high absenteeism level and staff turnover, and violence in the workplace. (Giorgi, et al, 2017).

Stress can be explained through different models, one of these is the so - called demand - control model. This model explains stress as the interaction between 'job characteristics, psychological demands and control degree over the tasks. In this way, it establishes four categories:

- High voltage, where the demands are high and there is a low control over them;
- Low voltage, where the demands are low and there is high control over them;
- Active workers, where there are high demands and high control; and finally,
- Passive workers, the situation in which the demands are low and at the same time there is a low control over such demands.

This model considers social support, as a moderating element in the interaction between the demands and the control level and establishes that learning occurs both when situations cataloged as demands or challenges occur, as well as having the capacity to make decisions. The ability to make decisions allows choosing the best way or strategy to cope with a stressor. If the control demands model is applied to the technostress, there would be a mismatch between the demands derived from the ICTs use and each user resources (Sauter, Murphy, Hurrell, & Levi, 1998, Salanova, Llorens, Cifre, & Nogareda, 2007, Charria, Sarsosa & Arenas, 2011).

Currently, the control concept in the demand - control model has been extended to other labor resources, considering that work conditions are categorized into labor demands and labor resources. In this regard, labor demands are characteristics of organizations and therefore all those factors present in the work, physical, social and organizational, that require an effort on the worker part in time to be done, and that costs entail physical or physiological and psychological. The main demands associated with the ICT use correspond to work overload, routine and monotony, role conflict and work-family conflict. On the other hand, labor resources are those protective, physical, psychological, social and organizational factors, which mainly contribute to reduce labor demands and their associated costs and stimulate personal development (Salanova, 2003, Salanova, Llorens, Cifre, & Nogareda, 2007, Orgambídez-Ramos, Pérez-Moreno & Borrego-Alés, 2015).

For Salanova, Llorens, Cifre, & Nogareda (2007) the information overload associated with the ICT use increases quantitative and qualitative workload, it is necessary to delve into what is related to labor resources. A very important issue is ICT implementation of strategies in the organizations, which can focus on technology or on the user. In this regard, the user-centered design causes greater psychosocial well-being, less stress and, on the other hand, a higher performance at work, as a result that ICT introduction reduces personal contact, and the possibility to receive emotional support, organization must provide the means for workers to expose their problems arising from changes in a working way and the skills required.

On the other hand, personal resources or the people characteristics cushion the negative high demands effects and lack of labor resources, such as certain personality characteristics, a resistant personality, and beliefs about individual and Self-efficacy in dealing with the technologies used, are key of self-efficacy that corresponds to 'beliefs in one's abilities to organize and execute the action courses required to produce certain achievements'.

Finally, the authors point out that technostress has the consequences and the consequences are psychosomatic complaints such as sleep problems, headaches, muscle aches, gastrointestinal disorders, as well as organizational damage such as absenteeism and performance reduction, especially due to non-use or misuse of ICTs in the workplace. Well, in the long term, technostress could end up developing also burnout (burning for work syndrome).

For Chavez-Orozco (2016) the so-called Burnout Syndrome or professional burnout, has become more important given the economic pressures derived mainly from industrialization, automation, globalization, and that have had a direct impact on the worker's health since they cannot adapt to the new rules imposed by the labor market. This Burnout manifests itself with psychological changes that increase in intensity from discontent and irritability to emotional outbursts, especially in professionals with a dependency relationship, mainly in the service provision area, such as teaching. A situation that is increased, if the work is performed in inappropriate conditions, excessive work hours, insecurity in the position, insufficient remuneration and lack of material or human resources essential for the proper execution of their tasks.

Technostress is a term that was first coined by the American psychologist Craig Brod in the 1980s as an adaptation disease originated by the lack of ability to deal with new tools and computer technology systems healthily, caused by the incompetence in the confrontation to the TIC.

What overtime has been widening to any negative impact on attitudes, thoughts, behaviors or physiology caused directly or indirectly by technology, given the increasing stress caused by the invasion in the daily life of mobile phones, e-mails, audio, image and video players or online access platforms to these. To which are added various related terms that are related to the term technostress, such as 'Information Fatigue Syndrome', Techno-addiction and Technophobia. All of them refer to technostress since this is a broad construct that harbors more specific ones. (Salanova, 2003). Lee, Chang, Lin & Cheng (2014), complement by pointing to technostress as 'a adaptation modern disease caused by the inability to cope with new computer technologies in a healthy way', which is related to the smartphones use, generating stress due to the information and communication overload experienced by end-users.

For Gaudioso, Turel & Galimberti (2017) technostress is formed in the technostress creators' presence and intensity (or techno-stressors), which exist in any workplace where computers are used. Even some technologies of invasive nature can lead employees to perceive technological invasion (a technological intrusion sense, which blurs the desired boundaries between work and other life domains). Technological stressors are conditions experienced within the extended organizational environment and create dynamics that can foster tension. Being recognized in the literature five technological stress key factors in organizations: technological overload, technological invasion, technological insecurity, technological uncertainty and technological complexity.

Also, for Seong-Tak & Park (2016) technostress influences job satisfaction only indirectly since there is a high relation with the conflict between work and family life. Unlike techno-stressors, in contrast, factors that relieve stress have a direct effect on job satisfaction, without playing a moderating role.

Also, organizations can improve their employees' information systems knowledge, which makes adaptation strategies easier. Secondly, another way to reduce the work exhaustion is by reducing technological stressors in the environment (banning emails after work hours can be a reducing technological invasion viable means, creating a culture of copying only relevant employees in emails and automating processes so that fewer people are involved it can reduce technology overload). Concluding that the stress dynamic and coping model applies to techno-stress context and stressing technological factors effects on the work, adverse results are mediated by tension facets and coping strategies. It is necessary to consider the stressors interaction, stress and coping strategies among employees, factors that organizations and employees can intervene. (Gaudioso, Turel and Galimberti, 2017)

Technostress and Improve Performance

Of course, technostress is directly connected to the low self-efficacy levels related to technology. Fulfilling self-efficacy, a moderating role in the technostress process, where there is a demands perception and lack of resources in current or future work with technology, and the belief users in their competencies to successfully face work with technology playing a crucial role in technostress development. Psychological processes mediate the effects of stressors on well-being, so that work-related stress can be considered as a process involving stressors or various kinds labor demands, stress consequences, and the person resources as of work, whose absence can become another stressor, and their presence can cushion the effects of damaging stressors. (Salanova-Soria, 2003).

Most organizations use some performance measure criteria as the basis for their incentive programs. In which are usually applied measures of yield to production, quality, processing time or other productivity indicators. Performance measures must be fair and coherent to reduce stress among the organization members, there are different measurement methods, from subjective estimates (conjecture) to the application of quantification work planned techniques (Sauter, Murphy, Hurrell, & Levi, 1998).

The legislation on occupational health has allowed the physical, hygienic and mechanical progressive risks control in companies. But, with psychosocial risks, it has meant greater difficulty, since they require a different nature methodology. These psychosocial factors are understood as any condition that the person experiences in their relationship with the organizational and social environment, work management product, organizational, environmental or individual aspects, which can potentially affect the workers well-being and health (both physical, psychic or social); these factors constitute a risk when under certain intensive conditions and exposure time, they generate stress and negatively affect the health of workers on an emotional, cognitive, behavioral and physiological level. At the organizational level, they are evident in variables such as absenteeism, turnover, accidents and low job performance (Charria, Sarsosa & Arenas, 2011).

Gaudioso, Turel and Galimberti (2017) acknowledge that Technostress negatively influences many employee work aspects, including: productivity, moral, intentions to quit work, reduce job satisfaction and reduce organizational commitment. Noting that in the research information systems field, it has been shown that technological factors increase the job burnout and its work exhaustion facet, presumably because they create a stress sense and a need to deal with stressors that deplete the employee's resources, feeling fatigued. But this effect is not direct and can be mediated by the tension they feel in employees and their coping strategies, a vision that is consistent with Lazaro's stress dynamics and coping theory (Tarafdar, Cooper & Stich, 2019).

In this regard, the authors note that people can apply coping actions, which can be classified into two groups based on their effectiveness and focus on solving the underlying stress problems. The first group includes adaptive coping strategies focused on the problems and functional. The second one includes maladaptive strategies that focus on inaction, disconnection and denial, which tend to be dysfunctional in the sense that they do not really solve personal problems. (Gaudioso, Turel and Galimberti, 2017).

TECHNOSTRESS IN CHILEAN UNIVERSITIES

Chile is a country where a neoliberal economy prevails, which during the last few years has been given a decline of the State in the regulation economic activities, generating a great opening to international trade, a social services privatization and high Internet connectivity. Thus, life develops under a political economy paradigm that over time has hardened its position on deregulation, established financial forms, empathy with globalization and the emphasis on economic growth, which has also led to a university privatization that stresses the concepts of state ownership and the public good, and places this sector with high dynamism and competition among its actors, an issue that due to legal changes must be accentuated in the coming years (Alarcón, 2017, Espinoza, 2017, Chilean Telecommunications Subsecretary, 2017, Ministry of Education - Chile, 2018, Rodrik, 2018, Vega, Valdes & Cruz, 2019).

For Schmal and Cabrales (2018), the Chilean university reality is characterized today by:

"... The objective reality existence, to 'knowledge society', to which the university must adapt Failure to adapt to this reality would limit its development and recognition by the markets it" must "attend to.

The need to improve university effectiveness and efficiency (productivity) by introducing a new organization and management forms, following the classic business management modes.

The academics precarious work through the increasing temporary contract schemes and evaluative instances to which they are subjected, together with the influence loss in the decision-making instances.

An accelerated massification based on a heterogeneous unregulated and increasingly private university offer, together with a high student indebtedness level.

An 'absent' State, without clarity regarding its role, which abandons the universities to their fate so that, on their own, they "autonomously" resolve what to do under the prevailing market rules.

A marked authoritarian character established in the dictatorship times by statutes where the students and officials are non-participation is consecrated, and a weakening in academics power. ... "

Thus, the new demands imposed by the teaching work exercise can produce various alterations to health, both physically and mentally. This is how stress at work is a consequence in which work systems are organized and turns out to be various pathologies mediator. Changes arisen, such as the new technologies incorporation, imply new risks for the worker, the organization where he works and society. Taking as supporting the most recent figures on psychosocial labor risk published by the Social Security Superintendence indicate that 2.4% of workplaces show a risk high level, with the education area having the risk the highest prevalence (7.5%). (Unda et al., 2016, Ministry of Health - Chile, 2017).

Evaluating Technostress in Chilean Universities

Through a quantitative approach study and non-random design, it is possible to collect by snowball sampling the opinion of 190 academics from Chilean universities in a transverse temporal instant obtaining a descriptive study that constitutes the first approach to this economy sector (Hernández, Fernández & Baptista, 2014), an issue that is relevant, given the social networks penetration in the country and although higher education in Chile is primarily face-to-face, it has begun to increase online education which should increase in the near future the use of educational technologies by Chilean university professors (Vega, Valdés & Cruz, 2019). Applying the Prevention Technical Note number 730 of the Spain National Institute for Safety and Hygiene at Work for measuring technostress (Salanova, Llorens, Cifre, & Nogareda, 2007), which allows the analysis of technological stress based on four theoretical constructs: skepticism, fatigue, anxiety and inefficacy. Validating the internal reliability of the instrument applied by calculating Cronbach's Alpha (Puentes-Martínez, & Díaz-Rábago, 2019, Murguia-Ramirez, Pozos-Radillo, & Plascencia-Campos, 2019).

Skepticism corresponds to a doubtful or distrustful attitude, towards knowledge declared as fact or truth or efficacy of something. It can also be defined as a disposition to disbelief in general or towards an object. Skepticism is related to the learning process and the search for knowledge and manifests itself in people who question information and its sources, who need to have more evidence to support their decisions. In the professional field, skepticism is influenced by the integrity and the individual motivation and, is understood as the objective attitude adoption, using an inquisitive mind, with a skeptical approach in decision making, considering previously having convincing evidence and critical evaluation. Therefore, skepticism can contribute to the increase of quality in an organization. In skepticism, self-confidence influences personal initiative to act on information that is considered questionable, contributing to the personal idea's assessment (Royal Spanish Academy, 2014a, Rotondo, 2015, Holley, 2016, Charron & Lowe 2008).

Anxiety is defined as an agitation state, restlessness or anxiety. It corresponds to a trait that is the personality part and of the emotional individual temperament, which predisposes him to present an anxious mood. There are two dimensions related to anxiety. The first is called "anxiety reactivity", and it is related to the intensity experienced by an anxious state an individual submitted to stressors. The second dimension is labeled "anxiety perseverance" and refers to the anxious reaction persistence caused by stressors. Then, somatic anxiety can be distinguished, related to more automatic emotional regulation processes, and cognitive anxiety, reflected in more conscious and lasting regulation processes. Anxiety is characterized by a hyperactivation physiological state, with an increased activity of autonomic nervous system with various manifestations. There is evidence that demonstrates that, at the onset of anxiety reactions, there is greater activation of the limbic system and, on the other hand, a reduction in the activation of superior level cortical structures in the perseverance of these reactions. Anxious people tend to have tremors, panic symptoms, worry, nervousness and greater emotionality (Royal Spanish Academy, 2014b, Rudaizky & MacLeod, 2014, Renner, Hock, Bergner-Köther & Laux, 2018).

Finally, inefficiency is defined as efficiency and lack of activity. It is related to incompetence feelings, with the reduction of performance and productivity. Inefficiency seems to be negatively related to efficiency, being opposite poles in a continuum. Exhaustion states, physical and emotional people resources, can be inefficiency at work predictors through a negative response to various aspects of this. Stressors presence within an organization and the lack of support from it towards people who work in

Table 1. Technostress theoretical constructs by NTP730

Theoretical constructs	Components
Skepticism	S1. With the time passage, technologies interest me less and less
	S2. Every time I feel less involved in the use of ICT
	S3. I am more skeptical about the technology's contribution in my work
	S4. I doubt the working meaning with these technologies
Fatigue	F1. I find it difficult to relax after a workday using them
	F.2 When I finish working with ICT, I feel exhausted
	F3. I'm so tired when I just work with them that I cannot do anything else
	F4. It is hard to concentrate after working with technologies
Anxiety	A1. I feel tense and anxious when working with technologies
	A2. It scares me to think that I can destroy a lot of information by the improper use
	A3. I doubt when using technologies for fear of making mistakes
	A4. Working with them makes me feel uncomfortable, irritable and impatient
Inefficacy	I1. In my opinion, I am inefficient using technologies
	I2. It is difficult to work with information and communication technologies
	I3. People say that I am inefficient using technologies
	I4. I am unsure of finishing my tasks well when I use ICT

Source: Salanova, Llorens, Cifre, & Nogareda (2007).

it, favors the exhaustion emergence of states leading to inefficiency (Royal Spanish Academy, 2014c, Schaufeli & Salanova, 2007, Xu & Yang, 2018).

Constructs that in turn are broken down into four sub-composition elements, as detailed in table 1.

The snowball sampling starts with two origins located in the Metropolitan Region and the Bío Bío, which accounted for 51% and 12% of university academics in the country (National Education Council, 2019). Getting answers from teachers who work mainly in the Regions: Metropolitan of Santiago (66, 34.7%), Bío Bío (71, 37.4%), Valparaíso (33, 17.4%), Maule (8, 4.2%), from Araucanía (5, 2.6%), from Los Lagos (2, 1.1%) and from Antofagasta (2, 1.1%) and academics who perform their work mainly in an online way for students from different regions (3, 1.6%).

Although the work nature accomplished by these academics is mainly carried out during the day (154, 81.1%), accompanied by 16.3% (31) working in daytime and a lower percentage working asynchronously online (5, 2.6%). But 58.9% (112) work only in one university, reaching 30.5% (58) those who work in two universities and even 10.5% (20) are working in three or more higher education institutions. Information that is complemented with the information presented in Figure 1 about the weekly dedication to the academic activity.

As shown in Figure 1, just over a third of the academics surveyed (65, 34.2%) dedicate more than 39 hours to this type of work. From the resulting data, also allows to clear that these cases do not necessarily involve the academic activity in a single university, because in these cases only 72% (47) are in that working condition, which could be understood as a full-time professor, in an only higher education institution, 25% of the cases total surveyed.

Figure 1. Weekly dedication as an academic (in hours per week)
Source: Self-made, 2019

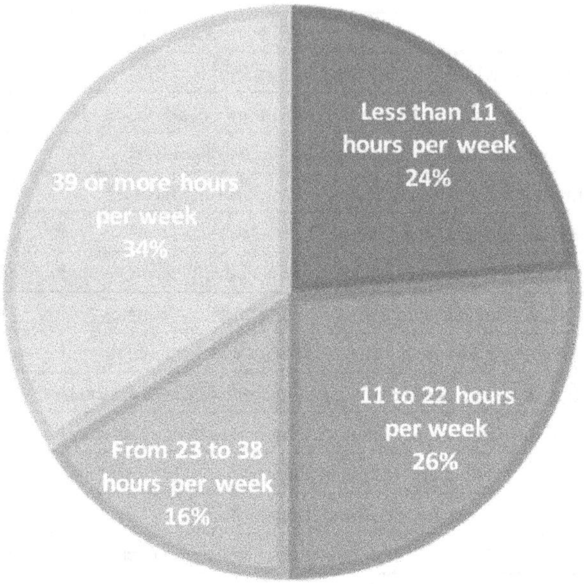

Regarding study level in which these academics perform a high percentage (158, 83.2%) they work in undergraduate teaching in professional careers, mostly in the areas: Education (30%), Administration and Commerce (21%), Health (14%), Social Sciences (12%) and Technology (10%). Being his formation in a Postgraduate a high percentage, mainly master's degree (62%) and to a lesser extent Ph.D. (25%), although still prevails 12% of academics that only have the academic degree (graduate) and a small percentage additionally with technical and professionals training levels. And whose age ranges are reflected in Figure 2, where academics of 44 and fewer years old predominate, but there is ample the presence of all the age groups.

While table 2 shows low technostress levels in its four components (Skepticism, Fatigue, Anxiety and Inefficacy) is slightly more pronounced the result obtained in the fatigue case, with a 2 value on a scale from 0 to 6, what accounts for what realizes that fatigue itself is a tiredness state or exhaustion caused not only by the mental demands derived from the ICT use, but also the other working conditions product, such as environmental factors, the social climate and organizational work, and psychosocial factors. Therefore, the fatigue state would not be produced by a direct cause of a specific stressor, but by multiple combining stressors. For example, inadequate lighting conditions in the workplace, or noise levels above the recommended, will affect the interaction between the ICT use and the user, fatigue is the result of the interaction between the two, and not necessarily the use of ICT itself, a situation that can be presented among the sample of academics consulted.

Detailed below is the statistical description of the 16 theoretical constructs used in the table 3, with averages ranging between 0.67 and 1.87, equivalent to 1 and 2 points in the discrete terms scale and therefore equivalent to the concepts 'Almost nothing' (a couple of times a year) and 'Rarely' (once a month) respectively.

Figure 2. Age ranges of the academics surveyed (in years old)
Source: Self-made, 2019

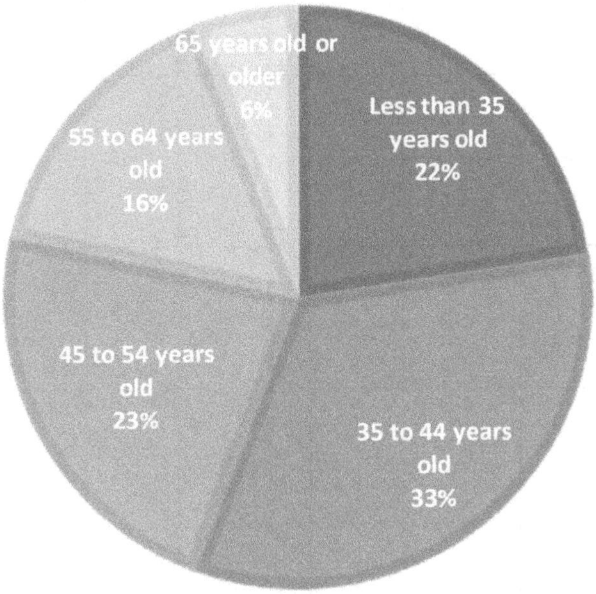

Regarding the internal reliability of the consultation instrument used (NTP730), to measure technostress in Chilean university professors, the 190 valid cases (without exclusions) were processed, achieving Cronbach's Alpha values very close to the maximum value of 1, such as it is shown in table 4, to which the statistics presented in table 5 are greater added.

RECOMMENDATIONS

It is recommended the identification in a proactive and participatory way, of the academic's work conditions that can lead to stressors. In this sense, emphasize all those conditions that generate fatigue associated with ICT use. On the other hand, it is necessary to know the individual capacities in the technologies used by academics, and the ICT most frequently used complexity.

On the other hand, it is recommended to acquire ICT based on the user-centered design, so that learning in the new technologies use is a friendly and easy-to-understand process. Besides, it is essential to generate formal training when it is required, so that users have the necessary resources to deal efficiently with the use of new technologies.

FUTURE RESEARCH DIRECTIONS

For future investigations, it is necessary to expand the sample, to reach national representation, it will be able to carry out a correlational study. On the other hand, it is also essential to apply the survey to other university academic community levels, such as students, administrative officials and academic managers, to advance in the knowledge of the ICT use influence in the different roles that are fulfilled in the academy.

Table 2. Technostress evaluation in Chilean university professors

Valuation total by response (as a percentage)	NOTHING Never 0	ALMOST NOTHING A couple of times a year 1	RARELY Once a month 2	SOMETIMES A couple of times a month 3	ENOUGH Once a week 4	OFTEN A couple of times a week 5	ALWAYS Everyday 6	Weighted Mean
S1. With the time passage, technologies interest me less and less	47	8	12	9	4	10	11	**2**
S2. Every time I feel less involved in the use of ICT	51	12	14	9	4	7	5	**1**
S3. I am more skeptical about the technology's contribution to my work	53	17	9	11	4	4	2	**1**
S4. I doubt the working meaning with these technologies	54	19	12	7	4	4	0	**1**
Skepticism								**1**
F1. I find it difficult to relax after a workday using them	37	18	13	14	7	7	4	**2**
F.2 When I finish working with ICT, I feel exhausted	33	17	18	15	6	8	3	**2**
F3. I'm so tired when I just work with them that I cannot do anything else	39	21	13	15	5	6	2	**2**
F4. It is hard to concentrate after working with technologies	41	22	15	9	6	5	3	**1**
Fatigue								**2**
A1. I feel tense and anxious when working with technologies	35	27	16	8	5	7	3	**2**

continues on following page

Table 2. Continued

Valuation total by response (as a percentage)	NOTHING Never 0	ALMOST NOTHING A couple of times a year 1	RARELY Once a month 2	SOMETIMES A couple of times a month 3	ENOUGH Once a week 4	OFTEN A couple of times a week 5	ALWAYS Everyday 6	Weighted Mean
A2. It scares me to think that I can destroy a lot of information by the improper use	47	20	14	5	6	5	3	**1**
A3. I doubt when using technologies for fear of making mistakes	50	23	14	6	3	4	1	**1**
A4. Working with them makes me feel uncomfortable, irritable and impatient	56	18	14	6	3	2	1	**1**
Anxiety								**1**
I1. In my opinion, I am inefficient using technologies	52	24	8	8	4	2	2	**1**
I2. It is difficult to work with information and communication technologies	44	26	13	11	3	3	1	**1**
I3. People say that I am inefficient using technologies	66	18	7	4	1	3	1	**1**
I4. I am unsure of finishing my tasks well when I use ICT	56	16	13	5	4	5	1	**1**
Inefficacy								**1**

Data Source: Self-made (2019).

Table 3. Descriptive Statistics of Technostress theoretical constructs evaluation in Chilean university professors

	N	Minimum	Maximum	Mean	Std. Deviation
S1	190	0	6	1,87	2,188
S2	190	0	6	1,43	1,855
S3	190	0	6	1,15	1,577
S4	190	0	5	,97	1,366
F1	190	0	6	1,71	1,810
F2	190	0	6	1,80	1,746
F3	190	0	6	1,52	1,645
F4	190	0	6	1,42	1,646
A1	190	0	6	1,52	1,658
A2	190	0	6	1,28	1,666
A3	190	0	6	1,02	1,363
A4	190	0	6	,91	1,304
I1	190	0	6	,99	1,412
I2	190	0	6	1,16	1,399
I3	190	0	6	,67	1,230
I4	190	0	6	1,01	1,484
Valid N (listwise)	190				

Data Source: Self-made (2019).

Table 4. Reliability Statistics

Cronbach's Alpha	Cronbach's Alpha Based on Standardized Items	N of Items
,941	,946	16

Data Source: Self-made (2019).

Table 5. Reliability: Summary Item Statistics

	Mean	Minimum	Maximum	Range	Maximum / Minimum	Variance	N of Items
Item Means	1,278	,674	1,874	1,200	2,781	,121	16
Item Variances	2,567	1,512	4,788	3,276	3,167	,683	16
Inter-Item Covariances	1,281	,756	2,838	2,082	3,753	,164	16
Inter-Item Correlations	,522	,247	,882	,635	3,573	,022	16

Data Source: Self-made (2019).

The educational contexts exploration with high exposure to stressors, such as e-learning and blended learning, it is important, given that in both contexts the ICT use which means that how interaction between educational content and learning occurs: the user

Finally, the work conditions study, such as organizational, physical, mental factors and environmental conditions, is essential, because of all these determine, in part, the interaction between the ICT and the user. It is necessary to know what work factors support this interaction, and which have the opposite effect.

CONCLUSION

This chapter allows us to understand the technostress level to which the Chilean university academics are exposed. It is concluded that there is low exposure to technostress in the sample consulted, in its four components (skepticism, fatigue, anxiety and ineffectiveness), the exposure to the techno fatigue is slightly greater concerning the other components.

It is necessary to study in great depth the stressors influence on Chilean higher education academics, extending to the all educational community (officials, students, authorities) focusing not only on ICT itself but also on the factors or work conditions that influence the interaction between these and the users.

ACKNOWLEDGMENT

The researchers of this study are both grateful to *Fundación Escuela de Asuntos Internacionales* for institutional sponsorship provided in the fields of Educational Quality Management and Higher Education Studies.

REFERENCES

Alam, M. A. (2016). Techno-stress and productivity: Survey evidence from the aviation industry. *Journal of Air Transport Management*, *50*, 62–70. doi:10.1016/j.jairtraman.2015.10.003

Alarcón, J. (2017). The rules of our game: Neoliberal privatization of education in Chile. *Praxis Educativa (Santa Rosa)*, *12*(3), 690–707. doi:10.5212/PraxEduc.v.12i3.001

Amorim-Santino, T., Ferreira-Tomaz, A., & Gomes de Lucena, N. M. (2017). Influence of occupational fatigue in the work ability of professors. *Ciencia & Trabajo*, *19*(59), 86–90. doi:10.4067/S0718-24492017000200086

Arquero, J. L., & Donoso, J. A. (2013). Docencia, investigación y burnout: El síndrome del quemado en profesores universitarios de contabilidad. *Revista de Contabilidad*, *16*(2), 94–105. doi:10.1016/j.rcsar.2013.04.001

Camargo-Mayorga, D. A. (2016). Motivations of Teaching Work: A Case Study of Two Public Accounting Programs in Bogota. *Cuadernos de Contabilidad*, *17*(44), 421–448. doi:10.11144/Javeriana.cc17-44.mlde

Charria, V. H., Sarsosa, K. V., & Arenas, F. (2011). Occupational psychosocial risk factors: methods and assessment tools. *Revista Facultad Nacional de Salud Pública, 29*(4), 380-391. Available in: http://www.redalyc.org/articulo.oa?id=12021522004

Charron, K. F., & Lowe, D. J. (2008). Skepticism and the Management Accountant: Insights for Fraud Detection. *Management Accounting Quarterly, 9*(2), 9–15. Retrieved from https://www.imanet.org/insights-and-trends/management-accounting-quarterly/maq-index/2008/winter-2008?ssopc=1

Chávez-Orozco, C. A. (2016). Burnout syndrome in university teachers. *INNOVA Research Journal, 1*(9), 77–95. doi:10.33890/innova.v1.n9.2016.55

Chilean Telecommunications Undersecretary. (2017). *IX Internet Access and Usage Survey*. Government of Chile.

Chu, H. C., & Kuo, T. (2015). Testing Herzberg's two-factor theory in educational settings in Taiwan. *The Journal of Human Resource and Adult Learning, 11*(1), 54-65. Available in: http://www.hraljournal.com/Page/10%20HuichinChu&TsuiYangKuo.pdf

Espinoza, O. (2017). Privatization of higher education in Chile: consequences and lessons learned. *Ec-coS– Revista Científica*, (44), 175-202. DOI: . doi:10.5585/eccos.n44.8070

Fernández-López, J. A., Siegrist, J., Rödel, A., & Hernández-Mejía, R. (2003). Stress at work: a new risk factor. What do we know and what can we do? *Atención Primaria, 31*(8), 469-558. Available in: https://www.elsevier.es/es-revista-atencion-primaria-27-pdf-13047737

García, L. B. (2017). The academics in the Argentinean public university: Changes, tensions and challenges. *Espacios en Blanco. Serie Indagaciones, 27*(1), 87–110. Retrieved from http://ref.scielo.org/ptgy3t

García, L. B. (2017b). Itinerary of the construction of academic profession in Argentina. *Integración y Conocimiento, 7*(2), 206-225. Retrieved from: https://revistas.unc.edu.ar/index.php/integracionyconocimiento/article/view/18707

García, M. M., Iglesias, S., Saleta, M., & Romay, J. (2016). Psychosocial risks in university education teachers: Diagnosis and prevention. *Journal of Work and Organizational Psychology, 32*, 173–182. doi:10.1016/j.rpto.2016.07.001

Gaudioso, F., Turel, O., & Galimberti, C. (2017). The mediating roles of strain facets and coping strategies in translating techno-stressors into adverse job outcomes. *Computers in Human Behavior, 69*, 189–196. doi:10.1016/j.chb.2016.12.041

Giorgi, G., Arcangeli, G., Perminiene, M., Lorini, C., Ariza-Montes, A., Fiz-Perez, J., ... Mucci, N. (2017). Work-Related Stress in the Banking Sector: A Review of Incidence, Correlated Factors, and Major Consequences. *Frontiers in Psychology, 8*, 2166. doi:10.3389/fpsyg.2017.02166 PMID:29312044

Hernández, R., Fernández, C., & Baptista, P. (2014). Research Methodology (6th ed.). McGraw-Hill.

Holley, S. (2016). *The relationship between professional skepticism and critical thinking of accounting managers: A quantitative study*. Minneapolis, MN: Capella University.

International Labour Office. (2013). *Stress prevention at work, control points: Best practices for the stress prevention in the workplace*. Ginebra: Oficina Internacional del Trabajo. Available in: https://www.ilo.org/wcmsp5/groups/public/@dgreports/@dcomm/@publ/documents/publication/wcms_251057.pdf

International Labour Organization. (2016). *Workplace Stress. A collective challenge world day for safety and health at work*. Geneva: International Labour Organization. Available in: https://www.ilo.org/safework/info/publications/WCMS_466547/lang--en/index.htm

Kruel-Goebel, D., & Carlotto, M.S. (2019). Socio-demographic, labor and psychosocial predictors of Burnout Syndrome in distance education teachers. *Avances en Psicología Latinoamericana*, 37(2), 295-311. doi:10.12804/revistas.urosario.edu.co/apl/a.6886

Lara-Sotomayor, J. E., & Pando-Moreno, M. (2014). Mobbing and Symptoms of Stress in Public Sector University Faculty. *Ciencia & Trabajo*, *16*(49), 43–48. doi:10.4067/S0718-24492014000100008

Lee, Y. K., Chang, C. T., Lin, Y., & Cheng, Z. H. (2014). The dark side of smartphone usage: Psychological traits, compulsive behavior and technostress. *Computers in Human Behavior*, *31*, 373–383. doi:10.1016/j.chb.2013.10.047

Lew, F. L., & Qu, X. (2014). Effects of mental fatigue on biomechanics of slips. *Ergonomics*, *57*(12), 1927–1932. doi:10.1080/00140139.2014.937771

Ministry of Education - Chile. (2018). *Law 21,091 'About Higher Education'.* Available in: http://bcn.cl/25b7u

Ministry of Health. (2017). *Protocol for surveillance of psychosocial risks at work*. Government of Chile.

Molina-Sabando, K., & García-Lucas, C. A. (2018). Relationship between stress and the affective area in the teachers of the Technical University of Manabí. *Espirales revista multidisciplinaria de investigación*, *2*(16). Available in: http://www.revistaespirales.com/index.php/es/article/view/233

Murguia-Ramirez, A. C., Pozos-Radillo, B. E., & Plascencia-Campos, A. R. (2019). Work stress and its relationship with socio-labor factors in teachers of a public preparatory school and of a private one. *Revista Cubana de Salud y Trabajo*, *20*(1), 52–57. Retrieved from http://revsaludtrabajo.sld.cu/index.php/revsyt/article/view/81

Orgambídez-Ramos, A., Pérez-Moreno, P. J., & Borrego-Alés, Y. (2015). Role stress and job satisfaction: Examining the mediating role of work engagement. *Journal of Work and Organizational Psychology*, *31*, 69–77. doi:10.1016/j.rpto.2015.04.001

Pereira, F., Grützmann, T., & Novello, T. (2019). Mapping Research on Tecno Stress in Mathematics Teachers. *RELACult - Revista Latino-Americana de Estudos em Cultura e Sociedade, 5*(4). doi:10.23899/relacult.v5i4.1234

Pérez-Carpio, J. E., Turpo-Chaparro, J. E., & López-Gonzales, J. L. (2019). Psychosocial risk factors and work stress in university teachers. *Revista Espacios, 40*(19). Retrieved from: https://www.revistaespacios.com/a19v40n19/19401913.html

Puentes-Martínez, L., & Díaz-Rábago, A. B. (2019). Reliability and construct validity of the Perceived Stress Scale in medical students. *Revista de Ciencias Médicas de Pinar del Río, 23*(3), 373–379. Retrieved from http://ref.scielo.org/kbhqym

Pujol-Cols, L. J. (2018). Core self-evaluations and autonomy: a study of their direct and interactive effects on work engagement among highly skilled Argentinian professionals. *Estudios Gerenciales, 34*(149), 361-372. http://ref.scielo.org/6494gq

Pujol-Cols, L. J., & Arraigada, M. (2017). Psychometric properties of the Copsoq-Istas Psychosocial Risk Questionnaire 21 in Argentinian university teachers. *Cuadernos de Administración, 30*(55), 97-125. Retrieved from: http://ref.scielo.org/d8qmv2

Pujol-Cols, L. J., & Lazzaro-Salazar, M. (2018). Psychosocial risks and job satisfaction in Argentinian scholars: Exploring the moderating role of work engagement. *Work and Organizations Psichology Magazine, 34*(3), 145–156. doi:10.5093/jwop2018a17

Renner, K. H., Hock, M., Bergner-Köther, R., & Laux, L. (2018). Differentiating anxiety and depression: The State-Trait Anxiety-Depression Inventory. *Cognition and Emotion, 32*(7), 1409–1423. doi:10.1080/02699931.2016.1266306

Rodrik, D. (2018). Rescue the economy of neoliberalism. *Letras Libres*, (196), 12-17. Available in: https://www.letraslibres.com/espana-mexico/revista/rescatar-la-economia-del-neoliberalismo

Rotondo, A. (2015). Disagreement and Intellectual Skepticism. *Australasian Journal of Philosophy, 93*(2), 251–271. doi:10.1080/00048402.2014.986746

Royal Spanish Academy. (2014a). *Dictionary of the Spanish language* (23rd ed.). Retrieved from: https://dle.rae.es/?id=GDlmBBp

Royal Spanish Academy. (2014b). *Dictionary of the Spanish language* (23rd ed.). Retrieved from: https://dle.rae.es/?id=2l0oQtn

Royal Spanish Academy. (2014c). *Dictionary of the Spanish language* (23rd ed.). Retrieved from: https://dle.rae.es/srv/search?m=30&w=ineficacia

Rudaizky, D., & Macleod, C. (2014). Anxiety reactivity and anxiety perseveration represent independent dimensions of anxiety vulnerability: An in vivo study. *Anxiety, Stress, and Coping, 27*(4), 361–375. doi:10.1080/10615806.2013.853047

Salanova, M., Llorens, S., Cifre, E., & Nogareda, C. (2007). *El tecnoestrés: concepto, medida e intervención psicosocial.* Nota Técnica de Prevención, 730, 21ª Serie. National Institute for Safety and Hygiene at Work. Available in: http://www.want.uji.es/download/el-tecnoestres-concepto-medida-e-intervencion-psicosocial/

Salanova-Soria, M. (2003). Working with technologies and coping with technostress: The role of efficacy beliefs. *Revista de Psicología del Trabajo y de las Organizaciones, 19*(3), 225–246.

Sauter, S. L., Murphy, L. R., Hurrell, J. J., & Levi, L. (1998). *Health and Safety at Work Encyclopedia. Psychosocial and organizational factors.* Capítulo 34. Available in: http://www.insht.es/InshtWeb/Contenidos/Documentacion/TextosOnline/EnciclopediaOIT/tomo2/34.pdf

Schaufeli, W. B., & Salanova, M. (2007). Efficacy or inefficacy, that's the question: Burnout and work engagement, and their relationships with efficacy beliefs. *Anxiety, Stress, and Coping*, *20*(2), 177–196. doi:10.1080/10615800701217878

Schmal, R., & Cabrales, F. (2018). The challenge of university governance: The Chilean case. *Ensaio: Avaliação e Políticas Públicas em Educação*, *26*(100), 822–848. doi:10.15900104-40362018002601309

Seong-Tak, O., & Park, S. (2016). A Study of the Connected Smart Worker's Techno-Stress. *Procedia Computer Science*, *91*, 725–733. doi:10.1016/j.procs.2016.07.065

Seyle, H. (1936). A Syndrome produced by Diverse Nocuous Agents. *Nature*, *138*(3479), 32. doi:10.1038/138032a0

Szpitalak, M., & Polczyk, R. (2014). Mental fatigue, mental warm-up, and self-reference as determinants of the misinformation effect. *Journal of Forensic Psychiatry & Psychology*, *25*(2), 135–151. doi:10.1080/14789949.2014.895024

Tarafdar, M., Cooper, C. L., & Stich, J. F. (2019). The technostress trifecta - techno eustress, techno distress and design: Theoretical directions and an agenda for research. *Information Systems Journal*, *29*(1), 6–42. doi:10.1111/isj.12169

Unda, S., Uribe, F., Jurado, S., García, M., Tovalín, H., & Juárez, A. (2016). A scale development to assess the psychosocial risk factors in the university professors work. *Journal of Work and Organizational Psychology*, *32*, 67–74. doi:10.1016/j.rpto.2016.04.004

Vega, A., Rojas, M., & Salazar, G. (2018). University Social Responsibility: Recent Contributions to the Development of Small Businesses in Chile. *Revista Venezolana de Gerencia*, *23*(1), 328-345. Available in: http://www.produccioncientifica.luz.edu.ve/index.php/rvg/article/view/23919

Vega, A., Valdés, M., & Cruz, M. (2019). Challenges for the creation of an international online university in a controversial environment: Chilean higher education system case. In *Handbook of Research on Challenges and Opportunities in Launching a Technology-Driven International University*. Hershey, PA: IGI Global. doi:10.4018/978-1-5225-6255-9.ch003

Vega, Martínez, & Morales. (2017). Social movement and inequity in access to Higher Education in Chile: the difficult path towards structural reform In A. Vega & P. Andreucci (Eds.), *From Social Conflict to Global Indignation*. Santiago de Chile: RIL Editores.

Vergara-Mendoza, K. Z., Carabajo-Romero, I. R., & Leal-Mariduеña, I. A. (2017). The level of stress in the teachers of the UNEMI. *Dominio de las Ciencias, 3*(2), 405-425. Retrieved from: http://dominiodelasciencias.com/ojs/index.php/es/article/view/337

Xu, Z., & Yang, F. (2018). The impact of perceived organizational support on the relationship between job stress and burnout: A mediating or moderating role? *Current Psychology (New Brunswick, N.J.)*, 1–12. doi:10.100712144-018-9941-4

ADDITIONAL READING

Apud, E., & Oñate, E. (2015). Criteria for participatory ergonomics to improve the working life quality. In L. Godoy & Ansoleaga, E. (Ed), A field in tension or tension between fields: Organizational Psychology and Labor in Ibero-America. Santiago, Chile: RIL editores.

Bozoglan, B. (2018). *Psychological, Social, and Cultural Aspects of Internet Addiction* (pp. 1–390). Hershey, PA: IGI Global; doi:10.4018/978-1-5225-3477-8

Grant, M. C. (2018). *Equity, Equality, and Reform in Contemporary Public Education* (pp. 1–329). Hershey, PA: IGI Global; doi:10.4018/978-1-5225-4960-4

Hughes, R., Kinder, A., & Cooper, C. L. (2019). *The Wellbeing Workout: How to manage stress and develop resilience*. Basingstoke: Palgrave Macmillan; doi:10.1007/978-3-319-92552-3

Karwowski, W., Ahram, T., & Nazir, S. (2019). *Advances in Human Factors in Training, Education, and Learning Sciences. AHFE 2019. Advances in Intelligent Systems and Computing* (Vol. 963). Cham: Springer; doi:10.1007/978-3-030-20135-7

Longo, L., & Leva, M. C. (2018). *Human Mental Workload: Models and Applications*. Amsterdam: Springer; doi:10.1007/978-3-030-14273-5

Loriol, M. (2019). *Stress and Suffering at Work: The Role of Culture and Society*. Basingstoke: Palgrave Macmillan; doi:10.1007/978-3-030-05876-0

McShane, S.L., Olekalns, M., Newman, A.H., & Martin, A. (2019). *Organisational behaviour: emerging knowledge, global insights*. Sydney, N.S.W.: McGraw-Hill Education.

Nair, S. R., & Saiz-Álvarez, J. M. (2019). *Ethics, Entrepreneurship, and Governance in Higher Education*. Hershey, PA: IGI Global; doi:10.4018/978-1-5225-5837-8

Santoro, D. A. (2018). *Demoralized. Why Teachers Leave the Profession They Love and How They Can Stay*. Cambridge, MA: Harvard Education Press.

Yan, Z. (2019). *Analyzing Human Behavior in Cyberspace* (pp. 1–333). Hershey, PA: IGI Global; doi:10.4018/978-1-5225-7128-5

KEY TERMS AND DEFINITIONS

Asynchronous Online Education: It is an online education form where communication is done asynchronously, that is, through non-immediate networks and without the need for people to be connected at the same time. The best example to understand the asynchronous communication is the electronic mail or a forum in which a query is left and can be solved in the following hours.

Ergonomics: The term ergonomics derives from the Greek words 'ergo' and 'nomos', where ergo means "work" and, nomos means "laws", therefore in the simple sense, ergonomics refers to "the laws of labor". Now, the ergonomics discipline is responsible for studying the interaction between the human being and all the elements that make up their particular work situation, so that the demands or this demands, do not exceed the people capabilities, ensuring a life quality optimal and efficiency.

Liquid Education: It is a 'liquid modernity' conceptual variant of the sociologist and philosopher Zygmunt Bauman, applied by him to the education field. So, Bauman makes reference to how human consciousness regarding the dominant instability in today's society, forces to develop an immediacy culture, where education should adapted be fast enough to integrate into a world that changes in continuous time.

Mental Workload: It refers to the cognitive, mental or intellectual type work demands. The mental workload is influenced both by the work demands and the environment where it is developed, as well as by individual factors.

Stress: It is an organism adaptive response that allows to respond to environment different demands. Stress is naturally necessary for survival, however, if it is maintained over time, it can generate negative effects on health.

Technology: It is the applied science to the concrete problems resolution that facilitate the goods or services design and creation that facilitate human adaptation to the surrounding environment and the humanity essential needs and desires satisfaction. Although there are many technologies and very different from each other, as a theoretical discipline technology studies the knowledge common to all technologies. Although it is common to use the term technology in singular both to refer to the set of all, as well as to one of them in specific.

Ubiquity: It is the ability to be present everywhere at the same time, originally associated with a divine gift. But thanks to mobile technology and virtual and simultaneous presence in various social networks is understood as a gift technologically acquired by humans to be able to be present at any place and time.

Chapter 9
Artificial Intelligence for Evaluating the Mental Workload of Air Traffic Controllers

Tetiana Shmelova
https://orcid.org/0000-0002-9737-6906
National Aviation University, Ukraine

Yuliya Sikirda
https://orcid.org/0000-0002-7303-0441
Flight Academy, National Aviation University, Ukraine

ABSTRACT

In this chapter, the authors propose the application of artificial intelligence (namely expert system and neural network) for estimating the mental workload of air traffic controllers while working at different control centers (sectors): terminal control center, approach control center, area control center. At each air traffic control center, air traffic controllers will perform the following procedures: coordination between units, aircraft transit, climbing, and descending. So with the help of the artificial intelligence (AI) and its branches expert system and neural network, it is possible to estimate the mental workload of dispatchers for a different number of aircraft, compare the workload intensity of the air traffic control sectors, and optimize the workload between sectors and control centers. The differentiating factor of an AI system from a standard software system is the characteristic ability to learn, improve, and predict. Real dispatchers, students, graduate students, and teachers of the National Aviation University took part in these researches.

INTRODUCTION

Air transport industry plays a major role in the world economic activity and to maintain a safe and efficient operation of aviation enterprises. International Civil Aviation Organization (ICAO) in its recent documents extended and defined new approaches for achieving the main goals of ICAO that is,

DOI: 10.4018/978-1-7998-1052-0.ch009

enhancing the effectiveness of the global aviation security and improving the practical and sustainable implementation of preventive aviation security measures such as the development of security culture and human capability, improving and enhancing technological resources, oversight and quality assurance, etc. (ICAO, 2018). The Artificial Intelligence (AI) document "White paper" of IATA (International Air Transport Association) presents the results of IATA research and development activities on AI in collaboration with airlines. The new technologies of AI can be clustered in the following capabilities, such as: Machine learning (ML), Natural Language Processing (NLP), Expert Systems, Vision, Speech, Planning, Robotics (IATA, 2016).

The efficiency and safety of the operation of the systems depend to a high degree on the quality of a human operator's decisions that in its turn is guided by the factors of education, competence, working conditions, experience, and versatility of application of modern-day information and data processing technologies and others. So it is necessary for aviation to maximize the use of new technology such as AI. The authors offer the application of Artificial Intelligence (Expert System and Neural Network) for estimating the mental workload of air traffic controllers while working at different control centers (sectors).

The following can be said about the advantages of Aviation and Air Traffic Control (ATC). Aviation became an independent part of a human being. Over the last decades, there is a tendency of increase of air traffic flows over the world. Also, aviation is a vital part of the increasingly globalized world economy, facilitating the growth of international trade, tourism, and international investment, and connecting people across continents. Air traffic is a many-sided process:

- Cargo transfer;
- Private aviation;
- Passenger transfer;
- Flight training;
- Business aviation;
- Air show;
- Search and rescue service;
- Testing flights;
- Military flights.

Air traffic must be controlled therefore ATC is an integral and very important part of each flight. Aircraft are safely separated in the sky as they fly and at the airports where they land and take off again – air traffic control takes care of this. In Europe, ATC is done by the air traffic control centers located in each country, which guide aircraft to and from airports. The main actor in these centers is the controller. Air traffic controller (ATCO) – is a person authorized to provide air traffic control services (Federal Aviation Administration [FAA], 2014). Each aircraft during the flight is served by ATCO according to defined rules. ATCO is responsible as for aircrew so for passengers and at the same time for their safety. And a question arises, how many aircraft (ACFT) may be under control simultaneously in order to provide safety for passengers and aircrew members? The answer is capacity which is calculated for each zone. As each zone has a different number of ACFT simultaneously and at the same time different sizes, it is important to define the capacity of each zone. Hence, the capacity of the zone is defined as a number of ACFT which are served at the same time by controllers in a certain zone taking into account probable delays and time needed for them. Delays occur on the airfield whenever two or more aircraft seek to use a runway, taxiway, gate, or any other airside facility at the same time. One must wait while the other is accommodated. If all users of the airfield sought service at evenly spaced intervals, the airfield could accommodate them at a rate determined solely by the time required to move them through the facility. Aircraft, however, arrive and leave not at a uniform rate but somewhat randomly, which means that delay can occur even when demand is low in relation to capacity. Further, the probability of the simultaneous need for service increases rapidly with traffic density, so that the average delay per aircraft increases exponentially as demand approaches throughput capacity. When demand exceeds capacity, there is an accumulation of aircraft awaiting service that is directly proportional to the excess of demand over capacity (Georgia & Barbara, 1997). The capacity of the zone connects with the capacity of each separate controller and with his workload. He provides a service which requires some human efforts.

But as human resources are limited, the level needed for a specific task can exceed the amount available. These problems are conceptually presented as a human factor (HF) problem (ICAO, 1993). A given task will not produce the same workload level for all ATCOs. Rather, workload depends on his experience with the task, training and relevant skill levels. A task can even produce different workload for the same controller at a different time depending on his state when the task must be performed. The workload of the controller also depends on the time which is needed for ACFT flight through the zone, time which is needed for service of single ACFT according to defined rules and procedures, technical equipment, meteorological conditions.

Therefore, the *workload* is an individual experience and workload, in many cases, may be a key factor for the whole zone. Hence, the quality and effectiveness of ATC system functioning are tightly connected with the quality and effectiveness of ATCO work, his reliability, and capacity (ICAO, 2002).

While discussing the problems connected with the human factor, it is necessary to pay attention to the most important aspects as tasks performed by each separate ATCO (human-procedure), equipment that he uses (human-equipment) and the influence of system elements on safety and effectiveness of system functioning (human-environment). In solving problems in the sphere of the human factor it is well to bear in mind that causal link may be not the same that is why the most successive in particular problems solving may be different from one another. In practice, typical for both categories the presence of any mismatch between human and system which may be solved either in the system or human changing or the one and the other changing.

Air traffic control, in general, is challenged by ever more data sources, information flows, control needs, cost pressures, and environmental requirements. Not to mention the increase in air traffic itself. Automatization is an important solution to these challenges. Performance capabilities of ATCO become bigger according to the evolution of technical equipment. One of the main reasons for equipment development, in the sphere of technique and navigation, is obtaining more reliable and timely data about position of ACFT, their intentions, flight levels and speed of flights.

Automatization is followed by the next objectives (ICAO, 1993, 1998; Arkhangelskiy & Bohaenko, 2000):

- essential to use resources, which provide additional information and at the same time don't change the present method of work procedure;
- essential to perform partial or total automatization for the accomplishment of the mission, which doesn't need expert estimation, for example, passing data connected with ATC through datalink or usage of SSR;
- essential to use the equipment for obtaining information, implementation of which change the methods of controllers work procedure, for example, ADS-B;

- essential to provide automatization during performance so-called experts tasks with the help of expert system or resources which give the possibilities to evaluate and coordinate conflict-free trajectory of ACFT movement in a single and complex system "air-ground".

ATC is very dynamic and continuously broadening the sphere of human activity. It is very hard to foresee the future development of ATC because it may not depend on factors connected with ATC, for example, global or national economic conditions, presence of aviation fuel and its cost, and how passengers evaluate the safety of flights. Nevertheless all forecasts say that expected increase of air traffic volume in a long-term perspective will be so significant that the most part of existing ATC systems must be changed to new and developed ones or their capacity must be increased, that's why it is necessary to improve them because they were not developed for such volume of air traffic.

The volume of air traffic is continuously increasing. The time needed for ACFT servicing changes all the time. This leads to delays. Delays tightly connected with ATCO workload and ATCO capacity. ATCO capacity and workload tightly connected with the workload of the defined zone. That is why it is very important to evaluate capacity and workload in order to avoid conflict situations, traffic congestion, controllers overload, misunderstanding between pilots and controllers, delays of traffic and to promote the safe, orderly and expeditious flow of air traffic.

The goal of the research – to develop the methodology of ATCO mental workload evaluating and to suggest an algorithm of ATCO workload estimation taking into account the characteristics of the service procedures and intensity of air traffic using AI. As said before, aviation is a dynamic system which needs development and improvement. As peoples demands to fly increase the aviation personnel has to provide safe transfer for them from airdrome of departure to aerodrome of destination, where controllers play great roles. And it is necessary for aviation providers to create such conditions for controllers in which they can provide the safe, orderly and expeditious flow of air traffic.

BACKGROUND

Statistical data show that human errors account for up 80% of all causes of aviation accidents (Leychenko, Malishevskiy, & Mikhalic, 2006; Kulik, Kharchenko, & Lutskii, 2008; Aviation Accident Statistics, 2019). The existing approaches to checking separate aspects (psychophysiological, behavioral, ergonomic, professional, etc.) do not consider the functional state of H-O in the conditions of the dynamic change of external and internal factors (ICAO, 2013). Aviation systems with its complex interrelation between a man and technologies have been evolved towards complex STS. The evolutions of Human Factor's models are presented (from 1972 to the present time) in Table 1. The authors present five stages of the evolution of the human factor's models associated with the appearance of new system components and the diagnosis of operator errors (Kharchenko, Shmelova, & Sikirda, 2016, 2018):

I stage "Professional skills of H-O / Interaction of H-O's / Definition of H-O's errors".
II stage "Cooperation in team / Interaction of H-O's in team / Error detection".
III stage "Influence of Culture / Safety / Error prevention".
IV stage "Safety / Efficiency / Minimization of errors".
V stage "Artificial Intelligence Systems / Analyze, detection, prevention, and minimization of errors".

Table 1. Evolution of human factor's models

Years	Model	Content of model	Content of stage of evolution human factor's model	Number of stage
1972	SHEL	Software (procedures) - Hardware (machines) - Environment - Liveware	Professional skills Interaction Errors	I
1990	Reason's "Swiss Cheese Model"	Active errors - Latent errors - Windows of opportunity - Causation chain		
1993	SHELL	Software (procedures) - Hardware (machines) - Environment - Liveware - Liveware (humans)		
1999	CRM	Crew - Resource - Management	Cooperation in team Interaction in team Error detection	II
2000	TEM	Threat and Error - Management		
2000	MRM	Maintenance - Resource - Management		
2004	SHELL-T (SHELL-Team)	Software (procedures) - Hardware (machines) - Environment – Liveware - Liveware (humans) - Team		
2004	SCHELL model and CRM	Software (procedures) – Culture - Hardware (machines) - Environment - Liveware - Liveware (humans)	Culture Safety Error prevention	III
2004	LOSA	Line - Operation - Safety - Audit		
2009	HEAD	Human - Environment - Analysis - Design		
2010	HFACS	Human Factors - Accident - Classification - System		
2012	SMS	Safety Management System Safety Balance Models Collaborative Decision Making Artificial Intelligence	Safety Efficiency Minimization of errors	IV
2016	AI CDM SWIM FF-ICE	Artificial Intelligence Collaborative Decision Making System-Wide Information Sharing and Management Flight & Flow Information for a Collaborative Environment	Artificial Intelligence Systems Analyze, detection, prevention, and minimization of errors	V

The global air traffic management (ATM) operational concept presents the ICAO vision of an integrated, harmonized and globally interoperable ATM system. The planning horizon is up to and beyond 2025 (ICAO, 2005). The integration of the concept components may be balanced to achieve different expected outcomes. All concept components must be present in each State's or region's ATM system to some degree. That is not to say that any particular component will be used as a major contributor to an outcome in a particular State or region, or that a great deal of automation or technology will be required to deliver against that component; however, they must be considered at each evolutionary stage. Safety can never fall below minimum acceptable levels. In fact, it should be argued that any change to the ATM system for an outcome not directly aimed at enhancing safety should, nonetheless, strive to achieve its net increase (Figure 1).

The safety balance model indicates that, on the whole, the system needs to retain a safety tension to achieve an acceptable level of safety. The ATM system is based on the provision of services. This framework considers all resources: airspace, aerodromes, aircraft, and humans, to be part of the ATM system. The description of the concept components is based on realistic expectations of human capabili-

Figure 1. Safety balance model (ICAO, 2005)

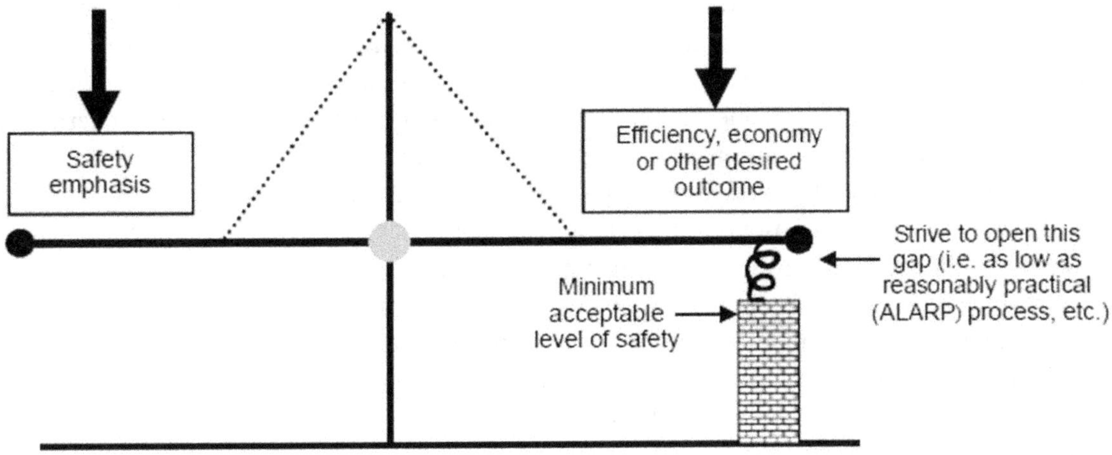

ties and the ATM infrastructure at any particular time in the evolution to the ATM system described by this operational concept and is independent of reference to any specific technology.

Efficiency addresses the operational and economic cost-effectiveness of gate-to-gate flight operations from a single-flight perspective. The effectiveness is the measure for decision-making how the system provides the desired output or not. Being effective means producing the right output in terms of quantity and quality. When the system is ineffective, the system is out of control and it needs a major correction.

When determining the optimal mental download of the controller, it is important to find the balance between flight safety (the number of ACFT under the control) and the efficiency/cost of service (the number of ATCO). Minimum cost with maximum safety by Wald criterion (Kharchenko, Shmelova, & Sikirda, 2012):

$$\mathrm{C}_{opt} = \max_{i} \min_{j} C_{ij} . \tag{1}$$

The process of functioning of Air Traffic Service (ATS), and consequently controller's activity in this process is performing tightly connected with the outside environment. That's, while evaluation of ATCO workload and quality of his activity, very important take into account the influence of different factors (F).

It is possible to list many factors, which have an influence on the quality of ATCO performance. Depending on the nature and source of appearance these factors may be divided into groups:

F_{h}, directly associated with human as subject in the system of management;
F_{t}, associated with the functioning of technique in the process of ATC;
F_{e}, characterize the influence of environment on the process of controllers activity.

To the group F_h is referred to so-called personality factors (causes), which is typical to ATCO or directly connected with him (the level of training, length of work). Then must be moral-political and age-related factors. The sizable role is played by human factors and factors connected with ATCO's activity – the complexity of given functions, labor routine and so on.

To the group F_t is referred to factors, which is connected with characteristics of surety (concerning techniques) and also how these characteristics influence on ATCO activity. In this case, under technical failure is realized action, where is present partial or whole loss or changing in technological capabilities which lead to the considerable reduction or complete loss in its performance capabilities. The negative influence even of functional techniques on the quality of the controller's performance is determined by non-observance of ergonomic requirements while manufacturing of facilities.

To the group F_e is referred to conditions in which ACFT performed the flights, intensity of air traffic, time of flights, presence of restrictions during flights, characteristics of zones, meteorological conditions (including microclimate on controller's working place), etc. In such a manner, the quality of the controller's performance depends on certain factors which may be taken into account and eliminated. The next step in the evaluation of affecting factors was a research of so-called engineering-psychological factors. In general case under engineering-psychological factors is realized variables which have an influence on the result of human-operator activity in the systems of management, and consequently the reliability and efficiency of these systems.

The research shows that among the complex of factors the most influence on quality the following:

- the correspondence of algorithm of the controller's activity with his psychological characteristics (type, character, sequence, and complexity of performing functions, allocation of function between him and technique);
- the controller's proficiency, the level of his main skills, knowledge, the experience of practical work;
- the correspondence between equipment on working place and his psychological characteristics, and also the level of agreement of these characteristics with the technical process of ATCO activity;
- the conditions of the outside environment on the working place (air temperature, its clearance, humidity, noise in the building), it means microclimate and work conditions;
- the organization of the working process (duration of continuous operation, the character of rest, periodicity of working shifts, etc.).

As the controller's activity may be examined in general as complex of processes connected with information, then principal attention must be paid to information processes. In this case among all ergonomic abilities of ATCO, the most interest is a perception of information while visual, aural and sensitive channels and also psychological processes (attention, memory, and thinking) and locomotor functions (speed, accuracy, and coordination of movements). Practically, each of these functions has well-defined the threshold meaning which consequently influences on the efficiency of ATCO functionality. Specifically, while running events directed on the perfection of the ATC system and automatization processes, it is efficient to consider these threshold meanings of human-operator and evaluate the workload of ATCO essentially on the processes of information overload.

Air traffic controller workload is considered to be an important limiting factor to the growth of air traffic. The difficulty of an air traffic control task can be analyzed through examining the problem's solution space, that is, all possible vector commands that satisfy the constraints of safety, productivity, and efficiency. On the basis of different information sources (e.g., radar screen, paper or electronic flight progress strips, radio and interphone communication), air traffic controllers have to control complex, dynamic, and time-constraint traffic situations in order to identify potential conflict and risky relationships between aircraft and to be able to resolve them. Therefore, they have to perceive, comprehend, and anticipate multiple characteristics and flight paths of many aircraft while new incoming aircraft create new traffic relationships for evaluation.

The workload of a controller must be accurately assessed to permit optimum efficiency. If it is too high for too long, they may be overstretched. If it is too low for too long, this not only constitutes an inefficient application of resources but is likely to increase the chances of a controller becoming distracted from their primary task.

An overworked controller may:

- have difficulty maintaining situational awareness
- overlook a developing unsafe situation
- make errors of judgment
- become confused
- be unable to cope with a sudden increase in workload

The theme of mental workload evaluating was also considered in students' thesis "Methodology of workload estimation of control", "Determination of conditional workload of air traffic controller taking into account the complication of technological procedures" and "Interpretation of conditional workload of air controller in graph" (Shmelova, Stasiuk, & Bondarev, 2013; Bilko, 2015; Shmelova, Stasiuk, & Poluhovich, 2013a, 2013b).

METHODOLOGY OF EVALUATING OF MENTAL WORKLOAD OF AIR TRAFFIC CONTROLLERS

In the areas of high intensity of air traffic the main aspect of efficiency for definition the number of ATC sectors may be the controller's mental workload in the control zone. As workload, is used the measure in terms of complex criteria, which takes into account the number of ACFT, which are simultaneously present in the zone and consumption which controllers spend on the ACFT service during defined time interval τ (for one hour, during their shift, etc.) (Shmelova & Paukov, 2007).

The number of ACFT which are simultaneously present in the zone depends on the size of the zone S and intensity of incoming air traffic λ (2):

$$N=\lambda * S. \tag{2}$$

As a criterion for evaluating the ATC mental workload is used a complex criterion, which includes the intensity of air traffic (the number of aircraft during the time) λ; time τ; difficult of service procedures for an aircraft ω_i.

Total ATCO mental workload for the certain time interval τ (3):

$$F_{\Sigma} = \sum_{i=1}^{n} \omega_i \lambda \tau , \tag{3}$$

where ω_i – is a weight coefficient, which takes into account labor expenditure on servicing of one ACFT and depends on the character of procedure; significance coefficient on servicing of ACFT *i*-th type of flight; λ – is an intensity of air traffic; and τ – is a time interval.

It has been determined that a flight stage, every zone, where air traffic service is provided, has the different technology of work and individual instructions for procedures. The weight coefficients of service procedures difficult are calculated with Expert Judgment Method (EJM) or method of expert estimations. EJM is a structured communication technique, originally developed as a systematic, interactive forecasting method which relies on a panel of experts. The experts answer questionnaires in two or more rounds. After each round, a facilitator provides an anonymous summary of the experts' forecasts from the previous round as well as the reasons they provided for their judgment. Thus, experts are encouraged to revise their earlier answer in light of the replies of other members of their panel. It is believed that during this process the range of the answers will decrease and the groups will coverage towards the "correct" answer. Finally, the process is stopped after a predefined stop criterion (e.g. the number of rounds, achievement of consensus, and stability of results) and the mean or average scores of the final rounds determine the results (Velychko, Kolomiyets', Hordiyenko, Karpenko, & Haber, 2015; Kurtov, Polikashyn, Potikhens'kyy, & Aleksandrov, 2017).

The algorithm of evaluating the ATCO mental workload using EJM (Figure 2):

1. Questionnaires for experts: m – is a number of experts, $m \geq 30$.
2. The matrix of individual preferences: R_i – is a system of preferences of *i*-expert, $i = \overline{1,m}$.
3. The matrix of group preferences $R = R_j$ (4):

$$R = R_j = R_{gr} = \frac{\sum_{i=1}^{m} R_i}{m}. \tag{4}$$

where $R = R_j = R_{gr}$ – is an experts' group opinion, $j = \overline{1,n}$; n – is a number of service procedures; m – is a number of experts; R_i – is a system of preferences of *i*-expert.

4. Coordination of expert's opinion.
   4.1. Calculation of dispersion D (5):

$$D = \frac{\sum_{i=1}^{m} (R_{gr} - R_i)^2}{m-1}. \tag{5}$$

   4.2. Calculation of square average deviation σ (6):

$$\sigma = \sqrt{D}. \tag{6}$$

   4.3. The coefficient of the variation ν (7):

$$v = \frac{\sigma}{R_{gr}} \cdot 100\% . \tag{7}$$

If $\nu \leq 33\%$ then the opinion is concerted and system of the expert group has been obtained. If $\nu > 33\%$ then it is necessary to calculate Kendal's concordation coefficient:

5. Kendal's concordation coefficient W (8):

$$W = \frac{12S}{m^2(n^3 - n) - m\sum_{i=1}^{m} T_i}; \tag{8}$$

$$S = \sum_{j=1}^{n} \left(\sum_{i=1}^{m} R_{ij} - \overline{R}\right)^2 ;$$

$$T_i = \sum_{i=1}^{m} (t_i^3 - t_i);$$

$$\overline{R} = \frac{1}{n} \sum_{j=1}^{n} \left(\sum_{i=1}^{m} R_{ij}\right),$$

where S – is a generalized dispersion; ti – is a number of the same ranks in the i-row which fixed the i-expert.

Kendal's concordation coefficient must be within the limits $0{,}7 < W \leq 1$. If $W < 0{,}7$ it is necessary to repeat the interrogation.

6. Compare the system of preferences R_{gr} and R_i, $i = \overline{1, m}$ with the help of rating correlation coefficient R_s (Spearman's coefficient) (9):

$$R_S = 1 - \frac{6\sum_{j=1}^{n} (R_{gr} - R_i)^2}{n(n^2 - 1)} . \tag{9}$$

7. The significance of the calculations.
   7.1. The significance of the calculation of Kendal's coordination coefficient W, criterion χ^2 (10):

$$\chi_f^2 = \frac{S}{\frac{1}{2}m(n+1) - \frac{1}{12(n-1)} \sum_{j=1}^{n} R_j} > \chi_t^2, \tag{10}$$

where χ_f^2 – is a factual value of the variable; χ_t^2 – is a table value of the variable.

7.2. The significance of the calculation of Spearman's coefficient R_s with using Student's t – criterion (11):

$$t_{critical} = R_s \sqrt{\frac{n-2}{1-R_s^2}} > t_{st}, . \tag{11}$$

where n – is a number of service procedures; t_{st} – is a tabulated value while the number of degrees of freedom $f = n–2$ and error $\alpha = 5\%$.

8. Weight coefficients w_j of service procedures (12):

$$w_j = \frac{Cj}{\sum_{j=1}^{n} C_j}; \tag{12}$$

$$\sum_{j=1}^{n} w_j = 1,$$

where n – is a number of service procedures; $C_j = 1 - \frac{R-1}{n}$ – are the estimates, $j = \overline{1,n}$.

9. Graph of results of the calculation.
10. Total ATCO mental workload for the certain time interval τ (13):

$$F_{\Sigma} = \sum_{i=1}^{n} \omega_i \lambda \tau, \tag{13}$$

where ω_i – is a weight coefficient, which takes into account labor expenditure on servicing of one ACFT and depends on the character of procedure; significance coefficient on servicing of ACFT i-th type of flight; λ – is an intensity of air traffic; and τ – is a time interval.

Figure 2. Block-scheme of the algorithm of EJM

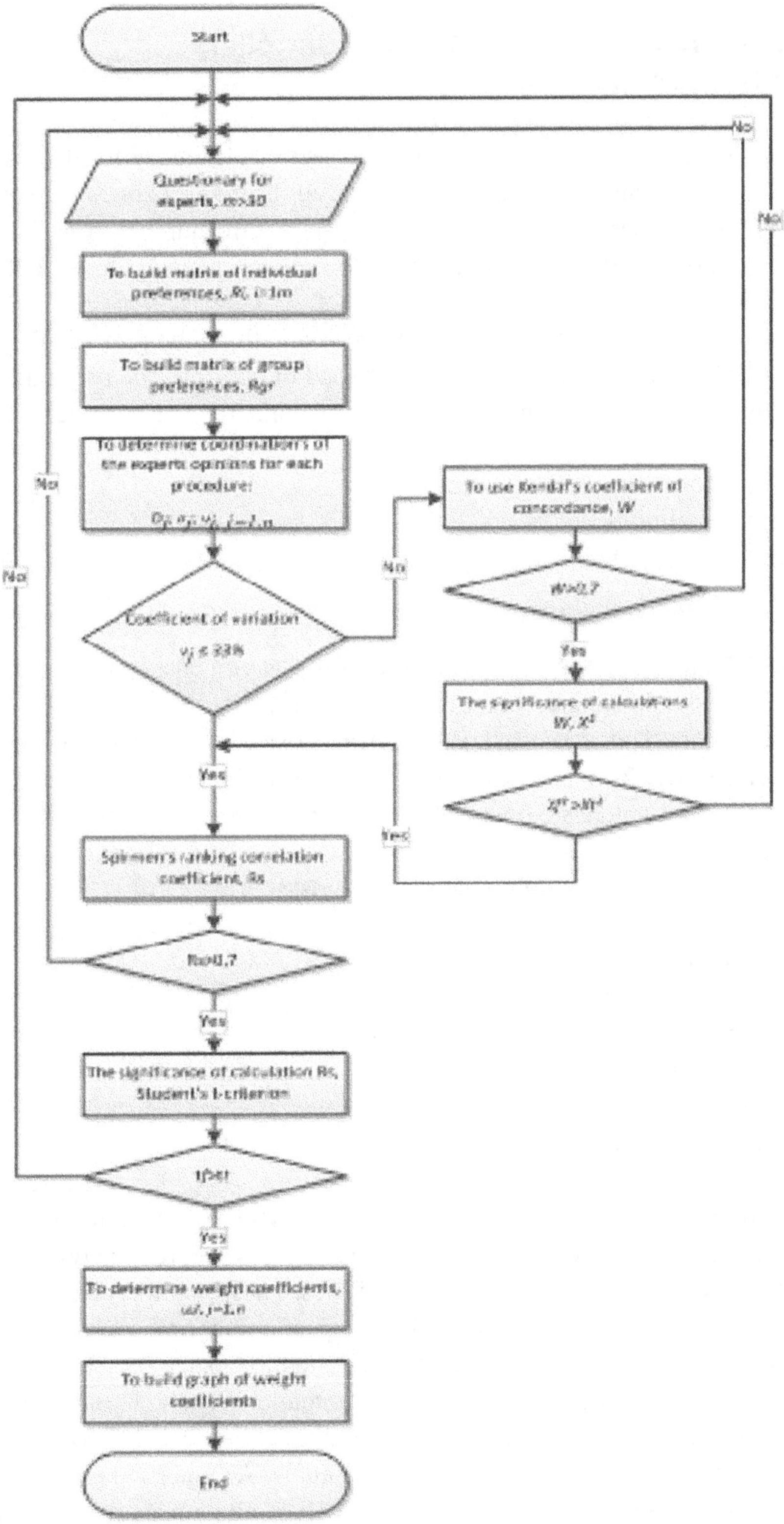

ILLUSTRATIVE EXAMPLES

Evaluating Mental Workload of Air Traffic Controllers Depending on the Service Procedures

In the areas of high intensity of air traffic, the main aspect of efficiency for determining the number of ATC sectors may be the controller's mental workload in the control zone. As workload, is used the measure in terms of complex criteria, which takes into account the number of ACFT, which are simultaneously present in the zone and consumption which controllers spend on the ACFT service during the defined time interval (for one hour, during their shift, etc.).

The complexity of ATCO workload has been estimated with the help of EJM's algorithm and MS Excel program in Master's thesis "Evaluation of workload of control zone using the method of expert assessments" (Stasiuk, 2014). Approach procedures were compared that include:

- coordination of information with adjacent sectors
- control of climbing aircraft
- control of descending aircraft
- control of transit aircraft

The Area Control Center (ACC) provides radar coverage over vast distances at set altitudes. Depending on the location, aircraft should contact center between 8000 and 41000 feet (FL80-FL410). The Center handles mainly IFR flights. This is because VFR traffic doesn't regularly tend to fly at great altitudes. ACC typically accepts traffic from and passes traffic to, a Terminal Control Center, like an Approach, or of another Center. Most Centers are operated by the national governments of the countries in which they are located (ICAO, 2007).

ACC will normally provide these following instructions:

- give "fly direct waypoints"
- altitude changes and descents
- give STAR's if needed
- instruct pilots to fly into a holding pattern
- give speed instructions
- give IFR clearances for pilots departing at uncontrolled fields and flying IFR

ACC can be subdivided into sectors. Each sector will be working on a radio frequency. Each sector also has secure landline communications with adjacent sectors, approach controls, areas, ARTCCs, flight service centers, and military aviation control facilities. These landline communications are shared among all sectors that need them and are available on a first-come, first served basis. Aircraft passing from one sector to another shall be handed off and requested to change frequencies to contact the next sector controller. Sector boundaries are specified by aeronautical charts. The communications between pilots and ATCOs are done via radio, usually VHF AM bands (between 118 MHz and 137 MHz). The frequencies are published in aeronautical charts and manuals. As a normal procedure, when a pilot is told to change to another controller, the new frequency will be announced. In addition, Center controllers also are connected electronically to other Centers. This connection allows controllers to be linked to the electronic traffic management system. Radar is used to monitor and give instructions to the traffic. Usually, Center controllers give "direct to waypoint" instructions. This waypoint can be GPS fixes or Radio Navigation beacons (NAVAIDS) like VOR's or NDB's. Center controllers also assign Standard Terminal Arrival Routes (STARs) and/or the runway for landing at the destination airport. In the Airspace over the oceans, there is no Radar Coverage, so the procedures to manage the air traffic are different from the normal airspace. In Oceanic Airspace controllers estimate the position of the traffic from pilot reports and computer models, as is impossible to have a picture of what is happening. For Oceanic flights pilots need special clearance, also the communications are done using HF radio because of its greater propagation over long distances (ICAO, 2007).

The first step of EJM are the matrixes of individual and group preferences (Tables 2, 3).

Figure 3 shows that the highest ATCO mental workload at ACC corresponds to descend procedures.

The sum of the controller's expenditure during time τ (τ=1 hour), λ - is the intensity of incoming air traffic depending on the type of procedure $\lambda_1 = 10$, $\lambda_2 = 3$, $\lambda_3 = 7$, $\lambda_4 = 12$. Using the formula (3) defines the aggregate expenditure on performing different procedures:

$F_\Sigma = 0.12*10+0.34*3+0.36*7+0.18*12 = 1.2+1.02+2.52+2.16 = 6.9$ imag. ACFT/hr.

Table 2. The matrix of individual preferences of expert number 1

Procedures	Transit	Climb	Descend	Coordination	Σr	R	R
Transit		0	0	0	0	4	4
Climb	1		0.5	1	2.5	1; 2	1.5
Descend	1	0.5		1	2.5	1; 2	1.5
Coordination	1	0	0		1	3	3

Table 3. The matrix of group preferences that has been obtained using MS Excel

Experts	Procedures			
	Transit	Climb	Descend	Coordination
1	4	1.5	1.5	3
…	…	…	…	…
30	4	2	1	3
R_{grj}	3.8	1.6	1.4	3.2
D_j	0.075	0.05	0.05	0.075
σ_j	0.273861	0.223607	0.223607	0.273861
ν_j	7.206876	13.97542	15.97191	8.558165
C_j	0.3	0.85	0.9	0.45
w_j	0.12	0.34	0.36	0.18

Figure 3. Estimation of multi-criteria decision with the help of EJM and recommendations for the description of ATC procedures

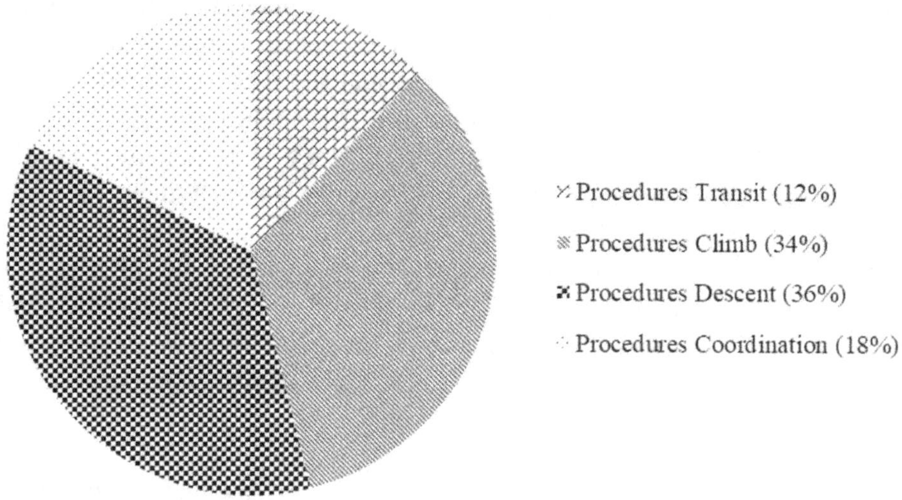

With the help of Expert System actual indicators of ATCO mental workload are compared with the normative ones and it is concluded that it is expedient to reduce the workload on the controller by optimizing air traffic flows, streamlining the structure of the airspace, improving technical support and technologies, etc.

Evaluating Mental Workload of Air Traffic Controllers Depending on the Airspace Zone

ATCO Simulation Training is one of the major components in the preparation of ATC students (European Organization for the Safety of Air Navigation [Eurocontrol], 2004a). Before beginning the exercises on the simulator (different zones and difficulties) intended ATC they must have appropriate knowledge, according to theoretical practices – Pre-Simulation Training. Theoretical knowledge is the basis for the admission of the ATCO to Simulation Training. Since the student must master before this list of disciplines, which is regulated of Educational Plan (Curriculum). Education plan – is the educational program with additional information. It details (for each exercise) the type of events that occur during the period of training necessary teaching materials, methods of preparation. It also contains the time scale, which will be performed the exercise.

According to Eurocontrol's requirements, the Basic Training of student consists of two phase (Eurocontrol, 2004b):

1. Theoretical education.
2. Practical education (practical training on Simulator).

The purpose of basic education is to provide students the basic knowledge and practical skills of ATM needed for further rating training to obtain a certificate ATC student.

Program of ATC Basic Training has the list of discipline such as ATM, Navigation, Human Factors, etc. ([Eurocontrol, 2015). Basic Training includes to Pre-Simulation Training and determines whether a student ready to Simulation Training or not (Figure 4).

Firstly, the student should fix to learn a number of these disciplines. After that it's seen: if the student has an acceptable level in these disciplines he/she ready to Simulation Training, if no – not ready. Simulation Training included three zones according to normative documents: CTR, TMA, and CTA (ICAO, 2007). Each of the zones has the list of exercise with different difficulties, it depends only from the number of the lesson. The organization of the airspace over the given area should be arranged so that it corresponds to operational and technical considerations only. In addition, aerodromes, where ATC is provided, should be designated as controlled aerodromes.

According to ICAO requirements, the Ukrainian ATS airspace has been classified and designated for the following classes: class C and class D (Ministry of Transport of Ukraine, 2003) (Table 4).

Figure 4. The interconnection between pre-simulation training of student and simulation training

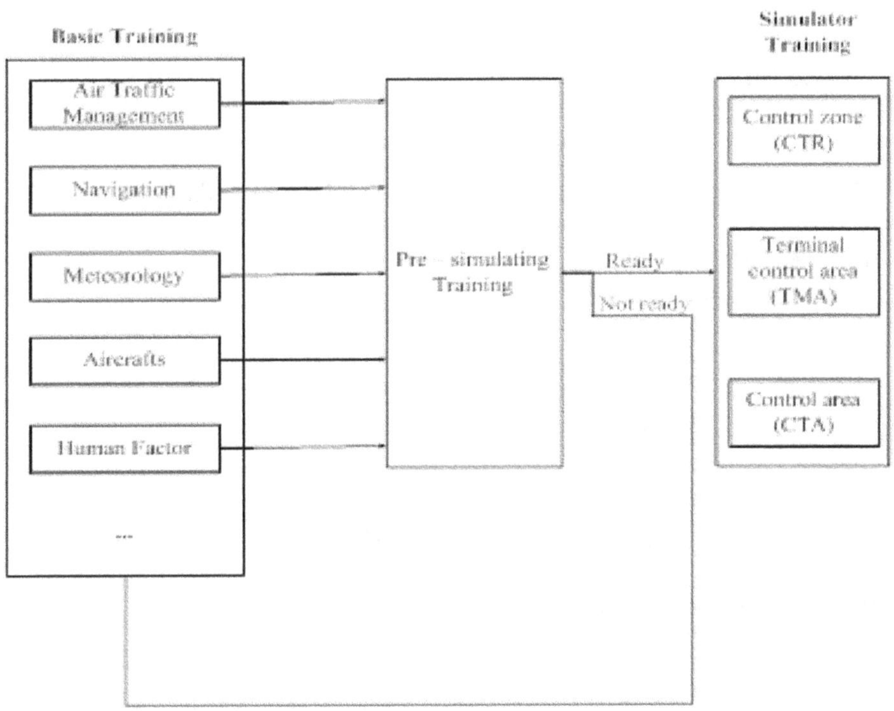

Table 4. Implementation of airspace classes in Ukrainian airspace

N°	Class of Airspace	Zones of Airspace	Restrictions
1	D	CTR	1500-2900 m
2	D (except Boryspil TMA, where class C is applied due to high traffic volumes)	TMA	D (1500-2900 m) and C (2900 m – Fl 660)
3	D and C	CTA	D (1500-2900 m) and C (2900 m – Fl 660)

For estimation complexity of the exercises in the system of Pre-Simulation Training, it is necessary to find weight coefficients, which characterize the complexity of airspace zones. Assessments of the complexity of airspace zones with using the algorithm of estimation of the complexity of the tasks in the Pre-Simulation Training have been obtained (Shmelova, Lazorenko, & Bilko, 2014; Bilko, 2015; Shmelova, Sikirda, & Jafarzade, 2019):

1. Questionnaires for experts – ATCOs with working experience.
2. The matrix of individual preferences. Evaluation of complexity of airspace zones (CTR, TMA, and CTA): R.

R_i has been obtained, $i = \overline{1, m}$, where m – is a number of experts; R_i – is a system of preferences of i-expert. For example, $R_i = R_{iTMA} \succ R_{iCTA}, R_{iCTR}.1,m$

3. The matrix of group preferences for CTR has been obtained:

$$R_{grCTR} = \frac{\sum_{i=1}^{m} R_{iCTR}}{m} = 2,64.$$

Average value R_{gr} for TMA and CTA have similar calculations (Table 5).

4. Concordance of expert's opinion.
   4.1. Calculation of dispersion D:

$$D_{! TR} = \frac{\sum_{i=1}^{m} (R_{grCTR} - R_{iCTR})^2}{m-1} = 0,401099.$$

Calculations for TMA and CTA would be the same variant (Table 5).

4.2. Calculation of square average deviation σ:

$$\sigma_{CTR} = \sqrt{D_{CTR}} = 0,633324.$$

Calculations for TMA and CTA would be the same variant (Table 5).

4.3. The coefficient of the variation ν:

$$\nu_{CTR} = \frac{\sigma_{CTR}}{R_{grCTR}} \cdot 100\% = 23,9636\%.$$

Table 5. The matrix of group preferences

Coordination of Expert's Opinion	CTR	TMA	CTA
	x_1	x_2	x_3
R_{gr}	2.642857	1.142857	2.214286
D_i	0.401099288976	0.131868480769	0.335164576356
σ_i	0.633324	0.363137	0.578934
ν_i, %	23.9636	31.77445	26.14542

Variation for TMA and CTA have similar calculations (Table 5).

If $\nu_{\text{CTR,TMA,CTA}} \leq 33\%$ then the opinion is concerted and the system of the expert group has been obtained. For example, $R_{gr} = R_{TMA} \succ R_{CTR} \succ R_{CTA}$.

Calculations show that opinion is concerted and it is necessary to obtain weight coefficients of complexity for airspace zones.

5. Weight coefficients of complexity (Table 6):

$w_1 = w_{\text{CTR}}$ – weight coefficient for CTR zone;

$w_2 = w_{\text{TMA}}$ – weight coefficient for TMA zone;

$w_3 = w_{\text{CTA}}$ – weight coefficient for CTA zone.

6. Graphical presentation of weight coefficients of CTR, TMA, and CTA (Figure 5).

Calculations have been performed with using computer program MS Excel.

Integrated estimation of tasks Q_{jl} with j-level of complexity in air traffic control for n-zones (14):

$$Q_{jl} = \sum_{j=1}^{n} \sum_{l=1}^{L} w_j q_l, \tag{14}$$

where q_l – is an estimation of the task with given complexity and type of airspace zone (CTR, TMA, and CTA); and w_j – is a weight coefficient (complexity of airspace zone); l – is a level of the task.

So, we can see that the most difficult zone of an airspace according to the opinion of the expert is the Terminal Control Area ($w_{\text{TMA}} = 0.475786$).

Table 6. The results of the calculation of weight coefficients

N°	Zone	R_{gr}	C_j	w_j
1	CTR	2.642857	0.453333	0.226161
2	TMA	1.142857143	0.953333	0.475786
3	CTA	2.214285714	0.596667	0.298053

Figure 5. Weight coefficients of zones' importance

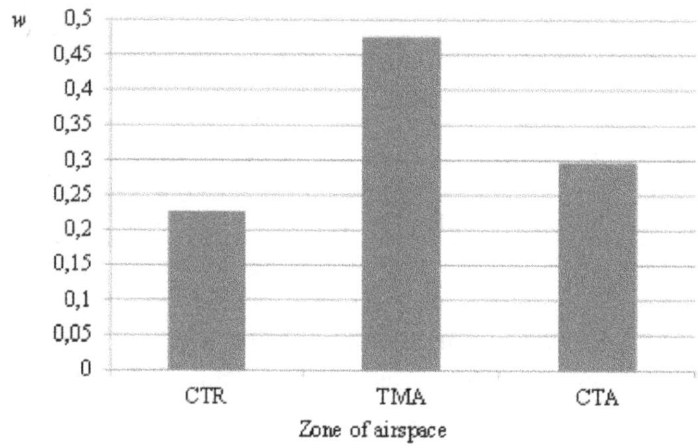

In the future, ATC instructor would take into account this expert's opinion for determination of a task according to difficulty. Integrated estimation for implementation of the task with complexity characteristic of airspace zone has been calculated with the help of the additive aggregation method. For automating estimation of Pre-Simulation Training on initial stage the neural network of multilayer type has been built (Shmelova, Lazorenko, & Bilko, 2014; Bilko, 2015; Shmelova, Sikirda, & Jafarzade, 2019).

Neural Network Model for Admission of ATC Students to Simulation Training

Contracting States shall take the appropriate measures to ensure that ATC student does not constitute a hazard to air navigation. A Contracting State shall not permit ATC student to receive instruction in an operational environment unless that ATC student holds a current Class 3 Medical Assessment. Before issuing an ATC license, a Contracting State shall require the applicant to meet the requirements of and the requirements of at least one of the ratings. Unlicensed State employees may operate as ATCOs on condition that they meet the same requirements (ICAO, 2016a, 2016b).

Four-layers neural network model for evaluating correctness and timeliness of decision making by air traffic controller during the Pre-Simulation Training has been built and its parameters have been obtained (Shmelova, Sikirda, Zemlyanskiy, Danilenko, & Lazorenko, 2016; Bilko, 2015; Shmelova, Sikirda, & Jafarzade, 2019). The first layer (input) includes exercises that perform student to solve potentially conflict situation, the second layer (hidden) depends physiological characteristics of student, the third layer (hidden) takes into account the complexity of the exercise depending on the number of potential conflict situations, the fourth layer (output) – is assessment of student during performance of exercise. Neural network model also has additional inputs (Bias) that including restrictions on calculating parameters.

Figure 6 represents the neural network for admission of ATC student to Simulation Training by the number of hours and level of training. It is the multilayer perceptron with three hidden layers:

- the input – are the disciplines of Pre-Simulation Training
- the first layer (input) – is a calculation of hours on theoretical training in accordance with the student's knowledge evaluation
- the second layer – are the restrictions on the given number of hours (hidden layer)

- the third layer – are the restrictions on passing hours (hidden layer)
- the fourth layer – are the restrictions on student's assessments (hidden layer)
- the output – is an admission / not admission of ATC student to Simulation Training

Threshold activation functions have been obtained according to requirements of hours and level of training marks (discipline) in compliance with the assessment criterion of tasks.

ATC student's Pre-Simulation Training consists of 5 disciplines (number depends on the teacher):

1. Navigation (NAV).
2. Air Traffic Management (ATM).
3. Meteorology (MET).
4. Human Factors (HF).
5. Aircrafts (ACFTs).

For each discipline, the student has a task (test) that he must perform in a given time. Therefore to be admitted he/she needs to deal with three barriers or three hidden layers (Figure 6):

1. The specified number of hours in the study of disciplines, which regulates as educational plan (T).
2. Time of task/test completed (t_{compl}).
3. Test mark (w_i).

Figure 6. Neural network for admission of ATC student to simulation training by the number of hours and level of training

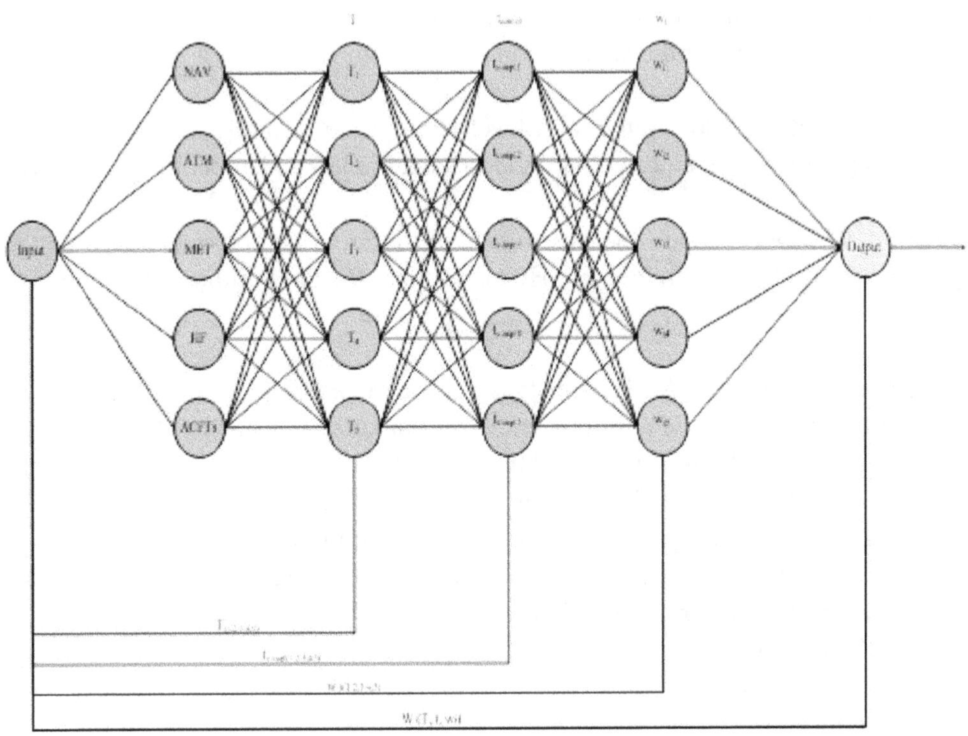

If a student is unable to cope with these three hidden layers he\she returns to the initial stage. And try to pass again for admission to training.

All positions of assessment criteria have been prescribed and must be used in a proper way as given below:

1. To take duty and workplace preparation.
2. An ability to follow the prescribed standard phraseology (excepting tasks with emergency and urgency situations).
3. Coordination with adjacent ATC units and other kinds of aerodrome service provision units.
4. Handling of procedural control.
5. Handling of visual control.
6. Daily flight plan conduction.
7. Execution of traffic massages timesheets.
8. Timeliness and accuracy of decision making in ATC.
9. Compliance with safety in ATC.
10. Performing of console operations.

Some of the criteria might not be used in order to which are chosen by a supervisor before training. During Pre-Simulation Training it is necessary to take into account that abilities and skills of ATC are evaluating feedback.

The applicant shall have completed an approved training course and not less than three months of satisfactory service engaged in the actual control of air traffic under the supervision of an appropriately rated air traffic controller. The applicant shall have:

a) satisfactorily completed an approved training course;
b) provided, satisfactorily, under the supervision of an appropriately rated ATC.

The applicant shall have demonstrated, at a level appropriate to the privileges being granted, the skill, judgment, and performance required to provide a safe, orderly and expeditious ATS (ICAO, 2012, 2016a, 2016b).

With the help of Microsoft Excel, the neural network model that correctly maps the input to the output using historical data has been created. Historical data for the building of neural network table for admission of student:

1. Dendrites (input) – Navigation, Air Traffic Management, Meteorology, Human Factors, and Aircrafts. It is a set of main disciplines, which ATC student must know before Simulation Training.
2. Ranks (R_i) – previously obtained with the help of EJM.
3. Estimates (C_i) – necessary value for obtaining weight coefficients.
4. Weight coefficients (w_j) – weight coefficient for each discipline.
5. Specified number of hours in study of disciplines which regulates by Educational Plan (T).
6. Estimated number of hours for preparation ($w_j\, x_i$).
7. Time of task/test completed (t_{compl}).
8. Time for tests in minutes.
9. Maximum time for tests.

10. Admission of time for testing.
11. Test mark (w_i)
12. Minimum score.
13. Admission according to the mark.
14. True/False – a logic function of Microsoft Excel.

The model can be used to produce the output – admission to the ATC Simulation Training (when output is unknown). Firstly, there is a measurement – student readiness for all criteria of Pre-Simulation Training tests. The student has attended a sufficient number of lessons; runs out of time passing tests and got a positive assessment (Figure 7).

If the student did not attend all lessons on ATM, he/she is not ready for Simulation Training. Despite that the other criteria – specified number of hours in studying disciplines and got the good marks of the test performance (Figure 8).

When the student runs out of time – tests Navigation and Aircrafts – 60 minutes, but he/she knew all the answers and got positive marks, also is not ready (Figure 9).

If the student got a bad mark on Human Factors he isn't ready to Simulation Training (Figure 10).

This automatically process shows a ready student or not ready to simulator training, using three types of the barrier – hidden layer in the neural network model.

FUTURE RESEARCH DIRECTIONS

It is relevant to adapt the developed methodology of ATCO mental workload evaluating for others Air Navigation System's human-operators: pilots, Unmanned Aerial Vehicles operators, flight dispatchers, rescuers, specialists of aviation security, etc. that will allow increasing the quality of their professional activity.

Figure 7. The student is ready to simulation training (screenshot of Microsoft Excel)

№ п п	Input (dendrites)	Ranks Ri	Estimates Ci	Weight coefficients (*synapse*) wj	Specified number of hours in study of disciplines, which regulates as educational Plan (T)	Estimated number of hours for preparation wj Xi (*axons*)	Time of task test completed (t_{compl})	Maximum time for tests (min)	Admission of time for testing	Test mark (wi)	Minimum score	Admission according to mark
1	Navigation	2	0,8	0,266666667	90	24	55	55	Ready	90	60	Ready
2	Air Traffic Management	1	1	0,333333333	89	29,6666667	55	55	Ready	80	60	Ready
3	Meteorology	3	0,6	0,2	233	46,6	55	55	Ready	70	60	Ready
4	Aircrafts	4	0,4	0,133333333	162	21,6	55	55	Ready	80	60	Ready
5	Human Factor	5	0,2	0,066666667	611	40,7333333	40	55	Ready	60	60	Ready
	Minimum Estimated coeff	161,2	3	1		162,6			ИСТИНА			ИСТИНА
					Function of activation	Ready						

Figure 8. The student isn't ready to simulation training according to discipline "ATM" (screenshot of Microsoft Excel)

№ п/п	Input (dendrites)	Ranks Ri	Estimates Ci	Weight coefficients (*synapse*) wj	Specified number of hours in study of disciplines, which regulates as educational Plan (T)	Estimated number of hours for preparation wj Xi (*axons*)	Time of task test completed (t_{compl})	Maximum time for tests (min)	Admission of time for testing	Test mark (wi)	Minimum score	Admission according to mark
1	Navigation	2	0,8	0,266666667	90	24	55	55	Ready	90	60	Ready
2	Air Traffic Management	1	1	0,333333333	70	23,3333333	55	55	Ready	80	60	Ready
3	Meteorology	3	0,6	0,2	233	46,6	55	55	Ready	70	60	Ready
4	Aircrafts	4	0,4	0,133333333	162	21,6	55	55	Ready	80	60	Ready
5	Human Factor	5	0,2	0,066666667	611	40,7333333	40	55	Ready	60	60	Ready
	Minimum Estimated coeff	161,2	3	1		156,266667			ИСТИНА			ИСТИНА
					Function of activation	Not ready						

Figure 9. The student isn't ready to simulation training according to time for tests (screenshot of Microsoft Excel)

№ п/п	Input (dendrites)	Ranks Ri	Estimates Ci	Weight coefficients (*synapse*) wj	Specified number of hours in study of disciplines, which regulates as educational Plan (T)	Estimated number of hours for preparation wj Xi (*axons*)	Time of task test completed (t_{compl})	Maximum time for tests (min)	Admission of time for testing	Test mark (wi)	Minimum score	Admission according to mark
1	Navigation	2	0.8	0.266666667	90	24	60	55	Not ready	90	60	Ready
2	Air Traffic Management	1	1	0.333333333	89	29.6666667	55	55	Ready	80	60	Ready
3	Meteorology	3	0.6	0.2	233	46.6	55	55	Ready	70	60	Ready
4	Aircrafts	4	0.4	0.133333333	162	21.6	60	55	Not ready	80	60	Ready
5	Human Factor	5	0.2	0.066666667	611	40.7333333	40	55	Ready	60	60	Ready
	Minimum Estimated coeff	161.2	3	1		162.6			ЛОЖЬ			ИСТИНА
					Function of activation	Ready						

Figure 10. The student isn't ready to Simulation Training according to mark (screenshot of Microsoft Excel)

№ п п	Input (dendrites)	Ranks Ri	Estimates Ci	Weight coefficients (*synapse*) wj	Specified number of hours in study of disciplines, which regulates as educational Plan (T)	Estimated number of hours for preparation wj Xi (*axons*)	Time of task'test completed ([illegible])	Maximum time for tests (min)	Admission of time for testing	Test mark (wi)	Minimum score	Admission according to mark
1	Navigation	2	0,5	0,266666667	90	24	55	55	Ready	90	60	Ready
2	Air Traffic Management	1	1	0,333333333	89	29,6666667	55	55	Ready	80	60	Ready
3	Meteorology	3	0,6	0,2	233	46,6	55	55	Ready	70	60	Ready
4	Aircrafts	4	0,4	0,133333333	162	21,6	55	55	Ready	80	60	Ready
5	Human Factor	5	0,2	0,066666667	611	40,7333333	40	55	Ready	59	60	Not ready
	Minimum Estimated coeff	161,2	3	1		162,6			ИСТИНА			ЛОЖЬ
					Function of activation	Ready						

It is our belief, that the methodology of mental workload evaluating can be used for improving the professional activity of specialists in any technogenous production (hydraulic engineering, chemical and military industries, gas and oil pipelines, nuclear power plants and transport, etc.).

What's Next?

On the next steps we are planning to use the methodology of ATCO mental workload evaluating in the System for control and forecasting the development of emergency situations on the base of Artificial Intelligence System (AIS) / Decision Support System (DSS) / Expert System (ES) that taking into account the influence of the professional factors (knowledge, habits, skills, experience) as well as the factors of non-professional nature (individual-psychological, psycho-physiological and socio-psychological) on the decision making process by human-operator of Air Navigation System.

CONCLUSION

Aviation became a vital part of our everyday life. ATC is the organization of aircraft movements in airspace, including methods and procedures used to manage and safeguard air traffic. Since air traffic is shared by all countries in the world, it is obvious that flight rules and organization should be standardized in some way so all the pilots in the world follow the same procedures independently of the country or the region in which they are flying.

Each aircraft during the flight is served by ATCO according to defined rules. ATCO is responsible as for aircrew so for passengers. But how many ACFT may be under control simultaneously? In these cases capacity is considered. Hence, the capacity of the zone is defined as a number of ACFT which are served at the same time by controllers in a certain zone taking into account probable delays and time needed for them.

The capacity of the zone connects with the capacity of each separate controller and with his mental workload. He provides a service which requires some human efforts. As human resources are limited, the level needed for a specific task can exceed the amount available. A given task will not produce the same workload level for all ATCOs. Rather, workload depends on his experience with the task, training and relevant skill levels. A task can even produce different workload for the same controller at a different time depending on his state when the task must be performed. The workload of the controller also depends on the time which is needed for ACFT flight through the zone, time which is needed for service of single ACFT according to defined rules and procedures, technical equipment, meteorological conditions. Therefore, the workload is an individual experience and workload, in many cases, may be a key factor for the whole zone. Hence, the quality and effectiveness of ATC system functioning are tightly connected with quality and effectiveness of ATCO work, his reliability, and capacity.

Also, analyzing factors, which influence on controllers´ mental workload, the next conclusion may be done: workload depends not just on the intensity of flights but also on the quality of technical equipment on controllers' working place, in other words, on the level of automatization, and on the difficult of service procedures.

Using the method of experts' estimation, according to the questionnaires (among climbing, descending, transit, and coordination), the procedure where it needs more expenditure from operators was defined (descending). And, consequently, was defined the number of ACFT per hour. With the help of Expert System actual indicators of ATCO mental workload are compared with the normative ones and defined either controller has overload or not.

The results can be used in sectorization of airspace, in order to estimate the workload of ATCO (because the present method does not take into account the difficult of service procedures, just intensity of flight). Although it can be used in simulators, during ATCO training. If we take into account the controller's workload we will solve many problems. For example, flights will be distributed in such a way that controllers' boring and workload will be decreased. Controllers encountered with different procedures during the work, and estimation of conditional workload will lead to effective work and safety of flights.

Automation can also increase workload due to demands on vigilance. These findings suggest that further implementation of automation in air traffic control systems must be preceded by systematic analysis of the impact of new technologies on controller workload and vigilance.

Before becoming ATCO candidates must possess certain skills as practical and theoretical education. Practical education consists of appropriate task on Simulator: change management area (CTR, TMA, and CTA); the intensity of traffic; regulation of potential conflict situation in real time. Theoretical education consists of the list of basic discipline, which ATC student must know because it is a key aspect of the preparation of the ATCO to Simulation Training. Without some knowledge, they cannot manage air traffic safely.

With the help of EJM the difficulty of ATC operations (tasks) has been determined. Using expert's opinion and criterion of weight coefficients, the complexity of airspace zones for operation on Initial Training, such as Simulator Practice, has been defined. Neural network for admission of ATC students to Simulation Training by the number of hours and level of training, which consists of five basic disciplines (Navigation, ATM, Meteorology, Human Factors, Aircrafts) and has three hidden layers (specified number of hours in study of disciplines, which regulates as educational plan; time of task\test completed; test mark), has been built. Estimation of multi-criteria decision with the help of EJM has been done and recommendations for the description of ATC procedures have been given.

Using AI methods as Expert Systems on the phase of Initial Training increases the efficiency of Simulation Training through interactive evaluation of mental workload of ATC student. Performance of exercises accompanies by comments, displaying results, assessments of the students and feedback. With using information about the difficulty of ATC zones and ATC procedures instructor may increase the number of hours of training and reorganize educational plan.

REFERENCES

Arkhangelskiy, V., & Bohaenko, I. (2000). *Man-machine automation systems: quality, safety and reliability management*. Kiev: Kiev Automation Institute.

Aviation Accident Statistics. (2019). *National Transportation Safety Board*. Retrieved from www.ntsb.gov/aviation/ aviation.htm

Bilko, A. (2015). *Neural network model of student admission in Air Traffic Controller simulator training* (Master's thesis). Kyiv: National Aviation University.

European Organization for the Safety of Air Navigation (Eurocontrol). (2004a). ATM Services' Personnel (2nd ed.). ESARR 5. Belgium, Brussels: Author.

European Organization for the Safety of Air Navigation (Eurocontrol). (2004b). *EATM Training Progression and Concepts*. Brussels, Belgium: Author.

European Organization for the Safety of Air Navigation (Eurocontrol). (2015). *Specifications for the ATCO Common Core Content Initial Training* (2nd ed.). Brussels, Belgium: Author.

Federal Aviation Administration. (2014). *Pilot/Controller Glossary*. Washington, DC: Author.

Georgia, A. P., & Barbara, J. P. (1997). *Flight to the future: human factors in air traffic control*. Washington, DC: National Academies Press.

IATA. (2016). Retrieved from https://www.iata.org/publications/Pages/AI-white-paper.aspxInternational

International Civil Aviation Organization. (1993). *Human Factors Digest No. 8: Human Factors in Air Traffic Control. Cir. 241*. Montreal, Canada: Author.

International Civil Aviation Organization. (1998). Human Factors Training Manual (1st ed.). Doc. ICAO 9683-AN/950. Canada, Montreal: Author.

International Civil Aviation Organization. (2002). Human Factors Guidelines for Safety Audits Manual (1st ed.). Doc. ICAO 9806-AN/763. Canada, Montreal: Author.

International Civil Aviation Organization. (2005). *Global Air Traffic Management Operational Concept. Doc. ICAO 9854-AN/458*. Montreal, Canada: Author.

International Civil Aviation Organization. (2007). Air Traffic Management (15th ed.). Doc. ICAO 4444-ATM/501. Canada, Montreal: Author.

International Civil Aviation Organization. (2012). *Manual on the Approval of Training Organizations. Doc. ICAO 9841-AN/456*. Montreal, Canada: Author.

International Civil Aviation Organization. (2013). Safety Management Manual (SMM) (3rd ed.). Doc. ICAO 9859-AN/474. Canada, Montreal: Author.

International Civil Aviation Organization. (2016a). Manual on Air Traffic Controller Competency-based Training and Assessment (1st ed.). Doc. ICAO 10056-AN/519. Canada, Montreal: Author.

International Civil Aviation Organization. (2016b). *Procedures for Air Navigation Services – Training (PANS-TRG). Doc. ICAO 9868*. Montreal, Canada: Author.

International Civil Aviation Organization. (2018). *Potential of Artificial Intelligence (AI) in Air Traffic Management (ATM)*. In Thirteenth Air Navigation Conference ICAO, Montréal, Canada.

Kharchenko, V., Shmelova, T., & Sikirda, Y. (2016). *Decision-making in socio-technical systems: monograph*. Kyiv: National Aviation University.

Kharchenko, V., Shmelova, T., & Sikirda, Y. (2018). Methodology of research and training in air navigation socio-technical system. *Proceedings of the National Aviation University, 1*, 8–23.

Kulik, N., Kharchenko, V., & Lutskii, M. (2008). *Encyclopedia of aviation safety*. Kyiv: Technology Publ.

Kurtov, A., Polikashyn, O., Potikhens'kyy, A., & Aleksandrov, V. (2017). Expert assessments. "Delphy" method as technology of administrative decision making. *Collections of Scientific Works of the Kharkiv National University of Air Force, No., 1*(50), 118–122.

Leychenko, S., Malishevskiy, A., & Mikhalic, N. (2006). *Human factors in aviation: monograph in two books. Book 1st*. Kirovograd: YMEKS.

Ministry of Transport of Ukraine. (2003). *About Approving the Flight Rules of Aircrafts and Air Traffic Services in the Classified Airspace of Ukraine*. Kyiv: Author.

Shmelova, T., Lazorenko, V., & Bilko, A. (2014). Estimation of pre-simulating training tasks complexity. *Proceedings of the National Aviation University, No., 1*(62), 17–22.

Shmelova, T., & Paukov, O. (2007). Determination of conditional loading of the air traffic controller taking into account the complexity of the technological procedures. In *Materials of VII International Scientific Conference of Students and Young Scientists "Flight-2007"*. Kyiv: National Aviation University.

Shmelova, T., Sikirda, Yu., & Jafarzade, T. (2019). Artificial neural network for pre-simulation training of air traffic controller. In T. Shmelova, Yu. Sikirda, N. Rizun, & D. Kucherov (Eds.), *Cases on modern computer systems in aviation* (pp. 27–51). Hershey, PA: IGI Global. doi:10.4018/978-1-5225-7588-7.ch002

Shmelova, T., Sikirda, Yu., Zemlyanskiy, A., Danilenko, O., & Lazorenko, V. (2016). Artificial neural network for air traffic controller's pre-simulator training. *Proceedings of the National Aviation University, No., 3*(68), 13–23.

Shmelova, T., Stasiuk, O., & Bondarev, D. (2013). Methodology of workload estimation. In *All-Ukrainian Scientific and Practical Conference of Young Scientists and Students*. In *Problems of navigation and traffic control*. Kyiv: National Aviation University.

Shmelova, T., Stasiuk, O., & Poluhovich, O. (2013a). Determination of conditional workload of air traffic controller taking into account the complication of technological procedures. In *All-Ukrainian Scientific and Practical Conference of Young Scientists and Students*. In *Problems of navigation and traffic control*. Kyiv: National Aviation University.

Shmelova, T., Stasiuk, O., & Poluhovich, O. (2013b). Interpretation of conditional workload of air controller in graph. In *All-Ukrainian Scientific and Practical Conference of Young Scientists and Students*. In *Problems of navigation and traffic control*. Kyiv: National Aviation University.

Stasiuk, O. (2014). *Evaluation of workload of control zone using the method of expert assessments* (Master's thesis). Kyiv: National Aviation University.

Velychko, O., Kolomiyets', L., Hordiyenko, T., Karpenko, S., & Haber, A. (2015). *Group expert assessment and axperts' competence: monograph*. Odesa: Aprel Publ.

KEY TERMS AND DEFINITIONS

Air Traffic Control (ATC): A service provided for the purpose of preventing collisions between aircraft and on the maneuvering area between aircraft and obstructions and expediting and maintaining an orderly flow of air traffic.

Air Traffic Controllers (ATCs): Are the coordinators of the movement of aircraft to maintain safe distances between them. Air traffic controllers typically do the following: monitor and direct the movement of aircraft on the ground and in the air; control all ground traffic at airport runways and taxiways; issue landing and takeoff instructions to pilots; transfer control of departing flights to other traffic control centers and accept control of arriving flights; inform pilots about weather, runway closures, and other critical information; alert airport response staff in the event of an aircraft emergency.

Air Traffic Management (ATM): The dynamic, integrated management of air traffic and airspace including air traffic services, airspace management, and air traffic flow management—safely, economically, and efficiently—through the provision of facilities and seamless services in collaboration with all parties and involving airborne and ground-based functions.

Air Traffic Service (ATS): A generic term meaning variously, flight information service, alerting service, air traffic advisory service, air traffic control service (area control service, approach control service or aerodrome control service).

Aircraft (ACFT): Is a flying vehicle maintained in the atmosphere due to interaction with air, other than interaction with air reflected from the earth surface or water.

Area Control Center (ACC): Is a facility responsible for controlling aircraft flying in a particular volume of airspace (a Flight Information Region) at high altitudes between airport approaches and departures.

Artificial Intelligence System (AIS): Was a distributed computing project undertaken by Intelligence Realm, Inc. with the long-term goal of simulating the human brain in real time, complete with artificial consciousness and artificial general intelligence.

Decision Support System (DSS): Is the interactive computer system intended to support different types of activity during the decision making including poorly structured and unstructured problems.

European Organization for the Safety of Air Navigation (Eurocontrol): Is an international organization working to achieve safe and seamless air traffic management across Europe.

Expert Judgment Method (EJM): Is the procedure for obtaining an assessment of the problem based on the opinion of specialists (experts) for the purpose of subsequent decision making (choice).

Expert System (ES): Is a computer system that emulates the decision-making ability of a human expert.

International Civil Aviation Organization (ICAO): It codifies the principles and techniques of international air navigation and fosters the planning and development of international air transport to ensure safe and orderly growth.

Zones of Airspace: 1. *Control Zone (CTR):* A controlled airspace extending upwards from the surface of the earth to a specified upper limit. 2. *Terminal Control Area (TMA):* A control area normally established at the confluence of ATS Routes in the vicinity of one or more major aerodromes. 3. *Control Area (CTA):* A controlled airspace extending upwards from a specified limit above the earth to a specified upper limit.

Section 3
Performance Evalutation

Chapter 10
Indicators for Measuring Changeover Activities:
Operationalization of 4Ps model of Changeovers

Yuridia Vega
https://orcid.org/0000-0001-5229-9655
Autonomous University of Ciudad Juarez, Mexico

Roberto Romero-López
https://orcid.org/0000-0003-0859-327X
Autonomous University of Ciudad Juarez, Mexico

Norma Alicia Barboza-Tello
https://orcid.org/0000-0002-1009-3672
Autonomous University of Baja California, Mexico

Alex Bernardo Pimentel-Mendoza
Autonomous University of Baja California, Mexico

Manuel Javier Rosel-Solis
https://orcid.org/0000-0002-3800-7094
Autonomous University of Baja California, Mexico

ABSTRACT

At present, the manufacturing industries require the implementation of more efficient and flexible fabrication processes to offer high-quality products. The changeover methodologies can be used to reduce the setup times, allowing the industries to be more competitive. The application of changeover methodologies is mainly influenced by the 4Ps model, which is composed of organizational and design factors, such as people, practices, product, and processes. However, this model is not useful in determining the relationship between each one of the Ps and the changeover activities. In this chapter, the authors have developed an exhaustive review of the references to establish the indicators to design an instrument composed of 79 items and divided into the five constructs of the 4P model, which was statistically validated using the Kendall W indicator and the Cronbach´s alpha indicator.

DOI: 10.4018/978-1-7998-1052-0.ch010

INTRODUCTION

Currently, in the industry, several factors such as the growing demand from markets and customers which demand higher quality products, have influenced the way by which organizations use their personnel, facilities, and administrative and production systems and be capable to respond to the need of manufacturing flexibility in relation to the variety of products and production volume at profitable costs. Recently Chabowski et al. (2016) detected through an analysis of causes, that a production line, does not reach the established required standards mainly because of changeover activities. Therefore, one of the key factors that allows an industry to be more productive is the reduction of build-up production times, achieved through the implementation of changeover methodologies. The literature reports that a significant number of companies have implemented the SMED methodology (Single Minute Exchange of Die) or its variations, combining it with lean manufacturing methodologies. However, in those reports are not consider the factors and variables that intervene in the production systems deployment, so the results are often not optimal. Researchers have to consider that the design and organizational factors play an important role because they are the basis of operational and administrative decisions within the companies. The production variables are identify and controlled flexibility and efficiency inside and outside the organization.

Reik et al. (2006), present a model of rapid changeover that considers organizational and design factors to support increased capacity and flexibility in manufacturing processes and thus respond timely to the customer's needs. This Theoretical Model shows the relation of positive influence and correlations between four factors: Product, Process, Human Resource (People) and Work Methods (Practice) and is called the model of the 4P's. In this model, the rapid changeover activities are understand as essential tasks such as disassembly, assembly, adjustments, and validation, involved in the production process and its accomplishment improves efficiency and facilities availability. On the other hand, the Process and Product factors are present at the initial stage of the productive processes and are directly relate to machine designs, use of tools, manufacturing systems, and products, and all the factors that can contribute to flexibility, simplify, through eliminating or adding elements that contribute to the capacity and stability of each system run. "People" and "Practices" factors are relate to the industry functioning, as they organize and use their resources to achieve greater profitability and competitiveness. Van Goubergen et al. (2002), suggest that the assignment of employees with specific skills and abilities influences the performance of their responsibilities and the provided resources.

As is shown, the model presents a great option to support the efficiency of changeover implementation. However, because this model is theoretical, the 4P factors cannot be explain just with these concepts, it requires the definition of measurable and observable variables and so to determine the degree of relationship that each of the P's has with the activities of the rapid changeover. In order to make sense of the 4P's model, a review has been realize from which variables were obtained and used to design an instrument of 79 items.

This chapter deals with the operationalization of the variables and the design and validation of an instrument that allows measuring for rapid changeover activities. The operationalization consisted of a descriptive analysis of each identified variable described through indicators. Then the measurement scale was define. From the described analysis, an instrument composed of 79 items was formulate. Each item gives six options to respond based on a Likert scale and represents each indicator. Finally, to obtain higher reliability of the gathered information is addressed the content validation and instrument reliability. The instrument was submit to the appreciation of six maintenance professionals to validate its content. The judges evaluated through a test the content validation of each instrument giving a relevance of 94%. The agreement of the experts was estimated using a Kendall hypothesis test (Olmos Rueda & Mas Torelló, 2018) obtaining a p-value of 0.029, indicating an acceptable relation between the judge's agreement and the relevance of the items. Additionally, Changeover activities were execute to estimate the reliability of the instrument, by a pilot run of 31 respondents from industries in the Tijuana, Baja California region. The reliability test was apply using the Cronbach alpha (α), whose coefficient values oscillate 0 to 1. The value closest to one indicates the highest degree of reliability of the instrument. In this analysis, we obtained a coefficient of 0.97 by the statistical software SPSS version 25. Therefore the instrument is reliable and feasible to apply it in the industry of the Baja California region and to test the relationships and correlations of the Reik's and 4P's model.

CONTINUOUS IMPROVEMENT TECHNIQUES IN THE MANUFACTURING INDUSTRY

Changeover Methodology

A changeover it is define as the set of activities executed to set up the materials and equipment necessary to manufacture a product having the quality and speed required (Reik, 2006). In Figure 1, is show the sequence of the changeover activities. The process starts when the manufacturing period of product "A" falls to zero. Then the "set up" period is execute, during this period all the accessories and equipment necessary to manufacture the product B, are install. Finally, starts the "run up" period, which lasts until the quality and production rates desired are reach again. Also, in Figure 1, shows the production losses during "set up" and "run up" periods.

Changeover activities are an essential tool of modern industries (Mileham, et al., 1999) to improve changeover times and at the same time increase the variety of products, and small volumes; they contribute to short time interventions that become economically viable.

4P's Model

On the other hand, Reik et al. (2006) presents a model of rapid changes that consider organizational and design factors to support the increase of capacity and flexibility in manufacturing processes to respond timely to the customer's needs (Reik et al., 2007). This Theoretical Model integrates, in turn, factors of Product design, Process Design, Human Resource (People) and Work Methods (Practice) and is known as the 4P's model as shown in Figure 2.

4P's model shows a positive influence and correlations between the constructs to solve the problem of the changeover activities effectiveness. However, to explain each P in the model is required the definition of measurable and observable variables. Figure 3, is shows the procedure for confirming factor analysis and establish the related hypotheses.

This chapter shows the first results for the validation of the model, which consists in the design and validation of a measurement instrument (Questionnaire) for data collection in the manufacturing sector in the state of Baja California, Mexico.

Figure 1. Shows the components of changeover process (Reik, et al., 2006)

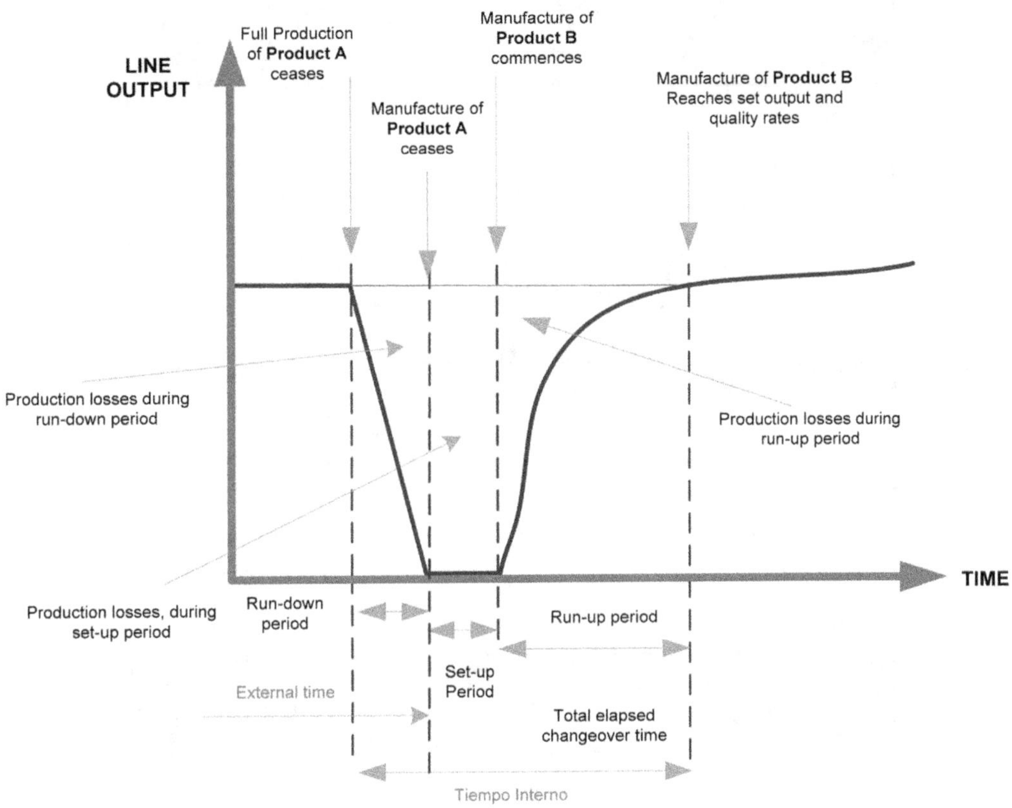

OPERATIONALIZATION OF 4P'S MODEL METHODOLOGY

Resources

1) Electronic databases. The first step consisted of an extensive review through several electronic databases and Journals such as IEEE, Elsevier, and Springer, among others; throwing 37 papers related to the analysis and applications of changeover methodologies. 73% of studied papers were published less than 5 years ago, and the others correspond to relevant references for the study.
2) Measurement instrument (Questionnaire): this step consisted on the instrument design from the review of the literature and the descriptive analysis of the variables that will be developed later, consisting of 79 items in 5 constructs: Changeover, processes, products, people, and practices.
3) Statistical programs. For the data processing and instrument, validation is used the software: *Statistical Package for the Social Sciences* (SPSS) version 25.

Figure 2. 4P's Theoretical Model for changeover activities (Reik et al., Part 2, 2006)

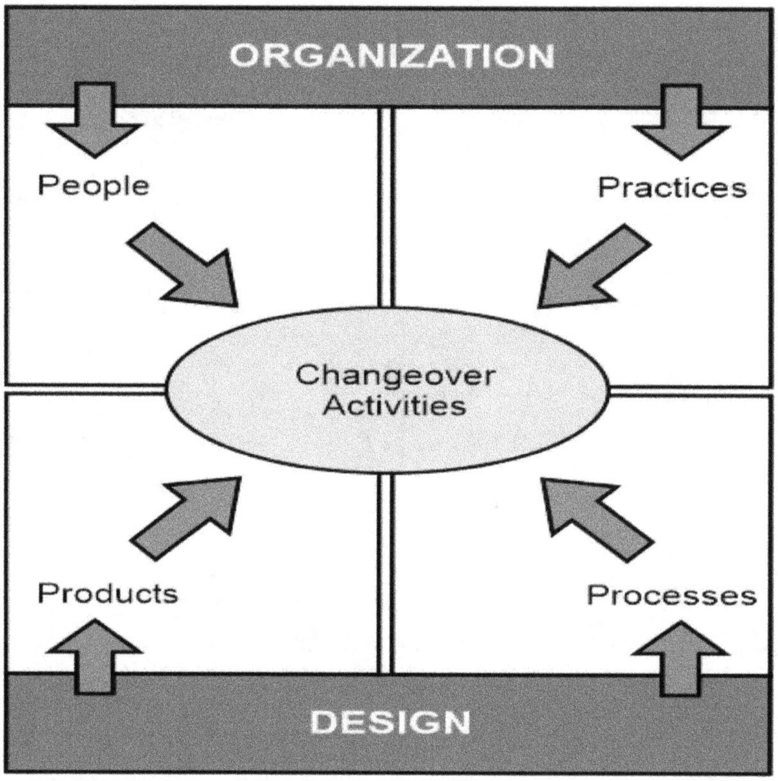

Methods

The initial model consists of 4 constructs, and a fifth construct was considered to identify the activities that make up the rapid changes and to evaluate the weights that they have on this construct, in the second stage of this investigation.0

1) **Variables Collection for each construct**. To identify the observable variables of five constructs and the changeover activities, 37 papers were select. Firstly, the variables that the authors highlighted as relevant in the application of rapid change methodologies were list using a matrix supported by Excel software. Then, all variables were group in each of the constructs empirically. Finally, were calculated the frequency and repetition percentage of each variable.
2) **Descriptive analysis of the variables (Operationalization)**. A descriptive analysis of the observable variables was realized for the characterization of the Theoretical 4P's model, considering the following 4 phases. (Cauas, 2015):
    - Representation of the concept of the latent variable (Construct). The construct is theoretically define, to be more understandable the relationship they have with the model.
    - Specification of each concept. The dimensions are recognize, being understand as the operative variables of the new model.
    - Selection of indicators. In this step, the observable indicators of the variables were select, now statistical methods can be apply.

Figure 3. Theoretical model of 4P's and their relationships. This model explains the six hypothetical positive relations for the efficient deployment of changeover activities.

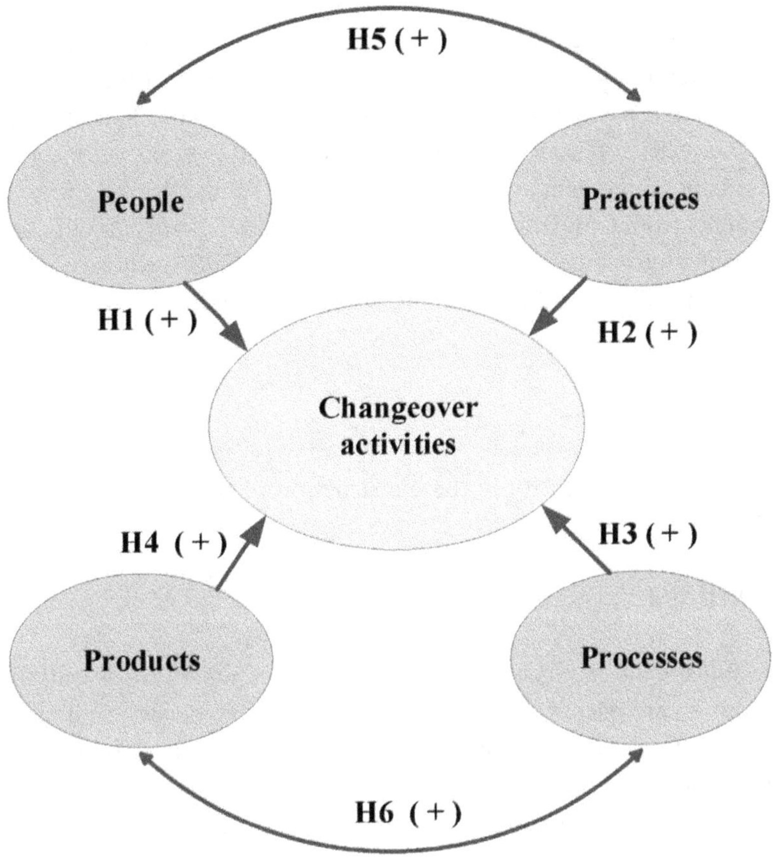

- Index: In this step, the criteria for measuring the indicators are establish, to determine their presence or absence, the respondent could choose between six options based on a Likert scale, from "totally disagree" to "totally agree".
- Design of the measuring instrument (Questionnaire). From the descriptive analysis of the variables, a questionnaire is formulate, composed of 79 questions divided into the 5 sections. A question was ask per indicator affirmatively, giving six options to answers according to the Lickert scale.
- Validation of the instrument. An analysis of the data validity and reliability of the questionnaire was develop to obtain higher reliability of the information gathered in the questionnaire. Data validation consisted of an evaluation of relevance of the items raised in the instrument, each indicator was evaluated using a scale from 1 to 6 points depending on the items relevance, where 1 is totally in disagreement, 2 strongly disagrees, 3 disagrees, 4 agrees, 5 strongly agrees, and 6 totally agrees, then, the relevance of the instrument was calculated using the following equation:

Relevance of the instrument = (Total Favorable Answers (4, 5, 6)) / (Total responses of the instrument)

In addition to these results, the reliability of the expert assessment was estimate through a statistical match test known as the Kendall's W Model. This model establishes that the following criteria must be met, W> 0 and the test statistic p-value <0.05 to obtain a matching value. This test is performed at a 95% reliability (Olmos & Mas, 2018) (Escobar & Cuervo, 2008), and it seeks to reject the null hypothesis, which states that there is no agreement among the evaluators. To test the reliability of the instrument a pilot run of 31 respondents from companies in the region was carried out, carrying out activities of rapid changes and the Cronbach alpha statistical test (α) was applied in SPSS, whose coefficient oscillates between 0 to 1, where the value closest to 1 is excellent, with $\alpha \geq 0.7$ being acceptable (Gómez et al., 2019).

VARIABLE IDENTIFICATION

Seven operational variables were identify in the construction of the changeover activities from the 37 papers selected for the factor's analysis.

Changeover Activities

Table 1 shows the variables of the changeover activities construct, which are essential tasks in the product changes and their execution are part of the efficiency of the change period, as it can be see, most of the authors highlight the separation of external and internal activities, adjustments and validation and control.

According to Reik, et al.(2006). In the 4P's model, these are affected by organizational and design factors. In the following section is described the operationalization of each construct.

Design Factors

It is necessary for the products designers and productive team to identify the variables involved in the changes of products to consider them from the early stages of design and contribute to efficiency in the production processes (Wiendahl, et al., 2007) also improves flexibility and production capacity and provides higher stability in product runs (McIntosh et al., 2000). These are considered instruments, tools,

Table 1. Variables of the changeover construct

Variable	Repetition rate	Repetition (%)
Adjustments	18	49
Assembly	15	41
Change planning	16	43
Disassembly	15	41
Mounting	16	43
Separation of internal and external activities	25	68
Validation and control	17	46

and products design, and production practices to improve the capacity for changeover (Reik, et al., part 2, 2006), allowing to simplify, eliminate or add elements to make model changes more efficient (Sugai et al., 2007). Table 2 shows the results of the analysis for the process construct, it can be observed that the variables with higher repetition rate and influence in changeover activities according to the authors are the "standardization", "exclusive tools of a manufacturer", "processes of changes manuals" and the "elements of settings used".

Regarding the evaluation of the "Product" construct, it has been find that the indicators more repetitive are "lot size", "cost price" and "quality specifications", as shown in table 3.

Organizational Factors

To be more productive, profitable and competitive, companies have to be committed to the effective use of resources and deploy the best practices, while maintaining a company-wide continuous improvement strategy. McIntosh, et al. (1996), analyze the works developed by Shigeo Shingo and determine that 36% of the difficulties in the changeover methodologies implementation are relate to aspects of an organizational type. Among the organizational factors, for instance, Van Goubergen, et al. (2002) reports that people performance depends mainly on their abilities and skills, as well as the use of the resources required to do the job. Table 4 presents more factors related to the construct "People".

Regarding the evaluation of the "Practice" construct, it has been found that the most frequent indicator are "organizational structure", "use of continuous improvement tools" and "Procedures tracking", as shows table 5.

Table 2. Construct "process" variables

Variable	Repetition rate	Repetition (%)	Variable	Repetition rate	Repetition (%)
Access to the machine or tools	18	49	Manual Process	19	51
Adjustment elements	19	51	Manufacturer's tools	26	70
Automation	11	30	Measurement (Times, losses, failures)	15	41
Cleaning	9	24	Modular Fixing System	3	8
Decreased effort	15	41	Monitoring equipment/ Scrap detection	9	24
Dependent task	3	8	Simplification	13	35
Driving	13	35	Standarization	30	81
Easily identify the pieces (color, engraving)	7	19	Subjection	4	11
Fast release devices	11	30	Systems tolerant to variation	3	8
Handling	9	24	Tools location	18	49
Lightweight materials	4	11	Transport of tools	16	43
Machine lines	4	11	Try and error systems	6	16
Maintenance	12	32	Universality	4	11

Table 3. Construct "product" variables

Variable	Repetition rate	Repetition (%)
Cost/price	14	38
Lot size	16	43
Product documentation	3	8
Quality specifications	12	32
Sizes variety	6	16
Standard product characteristics	8	22

Table 4. Construct "people" variables

Variable	Repetition rate	Repetition (%)
Commitment	9	24
Culture	5	14
Number of line workers	16	43
People's skills	21	57
Physical effort	4	11
Responsible for improvement projects	14	38
Specialization	14	38
Tasks quality	12	32
Teamwork (motivation, communication, leadership)	23	62
Training	27	73

Table 5. Construct "practice" variables

Variable	Repetition rate	Repetition (%)
Balance of workload	9	24
Company goals	7	19
Documented procedures	10	27
Environmental conditions	2	5
Organizational structure	28	76
Procedures tracking	11	30
Security	5	14
Supervision	13	35
Use of continuous improvement tools	18	49
Work sequence	9	24

Variable Operationalization

Because of this research, the following operationalization tables were obtain including the definition and characteristics of each indicator, as well as the scale used to measure them. Table 6 shows the operationalization and definitions corresponding to the changeover activities construct. It can be observed that the changeover activities construct is affected by 7 central activities described through a corresponding indicator.

The process construct is one of the most complex due to the number of activities and variables involved, in this research was find to be describe by 26 main activities, as is shown in table 7. This table presents the activities arranged alphabetically, a definition of each variable and how they can be measure.

The product construct is mainly influence by customer's specifications, standard characteristics and product cost as can be observed in table 8.

The People construct involves several activities related to social development such as motivation, commitment, leadership and communication; also, it must be consider the physical effort, employee's skills, specialization and training. In table 9, are show the activities studied in relation to people construct.

Table 6. Operationalization of the "changeover activities" construct

Variable	Definition	Indicator	Scale
Assembly	Parts that are coupled together or in several combinations to form the main component to produce product B.	Assembly time of the elements for the new product manufacture.	Interval
Disassembly	Includes the disintegration-useful parts linked to the last batch of product A, that is not required to manufacture a product B.	Time spent in dismantling or changing the elements unnecessary to fabricate a new product.	Interval
Mounting	It refers to the installation of the components in the machine or production equipment.	Installation time given to the clarity in the activities of location, orientation, temperature, speed, movements, cleaning, purging, etc.	Interval
Preparation: Planning the change	It is about ensuring that all the pieces, materials, utensils, etc. Are where they should be and prepared to work properly	Production Programs strategically planned and organized production. Control of external activities that have started in a timely manner.	Interval
Separation of activities in internals and externals	It refers to the classification of internal activities, which are the ones that require the team to be stop, affecting the productive time of the team. In addition, the external activities, which can be done with the machine in production, since they are executed outside the operation of the machine, not affecting the productive times.	Existence of classification and analysis of internal and external operations for the optimization of the changeover time	Interval
Settings / configuration	They are successive approximations for the achievement of manufacturing of the first pieces of product B.	Clearly in the criteria of adjustments in the process, to obtain the first good piece of product B.	Interval
Validation and control	They correspond to all the measurements and calibrations that must be carried out to begin the manufacture of product B, such as: centering, dimension adjustments, temperature measurements, pressure measurements, etc.	Existence of a validation and control of the set of adjusted values, as well as tests, quality controls and indicators of the set up.	Interval

The management of people is a key factor for achieving the goals of the organization, for which clear and well-structured work practices are required, in table 10 and efficiency in their activities.

MEASUREMENT INSTRUMENT DESIGN

Once the 5 constructs were operationalized, the measurement instrument was designed (questionnaire), being structured with 79 items, these items were written as affirmative statements, with the purpose that the research subject gave their degree of agreement or disagreement to the statement. For the measurement, a Likert scale of six categories (1 to 6) was used, where the value of 6 means totally in agreement and 1 totally disagrees. The constructs were construct in the following way:

- Construct "Activities of rapid changes", which refers to those tasks necessary to make the change, is integrated by 8 items.
- Construct "Processes", corresponding to a design factor, which refers to the technical and operative conditions of the machines, tools and production systems, was integrated into 26 items.

Table 7. Operationalization of the "process" construct

Variable	Definition	Indicators	Scale
Automation	Implementation of technologies and intelligent systems to manipulate, operate and control the equipment in the changeover. To exclude human activities that require greater effort or risks to the operators.	Change times in automated change processes.	Interval
Cleaning	Includes all the actions taken to keep organized and clean the workplace, equipment, machinery or tools. For example: remove oil, lubricants or dust; disinfect, sweep, vacuum and others.	Cleaning control of equipment, tools and work area.	Interval
Dependent tasks	Those tasks that depend on others to be performed	Independent tasks are performed which facilitate the simultaneous work between operators to speed up the change.	Interval
Adjustments elements	Accessories that assure dimensional requirements in the assembly of two pieces that adjust independently of their shape.	The equipment uses elements of adjustment such as single turn screws, one movement or combined methods, torque tools, washers, etc.	Interval
Equipment or tools access	The path taken from point A to point B to transport everything is required to perform the tasks of change.	It means clean access for transportation and equipment handling to make product changes.	Interval
Error proof systems	The mechanism that prevents human errors in processes from becoming defects. Fault-free mechanism (poka-yoke).	Error test systems (poka-yoke) are use to prevent errors and guarantee quality and security in activities of change.	Interval
Fastening devices	Devices with the purpose of keeping two or more elements tied to facilitate tasks.	Use fastening devices to keep objects fixed with minimum effort.	Interval
Handling	Refers to facility of modifications and withdraw of tools, pieces or equipment after being employ.	Use few change components.	Interval
Identification of pieces (color, engraving)	Refers to the easiness to recognize or differentiate necessary elements in the change. Normally they are classified or identified by color, finishing, etc.	Elements are classify and identify. Through visual inspection, you can know if there are the materials or tools necessary to carry out the change.	Interval
Materials light weighting	Refers to the use of low-density materials in modern molding design technologies, as well as in the manufacturing materials, in order to facilitate transport, handling, assembly, disassembly and maintenance that ensure accuracy and mechanical properties in production, that is, without sacrificing the quality parameters of the final product.	Lightweight materials are using in molds and equipment to facilitate the installation, transport and maintenance.	Interval
Location tools	Physical place where tools, parts or accessories are located for the changeover activities.	Control and organization of tools, parts and accessories necessaries to perform the tasks of the machine and/or equipment.	Interval
Machine lines	Structure where the equipment interconnects and share functional relations in the manufacturing process of a good, affecting in the times of change.	Production process configuration such as workshop, work centers, production in line, modular manufacturing, continuous manufacturing, etc.	Interval
Maintenance	Set of activities developed with the objective of ensure that any asset (machinery, instrument, etc.) continues to perform the desired functions.	There are maintenance plans and controls for equipment and tools	Interval

continues on following page

Table 7. Continued

Variable	Definition	Indicators	Scale
Manipulation	Refers to the actions taken by persons to alter or modify equipment, tools or others, needed to start-up of the productive processes.	Mechanisms and controls to assure and keep the precision in replacement parts and to guarantee the product quality.	Interval
Manual process	Set of activities developed manually by operators through traditional tools in a process of change.	Change times in manual activities.	Interval
Manufacturer´s tools	Tools and accessories that are property of the equipment manufacturers and cannot be replace or manipulate without its control.	Available equipment to handle accessories and tools that are exclusive of the manufacturer.	Interval
Measurement (Times, losses, failures)	Process by which a set of data is generated to evaluate objectively the performance of the tasks of change, for example: change times, wastes due to quality, quantity of failures, stoppages, etc.	Measurement and monitoring of indicators such as times of changes and resources used to start up the new product.	Interval
Minimize the effort	Requirement of the design to minimize movements, transportations and physical efforts by the operator when making a change in order to avoid accidents or work injuries.	Identification of complex and unsecure elements in the processes of change.	Interval
Modular fixing system	System that facilitate fixation of pieces, working material for a better manipulation, increase precision in assembly of product B.	Modular fixation systems are used to facilitate the assembly of machine parts.	Interval
Monitoring equipment/Scrap detection	Devices installed in strategic zones of the process that allow the record or detection of failures by means of sensors to supervise tasks in the process and avoid equipment faults or waste.	Failure control and waste separation and control.	Interval
Quick release devices	Devices that allow coupling or uncoupling of components in a simpler and safer way.	Quick release devices that facilitate change activities are present.	Interval
Simplification	Action of making the task easier.	a) Few mechanisms to perform activities of change exists and whole pieces' change or pipe connections are not necessary. b) Tools have few accessories and minimum manual tools are using in activities of change.	Interval
Standardization	Unification of components, tools, materials and others that are used in different processes in order to save money and time in the tasks of change.	Standardization of parts, tools, components, etc.	Interval
Tool Transportation	They are special elements for loading, used for the transportation of material, molds and tools, easily and safely to the work place, for example: Pallet Jack, cranes, forklifts, accessories carts, etc.	It has special transport elements to move materials and tools, such as Pallet Jack, portable cranes, accessories cart and transporters.	Interval
Universality	Attribute that allows tools, accessories, fixtures and pieces to be the same for all the processes.	Use of universal parts, tools and fixtures in different processes	Interval
Variation tolerant systems	System or equipment capable to work with more than one product model, adapting to their dimensions, weight, etc.	Identify equipment that can handle different product configuration.	Interval

Table 8. Operationalization of the "Product" construct

Variable	Definition	Characteristics	Scale
Lot Size	Refers to the quantity of pieces or products that are processed in the production system, which is fundamental for resource planning and influences the time and cost of configuration.	The size of lot affects the times of changeover activities.	Interval
Product Documentation	Documents including product details and their manufacture, as well as plans, drawings, work routs, materials, costs, manufacturing time, among others.	Clear product specifications (plans, drawings), which facilitate model changes.	Interval
Variety of sizes	Products differ in sizes but are part of the same family of products. Product A is of different size than product B. Is consider a minor configuration when the piece is part of the same family.	The unitary volume of the product (size) influences changeover activities.	Interval
Quality specifications	They are the technical specifications of the products, services and manufacturing processes to meet the client needs. These parameters are monitor along the manufacturing process.	a) The product quality specifications affect the times of rapid changes b) The different configurations of the products have an effect in the times of rapid changes.	Interval
Standard characteristics of product	They are the characteristics or attributes of the products and are link to client specifications. Managing different product implies more time in the process of change, starting with the acquisition of the materials, preparing the equipment in a specific way, documentation, storing and saving all the previous product components, etc.	a) The characteristics of the product (components, dimensions, forms, functions, parameters) influence in the times of rapid changes. b) The variety of products have an effect in the times of rapid changes.	Interval
Product cost	Investment on the manufacturing of the product, which is composed of the cost of labor, materials and indirect costs (amortization of machinery, indirect labor, fuel, etc.).	Perform improvement actions to reduce manufacturing costs of products.	Interval

- Construct "Product", the other P of Design, which have to do with the conditions and characteristics of the product in the impact of the activities of rapid changes, was integrated by 7 items.
- Construct "People", which is part of the factors of the organization, and refers to the indicators that have to do with the human factor, 17 items integrated this.
- 21 items formed construct "Practice", second P of the organization, which corresponds to the practices performed by the company for the achievement of improvement projects.
- Finally, a block of general questions was add such as company sector, hierarchical position, size of the company, among others, with the purpose of carrying out a descriptive study to determine areas of opportunity in the different sectors. The designed measurement instrument is aim at the personnel of the companies that are involved in the activities of model changes.

Pilot Test

A pilot test was carried out in manufacturing companies in the Tijuana Baja California region, which carry out rapid change activities, this was carried out through a non-probabilistic sample, since the application of the instrument depended on the accessibility of the company, in the following table 11, It shows the distribution of the 31 surveys applied, the company turns, the number of surveys applied and the percentage of participation that was taken from each industrial sector.

Table 9. Operationalization of the "people" construct

Variable	Definition	Indicators	Scale
Commitment	Capacity that a person has to become aware of the importance that exists in fulfilling something previously agreed before.	The personnel in charge of carrying out the activities is committed and understands clearly the importance of carrying out the activity in the shortest time.	Interval
Number of operators	Persons assigned to the management and control of operational parameters in the production process. This assignment arises from an analysis of operations.	The number of people involved in rapid change activities is enough to achieve efficiency in times of change	Interval
People's skills	The skill or ability that a person must carry out and successfully, a certain activity or work.	a) The team in charge of model changes has professional skills and experience. b) People involved in rapid change activities have the capacity and willingness to perform various tasks in the processes of change (poly functionality).	Interval
Physical effort	Activity in which, in response to the demands of a task, the operator sets up a series of resources / capacities / abilities, etc. in order to satisfy the requirements that are required.	The workload of the people involved in the team is adequate.	Interval
Quality of the tasks	Efforts made by people to meet the characteristics required in the team, product or organization, efficiently and productive.	a) The quality with which the individual tasks are perform in the sequence of activities of the changeover influences the time in which the team is available to run the model without generating waste and fulfilling the requirements. b) The workers' culture (values, beliefs, customs, knowledge, etc.) have a positive influence on the quality of tasks, teamwork and motivation.	Interval
Responsible for improvement projects	The leader in continuous improvement projects, who actively participates with the people to achieve productivity and efficiency of the processes.	The person responsible for directing, managing or administering rapid change projects collaborate in planning, monitoring, resource management, supervision, coordination of personnel, generate statistics, solve incidents and problems and communicate results efficiently.	Interval
Specialization	It refers to the extensive knowledge that a person has of a specific topic or work, which implies limitations for the change of roles or support with multiple tasks.	Identify people with more specialization in the performance of tasks.	Interval
Teamwork (motivation, communication, leadership)	It is the union of two or more people, who share efforts, attitudes, skills and knowledge in the work to achieve a common goal, requires leadership and effective communication. An efficient and harmonious union increases motivation and retains talent in the company.	a) The staff works in, sharing knowledge and skills, which is reflect in the reduction of time of tasks and greater efficiency of work. b) Staff motivation positive impact on the performance of activities of rapid change, mainly in the quality of their work. c) The verbal, written and visual communication between the people involved in the activities of rapid changes is an important factor for the accomplishment of the tasks. d) The leadership of those responsible for rapid change projects motivate people and clarify the objectives for a favorable performance.	Interval
Training	These labor education activities prepare the worker, with the purpose of being able to develop a position or function within an organization, with greater efficiency.	a) The people involved in implementing the changeover have a training program to handle the equipment and use tools. b) All those involved in the implementation of changeover know the process of product changes. c) The persons in charge of changeover know the operation and maintenance of the tools and equipment.	Interval

Table 10. Operationalization of the practice construct

Variable	Definition	Indicators	Scale
Organizational structure	It is the way in which each member of an organization takes a role in the activities that are done to achieve the goals and objectives set. This structure allows establishing rules of action, allocation of resources, efficiency in tasks and measuring the performance of the organization, for the improvement of technical and administrative processes.	a) There is a clear organizational structure that allows each person know their role and responsibilities. b) Top management supports the implementation of rapid change projects. c) There is a specific area or group for the continuous improvement of the company's processes, and from there the problems and the reduction of equipment times are consider and addressed.	Interval
Processes documented	It is the detailed documentation of the activities developed in a work environment; they represent the action guides and avoid operational errors, such as factors of time, effort, security, among others.	a) The company has a culture of quality assurance and documents have their operational processes. b) Every improvement actions are document and the procedure of the task is update. c) The times of the tasks or activities have been identify, documented, assigned and measured, which facilitates the development and avoids errors. d) There are controls for measuring and controlling incidents, readjustments, failures, etc., which facilitates process improvement actions.	Interval
Supervision	Set of activities (assessment, guidance, advice, monitoring, inspection, etc.) that a person exercises in relation to others, over which he has some authority within the organization.	The responsible person directs, manages, collaborates, follows up, guides, coordinates the staff, generates statistics, solves problems and communicates the results efficiently.	Interval
Procedures tracking	Set of actions to verify the correct execution of the activities, previously documented, so that they can be measured and take appropriate actions to the process. The staff follows systematically the tasks contained in the documents.	S and follow procedures in the order and sequence indicated in tasks change.	Interval
Work sequence	It consists of activities that are executed together with the time (hours) / priorities and other dependencies that determine the order of the process.	a) Identify the activities / tasks that have immediate origin. b) There is a procedure to change the daily production plan so as not to affect the resources of the company.	Interval
Use of tools for continuous improvement	These tools are useful to look for weak points in the processes, products or services developed. Some focus on identifying the areas of improvement with the highest priority, to minimize time and make the necessary changes.	a) In the process of improvement, tools are used for the analysis of how 5 whys, Pareto diagrams, cause-effect diagrams, PDCA cycle, and control charts, among others that help to identify areas of opportunity in change activities. b) Complementary techniques are used to improve processes such as 5's, Poke Yoke, Just in Time, TPM, Kanban, DMAIC, Value Chain Mapping, Standardized Work, Kaizen, among others that support the efficiency of change times. c) The implementation of several methodologies of continuous improvement at the same time drive the activities of rapid change.	Interval

continues on following page

Table 10. Continued

Variable	Definition	Indicators	Scale
Environment	Are the conditions present in the environment where the product or service provision is obtain that influence the motivation, satisfaction and quality of the tasks?	Identify the best conditions for the work environment.	Interval
Objectives of the company	It refers to the goals that a company aims to achieve in a given period of time and with the resources available.	a) There are strategic objectives to reduce change times, increase the availability of the machine or equipment and reduce costs related to exchange activities. b) There are established objectives to reduce waste caused by rapid change activities. c) There is financial support for the implementation of improvements in the equipment, tools, work area, etc. that simplifies and improves the quality	Interval
Security	It is a set of techniques and procedures applied in the labor areas, in order to minimize or eliminate the risks derived from the work.	a) Availability of protective equipment for the safety of the personnel that performs the tasks. b) Only the tools, materials and means of control established to make the change are used.	Interval
Balance of workload	It is the amount of responsibility or tasks assigned to an area or staff, which must be relate to the capacity and number of activities to be developed, to achieve efficiency and a favorable work environment.	The roles of people who participate in rapid change activities are assign according to their experience, knowledge and skills, which allows for greater results in the process.	Interval

Table 11. Participation of types of companies in the pilot test

Industrial Sector	Surveyed	% participation
Medical	7	23%
Aeroespace	6	16%
Alimentary	2	6%
Electronics	3	10%
Metalworking	8	26%
Automotive	4	19%
Total	**31**	**100%**

The subject of study within the company was select as that person who was relate to the change process, considering in the analysis managers, engineers, technicians, supervisors and operators, since all of them have influence with the variables that are analyze in questionnaire. In this pilot, 61.29% was represent by responses from technicians, who have a greater impact on the product startup process as shown in figure 4.

Validation of the Instrument

The measurement instrument is presented to 2 types of analysis to measure its performance, the first call, the duration of the content and a second reliability of the instrument.

Figure 4. Distribution of respondent results according to the role in the change process

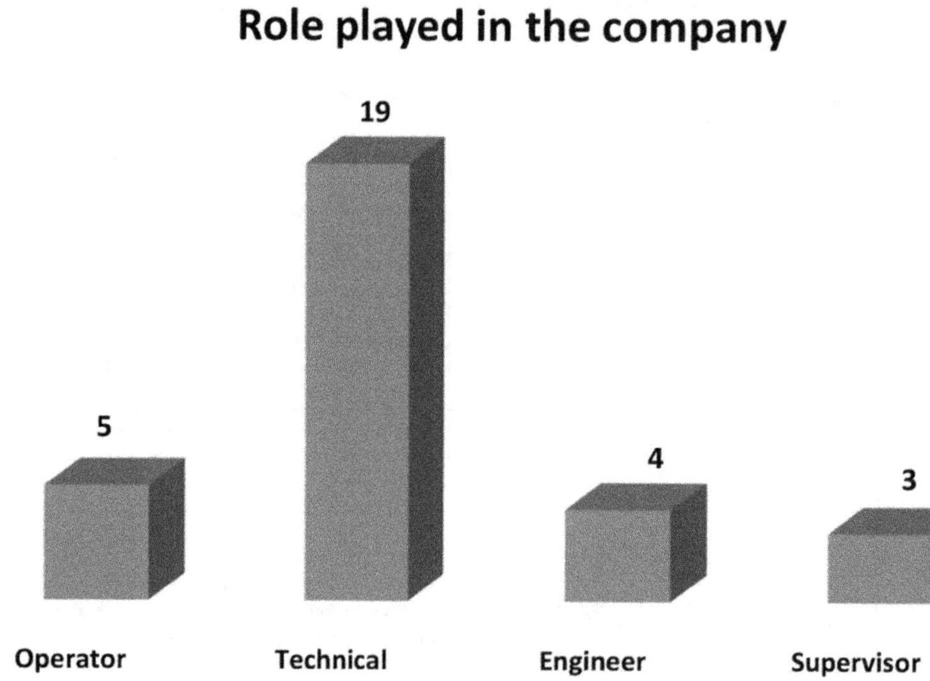

The validity of content. It consisted in an evaluation of the importance of the elements raised in the instrument by 6 experienced judges, with more than 10 years of experience in the activities of changes in the manufacture industry of the region, where it was evaluated with an escalation from 1 to 6 points the relevance of the questions. In the following figure 5, you can see the scores given by each evaluator to each of the questions, clearly noting that the majority is above 4 points.

The total answers that obtained a score greater than or equal to 4 points were count, with the objective of calculating the total relevance of the measurement instrument, obtaining a total relevance of 94.93%, according to equation 1. What we can conclude, that the evaluators consider the questions contained in the questionnaire relevant

$$Relevance\ of\ the\ instrument = \frac{450}{474} = 0.9493 \times 100 = 94.93\% \tag{1}$$

To give more confidence to the design of the instrument, an agreement of expert judgment was analyze, through the Kendall test, which contrasts two statistical hypotheses with a 95% reliability. The hypotheses are evaluate by the P-value. Where values below 0.05 provide strong evidence to reject the null hypothesis and consequently accept the alternate, together with this we obtain the coefficient of W of Kendall that measures the strength of the agreement (W> 0) closest to 1 greater concordance.

Expert Judgment Concordance Hypothesis:

H_0, There is no significant agreement among the evaluators regarding the items contained in the 4Ps measurement instrument for changeovers.

Figure 5. Score of the evaluators to the questionnaire items

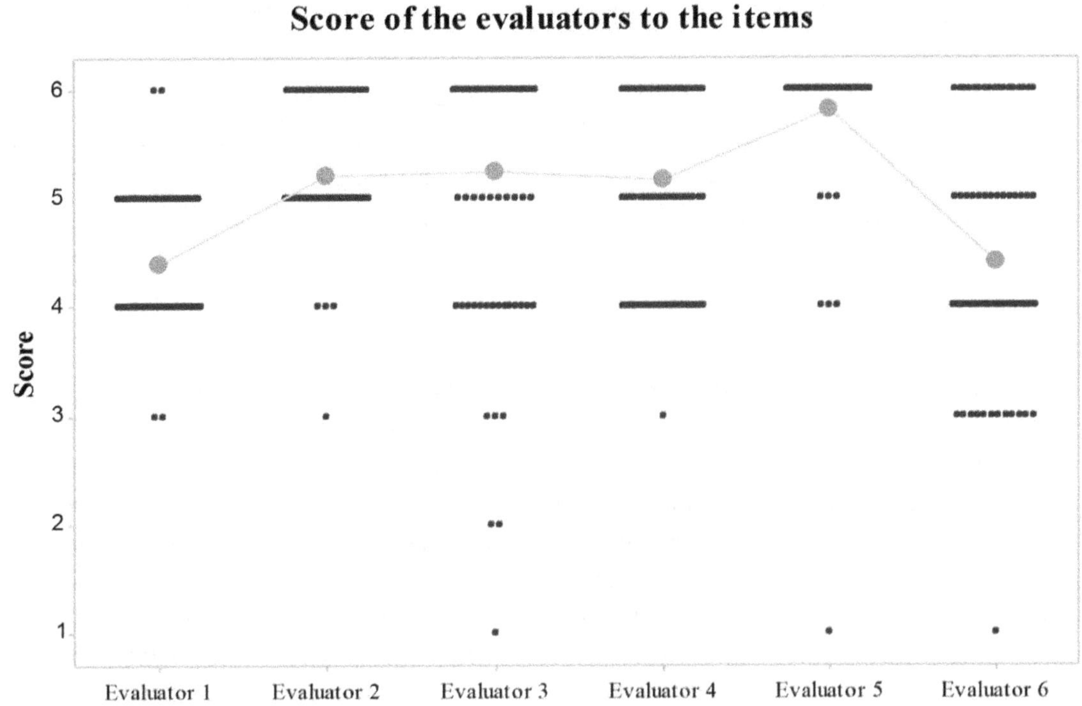

H_A, There is a significant agreement among the evaluators in relation to the items contained in the 4Ps measurement instrument for changeovers.

Table 12, is shows a P value of 0.029, indicating that there is enough statistical evidence to reject the null hypothesis (H_0) and conclude through the alternative hypothesis (HA), that there is a significant agreement between the evaluators in relation to the questions contained in the instrument with a weight of W = 0.2208

Reliability of the Instrument. From the data obtained in the pilot test, in SPSS the reliability of the instrument was analyze through the Cronbach alpha statistic, resulting in a value of 0.974 with the 79 items analyzed. What the instrument is quite consistent to measure the 4Ps of rapid change activities. Gómez, et al., (2019), mentions that the closer the Cronbach coefficient is to 1, the more reliable the instrument is, being acceptable greater than 0.7. The following table 13 shows the Cronbach coefficients by construct, being reliable to gather information to validate the hypotheses of the model of the 4Ps, defined in Figure 2.

Table 12. Kendall concordance indicators of changeover instrument

W	Chi-square	Freedom degrees	P-Value
0.220807	103.338	78	0.029

Table 13. Reliability indicators by construct of the 4Ps model

Construct	Cronbach Alpha
Changeover activities	0.872
Process	0.934
Product	0.763
People	0.910
Practice	0.934

CONCLUSION

The needs of the productive sectors to be more efficient in the application of methodologies to improve their processes, is increasingly necessary. With more demanding markets, a modern manufacturing is required that involves the manufacture of small lots and a great variety of product models; this implies that the times of changes have to be shorter and, to the same extent, reduce the costs associated with them, so. Therefore, it is necessary to know the relative effect of the factors that influence these activities. Design factors and organizational factors play an important role because they are the basis of operational and administrative decisions within the company, as Reik proposes in its model of the 4Ps. As a result, this article shows the design of a measurement instrument, based on the operationalization of each of the P's so that, in this way, improvement strategies are made to reduce the model change times.

The results presented correspond to the first stage of the research project, which is the design and validation of the measuring instrument for rapid change activities, as seen in the results of the evaluations, the instrument is relevant for changeover experts and complies Kendall's statistical hypothesis of agreement, in addition to having internal reliability, which was demonstrated with the Cronbach's alpha of 0.974 when conducting the pilot test in the industrial sector of Baja California. In the following stages of this project, the instrument will be applied to a sample of at least 300 people, and the statistical hypotheses of relations of the Reik model will be demonstrated, by means of a confirmatory analysis with the technique of structural equations.

FUTURE RESEARCH DIRECTIONS

In the future work, the validation of the statistical 4P's Changeover Model, the use of Structural Equations to find the relationships and the weights of each hour will be presented. The changeover activities, which will be a contribution to the theoretical model of Reik and a useful tool for continuous improvement for companies in the region.

ACKNOWLEDGMENT

Yuridia Vega appreciates the economic support and the facilities given by the Autonomous University of Baja California to execute this research.

REFERENCES

Abhijeet, Abhishek, Akash, Abhishek, & Swapnil. (2016). *Set up time reduction by using SMED and Kaizen approach.* Academic Press.

Adanna, I. W., & Shantharam, A. (2013). *Improvement of Setup Time and Production Output with the use of Single Minute Exchange of Die Principles.* Academic Press.

Bajpai, J. D. (2014). SMED (Single-Minute Exchange of Die) methodology in Garment manufacturing Industry : Case study in reducing Style Change over. *Time*, 1–7.

Benjamin, S. J., Murugaiah, U., & Marathamuthu, M. S. (2013). The use of SMED to eliminate small stops in a manufacturing firm. *Journal of Manufacturing Technology Management, 24*(5), 792–807. doi:10.1108/17410381311328016

Cakmakci, M., & Karasu, M. K. (2007). Set-up time reduction process and integrated predetermined time system MTM-UAS: A study of application in a large size company of automobile industry. *International Journal of Advanced Manufacturing Technology, 33*(3–4), 334–344. doi:10.100700170-006-0466-x

Cauas, D. (2015). *Definición de las variables, enfoque y tipo de investigación* (No. Recuperado el Vol. 15). Universidad Nacional Abierta y a Distancia (UNAD). Retrieved from http://www.mecanicahn.com/personal/marcosmartinez/seminario1/los_pdf/l-Variables.pdf

Chabowski, P., Rewers, P., & Trojanowska, J. (2016). Impact of shortening changeover times on manufacturing flexibility. *Technological Forum 2016*, 1–7.

Costa, E., Sousa, R., Bragança, S., & Alves, A. (2013). An industrial application of the SMED methodology and other lean production tools. *4th International Conference on Integrity, Reliability and Failure of Mechanical Systems, 1*(i), 1–8. 10.13140/2.1.2099.5525

Dave, Y., & Sohani, N. (2012). Single Minute Exchange of Dies: Literature Review. *International Journal of Lean Thinking, 3*(2), 27–37.

Escobar Pérez, J., & Cuervo Martínez, Á. (2008, Jan.). Validez de contenido y juicio de expertos: una aproximación a su utilización. *Avances En Medición*, 27–36. doi:10.1016/j.eatbeh.2007.10.005

Faccio, M. (2013). Setup time reduction: SMED-balancing integrated model for manufacturing systems with automated transfer. *IACSIT International Journal of Engineering and Technology, 5*(5), 4075–4084.

Gade, P. A., Chavan, R. G., & Bhavsar, D. N. (2016). Reduction In Setup Time By Single Minute Exchange Of Dies (SMED) Methodology. *International Journal of Scientific & Technology Research, 5*(06), 6–8.

Gaikwad, S. P., Avhad, S. S., Pawar, S. S., & Thorat, P. R. (2015). Reduction in Setup time on Rubber Moulding Machine using SMED Technique. *International Journal of Engineering Research & Technology, 4*(04), 169–173.

García Torres, A., & Hernández, M. F. M. (2013). Reducción de tiempos de set-up a través de la técnica SMED en una línea. XII Encuentro. *Participación de La Mujer En La Ciencia*, (1985), 1–5.

Gómez del Pulgar García Madrid, M., Hernández-Iglesias, S., Crespo Cañizares, A., Pérez Martín, A. M., González Jurado, M. A., & Beneit Montesinos, J. V. (2019). Fiabilidad de una escala para la evaluación de competencias enfermeras: estudio de concordancia. *Educación Médica*. doi:10.1016/j.edumed.2018.12.002

Guzmán Ferradás, P., & Salonitis, K. (2013). Improving changeover time: A tailored SMED approach for welding cells. *Procedia CIRP*, *7*, 598–603. doi:10.1016/j.procir.2013.06.039

Hicks, B. J., & Matthews, J. (2010). The barriers to realising sustainable process improvement: A root cause analysis of paradigms for manufacturing systems improvement. *International Journal of Computer Integrated Manufacturing*, *23*(7), 585–602. doi:10.1080/0951192X.2010.485754

Karim, R. (2013). Impact of Changeover time on productivity: A case study. *International Journal of Engineering & Technology IJET-IJENS*, *13*(06), 42–48.

Kumar, V., & Bajaj, A. (2015). The Implementation of Single Minute Exchange of Die with 5 ' S in Machining Processes for reduction of Setup Time. *International Journal on Recent Technologies in Mechanical and Electrical Engineering*, *2*(2), 32–39.

Madhav, R. (2016). *Managing changeover waste in manufacturing plants when using single minute exchange of dies*. University of Johannesburg.

Mcintosh, R., Culley, S., Gest, G., Mileham, T., & Owen, G. (1996). An assessment of the role of design in the improvement of changeover performance. *International Journal of Operations & Production Management*, *16*(9), 5–22. doi:10.1108/01443579610125552

McIntosh, R. I., Culley, S. J., Mileham, A. R., & Owen, G. W. (2001). Changeover improvement: A maintenance perspective. *International Journal of Production Economics*, *73*(2), 153–163. doi:10.1016/S0925-5273(00)00170-5

Mileham, A. R., Culley, G. W., Owen, G. W., & McIntosh, R. I. (1999). Rapid changeover - a prerequisite for responsive manufacture. *International Journal of Operations & Production Management*, *19*(8), 785–796. doi:10.1108/01443579910274383

Mileham, A.R, Culley, S. J., Owen, G. W., Newnes, L. B., & Giess, M. D. (2005). *The impact of run-up in ensuring Rapid Changeover*. Academic Press.

Morales Méndez, J., & Silva Rodríguez, R. (2015). Set-up reduction in an interconnection axle manufacturing cell using SMED. *International Journal of Advanced Manufacturing Technology*, *84*(9–12), 1907–1916. doi:10.100700170-015-7845-0

Musa, M. A., Ibrahim, A. M., Ravi, S., Abidin, Z. F. Z., & Wan Mat, W. A. (2013). A case study and analysis of setup reduction for stamping dies - SMED approach. *Global Engineers & Technologists Review*, *4*(1), 1–9.

Olmos Rueda, P., & Mas Torelló, Ó. (2018). Validación de AUTOCOM: Autoevaluación de las competencias básicas de jóvenes en el marco de programas formativos de segunda oportunidad. *Revista Electrónica de Investigación Educativa*, *20*(4), 49. doi:10.24320/redie.2018.20.4.1674

Palanisamy, S., & Siddiqui, S. (2013). Changeover Time Reduction and Productivity Improvement by Integrating Conventional SMED Method with Implementation of MES for Better Production Planning and Control. International Journal of Innovative Research in Science. *Engineering and Technology*, *2*(12), 7961–7974.

Pawar, G. J., Sirdeshpande, N. S., Atram, A. B., & Patil, P. R. (2014). Reduction in setup change time of a machine in a bearing manufacturing plant using SMED and ECRS. *International Journal of Engine Research*, *3*(5), 321–323. doi:10.17950/ijer/v3s5/506

Pawłyszyn, I., Agnieszka, S., & Hadaś, Ł. (2014). Application of Smed Methodology in a Printing-House. *Research in Logisb*, *4*(4), 357–368.

Pinto, J. P. (2008). Lean Thinking - Introdução ao pensamento magro. *Comunidade Lean Thinking*, *159–163*. doi:10.1002/9780470759660.ch27

Reik, M., McIntosh, R., Owen, G., Mileham, A., & Culley, S. (2005). The development of a systematic design for changeover methodology. *International Conference on Engineering Design, ICED'05*, 1–26.

Reik, M., Owen, G., Cully, S., McIntosh, R., & Mileham, T. (2007). Integrating product and manufacturing systems design to minimise changeover losses. *International Conference on Engineering Design, ICED'07, 441*, 1–9. Retrieved from http://opus.bath.ac.uk/1551/

Reik, M. P., Mcintosh, R. I., Culley, S. J., Mileham, A. R., & Owen, G. W. (2006). A formal design for changeover methodology. Part 1: Theory and background. *Proceedings of the Institution of Mechanical Engineers. Part B, Journal of Engineering Manufacture*, *220*(8), 1225–1235. doi:10.1243/09544054JEM527

Reik, M. P., McIntosh, R. I., Culley, S. J., Mileham, A. R., & Owen, G. W. (2006). A formal design for changeover methodology. Part 2: Theory and background. *Proceedings of the Institution of Mechanical Engineers. Part B, Journal of Engineering Manufacture*, *220*(8), 1225–1235. doi:10.1243/09544054JEM527

Riippa, L. (2016). *Measuring and Improving Production Efficiency of Paint Filling and Packing Line*. LUT School of Business and Management Industrial.

Rodríguez Méndez, R., Sánchez Partida, D., Martínez Flores, J. L., & Arvizu Barrón, E. (2015). A case study: SMED & JIT methodologies to develop continuous flow of stamped parts into AC disconnect assembly line in Schneider Electric Tlaxcala Plant. *IFAC-PapersOnLine*, *48*(3), 1399–1404. doi:10.1016/j.ifacol.2015.06.282

Schreuder, N. W. (2014). *Maximizing flexibility through minimizing changeover time*. Universiteit Twente. Retrieved from http://essay.utwente.nl/65172/

Singh, J., & Brar, G. S. (2017). Process improvement and setup time reduction in manufacturing industry : A case study. *IJAMR*, *9*(1), 15–23.

Stadnicka, D. (2015). Setup analysis: Combining SMED with other tools. *Management and Production Engineering Review*, *6*(1), 36–50. doi:10.1515/mper-2015-0006

Sugai, M., McIntosh, R. I., & Novaski, O. (2007). Metodologia de Shigeo Shingo (SMED): Análise crítica e estudo de caso. *Gestão & Produção*, *14*(2), 323–335. doi:10.1590/S0104-530X2007000200010

Teran Somohano, A., & Smith, A. E. (2013). A setup reduction methodology from lean manufacturing for development of meta-heuristic algorithms. *2013 IEEE Congress on Evolutionary Computation, CEC 2013*, 3132–3139. 10.1109/CEC.2013.6557952

Van Goubergen, D., & Van Landeghem, H. (2002). Rules for integrating fast changeover capabilities into new equipment design. *Robotics and Computer-integrated Manufacturing*, *18*(3), 205–214. doi:10.1016/S0736-5845(02)00011-X

Wiendahl, H. P., ElMaraghy, H. A., Nyhuis, P., Zäh, M. F., Wiendahl, H. H., Duffie, N., & Brieke, M. (2007). Changeable Manufacturing - Classification, Design and Operation. *Annals of the CIRP*, *56*(2), 783–809. doi:10.1016/j.cirp.2007.10.003

Chapter 11

Determination of the Critical Success Factors of Philosophies, Techniques, and Tools for Continuous Improvement Applied in the Service Sector

Karla F. Madrigal
Universidad Autonoma de Ciudad Juarez, Mexico

Salvador A. Noriega Morales
https://orcid.org/0000-0001-7813-5835
Universidad Autonoma de Ciudad Juarez, Mexico

Erwin Martinez Gomez
https://orcid.org/0000-0002-7753-2545
Universidad Autonoma de Ciudad Juarez, Mexico

Vianey Torres-Arguelles
https://orcid.org/0000-0003-0978-3796
Universidad Autonoma de Ciudad Juarez, Mexico

Roberto Romero López
https://orcid.org/0000-0003-0859-327X
Universidad Autonoma de Ciudad Juarez, Mexico

ABSTRACT

At the global level, the service industry represents a critical component for the economy and its growth trend is above of the other sectors. This sector alone is responsible for 63% of the gross domestic product and 45.5% of labor occupation worldwide. Despite its role in modern economies, the sector receives very little attention. In the literature, the authors have found the efforts that have been made to increase the efficiency and productivity of this type of organizations: adapting philosophies, tools, and/or techniques that were born to achieve this goal in the manufacturing industry, such as Lean manufacturing, total quality management, six sigma, lean six sigma, among others. The objective of this study is to perform an exhaustive literature review of the critical success factors reported in diverse studies of the implementation of these tools or philosophies in the service sector, as well as their differences, similarities, and results.

DOI: 10.4018/978-1-7998-1052-0.ch011

INTRODUCTION

In the last three decades there has been a continuous evolution of the services sector in the developed economies modifying the structure of employment and the generation of added value (Maroto Sánchez, 2010).

The services are the main income source of developed economies as well as the major employment generators (Piercy & Rich, 2009), representing 63% of the world´s gross domestic product. With regard to the gross domestic product generated by this sector, Table 1 shows the percentage that contributes to the gross domestic product of some of the most important economies in the world. As you can notice in this information, this sector also plays an important role in developing economies.

Regarding generation of jobs, this sector represents 70% of the total in the developed economies (Maroto Sánchez, 2010).

The efficiency and the effectiveness are starting to grasp greater importance within the organizations of this kind (Suárez-Barraza, Smith, & Dahlgaard-Park, 2012), because these can be a key factor for the country's growth and economic competitiveness.

Despite the important role it has in modern economies, the sector receives little attention in all aspects. According with Piercy and Rich (2009) the services quality does not meet the level required by customers. The traditional perception of services as unproductive remains a paradigm in today's society (Maroto Sánchez, 2010). Therefore the productivity in this sector is far below when compared to that of the manufacturing industry, e.g. in the 1981 – 1990 period the growth factor of the services sector was 0.1% yearly compared to the 3% of the manufacturing industry (Suárez-Barraza, Smith, & Dahlgaard-Park, 2012).

On the other hand, globalization represents a challenge for the survival of every organization of any kind because of the intense competition, consequently, they are searching new approaches to improve efficiency as well as to remain as market leaders. These organizations are faced with different challenges for instance; cost reduction, quality improvement, flexibility for changes, delivery time reduction, among others, all of which obliges organizations to innovate the way how they execute their processes.

The manufacturing industry has been the pioneer to face these challenges (Hadid & Afshin Mansouri, 2014). Thus, they have invested in the systemic exploration of process improvement opportunities, cost reduction, and efficiency improvement. As a result, numerous innovative tools and philosophies have been developed (De Koning, Does, & Bisgaard, 2008). Philosophies and methodologies based on continuous improvement, in quality, and also in productivity, for instance: Lean Manufacturing, Total Quality Management, Six Sigma, Lean Six Sigma.

Table 1. GDP by sector of origin

PPP GDP 2017	Agriculture	Industry	Service
European Union	1,6%	25,1%	70,9%
United States	0,9%	19,1%	80,0%
China	7,9%	40,5%	51,6%
India	15,4%	23,0%	61,5%
Mexico	3,6%	31,9%	64,5%

Source: https://www.cia.gov/library/publications/resources/the-world-factbook/fields/214.html#XX

As a consequence of the success of these philosophies and methodologies, the service sector has adapted/tailored them with the purpose of increasing efficiency and productivity of their organizations.

The objective of this study is to identify which tools or philosophies or both developed for the manufacturing industry are being employed in the service sector, in addition, to review the critical success factors reported in diverse studies of the implementation of these tools or philosophies in the service sector, as well as their differences, similarities, and results.

To achieve the objective of this study, a literature review was carried out which focused on the search and analysis of the information, in the period of the year 2000 to date. The search was conducted in various databases, such as Elsevier, IIIE, Emerald, EBSCO, Springer, mainly; In addition, the academic Google database was used as a more general reference. The information on which the results are obtained was limited to the free access articles.

The search was divided into several stages, each one focused on a specific tool and / or technique. In this way the articles found in the following categories were classified; lean services, "six sigma", "lean six sigma", "TQM", and others. The keywords used in the search were one or the combination of several of the following; "Lean", "service sector", "service industry", "six sigma", "lean six sigma", "TQM", "productivity", "CSF", "methodologies", "framework, trying in all searches to include the words "services sector" or "service industry".

Background

The service sector has seen the need to improve its efficiency to become competitive, for this reason it has used the tools / philosophies for continuous improvement that were developed for the manufacturing industry (Madrigal, Martinez, Torres-Arguelles, & Beltran, 2017). The manufacturing tools or philosophies utilized in the services sector found in the literature research were as follows: Lean Six Sigma, Lean Services, Total Quality Management, and Six Sigma; quality practices, and specific tools are considered in the "Other" category. Figure 1 shows the classified papers.

The majority of reported articles correspond to the philosophy known as "lean services" 65 out of a universe of 188 papers corresponds to this category.

Additionally, a relevant information is to determine what are the type of businesses most researched about this subject. The business type were classified as follows: a) healthcare, b) airports/airlines, c) hospitality, d) retailers (supermarkets), e)telecommunications, f) information technologies, g) public sector/government, h) logistics services, i) financial services, j) information services, k)call centers, l) consulting services.

The type of business representing the highest number of cases of study is about the deployment of these tools and philosophies in the medical industry with a 36%, followed by information technologies with a 12%. In third place with 11% financial services, followed by the public sector with a 10% and hospitality industry representing 9%. The rest of the categories are situated in the 1% to 5% threshold.

The following part shows what is found in the literature for each of these tools and / or philosophies in the service sector.

In the case of the philosophy of Lean Services, the topics reported in the literature were; 1) case studies with a total of 42 articles, 2) Definitions, frameworks of Lean Services with 8 articles, 3) Implementation of Lean in services with 6 articles, 4) Literature review with 4 articles and finally 5) Lean assessment with 3 papers. Within the case studies the most mentioned organizations correspond to healthcare in the first place with 18 articles, followed by information technologies and the public sector with 6 and

Figure 1. Number of papers by category

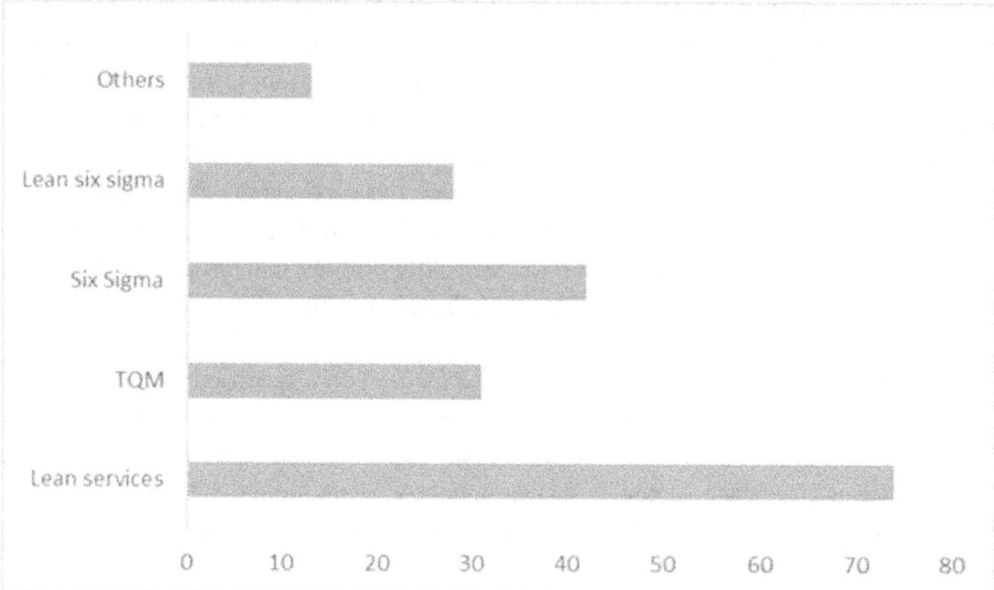

5 articles respectively. The country that is mentioned most in the works was UK, and there are articles from Colombia, Malaysia, Mexico, United States, Spain, Italy, India, Colombia and Switzerland all of them with a single mention. Among these works, a total of 3 articles were found where statistics are used to establish relationships between the factors and the implementation of lean services. Among the techniques mentioned are Structural Modeling Equation with two articles (G. K. Kundu & Bairi, 2014; Noori, 2015) and another article where it is mentioned Partial Least Square - Structural Model Equation (Hadid, Mansouri, & Gallear, 2016).

In the case of the TQM tool, the topics mentioned in the 31 articles found were: 1) critical success factors in the implementation of TQM for organizations with 7 articles, 2) theory on TQM in services with 5 articles, 3) Comparisons between TQM in services and manufacturing with 5 jobs, 4) revisions of literature with 3, 5) cases of implementation studies and TQM barriers in services with 2 jobs each. The countries mentioned in the articles correspond to Sweden, Singapore, India, Malaysia, Greece, Australia and Kosovo. Something important to note is that within these works a total of 8 articles were found where some modeling is mentioned using statistical techniques, such as Structural Modeling equations (Fotopoulos & Psomas, 2010; Gustafsson, Nilsson, & Johnson, 2003; Prajogo & I., 2005), correlation and regression analysis (Ooi, Lin, Tan, & Chong, 2011) and interpretative structural modeling approach (Talib, F., Rahman, Z., & Qureshi, 2011; Talib, Rahman, & Qureshi, 2011).

In the case of Six Sigma the topics mentioned in the articles were; 1) cases of study with 20 works, 2) Six sigma in services with 13 papers, 3) critical success factors with 5 and finally 4) literature review with 2 papers. Among the case studies, the type of organizations analyzed was first financial services with 6 articles followed by healthcare with 5 articles on this topic. Another aspect that stands out from this revision are the countries in which the studies were carried out, among which are Singapore, Great Britain, Mexico, Brazil, Qatar and Lebanon. Finally, two articles were found that use statistical techniques to establish relationships. One of these studies uses structural equation modeling to establish the relationships between the critical factors of success and the performance of the organization (Marzagao & Carvalho, 2016). The other work uses the exploratory factor analysis to understand the dependency relations among the facilitating factors in the implementation of Six Sigma (De Carvalho, Ho, & Pinto, 2014).

In the case of Lean Six sigma, the main topics mentioned in the articles were: 1) study cases with 15 papers, 2) critical success factors for the implementation of LSS with 3 articles, 3) theory of LSS in services with 2 articles, 4) literature review, frameworks and critical failure factors with one work each. The countries mentioned in the articles are Mexico, Nigeria, Southern Europe, and Holland. In these articles only qualitative studies stand out in some cases, we do not find the use of statistics to establish relationships between the factors and the implementation of LSS in services.

In summary, the largest volume of articles corresponds to case studies with a total of 79. These articles discuss specific cases, most of them reporting results from a single organization.

With respect to the type of organizations analyzed the healthcare industry is the most analyzed type of business as a result of the high variety and quantity of operations performed, financial services come after because the information technologies have played a key role in the development of this sector, additionally, the market has expanded to a global level.

There were a few studies that discuss of models that explain the relationships between the different factors and the performance of the organization, where this topic has been explored the most is in the paper's referents to TQM. On the other hand, there are few countries in which this type of studies was developed with the main contributor to the UK and other European countries.

PHILOSOPHIES, TECHNIQUES AND TOOLS FOR CONTINUOUS IMPROVEMENT APPLIED IN THE SERVICE SECTOR

Lean Thinking in the Sector Services ("Lean Services")

The word "lean" commonly refers to the term "lean manufacturing" or lean production which is characterized by the use of fewer resources to produce, when compared to that of mass production (Wahab, Mukhtar, & Sulaiman, 2013). According to several authors, lean manufacturing is considered as a technique for waste reduction, but in practice, it maximizes the product value through waste elimination (Sundar, Balaji, & Satheesh Kumar, 2014).

The mains goals of lean manufacturing implementation in a production organization are; increase productivity, quality improvement, delivery time reduction, and reduce cost. The term "lean service" was introduced in the 90's describing lean thinking implementation in the services industry (Asnan, Nordin, & Othman, 2015). "Lean service" is necessary in order to eliminate waste from the service creation process aiming cost reductions and better services can be provided according to the customer requirements (Qu et. al; 2011 cited by Asnan et.al; 2015).

The level reached by lean thinking in the services sector represents a challenge for every organization as a consequence of the deep mindset change in operations required in the field service (Andrés-López, González-Requena, & Sanz-Lobera, 2015). The primary challenges in the Lean deployment in the service sector are the lack of awareness about all the benefits of the implementation and the fear that the identification of waste and inefficiency can interfere and change the way the service is provided (Gupta, Sharma, & Sunder M., 2016).

In literature, an assortment of study cases about this application can be found being the utmost common one that of the medical industry, followed by the information technologies, education, financial services and public sector, among other sectors.

TQM ("Total Quality Management") in the Service Sector

TQM is the set of management practices applicable to every organization, these practices assure that the organization accomplishes or exceeds the customer expectations consistently (Talib, Rahman, & Qureshi, 2012). TQM is the art of managing an entirety in order to achieve excellence (Talib & Rahman, 2016).

This technique was developed in the manufacturing industry in the 80's. Despite the TQM origin was in the manufacturing industry, it is strongly believed that the principles and practices are equally relevant for the service sector since both of them make use of facilities as their inputs in order to satisfy and exceed customer expectations (Talib et al., 2012). Considering that the main goal of every service operation is to satisfy and exceed customer expectations (Raja, Raju, & Srivatsa, 2015), the TQM philosophy also shares the same goal.

The emergence of the TQM philosophy in the service industry occurred two decades ago (Talib & Rahman, 2012). Recent literature reveals that TQM investigations in the service sector have been focused on very specific environments, for instance; hospitals, education, hotels, restaurants and tourism, banks and software development companies, among others (Talib, Rahman, & Qureshi, 2013).

Six Sigma in the Service Sector

Six Sigma philosophy can be summarized as the improvement in business processes capacity via statistic methods to identify, reduce, or eliminate completely the process variation (Ozkan, Rubio, Hassan, & Davis, 2017).

Six Sigma has two deployment models namely DMAIC (Define, measure, analyze, improve, and control) and DMADV (Define, measure analyze, design, and verify). DMAIC is utilized to improve existent processes, whereas DMADV is used to develop a new process or design new products that meet the six sigma quality levels. (Kim, Kim, & Chung, 2010). As a result, the application to production processes was evident and only manufacturing organizations adopted this philosophy (Ozkan et al., 2017).

Currently, the six sigma philosophy has extended to services organizations (Ozkan et al., 2017). Within the service sector, six sigma offers a disciplined approach to improve the effectivity of services (fulfill the desirable attributes of the service) as well as their efficiency (time and costs). The target is the reduction of non-value added activities and variation in central processes in order to achieve the improvement in service performance (Jiju Antony, 2004).

The target of the six sigma philosophy in service processes is to understand the cause of defects in order to visualize improvements that aid in the reduction of occurrence of these defects, thus improving the customer experience so do as their satisfaction (Jiju Antony, Antony, Kumar, & Cho, 2007).

Common applications in the service sector are hospitals, banks, call centers, and more recently education and hotel industry (Ayon Chakrabarty & Tan, 2007).

Currently, several organizations either manufacturers or public private service providers, small or large scale, are utilizing six sigma. Besides GE and Motorola who were the first and biggest companies to adopt this philosophy, other companies such as American Express, Boeing, Caterpillar, Fidelity investments, Honeywell International, J.P. Morgan, Chase, to name a few, are using this philosophy in a great diversity of projects (Nakhai & Neves, 2009).

Lean Six Sigma in the Service Sector

Lean Six Sigma is a combination of six sigma and lean manufacturing. Lean six sigma make use of tools from both philosophies in order to obtain the best practices from both of them, increasing rapidness and precision of improvements implemented (Laureani, 2011).

Lean six sigma methodology not only reduces waste, but also establishes a framework for cultural organization change (Sarkar, Mukhopadhyay, & Ghosh, 2013). Lean six sigma focuses on quality and continuous improvement and establish itself with the participation of all the employees in the organization (Tsironis & Psychogios, 2016).

Lean six sigma has been applied in the manufacturing industry and in some cases in service organizations resulting in valuable results from this implementation (Tsironis & Psychogios, 2016). The popularity of Lean six sigma in the service sector is increasing due to the improvement in the process performance (Sarkar et al., 2013).

In service organizations, "lean" is perceived as a methodology that reduces waste in terms of time, thus allowing the process to be more efficient. This methodology requires a process analysis as seen from the customer perspective to eliminate waste and inefficiency. Then again, six sigma focuses on refining the process, reducing variability in order to achieve the same result 99.999% of the time (six sigma), (Delgado, Ferreira & Castelo, 2010).

There are several challenges when implementing lean six sigma in the service sector, e.g. Data collection difficulties, processes dynamism, and the reporting of results analysis using service jargon instead of statistical. These are the most important challenges (Lameijer, Veen, Does, & De Mast, 2016).

Common applications in the service sector are, for instance, in the medical industry and financial services. Other limited applications can be found in call centers, human resource departments and customer service centers (Delgado, et al., 2010).

CRITICAL SUCCESS FACTOR IN THE IMPLEMENTATION OF CONTINUOUS IMPROVEMENT TOOLS IN THE SERVICE INDUSTRY

The CSF methodology is a procedure that attempts to make explicit those few key areas that dictate managerial or organizational success and was first introduced by John Rockart (Boynton & Zmud, 1986). Según Rockart (1981) the critical success factors are the limited number of areas in which positive results will ensure successful competitive performance for the organization.CFSs include issues vital to an organization´s current operating activities and its future success (Boynton & Zmud, 1986).

In the literature review, the key success factors for each continuous improvement tool utilized in the service sector are shown.

Critical Success Factors for Lean in Services

From the 74 publications found for lean services, only nine of them approached the subject of critical success factors for the lean implementation in services. Out of these nine articles, three of them approach the subject of critical factors in hospitals, three in the public sector, two in the field of information technologies, and one of them consider the perspective of the SMES, without specifically specifying the field. The information found is shown in Table 2.

Table 2. Critical success factors for lean in services

Critical success factors	References
Top Management commitment	(G. Kundu & Manohar, 2012),(Z. Radnor, Walley, Stephens, & Bucci, 2006),(Suárez-Barraza & Ramis-Pujol, 2010)
Management involvement and support	(G. Kundu & Manohar, 2012), (Noori, 2015), (Kollberg, Dahlgaard, & Brehmer, 2006), (Suárez-Barraza & Ramis-Pujol, 2010)
Management leadership	(G. Kundu & Manohar, 2012), (Kobus & Westner, 2015), (Achanga, Shehab, Roy, & Nelder, 2006), (Zoe Radnor & Boaden, 2008), (Suárez-Barraza & Ramis-Pujol, 2010)
Communication	(G. Kundu & Manohar, 2012), (Kobus & Westner, 2015), (Kollberg et al., 2006), (Zoe Radnor & Boaden, 2008),
Organizational culture	(G. Kundu & Manohar, 2012), (Z. Radnor et al., 2006)
Training and education	(G. Kundu & Manohar, 2012), (Kobus & Westner, 2015)
Financial Capability	(G. Kundu & Manohar, 2012), (Kobus & Westner, 2015), (Achanga et al., 2006)
Measurement Framework	(G. Kundu & Manohar, 2012)
Strategic orientation	(Noori, 2015)
Culture role	(Noori, 2015), (Kobus & Westner, 2015), (Zoe Radnor & Boaden, 2008),
Implementation process	(Noori, 2015), (Kobus & Westner, 2015)
Implementation team	(Noori, 2015), (Kobus & Westner, 2015), (Kollberg et al., 2006)
Employee involvement	(Kobus & Westner, 2015)
Clear vision/long term focus	(Kobus & Westner, 2015)
Customer focus	(Kobus & Westner, 2015), (Z. Radnor et al., 2006)
Existing skills	(Kobus & Westner, 2015), (Achanga et al., 2006),
Organizational changes	(Kobus & Westner, 2015)
Performance management	(Kobus & Westner, 2015)
Holistic approach	(Kobus & Westner, 2015),(Suárez-Barraza & Ramis-Pujol, 2010)
Organizational structure	(Achanga et al., 2006),(Dahlgaard, Pettersen, & Dahlgaard-Park, 2011)
Ability of lean concept adaptation	(Dahlgaard et al., 2011)
Organizational readiness	(Z. Radnor et al., 2006), (Zoe Radnor & Boaden, 2008)
Adequate resources	(Z. Radnor et al., 2006), (Zoe Radnor & Boaden, 2008)
Strategic approach	(Z. Radnor et al., 2006)
Effective implementation of best HRM practices	(Suárez-Barraza & Ramis-Pujol, 2010)
Establishing a system for measuring service process performance	(Suárez-Barraza & Ramis-Pujol, 2010)
The service is outcome/customer/stakeholder-oriented	(Suárez-Barraza & Ramis-Pujol, 2010)
Focus on the simple and practical	(Suárez-Barraza & Ramis-Pujol, 2010)

Regardless of the number of publications where lean is mentioned as a strategy to improve performance in service organizations, the critical factors topic has been explored shallowly, there was no publication found describing the general critical factors for the implementation in this sector. The research investigates the critical factors from the point of view of the organization where the investigation was conducted. Leadership or management leadership factor was the most repeated factor, followed by management involvement and top management commitment in second place. Communication is also a factor mentioned in several publications as leading to success in lean implementation. The factors of financial capability, implementation team, and culture role where stated in three out of nine articles.

Critical Success Factors for TQM in Services

From 31 publications found for TQM in services 11 of them were focused on the success key factors subject. While three articles discuss factors at a general level for services. Regarding studies focused in specific service sector fields, one study was focused on the airline industry in India and one in the hotel industry in Kosovo. Also, two articles reviewed perform an analysis of critical factors amongst manufacturing industry and services, finally, four articles mentioned different sectors without specifying field or type of businesses. Table 3 show more detailed information.

Among the most mentioned factors are customer focus and training and education found in nine out of eleven publications. Then with eight counts each, we have top management commitment and teamwork and involvement. It is noticeable the importance of the management commitment, the teamwork, and involvement in the organization. The employee involvement factor is found in seven publications, reaffirming yet again that employees play a key role in the implementation success. The following repeated factor is supplier partnership, consequently, suppliers have to be a part of this process. Customer satisfaction was mentioned in 50% of the aforementioned publications since TQM considers the customer as a fundamental part. Continuous improvement, employee encouragement, benchmarking, and leadership was found in five studies out of eleven. Communication and recognition and awards were mentioned in 4 studies. Amongst these publications, there was a greater coincidence in terms utilized in the key factors, this due to the studies not focusing in a particular field or area.

Critical Success Factor for Six Sigma in Services

The authors reviewed 41 articles focusing in six sigma in the service sector, moreover, 19 articles were found approaching the subject of key success factors out of these 41, hence, this was the subject with the most subject related publications from all the continuous improvement tools reviewed. We found 13 studies focusing on key factors for the service sector, that were analyzed from a point of view of financial services, health industry, hotel sector, public sector, construction industry, engineering services, and consulting services. Four of these studies analyzed both the services sector as well as the manufacturing industry. Additionally, three publications do not specify the type of sector where the investigation took place and only disclose their information as key factors for the implementation of six sigma projects. Detailed information is presented in Table 4.

Amongst the most repeated factors in all the research, we can find training and education in first place with 13 counts followed by top management commitment with 12. Cultural change appears 10 times so do as customer focus. The next factor with an incidence of 9 counts has to do with the organization strategy; a binding strategy with six sigma target. Then, showing seven times each we have management involvement and support, project management skills, and organization infrastructure; with 6 incidences teamwork, SS projects selection/prioritization, understand SS methodology, and companywide commitment. SS tools and techniques, linking SS to HR rewards were found in 5 studies, process management and project management and reviews found repeated in 4 articles, the rest of the factors were mentioned in less than three occasions.

Table 3. Critical success factors for TQM in services

Critical success factors	References
Top management commitment	(Antony, J., Fergusson, C., Warwood, S., & Hing Yee Tsang, 2004), (Talib & Rahman, 2010), (Singh, 2013), (Talib, F. & Rahman, 2010), (Kumar, R., Garg, D., & Garg, 2011), (Hietschold, Reinhardt, & Gurtner, 2014), (Aquilani, Silvestri, Ruggieri, & Gatti, 2017), (Sila & Ebrahimpour, 2003)
Top management support	(Brah, Wong, & Rao, 2000), (Fotopoulos & Psomas, 2010)
Continuous improvement	(Antony, et al., 2004), (Talib & Rahman, 2010), (Singh, 2013), (Kumar, et al., 2011), (Sila & Ebrahimpour, 2003)
Teamwork and involvement	(Antony, et al., 2004), (Singh, 2013), (Talib, F. & Rahman, 2010), (Kumar, et al., 2011), (Zylfijaj, R., & Pira, 2017), (Aquilani et al., 2017), (Hietschold et al., 2014), (Sila & Ebrahimpour, 2003)
Customer focus	(Antony, et al., 2004), (Talib & Rahman, 2010), (Talib, F. & Rahman, 2010), (Brah et al., 2000), (Fotopoulos & Psomas, 2010), (Zylfijaj, R., & Pira, 2017), (Aquilani et al., 2017), (Hietschold et al., 2014), (Sila & Ebrahimpour, 2003)
Training and education	(Antony, et al., 2004), (Talib & Rahman, 2010), (Singh, 2013), (Talib, F. & Rahman, 2010), (Brah et al., 2000), (Kumar, et al., 2011), (Zylfijaj, R., & Pira, 2017), (Aquilani et al., 2017), (Sila & Ebrahimpour, 2003)
Quality systems and policies	(Antony, et al., 2004)
Communication	(Antony, et al., 2004), (Talib, F. & Rahman, 2010), (Kumar, et al., 2011), (Zylfijaj, R., & Pira, 2017), (Singh, 2013), (Hietschold et al., 2014)
Supplier partnership/ Supplier quality management	(Antony, et al., 2004), (Hietschold et al., 2014), (Talib & Rahman, 2010), (Brah et al., 2000), (Aquilani et al., 2017), (Sila & Ebrahimpour, 2003)
Measurement and feedback	(Antony, et al., 2004), (Kumar, et al., 2011), (Aquilani et al., 2017)
Cultural change	(Antony, et al., 2004)
Employee involvement	(Talib & Rahman, 2010), (Singh, 2013), (Talib, F. & Rahman, 2010), (Brah et al., 2000), (Fotopoulos & Psomas, 2010), (Aquilani et al., 2017), (Sila & Ebrahimpour, 2003)
Employee encouragement	(Talib & Rahman, 2010), (Singh, 2013), (Talib, F. & Rahman, 2010), (Brah et al., 2000), (Zylfijaj, R., & Pira, 2017)
Quality information and performance measurement	(Talib & Rahman, 2010), (Fotopoulos & Psomas, 2010)
Benchmarking	(Singh, 2013), (Talib, F. & Rahman, 2010), (Brah et al., 2000), (Hietschold et al., 2014),29(Sila & Ebrahimpour, 2003)
Quality culture	(Singh, 2013), (Hietschold et al., 2014)
Improved service quality	(Singh, 2013), (Fotopoulos & Psomas, 2010)
Process improvement	(Singh, 2013), (Brah et al., 2000)
On time performance	(Singh, 2013)
Increased load factor	(Singh, 2013)
Customer satisfaction	(Singh, 2013), (Talib, F. & Rahman, 2010),(Kumar, et al., 2011), (Fotopoulos & Psomas, 2010), (Aquilani et al., 2017), (Hietschold et al., 2014)
Recognition and award	(Talib, F. & Rahman, 2010), (Brah et al., 2000), (Kumar, et al., 2011), (Hietschold et al., 2014)
Leadership/supervisory leadership	(Antony, et al., 2004), (Talib, F. & Rahman, 2010), (Hietschold et al., 2014), (Aquilani et al., 2017), (Sila & Ebrahimpour, 2003)
Product/Service design	(Brah et al., 2000), (Aquilani et al., 2017), (Sila & Ebrahimpour, 2003)
Cleanliness and organization.	(Brah et al., 2000)
Quality tools and techniques	(Fotopoulos & Psomas, 2010)

continues on following page

Table 3. Continued

Critical success factors	References
Protection of natural and social environment	(Fotopoulos & Psomas, 2010), (Hietschold et al., 2014)
Process and data quality management	(Fotopoulos & Psomas, 2010)
Human resource management (HRM)	(Aquilani et al., 2017), (Hietschold et al., 2014), (Sila & Ebrahimpour, 2003)
Strategic planning	(Aquilani et al., 2017), (Hietschold et al., 2014), (Sila & Ebrahimpour, 2003)
Role of quality department	(Aquilani et al., 2017)
Employee relations	(Aquilani et al., 2017)
Process management	(Aquilani et al., 2017), (Hietschold et al., 2014), (Sila & Ebrahimpour, 2003)
Information and analysis	(Sila & Ebrahimpour, 2003)

Table 4. Critical success factors for Six Sigma in services

Critical success factors	References
Top Management commitment	(Chakrabarty & Chuan, 2009), (A. Chakrabarty & Tan, 2008), (Chakrabarty & Tan, 2007), (Sabry, 2014), (Ayon Chakrabarty & Tan, 2006), (Jones & Johnson, 2007), (J. Antony, 2006), (Chakraborty, 2013), (Banuelas Coronado & Antony, 2002), (Salaheldin & Abdelwahab, 2009), (Antony & Banuelas, 2002)
Management involvement and support	(Jiju Antony et al., 2007), (Chakraborty, 2013), (A. Chakrabarty & Tan, 2008), (Banuelas Coronado & Antony, 2002), (Jones & Johnson, 2007), (Salaheldin & Abdelwahab, 2009), (Antony & Banuelas, 2002)
Committed leadership	(Niyazmetov & Keoy, 2011), (Jones & Johnson, 2007), (J. Antony, 2006)
Quality-driven culture	(Sabry, 2014)
Organizational culture	(Niyazmetov & Keoy, 2011)
Strategic alignment	(Niyazmetov & Keoy, 2011)
Morale and participation	(Jones & Johnson, 2007)
Teamwork	(Sabry, 2014), (A. Chakrabarty & Tan, 2008), (Chakraborty, 2013), (Niyazmetov & Keoy, 2011), (Jones & Johnson, 2007), (J. Antony, 2006)
Project management	(A. Chakrabarty & Tan, 2008), (Marzagao & Carvalho, 2016), (Jiju Antony et al., 2007), (Jiju Antony, 2004), (Banuelas Coronado & Antony, 2002), (J. Antony, 2006), (Antony & Banuelas, 2002)
Training and education	(Chakrabarty & Chuan, 2009), (A. Chakrabarty & Tan, 2008), (Chakrabarty & Tan, 2007), (Sabry, 2014), (Jiju Antony et al., 2007), (Jiju Antony, 2004), (A. Chakrabarty & Tan, 2007), (Chakraborty, 2013), (Ayon Chakrabarty & Tan, 2006), (Niyazmetov & Keoy, 2011), (Banuelas Coronado & Antony, 2002), (Salaheldin & Abdelwahab, 2009), (J. Antony, 2006)
SS Training	(J. Antony, 2006)
Link SS targets and customer satisfaction	(Banuelas Coronado & Antony, 2002), (J. Antony, 2006), (Antony & Banuelas, 2002)
Binding strategy with SS targets	(A. Chakrabarty & Tan, 2008), (Jiju Antony et al., 2007), (Jiju Antony, 2004), (Chakraborty, 2013), (Ayon Chakrabarty & Tan, 2006), (Leyer & Chakrabarty, 2011), (Banuelas Coronado & Antony, 2002), (J. Antony, 2006), (Antony & Banuelas, 2002)
Prior experience in implementing similar quality Initiatives	(Ayon Chakrabarty & Tan, 2006)

continues on following page

Table 4. Continued

Critical success factors	References
Measure the success in terms of financial benefits	(Chakrabarty & Tan, 2007), (Ayon Chakrabarty & Tan, 2006), (Leyer & Chakrabarty, 2011)
SS Financial Accountability	(Jiju Antony et al., 2007), (Jiju Antony, 2004), (J. Antony, 2006)
Communication	(Banuelas Coronado & Antony, 2002)
Selection of SS staff	(Leyer & Chakrabarty, 2011), (Jones & Johnson, 2007)
SS Projects Selection/Prioritization	(A. Chakrabarty & Tan, 2008), (Jiju Antony et al., 2007),(Banuelas Coronado & Antony, 2002), (Jones & Johnson, 2007), (J. Antony, 2006), (Antony & Banuelas, 2002)
SS Tools & Techniques	(A. Chakrabarty & Tan, 2008), (Sabry, 2014), (De Carvalho et al., 2014), (Banuelas Coronado & Antony, 2002), (Salaheldin & Abdelwahab, 2009)
Organization Infrastructure	(A. Chakrabarty & Tan, 2008), (Sabry, 2014),7(Jiju Antony et al., 2007), (Ayon Chakrabarty & Tan, 2006), (Niyazmetov & Keoy, 2011), (Banuelas Coronado & Antony, 2002), (Antony & Banuelas, 2002)
Extending SS to Supply Chain	(A. Chakrabarty & Tan, 2008), (Sabry, 2014), (Antony & Banuelas, 2002)
Linking SS to HR Rewards	(A. Chakrabarty & Tan, 2008), (Jiju Antony et al., 2007), (Jiju Antony, 2004), (Niyazmetov & Keoy, 2011), (Antony & Banuelas, 2002)
Customer satisfaction	(Leyer & Chakrabarty, 2011)
Cultural change	(Chakrabarty & Chuan, 2009), (A. Chakrabarty & Tan, 2008), (Chakrabarty & Tan, 2007), (Jiju Antony et al., 2007), (A. Chakrabarty & Tan, 2007), (Chakraborty, 2013), (A. Chakrabarty & Tan, 2008),36,40(J. Antony, 2006), (Antony & Banuelas, 2002)
Understand SS methodology	(A. Chakrabarty & Tan, 2008), (Marzagao & Carvalho, 2016), (Jiju Antony et al., 2007), (Jiju Antony, 2004), (J. Antony, 2006), (Antony & Banuelas, 2002)
Strategic quality planning	(Sabry, 2014)
Process management	(Chakrabarty & Tan, 2007), (Sabry, 2014), (De Carvalho et al., 2014), (Salaheldin & Abdelwahab, 2009)
Product design	(Sabry, 2014)
Employee satisfaction	(De Carvalho et al., 2014)
Employee relation/empowerment	(Sabry, 2014), (De Carvalho et al., 2014)
Benchmarking	(Sabry, 2014)
Role of quality department	(Ayon Chakrabarty & Tan, 2006)
Customer focus	(Chakrabarty & Chuan, 2009), (A. Chakrabarty & Tan, 2008), (Chakrabarty & Tan, 2007), (Jiju Antony et al., 2007), (Jiju Antony, 2004), (A. Chakrabarty & Tan, 2007), (Chakraborty, 2013), (Ayon Chakrabarty & Tan, 2006), (Niyazmetov & Keoy, 2011), (Jones & Johnson, 2007)
Organization readiness	(Chakrabarty & Chuan, 2009), (A. Chakrabarty & Tan, 2007), (Chakraborty, 2013)
Company wide-commitment	(Chakrabarty & Chuan, 2009), (A. Chakrabarty & Tan, 2008), (Jiju Antony et al., 2007), (Jiju Antony, 2004), (Chakraborty, 2013), (Jones & Johnson, 2007)
Goal based approach	(A. Chakrabarty & Tan, 2008), (Jones & Johnson, 2007)
Selections of team member	(A. Chakrabarty & Tan, 2008), (Jones & Johnson, 2007), (J. Antony, 2006)
Clear performance metrics	(A. Chakrabarty & Tan, 2008), (Chakrabarty & Tan, 2007), (Sabry, 2014), (A. Chakrabarty & Tan, 2007), (Chakraborty, 2013),(Ayon Chakrabarty & Tan, 2006), (Niyazmetov & Keoy, 2011), (Salaheldin & Abdelwahab, 2009)
Project tracking and reviews	(A. Chakrabarty & Tan, 2008), (Jiju Antony et al., 2007), (Jiju Antony, 2004), (Antony & Banuelas, 2002)
Six Sigma project manager Competencies	(Marzagao & Carvalho, 2016)

continues on following page

Table 4. Continued

Critical success factors	References
Audits	(Sabry, 2014)
Production	(Sabry, 2014)
Resources	(Salaheldin & Abdelwahab, 2009)

Table 5. Critical success factors for Lean Six Sigma in services

Critical success factors	References
Top Management commitment	(Delgado, Ferreira, & Castelo Branco, 2010), (Näslund, 2013),(Laureani & Antony, 2012), (Lande, Shrivastava, & Seth, 2016), (Jiju Antony, Krishan, Cullen, & Kumar, 2012)
Management involvement and support	(Tsironis & Psychogios, 2016), (Psychogios, Atanasovski, & Tsironis, 2012), (Lande et al., 2016), (Jiju Antony et al., 2012)
Committed leadership	(Tsironis & Psychogios, 2016), (Laureani & Antony, 2012), (Lande et al., 2016), (Jiju Antony et al., 2012)
Quality-driven culture	(Tsironis & Psychogios, 2016), (Psychogios et al., 2012)
Organizational culture	(Näslund, 2013), (Laureani & Antony, 2012), (Jiju Antony et al., 2012)
Strategic alignment	(Näslund, 2013)
Morale and participation	(Näslund, 2013)
Teamwork	(Tsironis & Psychogios, 2016)
Project management skills	(Näslund, 2013), (Laureani & Antony, 2012)
Training and education /Quality-driven training /LSS Training	(Näslund, 2013),(Delgado et al., 2010), (Tsironis & Psychogios, 2016), (Psychogios et al., 2012), (Laureani & Antony, 2012), (Jiju Antony et al., 2012)
Link LSS targets and customer satisfaction	(Tsironis & Psychogios, 2016), (Laureani & Antony, 2012), (Lande et al., 2016)
Binding strategy with LSS targets	(Tsironis & Psychogios, 2016), (Laureani & Antony, 2012), (Lande et al., 2016)
Supportive technical systems /Supportive performance management and IT systems	(Tsironis & Psychogios, 2016), (Psychogios et al., 2012)
Clear targets of LSS projects	(Tsironis & Psychogios, 2016)
Prior experience in implementing similar quality Initiatives	(Tsironis & Psychogios, 2016), (Psychogios et al., 2012)
Link performance management system with LSS	(Tsironis & Psychogios, 2016)
Project driven approach	(Delgado et al., 2010)
Measure the success in terms of financial benefits	(Delgado et al., 2010)
LSS Financial Accountability	(Laureani & Antony, 2012)
Communication	(Laureani & Antony, 2012), (Lande et al., 2016), (Jiju Antony et al., 2012)
Awareness	(Laureani & Antony, 2012)
Selection of LSS staff	(Laureani & Antony, 2012)
Data Based Approach	(Laureani & Antony, 2012)
LSS Projects Selection/Prioritization	(Laureani & Antony, 2012), (Psychogios et al., 2012), (Lande et al., 2016), (Jiju Antony et al., 2012)

continues on following page

Table 5. Continued

Critical success factors	References
LSS Tools & Techniques	(Laureani & Antony, 2012), (Jiju Antony et al., 2012)
Organization Infrastructure	(Laureani & Antony, 2012)
Extending LSS to Supply Chain	(Laureani & Antony, 2012), (Lande et al., 2016)
Linking LSS to HR Rewards	(Laureani & Antony, 2012), (Lande et al., 2016)
Customer satisfaction	(Psychogios et al., 2012), (Lande et al., 2016)
Cultural change	(Lande et al., 2016)
Understand LSS methodology	(Lande et al., 2016)
Strategic quality planning	(Lande et al., 2016)
Process management	(Lande et al., 2016), (Jiju Antony et al., 2012)
Product design	(Lande et al., 2016)
Inventory control	(Lande et al., 2016)
Employee satisfaction	(Lande et al., 2016)
Employee relation/empowerment	(Lande et al., 2016)
Benchmarking	(Lande et al., 2016)
Role of quality department	(Lande et al., 2016)
Organization readiness	(Jiju Antony et al., 2012)

Critical Success Factor for Lean Six Sigma in Services

In the literature review, we could find a total of 28 papers referring to lean six sigma in the service sectors from which seven approach the subject of key success factors. Four of these studies discuss the key factors within the service sector, one of them in the telecommunications area, another in the financial services area, and other in the higher education institute. Another paper discusses factors for both services and manufacturing as well. Finally, one publication examines the critical factors in SMEs, in which the factors for both lean tools as well as six sigma are visited separately. Detailed information is shown in Table 5.

The most repeated factor in studies was training and education, followed by top management commitment and management involvement and support. Other factors appearing in at least 50% of the publications were committed leadership and LSS projects selection/prioritization. Other factors mentioned several times where organizational culture, communication, link LSS targets and customer satisfaction, and binding strategy with LSS targets.

Proposed Critical Success Factor for Continuous Improvement Tools in Services

According to the literature reviewed 35 different CSF were found for TQM, 28 CFS for LS, 44 CSF for SS and 40 for LSS.

The three most repeated factors were: top management commitment is mentioned in 89% of the papers, training and education are mentioned in 74% of the papers, while customer focus was mentioned in 66% of the articles. Figure 2 shows a summary of the factors by frequency with the most appearances in the literature amongst the philosophies.

Figure 2. Critical success factor by frequency

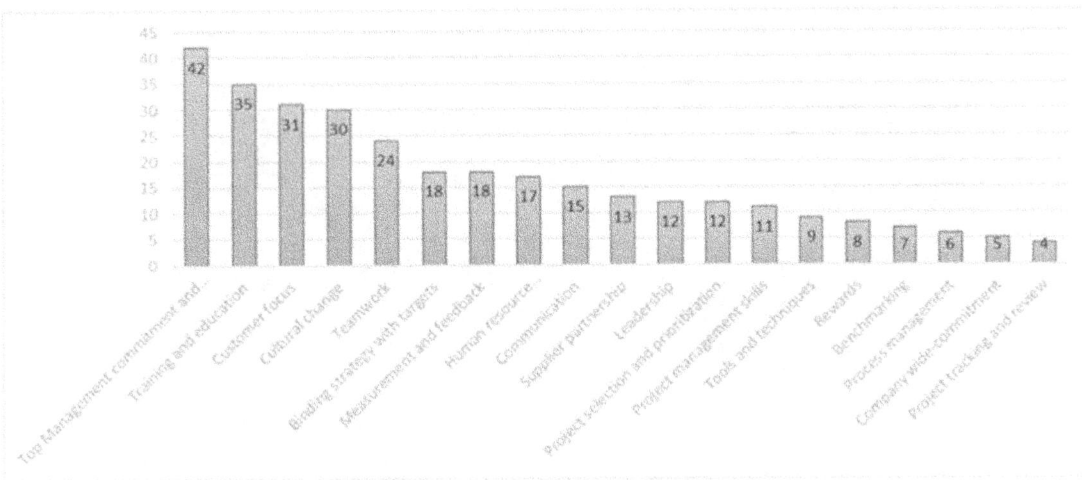

The factors mentioned across all of the continuous improvement tools were top commitment management, training and education, leadership, communication and cultural change.

Other factors mentioned in three of the tools reviewed with a considerable number of mentions within the literature are: Leadership, teamwork, customer focus, process management, supplier partnership, customer satisfaction, tools and techniques, and rewards. On the other hand, factors only mentioned in the tools Lean six sigma and six sigma were detected, due to the similarity of both tools that search for continuous improvement through projects, the factors among this category are; project management skills, binding strategy with targets, project selection, and prioritization.

The literature review shows different outcomes of CSF (critical success factors) according to the continuous improvement tool being analyzed as well as the kind of organization in which the study was conducted. Several of these factors might be classified in broader categories, moreover, these can be validated independently of the continuous improvement tool and the organization type, on the other hand, other factors cannot be generalized since they are linked by nature to the tool or to the organization type. Certain authors state that there are no differences among CFS found in the service sector and CSF from the manufacturing industry, as opposed to a number of authors stating that there are differences between these two kinds of factors.

Figure 3 shows the most CSF mentioned by percentage of the total. In the section of others are grouped those factors that had less than 2% of repetitions.

According to the literature review, the following CSFs were found as the most frequent, therefore they are considered as the proposed:

- Top management commitment
- Training and education
- Customer Focus
- Cultural change
- Teamwork
- Binding strategy with targets
- Measurement and Feedback

Figure 3. Critical success factor most mentioned by percentage of the total

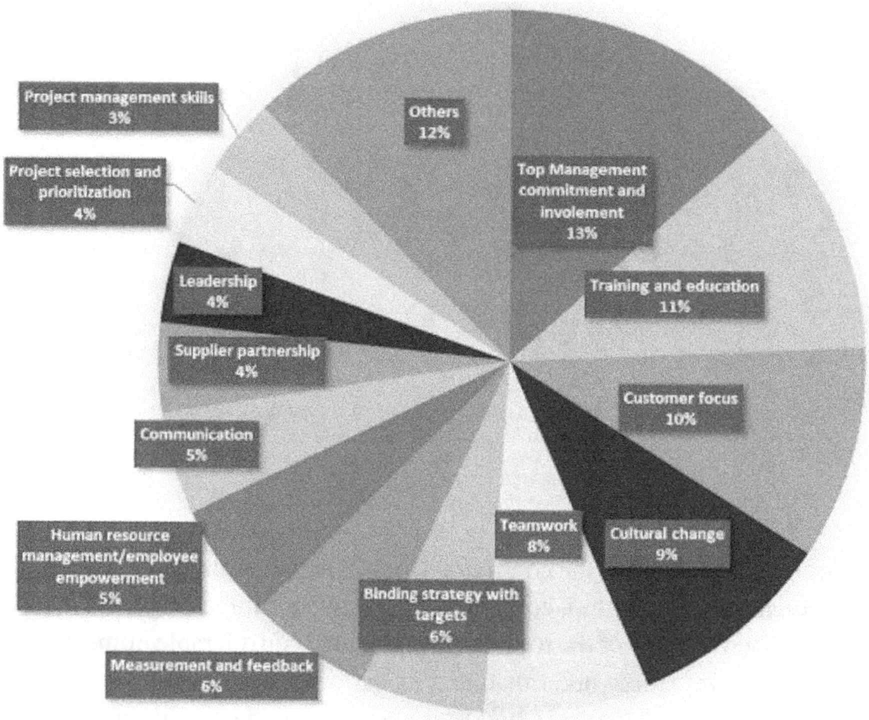

- Employees empowerment
- Communication
- Supplier partnership
- Leadership
- Projects selection and prioritization
- Project management skills
- Tools and techniques
- Recognitions and rewards
- Benchmarking
- Process management

FUTURE RESEARCH DIRECTIONS

The search for continuous improvement in organizations has become a common denominator for the increase in productivity. The subject of continuous improvement in services has been explored in the literature, however, we think authors can seek to deepen in such topics as the quantification of the benefits of these implementations, the relationships between the factors that guarantee the success of said implementations, how to carry out studies in more countries and in different types of organizations.

CONCLUSION

Globalization has forced organizations of all sectors to seek new ways to achieve high levels of efficiency and thus remain competitive in the markets. The services sector has been modernized and now enters the scope of global competition due to the advances in information technologies. This has led the sector to adopt philosophies that other sectors have used to improve their productivity. In the literature review, diverse studies have been found on the use of tools such as Lean, Six Sigma, TQM, and Lean Six Sigma that were developed initially for manufacturing and that have been adapted to be applied in this sector.

In the literature, there are a wide variety of studies aiming to explain how the implementations were carried out, moreover, we found studies applied in healthcare, airports, hotels, supermarkets, telecommunications, information technologies, public sector, logistic services, banks, information services, call centers and consulting services in all the different tools. Despite the great number of publications related to the subject in matter, there are still significant gaps in the information, especially in reference to the benefits granted by the usage of these tools, we found a necessity to quantify the benefits obtained as well to explore and clarify the concepts and metrics applicable to this sector, also, define the impact of the implementation of these practices in the organization global performance.

The critical success factors are a piece of fundamental information aiding to ease the implementation of continuous improvement programs at any organization, it is necessary to emphasize the compliance of all aspects mentioned in the CSF in order to attain a greater success possible for the implementation of these continuous improvement programs. In the literature review about CSF, we found scarce information on this subject. A large majority of information or cases of study were found in lean, specifically in health care. Also, it is noticeable that very few countries are mentioned in the studies, hence, we can argue that it is necessary to conduct studies in more countries as well as in different types of organizations. On the other hand, a gap is perceived regarding the influence of each one of the critical success factors and its correlation in order to achieve a successful implementation. This study can serve as a starting point to explore and perform an empirical investigation on the subject.

In the literature, there are two main problems in the theory of knowledge in this field, which are the wide range of results on the CSFs for effective and successful deployment of continuous improvement tools and lack of agreement among experts about not no reasonably satisfactory explanations about the causes of failure or success factors counterpart. It can be concluded that the theory is incomplete and has faults of organization and thus its explanatory power is not enough. It's a working theory has contradictions that must be resolved to build a substantive theory, (Bunge, 2004). Therefore, in this research will identify more precisely the related CFS dimension that characterizes the successful deployment of continuous improvement tools.

REFERENCES

Achanga, P., Shehab, E., Roy, R., & Nelder, G. (2006). Critical success factors for lean implementation within SMEs. *Journal of Manufacturing Technology Management*, *17*(4), 460–471. doi:10.1108/17410380610662889

Andrés-López, E., González-Requena, I., & Sanz-Lobera, A. (2015). Lean Service: Reassessment of Lean Manufacturing for Service Activities. *Procedia Engineering, 132*, 23–30. doi:10.1016/j.proeng.2015.12.463

Antony, J. (2004). Six Sigma in the UK service organisations: Results from a pilot survey. *Managerial Auditing Journal, 19*(8), 1006–1013. doi:10.1108/02686900410557908

Antony, J. (2006). Six sigma for service processes. *Business Process Management Journal, 12*(2), 234–248. doi:10.1108/14637150610657558

Antony, J., Antony, F. J., Kumar, M., & Cho, B. R. (2007). Six sigma in service organisations: Benefits, challenges and difficulties, common myths, empirical observations and success factors. *International Journal of Quality & Reliability Management, 24*(3), 294–311. doi:10.1108/02656710710730889

Antony, J., & Banuelas, R. (2002). Key ingredients for the effective implementation of Six Sigma program. *Measuring Business Excellence, 6*(4), 20–27. doi:10.1108/13683040210451679

Antony, J., Fergusson, C., Warwood, S., & Hing Yee Tsang, J. (2004). Comparing total quality management success factors in UK manufacturing and service industries: Some key findings from a survey. *Journal of Advances in Management Research, 1*(2), 32–45. doi:10.1108/97279810480000363

Antony, J., Krishan, N., Cullen, D., & Kumar, M. (2012). Lean Six Sigma for higher education institutions (HEIs). *International Journal of Productivity and Performance Management, 61*(8), 940–948. doi:10.1108/17410401211277165

Aquilani, B., Silvestri, C., Ruggieri, A., & Gatti, C. (2017). A systematic literature review on total quality management critical success factors and the identification of new avenues of research. *The TQM Journal, 29*(1), 184–213. doi:10.1108/TQM-01-2016-0003

Asnan, R., Nordin, N., & Othman, S. N. (2015). Managing Change on Lean Implementation in Service Sector. *Procedia: Social and Behavioral Sciences, 211*, 313–319. doi:10.1016/j.sbspro.2015.11.040

Banuelas Coronado, R., & Antony, J. (2002). Critical success factors for the successful implementation of six sigma projects in organisations. *The TQM Magazine, 14*(2), 92–99. doi:10.1108/09544780210416702

Boynton, A. C., & Zmud, R. W. (1986). An Assessment of Critical Success Factors. *Sloan Management Review, 25*, 17–27.

Brah, S. A., Wong, J. L., & Rao, B. M. (2000). TQM and business performance in the service sector: A Singapore study. *International Journal of Operations & Production Management, 20*(11), 1293–1312. doi:10.1108/01443570010348262

Bunge, M. (2004). La investigación científica. Su estrategia y su filosofía (Tercera ed). siglo xxi Editores S.A. de C.V.

Chakrabarty, A., & Tan, K. C. (2006). Applying six-sigma in the service industry: A review and case study in call center services. *ICMIT 2006 Proceedings - 2006 IEEE International Conference on Management of Innovation and Technology, 2*, 728–732. doi:10.1109/ICMIT.2006.262316

Chakrabarty, A., & Chuan Tan, K. (2007). The current state of six sigma application in services. *Managing Service Quality, 17*(2), 194–208. doi:10.1108/09604520710735191

Chakrabarty, A., & Kay Chuan, T. (2009). An exploratory qualitative and quantitative analysis of Six Sigma in service organizations in Singapore. *Management Research News, 32*(7), 614–632. doi:10.1108/01409170910965224

Chakrabarty, A., & Tan, K. C. (2007). A survey on Six Sigma implementation in Singapore service industries. *IEEM 2007: 2007 IEEE International Conference on Industrial Engineering and Engineering Management*, 1428–1432. 10.1109/IEEM.2007.4419428

Chakrabarty, A., & Tan, K. C. (2008). Case study analysis of six Sigma in Singapore service organizations. *5th International Conference Service Systems and Service Management - Exploring Service Dynamics with Science and Innovative Technology, ICSSSM'08*. 10.1109/ICSSSM.2008.4598532

Chakraborty, A. (2013). An empirical analysis on Six Sigma implementation in service organisations. *International Journal of Lean Six Sigma*. doi:10.1108/20401461311319338

Dahlgaard, J., Pettersen, J., & Dahlgaard-Park, S. M. (2011). Quality and lean health care: A system for assessing and improving the health of healthcare organisations. *Total Quality Management & Business Excellence, 22*(6), 673–689. doi:10.1080/14783363.2011.580651

De Carvalho, M. M., Ho, L. L., & Pinto, S. H. B. (2014). The Six Sigma program: An empirical study of Brazilian companies. *Journal of Manufacturing Technology Management, 25*(5), 602–630. doi:10.1108/JMTM-04-2012-0045

De Koning, H., Does, R. J. M. M., & Bisgaard, S. (2008). Lean Six Sigma in financial services. *Int. J. Six Sigma and Competitive Advantage, 4*(1), 2014–11. doi:10.1504/IJSSCA.2008.018417

Delgado, C., Ferreira, M., & Castelo Branco, M. (2010). The implementation of lean Six Sigma in financial services organizations. *Journal of Manufacturing Technology Management, 21*(4), 512–523. doi:10.1108/17410381011046616

Fotopoulos, C. V., & Psomas, E. L. (2010). The structural relationships between TQM factors and organizational performance. *The TQM Journal, 22*(5), 539–552. doi:10.1108/17542731011072874

Gupta, S., Sharma, M., & Sunder, M. V. (2016). Lean services: A systematic review. *International Journal of Productivity and Performance Management, 65*(8), 1025–1056. doi:10.1108/IJPPM-02-2015-0032

Gustafsson, A., Nilsson, L., & Johnson, M. D. (2003). The role of quality practices in service organizations. *International Journal of Service Industry Management, 14*(2), 232–244. doi:10.1108/09564230310474183

Hadid, W., & Afshin Mansouri, S. (2014). The lean-performance relationship in services: A theoretical model. *International Journal of Operations & Production Management, 34*(6), 750–785. doi:10.1108/IJOPM-02-2013-0080

Hadid, W., Mansouri, S. A., & Gallear, D. (2016). Is lean service promising? A socio-technical perspective. *International Journal of Operations & Production Management, 36*(6), 618–642. doi:10.1108/IJOPM-01-2015-0008

Hietschold, N., Reinhardt, R., & Gurtner, S. (2014). Measuring critical success factors of TQM implementation successfully – a systematic literature review. *International Journal of Production Research*, *52*(21), 6254–6272. doi:10.1080/00207543.2014.918288

Jones, B., & Johnson, R. T. (2007). Six Sigma Literature: A Review and Agenda for Future Research. *Quality and Reliability Engineering International*, *23*, 517–543. doi:10.1002/qre

Kim, Y., Kim, E. J., & Chung, M. G. (2010). A Six Sigma-based method to renovate information services: Focusing on information acquisition process. *Library Hi Tech*, *28*(4), 632–647. doi:10.1108/07378831011096286

Kobus, J., & Westner, M. (2015). Lean Management of IT organizations: Implementation success factors and theoretical foundation. *2015 Americas Conference on Information Systems, AMCIS 2015*, (1), 1–17. Retrieved from https://www.scopus.com/inward/record.uri?eid=2-s2.0-84963611888&partnerID=40&md5=eb6d634f3f27a6c1b330677df9b3ec3b

Kollberg, B., Dahlgaard, J. J., & Brehmer, P. (2006). Measuring lean initiatives in health care services: Issues and findings. *International Journal of Productivity and Performance Management*, *56*(1), 7–24. doi:10.1108/17410400710717064

Kumar, R., Garg, D., & Garg, T. K. (2011). TQM success factors in North Indian manufacturing and service industries. *The TQM Journal*, *23*(1), 36–46. doi:10.1108/17542731111097470

Kundu, G., & Manohar, B. (2012). Critical success factors for implementing lean practices in it support services. *International Journal of Qualitative Research*, *6*(4), 301–312. Retrieved from http://www.ijqr.net/journal/v6-n4/1.pdf

Kundu, G. K., & Bairi, J. (2014). A scale for measuring the applicability of lean practices in IT support services. *Journal of Enterprise Information Management*, *27*(5), 623–643. doi:10.1108/JEIM-02-2013-0005

Lameijer, B. A., Veen, D. T. J., Does, R. J. M. M., & De Mast, J. (2016). Perceptions of Lean Six Sigma: A Multiple Case Study in the Financial Services Industry. *The Quality Management Journal*, *23*(2), 29–56. doi:10.1080/10686967.2016.11918470

Lande, M., Shrivastava, R. L., & Seth, D. (2016). Critical success factors for Lean Six Sigma in SMEs (small and medium enterprises). *The TQM Journal*, *28*(4), 613–635. doi:10.1108/TQM-12-2014-0107

Laureani, A. (2011). Lean Six Sigma in the Service Industry. *Advanced Topics in Applied Operations Management*. Retrieved from http://cdn.intechopen.com/pdfs-wm/31666.pdf

Laureani, A., & Antony, J. (2012). Critical success factors for the effective implementation of Lean Sigma Results from an empirical study and agenda. *International Journal of Lean Six Sigma*, *3*(4), 274–283. doi:10.1108/20401461211284743

Leyer, M., & Chakrabarty, A. (2011). Implementing a Six Sigma initiative in financial service companies. *2011 IEEE International Conference on Quality and Reliability, ICQR 2011*, 521–525. 10.1109/ICQR.2011.6031594

Madrigal, K., Martinez, E., Torres-Arguelles, V., & Beltran, E. (2017). Critical Success Factors of Continuous Improvement Tools in Service Industry. In 2017 Annual SISE Conference (Ed.), *Proceeding of the 6th Annual World Conference of the Society for Industrial and Systems Engineering*. Academic Press.

Maroto Sánchez, A. (2010). Growth and productivity in the service sector: the state of the art. *Institute of Social and Economic Analysis. WP 07/2010*, (7), 50. Retrieved from http://www.iaes.es/iuaes_sp/publicaciones.htm%0Ahttp://dialnet.unirioja.es/servlet/articulo?codigo=3247453&orden=260167&info=link%5Cnhttp://dialnet.unirioja.es/servlet/extart?codigo=3247453

Marzagao, D. S. L., & Carvalho, M. M. (2016). Critical success factors for Six Sigma projects. *International Journal of Project Management*, *34*(8), 1505–1518. doi:10.1016/j.ijproman.2016.08.005

Nakhai, B., & Neves, J. S. (2009). The challenges of six sigma in improving service quality. *International Journal of Quality & Reliability Management*, *26*(7), 663–684. doi:10.1108/02656710910975741

Näslund, D. (2013). Lean and six sigma - critical success factors revisited. *International Journal of Quality and Service Sciences*, *5*(1), 86–100. doi:10.1108/17566691311316266

Niyazmetov, T., & Keoy, K. H. (2011). Developing a capability model of Six Sigma implementation: A comparative study of CSF of Six Sigma implementation between manufacturing and service sectors in Uzbekistan. *International Journal of the Built Environment and Asset Management*, *1*(1), 14. doi:10.1504/IJBEAM.2011.044127

Noori, B. (2015). The critical success factors for successful lean implementation in hospitals. *International Journal of Productivity and Quality Management*, *15*(1), 108–126. doi:10.1504/IJPQM.2015.065987

Ooi, K.-B., Lin, B., Tan, B.-I., & Chong, A. Y.-L. (2011). Are TQM practices supporting customer satisfaction and service quality? *Journal of Services Marketing*, *25*(6), 410–419. doi:10.1108/08876041111161005

Ozkan, B., Rubio, J. F., Hassan, M. K., & Davis, J. R. (2017). Six Sigma, stock returns and operating performance. *Management Research Review*, *40*(3), 331–351. doi:10.1108/MRR-12-2015-0291

Piercy, N., & Rich, N. (2009). Lean transformation in the pure service environment: The case of the call service centre. *International Journal of Operations & Production Management*, *29*(1), 54–76. doi:10.1108/01443570910925361

Prajogo, & I., D. (2005). The comparative analysis of TQM practices and quality performance between manufacturing and service firms. *International Journal of Service Industry Management, 16*(3), 217–228. doi:10.1108/09564230510601378

Psychogios, A. G., Atanasovski, J., & Tsironis, L. K. (2012). Lean Six Sigma in a service context: A multi-factor application approach in the telecommunications industry. *International Journal of Quality & Reliability Management*, *29*(1), 122–139. doi:10.1108/02656711211190909

Radnor, Z., & Boaden, R. (2008). Editorial: Lean in public services - Panacea or paradox?: Does lean enhance public services? *Public Money & Management*, *28*(1), 3–7. doi:10.1111/j.1467-9302.2008.00610.x

Radnor, Z., Walley, P., Stephens, A., & Bucci, G. (2006). Evaluation of the lean approach to business management and its use in the public sector. *Scottish Executive Social Research, 20.*

Raja, V., Raju, R., & Srivatsa, S. (2015, Sept.). A review of the quality evolution in various organisations. *Total Quality Management & Business Excellence*, 1–15. doi:10.1080/14783363.2015.1082421

Sabry, A. (2014). Factors critical to the success of Six-Sigma quality program and their influence on performance indicators in some of Lebanese hospitals. *Arab Economic and Business Journal*, *9*(2), 93–114. doi:10.1016/j.aebj.2014.07.001

Salaheldin, S. I., & Abdelwahab, I. S. (2009). Six Sigma Practices in the Banking Sector in Qatar. *Global Business & Management Research*, *1*(1), 23–35. Retrieved from http://search.ebscohost.com/login.aspx?direct=true&db=bth&AN=42988759&site=eds-live

Sarkar, S. A., Mukhopadhyay, A. R., & Ghosh, S. K. (2013). Improvement of claim processing cycle time through Lean Six Sigma methodology. *International Journal of Lean Six Sigma*, *4*(2), 171–183. doi:10.1108/20401461311319347

Sila, I., & Ebrahimpour, M. (2003). Examination and comparison of the critical factors of total quality management (TQM) across countries. *International Journal of Production Research*, *41*(2), 235–268. doi:10.1080/0020754021000022212

Singh, A. K., & Sushil. (2013). Modeling enablers of TQM to improve airline performance. *International Journal of Productivity and Performance Management*, *62*(3), 250–275. doi:10.1108/17410401311309177

Suárez-Barraza, M. F., & Ramis-Pujol, J. (2010). Implementation of Lean-Kaizen in the human resource service process. *Journal of Manufacturing Technology Management*, *21*(3), 388–410. doi:10.1108/17410381011024359

Suárez-Barraza, M. F., Smith, T., & Dahlgaard-Park, S. M. (2012). Lean Service: A literature analysis and classification. *Total Quality Management & Business Excellence*, *23*(3–4), 359–380. doi:10.1080/14783363.2011.637777

Sundar, R., Balaji, A. N., & Satheesh Kumar, R. M. (2014). A review on lean manufacturing implementation techniques. *Procedia Engineering*, *97*, 1875–1885. doi:10.1016/j.proeng.2014.12.341

Talib, F., & Rahman, Z. (2010). Studying the Impact of Total Quality Management in Service Industries. *International Journal of Productivity and Quality Management*, *6*(2), 249–268. doi:10.1504/IJPQM.2010.034408

Talib, F., & Rahman, Z. (2010). Critical Success Factors of TQM in Service Organizations: A Proposed Model. *Services Marketing Quarterly*, *31*(3), 363–380. doi:10.1080/15332969.2010.486700

Talib, F., & Rahman, Z. (2012). Total quality management practices in manufacturing and service industries: A comparative study. *International Journal of Advanced Operations Management*, *4*(3), 155. doi:10.1504/IJAOM.2012.047634

Talib, F., Rahman, Z., & Qureshi, M. N. (2011). Analysis of interaction among the barriers to total quality management implementation using interpretive structural modeling approach. *Benchmarking: An International Journal*, *18*(4), 563–587. doi:10.1108/14635771111147641

Talib, F., Rahman, Z., & Qureshi, M. N. (2011). An interpretive structural modelling approach for modelling the practices of total quality management in service sector. *International Journal of Modelling in Operations Management, 1*(3), 223–250. doi:10.1504/IJMOM.2011.039528

Talib, F., Rahman, Z., & Qureshi, M. N. (2012). Total quality management in service sector : A literature review. *International Journal of Business Innovation and Research, 6*(3), 259–301. doi:10.1504/IJBIR.2012.046628

Talib, F., Rahman, Z., & Qureshi, M. N. (2013). An empirical investigation of relationship between total quality management practices and quality performance in Indian service companies. *The International Journal of Quality & Reliability Management, 30.*

Tsironis, L. K., & Psychogios, A. (2016). Road towards Lean Six Sigma in service industry : A multi-factor integrated framework. *Business Process Management Journal, 22*(4), 812–834. doi:10.1108/BPMJ-08-2015-0118

Wahab, A. N. A., Mukhtar, M., & Sulaiman, R. (2013). A Conceptual Model of Lean Manufacturing Dimensions. *Procedia Technology, 11*, 1292–1298. doi:10.1016/j.protcy.2013.12.327

Zylfijaj, R., & Pira, B. (2017). Assessment of critical success factors of TQM culture in hospitality sector in Kosovo. *International Journal of Research in Business and Social Science, 6*(1), 65–77.

ADDITIONAL READING

Benítez Rodríguez, L., Romero Lamorú, I., & Solís Corvo, M. (2016). Bondades de las ecuaciones estructurales en el manejo de la satisfacción percibida en el restaurante El Aljibe. *Economia y Desarrollo, 157*(2), 50–59.

Cruz, A. D., Martínez, E. E. V., Torres, F. R., & Hincapié, J. M. M. (2017). Gestión Tecnológica en Restaurantes: Desarrollo y Validación de un Instrumento de Medición (Technology Management in Restaurants: Development and Validation of a Measuring Instrument). *GECONTEC: Revista Internacional de Gestión del Conocimiento y la Tecnología, 5*(2), 23–40.

Del Carmen, M. (2018). Factorial analysis of the elements that compose the training in the small and medium enterprises of the Industrial sector. *Management, 22*(2), 42–59. doi:10.2478/manment-2018-0022

Farooq, M. S., Salam, M., Fayolle, A., Jaafar, N., & Ayupp, K. (2018). Impact of service quality on customer satisfaction in Malaysia airlines: A PLS-SEM approach. *Journal of Air Transport Management, 67*, 169–180. doi:10.1016/j.jairtraman.2017.12.008

Ferreira, H. P., & Fernandes, P. O. (2015). Identification of critical success factors that maximise customers' satisfaction: Multivariate analysis. *Tourism & Management Studies, 1*(11), 164–172.

Kido Cruz, M. T., Díaz Carrión, I. A., & Kido Cruz, A. (2018). La satisfacción del comensal como elemento clave del binomio gastronomía-turismo en Tijuana. *Estudios sociales (Hermosillo, Son.), 28*(51).

Pinto, S. M., Ramírez, P. E., & Grandón, E. E. (2017). Antecedentes del Éxito de los Sistemas de Planificación de Recursos Empresariales en las Grandes Empresas Chilenas: Un Modelo Factorial Exploratorio. *Información Tecnológica*, *28*(3), 139–146. doi:10.4067/S0718-07642017000300015

Psomas, E. (2016). The underlying factorial structure and significance of the Six Sigma difficulties and critical success factors: The Greek case. *The TQM Journal*, *28*(4), 530–546. doi:10.1108/TQM-04-2015-0049

Silva, B. B., Mergulhão, R. C., Favoretto, C., & Mendes, G. H. (2019). Critical success factors of Six Sigma implementations in companies in Brazil. *International Journal of Lean Six Sigma*, *10*(1), 143–160. doi:10.1108/IJLSS-01-2018-0008

Yadegaridehkordi, E., Nilashi, M., Nasir, M. H. N. B. M., & Ibrahim, O. (2018). Predicting determinants of hotel success and development using Structural Equation Modelling (SEM)-ANFIS method. *Tourism Management*, *66*, 364–386. doi:10.1016/j.tourman.2017.11.012

KEY TERMS AND DEFINITIONS

Critical Success Factors (CSF): Elements that are needed so that the efforts in the implementations of methods are successful.

Lean Services (LS): It is a philosophy that is based on the elimination of waste in the service sector.

Lean Six Sigma (LSS): It is a philosophy that focuses on the elimination of waste and the processes control to improve the productivity of organizations.

Service Sector: It is the sector where the organizations that produce intangible goods are grouped.

Six Sigma (SS): It is a philosophy that focuses on the processes control to improve the efficiency of organizations.

Total Quality Management (TQM): It is a management practice that focuses on exceeding customer expectations.

Chapter 12
Determination of the Critical Success Factors (CSF) in the Implementation of Six Sigma (SS) and Its Sustainable Benefits:
Content Validity and Internal Consistency of the Measurement Instrument

Aida López
https://orcid.org/0000-0002-8856-0779
Universidad Autónoma de Baja California, Mexico

Jesús A. Hernández Gómez
https://orcid.org/0000-0003-2325-2051
Universidad Autónoma de Ciudad Juárez, Mexico

Karla I. Velázquez Victorica
https://orcid.org/0000-0002-8073-6119
Universidad Autónoma de Baja California, Mexico

Vianey Torres Argüelles
https://orcid.org/0000-0003-0978-3796
Universidad Autónoma de Ciudad Juárez, Mexico

Salvador Noriega Morales
https://orcid.org/0000-0001-7813-5835
Universidad Autónoma de Ciudad Juárez, Mexico

Luz del Consuelo Olivares Fong
https://orcid.org/0000-0003-3790-6810
Universidad Autónoma de Baja California, Mexico

ABSTRACT

Currently, organizations seek to position themselves in the market as the most competitive and profitable in their branch, through the continuous improvement of their processes, products, and/or services, applying various techniques, tools, and methodologies. Particularly in this chapter, focus on Six Sigma (SS) will be shown, a strategy used in companies to achieve competitive objectives, continuously improving processes. In this sense, it is considered important to identify and know the main factors that are involved in its implementation. Likewise, the organizations are presenting a culture towards the sustainability and the environmental care, derived from this, the methodology used to develop a measurement instrument that allows to identify the CSF in the implementation of SS, the sustainable benefits that can be achieve with correct implementation, the procedure used for the validation of the content of the instrument, the validity of internal consistency and the obtained results.

DOI: 10.4018/978-1-7998-1052-0.ch012

INTRODUCTION

As is already known, organizations are in search of competitiveness, continuous improvement, profitability and recently of sustainable development and the environmental care, for the achievement of these strategic objectives supported by various techniques, tools and methodologies that help them to lead the path of success. Of the diverse techniques that exist for the continuous improvement of the processes, products and services; this chapter will present an approach towards Six Sigma (SS), used mostly in organizations to achieve competitive objectives, continuously improving the processes developed within it, in this sense, for Tlapa, Limon, García-Alcaraz, Baez and Sánchez (2016) the adoption of SS has increased significantly in those organizations that seek to apply best practices to increase or maintain competitiveness.

Therefore, it is necessary to identify the main factors that are immersed in the deployment of SS, which support successful implementation, the literature reports them as Critical Success Factors, and are defined by O'Sullivan (2009) as variables once identified and managed by the organization, they lead to success and the goals planned, while Suarez Amaya and Díaz Barrios (2013) define them as all those actions, capacities, resources, advantages, knowledge and skills that constitute a competitive advantage, while for Amberg, Fischl, and Wiener (2005), they are a limited number of areas in which the results is satisfactory, ensure a successful competitive performance for the organization, those characteristics, conditions or variables that, when maintained a properly management can have a significant impact on the company success that competes in a particular industry and as a this factors that, if addressed significantly improve the project implementation.

It is important to indicate that, in relation to the CSF, the literature reports a great variety, because each case study reports what for them represented a factor of success in the deployment of SS. Initially, a total of 145 factors were located through the literature review, from which a detailed analysis was carried out to identify and select the main ones to integrate this research. In another sense, in the recent literature Cherrafi et al., (2016), Faulkner and Badurdeen, (2014) there is a tendency for organizations to give priority to projects that include an evaluation or improvement of the environmental impact on the processes or product development.

In terms of the various benefits that can be obtained by properly deploying the SS strategy, sustainability is one of these, so organizations that implement continuous improvement and Green principles simultaneously consider having a better performance (Chugani, Kumar, Garza -Reyes, Rocha-Lona and Upadhyay, 2017). In this sense Dües, Tan, and Lim (2013), mention that only a group of environmental experts and researchers have investigated until now the relationship between the aspects of continuous improvement practices and Green.

In relation to sustainable benefits, Alhuraish, Robledo, and Kobi (2017) mention that a competitive advantage is achieved when companies maintain practices consistent with sustainable development strategies and, as such, control waste and the implementation of practices that are environmental and socially responsible.

With respect to the link between SS and sustainable development, there is the impression that SS can indirectly influence sustainable development through the application of its tools to environmental management systems, Sagnak and Kazancoglu (2016) and Camia et al., (2009).

Taking into account the above, it is considered pertinent and necessary to generate a measurement instrument that allows to identify the CSFs considered by the organizations that have developed SS, as well as to prove the relationship between the development of SS and the sustainability positive results.

For this, first, a literature review was developed, taking into account mainly articles that presented results on the implementation of SS and those that mentioned sustainable results from its deployment.

Once the CSFs were identified, the constructs to be evaluated were defined, the variables were operationalized and with these elements the research instrument was constructed.

The instrument was subjected to content validations through expert judgment and validation of internal consistency. The results of these procedures are described in detail in later sections of this chapter.

BACKGROUND

Contextualization of Six Sigma (SS)

At the present time, companies seek to be recognized through the development of competitive strategies that position them closer to achieving the objectives, according to M. Juran cited by Gutierrez Pulido (2014) it is important consider the quality trilogy to achieve quality in products and processes, the Juran trilogy considers the interaction of three universal processes of quality management, which are plan, control and improve; this trilogy remains in force, as organizations continue to aim at things better, faster and at a cheaper cost. Seeking compliance with the aforementioned and in relation to quality improvement, SS is one of the main strategies for continuous improvement used in large organizations that pursue total quality control and the achievement of objectives and goals.

Kaouro Ishikawa cited by Gutierrez Pulido (2014), was a great precursor of quality in Japan, due to its contribution with innovative ideas for quality, for example the DEMING quality circle, cause-effect diagram, known as Ishikawa diagram. This philosophy of total quality control took importance in Japan and establishes that all areas are responsible for quality, led it by senior management and management in charge of large organizations, these leaders seek to take advantage of competitive strategies that allow them to reach all the metrics, it is here that SS has a place as a competitive strategy that comes to strongly support to achieve the organizational objectives.

To understand the importance and usefulness of SS, it has been considered convenient to expose its beginning, evolution and development. In addition, the description of the concepts and definitions will allow the reader to contextualize SS as a competitive strategy.

SS is a strategy of continuous business improvement that has different meanings for different groups within an organization. Considering the entire company, it is a strategic initiative that seeks to achieve a significant improvement in business growth, capacity and customer satisfaction, Gutiérrez Pulido (2014). SS implies a change in the way of operating and making decisions, the strategy must be understood and supported from the highest levels of the organization, starting with the top leader.

Regarding the beginning of SS, Vinod, Devadasan, Sunil, and Thilak (2015) mention that SS emerged in Motorola in the mid-1980s, at that time it was possible to facilitate that companies achieve the desired profitability. Through this, SS was implemented in many parts of the world, the companies that carried out their implementation, they did it through the application of phases, known as DMAIC (Define, Measure, Analyze, Improve and Control), some companies that obtained significant financial benefits are General Electric, Motorola and Allied Signal (now Honeywell), (Swink & Jacobs, 2012).

SS has been defined by numerous authors in different ways, with the main objective of supporting companies towards competitiveness and profitability, achieving continuous improvement in their processes, products or services, in general terms and with the objective of knowing the different approaches to SS, some concepts identified in the literature will be retaken.

For Arturo Garza-Reyes, Flint, Kumar, Antony, and Soriano-Meier (2014) SS is considered one of the most important developments for quality management and process improvement of the last two decades, they mention that SS focuses on the critical quality characteristics of the product or process that are relevant to customers and that mainly seeks to identify and eliminate defects, errors or failures that may affect business processes or systems, in this sense, Arturo Garza-Reyes et al, Sagnak and Kazancoglu (2016), Acharya and Mathur (2016), Linderman, Schroeder, Zaheer, and Choo (2003) and Al-agha and Al-agha (2015) state that SS has three meanings, first, that it is a statistical measure of variation that when it is achieved, a process would produce 3.4 defects per million opportunities, second, which is a philosophy and management strategy that allows organizations to obtain lower costs, guaranteeing competitive operations and third that is a problem solving and improvement methodology that can be applied to all types of processes to eliminate the root cause of defects

For Furukawa, Cunha, Pedreira, & Marck, (2016), SS identifies the ability of the process to generate products within pre-established specifications, while Aslan (2005) mentions that defects in a process can be prevented if the variations are controlled and as SS focuses on the variations that cause defects in a process has been widely accepted, it also states that the SS methodology requires structured preparations and training courses.

SS is also defined as a business strategy that focuses on improving the understanding of customer requirements, commercial systems, productivity and financial performance (Mehrabi, 2012), meanwhile, Thakore, Dave, Parsana, and Solanki (2014) extend this definition, considering it as a quality initiative that reduces variations in a process and helps reduce the cost of the product and process, mentioning that the key strategy for the successful implementation of SS is that the industry that applies it must follow a correct methodology and the use of tools and techniques is done in such a way that it gives an effective solution to the respective problem.

Linderman, Schroeder and Choo (2006) mention that the SS approach to process improvement employs many objectives and that it provides an ideal context to study the relationship between objective theory and quality management, while Tjahjono et al., (2010) propose four interpretations that define SS, the first of them defines it as a set of statistical tools, the second as an operational management philosophy, the third as a business culture and finally as an analysis methodology that uses scientific methods.

Finally, Hoerl and Snee (2003) mention that the future of SS is brilliant. It is about improving and there will always be a need for improvement since we live in a dynamic and ever changing world with new customers' needs, new markets, innovation and social changes.

Relationship of SS With Sustainable Development

Recently it has been reported that organizations are presenting a trend towards sustainability and care for the environment, since environmental concern has become a concern for all, De Freitas, Costa, and Ferraz (2017). Sustainability has become a crucial element around the world, allowing the generation of profits and citizens live in a healthy environment at the same time.

Research has reported that if SS is properly implemented, it can generate sustainable benefits, although initially it has not been one of the objectives, so it is considered important to investigate existing theories and case studies that identify the way to relate a strategy of continuous improvement with sustainable benefits and environmental care.

For Zhang and Iru (2012), sustainable manufacturing is the creation of manufactured products through economically viable processes that minimize negative environmental impacts, conserving energy and natural resources simultaneously, improving the employee's safety, the community and products.

De Freitas, Costa, and Ferraz (2017) mention that sustainability has become, in recent decades, a very relevant issue for organizations, mainly due to the pressures generated by the interested parties and the change of thinking experienced by the society.

In relation to the sustainable benefits that can be obtained through the implementation of SS Vinodh, Arvind, and Somanaathan (2011) conducted a literature review in order to know the proven case studies that report environmental benefits and found that several companies they have successfully implemented continuous improvement principles (within which SS is found) to achieve sustainable benefits. With a correct implementation of SS, it is possible to produce fewer defects, therefore, less waste, improving the durability and reliability of the product; therefore, it increases the useful product life generating less negative impact on the environment.

Cherrafi et al., (2016), mention that, the possible integration of SS and sustainability has received increasing attention and that many academics and professionals have contributed to the research and development of this field, Fliedner (2008) mentions that many organizations have discovered that a byproduct of lean principles is an improved "green" or environmental performance, even when lean activities were not initiated for environmental reasons, it notes some examples of environmental benefits observed through the deployment of SS:

- Fewer defects that reduce the energy and resources needs; avoiding waste.
- It concentrates attention on reducing the conditions that cause accidents, spills and malfunctions, thus reducing solid and dangerous waste.
- Improving the product durability and reliability can increase the product useful life, reducing environmental impacts.

In the literature review has been observed the impact of SS on the care of the environment, Chugani et al (2017), Chiarini (2014), De Freitas and Costa (2017), Sagnak and Kazancoglu (2015) have positively linked the SS impact on energy issues, global warming, pollution and resources use, in addition, conducted research determine if the tools of continuous improvement reduce environmental impacts, obtaining positive results and recommending further research and increase sustainable processes within the organizations, so it is observed that when deploying SS projects, favorable results are obtained in sustainable terms and that, the relation to SS applications, the obtained contributions and benefits in the sustainable theme can achieve positive results on innovation and organizational sustainability.

Through the relationship identified between SS and the sustainable benefits and with the objective of deepening more in this research, in the elaboration of the measurement instrument it is considered a section to verify the existing relationship between SS and the sustainable benefits in the organizations that develop SS.

Identification of Critical Success Factors (CSF)

To carry out the search, the procedure suggested by Colicchia & Strozzi (2012) and Tranfield, Denyer, & Smart (2003) was taken into consideration. The main databases considered for the search and selection of the articles were EBSCO, ELSEVIER, EMERALD, SPRINGER and TAYLOR & FRANCIS, taking into account a period from 2013 to 2017, mainly, the keywords used were Six Sigma, Administrative strategy, Applications, Implementation areas, Critical success factors.

Through the various applications of SS, numerous critical factors for success have been identified; the literature suggests that these factors be taken into account in the continuous improvement projects developed in the organizations.

In that sense, the CSF that have been considered most relevant according to Júnior and Lima (2011) are the lack of alignment of the SS project with the objectives of the company, the quality of the projects did not meet the expectations of senior management, low participation of leaders and development of projects at inadequate times for the company, for Alhuraish, Robledo, and Kobi, (2017) CSF include communication, culture change and the commitment of top management, however, diverse authors, consider numerous critical factors for the development of SS projects in organizations, of which a generalized consensus has not been identified.

In the first stage of the research project, the objective was to search and select studies that explore the critical success factors in the development of SS projects in different organizations, where 145 factors were initially identified, of which the most relevant were selected for achieve the success of the implementation of SS.

In this sense, the literature has allowed to identify numerous factors that have been considered for the success of the implementation of SS, Table 1 shows 145 factors that were identified in the review, grouped into seven large groups named constructs, Senior Management Support, Strategy Implementation, Collaborative Team, Customer Relationship, Supplier Relationship, Education and Training, and that are considered critical success factors. It is important to mention that as a main contribution to the research, an additional construct was added to evaluate the sustainable benefits that can be obtained with a correct implementation of SS, which will be described later.

Finally, through the review and selection, the CSF considered in this research are *Senior Management Support, Strategy Implementation, Collaborative Team, Customer Relationship, Supplier Relationship, Education and Training.*

To design the measuring instrument (questionnaire), the grouping presented in the table was considered, as well as instruments used in various investigations; in the following section each construct and instrument integration are described in general, and will be measured through the observable variables (questions that conform the instrument). In this part of the investigation it is not appropriate to indicate specifically the questions that conform the instrument, since the investigation is still in final validation, however it is planned to make another writing where the final conclusion is given to the reader of research, as well as recommendations for future studies. In this sense, a way to guide those interested in the construction of the questionnaire, column "Similar Factors" (Table 1) and diverse researchers opinions were considered.

Table 1 was constructed based on an overview of the CSF considered in the literature and in various applications, giving a total of 145 factors, in the first investigation, later were grouped according to characteristics or because they had the same meaning but that the authors named them differently in their investigations, and those finally considered for the proposal instrument of this research.

Table 1. Group of the initial list of critical success factors

Group	Similar factors	Quantity
Senior Management Support	1. Executive commitment 2. Executive leadership and senior management commitment 3. Project selection and prioritization 4. Organizational infrastructure 5. Senior management involvement 6. Senior management support 7. Monitoring and evaluation of the project 8. Involvement and commitment of management 9. Commitment and participation of senior management 10. Leadership and commitment of senior management 11. Involvement and commitment of senior management 12. Project selection 13. Middle management commitment 14. Strong leadership and administrative commitment 15. Leadership 16. Administration support 17. Encouragement of employees 18. Evaluation 19. Leadership and support 20. Motivation 21. Leadership Participation 22. Vision and support of leaders 23. Leadership, team and focus 24. Leadership skills 25. Management commitment 26. Participation and commitment of management 27. Quality of projects do not meet the expectations of senior management 28. Recognitions or incentives of the company 29. Lack of logistics support 30. Lack of consideration of the human factor 31. Selection and start of projects 32. Project monitoring and measurements 33. Lack of communication between managers and workers 34. Lack of cooperation and trust between workers and managers 35. Project leadership 36. Responsibility	36

continues on following page

MEASUREMENT INSTRUMENT DESIGN

In relation to the importance of the implementation of SS and the varied results that have been reported in the literature, it is considered necessary to gather information that allows to establish the factors through which the possibilities of achieving success in the implementation can be increased, for this, a measurement instrument based on research and literature review was designed, which by means of reagents (items or questions), associated with each construct (section) measure those factors that those who implement SS consider most important to achieve success in the implementation, the instrument also includes a section with items related to the sustainable benefits obtained by the deployment of SS projects.

Table 1. Continued

Group	Similar factors	Quantity
Strategy Implementation	1. Adopting the philosophy 2. Zero defects mentality 3. Linking SS to the business strategy 4. Integration of SS with financial responsibility 5. Understanding the methodology 6. Understanding methods and tools 7. Understanding techniques and tools within SS 8. Structure of the SS role 9. Structured procedure in SS 10. SS focused on metrics 11. Establishment of the SS framework 12. Use of Six Sigma tools 13. Alignment of SS projects to business objectives 14. Integrating six sigma with the financial infrastructure 15. Bad selection of SS tools 16. Little knowledge of SS tools 17. SS techniques and practices 18. Lack of recognition of the need for SS projects 19. Lack of experience in SS projects 20. Development in DMAIC 21. Lack of recognition of the benefits of SS 22. Lack of a route model to guide implementation 23. Replicate the SS strategies of another organization 24. Lack of a development measurement system 25. Measurement 26. Process documentation 27. Regular audits 28. Process administration	28

continues on following page

Variables Operationalization

Senior Management Support

The participation and commitment of top management is one of the most important factors in the implementation of SS, since without the commitment and support the true importance of the initiative could be weakened, management must participate in the establishment, criteria and administration system, as well as participating in the projects, this should begin with the selection and prioritization of projects of SS, Tlapa, Limon, García-Alcaraz, Baez and Sánchez, (2016); Zu, Robbins and Fredendall, (2010); Ho, Chang and Wang, (2008); G. Dileep and S.S. Rau, (2009); Banuelas Coronado and Antony (2002).

Strategy Implementation

The implementation of the strategy for SS implies that the projects focus on the objectives of the organization and the commercial strategy and that the members have project management skills and a defined strategy to supervise and control projects.

The implementation of the strategy refers to the project execution, the project administration and monitoring of the results, Goldstein, (2001); Zu, Robbins and Fredendall, (2010); Flynn et al., (1995); Breyfogle et al. (2001); Ho, Chang and Wang, (2008); G. Dileep and S.S. Rau, (2009).

Table 1. Continued

Group	Similar factors	Quantity
Collaborative Team	1. Organizational Structures / Infrastructures 2. Team building 3. Team communication 4. Team involvement 5. Effective communication 6. Culture and organizational infrastructure 7. Based on the team 8. Participation of all staff 9. Clear definitions and understanding of the roles of all team members 10. Cooperation and communication 11. Adequate development of the human resources management system 12. Teamwork 13. Multifunctional work team 14. Lack of adequate development of the human resources management system / Lack of qualified personnel 15. Lack of multifunctional teamwork 16. Incompetence within the organizational structure 17. Selection of team members 18. Organizational understanding of work processes 19. Organizational flow adjustment 20. Capacity of key members 21. Lack of team autonomy 22. Few organizational capabilities 23. Clear roles in the project structure 24. Knowledge of the organizational structure 25. Full time dedication of black belts 26. Clear allocation of green belts 27. Attitude 28. Lack of commitment and employee participation 29. Green belts y black belts behavior characteristics 30. Worker resistance 31. Lack of perseverance 32. Lack of communication 33. Constant review of interest groups 34. Lack of employee empowerment 35. Interfunctional conflicts 36. Linking SS to human resources	36
Customer Relationship	1. Close relationships with customers 2. Customer focus 3. Participation and customer service 4. Relationship with the client 5. Business strategy based on customer demands 6. Adequate implementation of the client management system 7. Linking customer quality initiatives 8. Lack of proper implementation of the customer management system 9. Demand 10. Lack of relationship of the project objective with the main goals of the company and customer demand 11. Lack of understanding for different types of customers 12. Lack of communication with customers 13. Linking SS to the client	13

continues on following page

Table 1. Continued

Group	Similar factors	Quantity
Supplier Relationship	1. Close relationships with suppliers 2. Relationship with the supplier 3. Adequate development of the supplier management system 4. Linking quality initiatives to the supplier 5. Personal Quality of suppliers / Personnel Administration 6. Weak relationship with suppliers 7. Lack of communication with suppliers 8. Lack of influence on suppliers or lack of involvement of suppliers with the current implementation 9. Lack of supplier collaboration 10. Linking SS to providers 11. Lack of adequate development of the supplier management system 12. Lack of cooperation with suppliers	12
Education and Training	1. Training 2. Education and training 3. Knowledge transfer 4. Knowledge management 5. Parallel training / learning structure 6. Staff development 7. Development culture 8. Investment and training framework for trainers and mentors 9. Coordination with a knowledge management system 10. Understanding to start the project 11. Training 12. Lack of training and education 13. Bad selection of candidates for belt training 14. Training for master black belts and black belts 15. Mass training for yellow belts or White belts 16. Training for directors and employees 17. Lack of consultants and training in the market 18. Lack of formal training of managers 19. Lack of formal employee training 20. Six Sigma Training	20
	Total de factores =	**145**

Source: By the author

Collaborative Team

Teamwork is a fundamental element within SS. The collaborative team is characterized by members who know and fully understand the methodology, techniques and tools of SS, in addition, has the appropriate leadership, effective communication and team participation, the value of teamwork formed by teams multifunctional will create a sense of ownership, better communication, teamwork value and a general vision of the organization, Zu, Robbins and Fredendall, (2010); Banuelas Coronado and Antony, (2002); Aviation Week, (1998); Hurley and Hult, (1998).

Customers Relationship

The needs and expectations of the client are evaluated, customers are involved in quality improvement projects, customer satisfaction is measured and there is close contact with key customers. The processes must be established to monitor levels of customer satisfaction, receive customer feedback and resolve their concerns, Zu et al., (2010); Ho et al., (2008); G. Dileep and S.S. Rau, (2009); Zu et al., (2006), Banuelas Coronado and Antony, (2002).

Suppliers Relationship

A well-developed supplier management system, where the main criteria for selecting suppliers are based on quality aspects, has a positive impact on the success of the SS since the processes must be built to monitor the quality performance levels of the suppliers . The participation of suppliers in SS helps to provide a high quality of products and services to end customers, Zu et al., (2010); G. Dileep and S.S. Rau, (2009); Banuelas Coronado and Antony, (2002); Zu et al., (2006).

Education and Training

Training is the first essential step in preparing the implementation of the SS methodology, which allows establishing new goals, asking employees to face the change thinking and acting differently, performing new tasks and participating in new ones, the training is a crucial factor in the successful implementation of SS projects, Tlapa et al., (2016); Ho, Chang, and Wang, (2008), G. Dileep and S.S. Rau, (2009), Banuelas Coronado and Antony, (2002); Szeto and Tsang, (2005); Henderson and Evans, (2000).

Sustainability

Sustainability is part of the benefits that can be obtained through a correct implementation of the SS strategy, since the deployment of SS allows focusing on the reduction of defects to improve product quality, which helps reduce environmental waste (it means, the material, the consumption of water and energy and the generation of waste), while sustainable manufacturing is the creation of manufactured products through economically viable processes that minimize negative environmental impacts, conserving energy and resources simultaneously enhance the safety of employees, the community and products.

Content of the Measuring Instrument

The measuring instrument was composed of 39 items (reactive) in total, distributed in 7 sections (constructs) that supported the identification of the main CSF in the implementation of SS and its relationship with sustainability, in this sense, the table 2 shows the constructs that make up the instrument, as well as the items corresponding to each section, the first six constructs were defined with the objective of identifying the CSF, the construct *management support* consists of 7 items, *collaborative team* for 7 items, *relationship with clients* for 3 items, *relationship with suppliers* for 5 items, *education and training* for 3 items, *implementation of the strategy* for 8 items and finally the construct which measures the relationship of SS with Sustainability, *Sustainable benefits* was integrated by 6 items, giving the total of 39 in the whole instrument.

The questions that make up each construct were proposed taking as reference the 145 CSF shown in table 1, obtained from previously validated measuring instruments and applied in investigations similar to this one.

Table 2. Content of the measuring instrument

Construct	Items	Total per construct
Support to senior management:	1,2,3,4,5,6,7	7
Collaborative team	16,17,18,19, 20,21, 22	7
Relationship with customers	23,24,25	3
Relationship with suppliers	26,27,28,29,30	5
Education and training	31,32,33	3
Strategy implementation	8,9,10,11,12,13,14,15	8
Sustainable benefits	34,35,36,37,38,39	6
Total in the instrument		**39**

Source: By the author

STATISTICAL VALIDATION OF THE MEASUREMENT INSTRUMENT

Validation of the measurement instrument was carried out through content validation (Expert judgment) and internal consistency validation (Pilot sample, n = 30).

Content Validity

To carry out the content validity of the first version of the instrument, the evaluation was requested through expert judgment, for Escobar-Pérez & Cuervo-Martínez (2008) the expert judgment is an informed opinion of people who have experience in the subject, that are recognized as experts and that can give information, evidence, judgments and assessments, is this sense Corral (2009) mentions that through the expert judgment can be known the probability of probable error in the configuration of the instrument and that is intended have reasonably good estimates. Corral (2009) indicates that expert's judgments can be obtained by group methods or by a single expert and there are also different types of methods, such as the individual aggregate method, Delphi, nominal group technique and the consensus group method.

Validity of Internal Consistency

For Corral (2009), the validation of an instrument consists of quantifying the extent to which the items or reagents of an instrument are representative of the universe or trait that is to be measured, in this sense Escobar-Pérez & Cuervo-Martínez (2008) mention that the validity content is an important component in estimating validity because it provides evidence about construct validity and provides a basis for constructing parallel forms of a test in large-scale evaluation.

To evaluate the reliability in instruments with polycotomic responses, with likert scales, it is common to use the Cronbach's alpha coefficient, which can take values ranging from 0 to 1, where 0 means zero reliability and 1 means total reliability, which represents that the greater the linear correlation between the items, the higher the Cronbach's alpha, in this sense Corral (2009) refers to Sierra Bravo (2001); Orozco, Labrador and Palencia (2002) who mention that levels above 0.70 indicate a very strong and high reliability coefficient, likewise, Gómez, Toledo, Prado and Morales (2015) cite Lévy and Varela

(2003); Hair et al (2010), since they suggest a recommended minimum value of *0.75*, Gliem & Gliem (2003) refer to George and Mallery (2003), which indicates that a correlation coefficient greater than 0.90 is excellent for the validation of the instrument.

RESULTS

The results obtained are presented in the following sections, starting with the demographic description to whom the instrument will be applied (target population), followed by the results of the statistical validation of reliability of the instrument, made through the statistical analysis recommended by the literature.

TARGET POPULATION

The target population for the application of the measurement instrument will be the managers, supervisors, engineers of various areas and people who have experience and have participated in continuous improvement projects where they have applied SS belonging to the aerospace industry, in figure 1 it is observed the distribution of the companies shows that the highest concentration is in Tijuana and Mexicali, so it is expected that the answers tend to concentrate on both.

Table 3 shows the percentages of companies in the aerospace industry in Baja California, the cities with the greatest presence, mentioned previously.

Figure 1. Aerospace industry in Baja California
Source: By the author

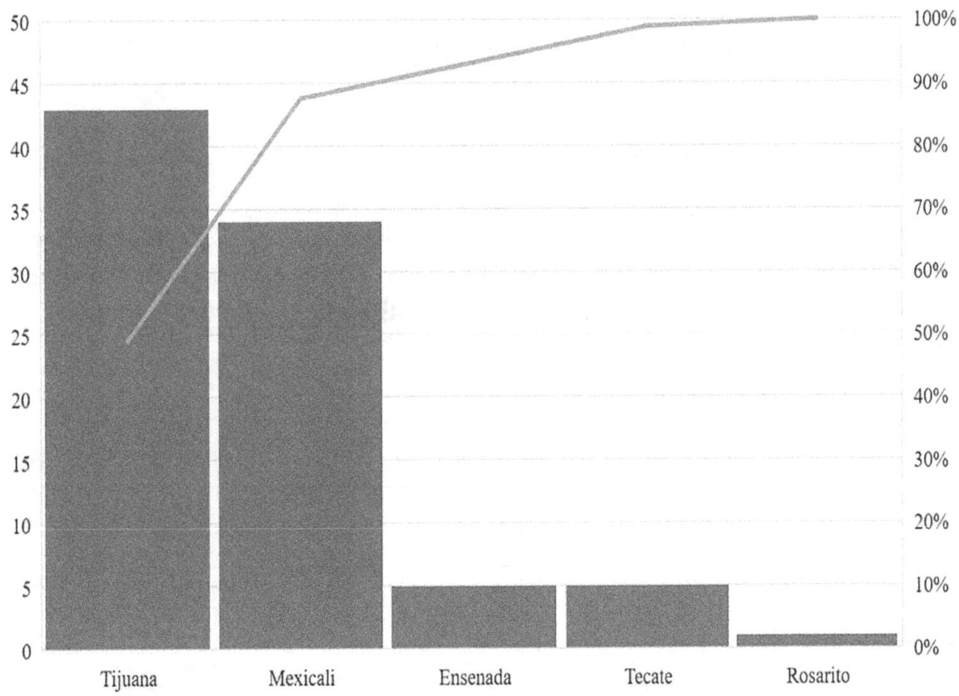

Table 3. Percentage distribution of the aerospace industry in Baja California

City	Tijuana	Mexicali	Ensenada	Tecate	Rosarito
Percentage distribution	48.86%	38.63%	5.68%	5.68%	1.13%

Source: By the author

RECOMMENDED STATISTICAL ANALYSIS

W of Kendall

To evaluate the reliability of the measurement instrument, 5 experts were asked to issue their opinion from two main characteristics that would allow us to improve the first version of the instrument, that is, the experts rated each of the items in relation to their clarity and relevance, in relation to *clarity*, a scale of 1 to 4 was used, where 1 is *the item is not clear* and 4 *the item is clear and adequate*, this part allowed to improve the writing of the items and identify if there were repeated items or that were being measured through others, as well as the elimination or modification of them, in relation to the *relevance* the scale used from 1 to 4 indicated the following, 1 *the item can be eliminated without affecting the dimension* and 4 *the item is very relevant and should be included,* in this sense it was possible to evaluate the agreement or the degree of agreement between the experts, through the evaluation of the coefficient of concordance W of Kendall, Escobar-Pérez & Cuervo-Martínez (2008) define it as a coefficient that is used to know the degree of association between the set of ranges *k* is particularly useful when the experts are asked to evaluate the items through ranges, for example from 1 to 4, as in our case. The minimum value that the coefficient can take is 0 and the maximum value is 1, which means that if the coefficient is 1 it indicates perfect agreement between the evaluators, if it is 0 it indicates that the agreement is not greater than expected by chance (there is no agreement between the evaluators).

In order to estimate the W of Kendall coefficient, the following research hypotheses were proposed:

Ho: There is no agreement between the evaluators.
Ha: There is significant agreement between the evaluators.

Based on this, the estimation was carried out, through the software SPSS 22, obtaining a **coefficient of agreement of *0.405***, although it is true that it is not an index that indicates a perfect agreement between the evaluators, however, the software showed **a level of significance of *0.000***, less than 0.05 defined in the hypothesis test, table 4.

Table 4. Coefficient of agreement

N	5
Kendall's W[a]	**.405**
Chi-Square	89.198
df	44
Asymp. Sig.	**.000**

Source: By the author

Considering Escobar-Pérez & Cuervo-Martínez (2008), it is concluded that there is significant agreement between the ranks assigned by the judges, so the measurement instrument passes the reliability assessment through expert judgment and is accepted the validity of content. Figure 2 shows the behavior of the answers given in the evaluations carried out by the evaluators, where it states the agreement in the answers assigned to each item in relation to the relevance indicated by each evaluator. As can be seen in the figure, the lines present a reasonable parallelism in almost all the items with the exception of the item 19; this is an indication that the evaluators have a concordance in the evaluated attributes for each item.

Cronbach's Alpha

To validate the instrument, we considered a sample of 30 individuals who have participated in SS projects, with experience and knowledge of the methodology, with the results obtained, the statistical validation of the instrument was made through the SPSS 22 software, the alpha of Cronbach was calculated for each of the constructs that make up the instrument, obtaining the results shown in table 5:

Finally, the Cronbach's alpha obtained for the complete instrument was ***0.959***, in the coefficients obtained it can be seen that the relationship with clients and education and training constructions have obtained the lowest rates within the whole instrument, *0.708* and *0.798* respectively, however, George and Mallery (2003) mention that indexes higher than 0.70 are acceptable within the validation of the instrument, so that with the reliability indices obtained, the internal consistency of the instrument is validated.

Figure 2. Comparison of responses between evaluators, content validity
Source: By the author

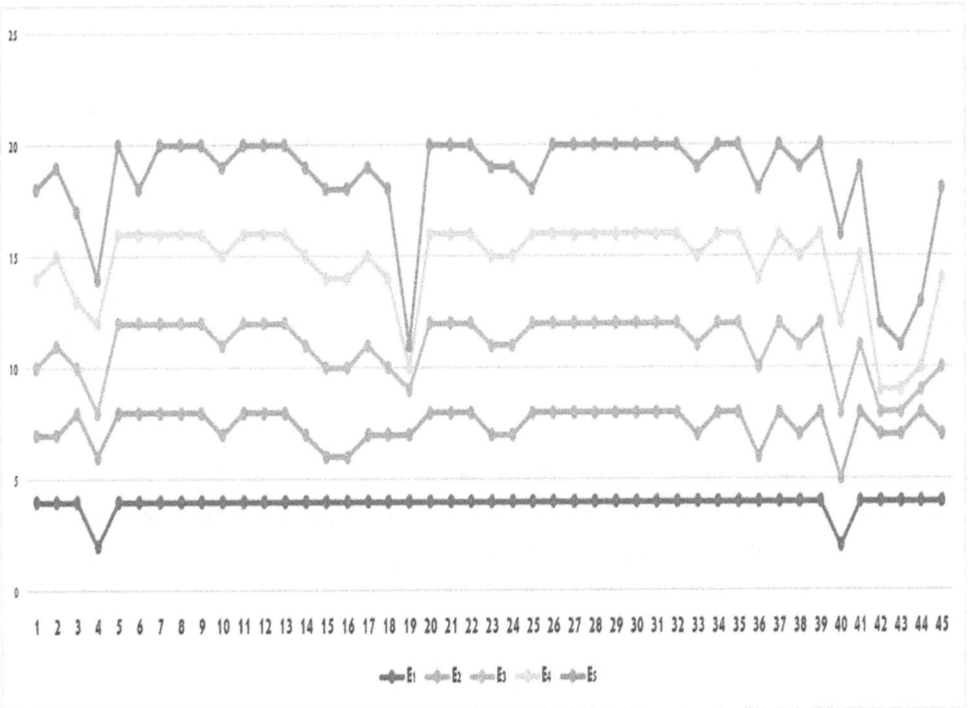

Table 5. Validity of internal consistency per construct

Construct to evaluate	Cronbach's Alpha
Management support	0.880
Strategy implementation	0.923
Collaborative team	0.864
Relationship with customers	0.708
Relationship with suppliers	0.805
Education and training	0.798
Sustainable benefits	0.896
Complete instrument	0.959

Source: By the author

RESULTS INTERPRETATION

In relation to the validation of content and according to Escobar-Pérez & Cuervo-Martínez (2008), the following is concluded:

Since the level of significance obtained in the hypothesis test is **0.000** and it is < **0.05**, the Ho is rejected, and it is concluded that **there is significant agreement between the evaluators**, so there is an agreement among the experts to validate the content of the instrument.

The values of Cronbach's Alpha show, for all constructs, an acceptable, good and excellent reliability of the instrument, since they exceed the minimum values recommended by George and Mallery (2003), which indicates that values between 0.70 and 0.79 will be acceptable, between 0.80 and 0.90 will be good and values greater than .90 will be excellent.

With the results obtained from the statistical evaluations made, considering the statistical coefficients mostly recommended for studies of this type in the literature, the content of the instrument is validated, so it can be applied in the target population and continue with the next phase of the investigation.

FUTURE RESEARCH DIRECTIONS

Although the utility and advantages that can be obtained with the implementation and development of SS are widely recognized in the literature, it is recognized that there are areas in which it can be deepened. During the literature review, certain gaps identified as an area of opportunity for researchers were identified, in this sense it is suggested that in future research it be deepened mainly in the areas of sustainability and environment, health and medicine, as well as document the practices that they are carried out in the services sector, in addition to this enriching the literature with case studies where models that support the development of projects are clearly developed, where factors that may have an impact on the achievement of the objectives of the project in an organization can be considered from the outset.

CONCLUSION

About the CSF, it is based that there are no satisfactory explanations, that they mention in which of them more attention should be paid, the resources that must be taken into consideration and how to achieve that the projects provide the desired results, besides, that there are few articles that emphasize quantitative research that includes mathematical models and that provides clear guidance for those who wish to develop and implement SS.

In the literature review, 145 CSFs were initially determined, which were analyzed and selected those considered most important for the achievement of the objectives. Through these it was possible to design the integrated measurement instrument for a total of 39 items grouped into 7 constructs, management support, strategy implementation, collaborative team, relationship with customers, relationship with suppliers, education and training and sustainable benefits

Although it is true, only with the knowledge of the CSF cannot ensure the achievement of the objectives set, it requires hard work where they are taken into account from the planning and prior to the execution of projects, in addition to a commitment of management throughout the execution process, as well as the participation of all members of the organization. In this sense the researchers report that, if the CSF are considered and taken into account from the planning and execution of SS can achieve better results and objectives, derived to this will take the organization and its leaders to improve continuous and consequently to achieve the success in the implementation.

Finally, the CSF that is sought to identify through the application of the instrument in the aerospace sector in Baja California, will be part of the main contribution of this research to the existing theory in the field of knowledge of the administration, also, it is considered that The factors considered are part of a precedent that will allow the managers of the organizations to identify, plan and schedule actions that allow them to achieve a successful implementation of SS as a competitive strategy.

REFERENCES

Acharya, A., & Mathur, A. (2016). A Study on Green Cloud Computing and Technologies. *International Journal of Advance Research in Engineering, Science & Technology, 2444*(6), 13–17.

Al-agha, O. I., & Al-agha, M. I. (2015). *Implementing Six Sigma Methodology in Industrial Control Systems*. Academic Press.

Alhuraish, I., Robledo, C., & Kobi, A. (2017). A comparative exploration of lean manufacturing and six sigma in terms of their critical success factors. *Journal of Cleaner Production, 164*, 325–337. doi:10.1016/j.jclepro.2017.06.146

Amberg, M., Fischl, F., & Wiener, M. (2005). Background of critical success factor research. *Evolution; International Journal of Organic Evolution, 17*(2), 12. Retrieved from http://www.international-outsourcing.de/CSF-Tool/docs/WorkingPaper_BackgroundCSF_Ambergetal._FINAL.pdf

Arturo Garza-Reyes, J., Flint, A., Kumar, V., Antony, J., & Soriano-Meier, H. (2014). A DMAIRC approach to lead time reduction in an aerospace engine assembly process. *Journal of Manufacturing Technology Management, 25*(1), 27–48. doi:10.1108/JMTM-05-2012-0058

Aslan, D. (2005). Çağrılı Derleme [Invited Review]. *Laboratuvar Tıbbında Altı-Sigma Kalite Yönetimi, 30*, 272–278.

Banuelas Coronado, R., & Antony, J. (2002). Critical success factors for the successful implementation of six sigma projects in organisations. *The TQM Magazine, 14*(2), 92–99. doi:10.1108/09544780210416702

Calia, R. C., Guerrini, F. M., & de Castro, M. (2009). The impact of Six Sigma in the performance of a Pollution Prevention program. *Journal of Cleaner Production, 17*(15), 1303–1310. doi:10.1016/j.jclepro.2009.05.001

Cherrafi, A., Elfezazi, S., Chiarini, A., Mokhlis, A., & Benhida, K. (2016). The integration of lean manufacturing, Six Sigma and sustainability: A literature review and future research directions for developing a specific model. *Journal of Cleaner Production, 139*, 828–846. doi:10.1016/j.jclepro.2016.08.101

Chiarini, A. (2014). Sustainable manufacturing-greening processes using specific Lean Production tools: An empirical observation from European motorcycle component manufacturers. *Journal of Cleaner Production, 85*, 226–233. doi:10.1016/j.jclepro.2014.07.080

Chugani, N., Kumar, V., Garza-Reyes, J. A., Rocha-Lona, L., & Upadhyay, A. (2017). International Journal of Lean Six Sigma Investigating the green impact of Lean, Six Sigma, and Lean Six Sigma: a systematic literature review Investigating the Green Impact of Lean, Six Sigma, and Lean Six Sigma: A Systematic Literature Review. *International Journal of Lean Six Sigma Iss International Journal of Lean Six Sigma Iss International Journal of Lean Six Sigma, 8*(8). doi:10.1108/IJLSS-11-2015-0043

Colicchia, C., & Strozzi, F. (2012). Supply chain risk management: A new methodology for a systematic literature review. *Supply Chain Management, 17*(4), 403–418. doi:10.1108/13598541211246558

Corral. (2009). Validez y confiabilidad de los instrumentos de investigación para la recolección de datos. *Revista Ciencias de La Educación, 19*(33), 228–247.

De Freitas, J. G., & Costa, H. G. (2017). Impacts of Lean Six Sigma over organizational sustainability. *International Journal of Lean Six Sigma, 8*(1), 89–108. doi:10.1108/IJLSS-10-2015-0039

de Freitas, J. G., Costa, H. G., & Ferraz, F. T. (2017). Impacts of Lean Six Sigma over organizational sustainability: A survey study. *Journal of Cleaner Production, 156*, 262–275. doi:10.1016/j.jclepro.2017.04.054

Dileep, G., & Rau, S. S. (2009). Applying Six-Sigma in Health Service: a Study of Critical Success Factors, Critical To Quality Characteristics and Key Performance Indicators in Medium Scale Hospitals. *Information Sciences & Computing, 3*(1), 25–31. Retrieved from http://journals-sathyabama.com/archives/iisc_abstract.php?id=37

Dües, C. M., Tan, K. H., & Lim, M. (2013). Green as the new Lean: How to use Lean practices as a catalyst to greening your supply chain. *Journal of Cleaner Production, 40*, 93–100. doi:10.1016/j.jclepro.2011.12.023

Escobar-Pérez, J., & Cuervo-Martínez, Á. (2008). Validez De Contenido Y Juicio De Expertos: Una Aproximación a Su Utilización. *Avances En Medición, 6*, 27–36.

Faulkner, W., & Badurdeen, F. (2014). Sustainable Value Stream Mapping (Sus-VSM): Methodology to visualize and assess manufacturing sustainability performance. *Journal of Cleaner Production, 85*, 8–18. doi:10.1016/j.jclepro.2014.05.042

Fliedner, G. (2008). Sustainability : a new lean principle. *Proceedings of the 39th Annual Meeting of the Decision Sciences Institute*, 3321–3326.

Furukawa, P. D., Cunha, I., Pedreira, M. D. G., & Marck, P. B. (2016). Environmental sustainability in medication processes performed in hospital nursing care. *Acta Paulista de Enfermagem, 29*(3), 316–324. doi:10.1590/1982-0194201600044

Gliem, J. A., & Gliem, R. R. (2003). *Calculating, Interpreting, and Reporting Cronbach's Alpha Reliability Coefficient for Likert-Type Scales*. doi:10.1109/PROC.1975.9792

Gómez, A. H., Toledo, C. E., Prado, J. M. L., & Morales, S. N. (2015). Factores críticos de éxito para el despliegue del mantenimiento productivo total en plantas de la industria maquiladora para la exportación en Ciudad Juárez: Una solución factorial. *Contaduría y Administración, 60*, 82–106. doi:10.1016/j.cya.2015.08.005

Ho, Y. C., Chang, O. C., & Wang, W. B. (2008). An empirical study of key success factors for Six Sigma Green Belt projects at an Asian MRO company. *Journal of Air Transport Management, 14*(5), 263–269. doi:10.1016/j.jairtraman.2008.05.002

Hoerl, B. R., & Snee, B. R. D. (2003). *YOUR The Future of Six Sigma*. Academic Press.

Júnior, C. H. M., & Lima, E. (2011). Descontinuidade de programas seis sigma: Um estudo comparativo de casos. *Revista de Gestão, 18*(4), 639–658. doi:10.5700/rege445

Linderman, K., Schroeder, R. G., & Choo, A. S. (2006). Six Sigma: The role of goals in improvement teams. *Journal of Operations Management, 24*(6), 779–790. doi:10.1016/j.jom.2005.08.005

Linderman, K., Schroeder, R. G., Zaheer, S., & Choo, A. S. (2003). Six Sigma: A goal-theoretic perspective. *Journal of Operations Management, 21*(2), 193–203. doi:10.1016/S0272-6963(02)00087-6

Mehrabi, J. (2012). Application of Six-Sigma in Educational Quality Management. *Procedia: Social and Behavioral Sciences, 47*, 1358–1362. doi:10.1016/j.sbspro.2012.06.826

O´Sullivan, C. (2009). *A study of critical success factors for regional*. Academic Press.

Sagnak, M., & Kazancoglu, Y. (2015). Integration of green lean approach with six sigma: An application for flue gas emissions. *Journal of Cleaner Production, 127*, 112–118. doi:10.1016/j.jclepro.2016.04.016

Suárez Amaya, W., & Díaz Barrios, J. (2013). *Factores criticos de èxito en la investigacion universitaria venezolana*. Academic Press.

Swink, M., & Jacobs, B. W. (2012). Six Sigma adoption: Operating performance impacts and contextual drivers of success. *Journal of Operations Management, 30*(6), 437–453. doi:10.1016/j.jom.2012.05.001

Thakore, R., Dave, R., Parsana, T., & Solanki, A. (2014). OPEN ACCESS A Review : Six Sigma Implementation Practice in Manufacturing Industries. *International Journal of Engineering Research and Applications, 4*(11), 63–69.

Tjahjono, B., Ball, P., Vitanov, V. I., Scorzafave, C., Nogueira, J., Calleja, J., ... Yadav, A. (2010). Six Sigma: A literature review. *International Journal of Lean Six Sigma*, *1*(3), 216–233. doi:10.1108/20401461011075017

Tlapa, D., Limon, J., García-Alcaraz, J. L., Baez, Y., & Sánchez, C. (2016). Industrial Management & Data Systems Six Sigma enablers in Mexican manufacturing companies: a proposed model Six Sigma enablers in Mexican manufacturing companies: a proposed model. *Data Systems*, *116*(5), 926–959. doi:10.1108/IMDS-06-2015-0265

Tranfield, D., Denyer, D., & Smart, P. (2003). Towards a Methodology for Developing Evidence-Informed Management Knowledge by Means of Systematic Review* Introduction: The need for an evidence-informed approach. *British Journal of Management*, *14*(3), 207–222. doi:10.1111/1467-8551.00375

Vinod, M., Devadasan, S. R., Sunil, D. T., & Thilak, V. M. M. (2015). Six Sigma through Poka-Yoke: A navigation through literature arena. *International Journal of Advanced Manufacturing Technology*, *81*(1–4), 315–327. doi:10.100700170-015-7217-9

Vinodh, S., Arvind, K. R., & Somanaathan, M. (2011). Tools and techniques for enabling sustainability through lean initiatives. *Clean Technologies and Environmental Policy*, *13*(3), 469–479. doi:10.100710098-010-0329-x

Zhang, M., & Iru, A. A. (2012). *Using Six Sigma To Achieve Sustianble Manufacturing*. Academic Press.

Zu, X., Fredendall, L. D., & Robbins, T. L. (2006). Organizational Culture and Quality Practices in Six Sigma. *The 2006 Annual Meeting of the Academy of Management*, 1–40. 10.5465/AMBPP.2006.27175447

Zu, X., Robbins, T. L., & Fredendall, L. D. (2010). Mapping the critical links between organizational culture and TQM/Six Sigma practices. *International Journal of Production Economics*, *123*(1), 86–106. doi:10.1016/j.ijpe.2009.07.009

Compilation of References

Abell, A., & Oxbrow, N. (2002). *Competing with knowledge*. London: Library Association Publishing.

Abhijeet, Abhishek, Akash, Abhishek, & Swapnil. (2016). *Set up time reduction by using SMED and Kaizen approach*. Academic Press.

Acevedo, G., Sánchez, J., Farias, M., & Fernández, A. (2013). Riesgos Psicosociales en el Equipo de Salud de Hospitales Públicos de la Provincia de Córdoba. *Ciencia & Trabajo*, *15*(48), 140–147. doi:10.4067/S0718-24492013000300006

Achanga, P., Shehab, E., Roy, R., & Nelder, G. (2006). Critical success factors for lean implementation within SMEs. *Journal of Manufacturing Technology Management*, *17*(4), 460–471. doi:10.1108/17410380610662889

Acharya, A., & Mathur, A. (2016). A Study on Green Cloud Computing and Technologies. *International Journal of Advance Research in Engineering, Science & Technology, 2444*(6), 13–17.

Adanna, I. W., & Shantharam, A. (2013). *Improvement of Setup Time and Production Output with the use of Single Minute Exchange of Die Principles*. Academic Press.

Ahsan, N., Abdullah, Z., Fie, D. G., & Alam, S. S. (2009). A study of job stress on job satisfaction among university staff in Malaysia: Empirical study. *European Journal of Social Sciences, 8*(1), 121-131.

Ahsan, N., Abdullah, Z., Fie, D. Y. G., & Alam, S. S. (2009). A Study of Job Stress on Job Satisfaction among University Staff in Malaysia: Empirical Study. *European Journal of Soil Science*, *8*(1), 121–131.

Ahsberg, E. (2000). Dimensions of fatigue in different working populations. *Scandinavian Journal of Psychology*, *41*(3), 231–241. doi:10.1111/1467-9450.00192 PMID:11041305

Ahsberg, E., Garnberale, F., & Kjellberg, A. (1997). Perceived quality of fatigue during different occupational tasks Development of a questionnaire Elizabeth Åhsberg, Francesco Garnberale. *Anders Kjellberg.*, *20*, 121–135.

Akinmayowa, J. T., & Kadiri, P. A. (2016). Stress Among Academic Staff in a Nigerian University. *Covenant Journal of Business and Social Sciences*, *6*(1), 73–91.

Akın, U., Baloğlu, M., & Karslı, M. D. (2014). Türkiye'deki Kadın Üniversite Yöneticilerinin Stres ve Kaygı Düzeylerinin İncelenmesi. *Eğitim ve Bilim*, *39*(174), 160–172.

Akyol, B., & Tanrisevdi, F. (2018). Academicians in Turkey: An Evaluation of Current Status of Academic Staff in Higher Education. *Higher Education Studies*, *8*(4), 129–138. doi:10.5539/hes.v8n4p129

Akyol, H. (2014). The Measuring Effect of Employee Satisfaction of Academic Staff to Employee Performance. *Journal of Social and Administrative Sciences*, *1*(1), 18–33. doi:10.1453/jsas.v1i1.119

Al-agha, O. I., & Al-agha, M. I. (2015). *Implementing Six Sigma Methodology in Industrial Control Systems*. Academic Press.

Alam, M. A. (2016). Techno-stress and productivity: Survey evidence from the aviation industry. *Journal of Air Transport Management*, *50*, 62–70. doi:10.1016/j.jairtraman.2015.10.003

Alarcón, J. (2017). The rules of our game: Neoliberal privatization of education in Chile. *Praxis Educativa (Santa Rosa)*, *12*(3), 690–707. doi:10.5212/PraxEduc.v.12i3.001

Albarrán, V., Geldres, V., Paredes, P., Ramírez, O., Ruiz, F., & Palomino, J. C. (2018). Validación de la batería de instrumentos para la evaluación de factores de riesgo psicosocial. *Horiz Med*, *18*(1), 59–67. doi:10.24265/horizmed.2018.v18n1.09

Alhuraish, I., Robledo, C., & Kobi, A. (2017). A comparative exploration of lean manufacturing and six sigma in terms of their critical success factors. *Journal of Cleaner Production*, *164*, 325–337. doi:10.1016/j.jclepro.2017.06.146

Álvarez, C. (2012). Riesgo psicosocial intralaboral y "burnout" en docentes universitarios de algunos países latinoamericanos. *Cuadernos de Administración*, *28*(48), 118–133. Retrieved from http://search.ebscohost.com/login.aspx?direct=true&db=fua&AN=86056250&lang=es&site=ehost-live

Amberg, M., Fischl, F., & Wiener, M. (2005). Background of critical success factor research. *Evolution; International Journal of Organic Evolution*, *17*(2), 12. Retrieved from http://www.international-outsourcing.de/CSF-Tool/docs/WorkingPaper_BackgroundCSF_Ambergetal._FINAL.pdf

Amorim-Santino, T., Ferreira-Tomaz, A., & Gomes de Lucena, N. M. (2017). Influence of occupational fatigue in the work ability of professors. *Ciencia & Trabajo*, *19*(59), 86–90. doi:10.4067/S0718-24492017000200086

Andrés-López, E., González-Requena, I., & Sanz-Lobera, A. (2015). Lean Service: Reassessment of Lean Manufacturing for Service Activities. *Procedia Engineering*, *132*, 23–30. doi:10.1016/j.proeng.2015.12.463

Ángel, D., & Camón, G. (2003). *Criterios objetivos para la evaluación de la carga de trabajo derivada de factores psicosociales y organizacionales*. Academic Press.

Ansoleaga Moreno, E., & Toro, J. P. (2010). Factores psicosociales laborales asociados a riesgo de sintomatología depresiva en trabajadores de una empresa minera. *Salud Trab*, *18*(1), 7–16.

Antoncic, B., & Zorn, O. (2004). The mediating role of corporate entrepreneurship in the organizational support-performance relationship: An empirical examination. *Managing Global Transitions*, *2*(1), 5.

Antony, J. (2004). Six Sigma in the UK service organisations: Results from a pilot survey. *Managerial Auditing Journal*, *19*(8), 1006–1013. doi:10.1108/02686900410557908

Antony, J. (2006). Six sigma for service processes. *Business Process Management Journal*, *12*(2), 234–248. doi:10.1108/14637150610657558

Antony, J., Antony, F. J., Kumar, M., & Cho, B. R. (2007). Six sigma in service organisations: Benefits, challenges and difficulties, common myths, empirical observations and success factors. *International Journal of Quality & Reliability Management*, *24*(3), 294–311. doi:10.1108/02656710710730889

Antony, J., & Banuelas, R. (2002). Key ingredients for the effective implementation of Six Sigma program. *Measuring Business Excellence*, *6*(4), 20–27. doi:10.1108/13683040210451679

Antony, J., Fergusson, C., Warwood, S., & Hing Yee Tsang, J. (2004). Comparing total quality management success factors in UK manufacturing and service industries: Some key findings from a survey. *Journal of Advances in Management Research*, *1*(2), 32–45. doi:10.1108/97279810480000363

Antony, J., Krishan, N., Cullen, D., & Kumar, M. (2012). Lean Six Sigma for higher education institutions (HEIs). *International Journal of Productivity and Performance Management*, *61*(8), 940–948. doi:10.1108/17410401211277165

Aoki, K. (2011). International Activity and Topics on "Ergonomic Principles related Mental Work Load (ISO 10075). *The Japanese Journal of Ergonomics*. doi:10.5100/jje.29.supplement_54

Aquilani, B., Silvestri, C., Ruggieri, A., & Gatti, C. (2017). A systematic literature review on total quality management critical success factors and the identification of new avenues of research. *The TQM Journal*, *29*(1), 184–213. doi:10.1108/TQM-01-2016-0003

Arabacı, B. (2010). The effects of depersonalization and organizational cynicism levels on the job satisfaction of educational inspectors. *African Journal of Business Management*, *4*(13), 2802–2811.

Arce, A., & Silvia, R. (2012). Factores organizacionales causantes del estrés en el trabajo y estrategias para afrontarlo. *Revista Venezolana de Gerencia (RVG)*, *17*(60), 611–634.

Ardıç, K. (2008). Tükenmişlik Sendromu Akademisyenler Üzerine Bir Uygulama (GOÜ Örneği). *Gazi Üniversitesi İktisadi ve İdari Bilimler Fakültesi Dergisi*, *10*(2), 69–96.

Arkan, Z., & Gürleyen, I. (2015). Europeanization of Education in Turkey. In A. Güney & A. Tekin (Eds.), *Europeanization of Turkish Public Policies* (pp. 164–177). London: Routledge. doi:10.4324/9781315733005-11

Arkhangelskiy, V., & Bohaenko, I. (2000). *Man-machine automation systems: quality, safety and reliability management*. Kiev: Kiev Automation Institute.

Arquer de, M. (1999). NTP 534: Carga mental de trabajo: factores. *Instituto Nacional de Seguridad e Higiene En El Trabajo*.

Arquer de, M. I. (1999). NTP 534: Carga mental de trabajo: factores. *Instituto Nacional de Seguridad e Higiene En El Trabajo*, 1–6. Retrieved from http://www.insht.es/InshtWeb/Contenidos/Documentacion/FichasTecnicas/NTP/Ficheros/501a600/ntp_534.pdf

Arquero, J. L., & Donoso, J. A. (2013). Docencia, investigación y burnout: El síndrome del quemado en profesores universitarios de contabilidad. *Revista de Contabilidad*, *16*(2), 94–105. doi:10.1016/j.rcsar.2013.04.001

Artazcoz, L. (2001). Factores de riesgo psicosocial y carga mental : ¿ estamos midiendo lo mismo o son conceptos diferentes? *Archivos de Prevencion de Riesgos Laborales*, *4*(3), 91–92.

Arturo Garza-Reyes, J., Flint, A., Kumar, V., Antony, J., & Soriano-Meier, H. (2014). A DMAIRC approach to lead time reduction in an aerospace engine assembly process. *Journal of Manufacturing Technology Management*, *25*(1), 27–48. doi:10.1108/JMTM-05-2012-0058

Arvey, R. D., Renz, G., & Watson, T. (1997). Individual differences in emotionality as predictors of job performance. In *Research in Personnel and Human Resources Management* (Vol. 15). Greenwich, CT: JAI.

Asensio-Cuesta, S., Bastante Ceca, M. J., & Diego Más, J. A. (2012). *Evaluación ergonómica de puestos de trabajo*. Retrieved from https://books.google.com.mx/books/about/EVALUACIÓN_ERGONÓMICA_DE_PUESTOS_DE_TR.html?id=v5kFfWOUh5oC&redir_esc=y

Aslan, D. (2005). Çağrılı Derleme [Invited Review]. *Laboratuvar Tıbbında Altı-Sigma Kalite Yönetimi*, *30*, 272–278.

Asnan, R., Nordin, N., & Othman, S. N. (2015). Managing Change on Lean Implementation in Service Sector. *Procedia: Social and Behavioral Sciences*, *211*, 313–319. doi:10.1016/j.sbspro.2015.11.040

Aviation Accident Statistics. (2019). *National Transportation Safety Board*. Retrieved from www.ntsb.gov/aviation/aviation.htm

Ayaz, H., Shewokis, P. A., Bunce, S., Izzetoglu, K., Willems, B., & Onaral, B. (2012). Optical brain monitoring for operator training and mental workload assessment. *NeuroImage*, *59*, 36–47.

Babazono, A., Mino, Y., Nagano, J., Tsuda, T., & Araki, T. (2005). A Prospective Study on the Influences of Workplace Stress on Mental Health. *Journal of Occupational Health*, *47*(6), 490–495. doi:10.1539/joh.47.490 PMID:16369111

Bailey, B. P., & Iqbal, S. T. (2008). Understanding changes in mental workload during execution of goal-directed tasks and its application for interruption management. *ACM Transactions on Computer-Human Interaction*, *14*(4), 1–28. doi:10.1145/1314683.1314689

Bajpai, J. D. (2014). SMED (Single-Minute Exchange of Die) methodology in Garment manufacturing Industry : Case study in reducing Style Change over. *Time*, 1–7.

Bang, H., & Reio, T. G. (2017). Análisis del papel del cinismo en la relación entre el burnout y el comportamiento de los trabajadores. *Revista de Psicología del Trabajo y de las Organizaciones*, *33*(3), 217–227. doi:10.1016/j.rpto.2017.07.002

Banuelas Coronado, R., & Antony, J. (2002). Critical success factors for the successful implementation of six sigma projects in organisations. *The TQM Magazine*, *14*(2), 92–99. doi:10.1108/09544780210416702

Bashiri, B., & Mann, D. D. (2015). Impact of Automation on Drivers' Performance in Agricultural Semi-Autonomous Vehicles. *Journal of Agricultural Safety and Health*, *21*(2), 129–139. doi:10.13031/jash.21.10977 PMID:26204788

Belkic, K. (2003). *The Occupational Stress Index: An Approach Derived from Cognitive Ergonomics and Brain Research for Clinical Practice*. Cambridge International Science Publishing.

Belkic, K., Landsbergis, P. A., Schnall, P. L., & Baker, D. (2004). Is job strain a major source of cardiovascular disease risk? *Scandinavian Journal of Work, Environment & Health*, *30*(2), 85–128. doi:10.5271jweh.769 PMID:15127782

Beltrán, C., Gónzalez, J., & Barraza Salas, J. (2013). Factores psicosociales y síndrome de burnout en trabajadores de la industria de la transformación de la masa, Tepic, México. *Revista Colombiana de Psiquiatría*, *42*(2), 167–172. doi:10.1016/S0034-7450(13)70003-9 PMID:26572811

Beltrán, C., Moreno, M., López, T., Estrada, J., & Torres, J. (2011). Factores psicosociales y patologías laborales en trabajadores de un sistema de transporte público urbano, México. *Revista Colombiana de Psiquiatría*, *40*(2), 266–278. doi:10.1016/S0034-7450(14)60123-2

Benavides, F., Gimeno, D., Benach, J., Martínez, J. M., Jarque, S., Berra, A., & Devesa, J. (2002). Descripción de los factores de riesgo psicosocial en cuatro empresas. *Gaceta Sanitaria*, *16*(3), 222–229. doi:10.1016/S0213-9111(02)71665-8 PMID:12057177

Benjamin, S. J., Murugaiah, U., & Marathamuthu, M. S. (2013). The use of SMED to eliminate small stops in a manufacturing firm. *Journal of Manufacturing Technology Management*, *24*(5), 792–807. doi:10.1108/17410381311328016

Berniker, E., & Mintzberg, H. (2006). Structure in Fives: Designing Effective Organizations. *Administrative Science Quarterly*. doi:10.2307/2393181

Bilko, A. (2015). *Neural network model of student admission in Air Traffic Controller simulator training* (Master's thesis). Kyiv: National Aviation University.

Birhanu, M., Gebrekidan, B., Tesefa, G., & Tareke, M. (2018). Workload Determines Workplace Stress among Health Professionals Working in Felege-Hiwot Referral Hospital, Bahir Dar, Northwest Ethiopia. *Journal of Environmental and Public Health, 2018*, 1–8. doi:10.1155/2018/6286010 PMID:30598668

Biron, C., Brun, J. P., & Ivers, H. (2008). Extent and sources of occupational stress in university staff. *Work (Reading, Mass.), 30*(4), 511–522. PMID:18725713

Biron, M., & Eshed, R. (2017). Gaps Between Actual and Preferred Career Paths Among Professional Employees: Implications for Performance and Burnout. *Journal of Career Development, 44*(3), 224–238. doi:10.1177/0894845316645664

Blanch, J., Sahagún, M., & Cervantes, G. (2010). Estructura factorial del cuestionario de condiciones de trabajo. *Revista de Psicología del Trabajo y de las Organizaciones, 26*(3), 175–189. doi:10.5093/tr2010v26n3a2

Bligård, L. O., & Osvalder, A. L. (2014). CCPE: Methodology for a combined evaluation of cognitive and physical ergonomics in the interaction between human and machine. *Human Factors and Ergonomics in Manufacturing, 24*(6), 685–711. doi:10.1002/hfm.20512

Blix, A. G., Cruise, R. J., Mitchell, B. M., & Blix, G. G. (1994). Occupational stress among university teachers. *Educational Research, 36*(2), 157–169. doi:10.1080/0013188940360205

Boet, S., Sharma, B., Pigford, A.-A., Hladkowicz, E., Rittenhouse, N., & Grantcharov, T. (2017). Debriefing decreases mental workload in surgical crisis: A randomized controlled trial. *Surgery, 161*(5), 1215–1220. doi:10.1016/j.surg.2016.11.031 PMID:28104293

Bones, K., Muntaner, C., Solar, O., Borrell, C., Bernales, P., & González, M., … Vallebuona, C. (2014). Social class, psychosocial occupational risk factors, and the association with self-rated health and mental health in Chile. *Cadernos de Saude Publica*. doi:10.1590/0102-311X00176213

Borg, G., Ljunggren, G., & Ceci, R. (1985). The increase of perceived exertion, aches and pain in the legs, heart rate and blood lactate during exercise on a bicycle ergometer. *European Journal of Applied Physiology and Occupational Physiology, 54*(4), 343–349. doi:10.1007/BF02337176 PMID:4065121

Borghini, G., Astolfi, L., Vecchiato, G., Mattia, D., & Babiloni, F. (2014). Measuring neurophysiological signals in aircraft pilots and car drivers for the assessment of mental workload, fatigue and drowsiness. *Neuroscience and Biobehavioral Reviews, 44*, 58–75. doi:10.1016/j.neubiorev.2012.10.003 PMID:23116991

Borman WC, Hanson M, Hedge J. (1997). Personnel selection. *Annu. Rev. Psychol., 48*, 299-337.

Borman, W. C., & Motowidlo, S. J. (1993). Expanding the criterion domain to include elements of contextual performance. Academic Press.

Borman, W. C., & Motowidlo, S. J. (1993). Expanding the criterion domain to include elements of contextual performance. In A. N. Schmitt & W. C. Borman (Ed.), Personnel selection in organizations (pp. 71–98). San Francisco: Jossey-Bass.

Bourbonnais, R., Brisson, C., Vinet, A., Vezina, M., Abdous, B., & Gaudet, M. (2006). Effectiveness of a participative intervention on psychosocial work factors to prevent mental health problems in a hospital setting. *Occup Environ Med, 63*(5), 335-342. Doi:10.1136/oem.2004.018077

Boynton, A. C., & Zmud, R. W. (1986). An Assessment of Critical Success Factors. *Sloan Management Review, 25*, 17–27.

Bradley, J., & Eachus, P. (1995). Occupational stress within a UK higher education institution. *International Journal of Stress Management, 2*(3), 145–158. doi:10.1007/BF01740300

Brah, S. A., Wong, J. L., & Rao, B. M. (2000). TQM and business performance in the service sector: A Singapore study. *International Journal of Operations & Production Management*, *20*(11), 1293–1312. doi:10.1108/01443570010348262

Brandes, P., Castro, S., James, M. S. L., Martinez, A. D., Matherly, T. A., Ferris, G. R., & Hochwater, W. A. (2008). The interactive effects of job insecurity and organiza- tional cynicism on work effort following a layoff. *Journal of Leadership & Organizational Studies*, *14*(3), 233–247. doi:10.1177/1071791907311967

Brookhuis, K. A., & de Waard, D. (2010). Monitoring drivers' mental workload in driving simulators using physiological measures. *Accident; Analysis and Prevention*, *42*(3), 898–903. doi:10.1016/j.aap.2009.06.001 PMID:20380918

Bruckmann, S., & Carvalho, T. (2018). Understanding change in higher education: An archetypal approach. *Higher Education*, *76*(4), 629–647. doi:10.100710734-018-0229-2

Budak, G., & Sürgevil, O. (2005). Tükenmişlik ve Tükenmíşliği Etkíleyen Örgütsel Faktörlerín Analízíne İlişkín Akademík Personel Üzerínde Bír Uygulama. *Dokuz Eylül Üniversitesi İİBF Dergisi*, *20*(2), 95–108.

Bunge, M. (2004). La investigación científica. Su estrategia y su filosofía (Tercera ed). siglo xxi Editores S.A. de C.V.

Burr, H., Albertsen, K., Rugulies, R., & Hannerz, H. (2010). Do dimensions from the Copenhagen Psychosocial Questionnaire predict vitality and mental health over and above the job strain and effort-reward imbalance models? *Scandinavian Journal of Public Health*, *38*, 59-68. DOI: . doi:10.1177/1403494809353436

Bushe, G. R. (1988). Cultural contradictions of statistical process control in A. *Journal of Management*, *14*(1), 19–31. doi:10.1177/014920638801400103

Byrne, A., Oliver, M., Bodger, O., Barnett, W. A., Williams, D., Jones, H., & Murphy, A. (2010). Novel method of measuring the mental workload of anaesthetists during clinical practice. *British Journal of Anaesthesia*, *105*(6), 767–771. doi:10.1093/bja/aeq240 PMID:20846966

Cain, B. (2004). A Review of the Mental Workload Literature. *NATO RTO-TR-HFM-121-Part-II*, (1998), 4-1-4–34. doi:10.14339/RTO-TR-HFM-121-Part-II

Cain, B. (2007). *A review of the mental workload literature*. Defence Research and Development Toronto.

Çakmak, E., Öztekin, Ö., & Karadağ, E. (2015). The effect of leadership on job satisfaction. In Leadership and Organizational Outcomes: Meta-Analysis of Empirical Studies. doi:10.1007/978-3-319-14908-0_3

Cakmakci, M., & Karasu, M. K. (2007). Set-up time reduction process and integrated predetermined time system MTM-UAS: A study of application in a large size company of automobile industry. *International Journal of Advanced Manufacturing Technology*, *33*(3–4), 334–344. doi:10.100700170-006-0466-x

Calderón Hernández, G., Serna Gómez, H., & Zuluaga Soto, J. (2013). Liderazgo y relaciones sociales en el trabajo como factor de riesgo psicosocial : Su incidencia sobre gestión humana en las Organizaciones. *Revista Diversitas - Perspectivas Psicológicas*, *9*(2), 409–423. Retrieved from http://aplicacionesbiblioteca.udea.edu.co:3628/ehost/detail/detail?vid=7&sid=9d93b370-38eb-4567-baeb-4c2cee3ce91f%40sessionmgr4002&hid=4209&bdata=Jmxhbmc9ZXMmc2l0ZT1laG9zdC1saXZl#AN=98258180&db=fua

Calia, R. C., Guerrini, F. M., & de Castro, M. (2009). The impact of Six Sigma in the performance of a Pollution Prevention program. *Journal of Cleaner Production*, *17*(15), 1303–1310. doi:10.1016/j.jclepro.2009.05.001

Callejón-Ferre, Á., Montoya-García, M., Pérez-Alonso, J., & Rojas-Sola, J. (2015). The psychosocial risks of farm workers in south-east Spain. *Safety Science*, *78*, 77–90. doi:10.1016/j.ssci.2015.04.015

Callejón-Ferre, A., Pérez-Alonso, J., Carreño-Ortega, A., & Velázquez-Martí, B. (2011). Indices of ergonomic-psychol-sociological workplace quality in the greenhouses of Almería (Spain): Crops of cucumbers, peppers, aubergines and melons. *Safety Science*, *49*(5), 746–750. doi:10.1016/j.ssci.2010.12.009

Camargo-Mayorga, D. A. (2016). Motivations of Teaching Work: A Case Study of Two Public Accounting Programs in Bogota. *Cuadernos de Contabilidad*, *17*(44), 421–448. doi:10.11144/Javeriana.cc17-44.mlde

Campbell, P. J. (1990). Modeling the performance prediction problem in industrial and organizational psychology. Handbook of Industrial and Organizational Psychology.

Campbell, J. P., McHenry, J. J., & Wise, L. L. (1990). Modeling job performance in a population of jobs. *Personnel Psychology*, *43*(2), 313–333. doi:10.1111/j.1744-6570.1990.tb01561.x

Cano-Climent, A., Oliver-Roig, A., Cabrero-García, J., de Vries, J., & Richart-Martínez, M. (2017). The Spanish version of the Fatigue Assessment Scale: Reliability and validity assessment in postpartum women. *PeerJ*, *5*, e3832. doi:10.7717/peerj.3832 PMID:28970968

Capano, G., & Piattoni, S. (2011). From Bologna to Lisbon: The Political Uses of the Lisbon 'script' in European Higher Education Policy. *Journal of European Public Policy*, *18*(4), 584–606. doi:10.1080/13501763.2011.560490

Çapri, B. (2006). Tükenmişlik Ölçeğinin Türkçe Uyarlaması: Geçerlik ve Güvenirlik Çalışması. *Mersin Üniversitesi Eğitim Fakültesi Dergisi*, *2*(1), 62–77. doi:10.17860/EFD.24817

Carayon, P., Smith, M. J., & Haims, M. C. (2007). Work Organization, Job Stress, and Work-Related Musculoskeletal Disorders. *Human Factors: The Journal of the Human Factors and Ergonomics Society*. doi:10.1518/001872099779656743

Cardy, R. L., & Dobbins, G. H. (1994). *Performance Appraisal: Alternative Perspectives*. Cincinnati, OH: Southwest.

Castor, M., MacLeod, I., Hanson, E., Svensson, E., Nählinder, S., Le Blaye, P., … Hilburn, B. (2003). GARTEUR Handbook of mental workload measurement. GARTEUR, Group for Aeronautical Research and Technology in Europe, Flight Mechanics Action Group FM AG13.

Cauas, D. (2015). *Definición de las variables, enfoque y tipo de investigación* (No. Recuperado el Vol. 15). Universidad Nacional Abierta y a Distancia (UNAD). Retrieved from http://www.mecanicahn.com/personal/marcosmartinez/seminario1/los_pdf/l-Variables.pdf

Çavuş, M. F., Gök, T., & Kurtay, F. (2007). Tükenmíşlík: Meslek Yüksekokulu Akademik Personelí Üzeríne Bír Araştırma. Ç.Ü. *Sosyal Bilimler Enstitüsü Dergisi*, *16*(2), 97–108.

Ceballos Vásquez, P., Paravic Klijn, T., Moreno, M. B., & Barriga, O. (2014). Validación De Escala Subjetiva De Carga Mental De Trabajo En Funcionarios/As Universitarios Validation of Subjective Mental Workload Scale in Academics Staff. *Ciencia y Enfermería*, *20*(2), 73–82. doi:10.4067/S0717-95532014000200008

Chabowski, P., Rewers, P., & Trojanowska, J. (2016). Impact of shortening changeover times on manufacturing flexibility. *Technological Forum 2016*, 1–7.

Chakrabarty, A., & Tan, K. C. (2006). Applying six-sigma in the service industry: A review and case study in call center services. *ICMIT 2006 Proceedings - 2006 IEEE International Conference on Management of Innovation and Technology*, *2*, 728–732. doi:10.1109/ICMIT.2006.262316

Chakrabarty, A., & Chuan Tan, K. (2007). The current state of six sigma application in services. *Managing Service Quality*, *17*(2), 194–208. doi:10.1108/09604520710735191

Chakrabarty, A., & Kay Chuan, T. (2009). An exploratory qualitative and quantitative analysis of Six Sigma in service organizations in Singapore. *Management Research News, 32*(7), 614–632. doi:10.1108/01409170910965224

Chakrabarty, A., & Tan, K. C. (2007). A survey on Six Sigma implementation in Singapore service industries. *IEEM 2007: 2007 IEEE International Conference on Industrial Engineering and Engineering Management*, 1428–1432. 10.1109/IEEM.2007.4419428

Chakrabarty, A., & Tan, K. C. (2008). Case study analysis of six Sigma in Singapore service organizations. *5th International Conference Service Systems and Service Management - Exploring Service Dynamics with Science and Innovative Technology, ICSSSM'08*. 10.1109/ICSSSM.2008.4598532

Chakraborty, A. (2013). An empirical analysis on Six Sigma implementation in service organisations. *International Journal of Lean Six Sigma*. doi:10.1108/20401461311319338

Charria, V. H., Sarsosa, K. V., & Arenas, F. (2011). Occupational psychosocial risk factors: methods and assessment tools. *Revista Facultad Nacional de Salud Pública, 29*(4), 380-391. Available in: http://www.redalyc.org/articulo.oa?id=12021522004

Charria, V., Sarsosa, K., & Arenas, F. (2011). Factores de riesgo psicosocial laboral : métodos e instrumentos de evaluación. *Revista Facultad Nacional de Salud Pública, 29*, 380–391. Retrieved from http://www.redalyc.org/articulo.oa?id=12021522004%5CnRevista

Charria, V., Sarsosa, K., & Arenas, F. (2011). Factores de riesgo psicosocial laboral; métodos e instrumentos de evaluación. *Rev. Fac. Nac. Salud Pública, 29*(4), 380–391.

Charron, K. F., & Lowe, D. J. (2008). Skepticism and the Management Accountant: Insights for Fraud Detection. *Management Accounting Quarterly, 9*(2), 9–15. Retrieved from https://www.imanet.org/insights-and-trends/management-accounting-quarterly/maq-index/2008/winter-2008?ssopc=1

Chávez-Orozco, C. A. (2016). Burnout syndrome in university teachers. *INNOVA Research Journal, 1*(9), 77–95. doi:10.33890/innova.v1.n9.2016.55

Cherrafi, A., Elfezazi, S., Chiarini, A., Mokhlis, A., & Benhida, K. (2016). The integration of lean manufacturing, Six Sigma and sustainability: A literature review and future research directions for developing a specific model. *Journal of Cleaner Production, 139*, 828–846. doi:10.1016/j.jclepro.2016.08.101

Che, X. X., Zhou, Z. E., Kessler, S. R., & Spector, P. E. (2017). Stressors beget stressors: The effect of passive leadership on employee health through workload and work–family conflict. *Work and Stress, 31*(4), 338–354. doi:10.1080/02678373.2017.1317881

Chiarini, A. (2014). Sustainable manufacturing-greening processes using specific Lean Production tools: An empirical observation from European motorcycle component manufacturers. *Journal of Cleaner Production, 85*, 226–233. doi:10.1016/j.jclepro.2014.07.080

Chilean Telecommunications Undersecretary. (2017). *IX Internet Access and Usage Survey*. Government of Chile.

Chirico, F. (2017). The forgotten realm of the new and emerging psychosocial risk factors. *Journal of Occupational Health, 59*(5), 433–435. doi:10.1539/joh.17-0111-OP PMID:28819083

Choe, P., Tew, J. D., & Tong, S. (2015). Effect of cognitive automation in a material handling system on manufacturing flexibility. *International Journal of Production Economics, 170*, 891–899. doi:10.1016/j.ijpe.2015.01.018

Choppin, J., Roth-McDuffie, A., Drake, C., & Davis, J. (2018). Curriculum ergonomics: Conceptualizing the interactions between curriculum design and use. *International Journal of Educational Research*, *92*, 75–85. doi:10.1016/j.ijer.2018.09.015

Chu, H. C., & Kuo, T. (2015). Testing Herzberg's two-factor theory in educational settings in Taiwan. *The Journal of Human Resource and Adult Learning, 11*(1), 54-65. Available in: http://www.hraljournal.com/Page/10%20HuichinChu&TsuiYangKuo.pdf

Chugani, N., Kumar, V., Garza-Reyes, J. A., Rocha-Lona, L., & Upadhyay, A. (2017). International Journal of Lean Six Sigma Investigating the green impact of Lean, Six Sigma, and Lean Six Sigma: a systematic literature review Investigating the Green Impact of Lean, Six Sigma, and Lean Six Sigma: A Systematic Literature Review. *International Journal of Lean Six Sigma Iss International Journal of Lean Six Sigma Iss International Journal of Lean Six Sigma*, *8*(8). doi:10.1108/IJLSS-11-2015-0043

Çiçek Sağlam, A. (2011). Akademik Personelin Sosyo-demografik Özelliklerinin Tükenmişlik Düzeyleri ile İlişkisi. *Mustafa Kemal Üniversitesi Sosyal Bilimler Enstitüsü Dergisi*, *8*(15), 407–420.

Cinaz, B., Arnrich, B., La Marca, R., & Tröster, G. (2013). Monitoring of mental workload levels during an everyday life office-work scenario. *Personal and Ubiquitous Computing*, *17*(2), 229–239. doi:10.100700779-011-0466-1

Clark, B. R. (2001). The Entrepreneurial University: New Foundations for Collegiality, Autonomy, & Achievement. *Higher Education Management*, *13*(2), 9–24.

Clark, B. R. (2004). *Sustaining Change in Universities: Continuities in case studies & concepts*. London: SRHE/OUP.

Claxton Bomme, S., & Fendley, M. (2018). A theoretical framework for evaluating mental workload resources in human systems design for manufacturing operations. *International Journal of Industrial Ergonomics*, *63*, 7–17. doi:10.1016/j.ergon.2016.10.007

CoHE. (2010). *National Qualifications Framework for Higher Education in Turkey*. Retrieved from https://tyyc.yok.gov.tr/?pid=31&dil=eng

CoHE. (2019). *"Yağmacı" Dergi Yayınlari Akademik Yükseltmelerde Kullanılamayacak*. Retrieved from https://www.yok.gov.tr/Sayfalar/Haberler/yagmaci-dergi-yayinlarina-onlem.aspx

Colicchia, C., & Strozzi, F. (2012). Supply chain risk management: A new methodology for a systematic literature review. *Supply Chain Management*, *17*(4), 403–418. doi:10.1108/13598541211246558

Colle, H. A., & Reid, G. B. (1999). Double trade-off curves with different cognitive processing combinations: Testing the cancellation axiom of mental workload measurement theory. *Human Factors*, *41*(1), 35–50. doi:10.1518/001872099779577327 PMID:10354805

Comité Mixto, O. I. T.-O. M. S. (1984). Factores psicosociales en el Trabajo: naturaleza, incidencia y prevención. *Oficina Internacional Del Trabajo, 1*, 1–85. Retrieved from http://biblioteca.uces.edu.ar/MEDIA/EDOCS/FACTORES_Texto.pdf

Conard, M. A., & Matthews, R. A. (2008). Modeling the stress process: Personality eclipses dysfunctional cognitions and workload in predicting stress. *Personality and Individual Differences*, *44*(1), 171–181. doi:10.1016/j.paid.2007.07.023

Corral. (2009). Validez y confiabilidad de los instrumentos de investigación para la recolección de datos. *Revista Ciencias de La Educación, 19*(33), 228–247.

Costa, E., Sousa, R., Bragança, S., & Alves, A. (2013). An industrial application of the SMED methodology and other lean production tools. *4th International Conference on Integrity, Reliability and Failure of Mechanical Systems, 1*(i), 1–8. 10.13140/2.1.2099.5525

Cox, T., & Griffiths, A. (1996). The assessment of psychosocial hazards at work. In Handbook of work and health psychology. Academic Press.

Cox, T., & Griffiths, A. J. (1996). The assessment of psychosocial hazards at work. In M.J. Schabracq, J. A. M. Winnubst, & C. L. Cooper (Eds.), Handbook of Work and Health Psychology (pp. 127-146). Academic Press.

D'Addona, D. M., Bracco, F., Bettoni, A., Nishino, N., Carpanzano, E., & Bruzzone, A. A. (2018). Adaptive automation and human factors in manufacturing: An experimental assessment for a cognitive approach. *CIRP Annals*, *67*(1), 455–458. doi:10.1016/j.cirp.2018.04.123

Dahlgaard, J., Pettersen, J., & Dahlgaard-Park, S. M. (2011). Quality and lean health care: A system for assessing and improving the health of healthcare organisations. *Total Quality Management & Business Excellence*, *22*(6), 673–689. doi:10.1080/14783363.2011.580651

Darr, W., & Johns, G. (2008). Work strain, health, and absenteeism: A meta-analysis. *Journal of Occupational Health Psychology*, *13*(4), 293–318. doi:10.1037/a0012639 PMID:18837626

Dave, Y., & Sohani, N. (2012). Single Minute Exchange of Dies: Literature Review. *International Journal of Lean Thinking*, *3*(2), 27–37.

de Arquer, I., & Nogareda, C. (2001). *Estimación de la carga mental de trabajo: el método NASA TLX*. Retrieved from http://www.prevencionintegral.com/Ntps/contenidoNTPS/ntp_544.pdf

De Carvalho, M. M., Ho, L. L., & Pinto, S. H. B. (2014). The Six Sigma program: An empirical study of Brazilian companies. *Journal of Manufacturing Technology Management*, *25*(5), 602–630. doi:10.1108/JMTM-04-2012-0045

De Castro, F., Place, J., Billings, D., Rivera, L., & Frongillo, E. A. (2015). Risk profiles associated with postnatal depressive symptoms among women in a public sector hospital in Mexico: The role of sociodemographic and psychosocial factors. *Archives of Women's Mental Health*, *18*(3), 463–471. doi:10.100700737-014-0472-1 PMID:25416532

De Freitas, J. G., & Costa, H. G. (2017). Impacts of Lean Six Sigma over organizational sustainability. *International Journal of Lean Six Sigma*, *8*(1), 89–108. doi:10.1108/IJLSS-10-2015-0039

de Freitas, J. G., Costa, H. G., & Ferraz, F. T. (2017). Impacts of Lean Six Sigma over organizational sustainability: A survey study. *Journal of Cleaner Production*, *156*, 262–275. doi:10.1016/j.jclepro.2017.04.054

De Koning, H., Does, R. J. M. M., & Bisgaard, S. (2008). Lean Six Sigma in financial services. *Int. J. Six Sigma and Competitive Advantage*, *4*(1), 2014–11. doi:10.1504/IJSSCA.2008.018417

De Waard, D. (1996). *The measurement of drivers' mental workload*. Groningen University, Traffic Research Center.

Delgado, C., Ferreira, M., & Castelo Branco, M. (2010). The implementation of lean Six Sigma in financial services organizations. *Journal of Manufacturing Technology Management*, *21*(4), 512–523. doi:10.1108/17410381011046616

De, M., Preciado-Serrano, L., Pozos-Radillo, E., Plascencia-Campos, A., & Colunga-Rodríguez, C. (2016). The Association of Psychosocial Risk Factors with the Burnout Syndrome in Dentists in Guadalajara, Jalisco Mexico. *Advances in Applied Sociology*, *6*(6), 81–89. doi:10.4236/aasoci.2016.63008

Demands, J., & De-, J. (2018). *Job Demands, Job Decision Latitude, and Mental Strain : Implications for Job Redesign Administrative Science Quarterly, 24*(2), 285–308.

Demerouti, E., Bakker, A., Nachreiner, F., & Ebbinghaus, M. (2002). From mental strain to burnout. *European Journal of Work and Organizational Psychology*, *11*(4), 423–441. doi:10.1080/13594320244000274

Demerouti, E., Veldhuis, W., Coombes, C., & Hunter, R. (2019). Burnout among pilots: Psychosocial factors related to happiness and performance at simulator training. *Ergonomics*, *62*(2), 233–245. doi:10.1080/00140139.2018.1464667 PMID:29648499

Deming, W. E. (1982). Quality productivity and competitive position. Massachusetts Institute of Technology.

DeNisi, A.S., & Peters, L.H. (1996). Organization of the information in memory and the performance appraisal process: Evidence from the field. *J. Appl. Psychol.*, *81*(6), 717-37.

DeNisi, A. S. (1997). *A Cognitive Approach to Performance Appraisal: A Program of Research.* London: Routledge.

Desai, T. P. (1993). Stress and mental workload: A study in an industrial organisation. *Indian Journal of Industrial Relations*, *28*(3), 258–273.

Dess, G., Lumpkin, G. A., & Eisner, A. (2008). *Strategic Management.* New York, NY: McGraw-Hill.

Diego-Mas, J. A., Poveda-Bautista, R., & Garzon-Leal, D. C. (2015). Influences on the use of observational methods by practitioners when identifying risk factors in physical work. *Ergonomics*, *58*(10), 1660–1670. doi:10.1080/00140139.2015.1023851 PMID:25735462

Dileep, G., & Rau, S. S. (2009). Applying Six-Sigma in Health Service: a Study of Critical Success Factors, Critical To Quality Characteristics and Key Performance Indicators in Medium Scale Hospitals. *Information Sciences & Computing, 3*(1), 25–31. Retrieved from http://journals-sathyabama.com/archives/iisc_abstract.php?id=37

Dillard, M., Warm, J., Funke, G., Funke, M., Finomore, V., & Matthews, G. … Parasuraman, R. (2014). The Sustained Attention to Response Task (SART) does not promote mindlessness during vigilance performance. *Human Factors.* doi:10.1177/0018720814537521

Dill, D. D. (2014). Public policy design and university reform: Insights into academic change. In C. Musselin & P. Teixeira (Eds.), *Reforming higher education* (pp. 21–37). Dordrecht: Springer. doi:10.1007/978-94-007-7028-7_2

Dües, C. M., Tan, K. H., & Lim, M. (2013). Green as the new Lean: How to use Lean practices as a catalyst to greening your supply chain. *Journal of Cleaner Production*, *40*, 93–100. doi:10.1016/j.jclepro.2011.12.023

Dul, J., Bruder, R., Buckle, P., Carayon, P., Falzon, P., Marras, W., ... van der Doelen, B. (2012). A strategy for human factors/ergonomics: Developing the discipline and profession. *Ergonomics*, *55*(4), 377–395. doi:10.1080/00140139.2012.661087 PMID:22332611

Duru, H. A., Ermiş, A., Akay, D., & Kurt, M. (2005). Bilgisayar Sektöründe Öznel Bir Yöntemle (Nasa-Tlx) Zihinsel İş Yükünün Ölçülmesi. *Teknoloji*, *8*(2), 173–180.

Duze, C. (2011). Job Stress, Workload, Academic Freedom and Quality Research in Nigerian Universities. *Academic Leadership: The Online Journal*, *9*(2), 1–10.

Edelman, L. F., Brush, C. G., & Manolova, T. S. (2002). The impact of human and organizational resources on small firm strategy. *Journal of Small Business and Enterprise Development*, *9*(3), 236–244. doi:10.1108/14626000210438562

EHEA. (2019). *European Higher Education Area and Bologna Process.* Retrieved from http://www.ehea.info/page-home-page

El-Batawi, M., Kalimo, R., & Cooper, C. (1988). Los factores psicosociales en el trabajo y su relación con la salud. *Organización Mundial de La Salud*, 1–106. Retrieved from http://apps.who.int/iris/bitstream/10665/37881/1/9243561022_spa.pdf

Emeç, Ş., & Akkaya, G. (2018). Sağlık Sektöründe Zihinsel İş Yükü Değerlendirmesi ve Bir Uygulama. *Ergonomics, 1*(3), 156–162.

Emil, S., & Akşab, Ş. (2018). Türkiye Yükseköğretiminde Araştırma Üniversitesi Kavramını Anlamak: Karşılaştırmalı Analiz. In C.T. Uğurlu, K. Beycioğlu, S. Koşar, H. Kahraman, & F. Köybaşı Şemin (Eds.), 13. Internatıonal Congress On Educational Administration E-Book (pp. 1-11). Sivas: Cumhuriyet Üniversitesi Yayıncılık.

Emil, S. (2018). Can world-class universities really exist in Turkey. In M. Rabossi, K. M. Joshi, & S. Paivandi (Eds.), *Pursuit of World-Class Universities: A Global Experience* (pp. 239–269). Studera Press.

Endsley, M. R., & Garland, D. J. (2000). *Situation Awareness Analysis and Measurement.* CRC Press. Retrieved from https://books.google.com.mx/books?id=WrJGDsjJakcC&lr=&hl=es&source=gbs_navlinks_s

Enterprise-project-management. (2019). *Enterprise project management.* Retrieved from CIO: https://www.cio.com/article/3277972/epmo-enterprise-project-management-office-explained.html

Erdoğan, E. (2011). *Etkili Liderlik, Örgütsel Sessizlik ve Performans İlişkisi.* Gebze Yüksek Teknoloji Enstitüsü.

Escobar Pérez, J., & Cuervo Martínez, Á. (2008, Jan.). Validez de contenido y juicio de expertos: una aproximación a su utilización. *Avances En Medición*, 27–36. doi:10.1016/j.eatbeh.2007.10.005

Escobar-Pérez, J., & Cuervo-Martínez, Á. (2008). Validez De Contenido Y Juicio De Expertos: Una Aproximación a Su Utilización. *Avances En Medición, 6*, 27–36.

Espinoza, O. (2017). Privatization of higher education in Chile: consequences and lessons learned. *EccoS– Revista Científica*, (44), 175-202. DOI: . doi:10.5585/eccos.n44.8070

Essiam, J. O., Mensah, M. E., Kudu, L. K., & Gyamfi, G. D. (2015). Influence of job stress on job satisfaction among university staff: Analytical evidence from a public university in Ghana. *International Journal of Economics. Commerce & Management, 3*(2), 1–15.

European Organization for the Safety of Air Navigation (Eurocontrol). (2004a). ATM Services' Personnel (2nd ed.). ESARR 5. Belgium, Brussels: Author.

European Organization for the Safety of Air Navigation (Eurocontrol). (2004b). *EATM Training Progression and Concepts.* Brussels, Belgium: Author.

European Organization for the Safety of Air Navigation (Eurocontrol). (2015). *Specifications for the ATCO Common Core Content Initial Training* (2nd ed.). Brussels, Belgium: Author.

Ewin, R. (1991). Moral Status of the Corporation. *Journal of Business Ethics, 10*(10), 749–756. doi:10.1007/BF00705709

Faccio, M. (2013). Setup time reduction: SMED-balancing integrated model for manufacturing systems with automated transfer. *IACSIT International Journal of Engineering and Technology, 5*(5), 4075–4084.

Farnacio, Y., Pratt, M., Marshall, E., & Graber, J. (2017). Are Workplace Psychosocial Factors Associated with Work-Related Injury in the US Workforce?: National Health Interview Survey, 2010. *Journal of Occupational and Environmental Medicine, 59*(10), e164–e171. doi:10.1097/JOM.0000000000001143 PMID:28991808

Faulkner, W., & Badurdeen, F. (2014). Sustainable Value Stream Mapping (Sus-VSM): Methodology to visualize and assess manufacturing sustainability performance. *Journal of Cleaner Production, 85*, 8–18. doi:10.1016/j.jclepro.2014.05.042

Federal Aviation Administration. (2014). *Pilot/Controller Glossary.* Washington, DC: Author.

Fedorikhin, A., Park, C. W., & Thomson, M. (2008). Beyond fit and attitude: The effect of emotional attachment on consumer responses to brand extensions. *Journal of Consumer Psychology, 18*(4), 281–291. doi:10.1016/j.jcps.2008.09.006

Fernández-López, J. A., Siegrist, J., Rödel, A., & Hernández-Mejía, R. (2003). Stress at work: a new risk factor. What do we know and what can we do? *Atención Primaria, 31*(8), 469-558. Available in: https://www.elsevier.es/es-revista-atencion-primaria-27-pdf-13047737

Fliedner, G. (2008). Sustainability : a new lean principle. *Proceedings of the 39th Annual Meeting of the Decision Sciences Institute*, 3321–3326.

Forcella, L., Di Donato, A., Coccia, U., Tamellini, L., Di Giampaolo, L., Grapsi, M., … Boscolo, P. (2007). Anxiety, job stress and job insecurity among teachers with indefinite or definite time contract. *Giornale Italiano Di Medicina Del Lavoro Ed Ergonomia, 29*(3 Suppl), 683–686. Retrieved from http://www.ncbi.nlm.nih.gov/pubmed/18409903

Fotopoulos, C. V., & Psomas, E. L. (2010). The structural relationships between TQM factors and organizational performance. *The TQM Journal, 22*(5), 539–552. doi:10.1108/17542731011072874

Fredrickson, B. L. (2001). The role of positive emotions in positive psychology: The broaden-and-build theory of positive emotions. *The American Psychologist, 56*(3), 218–226. doi:10.1037/0003-066X.56.3.218 PMID:11315248

Freudenberger, H. J. (1974). Staff Burn-Out. *The Journal of Social Issues, 30*(1), 159–165. doi:10.1111/j.1540-4560.1974.tb00706.x

Furukawa, P. D., Cunha, I., Pedreira, M. D. G., & Marck, P. B. (2016). Environmental sustainability in medication processes performed in hospital nursing care. *Acta Paulista de Enfermagem, 29*(3), 316–324. doi:10.1590/1982-0194201600044

Gade, P. A., Chavan, R. G., & Bhavsar, D. N. (2016). Reduction In Setup Time By Single Minute Exchange Of Dies (SMED) Methodology. *International Journal of Scientific & Technology Research, 5*(06), 6–8.

Gaikwad, S. P., Avhad, S. S., Pawar, S. S., & Thorat, P. R. (2015). Reduction in Setup time on Rubber Moulding Machine using SMED Technique. *International Journal of Engineering Research & Technology, 4*(04), 169–173.

Galy, E., Cariou, M., & Mélan, C. (2012). What is the relationship between mental workload factors and cognitive load types? *International Journal of Psychophysiology, 83*(3), 269–275. doi:10.1016/j.ijpsycho.2011.09.023 PMID:22008523

Galy, E., Paxion, J., & Berthelon, C. (2018). Measuring mental workload with the NASA-TLX needs to examine each dimension rather than relying on the global score: An example with driving. *Ergonomics, 61*(4), 517–527. doi:10.1080/00140139.2017.1369583 PMID:28817353

Gandi, J. C., Wai, P. S., Karick, H., & Dagona, Z. K. (2011). The role of stress and level of burnout in job performance among nurses. *Mental Health in Family Medicine, 8*(3), 181–194. PMID:22942900

García Torres, A., & Hernández, M. F. M. (2013). Reducción de tiempos de set-up a través de la técnica SMED en una línea. XII Encuentro. *Participación de La Mujer En La Ciencia*, (1985), 1–5.

García, L. B. (2017b). Itinerary of the construction of academic profession in Argentina. *Integración y Conocimiento, 7*(2), 206-225. Retrieved from: https://revistas.unc.edu.ar/index.php/integracionyconocimiento/article/view/18707

García, L. B. (2017). The academics in the Argentinean public university: Changes, tensions and challenges. *Espacios en Blanco. Serie Indagaciones, 27*(1), 87–110. Retrieved from http://ref.scielo.org/ptgy3t

García, M. M., Iglesias, S., Saleta, M., & Romay, J. (2016). Psychosocial risks in university education teachers: Diagnosis and prevention. *Journal of Work and Organizational Psychology, 32*, 173–182. doi:10.1016/j.rpto.2016.07.001

Garcia-Rojas, I., Choi, B., & Krause, N. (2015). Psychosocial job factors and biological cardiovascular risk factors in Mexican workers. *American Journal of Industrial Medicine*, *58*(3), 331–351. doi:10.1002/ajim.22410 PMID:25678459

Gartner, F. R., Nieuwenhuijsen, K., Van Dijk, F. J., & Sluiter, J. K. (2010). The impact of common mental disorders on the work functioning of nurses and allied health professionals: A systematic review. *International Journal of Nursing Studies*, *47*(8), 1047–1061. doi:10.1016/j.ijnurstu.2010.03.013 PMID:20444449

Gaudioso, F., Turel, O., & Galimberti, C. (2017). The mediating roles of strain facets and coping strategies in translating techno-stressors into adverse job outcomes. *Computers in Human Behavior*, *69*, 189–196. doi:10.1016/j.chb.2016.12.041

George, R. A., & Brief, A. P. (1992). Feeling good doing good: A conceptual analysis of the mood at work-organizational spontaneity relationship. *Psychological Bulletin*, *112*(2), 310–329. doi:10.1037/0033-2909.112.2.310 PMID:1454897

Georgia, A. P., & Barbara, J. P. (1997). *Flight to the future: human factors in air traffic control*. Washington, DC: National Academies Press.

Gezer, E., Yenel, F., & Şahan, H. (2009). Öğretim Elemanlarının Tükenmíşlík Düzeylerí ile Sosyodemografik Değíşkenlerí Arasındaki İlíşkí. *Uluslararası Sosyal Araştırmalar Dergisi*, *2*(6), 243–250.

Gholamreza, K. (2006). *Stress and anxiety for individuals and organizations*. Tehran: Reflections Publication.

Gil-Monte, P., Lopez-Vilchez, J., Luis Llorca-Rubio, J., & Sanchez Piernas, J. (2016). Prevalence of psychosocial risks in the justice administration staff of the valencian community (Spain). *Liberabit-revista de psicologia*.

Gil-Monte, P. R. (2012). Riesgos psicosociales en el trabajo y saud ocupacional. *Revista Peruana de Medicina Experimental y Salud Pública*, *29*(2), 237–241. doi:10.1590/S1726-46342012000200012 PMID:22858772

Giorgi, G., Arcangeli, G., Perminiene, M., Lorini, C., Ariza-Montes, A., Fiz-Perez, J., ... Mucci, N. (2017). Work-Related Stress in the Banking Sector: A Review of Incidence, Correlated Factors, and Major Consequences. *Frontiers in Psychology*, *8*, 2166. doi:10.3389/fpsyg.2017.02166 PMID:29312044

Glaser, D. N., Tatum, B. C., Nebeker, D. M., Sorenson, R. C., & Aiello, J. R. (1999). Workload & social support: Effects on performance and stress. *Human Performance*, *12*(2), 155–176. doi:10.1080/08959289909539865

Glazer, G., & Henry, M. S. (1994). Approaches to Conducting Faculty Workload Studies: A Case Study at Kent State University. *New Directions for Institutional Research*, *83*(83), 39–55. doi:10.1002/ir.37019948306

Gliem, J. A., & Gliem, R. R. (2003). *Calculating, Interpreting, and Reporting Cronbach's Alpha Reliability Coefficient for Likert-Type Scales*. doi:10.1109/PROC.1975.9792

Goh, T. Y. (1997). *Workload as a Stressor: Teachers' Perceptions of Work-related Stress and Its Sources* (Unpublished doctoral dissertation). International Islamic University, Malaysia.

Gómez del Pulgar García Madrid, M., Hernández-Iglesias, S., Crespo Cañizares, A., Pérez Martín, A. M., González Jurado, M. A., & Beneit Montesinos, J. V. (2019). Fiabilidad de una escala para la evaluación de competencias enfermeras: estudio de concordancia. *Educación Médica*. doi:10.1016/j.edumed.2018.12.002

Gómez, A. H., Toledo, C. E., Prado, J. M. L., & Morales, S. N. (2015). Factores críticos de éxito para el despliegue del mantenimiento productivo total en plantas de la industria maquiladora para la exportación en Ciudad Juárez: Una solución factorial. *Contaduría y Administración*, *60*, 82–106. doi:10.1016/j.cya.2015.08.005

Gómez, V. (2010). Assessment of Psychosocial Stressors at Work: Psychometric Properties of the Spanish Version of the ERI (Effort-Reward Imbalance) Questionnaire in Colombian Workers. *Revista de Psicología del Trabajo y de las Organizaciones*, *26*(2), 147–156. doi:10.5093/tr2010v26n2a6

González Gutiérrez, J. L., Jiménez, B. M., Hernández, E. G., & López, A. L. (2005). Spanish version of the Swedish Occupational Fatigue Inventory (SOFI): Factorial replication, reliability and validity. *International Journal of Industrial Ergonomics*, *35*(8), 737–746. doi:10.1016/j.ergon.2005.02.007

González Muños, E., & Gutiérrez Martinez, R. E. (2006). 2_Factor De Riesgo En Industria Electronica. *Revista Latinoamericana de Psicología*, *38*(2), 259–270. Retrieved from http://www.scielo.org.co/scielo.php?script=sci_arttext&pid=S0120-05342006000200003&lng=en&nrm=iso

González-Forteza, C., Juárez-López, C. E., Jiménez, A., Montejo-León, L., Rodríguez-Santisbón, U. R., & Wagner, F. A. (2017). Suicide behavior and associated psychosocial factors among adolescents in Campeche, Mexico. *Preventive Medicine*, *105*, 206–211. doi:10.1016/j.ypmed.2017.09.011 PMID:28917950

González-Muñoz, E., & Gutiérrez-Martínez, R. (2007). Contribution of mental workload to job stress in industrial workers. *Work (Reading, Mass.)*, *28*(4), 355–361. Retrieved from http://www.ncbi.nlm.nih.gov/pubmed/17522456 PMID:17522456

Goonetilleke, R. S., & Karwowski, W. (Eds.). (2018). *Advances in Physical Ergonomics & Human Factors*. Orlando, FL: Springer; doi:10.1007/978-3-319-60825-9

Gopher, D., & Donchin, E. (1986). *Workload: An examination of the concept*. Academic Press.

Gopher, D., & Donchin, E. (1986). Workload-an examination of the concept. In K. Boff, L. Kaufman, & J. Thomas (Eds.), *Handbook of Perception and Performance* (pp. 1–49). New York: Wiley.

Gracia-Camón, Á. (2003). *Criterios objetivos para la evaluación de la carga de trabajo derivada de factores psicosociales y organizacionales*. Academic Press.

Gray, C., Wilcox, G., & Nordstokke, D. (2017). Teacher mental health, school climate, inclusive education and student learning: A review. *Canadian Psychology*, *58*(3), 203–210. doi:10.1037/cap0000117

Griffin, J. M., Greiner, B. A., Stansfeld, S. A., & Marmot, M. (2007). The effect of self-reported and observed job conditions on depression and anxiety symptoms: A comparison of theoretical models. *Journal of Occupational Health Psychology*, *12*(4), 334–349. doi:10.1037/1076-8998.12.4.334 PMID:17953493

Guardia, J., Peró, M., & Barrios, M. (2008). Propiedades psicométricas de la batería de evaluación de riesgos psicosociales en la medianan y pequeña empresa. *Psicothema*, *20*(4), 939–944. PMID:18940107

Guelaud, F., Beauchense, M. N., Gautrat, J., & Roustrang, G. (1977). *Pour une analyse des conditions du travail ouvrier dans l'entreprise* (Vol. 11). Paris: Espirit.

Guelaud, F., Beauchesne, M. N., & Gautrat, J. Y. R. G. (1975). Pour une Analyse des Conditions du Travail Ouvrier dans l'Entreprise. *Economics and Politics*, *114/116*(257).

Guerrero, M., Jiménez, J., Ferrer, B., & Rivera, A. (2016). Un análisis psicosocial de la confianza en los grupos policiales: El caso de Cuernavaca (México). *Perfiles Latinoamericanos*, *24*(47), 151–174. doi:10.18504/pl2447-009-2016

Güilgüiruca, M., Meza, K., Góngora, R., & Moya, C. (2015). Factores de riesgo psicosocial y estrés percibido en trabajadores de una empresa eléctrica en Chile. *Medicina y Seguridad del Trabajo*, *61*(238).

Gupta, S., Sharma, M., & Sunder, M. V. (2016). Lean services: A systematic review. *International Journal of Productivity and Performance Management*, *65*(8), 1025–1056. doi:10.1108/IJPPM-02-2015-0032

Gürüz, K. (2012). Remuneration of Academic Staff in Turkish Universities. In P. G. Altbach, L. Reisberg, M. Yudkevich, G. Androushchak, & I. F. Pacheco (Eds.), *Paying the Professoriate: A Global Comparison of Compensation & Contracts* (pp. 297–307). New York: Routledge.

Gustafsson, A., Nilsson, L., & Johnson, M. D. (2003). The role of quality practices in service organizations. *International Journal of Service Industry Management*, *14*(2), 232–244. doi:10.1108/09564230310474183

Guzmán Ferradás, P., & Salonitis, K. (2013). Improving changeover time: A tailored SMED approach for welding cells. *Procedia CIRP*, *7*, 598–603. doi:10.1016/j.procir.2013.06.039

Guzzo, R. A., & Dickson, M. W. (1996). Teams in organizations: Recent research on performance and effectiveness. *Annual Review of Psychology*, *47*(1), 307–338. doi:10.1146/annurev.psych.47.1.307 PMID:15012484

Hadid, W., & Afshin Mansouri, S. (2014). The lean-performance relationship in services: A theoretical model. *International Journal of Operations & Production Management*, *34*(6), 750–785. doi:10.1108/IJOPM-02-2013-0080

Hadid, W., Mansouri, S. A., & Gallear, D. (2016). Is lean service promising? A socio-technical perspective. *International Journal of Operations & Production Management*, *36*(6), 618–642. doi:10.1108/IJOPM-01-2015-0008

Hagedoorn, J., & Cloodt, M. (2003). Measuring innovative performance: Is there an advantage in using multiple indicators? *Research Policy*, *32*(8), 1365–1379. doi:10.1016/S0048-7333(02)00137-3

Hancock, P. A., & Caird, J. K. (1993). Experimental evaluation of a model of mental workload. *Human Factors*, *35*(3), 413–429. doi:10.1177/001872089303500303 PMID:8244409

Hart, S., Staveland, L., Hancock, P., & Meshkati, N. (1988). *Human mental workload. Human mental workload* (Vol. 2). Retrieved from https://www.elsevier.com/books/human-mental-workload/hancock/978-0-444-70388-0

Hart, S. G. (2006). Nasa-Task Load Index (Nasa-Tlx). *20 Years Later. Human Factors and Ergonomics Society. Annual Meeting Proceedings*, *50*(9), 904–908.

Hart, S. G. (2006). Nasa-Task Load Index (NASA-TLX); 20 Years Later. *Proceedings of the Human Factors and Ergonomics Society Annual Meeting*, *50*(9), 904–908. doi:10.1177/154193120605000909

Hart, S. G., & Sta, L. E. (1988). *Human Mental Workload* (A. Hancock & N. Meshkati, Eds.). Elsevier Science Publishers.

Hart, S. G., & Staveland, L. E. (1988). Development of NASA-TLX (Task Load Index): Results of Empirical and Theoretical Research. *Advances in Psychology*, *52*(C), 139–183. doi:10.1016/S0166-4115(08)62386-9

Hart, S. M., & Warren, A. M. (2015). Understanding nurses' work: Exploring the links between changing work, labour relations, workload, stress, retention and recruitment. *Economic and Industrial Democracy*, *36*(2), 305–329. doi:10.1177/0143831X13505119

Harung, H. S., Heaton, D. P., & Alexander, C. N. (1999). Evolution of organizations in the new millennium. *Leadership and Organization Development Journal*, *20*(4), 198–206. doi:10.1108/01437739910277000

Hausser, J. A., Mojzisch, A., Niesel, M., & Schulz-Hardt, S. (2010). Ten years on: A review of recent research on the job demand-control (-support) model and psychological well-being. *Work and Stress*, *24*(1), 1–35. doi:10.1080/02678371003683747

Hayton, J. C. (2005). Competing in the new economy: The effect of intellectual capital on corporate entrepreneurship in high-technology new ventures. *R & D Management*, *35*(2), 137–155. doi:10.1111/j.1467-9310.2005.00379.x

Hayton, J. C., & Kelley, D. J. (2006). A competency-based framework for promoting corporate entrepreneurship. *Human Resource Management*, *45*(3), 407–427. doi:10.1002/hrm.20118

Hayton, J. C., & Zahra, S. A. (2005). Venture team human capital and absorptive capacity in high technology new ventures. *International Journal of Technology Management*, *31*(3/4), 256–274. doi:10.1504/IJTM.2005.006634

Hedge, J. W., & Borman, W. C. (1995). Changing conceptions and practices in performance appraisal. In The Changing Nature of Work. San Francisco: Jossey-Bass.

Heinze, T., Shapira, P., Rogers, J. D., & Senker, J. M. (2009). Organizational & institutional influences on creativity in scientific research. *Research Policy*, *38*(4), 610–623. doi:10.1016/j.respol.2009.01.014

Heponiemi, T., Kouvonen, A., Vanska, J., Halila, H., Sinervo, T., Kivimäki, M., & Elovainio, M. (2009). The Association of distress and sleeping problems with physicians' intentions to change profession: The moderating effect of job control. *Journal of Occupational Health Psychology*, *14*(4), 365–373. doi:10.1037/a0015853 PMID:19839657

Herazo, R. C., Ospina Serna, M., & Ramírez Henao, S. (2013). Factores psicosociales y organizacionales que afectan la productividad. Medellín: Universidad De Medellín: Facultad De Ciencias Económicas Y Administrativas Especialización en Gestión Del Talento Humano Y La Productividad.

Hernandez Arellano, J. L., Serratos Perez, J. N., Alcaraz, J. L. G., & Maldonado Macias, A. A. (2018). Assessment of Workload, Fatigue, and Musculoskeletal Discomfort Among Computerized Numerical Control Lathe Operators in Mexico. *IISE Transactions on Occupational Ergonomics and Human Factors*, *5*(2), 65–81. doi:10.1080/24725838.2017.1317301

Hernández, R., Fernández, C., & Baptista, P. (2014). Research Methodology (6th ed.). McGraw-Hill.

Hernández-Arellano, J. L., Aguilar-Duque, J. I., & Gómez-Bull, K. G. (2018). Methodology to Determine Product Dimensions Based on User Anthropometric Data. In J. L. García-Alcaraz, G. Alor-Hernández, A. A. Maldonado-Macías, & C. Sánchez-Ramírez (Eds.), New Perspectives on Applied Industrial Tools and Techniques (pp. 373–385). Cham, Switzerland: Springer International Publishing. doi:10.1007/978-3-319-56871-3_18

Hernandez-Arellano, J., Garcia-Alcaraz, J., Serratos-Perez, J., & Maldonado-Macías, A. (2016). Assessment of Workload, Fatigue, and Musculoskeletal Discomfort among Advanced Manufacturing Technology Operators in Mexico. A preliminary study. *IIE Transactions on Occupational Ergonomics and Human Factors*.

Hertzum, M., & Holmegaard, K. D. (2013). Perceived Time as a Measure of Mental Workload: Effects of Time Constraints & Task Success. *International Journal of Human-Computer Interaction*, *29*(1), 26–39. doi:10.1080/10447318.2012.676538

Hicks, B. J., & Matthews, J. (2010). The barriers to realising sustainable process improvement: A root cause analysis of paradigms for manufacturing systems improvement. *International Journal of Computer Integrated Manufacturing*, *23*(7), 585–602. doi:10.1080/0951192X.2010.485754

Hietschold, N., Reinhardt, R., & Gurtner, S. (2014). Measuring critical success factors of TQM implementation successfully – a systematic literature review. *International Journal of Production Research*, *52*(21), 6254–6272. doi:10.1080/00207543.2014.918288

Hill, S. G., Iavecchia, H. P., Byers, J. C., Bittner, A. C. Jr, Zaklade, A. L., & Christ, R. E. (1992). Comparison of Four Subjective Workload Rating Scales. *Human Factors: The Journal of the Human Factors and Ergonomics Society*, *34*(4), 429–439. doi:10.1177/001872089203400405

Hitt, M. A., Bierman, L., Shimizu, K., & Kochhar, R. (2001). Direct and moderating effects of human capital on strategy and performance in professional service firms: A resource-based perspective. *Academy of Management Journal*, *44*(1), 13–28.

Hoerl, B. R., & Snee, B. R. D. (2003). *YOUR The Future of Six Sigma*. Academic Press.

Holley, S. (2016). *The relationship between professional skepticism and critical thinking of accounting managers: A quantitative study*. Minneapolis, MN: Capella University.

Hong, S., Zhijian, J., & Baohua, M. (2003). Research on life-span of the population of intellectuals in Harbin Chinese. *Chin J Hosp Stat*, *10*, 8–16.

Hornsby, J. S., Kuratko, D. F., Shepherd, D. A., & Bott, J. P. (2009). Managers' corporate entrepreneurial actions: Examining perception and position. *Journal of Business Venturing*, *24*(3), 236–247. doi:10.1016/j.jbusvent.2008.03.002

Hornsby, J. S., Kuratko, D. F., & Zahra, S. A. (2002). Middle managers' perception of the internal environment for corporate entrepreneurship: Assessing a measurement scale. *Journal of Business Venturing*, *17*, 253.

Hornsby, J. S., Naffziger, D. W., Kuratko, D. F., & Montagno, R. V. (1993). An interactive model of the corporate entrepreneurship process. *Entrepreneurship Theory and Practice*, *24*(2), 9–24. doi:10.1177/104225879902400202

Ho, Y. C., Chang, O. C., & Wang, W. B. (2008). An empirical study of key success factors for Six Sigma Green Belt projects at an Asian MRO company. *Journal of Air Transport Management*, *14*(5), 263–269. doi:10.1016/j.jairtraman.2008.05.002

Hsieh, C. C., & Huisman, J. (2017). Higher education policy change in the European higher education area: Divergence of quality assurance systems in England and the Netherlands. *Research Papers in Education*, *32*(1), 71–83. doi:10.1080/02671522.2015.1129645

Huey, B. M., & Wickens, C. D. (1993). *Workload transition: Implications for individual and team performance*. National Research Council.

Huisman, J., Adelman, C., Hsieh, C. C., Shams, F., & Wilkins, S. (2012). Europe's Bologna Process & Its Impact on Global Higher Education. In D. K. Deardorff, H. d. Wit, J. Heyl, & T. Adams (Eds.), *The Sage Handbook of International Higher Education* (pp. 81–100). Thousand Oaks, CA: Sage. doi:10.4135/9781452218397.n5

Huisman, J., & Kaiser, F. (2002). A Comparative View on Policy Trends in Western European Higher Education. *German Policy Studies*, *2*(3), 1–23.

Hwang, S.-L., Yau, Y.-J., Lin, Y.-T., Chen, J.-H., Huang, T.-H., Yenn, T.-C., & Hsu, C.-C. (2008). Predicting work performance in nuclear power plants. *Safety Science*, *46*(7), 1115–1124. doi:10.1016/j.ssci.2007.06.005

IATA. (2016). Retrieved from https://www.iata.org/publications/Pages/AI-white-paper.aspxInternational

Iavicoli, S., Cesana, G., Dollard, M., Leka, S., & Sauter, S. (2015). Psychosocial Factors and Workers' Health and Safety. *BioMed Research International*, *2015*, 1–3. doi:10.1155/2015/628749 PMID:26634211

Idris, M.K. (2009). *Occupational Stress in Academic Life: A Study of Academics of Malaysian Public Universities* (PhD thesis). The University of Waikato, New Zealand.

IEA. (2000). *Definition of ergonomics*. International Ergonomics Association.

İnce, N. B., & Şahin, A. E. (2015). Maslach Tükenmişlik Envanteri-Eğitimci Formu'nu Türkçe'ye Uyarlama Çalışması. *Eğitimde ve Psikolojide Ölçme ve Değerlendirme Dergisi*, *6*(2), 385–399. doi:10.21031/epod.97301

Instituto Nacional de Estadística y Geografía (INEGI). (2017). ENH - Encuesta Nacional de los Hogares. Author.

Instituto Nacional de Seguridad e Higiene en el Trabajo (INSHT). (2003). *NTP 702: El proceso de evaluación de los factores psicosociales*. Insituto Nacional de Seguridad e Higiene en el Trabajo.

Instituto Nacional de Seguridad e Higiene en el Trabajo (INSHT). (2015). Algunas orientaciones para evaluar los factores de riesgo psicosocial (edición ampliada 2015). Madrid: Instituto Nacional de Seguridad e Higiene en el Trabajo (INSHT).

Instituto Nacional del Seguridad e Higiene en el Trabajo (INSHT). (2004). *El programa de ayuda al empleado (EAP): Intervención individual en la prevención de los riesgos psicosociales.* Madrid: Instituto Nacional del Seguridad e Higiene en el Trabajo.

Instituto Sindical de Trabajo. Ambiente y Salud (ISTAS). (2010). Manual del método CoPsoQ-istas21 (versión 1.5) para la evaluación y prevención de los riesgos psicosociales. Barcelona: Instituto Sindical de Trabajo, Ambiente y Salud.

International Civil Aviation Organization. (1993). *Human Factors Digest No. 8: Human Factors in Air Traffic Control. Cir. 241*. Montreal, Canada: Author.

International Civil Aviation Organization. (1998). Human Factors Training Manual (1st ed.). Doc. ICAO 9683-AN/950. Canada, Montreal: Author.

International Civil Aviation Organization. (2002). Human Factors Guidelines for Safety Audits Manual (1st ed.). Doc. ICAO 9806-AN/763. Canada, Montreal: Author.

International Civil Aviation Organization. (2005). *Global Air Traffic Management Operational Concept. Doc. ICAO 9854-AN/458*. Montreal, Canada: Author.

International Civil Aviation Organization. (2007). Air Traffic Management (15th ed.). Doc. ICAO 4444-ATM/501. Canada, Montreal: Author.

International Civil Aviation Organization. (2012). *Manual on the Approval of Training Organizations. Doc. ICAO 9841-AN/456*. Montreal, Canada: Author.

International Civil Aviation Organization. (2013). Safety Management Manual (SMM) (3rd ed.). Doc. ICAO 9859-AN/474. Canada, Montreal: Author.

International Civil Aviation Organization. (2016a). Manual on Air Traffic Controller Competency-based Training and Assessment (1st ed.). Doc. ICAO 10056-AN/519. Canada, Montreal: Author.

International Civil Aviation Organization. (2016b). *Procedures for Air Navigation Services – Training (PANS-TRG). Doc. ICAO 9868*. Montreal, Canada: Author.

International Civil Aviation Organization. (2018). *Potential of Artificial Intelligence (AI) in Air Traffic Management (ATM)*. In Thirteenth Air Navigation Conference ICAO, Montréal, Canada.

International Ergonomics Association (IEA). (2018). *Definition and Domains of Ergonomics | IEA Website*. Retrieved November 2, 2018, from http://www.iea.cc/whats/

International Labour Office (ILO). International Programme on Safety and Health at Work and the Environment & International Occupational Safety and Health Information Centre. SafeWork bookshelf. Geneva: ILO.

International Labour Office. (2013). *Stress prevention at work, control points: Best practices for the stress prevention in the workplace*. Ginebra: Oficina Internacional del Trabajo. Available in: https://www.ilo.org/wcmsp5/groups/public/@dgreports/@dcomm/@publ/documents/publication/wcms_251057.pdf

International Labour Organization. (2016). *Workplace Stress. A collective challenge world day for safety and health at work*. Geneva: International Labour Organization. Available in: https://www.ilo.org/safework/info/publications/WCMS_466547/lang--en/index.htm

Iraz, R., & Ganiyusufoglu, A. (2011). Örgütlerde Mesleki Tükenmişlik ve Akademisyenler Üzerinde Bir Uygulama. *SÜ İİBF Sosyal ve Ekonomik Araştırmalar Dergisi, 11*(21), 452–472.

ISO. (2012). *Quality management principles*. ISO.

Jackson, S. E. (1992). Consequences of group composition for the interpersonal dynamics of strategic issue processing. *Advances in Strategic Management*, *8*, 345–382.

Jackson, S. E. (1992). *Diversity in the Workplace: Human Resources Initiatives*. New York: Guilford.

Jackson, S. E., Brett, I. F., Sessa, V. I., Cooper, D. M., Julin, J. A., & Peyronnin, K. (1991). Some differences make a difference: Individual dissimilarity and group heterogeneity as correlates of recruitment, promotions, and turnover. *The Journal of Applied Psychology*, 675–689.

Jackson, S. E., & Dutton, J. E. (1988). Discerning threats and opportunities. *Administrative Science Quarterly*, *33*(3), 370–387. doi:10.2307/2392714

Jacobson, C. J. Jr, Bolon, S., Elder, N., Schroer, B., Matthews, G., Szaflarski, J. P., ... Horner, R. D. (2011). Temporal and subjective work demands in office-based patient care: An exploration of the dimensions of physician work intensity. *Medical Care*, *49*(1), 52–58. doi:10.1097/MLR.0b013e3181f53542 PMID:21164325

Jin, X., Zheng, B., Pei, Y., & Li, H. (2017). A Method to Estimate Operator's Mental Workload in Multiple Information Presentation Environment of Agricultural Vehicles. In D. Harris (Ed.), *Engineering Psychology and Cognitive Ergonomics: Performance, Emotion and Situation Awareness* (pp. 3–20). Vancouver: Springer; doi:10.1007/978-3-319-58472-0_1

Johnson, R. B., Onwuegbuzie, A. J., & Turner, L. A. (2007). Toward a definition of mixed methods research. *Journal of Mixed Methods Research*, *1*(2), 112–133. doi:10.1177/1558689806298224

Jones, B., & Johnson, R. T. (2007). Six Sigma Literature: A Review and Agenda for Future Research. *Quality and Reliability Engineering International, 23*, 517–543. doi:10.1002/qre

Juan, P., Hernández, A., Hernández, R. G., Yokasta, A., Vela, D. L. S., Valdés, E. S., ... Robledo, A. L. (2016). *Ergonomía cognitiva. Resultados cognitive ergonomics. Results De Un Taller De Capacitación Of A Training Workshop, 17*(3), 49–56.

Juárez, A. (2007). Psychosocial work factors associated to blood pressure and cardiovascular symptoms among Mexican nurses. *Salud Pública Mex*, *49*(2), 109-117.

Juárez, A. (2008). Percepción del control en la salud y bienestar laboral: Desarrollo de un modelo psicosocial. In J. F. Uribe (Ed.), Facultad de Psicología UNAM.

Juárez-García, A. (2007). La dimensión de fatiga-energía como indicador de presentismo: Validez de una escala en trabajadores mexicanos. *Ciencia & Trabajo*, *9*(24), 55–60. Retrieved from http://bases.bireme.br/cgi-bin/wxislind.exe/iah/online/?IsisScript=iah/iah.xis&src=google&base=LILACS&lang=p&nextAction=lnk&exprSearch=489174&indexSearch=ID

Jung, H. S., & Jung, H. S. (2001). Establishment of overall workload assessment technique for various tasks and workplaces. *International Journal of Industrial Ergonomics*, *28*(6), 341–353. doi:10.1016/S0169-8141(01)00040-3

Júnior, C. H. M., & Lima, E. (2011). Descontinuidade de programas seis sigma: Um estudo comparativo de casos. *Revista de Gestão*, *18*(4), 639–658. doi:10.5700/rege445

Kageyama, T., Matsuzaki, I., Morita, N., Sasahara, S. I., Satoh, S., & Nakamura, H. (2001). Mental health of scientific researchers I. Characteristics of job stress among scientific researchers working at a research park in Japan. *International Archives of Occupational and Environmental Health*, *74*(3), 199–205. doi:10.1007004200000200 PMID:11355294

Kakushi, L. E., & Évora, Y. D. M. (2014). Direct and indirect nursing care time in an Intensive Care Unit. *Revista Latino-Americana de Enfermagem*, *22*(1), 150–157. doi:10.1590/0104-1169.3032.2381 PMID:24553716

Kalimo, R., El-Batawi, M., & Cooper, C. L. (1988). *Los factores psicosociales en el trabajo y su.* Ginebra: OMS.

Karabay, M. E., Tezergil, S. A., & Köse, A. (2014). Does Motivation Mediate the Job Performance and Burnout? Evidence from Turkish Banking Sector. *American International Journal of Social Science*, *3*(6), 98–108.

Karadağ, M., & Cankul, İ. (2015b). Hemşirelerde Zihinsel İş Yükü Değerlendirmesi. *Anadolu Hemşirelik ve Sağlık Bilimleri Dergisi*, *18*(1), 26–34.

Karadağ, M., & Cankul, İ. H. (2015a). Hekimlerde Zihinsel İş Yükü Değerlendirmesi. *The Journal of Academic Social Science Studies*, *35*, 361–370.

Karatepe, O. M. (2013). The effects of work overload and work-family conflict on job embeddedness and job performance: The mediation of emotional exhaustion. *International Journal of Contemporary Hospitality Management*, *25*(4), 614–634. doi:10.1108/09596111311322952

Karim, R. (2013). Impact of Changeover time on productivity: A case study. *International Journal of Engineering & Technology IJET-IJENS*, *13*(06), 42–48.

Kar, S., & Suar, D. (2014). Role of burnout in the relationship between job demands and job outcomes among indian nurses. *Vikalpa*, *39*(4), 23–37. doi:10.1177/0256090920140403

Kawakami, N., & Tsutsumi, A. (2010). Job stress and mental health among workers in Asia and the World. *Journal of Occupational Health*, *52*(1), 1–3. doi:10.1539/joh.editorial1001 PMID:20154466

Kaygın, E., & Naktiyok, A. (2012). Tükenmişlik Ve İş Tatmini Arasındaki İlişki: Akademik Personel Üzerinde Bir Araştırma. *Çukurova Üniversitesi İktisadi ve İdari Bilimler Fakültesi Dergisi*, *16*(1).

Keratepe, O. M., & Uludag, O. (2008). Role Stress, Burnout and Their Effects on Frontline Hotel Employees' Job Performance: Evidence from Northern Cyprus. *International Journal of Tourism Research*, *10*(2), 111–126. doi:10.1002/jtr.645

Keser, A., & Yılmaz, G. (2014). Workload, Burnout, and Job Satisfaction Among Call Center Employees. *Sosyal Siyaset Konferansları Dergisi*, (66–67), 1–13.

Khan, F., Rasli, A., Yusoff, R., & Ahmad, A. (2015). Do Demographic Make a Difference to Job Burnout Among University Academicians? *International Journal of Economics and Financial Issues*, *5*(1), 229–237.

Khani Jazani, R., Salehi Sahlabadi, A., & Mousavi, S. S. (2018). Relationship Between Lean Manufacturing and Ergonomics. In S. Trzcielinski (Ed.), *Advances in Ergonomics of Manufacturing: Managing the Enterprise of the Future. AHFE 2017. Advances in Intelligent Systems and Computing* (pp. 162–166). Cham: Springer; doi:10.1007/978-3-319-60474-9_15

Kharchenko, V., Shmelova, T., & Sikirda, Y. (2016). *Decision-making in socio-technical systems: monograph.* Kyiv: National Aviation University.

Kharchenko, V., Shmelova, T., & Sikirda, Y. (2018). Methodology of research and training in air navigation socio-technical system. *Proceedings of the National Aviation University*, *1*, 8–23.

Kim, H. J., Shin, K. H., & Umbreit, W. T. (2007). Hotel job burnout: The role of personality characteristics. *International Journal of Hospitality Management*, *26*(2), 421–434. doi:10.1016/j.ijhm.2006.03.006

Kim, Y., Kim, E. J., & Chung, M. G. (2010). A Six Sigma-based method to renovate information services: Focusing on information acquisition process. *Library Hi Tech*, *28*(4), 632–647. doi:10.1108/07378831011096286

Kinman, G., & Jones, F. (2008). Effort-reward imbalance, over-commitment and work-life conflict: Testing an expanded model. *Journal of Managerial*, *23*(3), 236–251. doi:10.1108/02683940810861365

Kirchhof, A. L., Magnago, T. S., Camponogara, S., Griep, R. H., Tavares, J. P., Prestes, F. C., & Paes, L. G. (2009). Working conditions and social-demographic characteristics related to the presence of minor psychic disorders in nursing workers. *Texto & Contexto Enfermagem, 18*(2), 215–223. doi:10.1590/S0104-07072009000200003

Kirkman, B. L., & Rosen, B. (1999). Beyond Self-Management: Antecedents and Consequences of Team Empowerment. *Academy of Management Journal, 42*(1), 58–74.

Kobus, J., & Westner, M. (2015). Lean Management of IT organizations: Implementation success factors and theoretical foundation. *2015 Americas Conference on Information Systems, AMCIS 2015*, (1), 1–17. Retrieved from https://www.scopus.com/inward/record.uri?eid=2-s2.0-84963611888&partnerID=40&md5=eb6d634f3f27a6c1b330677df9b3ec3b

Koca, E. I., & Duru, D. G. (2017). Relationship between mental workload and photoplethysmography in the effect of physical performance. In *2017 Medical Technologies National Congress (TIPTEKNO)* (pp. 1-4). IEEE. 10.1109/TIPTEKNO.2017.8238094

Kokkinos, C. M. (2007). Job stressors, personality and burnout in primary school teachers. *The British Journal of Educational Psychology, 77*(1), 229–243. doi:10.1348/000709905X90344 PMID:17411497

Kollberg, B., Dahlgaard, J. J., & Brehmer, P. (2006). Measuring lean initiatives in health care services: Issues and findings. *International Journal of Productivity and Performance Management, 56*(1), 7–24. doi:10.1108/17410400710717064

Kolowich, L. (2015). *12 of the best marketing and advertising campaigns of all time*. Retrieved from Blog.hubspot.com

Kramer, A. F. (1991). Physiological metrics of mental workload: A review of recent progress. In D. L. Damos (Ed.), *Multiple-task performance* (pp. 279–328). London: Taylor & Francis.

Kristensen, T., & Borg, V. (2003). Copenhagen Psychosocial Questionnaire. *Mental Health*. doi:10.1177/1403494809353652

Kruel-Goebel, D., & Carlotto, M.S. (2019). Socio-demographic, labor and psychosocial predictors of Burnout Syndrome in distance education teachers. *Avances en Psicología Latinoamericana*, 37(2), 295-311. doi:10.12804/revistas.urosario.edu.co/apl/a.6886

Kudielka, B. M., Von Kanel, R., Gander, M. L., & Fischer, J. E. (2004). Effort - reward imbalance, overcommitment and sleep in a working population. *Work and Stress, 18*(2), 167–178. doi:10.1080/02678370410001731785

Kulik, N., Kharchenko, V., & Lutskii, M. (2008). *Encyclopedia of aviation safety*. Kyiv: Technology Publ.

Kumar, R., Garg, D., & Garg, T. K. (2011). TQM success factors in North Indian manufacturing and service industries. *The TQM Journal, 23*(1), 36–46. doi:10.1108/17542731111097470

Kumar, V., & Bajaj, A. (2015). The Implementation of Single Minute Exchange of Die with 5 ' S in Machining Processes for reduction of Setup Time. *International Journal on Recent Technologies in Mechanical and Electrical Engineering*, 2(2), 32–39.

Kundu, G. K., & Bairi, J. (2014). A scale for measuring the applicability of lean practices in IT support services. *Journal of Enterprise Information Management, 27*(5), 623–643. doi:10.1108/JEIM-02-2013-0005

Kundu, G., & Manohar, B. (2012). Critical success factors for implementing lean practices in it support services. *International Journal of Qualitative Research, 6*(4), 301–312. Retrieved from http://www.ijqr.net/journal/v6-n4/1.pdf

Kuratko, D. F., Hornsby, J. S., & Goldsby, M. G. (2004). Sustaining corporate entrepreneurship: Modeling perceived implementation and outcome comparisons at organizational and individual levels. *International Journal of Entrepreneurship and Innovation, 5*(2), 77–89. doi:10.5367/000000004773863237

Kuratko, D. F., Montagno, R. V., & Hornsby, J. S. (1990). Developing an intrapreneurial assessment instrument for effective corporate entrepreneurship. *Strategic Management Journal, 11*(5), 49–58.

Kurtov, A., Polikashyn, O., Potikhens'kyy, A., & Aleksandrov, V. (2017). Expert assessments. "Delphy" method as technology of administrative decision making. *Collections of Scientific Works of the Kharkiv National University of Air Force, No., 1*(50), 118–122.

Kutsal, D., & Bilge, F. (2012). Adaptation of Maslach burnout Inventory-student Survey: Validity and Reliability study. *World Applied Sciences Journal, 19*(9), 1360–1366.

Lahera, M., & Nogareda, C. (2009). El método del INSL para la identificación y evaluación de factores psicosociales, 1–6. Retrieved from papers3://publication/uuid/A9400361-817C-47B4-862D-9A95C1DC28D9

Lameijer, B. A., Veen, D. T. J., Does, R. J. M. M., & De Mast, J. (2016). Perceptions of Lean Six Sigma: A Multiple Case Study in the Financial Services Industry. *The Quality Management Journal, 23*(2), 29–56. doi:10.1080/10686967.2016.11918470

Lande, M., Shrivastava, R. L., & Seth, D. (2016). Critical success factors for Lean Six Sigma in SMEs (small and medium enterprises). *The TQM Journal, 28*(4), 613–635. doi:10.1108/TQM-12-2014-0107

Lara-Sotomayor, J. E., & Pando-Moreno, M. (2014). Mobbing and Symptoms of Stress in Public Sector University Faculty. *Ciencia & Trabajo, 16*(49), 43–48. doi:10.4067/S0718-24492014000100008

Laureani, A. (2011). Lean Six Sigma in the Service Industry. *Advanced Topics in Applied Operations Management.* Retrieved from http://cdn.intechopen.com/pdfs-wm/31666.pdf

Laureani, A., & Antony, J. (2012). Critical success factors for the effective implementation of Lean Sigma Results from an empirical study and agenda. *International Journal of Lean Six Sigma, 3*(4), 274–283. doi:10.1108/20401461211284743

Laurent, P., Pinte, S., Gerard-Guery, S., Wehrly, S., & Pamart, B. (2009). Use of the mos sf-36 questionnaire for carrying perceived health study among 4476 workers. Study carried out between 2007 and 2008. *Archives des Maladies Professionnelles et de l'Environnement, 70*(5), 525–538. doi:10.1016/j.admp.2009.03.002

Lawler, E.E., III, & Jenkins, G.D., Jr. (1992). *Strategic reward systems.* Academic Press.

Lazaro, C., Shinn, M., & Robinson, P. E. (1984). Burnout, Job Performance and Job Withdrawal Behaviors. *Journal of Health and Human Resources Administration, 7*(2), 213–234.

Lederer, P., Weltle, D., & Weber, A. (2001). Illness-related premature unfitness for work among civil servants in Bavaria - an evaluation in the social medical field. *Gesundheitswesen (Bundesverband der Arzte des Offentlichen Gesundheitsdienstes (Germany)), 63*(8–9), 509–513. doi:10.1055-2001-16688 PMID:11561198

Lee, C., An, M., & Noh, Y. (2015). The effects of emotional display rules on flight attendants' emotional labor strategy, job burnout and performance. *Service Business, 9*(3), 409–425. doi:10.100711628-014-0231-4

Lee, Y. K., Chang, C. T., Lin, Y., & Cheng, Z. H. (2014). The dark side of smartphone usage: Psychological traits, compulsive behavior and technostress. *Computers in Human Behavior, 31*, 373–383. doi:10.1016/j.chb.2013.10.047

Lee, Y., & Liu, B. (2003). Inflight workload assessment: Comparison of subjective and physiological measurements. *Aviation, Space, and Environmental Medicine, 74*(10), 1074–1084. Retrieved from https://www.ingentaconnect.com/content/asma/asem/2003/00000074/00000010/art00011 PMID:14556571

Lehr, D., Hillert, A., & Keller, S. (2009). What can balance the effort? Associations between effort-reward imbalance, overcommitment, and affective disorders in German teachers. *International Journal of Occupational and Environmental Health, 15*(4), 374–384. doi:10.1179/oeh.2009.15.4.374 PMID:19886348

Leka, S., Van Wassenhove, W., & Jain, A. (2015). Is psychosocial risk prevention possible? Deconstructing common presumptions. *Safety Science, 71*(Part A), 61–67. doi:10.1016/j.ssci.2014.03.014

Lew, F. L., & Qu, X. (2014). Effects of mental fatigue on biomechanics of slips. *Ergonomics, 57*(12), 1927–1932. doi:10.1080/00140139.2014.937771

Leychenko, S., Malishevskiy, A., & Mikhalic, N. (2006). *Human factors in aviation: monograph in two books. Book 1st.* Kirovograd: YMEKS.

Leyer, M., & Chakrabarty, A. (2011). Implementing a Six Sigma initiative in financial service companies. *2011 IEEE International Conference on Quality and Reliability, ICQR 2011*, 521–525. 10.1109/ICQR.2011.6031594

Linderman, K., Schroeder, R. G., & Choo, A. S. (2006). Six Sigma: The role of goals in improvement teams. *Journal of Operations Management, 24*(6), 779–790. doi:10.1016/j.jom.2005.08.005

Linderman, K., Schroeder, R. G., Zaheer, S., & Choo, A. S. (2003). Six Sigma: A goal-theoretic perspective. *Journal of Operations Management, 21*(2), 193–203. doi:10.1016/S0272-6963(02)00087-6

Liu, H. L., & Lo, V. (2018). An integrated model of workload, autonomy, burnout, job satisfaction, and turnover intention among Taiwanese reporters. *Asian Journal of Communication, 28*(2), 153–169. doi:10.1080/01292986.2017.1382544

Li, W.-C., Cao, J., Lin, J.-H., Braithwaite, G., & Greaves, M. (2017). The Evaluation of Pilot's First Fixation and Response Time to Different Design of Alerting Messages. In D. Harris (Ed.), *Engineering Psychology and Cognitive Ergonomics: Performance, Emotion and Situation Awareness* (pp. 21–31). Vancouver: Springer; doi:10.1007/978-3-319-58472-0_2

Loft, S., Sanderson, P., Neal, A., & Mooij, M. (2007). Modeling and Predicting Mental Workload in En Route Air Traffic Control: Critical Review and Broader Implications. *Human Factors: The Journal of the Human Factors and Ergonomics Society, 49*(3), 376–399. doi:10.1518/001872007X197017 PMID:17552304

Longo, L. (2012). Formalising Human Mental Workload as Non-monotonic Concept for Adaptive and Personalised Web-Design. In J. Masthoff, B. Mobasher, M. Desmarais, & R. Nkambou (Eds.), *User Modeling, Adaptation, and Personalization* (pp. 369–373). Berlin: Springer. doi:10.1007/978-3-642-31454-4_38

Longo, L. (2018). Experienced mental workload, perception of usability, their interaction and impact on task performance. *PLoS One, 13*(8), e0199661. doi:10.1371/journal.pone.0199661 PMID:30067747

Luceño Moreno, L., Martín García, J., Jáez Díaz, M., & Díaz Ramiro, E. M. (2005). Evaluación de factores psicosociales en el entorno laboral. *EduPsykhé:Revista de Psicología y Psicopedagogía, 4*(1), 19–42.

Lupien, S., McEwen, B. S., Gunnar, M. R., & Heim, C. (2009). Effects of stress throughout the lifespan on the brain, behavior and cognition. *Nature Reviews. Neuroscience, 10*(6), 434–445. doi:10.1038/nrn2639 PMID:19401723

Luthans, F., & Doh, J. (2012). *International Management: Culture, Strategy, and Behavior.* New York: McGraw-Hill.

Lysaght, R. J., Hill, S. G., Dick, A. O., Plamondon, B. D., & Linton, P. M. (1989). *Operator workload: Comprehensive review & evaluation of operator workload methodologies (No. TR-2075-3).* Analytics Inc. Willow Grove Pa. doi:10.21236/ADA212879

Lysaght, R., Ouellette-Kuntz, H., & Lin, C. J. (2012). Untapped potential: Perspectives on the employment of people with intellectual disability. *Work (Reading, Mass.), 41*, 409–422. doi:10.3233/WOR-2012-1318 PMID:22495411

Macdonald, J., & Levy, S. (2016). Ageism in the Workplace: The Role of Psychosocial Factors in Predicting Job Satisfaction, Commitment, and Engagement. *The Journal of Social Issues*, *72*(1), 169–190. doi:10.1111/josi.12161

Madhav, R. (2016). *Managing changeover waste in manufacturing plants when using single minute exchange of dies*. University of Johannesburg.

Madrigal, K., Martinez, E., Torres-Arguelles, V., & Beltran, E. (2017). Critical Success Factors of Continuous Improvement Tools in Service Industry. In 2017 Annual SISE Conference (Ed.), *Proceeding of the 6th Annual World Conference of the Society for Industrial and Systems Engineering*. Academic Press.

Magana, C., Hovey, J., Magana, C., Magaña, C., & Hovey, J. (2003). Psychosocial stressors associated with Mexican migrant farmworkers in the Midwest United States. *Journal of Immigrant Health*.

MAPFRE. (1975). *Ergonomía Práctica*. Retrieved from https://machete2000.files.wordpress.com/2012/05/mapfre-ergonomc3ada-prc3a1ctica.pdf

Ma, R., & Kaber, D. (2005). Situation awareness and workload in driving while using adaptive cruise control and a cell phone. *International Journal of Industrial Ergonomics*, *35*(10), 939–953. doi:10.1016/j.ergon.2005.04.002

Maroto Sánchez, A. (2010). Growth and productivity in the service sector: the state of the art. *Institute of Social and Economic Analysis. WP 07/2010*, (7), 50. Retrieved from http://www.iaes.es/iuaes_sp/publicaciones.htm%0Ahttp://dialnet.unirioja.es/servlet/articulo?codigo=3247453&orden=260167&info=link%5Cnhttp://dialnet.unirioja.es/servlet/extart?codigo=3247453

Marzagao, D. S. L., & Carvalho, M. M. (2016). Critical success factors for Six Sigma projects. *International Journal of Project Management*, *34*(8), 1505–1518. doi:10.1016/j.ijproman.2016.08.005

Maslach, C. (1976). Burned-out. *Human Behavior*, *5*(9), 16.

Maslach, C., & Goldberg, J. (1998). Prevention of burnout: New perspectives. *Applied & Preventive Psychology*, *7*(1), 63–74. doi:10.1016/S0962-1849(98)80022-X

Maslach, C., & Jackson, S. E. (1981). The Measurement of Experienced Burnout. *Journal of Occupational Behaviour*, *2*(2), 99–113. doi:10.1002/job.4030020205

Maslach, C., Schaufeli, W. B., & Leiter, P. M. (2001). Job burnout. *Annual Review of Psychology*, *53*(1), 397–422. doi:10.1146/annurev.psych.52.1.397 PMID:11148311

Matthews, G., Reinerman-Jones, L., Barber, D., & Abich, J. IV. (2015). The psychometrics of mental workload: Multiple measures are sensitive but divergent. *Human Factors*, *57*(1), 125–143. doi:10.1177/0018720814539505 PMID:25790574

Maykut, P., & Morehouse, R. (1994). *Beginning qualitative research: A philosophic & practical guide*. London: Falmer Press.

Mazur, L. M., Mosaly, P. R., Jackson, M., Chang, S. X., Burkhardt, K. D., Adams, R. D., … Marks, L. B. (2012). Quantitative Assessment of Workload and Stressors in Clinical Radiation Oncology. *International Journal of Radiation Oncology*Biology*Physics*, *83*(5), e571–e576. doi:10.1016/J.IJROBP.2012.01.063

McIntosh, R. I., Culley, S. J., Mileham, A. R., & Owen, G. W. (2001). Changeover improvement: A maintenance perspective. *International Journal of Production Economics*, *73*(2), 153–163. doi:10.1016/S0925-5273(00)00170-5

Mcintosh, R., Culley, S., Gest, G., Mileham, T., & Owen, G. (1996). An assessment of the role of design in the improvement of changeover performance. *International Journal of Operations & Production Management*, *16*(9), 5–22. doi:10.1108/01443579610125552

McIntyre, R. M., & Salas, E. (1995). Measuring and managing for team performance: Emerging principles from complex environments. In R. A. Guzzo & E. Salas (Eds.), *Team effectiveness and decision making in organizations*. San Francisco: Jossey-Bass.

McLean, L., Abry, T., Taylor, M., Jimenez, M., & Granger, K. (2017). Teachers' mental health and perceptions of school climate across the transition from training to teaching. *Teaching and Teacher Education*, *65*, 230–240. doi:10.1016/j.tate.2017.03.018

Meeus, M. T. H., & Oerlemans, L. A. G. (2000). Firm behavior and innovative performance: An empirical exploration of the selection-adaptation debate. *Research Policy*, *29*, 41–58. doi:10.1016/S0048-7333(99)00032-3

Mehrabi, J. (2012). Application of Six-Sigma in Educational Quality Management. *Procedia: Social and Behavioral Sciences*, *47*, 1358–1362. doi:10.1016/j.sbspro.2012.06.826

Mélan, C., & Cascino, N. (2014). A multidisciplinary approach of workload assessment in real-job situations: Investigation in the field of aerospace activities. *Frontiers in Psychology*. doi:10.3389/fpsyg.2014.00964 PMID:25232346

Mendenhall, W., Sincich, T., & Boudreau, N. S. (1996). *A second course in statistics: regression analysis* (Vol. 5). Upper Saddle River, NJ: Prentice Hall.

Michielsen, H. J., De Vries, J., & Van Heck, G. L. (2003). Fatigue Assessment Scale (FAS). *Springer Science+Business Media*, *5*, 1–406. doi:10.1007/978-1-4419-9893-4

Mileham, A.R, Culley, S. J., Owen, G. W., Newnes, L. B., & Giess, M. D. (2005). *The impact of run-up in ensuring Rapid Changeover*. Academic Press.

Mileham, A. R., Culley, G. W., Owen, G. W., & McIntosh, R. I. (1999). Rapid changeover - a pre-requisite for responsive manufacture. *International Journal of Operations & Production Management*, *19*(8), 785–796. doi:10.1108/01443579910274383

Miller, S. (2001). *Workload measures*. National Advanced Driving Simulator. Retrieved from http://www.nads-sc.uiowa.edu/publicationstorage/200501251347060.n01-006.pdf

Millhollan, C. (2009). *The journey to an enterprise project management office*. Paper presented at PMI® Global Congress 2009—North America, Orlando, FL.

Ministerio de la Protección Social. (2009). *Resolución 2566, Julio 7 del 2009: pro el cual se adopta la Tabla de Enfermedades Profesionales*. Bogotá: El Ministerio.

Ministerio de la Protección Social. (2010). *Batería de instrumentos para la evaluación de factores de riesgo psicosocial*. Retrieved from http://www.riesgopsicosocial.com.co/Bateria-riesgo-psicosocial.compressed.pdf

Ministry of Education - Chile. (2018). *Law 21,091 'About Higher Education'*. Available in: http://bcn.cl/25b7u

Ministry of Health. (2017). *Protocol for surveillance of psychosocial risks at work*. Government of Chile.

Ministry of Transport of Ukraine. (2003). *About Approving the Flight Rules of Aircrafts and Air Traffic Services in the Classified Airspace of Ukraine*. Kyiv: Author.

Minztberg, H. (1993). *Structure in fives: designing effective organizations*. London: Prentice-Hall International.

Miyake, S. (2001). Multivariate workload evaluation combining physiological and subjective measures. *International Journal of Psychophysiology*, *40*(3), 233–238. doi:10.1016/S0167-8760(00)00191-4 PMID:11228350

Mohammadian, Y., Malekpour, F., Malekpour, A., Zoghipour, S., & Malalekpour, K. (2015). Study on Mental Workload of Teachers and Its Correlation with Their Quality of Life. *J. Educ. Manage. Stud*, *5*(2), 144–149. Retrieved from www.science-line.com

Molina-Sabando, K., & García-Lucas, C. A. (2018). Relationship between stress and the affective area in the teachers of the Technical University of Manabí. *Espirales revista multidisciplinaria de investigación*, *2*(16). Available in: http://www.revistaespirales.com/index.php/es/article/view/233

Moncada, S., Llorens, C., Navarro, A., & Kristensen, T. S. (2005). ISTAS21: Versión en lengua castellana del cuestionario psicosocial de Copenhague (COPSOQ). *Arch Prev Riesgos Labor.*

Mondelo E., Barrau P. Ergonomía, P. R. (1999). *Edicions UPC Aula Politècnica / Etseib. Ergonomía 1 Fundamentos.* doi:10.1186/1748-717X-2-28

Morales Méndez, J., & Silva Rodríguez, R. (2015). Set-up reduction in an interconnection axle manufacturing cell using SMED. *International Journal of Advanced Manufacturing Technology*, *84*(9–12), 1907–1916. doi:10.100700170-015-7845-0

Moral, M., & Suárez, C. (2016). Factores de riesgo en el uso problemático de Internet y del teléfono móvil en adolescentes españoles. *Revista Iberoamericana de Psicología y Salud*, *7*(2), 69–78. doi:10.1016/j.rips.2016.03.001

Moray, N. (1979). Models and Measures of Mental Workload. Mental Workload. doi:10.1007/978-1-4757-0884-4_2

Moray, N. (1982). Subjective mental workload. *Human Factors*, *24*(1), 25–40. doi:10.1177/001872088202400104

Moray, N. (1989). Mental workload since 1979. *International Reviews of Ergonomics*, *2*, 123–150.

Moreno Jiménez, B., & Baéz León, C. (2010). *Factores y riesgos psicosociales, formas, consecuencias, medidas y buenas práctica* . Madrid: Universidad Autónoma de MAdrid.

Moreno, B. (2015). Ergonomía y Psicosociología. *Programa Técnico En Prevención de Riesgos Laborales - UGT*, *1*, 1689–1699. doi:10.1017/CBO9781107415324.004

Moreno-Jiménez, B., & Báez León, C. (2010). *Psychosocial factors and risks, forms, consequences, measures and good practices.* Instituto Nacional de Seguridad e Higiene En El Trabajo. doi:10.1016/0277-9536(85)90255-2

Moriarty, D., & Jarvis, S. (2014). A systems perspective on the unstable approach in commercial aviation. *Reliability Engineering & System Safety*, *131*, 197–202. doi:10.1016/j.ress.2014.06.019

Mo, S., & Shi, J. (2017). Linking Ethical Leadership to Employee Burnout, Workplace Deviance and Performance: Testing the Mediating Roles of Trust in Leader and Surface Acting. *Journal of Business Ethics*, *144*(2), 293–303. doi:10.100710551-015-2821-z

Mosier, K. L., Rettenmaier, P., McDearmid, M., Wilson, J., Mak, S., Raj, L., & Orasanu, J. (2013). Pilot–ATC Communication Conflicts: Implications for NextGen. *The International Journal of Aviation Psychology*, *23*(3), 213–226. do i:10.1080/10508414.2013.799350

Muñoz Rojas, D., Orellano, N., & Hernández Palma, H. (2018). Riesgo psicosocial: Tendencias y nuevas orientaciones laborales. *Psicogente*, *21*(40), 532–544. doi:10.17081/psico.21.40.3090

Murguia-Ramirez, A. C., Pozos-Radillo, B. E., & Plascencia-Campos, A. R. (2019). Work stress and its relationship with socio-labor factors in teachers of a public preparatory school and of a private one. *Revista Cubana de Salud y Trabajo*, *20*(1), 52–57. Retrieved from http://revsaludtrabajo.sld.cu/index.php/revsyt/article/view/81

Musa, M. A., Ibrahim, A. M., Ravi, S., Abidin, Z. F. Z., & Wan Mat, W. A. (2013). A case study and analysis of setup reduction for stamping dies - SMED approach. *Global Engineers & Technologists Review*, *4*(1), 1–9.

Mustapha, N. (2013). Measuring Job Satisfaction from the Perspective of Interpersonal Relationship and Faculty Workload among Academic Staff at Public Universities in Kelantan, Malaysia. *International Journal of Business and Social Science*, *4*(15), 120–124.

Nakhai, B., & Neves, J. S. (2009). The challenges of six sigma in improving service quality. *International Journal of Quality & Reliability Management*, *26*(7), 663–684. doi:10.1108/02656710910975741

Naktiyok, A., & Kaygın, E. (2012). Tükenmişlik ve İş Tatmini Düzeylerini Belirlemeye Yönelik Akademik Personel Üzerinde Bir Uygulama. *Sosyal ve Beşeri Bilimler Dergisi, 4*(1).

Naktiyok, A., & Karabey, C. N. (2005). İşkoliklik ve Tükenmişlik Sendromu. *Atatürk Üniversitesi İktisadi ve İdari Bilimler Dergisi*, *19*(2), 179–198.

Näslund, D. (2013). Lean and six sigma - critical success factors revisited. *International Journal of Quality and Service Sciences*, *5*(1), 86–100. doi:10.1108/17566691311316266

Negrete, B., & Garcia-Aurrecoechea, R. (2008). Psychosocial risk factors for illicit drug use in a sample of Mexican high school students. *Revista Panamericana de Salud Publica*, *24*(4), 223–232. PMID:19133170

Niedhammer, I., Sultan-Taïeb, H., Chastang, J., Vermeylen, G., & Parent-Thirion, A. (2012). Exposure to psychosocial work factors in 31 European countries. *Occupational Medicine*, *62*(3), 196–202. doi:10.1093/occmed/kqs020 PMID:22394680

Nikodijević, A., Labrović, J. A., & Đoković, A. (2012). Academic Burnout Among Students at Faculty of Organizational Sciences. *Management Journal for Theory and Practice Management*, (64), 47–53.

Niyazmetov, T., & Keoy, K. H. (2011). Developing a capability model of Six Sigma implementation: A comparative study of CSF of Six Sigma implementation between manufacturing and service sectors in Uzbekistan. *International Journal of the Built Environment and Asset Management*, *1*(1), 14. doi:10.1504/IJBEAM.2011.044127

Nogareda Cuixart, C., & Pérez Bilbao, J. (2012a). Factores Psicosociales: metodología de evaluación. *Notas Técnicas de Prevención*, 1–5. Retrieved from http://www.insht.es/InshtWeb/Contenidos/Documentacion/NTP/NTP/926a937/926w.pdf

Nogareda Cuixart, C., & Pérez Bilbao, J. (2012b). *NTP 926. Factores Psicosociales: metodología de evaluación*. Notas Técnicas de Prevención.

NOM035. S. (2018). *DOF: 23/10/2018*. Retrieved from https://www.dof.gob.mx/nota_detalle.php?codigo=5541828&fecha=23/10/2018&print=true

Noori, B. (2015). The critical success factors for successful lean implementation in hospitals. *International Journal of Productivity and Quality Management*, *15*(1), 108–126. doi:10.1504/IJPQM.2015.065987

Nübling, M., Stößel, U., Hasselhorn, H., Michaelis, M., & Hofmann, F. (2006). Measuring psychological stress and strain at work - Evaluation of the COPSOQ Questionnaire in Germany. *Psycho-Social Medicine*. PMID:19742072

Nygren, T. E. (1991). Psychometric properties of subjective workload measurement techniques: Implications for their use in the assessment of perceived mental workload. *Human Factors*, *33*(1), 17–33. doi:10.1177/001872089103300102

O´Sullivan, C. (2009). *A study of critical success factors for regional*. Academic Press.

O'Donnell, R. D., & Eggemeier, F. T. (1986). Handbook of Perception and Human Performance: Vol. 49. Workload Assesment Methodology. Academic Press.

O'Donnell, R. D., & Eggemeier, F. T. (1986). Workload assessment methodology. In K. R. Boff, L. Kaufman, & J. P. Thomas (Eds.), (pp. 42-1–42-49). Handbook of perception and human performance New York: Wiley.

Oficina Internacional del Trabajo (OIT). (1984). *Factores psicosociales en el trabajo: naturaleza, incidencia y prevención*. Ginebra: OIT.

Oficina Internacional del Trabajo (OIT). (1986). *Factores psicosociales en el trabajo: reconocimiento y control.* Ginebra: OIT.

Oficina Internacional del Trabajo Ginebra (OIT). (1984). *Factores Psicosociales en el Trabajo: Naturaleza, incidencia y prevención.* Ginebra: Oficina Internacional del Trabajo.

Oficina Internacional del Trabajo. (2012). *Guía del Formador SOLVE: Integrando la promoción de la salud a las políticas de SSt en el lugar de trabajo.* Ginebra: Valentina Forastieri.

Olmos Rueda, P., & Mas Torelló, Ó. (2018). Validación de AUTOCOM: Autoevaluación de las competencias básicas de jóvenes en el marco de programas formativos de segunda oportunidad. *Revista Electrónica de Investigación Educativa, 20*(4), 49. doi:10.24320/redie.2018.20.4.1674

Ooi, K.-B., Lin, B., Tan, B.-I., & Chong, A. Y.-L. (2011). Are TQM practices supporting customer satisfaction and service quality? *Journal of Services Marketing, 25*(6), 410–419. doi:10.1108/08876041111161005

Oppold, P., Rupp, M., Mouloua, M., Hancock, P., & Martin, J. (2012). *Design considerations to improve cognitive ergonomic issues of unmanned vehicle interfaces utilizing video game controllers.* Work. doi:10.3233/WOR-2012-0896-5609

Orgambídez-Ramos, A., Pérez-Moreno, P. J., & Borrego-Alés, Y. (2015). Role stress and job satisfaction: Examining the mediating role of work engagement. *Journal of Work and Organizational Psychology, 31*, 69–77. doi:10.1016/j.rpto.2015.04.001

Organización Mundial de la Salud (OMS). (2012). *Informe general por el Día Mundial de la Salud 2012: La buena salud añade vida a los años.* OMS.

Organización Mundial de la Salud (OMS). (2017). *Salud Mental.* Obtenido de https://www.who.int/mental_health/in_the_workplace/es/

Orozco-Solis, M., Colunga-Rodríguez, C., Preciado-Serrano, M., Ángel-González, M., Vázquez-Colunga, J., & Colunga-Rodríguez, B. (2017). Representación del autocuidado de la salud en el trabajo de conductores de autobús urbano de Guadalajara, México. *Cadernos de Saude Publica, 33*(3), e00139815. doi:10.1590/0102-311x00139815 PMID:28380145

Ortaş, İ. (2011). Ohio State Üniversitesinde Eğitim ve Araştırma. *Yükseköğretim Dergisi, 1*(1), 45–50.

Ortiz-Solis, M., Maldonado-Macias, A. A., Barajas-Bustillos, M. A., Arredondo-Soto, K., & Carrillo-Gutiérrez, T. (2018). Human Error Identification and Mental Workload Index Setting During a Computer Power Source Change Task: A Case Study. In *International Conference on Applied Human Factors and Ergonomics* (pp. 427-438). Springer.

Osorio-Escobar, M. (2011). El trabajo y los factores de riesgo psicosociales: Qué son y cómo se evalúan. *Revista CES Salud Pública, 2*(1), 74–79. Retrieved from http://revistas.ces.edu.co/index.php/ces_salud_publica/article/viewFile/1450/892

Otto, A., & Battaïa, O. (2017). Reducing physical ergonomic risks at assembly lines by line balancing and job rotation: A survey. *Computers & Industrial Engineering, 111*, 467–480. doi:10.1016/j.cie.2017.04.011

Ozkan, B., Rubio, J. F., Hassan, M. K., & Davis, J. R. (2017). Six Sigma, stock returns and operating performance. *Management Research Review, 40*(3), 331–351. doi:10.1108/MRR-12-2015-0291

P., H. (1982). ARBAN: A new method for analysis of ergonomic effort. *Applied Ergonomics, 13*(2), 82–86. Retrieved from http://ovidsp.ovid.com/ovidweb.cgi?T=JS&PAGE=reference&D=emed1a&NEWS=N&AN=1982164797

Palanisamy, S., & Siddiqui, S. (2013). Changeover Time Reduction and Productivity Improvement by Integrating Conventional SMED Method with Implementation of MES for Better Production Planning and Control. International Journal of Innovative Research in Science. *Engineering and Technology, 2*(12), 7961–7974.

Palliser, C. R., Firth, H. M., Feyer, A. M., & Paulin, S. M. (2005). Musculoskeletal discomfort and work-related stress in New Zealand dentists. *Work and Stress, 19*(4), 351–359. doi:10.1080/02678370500421064

Palmer, S., Cooper, C., & Thomas, K. (2003). *Creating a balance: managing stress.* Londres: British Library.

Palomo-vélez, G., Carrasco, J., Bastías, Á., Doris, M., & Jiménez, A. (2015). Factores de riesgo psicosocial y satisfacción laboral en trabajadoras estacionales de Chile. *Revista Panamericana de Salud Pública, 37*(7), 301–307. PMID:26208200

Panatik, S. S. B., Rajab, A., Shaari, R., Shah, I. M., Rahman, H. A., & Badri, S. K. B. Z. (2012). *Impact of Work-related Stress on Well-being among Academician in Malaysian Research University. 2012 International Conference on Education and Management Innovation*, Singapore.

Parasuraman, R., Sheridan, T. B., & Wickens, C. D. (2008). Situation awareness, mental workload, and trust in automation: Viable, empirically supported cognitive engineering constructs. *Journal of Cognitive Engineering and Decision Making, 2*(2), 140–160. doi:10.1518/155534308X284417

Pavlenko, S., & Bojan, C. (2014). Reclaiming the Idea of the University as a Possible Solution to Today's Crisis. *Center for Educational Policy Studies Journal, 4*(2), 91–104.

Pawar, G. J., Sirdeshpande, N. S., Atram, A. B., & Patil, P. R. (2014). Reduction in setup change time of a machine in a bearing manufacturing plant using SMED and ECRS. *International Journal of Engine Research, 3*(5), 321–323. doi:10.17950/ijer/v3s5/506

Pawłyszyn, I., Agnieszka, S., & Hadaś, Ł. (2014). Application of Smed Methodology in a Printing-House. *Research in Logisb, 4*(4), 357–368.

Peiro, J. (2013). *Desencadenantes del estrés laboral.* Universidad de València.

Pereira, F., Grützmann, T., & Novello, T. (2019). Mapping Research on Tecno Stress in Mathematics Teachers. *RELACult - Revista Latino-Americana de Estudos em Cultura e Sociedade, 5*(4). doi:10.23899/relacult.v5i4.1234

Pérez Bilbao, J., & Nogareda Cuixart, C. (2012). *Factores psicosociales : metodología de evaluación.* Instituto Nacional de Seguridad e Higiente En El Trabajo.

Pérez-Carpio, J. E., Turpo-Chaparro, J. E., & López-Gonzales, J. L. (2019). Psychosocial risk factors and work stress in university teachers. *Revista Espacios, 40*(19). Retrieved from: https://www.revistaespacios.com/a19v40n19/19401913.html

Perkins, J. A. (1973). Organisation & Function of the University. In J. A. Perkins (Ed.), *The University as an Organisation* (pp. 3–14). New York: McGraw Hill.

Petty, M., McGee, G., & Cavender, J. (2011). A Meta-Analysis of the Relationships Between Individual Job Satisfaction and Individual Performance. *Academy of Management Review.* doi:10.5465/amr.1984.4277608

Piercy, N., & Rich, N. (2009). Lean transformation in the pure service environment: The case of the call service centre. *International Journal of Operations & Production Management, 29*(1), 54–76. doi:10.1108/01443570910925361

Pimenta, A., Goncalves, S., Carneiro, D., Fde-Riverola, F., Neves, J., & Novais, P. (2015). Mental workload management as a tool in e-learning scenarios. In *2015 International Conference on Pervasive and Embedded Computing and Communication Systems (PECCS)* (pp. 25–32). Angers, France: Academic Press.

Pinchot, G. (1985). *Intrapreneuring: Why You Do not Have to Leave the Corporation to Become an Entrepreneur*. New York, NY: Harper, and Row.

Piñeda Geraldo, A., & Montes Paniza, G. (2014). ERGONOMÍA AMBIENTAL: Iluminación y confort térmico en trabajadores de oficinas con pantalla de visualización de datos. *Rev. Ingeniería. Matemáticas y Ciencias de La Información, 1*(2), 49–71.

Pines, A. M., & Aronson, E. (1988). *Career burnout: Causes and cures*. New York: Free press.

Pinheiro, R., Geschwind, L., Ramirez, F. O., & Vrangbæk, K. (Eds.). (2016). *Towards a comparative institutionalism: Forms, dynamics and logics across the organizational fields of health care & higher education*. Emerald Group Publishing Limited. doi:10.1108/S0733-558X201645

Pinto, J. P. (2008). Lean Thinking - Introdução ao pensamento magro. *Comunidade Lean Thinking, 159–163*. doi:10.1002/9780470759660.ch27

Piotet, F., & Mabile, J. (1984). *Conditions de travail, mode d'emploi ANACT [Agence nationale pour l'amélioration des conditions de travail]*. Academic Press.

Plane Crash Info. (2013). *Accident statistics*. Retrieved February 1, 2019, from http://planecrashinfo.com/cause.htm

Plummer, P., & Taylor, M. (2004). Entrepreneurship and human capital. *Journal of Small Business and Enterprise Development, 11*(4), 427–439. doi:10.1108/14626000410567071

Pollock, T., Whitbred, R., & Contractor, N. (2006). Social information processing and job characteristics. *Human Communication Research, 26*(2), 292–330. doi:10.1111/j.1468-2958.2000.tb00759.x

Pool, S. W. (2000). The learning organization: Motivating employees by integrating TQM philosophy in a supportive organizational culture. *Leadership and Organization Development Journal, 21*(8), 373–378. doi:10.1108/01437730010379276

Porter, S. R., & Umbach, P. D. (2001). Analyzing Faculty Workload Data Using Multilevel Modeling. *Research in Higher Education, 42*(2), 171–196. doi:10.1023/A:1026573503271

Portoghese, I., Galletta, M., Coppola, R. C., Finco, G., & Campagna, M. (2014). Burnout and workload among health care workers: The moderating role of job control. *Safety and Health at Work, 5*(3), 152–157. doi:10.1016/j.shaw.2014.05.004 PMID:25379330

Prajogo, & I., D. (2005). The comparative analysis of TQM practices and quality performance between manufacturing and service firms. *International Journal of Service Industry Management, 16*(3), 217–228. doi:10.1108/09564230510601378

Psychogios, A. G., Atanasovski, J., & Tsironis, L. K. (2012). Lean Six Sigma in a service context: A multi-factor application approach in the telecommunications industry. *International Journal of Quality & Reliability Management, 29*(1), 122–139. doi:10.1108/02656711211190909

Puentes-Martínez, L., & Díaz-Rábago, A. B. (2019). Reliability and construct validity of the Perceived Stress Scale in medical students. *Revista de Ciencias Médicas de Pinar del Río, 23*(3), 373–379. Retrieved from http://ref.scielo.org/kbhqym

Pugh, D. (1991). Organizational Behaviour. London: Prentice Hall International (UK) Ltd.

Pujol-Cols, L. J. (2018). Core self-evaluations and autonomy: a study of their direct and interactive effects on work engagement among highly skilled Argentinian professionals. *Estudios Gerenciales, 34*(149), 361-372. http://ref.scielo.org/6494gq

Pujol-Cols, L. J., & Arraigada, M. (2017). Psychometric properties of the Copsoq-Istas Psychosocial Risk Questionnaire 21 in Argentinian university teachers. *Cuadernos de Administración, 30*(55), 97-125. Retrieved from: http://ref.scielo.org/d8qmv2

Pujol-Cols, L. J., & Lazzaro-Salazar, M. (2018). Psychosocial risks and job satisfaction in Argentinian scholars: Exploring the moderating role of work engagement. *Work and Organizations Psichology Magazine*, *34*(3), 145–156. doi:10.5093/jwop2018a17

Pulakos, E. D., White, L. A., Oppler, S. H., & Borman, W. C. (1989). Examination of race and sex effects on performance ratings. *The Journal of Applied Psychology*, 74.

Radnor, Z., Walley, P., Stephens, A., & Bucci, G. (2006). Evaluation of the lean approach to business management and its use in the public sector. *Scottish Executive Social Research, 20.*

Radnor, Z., & Boaden, R. (2008). Editorial: Lean in public services - Panacea or paradox?: Does lean enhance public services? *Public Money & Management*, *28*(1), 3–7. doi:10.1111/j.1467-9302.2008.00610.x

Rahayu, S. N., Norazan, M. N., Az'lina, A. H., Adriana, I., Nornadiah, M. R., & Naslina, A. N. N. (2012). Determining the Significant Factors Affecting the Physical and Mental Components of Academicians Using Robust Linear Regression Models. *International Journal of Mathematical Models And Methods in Applied Sciences*, *7*(1), 30–37.

Raja, V., Raju, R., & Srivatsa, S. (2015, Sept.). A review of the quality evolution in various organisations. *Total Quality Management & Business Excellence*, 1–15. doi:10.1080/14783363.2015.1082421

Rana, H. (2016). Impact of Student's Burnout on Academic Performance/Achievement. *Journal of Academic Research, 3*(2), 159–174.

Raziq, A., & Maulabakhsh, R. (2015). Impact of Working Environment on Job Satisfaction. *Procedia Economics and Finance*, *23*, 717–725. doi:10.1016/S2212-5671(15)00524-9

Realyvásquez, A., Maldonado-Macías, A. A., García-Alcaraz, J. L., & Blanco-Fernández, J. (2015). Effects of organizational macroergonomic compatibility elements over manufacturing systems' performance. *Procedia Manufacturing, 3*, 5715–5722. doi:10.1016/j.promfg.2015.07.807

Reid, G. B., & Nygren, T. E. (1988). The subjective workload assessment technique: A scaling procedure for measuring mental workload. *Advances in Psychology*, *52*, 185–218. doi:10.1016/S0166-4115(08)62387-0

Reik, M., Owen, G., Cully, S., McIntosh, R., & Mileham, T. (2007). Integrating product and manufacturing systems design to minimise changeover losses. *International Conference on Engineering Design, ICED'07, 441*, 1–9. Retrieved from http://opus.bath.ac.uk/1551/

Reik, M. P., Mcintosh, R. I., Culley, S. J., Mileham, A. R., & Owen, G. W. (2006). A formal design for changeover methodology. Part 1: Theory and background. *Proceedings of the Institution of Mechanical Engineers. Part B, Journal of Engineering Manufacture*, *220*(8), 1225–1235. doi:10.1243/09544054JEM527

Reik, M., McIntosh, R., Owen, G., Mileham, A., & Culley, S. (2005). The development of a systematic design for changeover methodology. *International Conference on Engineering Design, ICED'05*, 1–26.

Renault, R. (1976). Les profils de postes. Méthode d'analyse des conditions de travail. *Services Des Conditions de Travail.*

Renault, U. (1976). *Método Renault*. Retrieved from https://books.google.com.mx/books/about/Lesœ_profils_de_postes.html?id=TrcYvwEACAAJ&redir_esc=y

Renner, K. H., Hock, M., Bergner-Köther, R., & Laux, L. (2018). Differentiating anxiety and depression: The State-Trait Anxiety-Depression Inventory. *Cognition and Emotion*, *32*(7), 1409–1423. doi:10.1080/02699931.2016.1266306

Richard, G. V., & Krieshok, T. S. (1989). Occupational stress, strain, and coping in university faculty. *Journal of Vocational Behavior*, *34*(1), 117–132. doi:10.1016/0001-8791(89)90068-7

Riippa, L. (2016). *Measuring and Improving Production Efficiency of Paint Filling and Packing Line*. LUT School of Business and Management Industrial.

Rizzo, L., & Longo, L. (2017). Representing and Inferring Mental Workload via Defeasible Reasoning: a Comparison with the NASA Task Load Index and the Workload Profile. In *1st Workshop on Advances In Argumentation In Artificial Intelligence* (pp. 126–140). Bari, Italy: Academic Press. Retrieved from https://arrow.dit.ie/scschcomcon/216

Robbins, S. P., & Judge, T. A. (2011). *Organizational Behavior*. Pearson Education Inc.

Robin, D. P., Giallourakis, M., David, F. R., & Moritz, T. E. (1989). A Different Look at Codes of Ethics. *Business Horizons*, *32*(1), 66–73. doi:10.1016/0007-6813(89)90028-1

Rodríguez Méndez, R., Sánchez Partida, D., Martínez Flores, J. L., & Arvizu Barrón, E. (2015). A case study: SMED & JIT methodologies to develop continuous flow of stamped parts into AC disconnect assembly line in Schneider Electric Tlaxcala Plant. *IFAC-PapersOnLine*, *48*(3), 1399–1404. doi:10.1016/j.ifacol.2015.06.282

Rodríguez, E., Sánchez-Gómez, J., Dorado, H. A., & Ramírez, J. M. (2015). Factores de Riesgo Psicosocial Intralaboral y Grado de Estrés en Docentes Universitarios. *Revista Colombiana de Salud Ocupacional*, *4*(2), 12–17. Retrieved from http://revistasojs.unilibrecali.edu.co/index.php/rcso/article/view/111

Rodríguez, I., González, G., & Carbonen, S. (2007). El modelo AMIGO y la metodología PREVENLAB-Psicosocial. Aportaciones y retos en la prevención de los riesgos psicosociales. *Seguridad y Salud en el Trabajo*, *42*, 18–25.

Rodrik, D. (2018). Rescue the economy of neoliberalism. *Letras Libres*, (196), 12-17. Available in: https://www.letraslibres.com/espana-mexico/revista/rescatar-la-economia-del-neoliberalismo

Roozeboom, M. B., Houtman, I., & Van den Bossche, S. (2008). Monitoring Psychosocial Risks at work. In S. Leka & T. Cox (Eds.), The European Framework for psychosocial Risk, (pp. 17-36). Academic Press.

Rossman, G. B., & Wilson, B. L. (1985). Numbers and words: Combining quantitative and qualitative methods in a single large-scale evaluation study. *Evaluation Review*, *9*(5), 627–643. doi:10.1177/0193841X8500900505

Rostami, Z., & Abedi, M. R., B., S. W., Ahmadi, S. A., & Sadeghi, A. H. (2013). The Psychometric Characteristics of Maslach Burnout Inventory Student Survey: Among Students of Isfahan University. *Zahedan Journal of Researches in Medical Sciences*, *16*(9), 29–32.

Rotondo, A. (2015). Disagreement and Intellectual Skepticism. *Australasian Journal of Philosophy*, *93*(2), 251–271. doi:10.1080/00048402.2014.986746

Rouse, W. B., Edwards, S. L., & Hammer, J. M. (1993). Modeling the dynamics of mental workload and human performance in complex systems. *IEEE Transactions on Systems, Man, and Cybernetics*, *23*(6), 1662–1671. doi:10.1109/21.257761

Royal Spanish Academy. (2014a). *Dictionary of the Spanish language* (23rd ed.). Retrieved from: https://dle.rae.es/?id=GDlmBBp

Royal Spanish Academy. (2014b). *Dictionary of the Spanish language* (23rd ed.). Retrieved from: https://dle.rae.es/?id=2l0oQtn

Royal Spanish Academy. (2014c). *Dictionary of the Spanish language* (23rd ed.). Retrieved from: https://dle.rae.es/srv/search?m=30&w=ineficacia

Rubén, A., Marchetti, N., Villalón, M., Hirmas, M., & Pastorino, M. S. (2010). Adaptación y análisis psicométrico de un cuestionario para evaluar riesgos psicosociales en el trabajo en Chil: Versión media del CoPsoQ. *Revista Chilena de Salud Pública, 13*(1), 7–16. doi:10.5354/0717-3652.2009.652

Rubio Valdehita, S., Díaz Ramiro, E. M., Martín García, J., & Luceño Moreno, L. (2010). La carga mental como factor de riesgo psicosocial. Diferencias por baja Laboral TT - Mental workload as a psychosocial risk factor. Differnces based on sick leave. *Ansiedad y Estrés.*

Rubio-Valdehita, S., López-Núñez, M. I., López-Higes, R., & Díaz-Ramiro, E. M. (2017). Desarrollo del cuestionario CarMen-Q para evaluar la carga mental de trabajo. *Psicothema, 29*(4), 570–576. doi:10.7334/psicothema2017.151 PMID:29048320

Rudaizky, D., & Macleod, C. (2014). Anxiety reactivity and anxiety perseveration represent independent dimensions of anxiety vulnerability: An in vivo study. *Anxiety, Stress, and Coping, 27*(4), 361–375. doi:10.1080/10615806.2013.853047

Rugulies, R., Bultmann, U., Aust, B., & Burr, H. (2006). Psychosocial work environment and incidence of severe depressive symptoms: prospective findings from a 5-year follow-up of the Danish work environment cohort study. *J Epidemiol, 163*(10), 877-887. Doi:10.1093/aje/kwj119

Ruíz García, E. (2005). *Idoate García.* MPF Cuestionario de Factores Psicosociales. Mini Psychosocial Factors.

Ruiz-Rabelo, J. F., Navarro-Rodriguez, E., Di-Stasi, L. L., Diaz-Jimenez, N., Cabrera-Bermon, J., Diaz-Iglesias, C., ... Briceño-Delgado, J. (2015). Validation of the NASA-TLX Score in Ongoing Assessment of Mental Workload During a Laparoscopic Learning Curve in Bariatric Surgery. *Obesity Surgery, 25*(12), 2451–2456. doi:10.100711695-015-1922-1 PMID:26459432

Sabry, A. (2014). Factors critical to the success of Six-Sigma quality program and their influence on performance indicators in some of Lebanese hospitals. *Arab Economic and Business Journal, 9*(2), 93–114. doi:10.1016/j.aebj.2014.07.001

Sagnak, M., & Kazancoglu, Y. (2015). Integration of green lean approach with six sigma: An application for flue gas emissions. *Journal of Cleaner Production, 127,* 112–118. doi:10.1016/j.jclepro.2016.04.016

Saito, Y., Kogi, K., & Kashiwagi, S. (1970). Factors Underlaying Subjective Feelings of Fatigue. *J Sci Lab, 46*(4), 204–224.

Salaheldin, S. I., & Abdelwahab, I. S. (2009). Six Sigma Practices in the Banking Sector in Qatar. *Global Business & Management Research, 1*(1), 23–35. Retrieved from http://search.ebscohost.com/login.aspx?direct=true&db=bth&AN=42988759&site=eds-live

Salanova, M., Llorens, S., Cifre, E., & Nogareda, C. (2007). *El tecnoestrés: concepto, medida e intervención psicosocial.* Nota Técnica de Prevención, 730, 21ª Serie. National Institute for Safety and Hygiene at Work. Available in: http://www.want.uji.es/download/el-tecnoestres-concepto-medida-e-intervencion-psicosocial/

Salanova-Soria, M. (2003). Working with technologies and coping with technostress: The role of efficacy beliefs. *Revista de Psicología del Trabajo y de las Organizaciones, 19*(3), 225–246.

Salas, E., & Maurino, D. (1988). *Human Factors in Aviation* (2nd ed.). San Diego, CA: Gulf Professional Publishing. Retrieved from https://books.google.com.mx/books?hl=es&lr=&id=Fi2Bqh_6fW4C&oi=fnd&pg=PT1&ots=wMOh3QytxD&sig=x3dUbOAfTX75N0IMXgX1faEwdxo&redir_esc=y#v=onepage&q&f=false

Salazar-Estrada, J., & Romero, N. (2013). Factores psicosociales del trabajador en la industria manufacturera en México. *Trabajo y Sociedad (Santiago del Estero), 20*, 119–129. Retrieved from http://www.unse.edu.ar/trabajoysociedad/20 SALAZAR ROMERO trabajador manufactura mexico.pdf

Sanchez-Lite,, A., Garcia,, M., & Domingo,, R. A. S. M. (2013). Novel Ergonomic Postural Assessment Method (NERPA) Using Product-Process Computer Aided Engineering for Ergonomic Workplace Design. *PLoS One, 12*. doi:10.1371/journal.pone.0072703 PMID:23977340

Sarkar, S. A., Mukhopadhyay, A. R., & Ghosh, S. K. (2013). Improvement of claim processing cycle time through Lean Six Sigma methodology. *International Journal of Lean Six Sigma, 4*(2), 171–183. doi:10.1108/20401461311319347

Sarsosa-Prowesk, K., Charria-Ortiz, V., & Arenas-Ortiz, F. (2014). Caracterizaci??n de los riesgos psicosociales intralaborales en jefes asistenciales de cinco cl??nicas nivel III de Santiago de Cali (Colombia). *Revista Gerencia y Politicas de Salud, 13*(27). doi:10.11144/Javeriana.rgyps13-27.crpi

Sauter, S. L., Murphy, L. R., Hurrell, J. J., & Levi, L. (1998). *Health and Safety at Work Encyclopedia. Psychosocial and organizational factors*. Capítulo 34. Available in: http://www.insht.es/InshtWeb/Contenidos/Documentacion/TextosOnline/EnciclopediaOIT/tomo2/34.pdf

Schaufeli, W. B., & Bakker, A. B. (2004). Job demands, job resources, and their relationship with burnout and engagement: A multi-sample study. *Journal of Organizational Behavior, 25*(3), 293–315. doi:10.1002/job.248

Schaufeli, W. B., & Greenglass, E. R. (2001). Introduction to special issue on burnout and health. *Psychology & Health, 16*(5), 501–510. doi:10.1080/08870440108405523 PMID:22804495

Schaufeli, W. B., & Salanova, M. (2007). Efficacy or inefficacy, that's the question: Burnout and work engagement, and their relationships with efficacy beliefs. *Anxiety, Stress, and Coping, 20*(2), 177–196. doi:10.1080/10615800701217878

Schaufeli, W. B., Salanova, M., Gonzalez-Roma, V., & Bakker, A. B. (2002). The Measurement of Engagement and Burnout: A Two Sample Confirmatory Factor Analytic Approach. *Journal of Happiness Studies, 3*(3), 71–92. doi:10.1023/A:1015630930326

Schiff, M., & Leip, L. (2019). The Impact of Job Expectations, Workload, & Autonomy on Work-Related Stress Among Prison Wardens in the United States. *Criminal Justice and Behavior, 46*(1), 136–153. doi:10.1177/0093854818802876

Schlegel, R. E. (1993). Driver mental workload. *Automotive ergonomics*, 359-382.

Schmal, R., & Cabrales, F. (2018). The challenge of university governance: The Chilean case. *Ensaio: Avaliação e Políticas Públicas em Educação, 26*(100), 822–848. doi:10.15900104-40362018002601309

Schmoldt, R. A., Freeborn, D. K., & Klevit, H. D. (1994). Physician burnout: Recommendations for

Schreuder, N. W. (2014). *Maximizing flexibility through minimizing changeover time*. Universiteit Twente. Retrieved from http://essay.utwente.nl/65172/

Schütte, S., Chastang, J., Malard, L., Parent-Thirion, A., Vermeylen, G., & Niedhammer, I. (2014). Psychosocial working conditions and psychological well-being among employees in 34 European countries. *International Archives of Occupational and Environmental Health, 87*(8), 897–907. doi:10.100700420-014-0930-0 PMID:24526111

Seaberg, J. R. (1998). Faculty Reports of Workload. *Journal of Social Work Education, 34*(1), 7–19. doi:10.1080/10437797.1998.10778901

Seçkiner, S. U., & Toraman, N. (2017). Bilişsel İşyükünü Belirlemek İçin Yeni Bir Model. *Mühendislik Bilimleri ve Tasarım Dergisi, 5*(1), 365–381.

Secretaría del Trabajo y Previsión Social (STPS). (2016). *Proyecto de Norma Oficial Mexicana Proy-Nom-035-Stps-2016.* Factores de Riesgo Psicosocial- Identificación Y Prevención.

Secretaría del Trabajo y Previsión Social (STPS). (2018). *Norma oficial mexicana NOM-035-STPS-2018: Factores de Riesgo Psicosocial en el Trabajo-Identificación, análisis y prevención.* STPS.

Secretaría del Trabajo y Previsión Social. (2018). *NORMA Oficial Mexicana NOM-035-STPS-2018, Factores de riesgo psicosocial en el trabajo-Identificación, análisis y prevención.* Author.

Selvarajan, T. T., Ramamoorthy, N., Flood, P. C., & Gutherie, J. P. (2007). The role of human capital philosophy in promoting firm innovativeness and performance: A test of a causal model. *International Journal of Human Resource Management, 18*(8), 1–70. doi:10.1080/09585190701502588

Seong-Tak, O., & Park, S. (2016). A Study of the Connected Smart Worker's Techno-Stress. *Procedia Computer Science, 91*, 725–733. doi:10.1016/j.procs.2016.07.065

Seyle, H. (1936). A Syndrome produced by Diverse Nocuous Agents. *Nature, 138*(3479), 32. doi:10.1038/138032a0

Shahzad, K., Mumtaz, H., Hayat, K., & Khan, M. A. (2010). Faculty Workload, Compensation Management and Academic Quality in Higher Education of Pakistan: Mediating Role of Job Satisfaction. European Journal of Economics. *Finance & Administrative Sciences, 27*, 111.

Sharan, D. (2012). Ergonomic workplace analysis (EWA). In Work. doi:10.3233/WOR-2012-0821-5366

Shete, S., & Wilkinson, A. (2017). Identifying demographic and psychosocial factors related to the escalation of smoking behavior among Mexican American adolescents. *Preventive Medicine, 99*, 146–151. doi:10.1016/j.ypmed.2017.02.018 PMID:28235542

Shmelova, T., & Paukov, O. (2007). Determination of conditional loading of the air traffic controller taking into account the complexity of the technological procedures. In *Materials of VII International Scientific Conference of Students and Young Scientists "Flight-2007".* Kyiv: National Aviation University.

Shmelova, T., Lazorenko, V., & Bilko, A. (2014). Estimation of pre-simulating training tasks complexity. *Proceedings of the National Aviation University, No., 1*(62), 17–22.

Shmelova, T., Sikirda, Yu., & Jafarzade, T. (2019). Artificial neural network for pre-simulation training of air traffic controller. In T. Shmelova, Yu. Sikirda, N. Rizun, & D. Kucherov (Eds.), *Cases on modern computer systems in aviation* (pp. 27–51). Hershey, PA: IGI Global. doi:10.4018/978-1-5225-7588-7.ch002

Shmelova, T., Sikirda, Yu., Zemlyanskiy, A., Danilenko, O., & Lazorenko, V. (2016). Artificial neural network for air traffic controller's pre-simulator training. *Proceedings of the National Aviation University, No., 3*(68), 13–23.

Shmelova, T., Stasiuk, O., & Bondarev, D. (2013). Methodology of workload estimation. In *All-Ukrainian Scientific and Practical Conference of Young Scientists and Students.* In *Problems of navigation and traffic control.* Kyiv: National Aviation University.

Shmelova, T., Stasiuk, O., & Poluhovich, O. (2013a). Determination of conditional workload of air traffic controller taking into account the complication of technological procedures. In *All-Ukrainian Scientific and Practical Conference of Young Scientists and Students.* In *Problems of navigation and traffic control.* Kyiv: National Aviation University.

Shmelova, T., Stasiuk, O., & Poluhovich, O. (2013b). Interpretation of conditional workload of air controller in graph. In *All-Ukrainian Scientific and Practical Conference of Young Scientists and Students.* In *Problems of navigation and traffic control.* Kyiv: National Aviation University.

Shultz, K. S., Wang, M., Crimmins, E. M., & Fisher, G. G. (2010). Age differences in the demand-control model of work stress an examination of data from 15 european countries. *Journal of Applied Gerontology*, *29*(1), 21–47. doi:10.1177/0733464809334286 PMID:20948986

Siegrist, J. (2008). Effort-reward imbalance and health in a globalized economy. *Scandinavian Journal of Work, Environment & Health*, 163–168.

Sila, I., & Ebrahimpour, M. (2003). Examination and comparison of the critical factors of total quality management (TQM) across countries. *International Journal of Production Research*, *41*(2), 235–268. doi:10.1080/0020754021000022212

Silva, A. A., De Souza, J. M., Borges, F. N., & Fischer, F. M. (2010). Health related quality of life and working conditions among nursing providers. *Revista de Saude Publica*, *44*(4), 718–725. doi:10.1590/S0034-89102010000400016 PMID:20676562

Singh, A. K., & Sushil. (2013). Modeling enablers of TQM to improve airline performance. *International Journal of Productivity and Performance Management*, *62*(3), 250–275. doi:10.1108/17410401311309177

Singh, J., & Brar, G. S. (2017). Process improvement and setup time reduction in manufacturing industry : A case study. *IJAMR*, *9*(1), 15–23.

Siu, O. L., Cooper, C. L., & Phillips, D. R. (2014). Intervention studies on enhancing work well-being, reducing burnout, and improving recovery experiences among Hong Kong health care workers and teachers. *International Journal of Stress Management*, *21*(1), 69–84. doi:10.1037/a0033291

Smartsheet. (2019). *The Complete Glossary of Project Management Terminology*. Retrieved from Smart Sheet: https://www.smartsheet.com/complete-glossary-project-management-terminology

Smith, L., Roman, A., Dollard, M. F., Winefield, A. H., & Siegrist, J. (2005). Effort-reward imbalance at work: The effects of work stress on anger and cardiovascular disease symptoms in a community sample. *Stress and Health*, *21*(2), 113–128. doi:10.1002mi.1045

Sonnentag, S., & Frese, M. (2002). Performance Concepts and Performance Theory. In S. Sonnentag (Ed.), *Psychological Management of Individual Performance*. John Wiley and Sons, Ltd. doi:10.1002/0470013419

Sontag, A., Vilagra, J., Moreira, H., Moro, A., Cruz, R., Reis, P., & Galvão, I. (2012). *Identification of the mental workload of public employees in the administrative sector at a public university*. Work. doi:10.3233/WOR-2012-0965-5828

Soto, K. C. A., Carrillo-Gutiérrez, T., Solís-Quinteros, M., & Hernández-Escobedo, G. (2018). A theoretical framework about the impact of human factors on manufacturing process performance. In *New Perspectives on Applied Industrial Tools and Techniques* (pp. 327–352). Cham: Springer. doi:10.1007/978-3-319-56871-3_16

Soto, K. C. A., Rivera, H. H., de la Riva Rodríguez, J., & Martínez, R. M. R. (2016). Effects of human factors in planning and production control activities in remanufacturing companies. In *Advances in Ergonomics of Manufacturing: Managing the Enterprise of the Future* (pp. 465–474). Cham: Springer. doi:10.1007/978-3-319-41697-7_41

Spector, P. E. (1997). *Job satisfaction: Application, assessment, causes, and consequences* (Vol. 3). Sage publications.

SSPC. (2013). *Yüksek öğretim istatistikleri, 2012-2013 öğretim yılı lisans eğitimi veren yükseköğretim programlarında görevli öğretim elemanlarının öğretim alanlarına göre sayıları*. Retrieved from http://www.osym.gov.tr/dosya/1-69402/h/13ogretimalanlisansogrencisay.pdf

Stadnicka, D. (2015). Setup analysis: Combining SMED with other tools. *Management and Production Engineering Review*, *6*(1), 36–50. doi:10.1515/mper-2015-0006

Stansfeld, S., & Candy, B. (2006). Psychosocial work environment and mental health--a meta-analytic review. *Scandinavian Journal of Work, Environment & Health, 32*(6), 443–462. doi:10.5271jweh.1050 PMID:17173201

Stanton, N., Hedge, A., Brookhuis, K., Salas, E., & Hendrick, H. (2005). Handbook of Human Factors and Ergonomics Methods. doi:10.1201/9780203489925

Stanton, N. A., Salmon, P. M., Walker, G. H., Baber, C., & Jenkins, D. (2018). *Human Factors Methods. A Practical Guide for Engineering and Design.* New York: Routledge.

Stasiuk, O. (2014). *Evaluation of workload of control zone using the method of expert assessments* (Master's thesis). Kyiv: National Aviation University.

Stén, J. C. E. (2018). The Petersburg Academy of Sciences as Seen by the Finnish Mathematician Anders Johan Lexell. *Transcultural Studies, 14*(2), 226–247. doi:10.1163/23751606-01402008

Steptoe, A., & Kivimäki, M. (2012). Stress and cardiovascular disease. *Nat Rev Cardiol.* DOI: . doi:10.1038/nrcardio.2012.45

Steven L., M. Lawrence, J., & Levi, L. (2001). Factores psicosociales y de organización. *O.I.T. Enciclopedia de Salud y Seguridad En El Trabajo.*, (2–3), 88.

Suárez Amaya, W., & Díaz Barrios, J. (2013). *Factores criticos de èxito en la investigacion universitaria venezolana.* Academic Press.

Suárez-Barraza, M. F., & Ramis-Pujol, J. (2010). Implementation of Lean-Kaizen in the human resource service process. *Journal of Manufacturing Technology Management, 21*(3), 388–410. doi:10.1108/17410381011024359

Suárez-Barraza, M. F., Smith, T., & Dahlgaard-Park, S. M. (2012). Lean Service: A literature analysis and classification. *Total Quality Management & Business Excellence, 23*(3–4), 359–380. doi:10.1080/14783363.2011.637777

Subramaniam, M., & Youndt, M. A. (2005). The influence of intellectual capital on the types of innovative capabilities. *Academy of Management Journal, 48*(3), 450–463. doi:10.5465/amj.2005.17407911

Sugai, M., McIntosh, R. I., & Novaski, O. (2007). Metodologia de Shigeo Shingo (SMED): Análise crítica e estudo de caso. *Gestão & Produção, 14*(2), 323–335. doi:10.1590/S0104-530X2007000200010

Sullivan, D. (1975). Competition in bio-medical science: Extent, structure, and consequences. *Sociology of Education, 48*(2), 223–241. doi:10.2307/2112477

Sundar, R., Balaji, A. N., & Satheesh Kumar, R. M. (2014). A review on lean manufacturing implementation techniques. *Procedia Engineering, 97*, 1875–1885. doi:10.1016/j.proeng.2014.12.341

Sweller, J., Van Merrienboer, J. J., & Paas, F. G. (1998). Cognitive architecture and instructional design. *Educational Psychology Review, 10*(3), 251–296. doi:10.1023/A:1022193728205

Swink, M., & Jacobs, B. W. (2012). Six Sigma adoption: Operating performance impacts and contextual drivers of success. *Journal of Operations Management, 30*(6), 437–453. doi:10.1016/j.jom.2012.05.001

Szpitalak, M., & Polczyk, R. (2014). Mental fatigue, mental warm-up, and self-reference as determinants of the misinformation effect. *Journal of Forensic Psychiatry & Psychology, 25*(2), 135–151. doi:10.1080/14789949.2014.895024

Talib, F., Rahman, Z., & Qureshi, M. N. (2013). An empirical investigation of relationship between total quality management practices and quality performance in Indian service companies. *The International Journal of Quality & Reliability Management, 30.*

Talib, F., & Rahman, Z. (2010). Critical Success Factors of TQM in Service Organizations: A Proposed Model. *Services Marketing Quarterly*, *31*(3), 363–380. doi:10.1080/15332969.2010.486700

Talib, F., & Rahman, Z. (2010). Studying the Impact of Total Quality Management in Service Industries. *International Journal of Productivity and Quality Management*, *6*(2), 249–268. doi:10.1504/IJPQM.2010.034408

Talib, F., & Rahman, Z. (2012). Total quality management practices in manufacturing and service industries: A comparative study. *International Journal of Advanced Operations Management*, *4*(3), 155. doi:10.1504/IJAOM.2012.047634

Talib, F., Rahman, Z., & Qureshi, M. N. (2011). An interpretive structural modelling approach for modelling the practices of total quality management in service sector. *International Journal of Modelling in Operations Management*, *1*(3), 223–250. doi:10.1504/IJMOM.2011.039528

Talib, F., Rahman, Z., & Qureshi, M. N. (2011). Analysis of interaction among the barriers to total quality management implementation using interpretive structural modeling approach. *Benchmarking: An International Journal*, *18*(4), 563–587. doi:10.1108/14635771111147641

Talib, F., Rahman, Z., & Qureshi, M. N. (2012). Total quality management in service sector : A literature review. *International Journal of Business Innovation and Research*, *6*(3), 259–301. doi:10.1504/IJBIR.2012.046628

Tarafdar, M., Cooper, C. L., & Stich, J. F. (2019). The technostress trifecta - techno eustress, techno distress and design: Theoretical directions and an agenda for research. *Information Systems Journal*, *29*(1), 6–42. doi:10.1111/isj.12169

Taris, T. W., Schreurs, P. J., & Van Iersel-Van Silfhout, I. J. (2001). Job stress, job strain, and psychological withdrawal among Dutch university staff: Towards a dualprocess model for the effects of occupational stress. *Work and Stress*, *15*(4), 283–296. doi:10.1080/02678370110084049

Team, T. J. I. T. D. (1992). *Estimación del riesgo al usar métodos de evaluación ergonómica de puestos de trabajo.* Academic Press.

Tejada, P., & Gómez, V. (2009). Factores psicosociales y laborales asociados al Burnout de psiquiatras en Colombia. *Revista Colombiana de Psiquiatría*, (38), 488–512.

Teran Somohano, A., & Smith, A. E. (2013). A setup reduction methodology from lean manufacturing for development of meta-heuristic algorithms. *2013 IEEE Congress on Evolutionary Computation, CEC 2013*, 3132–3139. 10.1109/CEC.2013.6557952

Thakore, R., Dave, R., Parsana, T., & Solanki, A. (2014). OPEN ACCESS A Review : Six Sigma Implementation Practice in Manufacturing Industries. *International Journal of Engineering Research and Applications*, *4*(11), 63–69.

Tjahjono, B., Ball, P., Vitanov, V. I., Scorzafave, C., Nogueira, J., Calleja, J., ... Yadav, A. (2010). Six Sigma: A literature review. *International Journal of Lean Six Sigma*, *1*(3), 216–233. doi:10.1108/20401461011075017

Tlapa, D., Limon, J., García-Alcaraz, J. L., Baez, Y., & Sánchez, C. (2016). Industrial Management & Data Systems Six Sigma enablers in Mexican manufacturing companies: a proposed model Six Sigma enablers in Mexican manufacturing companies: a proposed model. *Data Systems*, *116*(5), 926–959. doi:10.1108/IMDS-06-2015-0265

Toker, B. (2011). Burnout Among University Academicians: An Empirical Study on the Universities of Turkey. *Doğuş Üniversitesi Dergisi*, *12*(1), 114–127. doi:10.31671/dogus.2019.155

Toro, Á. F., Londoño Londoño, M. E., Sanin Posada, A., & Valencia Jáuregui, M. (2010). Modelo Analítico de Factores Psicosociales en Contextos. *Revista Interamericana de Psicología Ocupacional*, *29*(2), 95–137.

Tranfield, D., Denyer, D., & Smart, P. (2003). Towards a Methodology for Developing Evidence-Informed Management Knowledge by Means of Systematic Review* Introduction: The need for an evidence- informed approach. *British Journal of Management, 14*(3), 207–222. doi:10.1111/1467-8551.00375

Tsai, Y. (2011). Relationship between organizational culture, leadership behavior and job satisfaction. *BMC Health Services Research, 11*(1), 98. doi:10.1186/1472-6963-11-98 PMID:21569537

Tsang, P. S., & Vidulich, M. A. (2006). Mental workload and situation awareness. In G. Salvendy (Ed.), *Handbook of human factors & ergonomics* (pp. 243–268). New York, NY: Wiley. doi:10.1002/0470048204.ch9

Tsironis, L. K., & Psychogios, A. (2016). Road towards Lean Six Sigma in service industry : A multi-factor integrated framework. *Business Process Management Journal, 22*(4), 812–834. doi:10.1108/BPMJ-08-2015-0118

Tubbs-Cooley, H. L., Mara, C. A., Carle, A. C., & Gurses, A. P. (2018). The NASA Task Load Index as a measure of overall workload among neonatal, paediatric and adult intensive care nurses. *Intensive & Critical Care Nursing, 46*, 64–69. doi:10.1016/j.iccn.2018.01.004 PMID:29449130

Tucker, P., & Rutherford, C. (2005). Moderators of the relationship between long work hours and health. *Journal of Occupational Health Psychology, 10*(4), 465–476. doi:10.1037/1076-8998.10.4.465 PMID:16248693

Tümkaya, S., Çam, S., & Çavuşoğlu, İ. (2009). Tükenmíşlík Ölçeğí Kısa Versíyonunun Türkçe'ye Uyarlama, Geçerlík ve Güvenírlík Çalışması. Ç.Ü. *Sosyal Bilimler Enstitüsü Dergisi, 18*(1), 387–398.

Turgut, N., Karacalar, S., Polat, C., Kıran, Ö., Gültop, F., Kalyon, S. T., & Kaya, E. (2016). Uzmanlık Eğitimindeki Doktorlarda Tükenmişlik Sendromu. *Turk Anesteziyoloji ve Reanimasyon Dernegi Dergisi, 44*, 258–264. doi:10.5152/TJAR.2016.28000

Tytherleigh, M. Y., Jacobs, P. A., Webb, C., Ricketts, C., & Cooper, C. (2007). Gender, Health and Stress in English University Staff—Exposure or Vulnerability? *Applied Psychology, 56*(2), 267–287. doi:10.1111/j.1464-0597.2006.00254.x

Unda, S., Uribe, F., Jurado, S., García, M., Tovalín, H., & Juárez, A. (2016). Construction of a scale for assessing at work psychosocial risk factors in professors. *Revista de Psicología del Trabajo y de las Organizaciones, 32*(2), 67–74. doi:10.1016/j.rpto.2016.04.004

Unterbrink, T., Zimmermann, L., Pfeifer, R., Wirsching, M., Brähler, E., & Bauer, J. (2008). Parameters influencing health variables in a sample of 949 German teachers. *International Archives of Occupational and Environmental Health, 82*(1), 117–123. doi:10.100700420-008-0336-y PMID:18535835

Uribe, J. F. (2008). *Psicología de la Salud Ocupacional en México*. UNAM.

Üzüm, H., Yalçın, H. B., & Özen, G. B., & Yüktaşır. (2014). Akademik Yaşam ve Örgütsel Stresin Kaynakları. *Gazi Beden Eğitimi ve Spor Bilimleri Dergisi, 19*(1-4), 23–35.

Valdehita, S., Ramiro, E., García, J., & Moreno, L. (2010). La Carga Mental Como Factor De Riesgo Psicosocial. Diferencias Por Baja Laboral. *Ansiedad y Estrés*.

Valverde, M. (2007). Radiografía de los riesgos psicosociales. *Gestión práctica de riesgos laborales: integración y desarrollo de la gestión de la prevención, 34*, 32-35.

Van Acker, B. B., Parmentier, D. D., Vlerick, P., & Saldien, J. (2018). Understanding mental workload: From a clarifying concept analysis toward an implementable framework. *Cognition Technology and Work, 20*(3), 351–365. doi:10.100710111-018-0481-3

Van Goubergen, D., & Van Landeghem, H. (2002). Rules for integrating fast changeover capabilities into new equipment design. *Robotics and Computer-integrated Manufacturing*, *18*(3), 205–214. doi:10.1016/S0736-5845(02)00011-X

Van Vegchel, N., De Jonge, J., Bosma, H., & Schaufeli, W. (2005). Reviewing the effort-reward imbalance model: Drawing up the balance of 45 empirical studies. *Social Science & Medicine*, *60*(5), 1117–1131. doi:10.1016/j.socscimed.2004.06.043 PMID:15589679

Vaquero Álvarez, M., Álvarez Theurer, E., & Romero Saldaña, M. (2018). Influencia de las condiciones de trabajo sobre la incapacidad temporal por contingencias comunes. *Atencion Primaria*, *50*(4), 238–246. doi:10.1016/j.aprim.2017.03.011 PMID:28623010

Vash, S. (2019). *Why ethical people make unethical choices*. Retrieved from Harvard Business Review: https://oregonaudits.org/

Vedder, J., & Laurig, W. (2013). *Ergonomía: Herramientas Y Enfoques*. Enciclopedia de Salud y Seguridad En El Trabajo.

Vega Perez, J., Vargas Ramos, M., Amores Guevara, P., & Arias Tapia, S. (2017). Psychosocial risks and industrial safety in the textile laundries of pelileo canton. *Revista de comunicacion de la SEECI*. doi:10.15198eeci.2017.43.135-149

Vega, A., Rojas, M., & Salazar, G. (2018). University Social Responsibility: Recent Contributions to the Development of Small Businesses in Chile. *Revista Venezolana de Gerencia*, *23*(1), 328-345. Available in: http://www.produccioncientifica.luz.edu.ve/index.php/rvg/article/view/23919

Vega, Martínez, & Morales. (2017). Social movement and inequity in access to Higher Education in Chile: the difficult path towards structural reform In A. Vega & P. Andreucci (Eds.), *From Social Conflict to Global Indignation*. Santiago de Chile: RIL Editores.

Vega, A., Valdés, M., & Cruz, M. (2019). Challenges for the creation of an international online university in a controversial environment: Chilean higher education system case. In *Handbook of Research on Challenges and Opportunities in Launching a Technology-Driven International University*. Hershey, PA: IGI Global. doi:10.4018/978-1-5225-6255-9.ch003

Velychko, O., Kolomiyets', L., Hordiyenko, T., Karpenko, S., & Haber, A. (2015). *Group expert assessment and axperts' competence: monograph*. Odesa: Aprel Publ.

Vergara-Mendoza, K. Z., Carabajo-Romero, I. R., & Leal-Maridueña, I. A. (2017). The level of stress in the teachers of the UNEMI. *Dominio de las Ciencias, 3*(2), 405-425. Retrieved from: http://dominiodelasciencias.com/ojs/index.php/es/article/view/337

Vidulich, M. A., Field, M., & Tsang, P. S. (1987). Absolute magnitude estimation and relative judgement approaches to subjective workload assessment. *Proceedings of the Human Factors Society-3lst Annual Meeting*, 1057–1061.

Vidulich, M. A., & Tsang, P. S. (2012). Mental Workload and Situation Awareness. In G. Salvendy (Ed.), *Handbook of Human Factors and Ergonomics*. John Wiley and Sons, Ltd. doi:10.1002/9781118131350.ch8

Villalobos, G. (2005). *Diseño de un sistema de vigilancia epidemiológica de factores de riesgo psicosocial en el trabajo (Tesis doctoral)*. La Habana: Doctorado en Ciencias de la Salud, Escuela Nacional de Salud Pública.

Vinodh, S., Arvind, K. R., & Somanaathan, M. (2011). Tools and techniques for enabling sustainability through lean initiatives. *Clean Technologies and Environmental Policy*, *13*(3), 469–479. doi:10.100710098-010-0329-x

Vinod, M., Devadasan, S. R., Sunil, D. T., & Thilak, V. M. M. (2015). Six Sigma through Poka-Yoke: A navigation through literature arena. *International Journal of Advanced Manufacturing Technology*, *81*(1–4), 315–327. doi:10.100700170-015-7217-9

Virgolino, A. I., Coelho, A., & Ribeiro, N. (2017). The Impact of Perceived Organizational Justice, Psychological Contract, and the Burnout on Employee Performance: The Moderating Role of Organizational Support, in the Portuguese Context. *International Journal of Academic Research in Business and Social Sciences*, *7*(1), 241–263. doi:10.6007/IJARBSS/v7-i1/2604

Viswesvaran, C., & Ones, D. S. (2000). Perspectives on Models of Job Performance. *International Journal of Selection and Assessment*, *8*(4), 216–226. doi:10.1111/1468-2389.00151

von Humboldt, W. (1970). On the spirit & the organisational framework of intellectual institutions in Berlin. *Minerva*, *8*(2), 242–250.

Wahab, A. N. A., Mukhtar, M., & Sulaiman, R. (2013). A Conceptual Model of Lean Manufacturing Dimensions. *Procedia Technology*, *11*, 1292–1298. doi:10.1016/j.protcy.2013.12.327

Waldman, D. A. (1994a). Contributions of total quality management to the theory of work performance. *Academy of Management Review*, *19*(3), 510–536. doi:10.5465/amr.1994.9412271811

Waldman, D. A. (1994b). Designing performance management systems for total quality implementation. *Academy of Management Review*.

Wang, J. L., Schmitz, N., Dewa, C., & Stansfeld, S. (2009). Changes in perceived job strain and the risk of major depression: Results from a population-based longitudinal study. *American Journal of Epidemiology*, *169*(9), 1085–1091. doi:10.1093/aje/kwp037 PMID:19318611

Watson, J. D. (1968). *The Double Helix*. New York: Atheneum.

Westerheijden, D. F., Stensaker, B., Rosa, M. J., & Corbett, A. (2014). Next Generations, Catwalks, Random Walks & Arms Races: Conceptualising the Development of Quality Assurance Schemes. *European Journal of Education*, *49*(3), 421–434. doi:10.1111/ejed.12071

Whaley, W. J., Morrison, D. L., Payne, R. L., Fritschi, L., & Wall, T. D. (2005). Chronicity of psychological strain in occupational settings and the accuracy of the General Health Questionnaire. *Journal of Occupational Health Psychology*, *10*(4), 310–319. doi:10.1037/1076-8998.10.4.310 PMID:16248682

White, M. (2001). *Rivals: Conflict As the Fuel of Science*. London: Secker & Warburg.

Wickens, C. D. (2008). Multiple resources and mental workload. *Human Factors*, *50*(3), 449–455. doi:10.1518/001872008X288394 PMID:18689052

Wickens, C. D. (2017). Mental workload: assessment, prediction and consequences. In *International Symposium on Human Mental Workload: Models and Applications* (pp. 18-29). Springer.

Wickens, C. D., & Kramer, A. (1985). Engineering Psychology. *Annual Review of Psychology*, *36*(1), 307–348. doi:10.1146/annurev.ps.36.020185.001515

Wickens, C., Gordon, S., & Liu, Y. (2004). *An introduction to human factors engineering*. Pearson.

Wiegmann, D. A., & Shappell, S. A. (2017). *A Human Error Approach to Aviation Accident Analysis. The Human Factors Analysis and Classification System*. London: Routledge; doi:10.4324/9781315263878

Wiendahl, H. P., ElMaraghy, H. A., Nyhuis, P., Zäh, M. F., Wiendahl, H. H., Duffie, N., & Brieke, M. (2007). Changeable Manufacturing - Classification, Design and Operation. *Annals of the CIRP*, *56*(2), 783–809. doi:10.1016/j.cirp.2007.10.003

Wierwille, W. W., & Casali, J. G. (1983). A validated rating scale for global mental workload measurement applications. In *Proceedings of the Human Factors society Annual Meeting* (Vol. 27, No. 2, pp. 129-133). Los Angeles, CA: Sage Publications. 10.1177/154193128302700203

Winefield, A. H., Gillespie, N., Stough, C., Dua, J., Hapuarachchi, J., & Boyd, C. (2003). Occupational stress in Australian university staff: Results from a national survey. *International Journal of Stress Management, 10*(1), 51–63. doi:10.1037/1072-5245.10.1.51

Winefield, A. H., & Jarrett, R. (2001). Occupational stress in university staff. *International Journal of Stress Management, 8*(4), 285–298. doi:10.1023/A:1017513615819

Winwood, P. C., Winefield, A. H., Dawson, D., & Lushington, K. (2005). Development and validation of a scale to measure work-related fatigue and recovery: The Occupational Fatigue Exhaustion/Recovery scale (OFER). *Journal of Occupational and Environmental Medicine, 47*(6), 594–606. doi:10.1097/01.jom.0000161740.71049.c4 PMID:15951720

Woehr, D. J., & Roch, S. G. (1996). Context effects in performance evaluation: The impact of ratee sex and performance level on performance ratings and behavioral recall. *Journal of Management*, 705–720.

Wright, T. A., & Bonett, D. G. (1997). The contribution of burnout to work performance. *Journal of Organizational Behavior, 18*(5), 491–499. doi:10.1002/(SICI)1099-1379(199709)18:5<491::AID-JOB804>3.0.CO;2-I

Wright, T. A., & Cropanzano, R. (1998). Emotional exhaustion as a predictor of job performance and voluntary turnover. *The Journal of Applied Psychology, 83*(3), 486–493. doi:10.1037/0021-9010.83.3.486 PMID:9648526

Wung, S.-F., & Schatz, M. R. (2018). Critical Care Nurses' Cognitive Ergonomics Related to Medical Device Alarms. *Critical Care Nursing Clinics of North America, 30*(2), 191–202. doi:10.1016/j.cnc.2018.02.002 PMID:29724438

Xiao, Y., Li, W., Ren, Q., Ren, X., Wang, Z., Wang, M., & Lan, Y. (2015). Effects of mental workload on work ability in primary and secondary school teachers. *Chinese Journal of Industrial Hygiene and Occupational Diseases, 33*(2), 93–96. Retrieved from http://www.ncbi.nlm.nih.gov/pubmed/25916354 PMID:25916354

Xu, Z., & Yang, F. (2018). The impact of perceived organizational support on the relationship between job stress and burnout: A mediating or moderating role? *Current Psychology (New Brunswick, N.J.)*, 1–12. doi:10.100712144-018-9941-4

Yağcı, Y. (2010). A different view of the Bologna process: The case of Turkey. *European Journal of Education, 45*(4), 588–600. doi:10.1111/j.1465-3435.2010.01456.x

Yang, H., Hitchcock, E., Haldeman, S., Swanson, N., Lu, M., & Choi, B. … Baker, D. (2016). Workplace psychosocial and organizational factors for neck pain in workers in the United States. *American Journal of Industrial Medicine*. doi:10.1002/ajim.22602

Yang, X., Ge, C., Hu, B., Chi, T., & Wang, L. (2009). Relationship between quality of life and occupational stress among teachers. *Public Health, 123*(11), 750–755. doi:10.1016/j.puhe.2009.09.018 PMID:19883926

Yeşiltaş, M. D., & Ekici, E. (2017). İş Akış Deneyiminin Kişilik Özellikleri Ve İş Stresi İle İlişkisi: Akademik Personel Üzerine Bir Araştırma. *Çukurova Üniversitesi Sosyal Bilimler Enstitüsü Dergisi, 26*(1), 1-11.

Yıldırım, M. H., & İçerli, L. (2010). Tükenmişlik Sendromu: Maslach ve Kopenhag Tükenmişlik Ölçeklerinin Karşılaştırmalı Analizi. *Organizasyon ve Yönetim Bilimleri Dergisi, 2*(1), 1309–8039.

Yıldırım, Y., & Taşmektepligil, M. Y. (2011). Beden eğitimi ve spor yüksekokullarındaki görevli akademisyen personelin örgütsel stres ve tükenmişlik düzeyleri arasındaki ilişkinin incelenmesi. *Spormetre Beden Eğitimi ve Spor Bilimleri Dergisi, 9*(4), 131–140.

Ylipaavalniemi, J., Kivimäki, M., Elovainio, M., Virtanen, M., Keltikangas-Jarvinen, L., & Vahtera, J. (2005). Psychosocial work characteristics and incidence of newly diagnosed depression: A prospective cohort study of three different models. *Social Science & Medicine*, *61*(1), 111–122. doi:10.1016/j.socscimed.2004.11.038 PMID:15847966

Yoshitake, H. (1978). Three characteristic patterns of subjective fatigue symptoms. *Ergonomics*, *21*(3), 231–233. doi:10.1080/00140137808931718 PMID:27351

Young, M. S., Brookhuis, K. A., Wickens, C. D., & Hancock, P. A. (2015). State of science: Mental workload in ergonomics. *Ergonomics*, *58*(1), 1–17. doi:10.1080/00140139.2014.956151 PMID:25442818

Young, M. S., & Stanton, N. A. (2002). It's all relative: Defining mental workload in the light of Annett's paper. *Ergonomics*, *45*(14), 1018–1020. doi:10.1080/00140130210166816 PMID:12569059

Young, M. S., & Stanton, N. A. (2005). Mental workload. In N. A. Stanton, A. Hedge, K. Brookhuis, E. Salas, & H. W. Hendrick (Eds.), *Handbook of Human Factors & Ergonomics Methods* (pp. 390–400). London: Taylor & Francis.

Yücel, A. G., & Demir, S. B. (2018). Academic Incentive Allowance: Scientific Productivity, Threats, Expectations. *International Online Journal of Educational Sciences*, *10*(1), 39–55.

Yukl, G. (1989). Managerial Leadership: A Review of Theory and Research. *Journal of Management*, *15*(2), 251–289. doi:10.1177/014920638901500207

Yu, Y., Li, H., Umer, W., Dong, C., Yang, X., Skitmore, M., & Wong, A. Y. L. (2019). Automatic Biomechanical Workload Estimation for Construction Workers by Computer Vision and Smart Insoles. *Journal of Computing in Civil Engineering*, *33*(3), 04019010. doi:10.1061/(ASCE)CP.1943-5487.0000827

Zeitlin, L. R. (1995). Estimates of Driver Mental Workload: A Long-Term Field Trial of Two Subsidiary Tasks. *Human Factors: The Journal of the Human Factors and Ergonomics Society*, *37*(3), 611–621. doi:10.1518/001872095779049327

Zhang, M., & Iru, A. A. (2012). *Using Six Sigma To Achieve Sustianble Manufacturing*. Academic Press.

Zhao, X., Hsu, C.-Y., Chang, P.-C., & Li, L. (2016). A genetic algorithm for the multi-objective optimization of mixed-model assembly line based on the mental workload. *Engineering Applications of Artificial Intelligence*, *47*, 140–146. doi:10.1016/j.engappai.2015.03.005

Zu, X., Fredendall, L. D., & Robbins, T. L. (2006). Organizational Culture and Quality Practices in Six Sigma. *The 2006 Annual Meeting of the Academy of Management*, 1–40. 10.5465/AMBPP.2006.27175447

Zu, X., Robbins, T. L., & Fredendall, L. D. (2010). Mapping the critical links between organizational culture and TQM/Six Sigma practices. *International Journal of Production Economics*, *123*(1), 86–106. doi:10.1016/j.ijpe.2009.07.009

Zylfijaj, R., & Pira, B. (2017). Assessment of critical success factors of TQM culture in hospitality sector in Kosovo. *International Journal of Research in Business and Social Science*, *6*(1), 65–77.

About the Contributors

Arturo Realyvásquez-Vargas has studied Ergonomics since 2008. At the beginning, he contributed to this sicence developing an expert system to measure ergonomic compatibility of advanced manufacturing technology. Most recently, he developed the Macroergonomic Compatibility Questionnaire (MCQ), he proved that macroergonomic compatibility has positive effects on work systems performance, and he proposed the macroergonomic compatibility index (MCI). He has published and edited books in recognized publishers; moreover, he has published articles in journals indexed in the JCR. He is member of the National Researchers System of the CONACYT. Currently, he works as full time professor in Instituto Tecnológico de Tijuana. He offers the classes of Ergonomics, Operations Research, and Research Fundamentals.

Karina Arredondo-Soto studied Industrial Engineer at the Tijuana Institute of Technology where she continued studying a Master Degree in Industrial Engineering too; with a minor in Manufacturing. She has a Ph.D. in Industrial Engineering at the Ciudad Juarez Institute of Technology. She is a full-time teacher at the Autonomous University of Baja California since 2012 and an invited Professor at the Tijuana Institute of Technology since 2008. Her interest area is work studies to improve productivity in organizations through the collaborative work with the industrial regional sector.

* * *

Meltem Akca is an assistant professor in Alanya Alaaddin Keykubat University. She studies in major topics at organisational behaviour, psychology and management sciences.

Aide Aracely Maldonado-Macías actually work as a full time professor-investigator for the Autonomous University of Juarez Mexico, she is a member of the National System of Investigator in Mexico level II. Dr. Maldonado-Macías has published several papers in various international indexed journals and conference proceedings. She has been a member of the programme committee and scientific committee of several national and international conferences, in most cases also serving as referee. She is a certified professional in ergonomics in Mexico and she serves as Member of the Mexican Society on Ergonomics and the Society of Industrial Engineers. She also serves as Associate Editor of the AcademiaJournals.com journals and the Occupational Ergonomics Advances and Applications, IGI GLOBAL and Springer Editorial. She serves as referee for the International Journal of Advanced Manufacturing Technology and the World Conference of Industrial Engineering. She has also been evaluator and reviewer for research projects in Mexico. She has obtained the recognition with her research the best investigation in Industrial

Engineering in Mexico for the Tecnological Institute of Juarez México and has participated in the most prestigious International Conferences and Congresses on Ergonomics and Computers and Industrial Engineering. She has publications on indexed journals in her country and the International Journal of Advanced Manufacturing Technology and the International Journal of Industrial Engineering, Complexity, Sustainability, Industrial Ergonomics. Also has contributions in book chapters for prestigious editorials.

Nazlı Ayşe Ayyıldız Ünnü has been working as an Associate Professor in Ege University, Faculty of Economics and Administrative Sciences since 2015. She is the Chair of International Management Department and Coordinator of her home university's Human Resources Unit. She has been part of many consultancy projects in her home country (reorganization of FOB's, Designing HRM Systems). Her scholarly interests range widely from management & organization generally to HRM, Organizational Behavior and Gender Roles specifically. She has many articles published in national and international refereed journals. She got Young Academician Incentive Award 2015, which is given based on annual academic performance by a Scientific Committee at Ege University. Her research, conducted in collaboration with two colleagues, titled "Gender of Turkish Academia" was awarded by Turkish Researchers' Association in 2016. She was awarded a three-month scholarship, by DAAD to conduct a research in Trier University, entitled "The Dynamics of Academic Employment in The Light of Gender Roles: A Comparative Perspective on German and Turkish Universities".

Norma Barboza-Tello works at the Autonomous University of Baja California, Mexico, at the Bioengineering department where she focuses my research line on the digital processing of biosignals. She is currently doing one-year research stay at the Center for Nanoscience and nanotechnology at the Autonomous University of Mexico campus Ensenada where she develops activities related to the design of devices for quantum communication. She is an Electronics engineer graduated from the Technological Institute of Mexicali, Baja California, Mexico. She completed her Masters in Sciences in Optics at the Center for Scientific Research and Higher Education of Ensenada (CICESE), specializing in optoelectronics where she worked on the characterization of the refractive index dispersion of several ferroelectric materials. Finally, she completed her Ph.D. in optics with a specialty in optoelectronics where she worked in the design and manufacture of coherent light sources based on nonlinear optical processes.

Claudia Camargo Wilson is an engineer in electrical mechanics with electronics specialization by the School on Engineering, UABC. He did a Master's degree in Science and Industrial Engineering by the ITT. He has developed Quality Systems, he is an auditor for the norms: ISO17025:2005, ISO9001:2008 and TS16949:2009. He has collaborated in different academic and administrative functions for over 20 years in UABC; he has taken part in instrumentation, control and automatization projects. He is currently undertaking the Master in Solar Energy, SEAS. He has participated in agreements with the Industry and Public Institutions; he promotes science and education in previous education systems.

Carla Estrada-Muñoz has a M.Sc. in Ergonomics, Universidad de Concepción (Chile), Physical Therapist, Universidad de Concepción (Chile). His research interest are focused on work physiology, biomechanics, and psychosocial factors. She currently works as an academic collaborator at Ergonomics Department of the Universidad de Concepción (Chile). ORCID: https://orcid.org/0000-0002-4657-8751.

Emigdio Z. Flores-López is a full time professor and researcher working with Industrial Engineering Department, based at Instituto Tecnologico de Tijuana. He is a member of the National Researchers System. He completed his PhD at ITT in 2017 on novel methods for numerical optimization using evolutionary computation algorithms applied to academic and industrial problems. His current interests are data mining, numerical and stochastic optimization, theoretical and applied meta-heuristic algorithms, complexity analysis, fast learning, parallel programming and industrial applications.

Jorge García-Alcaráz is a full-time researcher of the Department of Industrial Engineering at the Autonomous University of Ciudad Juarez. He received a MSc in Industrial Engineering from the Colima Technology Institute (Mexico), a PhD in Industrial Engineering from Ciudad Juarez Technology Institute (Mexico) and a Postdoc from University of La Rioja (Spain). His main research areas are related to Multicriteria decision making applied to manufacturing, production process modeling and statistical inference. He is founding member of the Mexican Society of Operation Research and active member in the Mexican Academy of Industrial Engineering. Currently, Dr. Garcia is a National Researcher recognized by the National Council of Science & Technology of Mexico (CONACYT) and is working with group research from Colombia, Spain and Dominican Republic. Actually, Dr. Garcia is author/coauthor in around 120 journals, international conferences and congress.

Julio Cesar Gutierrez is an Industrial Engineer by the College of Engineering of the Center for Technical and Higher Education. He has a Master's Degree in Network Technologies and Information Technology from the Postgraduate College of the Center for Technical and Higher Education. I am currently a PhD student in the Master's and Doctorate in Science and Engineering program at UABC. He has collaborated in academic and administrative activities for 15 years at UABC. He evaluates psychosocial and ergonomic factors in the industrial and educational sector.

Mónica Gutierrez studied Industrial Engineering at the Technological Institute of Ciudad Jiménez during the period 2007-2011. Course the master's degree in Industrial Engineering during the period 2012-2014 at the Technological Institute of Ciudad Juarez, and is currently pursuing a Doctorate in Engineering Sciences in this Institution.

Jesús Hernandez holds a PhD in Administration Sciences from the Universidad Nacional Autónoma de México. Professor-researcher in the programs of PhD in Technology, Master in Industrial Engineering and in the Industrial and Systems Engineering of the Universidad Autónoma de Ciudad Juárez. He is a Member of the National System of Researchers (SNI) in México. His research interest on the study of critical success factors related to operational improvement strategies in the manufacturing industry.

Juan Hernández-Arellano is a researcher and a full time teacher of the Design Department at the Autonomous University of Ciudad Juarez, Mexico. His research interest are about industrial ergonomics, ergonomic product design, statistics applied to research ergonomics, and biomechanics. Dr. Hernandez have published numerous articles, books and books chapters in indexed Journals and Internationals books. Currently, Dr. Hernandez is the coordinator of the Advanced Engineering Doctorate in the Autonomous University of Ciudad Juarez.

Aida López received the Bs. Eng in Industrial Engineer in 2006, the Master of Science in 2013, at the Universidad Autónoma de Baja California, currently developing a postgraduate to obtain the PhD degree in Technology at the Universidad Autónoma de Ciudad Juárez. From 2006 to 2008 she worked in manufacturing companies in the areas of continuous improvement and quality and since 2009 she works for the Universidad Autónoma de Baja California. Currently, she is a Full time professor at the Engineering Faculty, Department of Industrial Engineering. Her research interest include: administration, organizational culture, modeling of structural equations based on statistical analysis and application of statistical techniques for multivariate organizational phenomena.

Juan López Barreras is an engineer in electrical mechanics with electronics specialization by the School on Engineering, UABC. He did a Master's degree in Science and Industrial Engineering by the ITT. He has developed Quality Systems, he is an auditor for the norms: ISO17025:2005, ISO9001:2008 and TS16949:2009. He has collaborated in different academic and administrative functions for over 20 years in UABC; he has taken part in instrumentation, control and automatization projects. He is currently undertaking the Master in Solar Energy, SEAS. He has participated in agreements with the Industry and Public Institutions; he promotes science and education in previous education systems.

Erwin Martínez is a professor and researcher on Engineering at The Technology Institute of the Autonomous University of Ciudad Juárez. PhD in Strategic Planning and Technology Management, by the Popular Autonomous University of the State of Puebla (UPAEP). His lines of research are Quality, Technological Management, Simulation of manufacturing processes, Planning and design of technologies and facilities His actual work is related to the determination of critical success factors for Six Sigma in the high technology industry in Ciudad Juarez, Mexico

Cristina Morales-Ochoa is currently working as full-time professor and researcher in Industrial Engineering Department at Instituto Tecnologico de Tijuana. She received her doctorate in Economic Sciences focusing in developing novel models for population migration analysis in local regions. She is an active member of the post-graduate program of Industrial Engineering. Her interests involve econometrics, enterprise economics, applied statistics, industrial processes optimization, productivity and quality management.

Salvador Noriega Morales is a professor and researcher at the Engineering and Technology Institute of the Autonomous University of Ciudad Juárez. Member of the National System of Researchers (SIN) level I. Ph. D in Sciences in Industrial Engineering from the Technological Institute of Ciudad Juárez. His research is focused on the deployment of Six Sigma projects and Lean Manufacturing. He has published more than 100 articles in national and international journals, these publications have more than 300 citations.

Jesús Everardo Olguín Tiznado is Industrial Engineer from the Huatabampo Technological Institute, Sonora, Mexico. Master of Science in Industrial Engineering from the Hermosillo Technological Institute, Sonora, Mexico. Doctor of Science in Industrial Engineering from the Autonomous University of Baja California, Ensenada Campus. Professor - Researcher of the Faculty of Engineering, Architecture and Design at the Autonomous University of Baja California, Ensenada Campus. He has developed in the area of occupational and environmental health, and in the modeling of optimization of industrial processes. He has collaborated in different academic and administrative functions for more than 14 years in the Autonomous University of Baja California. He has participated in research projects in occupational health, ergonomics, optimization of industrial processes through the modeling of stochastic approximation algorithms, among others. He has participated in agreements with Industry and Public Institutions; he promotes science and education in previous educational systems.

Luz Olivares Fong holds a Bachelor degree in Manufacturing Engineer by Centro de Enseñanza Técnica y Superior (CETYS – Universidad/Centro Politécnico Superior (Spain)); Master degree in Engineering by Instituto de Ingeniería, UABC; Virtual Diplomate in "Competencies for Education for Sustainable Development" by Universidad Autónoma de San Luis Potosí; Diplomate in "Manufacturing Management" by Centro de Enseñanza Técnica y Superior (CETYS – Universidad). Since 2006, professor at Facultad de Ingeniería-UABC, in 2014 assigned as full time professor in UABC. She has participated in projects of Innovation-Conacty. Interesting areas include engineering materials, manufacturing process, sustainable development and organizational behavior. She has work experience in industry, mainly in continuous improvement projects, training and process documentations for testing certification.

Alex Pimentel-Mendoza is a Mechanical Engineer with Masters in Sciences. Coordinator of the Educational Program of Mechatronic Engineering at the Autonomous University of Baja California. He is currently studying a Doctorate in Technology at the Autonomous University of Ciudad Juárez.

Rosa Reyes-Martínez has a Bachelor Degree in Industrial Engineering by the Technological Institute of Parral Chihuahua, Mexico. Her Master in Science in Industrial Engineering by the Technological Institute of Ciudad Juarez and her Doctorate in Labor Health Science by the University of Guadalajara.

Roberto Romero López is a profesor and researcher at the Engineering and Technology Institute of the Autonomous University of Ciudad Juárez . PhD in Administration Sciences by The Autonomous University National of Mexico (UNAM). He participates in production management, quality research and structural modeling.

Manuel Rosel-Solis Industrial and Systems Engineering from the Technological Institute of Sonora, with a Master of Science in Design and Manufacturing Processes at CETYS University. It has been developed in the School of Sciences of Engineering and Technology as Coordinator of the Industrial Design and Industrial Engineering programs. He is currently studying a Doctorate in Technology at the Autonomous University of Ciudad Juárez.

Jaime Sánchez-Leal is a Professor doing teaching and research, with a Ph. D. in Industrial Engineering from New Mexico State University. His areas of specialty include applied statistics, statistical quality control, and experimental optimization, design of experiments, response surface methodology and mathematical programming. He is author of two books of statistics and design of experiments and co-author of a number of national and international journal publications.

Burcu Şentürk is an associate professor in Ege University, Business Administration department. She holds a PhD in Politics form the University of York. Şentürk has published books and book chapters with IB Tauris, Routledge, Palgrave and İletişim Publishing. Her academic interests include gender, discrimination, and organizational studies.

Tetiana Shmelova, Ph.D., DSc., Professor of Department of Air Navigation Systems in National Aviation University (Ukraine). Thesis in the field of Scientific and Methodological Basis of Decision-Making in the Air Navigation System (2012). Areas of Scientific Interests: Mathematical Models of Decision-Making by Human operator, especially in Emergency Situation; Decision Support System; Research of Air Navigation system as Socio-technical system; Aviation Sociometry and Socionics; Management and Marketing in aviation; Information technology and Informatics of Decision-Making; Problems of Human factors in aviation. Author of more than 280 scientific books, articles and guides (about 200 articles is in Ukrainian and Russian, about 45 articles in English, 14 methodical manuals, 12 copyright certificates for computer programs), 6 monographs in fields of aviation, economics, mathematics, the theory of system. Teaching courses: Theory of decision-making, Mathematical Programming, Effectiveness of Air Traffic Management and UAVs.

Yuliya Sikirda is an Associate Professor of Management, Economy, Law and Tourism Department at the Flight Academy of National Aviation University. In 2001 has received a Master degree on specialty "Air Traffic Services" specialization "Air Traffic Control". In 2004 has got a diploma of PhD in Technical Sciences on specialty "Automated Control Systems and Advanced Information Technologies". In 2006 has received an attestat of Associate Professor of Management and Economy Department. Since 2014 is the member of the specialized scientific council for the defense of dissertations for PhD in Technical Sciences on the specialty "Navigation and Traffic Control". The author and co-author of about 180 scientific works, including three manuscripts and more than 40 articles in specialized scientific publications, three copyright certificates on computer programs, above 80 teaching and methodological works. Areas of scientific interests: increasing of the decision making efficiency by the human-operator of the Air Navigation System in flight emergencies; assessment of the influence of aviation enterprises' management environment factors on the activity of the Socio-technical System's operator. Teaching courses: "Introduction to the Specialty", "Transport and Transport Infrastructure", "Information Systems in Management", "Methodology of Scientific Researches", "Mathematical Modelling of Professional Tasks".

Mübeyyen Tepe Küçükoğlu is an Assistant Professor for International Trade at the Keşan Yusuf Çapraz School of Applied Sciences at the Trakya University. Her research interests relate to strategic management, sustainability and green innovation. Her research articles has been published, e.g. in Management Studies, Procedia-Social and Behavioral Sciences and also presented several proceedings in 10, 12. and 21. IAMB Conferences in Istanbul, Warsaw and Montreal. Currently, she is giving lectures on risk management, management and organization, crisis management and strategic management.

Vianey Torres Arguelles is a Full-time professor-researcher at the UACJ. Doctorate in Engineering and Master of Science from the Universidad Autónoma de Querétaro. Currently, he coordinates the Doctorate in Technology program. Her lines of research are technology, competitiveness, complexity.

Member of the consolidated academic body: Technological Planning and Ergonomic Design. She has carried out projects and published his results in articles in various national and international journals, in the topics of complex systems analysis and in process optimization.

Yuridia Vega Industrial Engineering from the Faculty of Engineering and Business UABC. He completed his Master's Degree in the same institution in the area of Engineering in the specialty Production-Quality. Currently a full-time professor at the School of Engineering and Technology Sciences of the UABC. He is currently studying a Doctorate in Technology at the Autonomous University of Ciudad Juárez.

Alejandro Vega-Muñoz has a Ph.D. in Business Studies, Universidad Antonio de Nebrija (Spain), M.Sc. in Industrial Engineering, Universidad de Concepción (Chile), B.Sc. in Port Engineering, Universidad Católica de la Santísima Concepción (Chile), and B.Sc. in Education, Universidad de Antofagasta (Chile). His research interests are focused on sectoral economics, international relations, economic geography and their relationship with economic development studies. He currently works as a Researcher in Universidad Autónoma de Chile (Chile), Foundation 'School of International Affairs' (Chile), PIIE Corporation (Chile), and Universidad Nacional de la Patagonia San Juan Bosco (Argentina). Member of SOCHIGEO (Sociedad Chilena de Ciencias Geográficas), and Professor at HEIs in Chile, Spain, Argentina, Peru and Honduras. ORCID: http://orcid.org/0000-0002-9427-2044.

Karla Velázquez Victorica holds a Bachelor degree in Industrial Engineer by Cetys Universidad, Master degree in engineering focus on Industrial Process by Universidad Autónoma de Baja California (UABC) and PhD in Science research area in Optimization and Statistical Quality Control by UABC. Currently is responsible of Industrial Engineer program in Facultad de Ingeniería in UABC. Since 2001 professor at Facultad de Ingeniería-UABC, in 2014 assigned as full time professor. She has participated in research projects focus in optimization and improving productive processes and services through statistical methodologies such design of experiments, Anova and Surface Response.

Eman Zabalawi from entrepreneurship to corporates, to academia. An experience of three angels journey that connects the needs and expectations of customers toward enterprise and its relation to project management that entitles SME to success. The final stage of Doctorate of Business Administration in young - human capital assets. Graduated from The University of Leicester (UK) in Excellency Management. I am a member of the Board of Directors of the Specialized Women – Arab League. and the President of the economic sector and investment. Member of Brands Owners Protection Group. Team leader for Habitat for Humanity. Fellowship for Higher Education Academy. And Fellowship in Innovation Association o Innovation Professionals.

Aarón Zárate Hernández is an electronics Engineer with an Electronics design background for Automotive and Home Appliances industries. He is currently working on a Data mining project for Road Safety purposes as a Master´s degree project for the Universidad Autonoma de Queretaro.

Index

Q

R

S

T

U

V

W

Y

Z

www.ingramcontent.com/pod-product-compliance
Lightning Source LLC
LaVergne TN
LVHW062138300926
849161LV00010B/2564